FREDERICK DELIUS AND
PETER WARLOCK

FREDERICK DELIUS
AND
PETER WARLOCK

A Friendship Revealed

Edited by
Barry Smith

OXFORD
UNIVERSITY PRESS

OXFORD

UNIVERSITY PRESS

Great Clarendon Street, Oxford OX2 6DP

Oxford University Press is a department of the University of Oxford.
It furthers the University's objective of excellence in research, scholarship,
and education by publishing worldwide in

Oxford New York

Athens Auckland Bangkok Bogotá Buenos Aires Calcutta
Cape Town Chennai Dar es Salaam Delhi Florence Hong Kong Istanbul
Karachi Kuala Lumpur Madrid Melbourne Mexico City Mumbai
Nairobi Paris São Paulo Singapore Taipei Tokyo Toronto Warsaw

and associated companies in Berlin Ibadan

Oxford is a registered trade mark of Oxford University Press
in the UK and certain other countries

Published in the United States
by Oxford University Press Inc., New York

British Library Cataloguing in Publication Data

Data available

Library of Congress Cataloging in Publication Data
Delius, Frederick, 1862–1934.
[Correspondence. Selections]
Frederick Delius and Peter Warlock : a friendship revealed /
edited by Barry Smith.
Includes bibliographical references and index.
1. Delius, Frederick, 1862–1934—Correspondence.   2. Warlock,
Peter, 1894–1930—Correspondence.   3. Composers—England—
Correspondence.   I. Warlock, Peter, 1894–1930.   II. Smith, Barry.
1939–   .   III. Title.
ML410.D35A4   2000   780'.92—dc21   [B]   98–30367
ISBN 0–19–816706–7

1 3 5 7 9 10 8 6 4 2

Typeset by Graphicraft Limited, Hong Kong
Printed in Great Britain
on acid-free paper by
TJ International Ltd., Padstow, Cornwall

To the memory of my parents,
Eric and Sibyl Smith

I value his letters to me among my most priceless treasures.

Heseltine to his mother, 13 December 1911

I thank you for the confidence you bestow upon me in writing me so thoroughly & frankly all about your life, thoughts & doings—It is a letter from a real & loving friend . . .

Delius to Heseltine, 2 January 1914

Acknowledgements

I SHOULD like to record my special thanks to Mr Stephen Lloyd for his scholarly advice and assistance in the preparation of this edition of letters. He has shared his immense knowledge of Delius and twentieth-century English music with unstinting generosity and must on many occasions have found me a frustrating intruder into the world of Delian scholarship. Thanks are also due to a number of people who have helped in various ways, notably Dr John Allison; Mr Felix Aprahamian; Mr Robert Beckhard; Mr Andrew Bentley; Mr Timothy Bestelink; Mr John Bishop, who kindly supplied the photographs; Mr Lewis Foreman; Dr Philip Hazel, who produced the musical examples; Ms Valerie Langfield; Mr James Poston; Mr Malcolm Rudland, secretary of the Peter Warlock Society; Mrs Margaret Selberg; Mr Martyn Swain; Mr Robert Threlfall; Mr Fred Tomlinson, formerly chairman of the Peter Warlock Society; Mr Michael Tuffin; Miss Ann-Marie Baker and Mrs Rosemary Florrimell of the Grainger Museum, University of Melbourne; Mr Hugh Cobbe, Mr Arthur Searle, and the staff of the Manuscripts Students' Room of the British Library; Mr David Fraser Jenkins of the Tate Gallery; Miss Leonie Twentyman-Jones, Mrs Lesley Hart, and the staff of the Manuscripts and Archives Department; Ms Alison Rubia and the staff of the South African College of Music Library of the University of Cape Town; and the ever-helpful and friendly staff of the South African Library, Cape Town. A special word of thanks is particularly due to Miss Linda Louw for her untiring help in proof-reading during the long process of transcribing and editing these letters. Acknowledgement is also made to the University of Cape Town Research Committee for a grant towards this project and to the executors of the estate of the late Cecil Gray for permission to quote from his book *Peter Warlock: A Memoir of Philip Heseltine*.

B.S.

Cape Town
1998

The author and publishers gratefully acknowledge the kind assistance from The Delius Trust and The Peter Warlock Society towards the publication of this book.

Contents

List of Illustrations

(between pp. 202 and 203)

Abbreviations

BL	London, British Library, Additional MS
Cape Town	Cape Town, University of Cape Town Library

Introduction

IT would appear that, on the whole, composers do not seem to show much enthusiasm when it comes to corresponding with their fellow composers. To be sure, examples of such correspondence certainly survive in libraries, archives, and private collections, but composers are generally not given to writing lengthy letters to each other, and certainly not on a regular, friendly basis over a long period of time. Such correspondence that does exist tends to be businesslike and usually short-lived. Therefore the correspondence between Frederick Delius and Philip Heseltine (Peter Warlock), if not perhaps unique, can certainly claim to be unusual in the annals of musical history.

The remarkable friendship between these two composers was sustained over a period of some nineteen years, during which time they exchanged a large number of letters, and it is particularly fortunate that both parties kept the correspondence and that all the letters should have eventually ended up in the British Library. At Heseltine's death, his letters to Delius were all with Delius, and presumably all Delius's to him were amongst Heseltine's papers. In his biography Cecil Gray thanks Delius for placing at his disposal 'the immense collection of letters he received from his friend . . . and for allowing me in addition to quote extensively from his own letters in reply . . .'.[1] Evidently Delius lent Gray the Heseltine side of the correspondence and Gray would naturally have had access, as biographer, to the Delius side, by that time in the possession of Heseltine's executor, Bernard van Dieren.

By the time Gray's book was published Delius had died and the Heseltine to Delius letters had obviously never been returned to Jelka (who died in 1935) nor to the Delius Trust, which arose on her death. Somehow they must have come into Bernard van Dieren's possession. On his death in 1936 his son inherited all the letters, eventually selling them off in two separate lots, the side from Delius to Heseltine being acquired by the British Library at a Sotheby's auction on 16 December 1964 (lot 395). When he disposed of the second lot (the letters from Heseltine to Delius) some three years later, the composer Elizabeth Poston (1905–87), in a determined bid to obtain memorabilia of a composer with whom she claimed a certain intimacy, unwittingly bid against the Delius Trust for these in a further Sotheby's auction on 16 May 1967 (lot 434). This led her to pay £1,500, considered by some to be well in excess of their market value at the time. In 1972 she told the Peter Warlock Society that the letters

---

[1] C. Gray, *Peter Warlock: A Memoir of Philip Heseltine* (London, 1934), 17.

would be published, but was unable to give a date.[2] Subsequently she delicately and politely avoided any requests from anyone wishing to see the letters and, as a result, for some sixty years Gray's selection was the only source of any of the Heseltine to Delius letters. There were even fears that she had left instructions that at her death they (together with other Heseltine material she possessed) should be destroyed. Fortunately this proved not to be the case and the correspondence was acquired by the British Library in 1993 to be finally united with the earlier set of letters.

Examined chronologically, these letters make for fascinating reading, particularly if they are seen in the context of the lives of the two composers and of British musical and social history in general. In the course of the correspondence one is able to trace the development and blossoming of the friendship as the two men slowly begin to rely on each other in different ways. At the same time, the reader is given an important and vivid picture of musical life in England and Europe, as many important figures of the day appear in the course of these pages. Vitally important, too, are the composers' comments on their own and each other's music.

These letters inevitably also reveal much about the two men themselves. Here are some of the most important letters Philip Heseltine ever wrote, particularly in his early days, and they tell us a great deal about him and his music. Heseltine came from a wealthy, upper middle-class background, his father dying when Philip was only 2. In 1903 his mother married Walter Buckley Jones, and although she kept on her house in Knightsbridge for a while, she and her young son moved to her new husband's large house near Abermule in rural Wales. She was to prove a dominating figure in Heseltine's life and it is not surprising that in these particular circumstances the young, insecure boy should turn to Delius, hero-worshipping him as a kind of father figure. As he gradually opens up, we see his tastes slowly developing as music becomes more and more an all-consuming passion. In these letters we also discover his enthusiasms, his likes and dislikes, as well as his curious passions and strange blind-spots and misjudgements. Heseltine's enigmatic personality is revealed in the many pages of his beautifully written prose. For him Delius was not only a father-figure but a trusted friend and confidante, and in his letters he poured out some of his innermost feelings on subjects as diverse as his family, his friends, his future career, music, religion, and sex. This collection of correspondence adds enormously to our knowledge of Delius as well. The older composer obviously enjoyed the role in which he suddenly found himself cast and dispensed advice and comment

[2] Malcolm Rudland and David Cox, 'Elizabeth Poston (1905–1987)', *Peter Warlock Society Newsletter*, 40 (Feb. 1988), 15.

with obvious relish. He was delighted by the attention, flattery, and adulation which welled from the young admirer and did not hesitate to take advantage of the opportunities that such a situation provided. Reading these letters, one is constantly amazed by how much Heseltine did for the older composer during his brief life. Here we discover just how much copying of scores and parts, proof-reading and correcting, transcription and making of vocal scores and other arrangements was actually done, often with lightning speed. In our age of instant photocopying, faxing, and e-mail, it is perhaps difficult to imagine just how important Heseltine's role was in assisting Delius during the early part of this century. In addition, when one takes into account Heseltine's personal anguishes and considerable problems at the time, it is amazing to see how readily and almost always speedily he responded to Delius's requests and demands. Occasionally, however, there is just the hint of impatience on Delius's part and one cannot help but feel that the young disciple is being pressurized beyond the call of either friendship or duty.

At the time of their meeting in 1911 Delius was 49 and Heseltine 16. Yet despite this considerable age difference, the two men had much in common which would eventually draw them together as kindred spirits. Both were from well-to-do backgrounds; both suffered parental disapproval of the musical profession; both were strongly anti-establishment and rebels by nature, and both were largely self-taught, developing their own unique musical language.

Delius's parents were German, his father having relocated to Bradford to work in the wool trade there. Despite the fact that he had musical interests, he strongly opposed his son's idea of a career in music, insisting that he follow in his footsteps. Having no interest, however, in the world of commerce, the young man set off for Florida in 1884 at the age of 22 to run an orange plantation. It was here that two lasting influences manifested themselves: the singing of the slaves on the plantation and a crash-course in composition from one Thomas F. Ward, an organist in Jacksonville. Having moved to Danville, Virginia, the following year, where he taught the violin, Delius travelled to New York City, where he remained briefly before returning to England in 1886. By this time his father had relented and he was allowed to enrol as a student at the Leipzig Conservatorium. But his student days were brief and he attended more concerts and opera performances than classes. By 1888 he was in Paris, where he moved in artistic circles that included such figures as Gauguin, Ravel, Munch, and Strindberg. A visit to Norway in 1887 resulted in an abiding passion for that country as well as cementing a friendship with Grieg, who managed to persuade Delius's father not to insist on his return to America.

Success as a composer came gradually. After a private performance of his 'Florida' suite in Leipzig (to an audience of two) in 1888, he composed his first operas,

Irmelin (1890–2), *The Magic Fountain* (1894–5), and *Koanga* (1896–7). A concert of his works which he gave in London in 1899, though a financial disaster, spurred him on to complete his orchestral work *Paris: The Song of a Great City*, which was performed at Elberfeld (1901) and Berlin (1902). Delius had by this time moved to Grez-sur-Loing, near Fontainebleau, where he lived with the painter Jelka Rosen, whom he had met in 1896 and eventually married in 1903. Two further operas were written between 1899 and 1902, *A Village Romeo and Juliet* and *Margot-la-Rouge*. Although his reputation in Germany was now established, it was not until 1907 that his works began to be heard with any regularity in England, where they were championed by Henry Wood and, in particular, Thomas Beecham.

The background to the friendship between Heseltine and Delius is an intriguing one. In 1910, rather as schoolboys today develop a craze for a certain pop-star or pop-group and cover the walls of their bedrooms with posters, the young Philip Heseltine's gradual interest in and eventual obsession with the music of Delius began to manifest itself. His first recorded reference to Delius appears in a letter to his mother from his preparatory school in Broadstairs. As early as 1908 he had written to his mother announcing his intention of obtaining Delius's autograph for Mr Brockway, his music master, who evidently collected composers' autographs. He hoped to do this through his uncle, Arthur Joseph Heseltine (1855–1930), a painter who lived in Marlotte and who knew Delius, who had been living close by at Grez-sur-Loing since 1897. Possibly it was Brockway's wish to obtain Delius's autograph that first attracted Heseltine's attention to his music, but, whatever the reason, the young boy's interest soon bordered on the obsessive and in his letters to his mother there are gradually increasing references to Delius and his music.

One of the visiting music teachers at Eton, the cellist Edward Mason (1878–1915), shared a common enthusiasm for Delius's music, a subject which the two discussed at great length. As Heseltine told his mother:

[Mason] is an enthusiast in the cause of that really great and (here in his native land only) much neglected composer Frederick Delius, whose works I positively adore; I am studying his operas and songs now with very great pleasure . . . although I have heard nothing of his music,[3] yet from what I can discover at the piano, I may say that so far as I have yet found, Delius comes the nearest to my own imperfect ideal of music . . . There is one little work of his: a part-song for voices unaccompanied, to words by Arthur Symons, 'On Craig Ddu' I think that song appeals to me as much as almost anything I have ever heard, by the way it *absolutely* catches the spirit of the Welsh hills and

---

[3] Heseltine had, in fact, heard Delius's *Lebenstanz* at a concert conducted by Enrique Arbós in the Albert Hall on 19 Jan. 1908. However, he later confessed to Delius that he had come away from the concert with no impression of the work whatever. (See Heseltine to Delius, 27 Sept. 1912.)

transfers it to music. I would give anything to hear it sung, as it seems to me nothing short of wonderful.[4]

At the time of writing this letter Heseltine was only 16, and although he had not yet heard a note of Delius's music, he had succeeded in studying the music from the scores he either possessed or borrowed. At the end of 1910 he was asking for a gift of money so that he could buy the score of *Brigg Fair*. By now his greatest desire was to hear the music itself:

Mr Mason lent me a copy of Delius's 'Sea Drift' which he is producing in London shortly: it is absolutely heavenly, and, to my mind, as near perfection almost as any music I have ever seen. What it must be with the proper orchestral colour! O that I could *hear* some Delius![5]

At last this wish was granted. On 16 June 1911 Beecham was due to conduct an all-Delius concert in Queen's Hall. Heseltine had heard all about it from Mason, who had shown him a copy of the *Songs of Sunset*, which were to be given their first London performance on this occasion. In a letter to his mother he wrote excitedly about this new discovery:

Mr Mason shewed me a copy of 'Songs of Sunset' last week, and though I only had half an hour's strum at it, I am absolutely raving over it: I consider it is one of if not quite the finest and most lovely pieces of music I have ever come across: it is very sad in character, but will be glorious when performed.[6]

His frustration increased as the day of the concert drew nearer:

Mr Mason was at Queen's Hall this afternoon when they were having a rehearsal for the Delius concert: Delius was there himself. I cannot tell you how *absolutely* tantalizing it is for me to hear them all talking about it—I who would give anything to hear one work of the composer whom I adore above all others.[7]

It is here that his enlightened Eton piano teacher, Colin Taylor, intervened and 'wangled permission'[8] from Heseltine's housemaster for the boy to attend the concert, an event which was to have a profound effect on his life. During the interval he met Delius, and the next day, completely under the music's spell, he wrote an ecstatic letter to the great man himself. The following day he wrote an equally ecstatic letter to his mother:

I have not yet got over Friday night—the recollections of that music and the impressions they made haunt me, and the more I study the score of 'Songs of Sunset' the more wonderfully beautiful they seem to me—standing absolutely apart from any other music

---

[4] Heseltine to his mother, 7 Oct. 1910, BL 57959.   [5] Heseltine to his mother, 12 Feb. 1911, ibid.
[6] Heseltine to his mother, 5 June 1911, ibid.   [7] Heseltine to his mother, 11 June 1911, BL 57960.
[8] C. Taylor, 'Peter Warlock at Eton', *Composer*, 14 (1964), 9–10.

in their loveliness. . . . I have never heard any music to touch it, and truly, words fail me to describe it at all—it is too divine. Colin Taylor enjoyed it immensely: he said he had not for a long time been so moved and described parts of the music by a singularly happy phrase, saying 'it was so beautiful that it almost hurt', which I think is an excellent description . . . Yes, Friday evening was the most perfectly happy evening I have ever spent, and I shall never forget it.[9]

Later in the same letter he included an uncannily prophetic sentence: 'I am quite sure music like that must have a very powerful influence on one's life.' From that first meeting at Queen's Hall began this remarkable and lasting friendship. Delius was obviously impressed by the young boy, commenting in a letter to Taylor on Heseltine's 'remarkable musical intelligence' and 'refreshing' enthusiasm.[10] Yet Cecil Gray, Heseltine's first biographer, was somewhat critical of the ensuing friendship:

That such a close and enduring friendship should exist between two people of such disparate ages may perhaps seem surprising, or at least unusual—Delius was a man of close on fifty when they met for the first time—but all his life Philip possessed the rare gift of being able to surmount the invisible barriers which ordinarily cut off one generation from complete intimacy with another; he was always able to establish as close a contact and as real an equality with persons much older and much younger than himself as with those of his own age. The relationship with Delius, however, was of a deeper and more comprehensive order than that of ordinary friendship; it comprised also that of master and disciple, and almost of father and son. In the years of Philip's adolescence, indeed, from sixteen onwards till about twenty-three, Delius was not merely his guide and mentor in questions of music and art generally, but also in the affairs of ordinary life, and it is admirable and touching to see from their correspondence how often Delius would lay aside his work in order to write long letters of help and advice to his young friend concerning religion, sex, the choice of a career, and all the hundred and one problems which beset adolescence. In return Delius found in Philip not only an indefatigable propagandist for his art, but also an invaluable assistant in such matters as making of transcriptions of orchestral scores, correcting proofs, and in innumerable other services of a similar nature.[11]

Another person who knew both men well was the colourful and controversial conductor Sir Thomas Beecham, himself an ardent champion of Delius's music. He too was critical of the friendship, writing in 1959:

Upon me the letters from both sides have always made an impression that is far from agreeable. The trouble began in 1913 when an anxious ex-schoolboy, beginning to look upon Frederick as an infallible guide, sought advice as to his immediate future. Frederick

[9] Heseltine to his mother, 18 June 1911, BL 57960.
[10] Delius to Taylor, 18 Dec. 1911, Cape Town BC76 A4.149.   [11] Gray, *Warlock*, 37.

gives his views in a letter dated January 11th, 1913, in which he advises his young friend to do exactly what he feels like doing, and to stick to it. If he considers that music is the only thing in the world which interests him, he should take it up to the exclusion of everything else. But he adds that everything depends on perseverance, for 'one never knows how far one can go'. This reads very pleasantly and would be harmless if there had not been a world of difference between the two men. Frederick, once he had escaped from Bradford, not only realized that music was everything on earth to him, but had the iron will to pursue his way towards a definite goal, without hesitations, misgivings, or complaints. By the time he had arrived at full manhood both his mind and character had hardened into moulds that nothing changed until the day of death. Philip was of quite a different type. At that time barely nineteen years of age, and of a mental development which he himself admitted was distinctly backward, he vaguely desired a career with all the intensity of a great longing and a fruitful imagination, but was entirely incapable of either following a fixed course, or doing some of those things which might have expedited the close of a long period of vacillating apprenticeship.[12]

Reading these critical words, one cannot help being reminded of the fact that Heseltine, in a letter to Delius, had referred to Beecham's operatic productions as 'becoming more and more inferior and artistically valueless'.[13] Beecham was certainly sensitive to such criticisms and also to the fact that Heseltine had that same year (1916) tried to plan an ultimately unsuccessful rival opera season. Small wonder then that Beecham's words on Heseltine are far from complimentary. In fact the following extract demonstrates just how patronizing Beecham could be. After discussing this opera saga in rather self-laudatory terms, his final paragraphs on the friendship of Heseltine and Delius become more and more uncomplimentary and judgemental:

. . . when I formed the English Opera Company which included most of the best singers in the country . . . I offered Philip a position on the musical staff. Here he would have had the opportunity of meeting a group of able and experienced persons, which after a while would have knocked some of the nonsense out of his head . . . He declined the offer. . . .

It is no part of my task to denigrate either the character or abilities of that strange being Philip Heseltine. As I have said I always recognised his undoubted gifts, and I did something on more than one occasion to help steer them towards some definite goal. He had a genuine gift for composition, but this did not manifest itself until several years later, when he produced a handful of songs and small choral works, in many ways equal to anything being turned out by his contemporaries in England. This side of his development, however, is not that with which I am at present concerned. It is the string of letters from him to Frederick beginning in 1913 and continuing until 1919, most of which contain a repetitious story of self-impotence, self-distrust and wandering intention. Hardly

[12] T. Beecham, *Frederick Delius* (London, 1959), 175.   [13] Heseltine to Delius, 11 Oct. 1916.

the most considerate sort of communication to inflict upon a great man, whose health at this time was far from normal, and who had enough troubles to occupy his mind without being harassed by those of others . . . The real culprit, if culprit there be in this tangled affair, is Frederick, who should never have committed the psychological blunder of preaching the doctrine of relentless determination and assertion of will to someone incapable of receiving it. It is hard to resist the impression that Philip's whole life would have been smoother, better ordered and increasingly rational if he had not devoted it wholly to the service in many forms of one art alone . . . The result was that for most of the time he did not really know what to do with himself, and worked off his self-discontentment by vilipending diatribes against nearly everyone around him.[14]

Brushing such criticism aside, the distinguished Warlock scholar Fred Tomlinson, in a succinct paragraph, neatly sums up the need to understand the vital importance of this friendship in Warlock's life and development:

It has been suggested that the friendship was harmful to Philip, and if Delius had never encouraged him his life might have gone differently. What would they want instead of Peter Warlock? A civil servant? If he had concentrated on one aspect to the exclusion of others, which would you choose? *The Curlew* or the *Peterisms*? *The Sackbut* or the lute transcriptions? *The English Ayre* or *Merry-go-down*? *Capriol* or the *Purcell Fantasias*? The carols or the limericks? All were part of Warlock, and the Delius friendship was a vital component.[15]

The observant reader will notice that, while in the earlier years there are a large number of letters, the correspondence slackens until in 1927 there are only two letters and in 1928 only one. The questions might legitimately be asked as to whether part of the correspondence has been lost or if Heseltine was visiting Delius so frequently that correspondence had become unnecessary. The truth is that there had been a slow drifting apart. It seems that both Delius and Jelka remained extremely fond of Heseltine but that he gradually began keeping them at a distance. In 1927 Jelka wrote saying 'we are disappointed that you did not come', while in 1928 we find Delius lamenting that it was 'an age since I heard anything from you'.

When Eric Fenby went to Grez in 1928 at the beginning of his period as Delius's amanuensis, he was well aware that the relationship had cooled. In his book, *Delius as I Knew Him*, he wrote:

. . . I burned with curiosity to meet that young man who had done so much for Delius since he was little more than a schoolboy—Philip Heseltine. Delius had made scant reference to him when I had enquired about him, and I gathered that there had been some slight estrangement between them, so I dropped the subject.

[14] Beecham, *Delius*, 176–9.   [15] F. Tomlinson, *Warlock and Delius* (London, 1976), 28.

and when Heseltine visited Grez, and Fenby had taken him out of the house:

We chatted affably enough, but by the time we had reached the pond I found myself wondering whether this could possibly be the same Heseltine who had written that glowing book about Delius and his work, for whenever there was an opening to attack the music he had once championed, he thrust his critical rapier in, hilt and all.[16]

In a talk given to the Delius Society, Fenby said:

Beecham had sent [Heseltine] to see whether Delius would be willing that he might prepare the Delius Festival in 1929 . . . This was a very embarrassing meeting because Delius had known that Heseltine had gone cool on his music. I once saw him coming out of a concert and I said, 'Aren't you staying for the Delius?' He said, 'Oh, no, I only came to hear the Haydn.' Delius received him very politely, and he told me, 'Now, I want you to be here, Eric, when he comes'. . . . Heseltine came twice only. On the second time he came, he said, 'Come on, Fenby, let's get out of this,' and he took me on to Moncourt. Both Delius and he were having words on that last visit which was very distressing. Unfortunately he was trying to plug Bartók's Fourth Quartet and Delius said he had never heard a more excruciating noise in all his life. I was there when it happened . . . It was always understood that if things reached that sort of stage, I was to intervene, so Phil and I went on to Moncourt.[17]

Fenby also tells us that before his (Fenby's) arrival Jelka had written to Heseltine 'asking him to come and live with them, but he had been unable to do so'.[18] No such letter has been found, and there may have been additional reasons, but no doubt the major reason for Heseltine's refusal was his increasing disenchantment with Delius's music.

Here, then, are all the surviving letters between Frederick Delius and Philip Heseltine printed in chronological order. A number of these have already appeared in print, notably in volume II of Lionel Carley's monumental *Delius: A Life in Letters 1909–1934*. However, at that time the Heseltine side of the correspondence was not available for study and his source for the Heseltine letters was of necessity the occasionally unreliable selection printed in Cecil Gray's *Peter Warlock: A Memoir of Philip Heseltine*. In this work Gray quotes, often at length, from Heseltine's letters to Delius to which he had access. He was, however, not past correcting what he considered to be infelicities of spelling, grammar, and punctuation as well as censoring uncomplimentary and unflattering remarks about people who were still alive at the time and deleting words which he thought might cause offence.

[16] Fenby, *Delius as I Knew Him* (London, 1936), 59.
[17] E. Fenby, 'Visitors to Grez', *Delius Society Journal*, 106 (Winter/Spring, 1991); repr. in S. Lloyd (ed.), *Fenby on Delius* (London, 1996), 115–16.
[18] Fenby, *Delius as I Knew Him*, 22.

Delius's punctuation and spelling are often highly eccentric, to say the least, and, despite his background and education at Eton and Oxford, Heseltine is also often guilty of curious errors and misspellings in his writing. In his early letters, for example, he often writes 'it's' instead of 'its' and 'do'nt' instead of 'don't'. After careful consideration I have avoided using [*sic*] lest its too constant appearance prove a source of irritation. The reader must accept in good faith that incorrect spellings, erratic punctuation, and unusual grammar are in the original letters and not the result of careless and shoddy proof-reading. A number of the letters in this volume are undated and the dates which appear in square brackets at the beginning are generally those obtained from the postmarks on the envelopes of the letters in question or from events referred to in other dated correspondence. Portions of the addresses in italics indicate headed or embossed notepaper.

Throughout his life Delius's wife, Jelka, assisted him with his correspondence, sometimes taking down the letters from his dictation, at other times writing them for him, especially towards the end of his life, when he became paralysed and blind. A number of letters in this collection, therefore, are from Jelka rather than from Delius himself, but are included as they nonetheless contain Delius's views and thoughts, information vital to understanding the friendship of the two composers. All letters are autograph, unless otherwise noted. For the sources see the Bibliography.

For the obvious reason of lack of space no attempt has been made to give anything like a full biographical background to the lives of either Delius or Warlock. Interested readers should look elsewhere for a fuller account of the lives and music of these two fascinating and remarkable men. A few brief biographical paragraphs, however, have been included at the beginning of each year, and these will, I hope, place the letters in some kind of context. Here I have followed the example set by Dr Lionel Carley in his indispensable two-volume anthology of Delius correspondence and to whom I acknowledge a considerable debt.

1911

1910 had been a depressing year of pain and illness for Delius. Whilst in Zürich in late May to hear a performance of *Brigg Fair*, he had consulted a specialist who suggested he spend a month at a sanatorium. It was there that he was diagnosed as having tertiary syphilis, and at the end of the year he entered another sanatorium in Dresden. Continuing illness at the beginning of 1911, however, prevented him from attending further performances (*Brigg Fair* in Berlin and *A Mass of Life* in Vienna) and he returned to Grez-sur-Loing in early March. In June he travelled to London together with Thomas Beecham and, although he was again ill during the journey, he soon recovered, attending a concert of his works conducted by Beecham in Queen's Hall on 16 June, the occasion on which he first met the young Philip Heseltine, then a 16-year-old schoolboy in his final year at Eton. In mid-July the Deliuses travelled to Norway where Delius went walking whilst Jelka painted. After a brief return to Grez at the end of August they went to Elberfeld in October to hear a performance of the *Mass*. During the remaining months of the year, which were spent at Grez, Delius completed *An Arabesque* and commenced work on *The Song of the High Hills*. New Year's Eve was spent in the company of Philip Heseltine's uncle, Arthur 'Joe' Heseltine, a painter in the nearby village of Marlotte, who dined with the Deliuses at Grez.

As early as 1908 Heseltine had begun to show an interest in Delius and his music, writing to his mother that he intended asking his uncle Joe for Delius's autograph. By the time he actually met the composer during the interval of that concert in 1911, he had developed an all-consuming passion for his music, having made some piano transcriptions of the orchestral works. From the day after that meeting the correspondence between the two began and was to continue right until Heseltine's death in 1930. Restless and unhappy at school, Heseltine persuaded his mother to let him leave Eton a year earlier than usual so that he could spend some time abroad in Germany, studying the piano and learning the language with a view to a possible career in the Civil Service. En route to Cologne he and his mother stayed a few days with Uncle Joe at Marlotte, during which time Heseltine was able to spend some time with Delius and so cement their growing friendship. Apart from his quick visit to Elberfeld, Delius remained at Grez for the rest of the year composing whilst Heseltine proceeded to settle down in Cologne, returning home briefly in December to spend Christmas with his family.

1

Philip Heseltine to Frederick Delius

June 17th [1911]   (c/o H. Brinton Esq)[1]
                                                         Eton College,
                                                         Windsor.

Dear M[r] Delius

I feel I must write and tell you how very much I enjoyed your concert last night,[2] though I cannot adequately express in words what intense pleasure it was to me to hear such perfect performances of such perfect music.[3] I hope you will not mind my writing to you like this, but I write in all sincerity, and your works appeal to me so strongly—so much more than any other music I have ever heard—that I feel I cannot but tell you what joy they afford me, not only in the hearing of them, and in studying vocal scores at the piano, (which, until last night, was my only means of getting to know your music)[4] but also in the impression they leave, for I am sure that to hear and be moved by beautiful music is to be influenced for good—far more than any number of sermons and discourses can influence.

It was extremely kind of you to see me in the interval, especially as you had so many friends to talk to. I am most grateful to you for allowing me to make your acquaintance, and I shall value it very highly.

If you would be so kind as to do me the honour of a visit in M[r] Beecham's motor, as you suggested, I should be overjoyed to see you and M[r] Beecham[5] any Tuesday, Thursday or Saturday afternoon, this or next month, (except Thursday July 6th and the following Saturday, when I shall be away), and I will show you everything you may wish to see in Eton and Windsor.

I was immensely struck by M[r] Beecham's magnificent conducting: I have never seen him conduct in a concert hall before, though I was lucky enough to hear him do all three Strauss operas.[6] I am so glad the concert was such a success.

[1] Hubert Brinton (1862–1940), Heseltine's housemaster at Eton.

[2] This was an all-Delius concert in Queen's Hall, 16 June 1911. Beecham conducted the Edward Mason Choir and the Beecham Symphony Orchestra (of 100 players) with soloists Julia Culp, Thorpe Bates, and Robert Maitland. The programme consisted of *Paris, Songs of Sunset* (first performance), *Dance Rhapsody*, and *Appalachia.*

[3] On Heseltine's impression of the concert, see also his letter to his mother of 18 June, quoted in the Introduction.

[4] Heseltine had told his mother the previous year: 'although I have heard nothing of his music, yet from what I can discover at the piano, I may say that so far as I have yet found, Delius comes the nearest to my own imperfect ideal of music.' Heseltine to his mother, 7 Oct. 1910, BL 57959.

[5] Thomas Beecham (1879–1961), English conductor and impresario.

[6] Beecham gave the first English performances of *Elektra* in Feb. 1910 (Covent Garden, with *A Village Romeo and Juliet*) and of *Feuersnot* in July 1910. *Salome* followed in Dec. 1910 (first English performance).

I cannot thank you enough for allowing me to meet you and for the most glorious evening I have ever spent:

Believe me
Your very sincere admirer
Philip Heseltine

2

Frederick Delius to Philip Heseltine

9, HANS PLACE,[7]
S. W.
[20 June 1911]

Dear Mr Heseltine

Let me thank you for your appreciative & sympathetic letter which gave me the greatest pleasure—If it is possible to arrange it I will come down to Eton next this week with Mr Beecham. If I should not be able to do so I should be delighted if you would visit me in Grez—Please remember me very kindly to your mother &

Believe me
Very sincerely yours
Frederick Delius

3

Philip Heseltine to Frederick Delius

25/11/11   Brüsselerstr. 98^{III}
(posted 27/11/11)   Cöln a/Rh

Dear Mr Delius

To my intense joy I managed to hear a performance of 'Brigg Fair' yester-day (24/11/11) in Coblenz! Thanks to kind Dr Fischer, I know whenever one

---

[7] This was the home of Frank Stoop, a wealthy art-collector and a friend of the Deliuses. His wife, Bertha, a music-lover, frequently held musical evenings at 9 Hans Place which the Deliuses often visited. Edith Buckley Jones owned 27 Hans Place until 1910 when it was acquired by Harrods department store.

of your works is going to be performed within reasonable distance of Cöln, so yesterday I took the first opportunity of hearing 'Brigg Fair', which I understand is given the most often in Germany.

By way of contrast to the music I was going to hear, my only fellow-passenger between Bonn and Coblenz in the train was an opera singer, who rehearsed the part of Mephistopheles from Gounod's 'Faust' in loud tones all the way! I cannot possibly tell you how much I enjoyed hearing 'Brigg Fair'; it is absolutely *marvellous*!—and it was a very great additional pleasure to me that I knew the score, although the actual performance entirely shattered my preconceived notion of the tempi: I am probably wrong, I expect, but I should be very interested to know whether your direction 'With easy movement: ♩. = 66' is best carried out by beating a rhythmical *one*-in-a-bar, or by *three* beats in a bar: the conductor at Coblenz[8] adopted the latter method, and I am *quite certain* his tempo was *considerably* slower than ♩. = 66: anyway, it seemed to me that by beating *three* the 'easy-going' of the movement was seriously impaired. But of course I do not know, since I have never heard the work before. The second 'easy movement' (section 22) seemed much nearer the proper time, but the next movement suffered, I thought, from a fault in the other direction:—the conductor just doubled the time, making a ♩ of 3/4 = a ♪ of 4/4 which, since the preceding movement was taken fairly fast, did not seem to carry out your direction '*Slow* —with solemnity', and the 'Maestoso' sounded positively hurried! The return to 3/8 was treated in much the same way as the first 3/8 movement. The orchestra, however, was good, except for some very shaky playing of the wind in the introduction.[9] Of course, I ought not to criticize the conductor, being no musician myself, but I hope you will forgive my doing so, since I am so *very* anxious to know all that I possibly can about your music, down to the correct *interpretations* of the scores. I would give anything to hear the work under Mr Beecham's direction: I could then be quite certain as to the right reading of it.

I was so sorry to hear from my uncle of his recent trouble in the divorce court.

Life here continues to be quite heavenly for me, the more so by contrast to the dull monotony of Eton and the depressing effect of being surrounded there by people whose chief ideal in life is to excel at football or some such thing!!

I am hearing a perfect deluge of music: the opera performances are very good indeed. 'Der Rosenkavalier' is played regularly once or twice a week to crowded

---

[8] Willem Kes (1856–1934), Dutch violinist and conductor.

[9] Heseltine wrote to Taylor of the performance, saying: 'I went to Coblenz last month to hear "Brigg Fair": such a performance! . . . In the "pastoral" introduction, I thought the flute and harp were playing in different keys! The woodwind were extremely bad in it, though, as a whole, the orchestra was good: but the conductor!!' Heseltine to Taylor, 6 Dec. 1911, BL 54197.

houses! I have heard it twice: it is very amusing and interesting musically in parts, but I must confess that three hours and a quarter of Strauss (*exclusive* of intervals between the acts!) is rather more than I altogether care for! Hearing 'Heldenleben' last night after 'Brigg Fair' filled me with disgust: the only part I liked at all was the 'Adversaries' section, which is distinctly *amusing*, though it almost rivals Schönberg in ugliness! Have you seen the three piano pieces by Schönberg? They are quite extraordinary, and, as I think, barbarous! I am told that is because he has *fourths* for the foundation of his tonal system, instead of thirds, as the ordinary major, minor & whole-tone scales have! About that I know nothing, nor do I wish to know. In the first of the piano pieces he experiments with *piano harmonics*! At least, that is what I suppose the confused muddle is meant to be!! Two specimens of English music have been given here lately—works as utterly different from each other as they could possibly be: Cyril Scott's Piano Sonata [1909] and—Sullivan's 'Mikado'!! I enjoyed them both, though the Sonata is difficult to grasp at one hearing: it struck me as being very fine all the same.

The last Gürzenich concert, consisting of French music, was exceedingly interesting: the programme contained Berlioz' 'Queen Mab', which I love, and a quite wonderful 'Image' of Debussy:—'Iberia', which I thought magnificently impressionistic and 'Stimmungsvoll'. The audience *hissed* at the end of it!! though they encored a quite appalling singer for Gounod and banal little chansons. I was glad to see that she received the worst critical notices I have ever read.

The 'Kölner Tageblatt' was splendid:—

. . . 'Einzelne aufsteigende Koloraturen liessen weniger an eine geschmeidige Sangeskehle, als an ein—Verzeihung—Aufstossen denken,'. . . . . !!!! [Some rising coloratura reminded one less of a supple singing throat, but rather of—pardon—belching] and this in spite of the fact that I am told that before singing, she fell on her knees in the Green-room and prayed for success, returning thanks afterwards in the same manner!!

I have just lately finished the scoring a suite of six numbers from Inghelbrecht's 'Nursery',[10] and so I have at present no *interesting* musical work, for I do not count piano finger exercises as music! I should very much like to make another piano arrangement of one of your works, since I found copying 'Brigg Fair' so very interesting and instructive. I am thinking of getting the score of 'In a Summer Garden' to do, as I do not know the work at all, but since you were kind enough to say that you thought my transcription of 'Brigg Fair' was not altogether bad,

[10] *La Nursery*, piano duets based on French folk songs by the French composer and conductor Désiré-Émile Inghelbrecht (1880–1965).

I venture to ask you first whether there is any other work I could do, either copying or arranging, that could be of use to you also, for I should consider it a very great honour to do the smallest service to you. If not, I shall get a copy of 'In a Summer Garden' and make a two-piano arrangement. We have two pianos in one room here, and it is much better than four hands on a single instrument. I found orchestration a very interesting study, especially after the very valuable advice you gave me at Grez. I cannot tell you what a difference that made to me: I *felt* that the work was quite different, after you had corrected the number I brought to you, and I re-scored all the numbers I had done previously. I am afraid, however, they are still very bad, as a beginner's work must inevitably be, but it gives me such pleasure to do—it is, I suppose, the next best thing to composing, which I *cannot* do, except by finding *every* chord at the piano, which is far from satisfactory! I hardly like to take advantage of your exceedingly kind offer to look over some of my work, when I have only such poor stuff to shew for it, but since you were good enough to say you would look over some, I should be overjoyed if you would allow me to send you perhaps one or two numbers of the 'Nursery' suite and a song or two—they are all very short, and you can burn them as soon as they arrive, if you like—I shall be quite content with the privilege of being allowed to send such nonsense to you.

I am looking forward immensely to the coming production of 'A Village Romeo and Juliet' at Elberfeld: I shall attend every performance, if I possibly can, as I have long known and loved the piano score of it.[11]

Please remember me very kindly to Mrs Delius. I hope you will not forget that *whenever* you feel inclined to visit Wales, my mother will be only too delighted if you will come and stay at our house in Montgomeryshire. I really think you would like Wales, and, I hope, find the Welsh people more attractive than the English! They are quite different . . . . If you could manage to come next August or September [1912] I should be quite overjoyed, since I shall be there then myself. However, please write to my mother *whenever* you would like to go, and we will take you Over the Hills and Far Away to the 'sweet solitude of purpling heather' and will shew you all the wild loveliness of Mid-Wales, and as many Craig-Ddu's (or 'Craigau Ddu' as I should say properly) as I can find on the map: in any case, we have many hills on which Symons[12] might have written his lovely poem.

---

[11] The planned performance evidently did not take place.

[12] Arthur Symons (1865–1945), English poet. In Dec. 1922 he stayed as a guest at Cefn Bryntalch for a week. Symons wrote an article on Petronius for the Sept. 1920 issue of *The Sackbut* and Heseltine later set several of his poems to music. He found him 'an interesting old bird full of anecdotes and reminiscence. He seems to have met everybody that's been anybody for the last half-century.' Heseltine to Taylor, 7 Dec. 1922, BL 54197.

. . . Now, I have let my pen run away with me, and have bored you with six pages of nonsense . . . . it is really too bad, but I always do it when I start writing a letter that is *not necessary*! Please forgive me for sending such a mess of ink—if, indeed, you have had the patience to read thus far! Please do not bother to answer, if you do not feel inclined to—I know your aversion to letter writing, and respect your feelings.

In conclusion, let me thank you again and again for your great kindness to me at Grez, and for introducing me to Dr Fischer, who has been extremely good to me . . . . it is more than I deserve by far.

Yours very sincerely,
Philip Heseltine

P.S. I hope my uncle has given you my Cöln doctor's prescription for biliousness, which I sent him for you: it has done me a great deal of good already, and is very simple—a mixture of apple, prune, almonds and oatmeal, put through a mincing machine and moistened with a little water, to be taken every morning before breakfast!

4
Frederick Delius to Philip Heseltine

Grez-sur-Loing
S & M
26 Nov 1911

Dear Mr Heseltine
I return you by the same post your transcription of 'Brigg Fair'—I have looked at it carefully again & find it exceedingly well done—In several places there are notes missing—& at times you might have made it rather fuller—With 2 pianos one need make no restrictions One ought at times, I think, to interpret rather freely in order to try & regive the orchestral effect—Let me know how you are getting on & what the professors give you to do—I suppose they are still teaching in the old, old fashion—Never lose your own criticism & dont be *imponirt* [over-impressed] & above all write as *much as possible*—

Sincerely yrs
Frederick Delius

5

Philip Heseltine to Frederick Delius

27/11/11   Brüsselerstr. 98 ᴵᴵᴵ
                                                                              Cöln

Dear Mʳ Delius

Curiously enough, I had just posted a long letter to you, when I came back
to find your letter awaiting me.

Thank you so much—it was very good of you to bother to look through
my transcription. I am sorry about the notes left out: I remember leaving out
some of the doubled notes in section 15, on the advice of my master at Eton,
Colin Taylor,[13] who likes 'pianistic' transcriptions of orchestral works, of the Liszt-
transcription order! Personally, I have always preferred the *literal* arrangement,
even if it gets a little unplayable!

I have not yet begun studying with the professors, since Dʳ Fischer thought
it would be better to wait until I knew more German. I am having piano lessons,[14]
but for five weeks now I have been given *nothing* but finger exercises to practise,
which, I am sorry to say, bore me horribly, since I have not the slightest wish
to become proficient on the piano![15]

I wonder when the 'old, old fashion' of teaching will be swept away by a practical revolution, as the old, old fashion of composing has been! It must surely
come soon . . Imagine a Conservatorium where the teachers expounded the use
of whole-tone scales theoretically, and harmony students were required to do
exercises in the art of *not-being-banal*—the reverse process, I take it, from the
present system of teaching 'harmony' and '*counterpoint*'!!

Did you read the essays Clutsam[16] wrote for the 'Musical Times' a short while
ago on 'The Whole Tone scale and it's practical use'?[17] I found them extraordin-

---

[13] Colin Taylor (1881–1973), English pianist, composer, and teacher. He was an assistant music master at Eton
from 1904 to 1914, and from 1921 to 1941 was on the staff of the South African College of Music in Cape Town.
An important collection of letters from Heseltine to Taylor is housed in the British Library, Add. MS 54197.

[14] Heseltine's piano teacher was Frau Lonny Epstein, a pupil of Carl Friedberg, the head of the piano department
at the Cologne Conservatorium.

[15] Heseltine had written earlier that month to his mother: 'I have discovered . . . that Fᵈ Bussius was quite right
all along in saying that I should do much better to have *private* lessons, and that the Conservatorium was no use to
anyone who was not going to stay *at least* 3 years. For the first year one learns *nothing*, except just getting used to the
routine, just as now, I learn nothing on the piano but finger exercises, done in the particular way they like at the Con.
Fᵈ B. agrees that lessons *entirely* devoted to finger exercises are not really useful for me, who am *not* going to become
a professional.' Heseltine to his mother, 12 Nov. 1911, BL 57960.

[16] George Howard Clutsam (1866–1951), Australian composer, pianist, and critic. He settled in London in 1889,
and acted as accompanist to Dame Nellie Melba. He began his composing career in the operatic field, later turning to
musical comedy.

[17] G. Clutsam, 'The Whole Tone Scale and its Practical Use', *Musical Times* (1910), 702–6 and 775–8.

arily interesting, especially in the examples of original chord-progressions, which I suppose he wrote himself.

You tell me to *write as much as possible* . . . . there is nothing in the world I should love better, but how am I to do it? If I *had* ideas, I could not write them down without a piano! The sum total of my 'compositions'—(I ought to say 'compilations' for they were all 'discovered' at the piano, and not connectedly at that)—amounts to six short songs! Three of them I have written in the last month, but it is such an unsatisfactory feeling that one must seek ideas at the piano!

If it were the reverse process, that I had ideas but could not write them down, I should not mind! But, alas, it is not!

If I am to make music my profession, which is of course, my great wish, I do not see what I can do except becoming a—critic! a writer *on* but not *of* music! But even for that, I am afraid I am not broad-minded enough, nor can I listen to *some* music with intelligence. It is utterly Philistine, I know, but the 'old masters' of classical music mean nothing to me! I suppose I am, therefore, no good at all:—Q.E.D.—and I have a thoroughly conventional life on the Stock Exchange!

However, the very *thought* of your music would always comfort me in a humdrum life.

I am, therefore, very sincerely yours in all gratitude,
Philip Heseltine

6
Frederick Delius to Philip Heseltine

Grez sur Loing
S & M
4 Dec 1911

Dear Mʳ Heseltine

Thank you so much for your warm & sympathetic letters which gave me the greatest pleasure—I am so glad you like the sound of Brigg Fair & am sorry you did not hear it conducted in a better way—What you say is perfectly correct—One must beat one in a bar—3 makes me shudder—Then again the slow section can scarcely be taken slow enough—The maestoso section must be taken solemly & not hurried—In other words it seems to have been a miserable

performance! It would interest me to read Clutsam's articles if you possess
them. I do not believe in any music constructed knowingly on any Harmonic
Scheme whatsoever. All the people who write about the Harmonic system or
try to invent other systems quarter tones etc. Dont seem to have anything to
say on Music—Systems are put together from the compositions of inspired musicians   Harmony is only a means of expression which is gradually develloping—
I dont believe in learning Harmony or counterpoint—There is no piano score
of the 'Summer Garden' as yet or of the 'Dance Rhapsody'—Do one of them
for 2 pianos[18]—& I will hear it when I next come to Germany—perhaps in
March—Send me the pieces you have orchestrated & I will be very glad to help
you—You have a great talent for Orchestration—that I could see from the 2
pieces you showed me—We should be delighted to come & see you in Wales
& we will try and arrange it for next September—or August—I should just love
to see Wild Wales again & of course you must be there to shew it me—I think
it is absurd that your teacher only gives you finger exercises—I would simply
tell him you did not come to Cologne for that purpose—If I were you I would
go to the best Theorist in Cologne & learn what you can from him—As a writer
& critic it may be of some use to you, as a composer none whatever—It is of
no importance whether you write at the piano or not—As long as you *feel* you
want to Express some emotion—*music is nothing else*—

I am working on a new choral work[19]—You must have thought very much
about Brigg Fair—as on the 25th I was quietly reading in my room when, suddenly, I could only think of Brigg Fair & I was obliged to get up & play it thro
& the rest of the evening it quite haunted me—Telepathy! Write me soon again

& Believe me
very sincerely yours
Frederick Delius

[18] The next year Heseltine was to tell Taylor: 'I should love to make a piano score of the "Dance Rhapsody", but
the scores are so fearfully expensive, and even when I told Delius last year that I wanted to make another transcription of one of his works, he never offered to lend me a copy of the score, so I had to buy the score of "In a Summer
Garden"—not that such a priceless work is not worth any money, but personally I cannot afford many scores at the
price. He told me before I transcribed "In a Summer Garden" that the Dance Rhapsody had never been done for
piano, which is very curious, for it would surely sell as a piano duet. He suggested that he might publish the arrangement of "In a Summer Garden".' Heseltine to Taylor, 10 Nov. 1912, BL 54197.
[19] *The Song of the High Hills*. Delius had recently completed *An Arabesque* (MS dated Autumn 1911).

7

Philip Heseltine to Frederick Delius

10/12/11   Brüsselerstr. 98 III
                                                                        Cöln

Dear Mr Delius,

I cannot tell you what great pleasure and interest your letter afforded me! It is very good of you to trouble to write to me at all, especially such a long and interesting letter as I received last week! Thank you also a thousand times for consenting to look through my little 'Nursery' scores—it is too kind of you, for I fear it will be unduly taking up your time to look through what is really not worth your bothering about. I sent them some while ago to Colin Taylor, but I have written to him and asked him to send them to you direct.[20] I feel indeed honoured that you should trouble to look at them.

I am so glad to know for certain about the tempi in 'Brigg Fair': I felt sure that the old man at Coblenz (who, by the way, looks a little like Hubert Parry!) knew nothing at all about it! Perhaps he did not understand the English directions on the score!

I enclose Clutsam's articles on the Whole-Tone Scale: I think they are very interesting, and that they will more or less coincide with what you very justly say about new 'systems', for, as Clutsam says, it is for the widening of the harmonic field, and not as a new and strange toy that the Tonal Scale will be of use in music. When I go home again, I will find and send you a little book recently published on the same subject: it is also interesting in tracing the origin of the scale, though Clutsam's is fuller. The other book quotes Purcell as the first to use a chord, which can only be analysed on the ground of the Whole-Tone Scale, so the book says, though its use was, of course, unintentional in that sense.

I am exceedingly interested in the incident of November 25th! I fear you would not have very much peace if the same thing occurred every time I thought of or played one of your works! As a matter of fact, I spent the whole evening of the 25th writing my first letter to you, which, although not finished until two days later, contained my description of the Coblenz concert in the first part, which I wrote on the 25th! I think it was undoubtedly telepathy, in which I believe very strongly, as also in many other occult and, at present, undeveloped

---

[20] Heseltine had written to Taylor: '[Delius] was also kind enough to say that he would be glad to look through my "Nursery" scores and give me a criticism of them, so when you have finished with them, will you please send them to him at Grez-sur-Loing, Seine et Marne, France, as that will save an extra postage?' Heseltine to Taylor, 6 Dec. 1911, BL 54197.

sciences, though many people laugh at them, because *they cannot themselves under-stand them*, owing to the fact that the necessary discoveries leading up to the developement of the science have not yet been made! It is extraordinary how many people immediately damn, as something utterly absurd, any new thing, which they cannot immediately grasp!—a quaint conceit, of which Anti-Wagnerianism is a capital example!!

I have lately been reading, with great delight, a fantastic and rather mysteri-ous book by Fiona MacLeod,[21] about Scotland and the real Celtic people: it is most fascinating, the style being, to my mind, particularly fine. It deals with all sorts of superstitions in a most convincing manner. From this book, by the way, are taken the words of Bax's[22] lovely 'Celtic Song-Cycle',[23] which I spoke to you about: I think your opinion of young England's music would rise if you knew that work! The words are beautiful enough to inspire any musician with fine thoughts.

I have not heard much music of note lately, except for two performances of a new opera by Karl von Kaskel,[24] 'Der Gefangene der Zarin',[25] a melodra-matic work, with music which is quite pleasant to listen to, although not very original, and in parts too reminiscent of Puccini! I suppose it's melodramatic qualities will make it popular, besides the fact that the composer is well known in Cöln, but I cannot imagine why such a thing should be put on here where comparatively few novelties are given!

The last 'new' opera I saw was Clutsam's 'Summer Night',[26] in London, which I consider a far finer and infinitely more original work. This is the second Kaskel novelty in the last year or 18 months!

Is your new opera[27] published or down for production yet? What would I not give to see *that* produced here!

I look forward with immense pleasure to your visit to us in Wales. My uncle told me you were very fond of Borrow's glorious book 'Wild Wales':[28] it is one of my most treasured possessions, which I have always by me, and read con-stantly, over and over again.[29]

---

[21] A nom de plume of the Scottish poet William Sharp (1855–1905). The book was *The Dominion of Dreams* (London, 1909).

[22] Arnold Bax (1883–1953), English composer. Norman O'Neill had already written to Delius about his music on 11 Nov. 1908.

[23] A set of five songs, composed July/Aug. 1904.

[24] Karl von Kaskel (1866–1943). He was a fairly successful composer living in Dresden and later in Munich who composed orchestral and piano pieces as well as songs and operas.

[25] First performed in Dresden, 1910.   [26] A one-act opera produced by Beecham in 1910.

[27] *Fennimore and Gerda* (1908–10).

[28] George Henry Borrow (1803–81), *Wild Wales: Its People, Language and Scenery*, 3 vols. (London, 1862), though Heseltine probably had the 1905 New Pocket Library edition.

[29] The month before Heseltine had written to his mother: 'I am constantly reading and re-reading chapters of George Borrows' immortal work "Wild Wales", which is quite one of my favourite books, and gives a most vivid picture of Wales and the Welsh people half a century ago, when they were *really* Welsh.' Heseltine to his mother, 12 Nov. 1911, BL 57960.

It is wonderful how Borrow caught the spirit of that heavenly country, and described it in such a delightful style. I simply adore Wales, and never tire of such a delicious picture of it! When you come to 'Cefn Bryntalch' you can visit Bala, Mallwyd, Machynlleth, Devil's Bridge, Plynlimmon and the three sources thereon, Llansilin, Llangollen, and many other places described by the inimitable Borrow, and you will, I am sure, enjoy them all the more by having read such living descriptions of them!

My plans for the future are taking definite shape: I really do not honestly *feel* that I could ever do enough in any branch of music to justify my adopting the career of a musician, though, of course, I shall continue to love and study music more and more, as my highest pleasure in life. I have found a far more attractive career than the Stock Exchange, so that, after I have learnt sufficient German here, I shall repair to Oxford, to study for the English Civil Service! At least, those are my plans at present.

I was highly delighted at what you said about my piano teacher! I am sure it is useless for anyone who is not going to study seriously for three years at least, to learn, from the foundations, any of these complicated 'methods', good as they may be for professional pianists! I have very little enthusiasm for playing the piano, except for the purpose of studying piano scores of operas and orchestral works.

I hope you will not be disturbed by any telepathic messages while you are working at your new choral work![30]

Please remember me to M^rs. Delius: I thank you again for all your kindness.

Yours very sincerely,
Philip Heseltine.

8
Frederick Delius to Philip Heseltine

[Grez-sur-Loing
Seine et Marne
13 December 1911]

Dear Mr Heseltine,

Many thanks for your nice letter & the Clutsam articles which I shall read with interest—Your music arrived also from England   Why did you not send

---

[30] *The Song of the High Hills*. Although the published score is dated 1911, this is possibly a misprint as the work was not completed until 1912.

the songs? Please give me the name of the book of Fiona Macleod as I should
like to get it—This in haste—I will write you again more fully—

very sincerely y^{rs}
Frederick Delius

Postcard.

9
Frederick Delius to Colin Taylor

Grez sur Loing
S[eine] & M[arne]
18 Dec 1911[31]

Dear Mr Taylor,
   Many thanks for your kind note & the music.[32]
Heseltine seems to me to have remarkable musical intelligence & also to be
very gifted—I like him very much & find his enthusiasm very refreshing—I
hope I shall have the pleasure of meeting you when I next come to England.

   I remain
   Sincerely yours
   Frederick Delius

10
Philip Heseltine to Frederick Delius

15/12/11   Brüsselerstr. 98 ^{III}
                                                                 Cöln

Dear Mr Delius
   I received your card last night, for which many thanks.
   I did not send the songs before, because, on second thoughts, I decided that
my only copies of them were illegible, and not worth deciphering, but since

---

[31] Cape Town BC76 A4.149.   [32] Heseltine's orchestrations of Inghelbrecht's *La Nursery.*

you kindly ask after them, I cannot resist the temptation of sending them this time, though please do not bother about them if you find them trying to the eyes![33]

I am sending you a Wagner calendar,[34] which I saw here a day or two ago and thought rather good: I hope it may interest you, and that you have not already had a copy.

The book by Fiona Macleod is called 'The Dominion of Dreams: and Under the Dark Star' (1 vol. Heinemann). You can get it at Galignani's Library, Paris, 224 Rue de Rivoli, where I got my copy of it.

I am suffering to-day from the extraordinarily depressing effect of Puccini's opera 'Madama Butterfly', which I saw last night! Though beautiful in a way, I think the piece is the most hysterically morbid and *unhealthy* thing I have ever seen: it made a most unpleasant impression on me!

I told my piano-teacher to day that I would have no more piano lessons next year! I simply cannot stand it any longer![35]

I am going to England on the 20th for three weeks: when I get home, I will try and find some photographs of Montgomeryshire scenery to send you, as an allurement!

I enclose a portrait, which I think is well worthy of a place in a *Wagner collection*!!

Yours very sincerely,
Philip Heseltine

---

[33] On 24 Jan. 1912 Heseltine wrote to Taylor: 'I sent eight songs to Delius (at his request—he little knew what he was in for!) and also my fair-copy of "In a summer garden" for 2 pianos, but beyond an acknowledgement on a post card, I have heard nothing further from him: I expect his disgust was, literally, too great for words!' Heseltine to Taylor, 24 Jan. 1912, BL 54197.

[34] On 13 Dec. 1911 Heseltine wrote to Taylor: 'I have discovered here a very original Calendar, which claims to give the life of Wagner in 365 pictures! . . . I cannot restrain myself from sending you one, as I think it is quite out of the ordinary!' Heseltine to Taylor, BL 54197.

[35] Heseltine wrote to Taylor early the following year: 'I have definitely abandoned piano lessons in Germany, as I could not stand them any longer! Also, it is impossible for me to work hard at a subject without enthusiasm for it, and my last course of "Klavierstunden" in Germany caused me to loathe the very idea of another! Besides, I shall not have time to keep up practising sufficiently, for when I have spare time to play the piano, I make myself acquainted with the divine works of Delius, and others (whose works one cannot always hear), and get to know them, even though I cannot *play* them properly.' Heseltine to Taylor, 24 Jan. 1912, BL 54197.

11

Frederick Delius to Philip Heseltine

[Grez-sur-Loing
Seine et Marne
22 December 1911]

Dear Heseltine—Thank you ever so much for your Wagner Calender   It is very interesting & contains lots that is new to me—I shall write you again about your music when I have a little more time—In the meantime I send you one of my photos & wish you a merry Xmas. Your uncle dines here on new years eve—Very sincerely y^{rs}

Frederick Delius

Postcard.

12

Philip Heseltine to Frederick Delius

28/12/11   *Cefn-Bryntalch*
                                 Abermule
                              Montgomeryshire

Dear Mr Delius

How can I thank you enough for the beautiful photograph, which reached me yesterday![36] It was *exceedingly* kind of you to send it me, and I shall prize it very highly indeed.

As you see, I am back again in lovely Wales, where I shall remain for a few weeks: I have been in that appalling county Essex in most uncongenial surroundings for the last week, so you can imagine my joy at returning here!

---

[36] Heseltine wrote to Taylor: 'I have had several long and extremely interesting letters from Delius lately, also a beautiful signed photograph of him! He is really a most awfully kind man.' Heseltine to Taylor, 27 Dec. 1911, BL 54197.

I have already completed a good deal of my 2 piano arrangement of 'In a Summer Garden', and shall continue it while I am here: I do not think it will take very long, and I find working at it quite absorbing!

I enclose the book I mentioned, about the Whole-Tone Scale. I was very interested to see in the Musical Times that an *Amateur orchestra* in Bolton are going to perform 'Paris'![37]

With best wishes for the New Year to you and Mrs. Delius, and again *very* many thanks for the photograph. I remain

Yours very sincerely
Philip Heseltine

[37] An entry on p. 739 of the Nov. 1911 edition of *Musical Times* reads: 'The Amateur Orchestra Society of this town [Bolton], under Mr Andrew Morris, will play Delius's "Paris" tone poem (probably for the first time in the County Palatine).'

1912

THE beginning of 1912 saw Delius at Grez working hard on *The Song of the High Hills*, a new work for chorus and orchestra which he wrote to Heseltine about in February. By 12 March the Deliuses were travelling yet again, this time to Berlin to hear a performance of *Paris* given by Oskar Fried. Moving on to Munich, they then took a brief holiday in Venice in April, returning to Munich to complete the business part of the trip. The visits to Munich had been occupied with unpleasant business dealings with the unsatisfactory music publisher Harmonie, a visit which necessitated consultations with lawyers and the eventual instituting of legal action. By August Universal Edition had replaced Harmonie as Delius's publisher. Towards the end of April the Deliuses were back home in Grez for some four months, where Delius continued to work on *The Song of the High Hills* before leaving for another holiday, this time at Arcachon on the west coast of France not far from Bordeaux. The next engagements were in England at the Birmingham Festival in October, where *Sea Drift* was to be performed. It was here that he and Heseltine met again. After that Delius travelled to London to hear performances of the *Dance Rhapsody* and the Piano Concerto. After a short spell in Grez in October he travelled yet again, this time to Berlin to hear Fried perform the *Lebenstanz* in its recently revised version. By the middle of December he was once more in Grez.

For Heseltine it was a busy, if somewhat unsettled, year. After a brief Christmas break (spent with his family in Wales and England) he returned to Cologne. By this time, however, he had given up his piano studies, having more or less accepted the fact that he would have to go on to university and end up in the civil service. His sojourn in Germany, however, was suddenly cut short when it was discovered that, to comply with the age-limit regulations, he would have to take the Oxford entrance examinations very much earlier than previously supposed. So, resigned at last to a non-musical career, Heseltine quickly settled down in March 1912 to cram Latin and Greek with the Reverend Clarence Rolt, the vicar of Chadlington, who soon moved, first to Hemel Hempstead for a short while in June and then on to the parish of Newbold Pacey, Warwickshire, in August, accompanied each time by his pupil. In September 1912 an article Heseltine had written on Schoenberg was published in the *Musical Standard*. This article of over 2,000 words is a quite remarkable piece of writing for a 17-year-old, notable also in that it was one of the first articles on the composer to appear in English. Although it was compiled chiefly from portions of

Schoenberg's book *Harmonielehre*, in it Heseltine was already showing signs of contempt for the British Musical Establishment. Delius, who was sent a copy, described it as 'very good & fair'.[1] The two men were able to meet at the Birmingham Festival in October when they spent some time together. At the beginning of December Heseltine took the Oxford scholarship examination. Although he was not elected to a scholarship, he was told by the Oxford authorities that he would be accepted in October the following year provided he passed Responsions. Despite his protests he was unable to escape the annual family Christmas party at his uncle Evelyn Heseltine's home in Essex.

13
Philip Heseltine to Frederick Delius

17/1/12   *Cefn-Bryntalch*
                                 Abermule
                                 Montgomeryshire

Dear Mr Delius

I am sending you the fair copy of my arrangement of your 'Summer Garden', and another song, though I feel quite ashamed of bombarding you with manuscripts in this way! The temptation, however, is great! The work of transcription has given me intense pleasure, and I am looking forward to playing it with 2 pianos at Cologne, whither I return at the end of this month. I will not weary you with any more superlatives: my admiration for your music literally 'grows by what it feeds on'[2] and is inexpressible in words—'But words are weak'![3]

There is deep snow here to-day, after three weeks of incessant rain! I hope you are not flooded out at Grez.

I have lately read a book—'The silent isle' by A. C. Benson[4]—which I think would interest you, since the author expresses precisely the same views as you told me you hold with regard to cultivating the individuality for the sake of art,

---

[1] Delius to Heseltine, 24 Sept. 1912.

[2] A misquote from *Hamlet*, I. ii. 143–5. 'Why, she would hang on him? as if increase of appetite had grown / By what it fed on.'

[3] From Ernest Dowson's poem 'A Valediction'. The correct quotation is 'But words are so weak'.

[4] Arthur Christopher Benson (1862–1925), Master of Magdalene College, Cambridge, author of essays and biographical studies. He was librettist for Elgar's *Coronation Ode*, and therefore of 'Land of Hope and Glory'.

and avoiding unsympathetic persons. The book is a very intimate and personal series of essays on all kinds of subjects, and, as I think, written in a perfectly delightful manner.

I am returning to Germany only for four months longer, as I find it necessary to return to England very soon to work for an Oxford scholarship examination.

I am much comforted by your having told me that the so-called 'rules' of music, such as harmony and counterpoint, are of little real value, since I shall not have time to learn them, while studying for a profession other than music, and also I am sure I should never have the patience to master them, knowing that the best music does not take them into account!

I made my first appearance in print this month, not, alas, with music, but with a miserable article in the 'Locomotive Magazine'![5]—quite the reverse of anything artistic!

With many further apologies for troubling you like this (as usual, I fear!) I remain

Yours very sincerely
Philip Heseltine

14
Frederick Delius to Philip Heseltine

Grez sur Loing
24 Feb. 1912

Dear Heseltine—

Forgive me for keeping you waiting so long—I have been very busy with a new work—The arrangement for 2 pianos of my 'Summer garden' I think is excellently done & I hope you will play it to me on my way thro' Cologne. I shall be in Germany in a fortnight—First Berlin & on my way back I hope to see you in Cologne—The only fault I find with the Orchestration of 'La Nursery' is that you employ by far too big an orchestra—The matter is too slight for such an enormous apparatus—Otherwise it is orchestrated with great taste— Your songs are beautiful. In one or two I have made slight alterations—only a

---

[5] P. A. Heseltine, 'The Van Railway', *The Locomotive* (Jan. 1912), 13–16. The article describes a railway in central Wales about a dozen miles up the Severn valley from Cefn Bryntalch.

suggestion mind—You come so persistently back to E flat in one of them—
Excuse this hasty scribble—

With kindest regards
I remain
Very sincerely yrs
Frederick Delius

15
Philip Heseltine to Frederick Delius

28. 2. 12.   Cologne

Dear Mr Delius

Thank you so much for your letter and return of my MSS. It was indeed
most kind of you to look through them, especially when you were busy with a
new work, and I am deeply grateful to you. I am only sorry that I have nothing better to show you, for my little songs, whatever their intrinsic merits or
demerits might be, are worthless in the one (to me) essential point—namely,
that they should be (and are not) spontaneous expressions of the composer—
in my case 'manufacturer' would be a more correct word! I have positively *no*
ideas in music—I cannot think in music, and if I could, my thoughts would
never assume definite shape—that is, I could never write down, or even play,
what I wanted to, though I cannot tell you how I *long* for some medium of
personal emotional expression—any kind of medium, through music, writing
or even personality[6] . . But I have none: though I *feel* so much,—the more, I
am inclined to think, because my feelings must be for ever pent up, and can
find no outlet in expression from this horrible *person* that encases them! In words,
spoken or written, in music, I can positively *get nothing out*! In this way, I often
long to be a 'disembodied spirit'!—so as to be rid, once and for all, of an apparatus for expression which *does not work*! . . . . I am afraid I am writing hopeless nonsense, but please forgive me: when I write to you, I somehow feel quite

---

[6] Heseltine had earlier described his method of composing to Taylor: 'My "composition" is rather ludicrous: the
only way I can produce anything at all is to strum chords at the piano until I light upon one which pleases me, whereupon it is imprisoned in a note-book. When a sufficient number of chords and progressions are congregated, I look
for a short and, if possible, appropriate poem to hang them on to. This found, more strumming has to ensue, until
there is about the same quantity of music as of poem. Then the voice part is added, and the whole passes for a "composition"! I should call it a "compilation"!' Heseltine to Taylor, 24 Jan. 1912, BL 54197.

different, and seem to say quite different things to what I could say to anyone else—though I have no right to inflict this kind of thing on you, but you have been so kind to me—I cannot help it! However, I will cease to bore you.

Alas! I shall not be in Germany in a fortnight's time—in fact I shall not be here next week! Since my love of music is so *unpractical*, I must take the next best work that comes along, and this being the English Civil Service, I shall have to sacrifice a good deal of what I should like to do, to what is necessary. I discovered last month that, to comply with the age-limit regulations, I shall have to enter for my first Oxford exam very much earlier than I had previously supposed—in fact at the end of the present year, and to prepare for it, I have quite as much, if not more, *classical* work before me than I can possibly cram into the succeeding nine months. On that account, therefore, most unwillingly, I must return to England and recommence study of 'the classics' at the beginning of next month! I leave here on Friday next. I shall, of course, return to Germany after this exam is over, and also during the vacations when I am at Oxford, but for the English Civil Service exam, for which I enter in five years' time, Classics and English are, of necessity, my chief subjects, German only counting one-tenth part of the total marks!

I am *extremely* sorry to miss seeing you here, as I had long been looking forward to your visit to Germany. But I continue to hope most ardently that you will come over and see us in Wales next August or September. I long to roam the wild hills with you, who *understand them*, who are in sympathy with them, as it were, and to whom they are not *merely* 'sights pleasing to the eye'!

I have crowded much music into this last month—chiefly opera: 'The Ring' complete, 'Die Meistersinger', 'Figaros Hochzeit', and other works I have heard with immense pleasure: also some pure 'hogwash' by Meyerbeer,[7] which is attracting enormous audiences because of its' elaborate staging! The text is equally absurd; amongst other things, Vasco di Gama is imprisoned for maintaining that he had discovered lands not mentioned in 'Holy Scriptures'!!!! (By the way, à propos 'Holy Scriptures', my classical tutor is a parson!![8] I anticipate some lively arguments, but trust I shall not be turned out of the house as a 'heretick'!!)

The Opera here is splendidly done—acting, singing and staging being alike excellent: but good novelties are very scarce. Dr Fischer published last week an open letter to the 'Festspiel' committee, in which he urged them to put 'A Village Romeo and Juliet' on the stage here.

I hope Mr Beecham will give another concert of your works this year: I suppose the new choral work will be ready soon. I am longing to hear more of your

---

[7] *L'Africaine.*   [8] The Revd Clarence Rolt.

music, after all the Strauss, etc, that I have heard here with interest, but not much real enjoyment.

I fear I am writing a terribly dull letter: please excuse too the scrawl: I am writing by moonlight, as they have turned all the gas off, it being nearly mid-night!—So I am not completely master of my pen!

It is really time I ceased this meandering epistle. I am afraid I am rather a letter-writing maniac, and I seldom have anything interesting to say, so please tell me if my letters become intolerably boring, as I really have no doubt they do, and I will cease them!

So, with many many thanks for all your goodness to me, and as many peti-tions that you will visit us in the summer,

I remain
Very sincerely yours
Philip Heseltine

16
Frederick Delius to Philip Heseltine

Grez sur Loing
S & M
11/3 1912

Dear Mr Heseltine

Thanks so much for your nice letter—Do not be afraid to write to me when you feel like it—I love to receive your letters & assure you that they are never a bore to me—If you dont always get a quick & lengthy reply please do not attribute it to lack of interest—it will be because I am occupied with some-thing very absorbing—If ever you want some advice from someone who really likes you & feels real interest in your welfare you can come to me without the slightest restraint—On any subject or question whatever I will tell you what I really think & I can assure you that very few people ever tell one what they really think—When they do they are always invaluable—We leave for Berlin tomorrow & shall be away about 18 days—It is so lovely here that I hate to go—The garden is full of daffodils, primroses scyllas⁹ & flowering fruit trees

---

⁹ Scilla, a genus of lilaceous plants.

—I should love to wander about the Welsh hills with you & hope to come to see you next September

With best love,
I remain
very sincerely yours
Frederick Delius

17
Philip Heseltine to Frederick Delius

25. 3. 12.   Chadlington
                                                                        Oxfordshire

Dear Mr Delius

Your kind letter cheered and delighted me more than any other letter I have ever received: I do not know how to thank you enough for your sympathy and goodness to me. You are indeed my best friend in the world: a little sympathy o'erleaps years of mere acquaintanceship. I can never, never be sufficiently grateful to you for your kindness, and I value your friendship more than words can say—and my words are so weak. Still, I find it a joy to express things even in such poor words, and, as you permit me, I shall often and often write to you, but please do not ever think that I expect you to answer my most insignificant letters, when I know that you are occupied with work for the world and all time. It is a joy and a great privilege to me to be allowed to write to you at all, and I cannot tell you what a glorious relief it is for me to be able to write to someone who I know will not misunderstand me, or laugh at me, and to cast off restraint.

I have lately been pouring these effusions into a kind of impression-book, kept for the purpose, and even that is refreshing. My motto I have taken from a little work of a very great friend of mine—an extraordinary combination of a dreamer and an athlete, a visionary and a 'sportsman' (hateful word!)! He writes:—

'I am sitting down to write I know not what. Often and often comes this desire to express my innermost thoughts, ideas hardly formed, vague longings as of one wandering through a land of shadows, hovering forever on the edge of truth, and forever being drawn back into the realities of life. Realities—? who knows, perchance these dreams are the more real and the facts of the world but shadows . . .'

I, too, feel every word of that, but I cannot express my innermost thoughts even as well as he can: and I believe that if the 'sporting' element were eliminated from him, he would have much to express, and the power to do so.

It always seems to me that sport (especially blood sport, one of the curses of this country) is the complete antithesis of all art! And yet lately a man, by name Kelly,[10] who was of great renown as an 'oar' at Eton and elsewhere, and won some big race at Henley, (champion of England, or something of that kind) has appeared in London as a pianist with immense success. He was formerly a pupil of Colin Taylor's I believe. Another pupil of Colin Taylor's—a small person who has been a choir boy at Eton for the last year or so[11]—has just won a scholarship for piano-playing, open to all England, at the Royal College of Music!

Colin Taylor is a splendid man: I owe most of my love for music to him.

The first Balfour Gardiner[12] concert seems to have been a great success: I would have given anything to have been there, to hear the works of Percy Grainger,[13] and the Dance Rhapsody again.[14] The Faero Island Ballad[15] must be enormously stirring! I think the words are quite delightful in their naïve simplicity, especially such verses as:

'Forth from the scabbard his sword he drew,
Hacked her lover in pieces two.'

which is one of the best things I've seen for a long time!

This place is exceedingly dull, but six hours work daily relieves the monotony; I have no consuming love for classics, but as a means to an end they are interesting enough, and I must say, people like Aeschylus and Plato are very fine indeed. The religeous atmosphere of the house is apt to be tedious at times,— in my pension in Cologne everyone was, happily, agnostic. But the parson here,

[10] Frederick Septimus Kelly (1881–1916), Australian pianist and composer. He was educated at Eton and Oxford (where he was known as a first-class oarsman) and later studied composition under Knorr at Frankfurt. He was killed in action in France.

[11] Morgan Nicholas (Heseltine wrote to Taylor: 'How splendid Nicholas getting that scholarship! It is awfully good, and I congratulate you on his performance.' Heseltine to Taylor, 6 Mar. 1912, BL 54197).

[12] Balfour Gardiner (1877–1950), English composer and promoter of concerts. Gardiner was particularly generous to Delius, easing his financial burden (from the lack of royalties from scores in the hands of German and Austrian publishers), by buying his house at Grez so that he could live there rent-free for the rest of his life. The contract was drawn up in Nov. 1923. He also assisted in the checking of proofs.

[13] Percy Grainger (1882–1961), Australian-born pianist and composer who studied at the Frankfurt Conservatorium. He became a great admirer of Delius's music.

[14] The programme for the first Balfour Gardiner Concert (13 Mar. 1912) consisted of: Bax, *Enchanted Summer*; Delius, *Dance Rhapsody* (No. 1); Grainger, *Irish Tune from County Derry* and *Faeroe Isles Dance*; Gardiner, *News from Whydah*; three works by Grainger (*Morning Song in the Jungle*, *Tiger! Tiger!*, *We have fed our seas for a thousand years*), and W. H. Bell, *The Baron of Brackley*.

[15] *Faeroe Isles Dance: Father and Daughter*, Grainger.

with whom I work, is exceedingly clever and interesting—really much too good for a parson, though one can't altogether get away from the parsonic atmosphere, and his sister has a positive mania for 'missions', and meetings of all kinds, on religeous subjects—meetings are held with the utmost regularity; almost daily there is some sort of religeous gathering. I suggested that she should form a literary society for the poorer people in the village, to read Shakespere and improve the mind generally, but was met with the reply that it was much better to stick to the 'working party' *for the encouragement of 'missions' in Canada*!!!! Canada, of all places under the sun! If you Christianize a savage, you do at least civilize him, as well as inculcating in him loads of useless nonsense: but spending time and money on civilized Britons in Canada—or, rather, not on them, but on a fetish you want them to accept—!!

You can imagine my feelings at this kind of remark—as also the type of person that makes it!

Still, I keep silence to avoid useless strife, as after all I have got to live here for the next 6 months or so. N.B. while this money is being squandered in Canada, men, women and children are starving in England, on account of a coal strike, which is itself the outcome of those excellent Christians, the coalowners!

I am beginning to hate all this mawkish, sentimental Christianity of misdirected efforts, and blind faith. Apart from the somewhat useless doctrines of 'redemption' and 'forgiveness of sin' and particulars of the next life, I admire the philosophy of Christ: but Christianity is a totally different thing. I think it is its' unquestioning smugness that makes it so hateful, and just points the difference between true philosophy as a guide to life, and 'religeon', which I suppose is founded on philosophy, but is completely tangled up in a network of useless if not pernicious dogmas, and has become a fetish in itself.

Most of these clever Christians have exceedingly clever and long-winded explanations of all these theories which appear so rotten, and I have no doubt that if I started arguing with this good priest here, I should be defeated in argument, without, however, being in the slightest bit convinced, if not made more hostile to Christianity by the very arguments that were meant to (and logically, I suppose, would) convince me of its' truth!

I should very much value your views on this subject, when you have time to write: not because I am distressed at the collapse of 'my faith' during the last 12 months!!—but because I find questions of this kind extremely interesting.

My private views are completely agnostic, though here and at home I have to play the part of a faithful Christian! At home I even read the lessons in church!! —such supremely idiotic tales, sometimes: I wonder how they have ever survived! If my mother suspected my real opinions, I should never hear the end of it! She even objects to my being a Socialist! A word against monarchy is like a red rag to a bull at home: the situation, however, is vastly amusing, as they never have a single argument *for* it!! Personally I believe Socialism (in which I do *not* include Communism as so many anti-Socialists do) is the only scheme which can save this country from the present entirely rotten state of affairs: the world hardly seems ripe for anarchy and individualism just yet, though I thoroughly agree with you in regarding the latter as an ideal scheme for 'Utopia' . . . But religeon and politics are distressing themes!

Have you ever come across the poems of Alfred Noyes?[16] I have been reading some lately with wild enthusiasm: I think they are some of the most beautiful I have ever seen. I expect you have read them: I thought them very striking.

I hope your Berlin concert[17] was a success, and also that you will give poor London another opportunity in the near future.

I must really stop this rigmarole—besides, my candle has almost burnt itself out!

Above all things, *please* do not ever think about bothering to answer: I am a bad hand at answering myself, though I have no excuse: I should have answered your last letter before, but, honestly, my feelings on receiving your letter were so exalted and overjoyed that I could hardly bring myself to an answer in cold, blank words of mine—which seems incongruous, since I so much desired to write to you and that without restraint, but I know you will understand: there is always the restraint in mere words, to a certain extent, unless one is a complete master of language, which I am far from being!

This letter is hopelessly inadequate for what I wanted to express, but forgive poor me who can do no better!

I am longing to see you again—in Wales.

Meanwhile I remain Yours in devotion and gratitude,
Philip Heseltine

PS. I experienced a certain type of English musical critic last week, in a manner that shows him up rather well! Having noticed an extremely caustic and bitter article in the 'Musical Times' about Arnold Schönberg,[18] which contained much would-be witticism and *no* information, I prepared another article, based on two papers from Dr Fischer's 'Musik-Zeitung' and Schönberg's own book, and wrote to the editor of the 'Musical Times' and asked him if he would like a little information about Schönberg, since judging by what he had printed about him he didn't seem to have any, and also adding that it

[16] Alfred Noyes (1880–1958), English poet.   [17] Oskar Fried conducted *Paris*.
[18] 'Occasional Notes', *Musical Times* (1912), 164. Amongst other things the editor wrote, 'We remind our readers that to our commonplace intelligences these manifestations of the newest Viennese spirit seem to be constructed, with fiendish ingenuity, out of the very antithesis and negation of music.'

would only be fair to Schönberg to publish a few facts about him after such a critical attack.

He replied (without even asking me to send the article for perusal) that *he did not know enough* of Schönberg's music to be able to decide in his own (rotten) mind whether S. was 'either sane or serious' and *therefore*, would not admit an 'appreciation' (as he called what I expressly told him was a plain statement of facts) into his paper! One gathers that ignorance warrants the complete damning of a new composer, though it forbids a fair consideration of his work!

Personally Schönberg's music strikes me as *utterly barbarous* beyond description, but I think he must be sincere or he would not bother to write music at all. Anyway he is probably a far better musician than Messrs W. G. McNaught[19] & Frederick Corder[20] who damn him!

18
Frederick Delius to Philip Heseltine

Grez sur Loing
(S&M)
April 28 1911 [i.e. 1912]

Dear Heseltine—

Your letter was forwarded on to me—I received it in Berlin some 3 weeks ago where I had gone en route for Munich & Venice[21]—Whilst in Berlin I heard 'Paris' excellently given by Oskar Fried—your letter gave me the greatest pleasure & I am so glad that you look upon me as a real friend—long acquaintanceship means nothing whatever—You are just going thro' what I have also gone thro' & I own that until I had become an entire disbeliever in any Life here-after I was constantly in a very unsatisfactory state of mind—Read *Nietzsche*[22]—the 'Anti Christ'—'Beyond good & evil'—Christianity is paralysing

---

[19] William McNaught (1849–1918), English writer, teacher, and choral conductor; editor of *Musical Times* from 1909.

[20] Frederick Corder (1852–1932), professor of composition at the Royal Academy of Music from 1888.

[21] The Deliuses travelled from Grez to Berlin on 12 Mar., after which they visited Munich and then moved on to Venice where they stayed at a palazzo rented by Lady Cunard.

[22] Friedrich Nietzsche (1844–1900), German philosopher. Selections from Nietzsche's *Also sprach Zarathustra* formed the text of Delius's *Mass of Life*. Both Frederick and Jelka were ardent Nietzscheans.

—If one is sincere it utterly unfits one for Life—If hypocritical one becomes hateful to oneself—And thenceforward one can only live amongst similar hypocrites—England & America have, I believe, the monopoly of such The moment you chuck all this rot over board Life becomes interesting—wonderful —& one gets a great desire to make something of it—*to live it to its full* One enjoys things more thoroughly—*one feels Nature*—there is no reason whatever for any doctrine or religion. Savages have superstitions which they form into a sort of religion & perform certain rites & we have nothing more with the exception that Priests invented a System to rule over Kings & the Kings used the system & the Priests to subdue the masses—the superstition often remains even when the belief in the System is gone—See table turning & spirit rapping etc—Be free—believe in Nature—it is quite enough & by far the most satis-factory standpoint—there is a great deal we do not understand—Every day one understands more—in a thousand years they will be considerably farther altho' I do not believe that certain things will ever be understood & why should they?—I cannot stand the moral atmosphere of England & therefore I live here—to send missions to China or Canada is merely ignorance & stupidity— When I come to see you in September we will talk about these things—I am but a poor writer—I stayed 12 days in Venice at the Palazzo of Lady Cunard[23] & enjoyed my stay altho' the weather was icy—the arrival at Venice at night & being fetched from the railway station in a gondola made a great impression on me—The celebrated paintings in the Churches & galleries with one or two exceptions I did not care for—I infinitely prefer modern painting to these old buffers with their saints, Jesuses & Virgin Marys—May I never see their faces again! I except a painting of the Crucifixion by Tintoretto[24]—Musical Criticism is another fraud—Our critics are nearly always composers who have failed & who have become bitter—Every musician of genius brings something which belongs entirely to himself & cannot be criticised by miserable failures who have stuck fast & crystalised Write to me soon again. I love receiving your letters —Our garden is too lovely just now & we were so happy to get back to Grez again We arrived last Wednesday Perhaps you will come over here in the summer we should be delighted to see you here again. I remain, with best love, your sincere friend

Frederick Delius

[23] Maud Lady Cunard (1872–1948), American-born, wealthy and brilliant hostess and patron of the arts. In 1895 she married Sir Bache Cunard Bt., a grandson of one of the founders of the Cunard Line, and was for a time Beecham's mistress. Her Grosvenor Square salon was an important centre of London society and many an aspiring musician, author, poet, and artist cultivated her.
[24] Jacopo Robusti Tintoretto (1518–94), Italian painter of the Renaissance. His *Crucifixion* (1565) is one of his most awe-inspiring works, described by Ruskin as 'beyond all analysis and above all praise'.

19

Philip Heseltine to Frederick Delius

May 5th 1912   Chadlington
                                                                           Oxon

Dear Mr Delius

Thank you a thousand times for your splendid letter which I received last
Tuesday: how *can* you say you are a poor writer? I cannot tell you what infinite
pleasure it gives me to receive your letters: it is *exceedingly* good of you to write
to me at all.

We must certainly talk of the matters you mention when you come over in
September: I shall be deeply interested to hear your views. Personally, I am inclined
to believe in future existences of some kind—of *what* kind is, of course, a profound mystery—though I do not think one should regulate one's life in this
world by a confident expectancy of just retribution in the next world. The old
Christian ideas of Heaven and Hell were, of course, quite fatuous, but that is
all done away with now. I am more inclined to believe in a chain of evolution-
ary existences (whether in this actual world or elsewhere), in which the soul, or
whatever one calls that part of oneself that is beyond the mere body, is constantly striving after an ideal—somewhat in the nature of a higher Buddhism.
I would sooner believe in complete annihilation than in Nietzsche's doctrine
of 'Eternal Recurrence', which seems to me a most unpleasant thought! Also,
it does not seem to *lead* anywhere: why should there be a 'thus far and no
further' in a timeless infinity? But as all theories of future existences are merely
speculative, everyone must, I suppose, believe what he likes . . I do not think,
however, that the work of such institutions as the Society for Psychical Research
is to be ignored, or that it may not lead to all-important discoveries in the future
which will throw light on much that is now obscure. I have read a book by
one J. M. Kennedy called 'The Quintessence of Nietzsche',[25] which, I must confess, did not impress me at all favourably, but of course one cannot form any
opinion of a man's philosophy from mere selections: I will certainly read the
books you mention.

Christianity is a very vast term: a great many of the so-called Christian
sects are only caricatures of Christianity: I see very little difference between the
Roman Catholic religeon and that of a primitive savage: the R. C's are, I think,

---

[25] John McFarland Kennedy, *The Quintessence of Nietzsche* (London, 1909).

the most degraded in their religeon and those chiefly responsible for the distorted ideas of Christianity: even their fellow-Christians admit that, e.g. George
Borrow and hosts of others. Of course there are things in the English sects
which are every bit as bad, but on the whole they are better, I think. Anyway,
there is none of the hypocritical nonsense-formulae of Ave Marias and Pater
Nosters and holy water and other bilge of that kind. Personally I loathe all
dogma, and churches and chapels and all the other paraphernalia of religeon: I
cannot see why ethics should be mixed up with religeon at all. There are certain things in the philosophy of Jesus that I admire immensely: but let it be a
philosophy and not a religeon! Kennedy quotes the following passage from
'Zarathustra', which I think is excellent:—'When I came unto men, then found
I them resting on an old infatuation: all of them thought they had long known
what was good and what was bad for men . . . . This somnolence did I disturb
when I taught that *no one yet knoweth* what is good and bad'. It is obvious
that everyone must have his own ideal, of whatever kind it be, and strive after
it. It is the smug self-confidence of Christians that I detest: if their schemes
are all so infallibly correct, let them demonstrate them and convince others,
for I am sure everyone would be willing to agree with them *if* they could prove
their superiority! 'If God has spoken, why is the universe not convinced?' as
Shelley quoted from somebody. As you say, Christianity is paralysing: but that
power of paralysing is most useful when applied to the criminal classes, as
it is by the 'Salvation Army' (mark the title!) and other kindred institutions,
with excellent effect! For in a country where there are laws, there must be a
fixed standard of some kind of morality, and so one may legitimately speak of
'criminals'.

I must admit, I dislike intensely Nietzsche's love of war, his taking Physical
Force as the foundation of everything (for this is how I understand him from
Kennedy's book, though as that is my only authority, please forgive me if I'm
mistaken). I cannot see that the question 'Who is to be master of the world'
matters two straws. That is the English aggressive-Tory-Conservative policy:
why should not each nation, each individual live his own life, without inter-
fering with or depending on anyone else? Personally I am an absolutely convinced Socialist, though that term is so loosely used nowadays that it is very apt
to be misunderstood.

The most satisfactory explanation of the Christian theory of *power* (not that
it need be Christian, but I met it in a book, written by a Christian and so it is
developed into a Christian theory) is that *all power is based on endurance*, and
that the whole of Nature's physical forces put together would be insufficient to
crush the *spirit of Man*—this, of course, postulates the existance of a soul or
spirit apart from the mere body.

Hence 'God' or whatever one calls the origin of Life, is merely the spirit of what *is ultimately good* (whether men know it to be good or not): this point is also found in Plato. On the other hand, there is 'Evil'—(Satan or the Devil or Mephistopheles!!) which consists not only of moral evil, but also of all misfortunes, such as disease, torture, death etc, with which God and the good are at enmity. But God has no physical power, either to compel or to avert: he is not the cause or even the approver of calamities: he can only help men to *conquer them by enduring them*, and coming off none the worse, except perhaps for the loss of the paltry human body. Of this Jesus was a typical example, who appeared to be none the worse three days after he was crucified! Such is the theory! I do not know enough to be able to judge whether it is at all plausible or not, but I thought it might interest you. It is the *only* theory that could make Christianity *rational*, even if every word in Christian literature were *proved* to be true! The old idea of a God of unlimited brute force and power to coerce, who yet allowed the existance of all the horrors that take place on this earth, and then came 'to die to redeem the world of sin' (whatever that means or ever did mean!!!) is, of course, unworthy of serious consideration.

The author of the theory I have stated above is my present tutor, but apparently the idea has been hinted at before: He quotes in his book[26] these lines of Shelley, which seem to bear on the point:—

'Gentleness, Virtue, Wisdom and Endurance,
These are the seals of that most firm assurance
Which bars the pit over Destruction's strength;
And if, with infirm hand, Eternity,
Mother of many acts and hours, should free
The serpent that would clasp her with his length,
These are the spells by which to reassume
An empire o'er the disentangled doom.
To suffer woes which Hope thinks infinite;
To forgive wrongs darker than death or night:
To defy Power, which seems omnipotent;
To love, and bear, to hope till Hope creates
From its' own wreck the thing it contemplates;
Neither to change, nor falter, nor repent;
This, like thy glory, Titan, is to be
Good, great and joyous, beautiful and free;
This is alone Life, Joy, Empire and Victory.'
(Prometheus Unbound: act 4)

[26] C. E. Rolt, *The World's Redemption* (London, 1913).

At the same time, there is something about Christianity—to my mind, at any rate—whether in itself, or the people who practise it, or their formulae, dogmas, creeds, churches, sunday-schools and sunday-dullness, and the thousands of other things connected with religeon, prayers, thanksgivings and, above all, those 'hymns', whose words and so-called music absolutely baffle description,—which is disgusting and loathsome in the highest degree: I suppose it is the servile spirit with relation to God, rather than the mere ethical code: I cannot quite define that something, but it is there, and very strong.[27]

The average Englishman, it strikes me, loves servility and grovelling, for all his boasted love of liberty, and states the fact pretty plainly by supporting such a disgusting system as an hereditary monarchy! The 'moral atmosphere' of England is certainly curious! I imagine, however, that the country is slowly recovering: I think we are now in a state of convalescence after the scourge of prudery, which came in an exaggerated form with the nineteenth century in England, just as British music has only of late years recovered from the equally disastrous scourge of Mendelssohnism! Mendelssohn and prudes go well together, I think!

Musical criticism does seem a queer thing, certainly! But I suppose there must be writers *on* music who are not writers *of* music. There is at least one critic in England who has not 'broken down' as a composer, namely George Clutsam: he is apparently going strong, and on May 17th will have the second of his so-called 'miniature-grand-operas'[28] produced, within three weeks of the production of the first! I liked his opera 'A Summer Night' very much indeed. Ernest Newman[29] and Robin Legge[30] seem to be good writers: the latter has given Balfour Gardiner's concerts the most enthusiastic notices I have ever read. Yesterday he published in the 'Daily Telegraph' an article on J. W. Davison,[31] the celebrated anti-Schumann anti-Wagner critic, which contained this apt limerick:—

> 'There was a J. W. D.
> Who thought a composer to be,
> But his muse would'nt budge,

[27] The Revd Mr Rolt strongly disapproved of Delius's increasing influence over the young Heseltine and wrote to Mrs Buckley Jones: 'Again Philip's admiration for Mr Delius is not without dangers. Mr Delius is, I have no doubt, far better than his theories (or he could not write good music) but the intimacy of a Nietzschian cannot be a good thing for a boy of his age.' Rolt to Edith Buckley Jones, 7 June 1912, BL 57964. He wrote again two months later: 'In fact Phil's theories in many matters (or at least in some) are quite unlike himself; & this is, I believe, due to the fact that he has imbibed them from Delius. . . . I am not necessarily blaming Delius for hating Christianity . . . But I do say that the harm which may be done by his influence to Phil now that the boy's mind is in a plastic state (& he has a very receptive & quite acute mind with, of course, absolutely *no* experience of life) is quite incalculable.' Rolt to Edith Buckley Jones, 5 Aug. 1913, ibid.
[28] *After a Thousand Years*, produced at the Tivoli in Apr. 1912.
[29] Ernest Newman (1868–1959), music critic, notably of the *Observer* (1919–20) and the *Sunday Times* (1920–58).
[30] Robin Legge (1862–1933), music critic of *The Daily Telegraph* (1906–31).
[31] James William Davison (1813–85), music critic of *The Times* (1864–79).

> So he set up as judge
> Over better composers than he.' (!)

I don't know whether you read the 'Musical Times': I was much amused to read in last month's issue the following, under the heading of 'Music in Manchester':—

'The past season has witnessed the laying of the Delius-bogey; this fearsome ultra-modernist has been represented by the 'Brigg Fair' and 'Appalachia' Variations, in addition to the 'Rhapsody', and the Manchester public has vigorously applauded, evidently finding him much to its' taste'.[32] (!!!!)

I am going to the first performance of Holbrooke's[33] 'Children of Don'[34] next month: I should dearly love to go up to London for Percy Grainger's concert this month, but I am afraid I shall not be able to do so. What you say about the 'old buffers' pleases me hugely!

Alfred Noyes' poems are published in two volumes by Blackwood: I expect you could get them at Galignani's in Paris. Two of the best books of English poetry I know are The Oxford Book of English Verse,[35] and the Dublin Book of Irish Verse, which are admirable selections of poetry of all periods, down to the present day. I wonder if you have come across them? Has my uncle shewn you the remarkable book of poems by Patrick McGill?[36] He seems to be distributing copies broadcast. He sent me a copy and I thought them exceedingly good . . . . . Is your new choral work set to an English text? I should be *most* interested to hear about it . . . . . . I seem to have written at great length again without very much point! Please forgive my lengthy dissertations on Christianity, etc: I really know so little that I have no right to hold views on such large subjects, only I am convinced that everyone, however ignorant, must make up his mind one way or the other, even if he alter it a hundred times, and that at no period of one's life can one be without opinions of some kind, however ignorant or absurd.

---

[32] *Musical Times* (1912), 264.   [33] Joseph Holbrooke (1878–1958), English composer.

[34] *The Children of Don* is the first part of an operatic trilogy of Wagnerian proportions called *The Cauldron of Annwyn*. It was first performed at the London Opera House on 15 June 1912 conducted by Nikisch. The London Opera house (on Kingsway) was built by Oscar Hammerstein in 1911 but abandoned after one unsuccessful season.

[35] Heseltine duly sent Delius a copy of *The Oxford Book of English Verse*. In an accompanying note he wrote: 'Here is the "Oxford Book"—too full of good things for me to make a selection for you. However, look particularly at the first thing in the book (no 1), the quaint 4-line (no 27), n°s 48, 121, 248, and all the Shakespeare lyrics. Of the moderns, see Bridge's "My delight and thy delight" (no 832). I will send you "A Shropshire Lad" and William Blake's poems in a day or so. The lyrics of the latter are wonderful for music.' Tomlinson, *Warlock and Delius*, 15. Tomlinson suggests that the book was sent by Heseltine to Delius as late as 1915.

[36] Patrick MacGill (1890–?), English poet. Heseltine had also written to Taylor about him: 'Have you come across the very remarkable ex-navvy poet Patrick MacGill, who is now private secretary to Canon Dalton, and lives at 4 The Cloisters, Windsor Castle? His verses are very remarkable indeed: until last year he was a poor navvy in the Caledonian R, but he seems to have picked up an enormous amount of knowledge, in spite of the fact, and must have a real gift for poetry. He is only 21.' Heseltine to Taylor, 24 May 1912, BL 54197.

If you really do not mind receiving letters like this, you are exceedingly kind, for it is an immense relief to be able to talk about these matters freely, especially with you, who can *really* give advice, and not merely quote so-called 'eternal laws' and 'divine commands' and that sort of thing!

I am rejoiced to think you are definitely coming in September. I'm afraid there's no chance of my coming to France this year. Good-bye for the present: this being the day of the week consecrated to Lethal dullness.

I have now to go and '*read the lessons*' for my parsonic tutor in church!!!!!!

It saves endless arguments, to go to church! But, Alas! hypocrisy! I am in such a mental muddle that I scarcely know what I really *do* believe!!

Please remember me very kindly to Mrs Delius.

Yours affectionately
Philip Heseltine

P.S. Just returned from the orgy of howls called '*divine service*'—think of it! It is somewhat trying to hear large numbers of voices shrieking forth dogmas half a tone below the note supplied for them by the organist, and this is what invariably occurs! Such divine sounds can, I suppose, only be appreciated by the noble army[37] of Schönbergians, or better still, those precious 'futurists' who assert that an octave contains *seventy-two notes* (!!) and write music accordingly!

20
Philip Heseltine to Frederick Delius

24. 5. 12.   Chadlington
                                                                 Oxon.

Dear Mr Delius

I wonder whether you were afflicted with a violent fit of the shudders last night about 9. o'clock—because at that hour 'Brigg Fair' was being positively *murdered* in Oxford by one Dr H. P Allen,[38] directing an amateur orchestra, augmented by wind players from the London Symphony Orchestra![39] I am

---

[37] cf. the *Te Deum Laudamus*, v. 9 ('The noble army of Martyrs praise Thee').

[38] Hugh Percy Allen (1869–1946), organist at New College, Oxford. He later became professor of music at Oxford, 1918–46, and director of the Royal College of Music, 1918–37.

[39] The concert took place in the Oxford Town Hall on 23 May, under the auspices of the Oxford Music Club. The programme also included the overture to *The Bartered Bride* (Smetana) and the overture to *A Midsummer Night's Dream* (Mendelssohn). Heseltine wrote to Taylor about the concert: 'Yet it was a very great treat to hear "Brigg Fair" again

perfectly furious about the performance: *three in a bar* just the same as at Coblenz, only *slower*, if anything!! It was too appalling: the orchestra played with little or no spirit, and the splendid climax just after $\boxed{14}$ was quite missed. $\boxed{22}$ and onwards was a trifle better, but still dragged, and, as before, $\boxed{26}$ and following sections were taken much too fast, with an entire absence of solemnity, and, incidentally, of expression. The trumpet, at section $\boxed{26}$, not content with playing 'f', and fiendishly out of tune, tried his best, for the first bar or so, to play his part twice as fast as even the conductor desired! Three in a bar, of course, where 'gaily' is marked, and at the lovely, lingering passage of descending sevenths, the wretched conductor entirely ignored the 'rallentando'—which made me particularly angry, since it was pure carelessness, and those four bars are very specially dear to me. The performance lasted exactly sixteen minutes.

It is horrible that such travesties of your work should appear before the public: the orchestra played badly, and I am sure no conductor, who had any idea of the spirit of the work could possibly beat three in a bar in the first movement. Dr Allen is organist of New College, Oxford, and is supposed to be a good musician: he is to share the conducting of the next Leeds festival with Nikisch!![40] However I would always go miles to hear any kind of performance of 'Brigg Fair': I will not weary you by repeating how much I love your works —how they seem to *speak* to me far more than any other music: it is no use attempting to say so in words: but you know what I feel. After 'Brigg Fair' came an exceedingly tedious symphony by Stanford (no 7: opus 124!!), reeking of the Victorian age! It is almost pathetic that such belated things continue to appear! A great deal of this symphony might have been written by Sullivan! Stanford conducted it himself. Afterwards came Beethoven's C minor, which I liked very much indeed, though I cannot understand the people who say Beethoven was by far the greatest musician that ever lived. I could not resist a wish that the Scherzo should lead into the opening bars of the 'Meistersinger' Overture, instead of into the proper finale!!

Percy Grainger's concert seems to have been a huge success: I should like to have been there. I am going to 'The Children of Don' next month.

You ought to be here next Monday for the 'Missionary pageant' (!) organized by the parson's sister—a mission-maniac of the most revolting order!!!!! The 'libretto' is enough to make a cat sick! I am getting about fed up with all this religeous tomfoolery.

at all, in spite of the performance: every time I hear a work of Delius, it seems more and more appealing, more *absolutely perfect*—to my mind, at least: I know no other music that appeals to me anything like as much as his does, and knowing Delius makes it even more lovely—if possible. I can never be too thankful for my good fortune in getting to know him.' Heseltine to Taylor, 24 May 1912, BL 54197.

[40] Artur Nikisch (1855–1922), Hungarian conductor and violinist. He conducted the first performances of *On Hearing the First Cuckoo in Spring* and *Summer Night on the River* at Leipzig on 23 Oct. 1913.

I am afraid I have no more news, as this place is still swamped in dullness, so I will subside for the present.

Yours affectionately
Philip Heseltine

Can nothing be done to prevent further travesties of 'Brigg Fair' being perpetrated? I believe Dʳ Allen conducts all over the country, and he might do it again. Awful thought!

21
Frederick Delius to Philip Heseltine

Grez sur Loing
(S&M)
23 June 1912

Forgive me, my dear, Heseltine, for leaving your interesting letters unanswered. I am working hard on a new Choral & Orchestral work & am already far advanced[41]—I consider Nietzsche the only free thinker of modern times & for me the most sympathetic one—He is at the same time such a poet. He feels nature. I believe, myself, in no doctrine whatever—& in nothing but in Nature & the great forces of Nature—I believe in complete annihilation as far as our personal consciousness goes—Matter, of course, is in an eternal state of change & evolution—In the great Scheme of Nature Man is no more important than a flie—Is Dʳ Allen a young man? I have noticed that only the young conductors understand my work. I did not have a fit of the shudders which shews me how little Dʳ Allen was in touch with me. At the end of next month I intend going to Norway for a 3 weeks walking tour in the mountains—Doesn't it tempt you? I love Norway & the Norwegian peasants. I consider Percy Grainger the most gifted English composer & the only one who writes English music—& he is an Australian—There is something of the old English robustness & vigor in his music[42]—that part of England which has long ago ceased to exist—or

---

[41] Probably *The Song of the High Hills*.
[42] Heseltine quoted this sentence in a letter to Taylor, 27 June 1912, BL 54197.

which has emigrated. Write me soon again & tell me all you are doing & thinking & believe me

Affectionately yours
Frederick Delius

The garden here is simply lovely now—

[Written on the back of the envelope] I do not know the Poems of Alfred Noyes?
Where can I get them—

22
Philip Heseltine to Frederick Delius

7. 7. 12.   4 Broadway
                                                      Hemel Hempstead

Dear Mr Delius

A thousand thanks for your most interesting letter, which was forwarded
to me here some days past. I left Chadlington on June 12th, and after a week
in London came on to this little town in Hertfordshire, 25 miles out of London, where my tutor is undergoing a 'cure' at a Eustace Miles[43] vegetarian diet
establishment, prior to beginning work in his new parish in Warwickshire,
which he will do in August. My fellow pupil and I are *not* partaking of nuts
and vegetables, needless to say! We have separate lodgings, and it is a great relief
to be out of a parsonage for a brief respite! The 'curé'[44] is a very meek and
harmless person, but, of course, frightfully bigoted, as they all are—I thought
at first he was more broadminded than the common run, but that was quite a
fallacy on my part. However, he affords endless amusement to his two pupils!
Thank goodness I have completely thrown off the shackles of Christianity—
'the Church'—(supposed to be one and the same thing, but really they are
quite different—the latter is much the worst). Church bells are jangling at this
moment, and giving me exactly the contrary impression to that with which
they are probably 'inspiring' the majority of their hearers all over the country.
When will that 'Messiah' come who will deliver the world from the bonds of
superstition and all the utter tomfoolery connected with Christianity? I suppose

---

[43] Eustace Miles (1868–1948), English educationalist and founder of the Normal Physical School. He wrote several
books on health and fitness.
[44] The Revd Clarence Rolt.

you will say to that 'Nietzsche has come as such, and the world has not received him', even as Christians say the same of Jesus to Jews who expect the coming of their Messiah—not that I wish to compare their respective merits by drawing the comparison: only that Christians are every bit as confident of the supreme excellence of Jesus' teaching as Nietzscheans are of Nietzsche, and Jews of Moses and Co. And *there* seems to be the deadlock! Personally I believe in a great part of the philosophy of Jesus (provided all the *religeous* element is thrown overboard), but a good deal of it, even then, is quite unoriginal. But as for the thing called 'the church'—I do not think there is any word in any language that can describe it's utter, childish, quibbling bilgewater nonsense, which it solemnly puts forward for it's adherents to swallow without question. A typical example is 'marriage with a deceased wife's sister'!! How anyone can 'get married' in a church I simply cannot understand. For what is 'getting married', I should like to know? It seems to me that, whatever it is, any third party is wholly superfluous, more especially if he be a canting priest with a book of formulae and directions!

Your tour in Norway sounds quite delightful, but I hope the grandeur of the fiords will not make Wales seem dull and uninteresting to you by comparison when you come in September. I am going home this week for about a fortnight, on my motor-cycle—a delightful mode of progression: I can almost entirely dispense with stuffy trains now—after which I shall spend August with the parson in Warwickshire, working away at the writings of fatuous windbags like Cicero, whose works' survival I lament almost daily. Classical study is frightfully tedious work, and I confess I cannot see the smallest particle of use in it: the languages are dead, and, as Patrick M°Gill says, 'Dead languages should be buried.' As for the subject-matter, it is very often absolutely worthless, except to antiquarians, and where there is interest and knowledge, translations would do just as well. Besides which, there is an indefinable 'classical spirit' which one meets in schoolmasters and professors, which seems to me something akin to the dogmatic, quibbling ideas of the theologist, and is therefore hateful. But still, until the whole educational scheme of the country changes, I suppose one must put up with it: I, for one, have no other opening for a profession, so must grind away as best I can for the next six years. I am always cursing my fate that, not being a mule that will take anything given to it without thought or question, I have been born without any capacity for doing anything useful, or artistic. If only I could write!—words or music—! After all, this classical work is just mechanical: anyone can do it with a little practise there is not a spark of creative ability evoked or cultivated. For writing Latin verses, which is supposed to be creative work, is only the baldest imitation—the more one can remember what real Roman poets have said on one's subject, even to interpolating their words and phrases, the better one's verses are considered to be! A precious lot of originality in that! But after all, I have very little to grumble at really: it is only because, like Icarus, I want to fly higher than I am able to: and I suppose I must regard his fate!

I am so very pleased to hear that 'Sea-Drift' is to be given at the Birmingham Festival: I look forward to the occasion with immense delight. I have heard quite a lot of music in London lately—including Clutsam's 'wordless mediaeval idyll', 'The Pool' at the Alhambra, Holbrooke's 'Children of Don', the Russian Ballet, with Balakirev's 'Thamar' (designed by Leon Bakst[45]) and the quite astounding 'L'Oiseau de Feu' of Stravinsky, and some English music at a 'Keats-Shelley matinée', which included some utter filth by Hubert Parry and Coleridge Taylor,[46] and a prelude to 'Adonaïs'[47] by Arnold Bax, which I believe was very good, but, according to the delightful English custom that prevails at London theatres, everyone talks at the top of their voice during any piece of music which is played while the curtain is down, so the piece was for the most part inaudible! I was very sorry, since I am particularly anxious to hear a work of Bax: his songs are among the most beautiful I know. One piece, however, Keats' 'La Belle Dame sans Merci', [Op. 31] for baritone and orchestra by Norman O' Neill,[48] I liked immensely: it is one of the best pieces of English music I have heard for some time. It had a stage setting, the first three verses being sung by 'a woodman', and the rest by the 'knight-at-arms'—Frederic Austin,[49] whom I admire very much indeed—as much as any English singer I have yet heard.

I did not like Holbrooke's opera very much: E. A. Baughan[50] said its' chief point was 'sheer musical loquacity', in which I think he was right. The libretto is quite preposterous, and about as much British as Chinese as far as the drama goes (nobody can follow the plot!), for all the big talk about an 'all-British opera'! Of course, the work would never have seen the light but for Lord Howard de Walden's[51] money, I suppose!

By the way, I read in some paper or other that it was rumoured that in the autumn there was going to be a season of opera in English, by English singers, in London, and *only* works by British composers to be performed! A fascinating report! Do you know if there is any foundation for it? Colin Taylor told me

---

[45] Léon Bakst (1866–1924), Russian painter and designer and an influential member of Diaghilev's circle.

[46] Samuel Coleridge-Taylor (1875–1912), English composer.

[47] The performance, conducted by Norman O'Neill, took place on 25 June 1912 at the Haymarket Theatre. The work was unpublished and the MS has been lost.

[48] Norman O'Neill (1875–1934), English composer and theatre music conductor/director who studied in Frankfurt. He composed incidental music for numerous productions, including *Mary Rose* and *The Bluebird*.

[49] Frederic Austin (1872–1952), English baritone and composer. He was the soloist in the first English and subsequent early performances of *Sea Drift*.

[50] Edward Algernon Baughan (1865–1938), English music critic and writer on music.

[51] Baron Howard de Walden (Thomas Evelyn Scott-Ellis) (1880–1946). He was the librettist for Joseph Holbrooke's operatic trilogy, *The Cauldron of Anwyn*.

that an exceedingly fine opera[52] had been written by one Gustav von Holst, who is said to be an Englishman in spite of his German name. I have never heard any of his music, but I expect you have.

Do you not find it somewhat depressing to think of Death as complete annihilation, while you are enjoying Life? It seems to me that the more one finds Life to be worth living, the more one must regret the prospect of sure and certain death to follow, if that death is to be as nothing. But if death is a mystery, and after-death a vast surprise, (in one's own imagination), that, I think, would make death far less formidable. I cannot adopt the attitude of contented resignation, which William Watson[53] suggests:—

> 'Not ours, say some, the thought of death to dread,
> Asking no heaven, we fear no fabled hell;
> Life is a feast, and we have banqueted:
> Shall not the worms as well?'

The last lines of his poem are significant, to my mind:—

> 'And, ah, to know not . . . . . .
> Whether 'tis ampler day divinelier lit
> Or joyless night without.'[54]

(I cannot quote quite correctly but that is its gist.)[55]

Personally, I do not find it painful merely *not to know* what comes next: an attitude of mysterious expectancy would be pleasant: but I should least of all like to lie on my death-bed in the sure and certain hope of being *Nothing* within a few moments.

I should say Dr Allen is between 40 and 50 years of age: he is said to be in sympathy with most modern music, but I should doubt the truth of such a reputation for him. I believe he busies himself a good deal with singing competitions. By the way, can the Willem Kes, who murdered 'Brigg Fair' at Coblenz,

---

[52] Probably Holst's three-act opera, *Sita* (1899–1906). It had received an honourable mention in the Ricordi competition, the result of which was announced in 1908.

[53] Sir William Watson (1858–1935). English poet.   [54] W. Watson, *The Great Misgiving*.

[55] The stanzas in question actually run as follows:

> 'Not ours,' say some, 'the thought of death to dread;
> Asking no heaven, we fear no fabled hell:
> Life is a feast, and we have banqueted—
> Shall not the worms as well?'

> And ah, to know not, while with friends I sit,
> And while the purple joy is passed about,
> Whether 'tis ampler day divinelier lit
> Or homeless night without;

be the same man who is said, in this month's 'Musical Times',[56] to have worked up the orchestra in Amsterdam to a very prominent position in Europe, before it was taken over by Mengelberg?[57]

The country is looking lovely just now: I am longing to be back in Wales —I shall be there next Friday until the end of the month. My address during August will be, I think, Newbold Pacy Vicarage, Warwickshire: it is conveniently close to Birmingham for the festival, and other music that goes on there. I am *so* looking forward to seeing you again in September, and to having some good long talks with you. I feel I can say so much more to you than anyone else I know: I cannot tell you how much I appreciate your kindness in listening to the paltry things I am doing and thinking. But enough of them, for the present.

Yours affectionately
Philip Heseltine

23
Frederick Delius to Philip Heseltine

Grez sur Loing
S & M
27 July 1912

My dear Heseltine—

I had such a lot of work to do—correcting proofs etc—that I decided not to go to Norway this summer—It would have been too late & I have not yet finished correcting proofs. We have hired a villa at Cap Ferret near Arcachon (on the coast)—from the 20th of August & we shall stay there, no doubt, until the end of September when I come to England for the Birmingham Festival.[58]—Now, should I come to see you before the Festival or After? Which would suit you the best? Sea-drift is on October 3rd & I must no doubt be in Birmingham about

---

[56] A. Kalisch, 'Willem Mengelberg', *Musical Times* (1912), 433–5. The relevant sentence read 'Three years later [Mengelberg] was chosen conductor and director of the Concertgebouw in Amsterdam, as successor to Willem Kes.'

[57] Willem Mengelberg (1871–1951), Dutch conductor. He conducted the first English performances of *On Hearing the First Cuckoo in Spring* and *Summer Night on the River* on 20 Jan. 1914 at Queen's Hall.

[58] Delius had been invited by Henry Wood to conduct the Festival performance of *Sea Drift* but declined because of his previous lack of success in conducting his works in England. He wrote to Bantock expressing reservations about the programming: 'On the Programme I see they have put it [*Sea Drift*] on the 4th day morning at the very end of a 4 hours Concert—Who is responsible for this friendly act?' (L. Carley, *Delius: A Life in Letters*, ii: *1909–1934* (Aldershot, 1988), 89). As a result of Delius's letter *Sea Drift* was performed on the third evening after Verdi's *Requiem*.

the 30th of Sept or Oct 1. for the last Rehearsal—Referring to your last letter
I want to tell you that Jesus—Nietzsche & Co are really the same natures—
Earnest, ardent & sincere natures protesting against human fraud & humbug: &
destroyers of doctrine—Neither of them had any system; both were destroyers
—These sort of intense natures seem to appear periodically—& in all parts of
the world—Jesus, coming at the time of the great Roman decadence—preached
naturally the negation of life—Nietzsche, coming at the end of the Roman Catholic
& Protestant church systems based on the negation of Life—preached Optim-
ism & the affirmation of Life—When this has had a good innings something
else will crop up—I do not find it depressing at all to look upon death as complete annihilation   It harmonises perfectly with my outlook on Life & I am
an optimist & I love life in all its forms   What do you believe? I dont mean—
what do you want to believe—but what you *really* believe—So many people
either deceive themselves or never dare to think the matter out to the end—
All that has been said about reincarnation—The higher spheres etc is simply
childish—Our soul is simply our brain & nervous system & can be entirely
destroyed before death—However enough of the subject—try to be yourself &
live up to your nature—Be harmonious—What ever ones nature be one ought
to develope it to its utmost limits & not be constantly trying to become someone else or be constantly trying to cork up ones nature: this leads to continual
dissatisfaction & to failure—I shall stay here until August the 19th & then we
go to Cap Ferret. The garden is lovely—but we are having quite a number of
thunderstorms this summer—

Affectionately yrs
Frederick Delius

24
Philip Heseltine to Frederick Delius

4. 8. 12.   *Whitney Rectory,*
                                             Hereford.

Dear Mr Delius
    Your letter has pursued me and tracked me down here. I cannot tell you how
overjoyed I am at the prospect of seeing you again so soon. Will you come to
us in September, *before* the festival? I am going to have the month of September

entirely free, so that if it makes no difference to you, that will be far the best time for me, since otherwise I should have to cut my holiday in two. *Do* come as early in September as you can, and stay as long as you can. I shall be going to the festival, of course, so that the end of your visit comes just at the right time. But do make the beginning as early as possible—yet I really ought not to be so importunate, as you must be frantically busy, and you may be frantically bored in Wales! However, I hope you will not be. To see our part of Wales properly (i.e. Mid-Wales), one must *walk* over the wild hills and moors, where there are no roads and scarcely any other human beings: the best thing to do is to go for two or three days walking, if one has the time, stopping at wayside inns en route. But even with our house as headquarters, one can see a great deal by motoring, and can do quite a lot walking: the best walk (which involves a certain amount of train journey too) is to follow the Severn to its source on the heights of Plynlimmon, which are absolutely wild and solitary: from these moors, one can see no cultivation, scarcely a tree or a house; only a rolling sea of green hills. But the best place for extensive walking is the great desert moorland of Maelienydd, which stretches for miles and miles of the most perfect scenery. But enough of words: I hope you will see all this for yourself. As to your best way of coming, I am uncertain of the times of the trains, but I will find out and let you know about them later on. If you leave Paris about 8.30 a.m. you can be in Welshpool by 10.30 the same night, and we can motor you from there. This, however, would mean a very early start: and perhaps Cap Ferret is out-of-the-way—I am afraid I have no idea where it is. Anyhow, we are four hours train-journey from London, and there are trains from London quite frequently —either Paddington or Euston. I hope Mrs Delius will come too. I am going back to my 'academic studies' to-morrow, until September 3rd: my address will be Newbold Pacey Vicarage, Warwick.

You certainly put me a poser to answer in your letter. I have not the least idea what I believe: I have not yet anywhere near enough knowledge of the scientific evidences on which the countless different beliefs are based. I can sift out a few things that I certainly do *not* believe, as being ridiculous, but otherwise I am absolutely open to conviction.

I hate present-day Christianity (whatever it may have been in time past), and hate it much more since living with a parson than before—because I know more about it since doing so. I also hate the parson, but I am sure that is not the reason. I am just starting to read Nietzsche's Beyond good and evil. Hitherto, my sole knowledge of Nietzsche is based on J. M. Kennedy's book about him, so that I really know very little about him. From that little, I admire his bold and splendid destructiveness more than his constructive theories. However, I find 'Beyond good and evil' extremely interesting. At the present time, with my exceedingly imperfect knowledge, I consider Bernard Shaw the most satisfactory person to trust in that I have come across: I think his conception of Man, and his ideas of the Life Force are really splendid: as a 'doctrine', if such it can be called, it seems to me quite magnificent. Besides, I admire Shaw exceedingly in other matters: I can never feel with Nietzsche when he desires to reduce all the lower orders of mankind to slavery, and let an aristocracy rule the world (if that really is what he is driving at). After all, if pity for the weak and helpless was the quintessence of everything that was bad, why did his disciple, J. M. Kennedy feel pity for Nietzsche when he went mad, referring to his madness as 'the saddest incident in his life'? But I suppose Nietzsche was talking parables more or less when he said that kind of thing. But I am absolutely in the dark about him, so have no right to discuss him.

It is, of course, very stupid to *fear* annihilation at death, for after all, there can be nothing to fear from a condition in which one *is* nothing, as in annihilation. But I should have thought that all who loved life would hope for its continuation after death, even if only as a dream in sleep. Do you believe in the Eternal Recurrence? As I said before, I do not know enough to believe anything: the Christian idea of *one* everlasting life is, of course, absurd and horrible at that. But there are many other ideas of reincarnation. Of course the important thing of all others is Life—here, while we have it, and not the speculative Life hereafter which may very likely not exist. But we must discuss these things: I have nothing to say on the subject, and so much to learn from you.

A friend of mine who conducts a small choral society in Surrey is going to practise your part-songs this season with a view to performing them at their little concert early next year, if they can master them. I am longing to hear the 'Midsummer Song' and 'On Craig Ddu': we must try and visit Craig Ddu when you are in Wales: there is one not far from us, but I do not know whether it is the right one. However, it does overlook the Vale of Llangollen, where Symons seems to have been when he wrote the little group of poems in which Craig Ddu occurs.

I must stop now—so, hoping to see you as soon as possible in September, I remain

Yours affectionately
Philip Heseltine

25

Frederick Delius to Philip Heseltine

Villa La Brise
Cap Ferret
par Arcachon
(Gironde) 22/8/1912

My dear Heseltine.

I am looking forward immensely to my visit to Wales. The scenery you describe must be beautiful & I love that sort of scenery; I was born on the Yorkshire moors & the love of the rough & solitary moorlands clings to me still. I shall try to be with you about the 23' or 4ᵗʰ of September—If it is possible I should prefer to travel right thro' the same day: I dont care how early I leave Paris— We shall stay here until the 14ᵗʰ or 15ᵗʰ of Sept & then return to Grez—My wife will stay in Grez as she wants to paint a good deal this Autumn—the summer has been abominable—The weather here is a little better but very unsettled— The place is lovely—Our Villa is situated on the bay of Arcachon in a pine forest & we have only to cross a strip of pine covered land to reach the Atlantic ocean & sands running to the horizon on both sides—There are no people here & we are entirely alone & undisturbed—Arcachon is 10 hours from Paris & from Arcachon one has to take a boat (a small steamer) to Cap Ferret, a jour- ney of another hour—so you see we are quite isolated—Bernard Shaw seems to me to be very much influenced by Nietzsche—Nietzsche seems to have given him the start—to have made him fruitful—But Nietzsche is ever so much deeper & ever so much more poetical & ever so much more daring—Bernard Shaw has a wonderfully clear mind but not much *feeling*—He is superficial like nearly all Irishmen—He is a clever—very clever polemist—Journalist— & what he *really* wants to do is to surprise you or make you laugh—or shock the 'bourgeois' just enough to avoid being put in prison—And then again *he is no artist whatever* —He is the 'Richard Strauss' of litterature—As soon as the problems his plays are written about are solved—or the abuses bettered) his plays will instantly become most uninteresting & worthless—The *preface is* by far the best part of his play. I know nothing of his conception of Man or of the Life Voice—Nietzsche does not want to reduce the lower order of mankind to slavery—They are in slavery & always have been in slavery, & will remain in slavery in spite of all theories to the contrary—The whole history of the world is the history of a few *individuals*—Coming back to our old subject let me assure you of one thing,

& of this you may be *perfectly certain*—In the year 2200 your self consciousness will be in exactly the same state as it was in 1820—*Your ego*—I believe in the Eternal recurrence of nothing whatever—Eternal change of matter is more likely—Let me know all about the trains—& believe me yrs affectionately

Frederick Delius

P.S. I should certainly like to enjoy good health & live for 3 or 400 years at least—Life is so interesting to me—

26
Philip Heseltine to Frederick Delius

6. 9. 12.   *Cefn-Bryntalch*
                                    Abermule
                              Montgomeryshire

Dear Mr Delius

I am afraid you cannot possibly get here from Paris in the day: there is no train to Montgomery leaving London later than 2.35 in the afternoon, and the earliest continental train does not arrive in London until after 3 o'clock. There are only two good trains here from London. You must come by the Great Western Railway:—

		a.m.	p.m.
LONDON (Paddington) dep.		11.5.	2.35
Montgomery	arr.	3.26	7.23
Abermule	arr.	. . . . .	7.30

The 11.5 is the better of the two: there are through Cambrian R^ys carriages on both: if you can find room in one of these carriages you will not have to change. Otherwise you must change at Shrewsbury and Welshpool. Montgomery and Abermule stations are 1 3/4 and 1 1/2 miles from here, respectively. The 11.5. does not stop at Abermule, but we can meet you with the car at Montgomery quite as well. I cannot tell you the times of the trains from Bourron to Paris, but here is a list of all the routes from Paris: I expect you will have no difficulty at all in getting a convenient train from Bourron.

	A.M.		P.M.
(1) PARIS (Nord) dep.	8.25		4.0
(crossing: Boulogne—Folkestone)			
LONDON (Charing X) arr.	3.25 p.m.		10.45 p.m.

	A.M.		P.M.	
(2) PARIS (Nord) dep.	9.50	12.0 noon	9.20	
(crossing: Calais—Dover)				
LONDON (Charing X) arr.	5.10 p.m.	7.25 p.m.	5.43 A.M.	
		(arrives at	(Charing X)	
		Victoria)		

	A.M.	P.M.
(3) PARIS (St Lazare) dep.	10.20	9.20
(crossing: Dieppe—Newhaven)		
LONDON (Victoria) arr.	7.0 p.m.	7.30 A.M.

	P.M.	
(4) PARIS (St Lazare)	dep. 7.48	This service does not run
(crossing: Havre—Southampton)		on Sunday nights: all the
		others are the same for
LONDON (Waterloo) arr.	9.0 A.M.	Sundays and Week-days.
(crossing lasts about 7. hours)		

You could come straight through by route n° 4, sleeping on the boat. I am looking forward immensely to seeing you on the 23rd or 24th, or any day before that date, if you possibly can come before. Just let me know what day and time you propose to come, and I will see that you and your luggage are met.

You seem to have hit upon a lovely spot at Cap Ferret. I hope your weather has begun to amend as ours has. I went up to London on Tuesday last[59] to hear the first performance in England of Five orchestral pieces by Arnold Schönberg: Wood brought them out at one of the promenade concerts.[60] I do not think he

[59] 3 Sept. 1912.
[60] 'Arnold Schönberg's "Five Orchestral Pieces", played for the first time on September 3, were described on the programme as "experiments in dissonance." Such they assuredly were; and while nobody could reasonably claim that he had not been fairly warned, almost everybody present seemed bewildered, if not shocked, at the degree to which Schönberg had carried his protest against all preconceived notions of music and harmony. . . . it sounded vague and disconnected, while most of the matter presented was ugly enough to suggest nothing but the distracting fancies of delirium. Schönberg's day has not dawned yet, and apparently "promenaders" are not in a hurry for it. The work began by provoking laughter, but this soon gave way to weariness.' 'The Promenade Concerts', *Musical Times* (1912), 660. The *Five Orchestral Pieces* were heard again at Queen's Hall on 17 Jan. 1914, this time with Schoenberg conducting the Queen's Hall orchestra.

will be appreciated for many years to come: the promenade audience seemed to find the music intensely humourous, but at the close their hisses were drowned by applause—presumably meant for the efforts of Sir Henry and his men. I cannot make head or tail out of his music, but I am sure he is perfectly sincere and that it means a great deal to him. I do not think it sounded nearly as bad as one would expect from all accounts of it: sometimes it was quite fascinating— one gets now and then, just a glimpse, as it were, of some weird, new country, and although one can only see it from a distance, there is a strange fascination in the idea of its further possibilities. But most of the while, the effect was as though each orchestral part was wandering about at it's own sweet will: one of the pieces is admittedly contrapuntal, and not harmonic, and every instrument seems to be treated as a solo. Families of instruments are not kept grouped together, so that the whole orchestration sounds very funny. There is a perfect pandemonium of sound when the composer becomes really noisy, and as he insists on keeping all the brass muted nearly all the time, the effect really does resemble a farmyard. But I expect his aim in writing thus was in reality far more artistic than that of Strauss when he wrote the 'Adversaries' in the 'Heldenleben' and the sheep-movement in 'Don Quixote'! I should very much like to meet someone who really could appreciate Schönberg's music!

I am sorry that you have no better opinion of Bernard Shaw than to class him with Richard Strauss! At least, he is sincere. One of his biographers, Holbrook Jackson,[61] denies that he was influenced by Nietzsche, saying that he had evolved his philosophy before he read any of Nietzsche's works.

Elgar seems to have taken a leaf out of Strauss' book by quoting copiously from his own works in 'We are the music-makers', which is described in this month's 'Musical Times'.

Wood is reported to have described Scriabine's 'Prometheus' as 'the last word in modernity'. Can this work possibly outdo Schönberg—?! Appalling thought! I have just got a lot of music by Balfour Gardiner, which I like very much: it is so cheery and vigorous.

Good bye for a few days.

Yours affectionately
Philip Heseltine

---

[61] Holbrook Jackson (1874–1948), English author. His biography of Shaw was published in 1907.

27
Philip Heseltine to Frederick Delius

7. 9. 12.   Cefn Bryntalch, Abermule

I find that you *can* come straight through in the day from Paris, on any day except Sunday, if you do not mind a nine-mile drive in an open car at 11 o'clock at night. If you come this way, we will meet you with the motor at Welshpool: the trains run as follows:—
(N.B. You *must* come by Boulogne, as the Calais train will not allow you enough time to get across London.)

		A.M.
PARIS (Nord)	dep.	8.25
(cross Boulogne—Folkestone)		
LONDON (Charing Cross)	arr.	3.25 P.M.
LONDON (Paddington)	dep.	6.5 P.M.
WELSHPOOL	arr.	10.20 P.M.

This is an excellent train, and you will find the journey very comfortable, if you do not mind a cold motor drive afterwards! The train does not go any further than Welshpool.

Yrs.
Philip Heseltine

Postcard.

28
Frederick Delius to Philip Heseltine

We return to Grez tomorrow

Villa la Brise
Cap Ferret
Arcachon

Wednesday [11 September 1912]

My dear Heseltine—

Many thanks for your letter & postcard & all the information about the trains I think the best way for me to travel will be as follows: leave Paris 4 P.M. & spend the night in London, take the 11.5 train in the morning & arrive at 3.26 Montgomery—I hope to be able to leave Grez on the 22nd inst & will write you again the exact date—When do you intend going to Birmingham? There is a rehearsal of Sea-drift on the 28th but I do not want to be so soon in Birmingham when I can be on the moors—Are you going for the first day?—What are they giving? I have ordered my room at the Queen's Hotel for the first *Oct* if it is Haendel or some other Oratorio & nothing new I shall not go to the concert[62]—consider that I have a fairly good opinion of Shaw to compare him to Strauss —Strauss is a wonderfully clever musician & has left his mark on his epoch —He is wanting in Soul & poetry & so is Shaw—They both interest me very much & I think Shaw extremely amusing, witty & clever—But I would not compare him to Ibsen[63] or Nietzsche—I know lots of Englishmen who would like to be compared with Strauss—I am looking forward immensely to my stay with you—Our stay here has been very successful & the weather quite good in comparison to other places—I am looking forward to Scriabines 'Prometheus' as all novelties interest me—I should very much like to hear Schonberg's music —He seems to be very *Academic*—à rebours—He writes after a system—He is perhaps the first musician who ever consequently wrote after a system that is

---

[62] Delius was to write critically to Jelka about some of the music he heard at the festival: 'Last night [1 Oct. 1912] I heard the "Musik Makers" Elgar & the Symphony of Sibelius—Elgars work is not very interesting—& very noisy—The chorus treated in the old way & very heavily orchestrated—It did not interest me—Sibelius interested me much more—He is trying to do something new & has a fine feeling for nature & he is also unconventional—Sometimes a bit sketchy & ragged   But I should like to hear the work again—He is a very nice fellow & we were together with Bantock before & after the Concert—Today I tried to hear the Mathew Passion but could not stand more than 40 minutes of it—I see now definitely that I have done for ever with this old music. It says nothing whatever to me—Beautiful bits—Endless recitations & Chorale   My goodness! how slow!' Delius to Jelka, 2 Oct. 1912 (Melbourne, Grainger Museum).

[63] Henrik Johan Ibsen (1828–1906), Norwegian dramatist and poet.

perhaps why it sounds so awful—No musical genius ever wrote a treatise on Harmony. affectionately y^{rs}

Frederick Delius

29
Philip Heseltine to Frederick Delius

20. 9. 12.   *Cefn-Bryntalch*
                              Abermule
                              Montgomeryshire

Dear Mr Delius

I am so dreadfully sorry to hear that you are ill, and that we shall not see you on Monday: it is most unfortunate, and a really bad cold is such a horrible thing—I am truly sorry for you. I hope you will be well enough to come later in the week: I should be terribly disappointed if you could not come after all, as I have been looking forward to your visit above everything, but of course it is very dangerous to run the least risk when one has only just recovered from a chill, and I should be very sorry if the Welsh climate were to make you bad again. The house is not situated on a bleak moor, though we can see a part of one from the windows. We are in the middle of the Severn valley, about 500 feet above sea-level. The post is just going, so I must stop now, but I will write another, longer letter to-morrow, and will send you a copy of my article on Arnold Schönberg published to-day in the 'Musical Standard'.[64] I think I told you about it's curious fate before! Please do not think for an instant that I am setting myself up as a critic!! The article was originally designed to instruct a miserable writer in the 'Musical Times' who suffered from a lamentable igno-rance of the *facts* of Schönberg's case, and it is practically only a plain statement of facts, drawn from the reliable source of a German article by one of his pupils.

Schönberg says in his book that he has no theory or system of composition for himself, and that he cannot explain his works by any theory whatever, as they are litterally *dictated* to him by his inspiration, or whatever you call it, and that he is powerless to alter a note of them afterwards to make them conform to any known theory! If it is true, it completely bears out what you once told

---

[64] P. A. Heseltine, 'Arnold Schönberg', *Musical Standard*, 21 Sept. 1912 (v. 38, no. 977), 176–8.

me in one of your letters, that systems are only put together from the compositions of inspired musicians. The question, however, still remains as to whether Schönberg is really inspired at all! Personally I see no reason why he should not be, although I admit I cannot understand a note of him myself!

I do hope you will get better *at once*, if not sooner!

Yours affectionately
Philip Heseltine

30
Philip Heseltine to Frederick Delius

22. 9. 12.   *Cefn-Bryntalch*
                                  Abermule
                                  Montgomeryshire

Dear Mr Delius

How are you getting on? I hope by the time you receive this you will have completely recovered. It is very sad to reflect that at this moment—4 o'clock on Sunday afternoon—you ought to be just arriving at the Gare du Nord en route for England, and in reality, are—sadder still—probably in bed and feeling very miserable. But I hope your attack has proved a very mild one. Influenza is such a horrible thing. I am sending you by the same post a copy of the number of the 'Musical Standard' which contains my article on Schönberg: also, enclosed therein, a panoramic photograph shewing this house, so that you may see that we are not perched upon the top of a cold, bleak and damp mountain! The photo is a few years old, and does not give you any idea of the distance one can see from the windows, as at least a dozen of the trees in front of the house have since been cut down. But it gives you a general idea of the place, so I hope you will not be frightened at any notion you may have formed about Wales! I know it has a bad reputation in the matter of weather and climate, but that really does not apply to this part of the country.

Colin Taylor has just left here after a week's visit: he is a very good musician and a most delightful person, quite one of my best friends. He has published a little music, in the way of songs, and small pieces, which is very nice, but he is too much bound by his having to teach the piano at Eton and Oxford to attempt anything big in the way of composition. His elder brother, L. Campbell

Taylor,[65] has a big reputation as a painter. Have you yet visited Uncle Joe's 'exhibition studio'? (!!!) Goodness knows how many studios he has got now!

I really know very little about Strauss, as I have only heard the four later operas, 'Heldenleben' and 'Don Quixote' and a few small things. But he does not appeal to me at all, though of course, he must be amazingly clever.

I have just received a very interesting book containing complete lists of the compositions (published or otherwise) of well over 100 British composers.[66] I dare say you have seen it.

The Birmingham Festival novelties are down, as follows:—

Elgar's choral work 'The Music-Makers') Sibelius' 4th Symphony	October 1st evening
Walford Davies' choral work, 'Song of the Sun'[67] Bantock's orchestral work, 'Fifine at the Fair'	October 2nd evening
Scriabine's 'Prometheus'	October 4th morning

so if you come here before the Festival, you need not leave until the afternoon of the 1st, as we are only two hours' train journey from Birmingham. The morning performance on the 1st is only 'Elijah', which, when it was staged as an opera, Ernest Newman described as 'funnier than "The Merry Widow" but the music isn't so good'! My mother will be at the Queen's Hotel: I shall stay with a friend[68] at Edgbaston, a suburb of Birmingham, but I shall probably be with my mother at the Queen's most of the time, as my friend is busy all day, being a solicitor, so I shall look forward eagerly to seeing something of you there, if by any sad mischance, you are unable to come here before then. But I sincerely hope that mischance will not occur! If, however, you find it impossible to come before the festival, *do* come afterwards if you possibly can. I am *so* much looking forward to seeing you again. Are you going to London to hear your pianoforte concerto at Queen's Hall on October 10th? I hope to be going with Colin Taylor, who is also exceedingly keen on your music. Now I *do* hope you are really better, and that I shall see you here before this week is out. So, with very best wishes for a very speedy recovery,

  I am yours affectionately
  Philip Heseltine

The weather here is quite lovely now.

[65] Leonard Campbell Taylor (1874–1969), English painter, brother of Colin Taylor. He studied at the John Ruskin School in Oxford, the St John's Wood Art School, and Royal Academy. His paintings are represented in the Tate, Manchester, and Sydney art galleries.
[66] Presumably the 1912 edition of the *Society of British Composers Yearbook*.
[67] *Song of St Francis*, Op. 36, for solo voices, chorus, and orchestra. This was hardly a subject likely to appeal to Delius.
[68] Almost certainly G. T. Leigh Spencer. He had lived in the village of Clifford, just across the river from Whitney-on-Wye, where Heseltine met him when visiting an aunt. Although Leigh Spencer was some years older than Heseltine, the two young men evidently enjoyed a lively friendship, as can be seen from their correspondence in BL 57946.

31
Frederick Delius to Philip Heseltine

Grez sur Loing
S&M
24/9/12

My dear Heseltine—

Your 2 letters & the Musical Standard arrived this morning—I have just got up & feel much better—but am afraid that I shall not be able to leave here before next Sunday—I feel terribly disappointed that I could not come to Wales & walk about the moors with you—I might perhaps be able to come for a day or 2 after the Festival if I feel alright—We will talk about it in Birmingham— Your Article on Schönberg is very good & fair—I know nothing of his music & am very keen to hear or see something—*Bring what you have to Birmingham* & we will go thro' it together—Bring also your arrangement of 'In a summer garden', which I want you to lend me for a short while I want to hear it & also to lend it to a musician in Frankfort who wants to play it.[69] I like your attitude towards music so much; your mind is so open—Of course the attitude of the critics is always stupid—Critics as a rule are musicians who have failed I know no exceptions. Clutsam is a man who for 25 years has tried to imitate every musician of repute & every style—Hoping by so doing to have a success— He has imitated from an American Coon song up to the 2 popular Composers Debussy & Strauss & music of all descriptions—But he himself (Clutsam) is a dead failure & he knows it—I mention Clutsam because he is an intelligent composer—the others are merely rotters—English rotters—which means rather more rotten than any other country's bar American—In no other country is there such talk about British composers etc. British music as a rule wont stand crossing the Channel—Music is a matter of temperament—Emotional music will be understood at once by emotional people—Intellectual music will be liked & understood by intellectual people & so on & soforth—I dont believe in the music you have to get accustomed to—That is what puts me out about Schönberg—you say yourself you cannot make head or tail of it—The attitude of reserving ones opinion vis a vis a new form of art is not always the best one, altho' it is the wisest one—we have to thank 'the reserving ones opinion attitude' for some of the most idiotic expressions of art—*The Futurists & the Cubists.*

---

[69] Delius later wrote to Jelka about his meeting with Heseltine at the festival: 'Heseltine & his mother are here— He is so nice & so enthusiastic—We played "In a summer garden" for 2 pianos this morning & he has done it really very well.' Delius to Jelka, 2 Oct. 1912 (Melbourne, Grainger Museum).

The public have become funky about giving their opinion—because the critics have made such terrible blunders—& quite a number of sensation seeking—opportunistic artistic rotters are taking advantage of it—I never once remember having made a mistake vis a vis a new work of music—When I first heard Chopin as a little boy of 6 or 7, I thought heaven had been opened to me—When also as a little boy I first heard the Humoresken of Grieg—a new world was opened to me again—When at the age of 23 I heard Tristan—I was perfectly overcome—also when I heard Lohengrin as a schoolboy. Beethoven always left me cold & reserved—Bach I always loved more—it seemed to me more spontaneous[70]—Brahms I never liked much & never shall—it is philistin music —altho' some of the chamber music is good—But to have to get accustomed to music is a fearfully bad sign—The sort of people who get accustomed to music are the unmusical & when once accustomed to it they will hear no other—All the music critics have got accustomed to music—to their great composer—I shall leave London for Birmingham on Oct 1st morning: I go to the Queen's Hotel & hope to see a lot of you—

Remember me to your mother most kindly

Believe me
Affectionately yours
Frederick Delius

32
Philip Heseltine to Frederick Delius

27. 9. 12.   *Cefn-Bryntalch*
                                    Abermule
                                    Montgomeryshire

Dear Mr Delius

Thank you so very much for your most delightful letter which I received yesterday: I am so very glad to think that you will probably be able to come here after the Festival, and I am looking forward intensely to seeing you in Birmingham. My mother and I shall arrive about 2.30 in the afternoon. I will bring the celebrated piano-pieces[71] of Schönberg: I have no other music of his,

---

[70] Heseltine quoted parts of this letter when writing to Taylor on 27 Sept. 1912, BL 54197.
[71] *Three Piano Pieces*, Op. 11 (1909, rev. 1924).

as it is useless for me to try to make head or tail of it. I should never recognize those orchestral pieces of his if I heard them again! You say you have not seen any of his pieces, but you surely remember playing through some songs by Anton von Webern at Dr Fischer's house? Schönberg is quite as horrible as those songs!; and of course he sounds *much* worse on the piano than when he is played by an orchestra!

I am very sorry the performance of Scriabine's 'Prometheus' has been cancelled. I do not think I shall go to any performance on the Friday, so if you are not staying for the 'Apostles' we can come back here together: my mother has only engaged rooms for the three nights, Tuesday, W'day and Thday. All that you say about appreciation of music interests me enormously: I always look at music from a purely emotional point of view. What appeals to me and thrills me to hear, I love: that is all I know about it. At the same time, I grow to like certain things more and more, as I become more and more familiar with them, either from repeated hearings, or study of the piano scores. For this reason, I consider a pianola a priceless help to the appreciation of new and difficult works, like those of Strauss, which I have no opportunities of hearing orchestrally, and which would probably bore me if I had to wade through the piano scores, as they do not appeal to me sufficiently.

I attribute a great deal of my love for music to a pianola which I heard very frequently when I was 12 years of age: it belonged to a master at the school where I was at the time. Before that time, I never took any *real* interest in music, although I had had piano lessons for some considerable time previously. I shall never forget the effect that some of Chopin's music, and Liszt's Rhapsodies had on me when I first heard them at that time. I have kept a record of all the music I have ever heard since 1906, and it is interesting to look back at the lists, and remember what appeal different works made to me when I heard them for the first time. I recall especially how I was *thrilled* by Chopin's G flat Etude, op 25, no 9, which I still love almost as much as any piano piece I know: also, by two little pieces by Schumann, 'Träumerei' and 'Grillen'.

I must admit, however, that when I heard 'A dance of life' in 1908, I came away with no impression of it whatever!—which, I think, shews that one's tastes—anyway when young—develop considerably with the advance of years. For you know what I felt when I studied your music two years afterwards: there was no need to 'get accustomed to it' then!

I'm afraid I like a great deal of modern British music very much! Only this week I have received the vocal score of a big choral work by a young Irish composer, which has thrilled me more than anything I have come across for a long time: I had not played it right through before I thought to myself 'Here is *real* music': to my mind, it is one of the most lovely things I have ever come across, but when it was performed in London, it was abused by every critic I read! The work is by Arnold Bax and is a setting of a scene from Shelley's 'Prometheus Unbound'.[72] In case you have not seen or heard it yet, I will bring it to Birmingham, as I am *sure* it would raise your opinion of the British composer; though, of course, there is a tremendous gulf between the Celtic, Irish tempera-ment and the English: the former is a thousand times more emotional. I know no British composer whose works appeal to me anything like so much as Arnold Bax.[73] Colin Taylor recently played me 'Handel in the Strand' by Grainger which I liked exceedingly, but I am still anxious to find a work by Grainger contain-ing really poetical feeling—as Bax's work does: British vigour and robustness are all very well for a time, but I think one can have too much of 'The Roast Beef of Old England' spirit! I do not know very much of Grainger's music, so I may have missed some of the best and most poetical. But of it's kind, I don't think 'Handel in the Strand' could be bettered: it is gloriously energetic and strong!

I am *so* looking forward to seeing you on Tuesday next.

Excuse haste: post is just going

Yours affectionately
Philip Heseltine

33
Frederick Delius to Philip Heseltine

[Grez, 29 September 1912]

Dear Heseltine

I forgot to tell you that I received the photo which is lovely & I do so hope that next summer I shall be able to come & stay with you & wander all about the country—this time I [am] afraid it will be impossible I have so much to do in London   Au revoir, in a day or 2. Affectionately

Frederick Delius

Picture postcard, Grez. Vue d'ensemble.

---

[72] *Enchanted Summer.* First performed on 13 Mar. 1912 at the first of the Balfour Gardiner concerts (and conducted by him) at Queens' Hall. The vocal score was published by Riorden, 1912.

[73] Bax was not Irish, as Heseltine seemed to think.

34
Philip Heseltine to Frederick Delius

Queens Hotel
Birmingham, October 4th 1912

Dear M[r] Delius,

I quite forgot to give you the names of the Celtic books you asked me about yesterday. They are:—

'The Dublin Book of Irish Verse'
Poems (two volumes) by W. B. Yeats[74]
'The Dominion of Dreams' by 'Fiona Macleod'.

I am sure you would like all of these, though, of course, modern Irish literature is fairly extensive, and there are any number of works by the same authors, or others of like temperament, which you would probably like just as well.

Will you please ask M[r] Balfour Gardiner if he will be kind enough to send the score of 'Lebenstanz' to me at Cefn Bryntalch, Abermule, Montgomeryshire, as I shall not be returning to the horrible priest for a week or so, and in the meanwhile, I might be getting on with the transcription at home.

I hope you have not frozen during your motor-drive to Berkshire![75] This fog here is getting thicker and thicker: it is enough to choke one!

It has been so very delightful, being here with you this week:[76] I have enjoyed it all most *tremendously*, and I am already looking forward to the 'Mass of Life' and 'Midsummer Song' in December (and, if at all possible for me to come, to the Concerto on Thursday next): and also to making acquaintance with 'Life's Dance' in the near future.

Yours affectionately
Philip Heseltine

---

[74] William Butler Yeats (1865–1939), Irish poet.   [75] Ashampstead, Berkshire, where Balfour Gardiner lived.
[76] Writing about the festival, Heseltine told Taylor: 'Delius is staying here: we see a lot of him. This morning he and I were taken to the Midland Institute of Music by its great professor, Granville Bantock, and we played through "In a Summer Garden" on two pianos: we also went through some Schönberg [*Three Piano Pieces*, Op. 11] together . . . I played him some Bax [*Enchanted Summer*], and he loved it.' Heseltine to Taylor, 2 Oct. 1912, BL 54197.

35
Frederick Delius to Philip Heseltine

[Grez, 21 October 1912]

My dear Heseltine

I received your letter & card in London—Many thanks—The Concerto was magnificently played by Szantó[77]—I left the day after (11ᵗʰ) & am here since last Saturday week & at work again   I was so glad to have seen something of you—We motored to Oxford & looked over the Colleges—We nearly got killed in the Motor car. The steering broke—luckily we were in a village & going slow—otherwise my career would have ended abruptly—With love

yrs ever
Frederick Delius

Remember me most kindly to your mother

Postcard.

36
Philip Heseltine to Frederick Delius

25. 11. 12.   Newbold Pacey Vicarage
                                                       Warwick

Dear Mʳ Delius

It was a great shock and a bitter disappointment to me to see in the 'Daily Telegraph' last Saturday that on December 7ᵗʰ the *Beecham wind-band* will give a concert in Queen's Hall: for I conclude therefrom that the promised performance of 'A Mass of Life' will not take place. It does seem a pity, but I hope that, at least, it is only postponed. What is the reason? I have seen nothing

---

[77] Theodor Szántó (1877–1934), Hungarian pianist and composer. He played Delius's Piano Concerto with Wood conducting at a concert in Queen's Hall on 10 October 1912. *The Times* described the concerto as the '2nd edition'. He was the work's dedicatee and was responsible for rewriting some of the solo part.

about it in the papers since a more or less official announcement of the performance in the 'Morning Post' six weeks ago, and I understood from what you said in Birmingham that the arrangements had already been made for it to take place. Shall you be coming over to England in any case next month? The 'Midsummer Song' will be performed—for the first time, I understand— at Windsor on Monday December 9th by the Windsor and Eton Madrigal Society, conducted by Sir Walter Parratt.[78] At least, they have been practising it for some time, though at first they were completely baffled by it, being accustomed to Bach and Palestrina, chiefly! However, I think it will be done, but Parratt is quite an old man, and not at all in sympathy with modern music, so I dare say the performance will not be first-rate.[79] Edward Mason[80] is going to do it in London next year, when I expect it will be sung much better. However, if you are in England, *do* come down to Windsor for the concert if you can. I shall be there, and if you care to come down early in the day, I will show you what little there is to see at Eton, if that interests you at all. I have to be in Oxford all next week till the 7th for an examination, and again on the 10th for another, so I am sandwiching a week-end at Eton with Colin Taylor between the two.

—What a narrow escape you must have had on your journey from Birmingham! You are indeed fortunate, and Mr Gardiner must be an uncommonly good motorist: you might have had a very serious accident. I received the score of 'Life's Dance' from Mr Gardiner, and worked at a piano score of it with enormous interest for ten days, at the end of which time my only regret was that it was finished![81] I enjoy transcription work immensely, though I am afraid that in this case my piano-version was a very bad one: I have never tackled so complex a score before, and the middle part I found exceedingly difficult.[82] I never

[78] Sir Walter Parratt (1841–1924), organist, St George's Chapel, Windsor, 1882–1924, professor of music, Oxford, 1908–18.

[79] Heseltine wrote to Taylor about the concert: 'I suppose the Windsor Madrigal Society's Concert is coming off alright on the 9th? I wrote to Delius last week and asked him to come down to Eton for the concert, if he would be in England, but I have not heard from him yet. My mother also wants to come for the concert. Where can one get tickets? Will you please let me know, as I had better get them before they are all swallowed up. . . . I hope we shall be able to induce Frederick the Great to come down on Monday the 9th, though I fear he may not be leaving France under the present circumstances.' Heseltine to Taylor, 1 Dec. 1912, BL 54197.

[80] Edward Mason (1878–1915), cellist and conductor; a member of the Grimson Quartet together with Frank Bridge. He had befriended Heseltine at Eton where he was an assistant music-teacher. He was also director and principal cellist of the New Symphony Orchestra with whom he conducted an annual concert of British music at Queen's Hall (much of it choral with his own choir) that included *Sea Drift* on 22 Mar. 1911 and *Midsummer Song* on 27 Feb. 1913. He was killed in action in France.

[81] Gardiner wrote to Heseltine: 'I shall not see your piano version of the Lebenstanz till I get back to Ashampstead, for it has not been sent on to me, though your letter has. I feel that I did not thank you half enough for undertaking the work. You yourself will realise how much it will facilitate the study of the score, & especially the apprehension of the big lines of it: indeed, an arrangement such as you have made is almost indispensable to a conductor producing the work for the first time.' Gardiner to Heseltine, 21 Oct. 1912, photocopy PWS Archives.

[82] Heseltine told Taylor: 'On Thursday evening [3 Oct. 1912] Balfour Gardiner turned up in his motor to hear "Sea-Drift", and I had a long conversation with him after the concert: he is an extremely nice person—very cheerful,

quite know whether it is better, when doing a transcription, to try to boil down the whole work into a playable piano piece—just giving a general *idea* of the whole work, omitting when necessary, and altering notes and figures for the sake of making the arrangement 'pianistic'—or to transcribe just as much as possible, note for note, which makes for an unplayable transcription, but, to my mind, gives a better idea of the original: it is certainly easier to make. Which way do you consider the best?

I enjoyed studying the music of 'Life's Dance' immensely and look forward to hearing it next year.[83] I think you told me you had altered the last part of it recently: it does not seem to correspond to the analysis written by Gilbert Webb[84] for the Albert Hall performance, and I do not quite understand its significance myself. The analysis mentions a 'downward glissando' for harps (which does not appear in the printed score), adding that from this point the music is plunged into gloom and despair, ending with a chord which signifies 'vagueness, incompleteness—death'. This does not seem to me to interpret the music at all, but by the absence of the 'glissando' mentioned, as well as one or two other small details, I conclude that the latter part is now quite different. I am glad the work had such a success in Berlin:[85] I read about it in the papers.

I am afraid this is a very dull and uninteresting letter: I have very little spare time, and what I have is very fully occupied with reading and writing, etc: however, after this wretched exam I hope to be freer. How useless all this Latin and Greek is! I have not forgotten your parting words in Birmingham 'Think more of your music than of your Latin'! But although I am constantly thinking and thinking about music, I can *do* nothing. I wouldn't mind if I could write anything, even the most hopeless hogwash and potboilers, so long as I was employed with music somehow: but, alas I cannot even do that.—I have been reading lately a very good book about Nietzsche, called 'Who is to be master

and "hearty". He wants me to make a piano score of Delius's orchestral work "Life's Dance" for him: he is going to perform it at his concerts next year. I have done about a quarter of it, but my progress with it is far from rapid, as it is frightfully complex: I am not surprised that B.G. wants a piano version, if he has to read such a score.' Heseltine to Taylor, 9 Oct. 1912, BL 54197. He wrote again to Taylor at the end of October: 'Delius' "Dance of Life" of which I made a piano score just lately, presented many difficulties arising from this question. Some pages of it are so fearfully complex, and *contrapuntal*—unusual for Delius—that it is simply impossible to reproduce them on the piano. It was most awfully interesting to transcribe, although it was rather hard work to make musical Bovril (for I cannot call it a "piano score" with any justice!) out of sixty pages of such tremendously full scoring.' Heseltine to Taylor, 28 Oct. 1912, BL 54197.

[83] Heseltine had written to Taylor about the work: 'The work was written as early as 1898, but has only just been published. It is quite in the well-known and absolutely original Delius "style", and there are some most *haunting* things in it. As a whole, however, I do not like it as well as the later works.' Heseltine to Taylor, 28 Oct. 1912, BL 54197.

[84] Francis Gilbert Webb (1853–1941), English music critic and organist. He wrote for various London newspapers and journals including the *Daily Telegraph*, *Observer*, *Sunday Times*, and *Musical Times*.

[85] 15 Nov. 1912, conducted by Oskar Fried.

of the world?' by A. M. Ludovici:[86] also some of 'Zarathustra' and 'Beyond Good and Evil': I find I can now understand and appreciate him much better than before. 'Zarathustra' is a magnificent book, but I cannot pretend to understand all of it yet. It requires very careful reading. There are some things, however, in which I do not think I shall ever agree with Nietzsche: for instance, his denial of pity, on principle (by 'pity' I do not mean the mawkish sentiment that passes for such so often, but the genuine article), and 'What is happiness? . . . *not* peace but war.' (quoted from the 'Antichrist' in J. M. Kennedy's book), and 'Man shall be trained for war and woman for the recreation of the warrior.' I *hate* war, and patriotism and jingoism in all its forms, intensely. Why should one want to get killed for a mere sentiment? However, having read so little of Nietzsche, I may find my notions as to these things mistaken when I come to read more of him. However one may differ from his views, everyone ought, I think, to admit that he was a very great man: one seems to feel his personality when reading his books. Most Christians, however, look upon him as a madman! Although nine out of ten never read him. His attitude towards Christianity would be quite new to most of them: for most modern opponents of Christianity turn first to historical facts like Huxley[87] and Darwin:[88] but Nietzsche goes straight to the point and denounces the whole scheme as rotten, and would, no doubt, continue to do so, even if Mr Jesus Carpenter and his gang were proved beyond all possible doubt to be God almighty and 'his chosen ones'!! This attitude of Nietzsche's is perfectly *splendid.*

I have to spend this Christmas with an uncle[89] (Uncle Joe's brother!) who is very religeous, and built a church in memory of my father! I wonder what he would say to Nietzsche!!! I am sure my mother thinks I am 'on the road to Hell' as pious Christians say: she is, unfortunately, quite out of sympathy with all modern ideas, which fact I, who am struggling to free myself from the quagmires of Christianity, convention and English 'respectability' in which I have hitherto been stuck fast, deplore greatly. It entails a great deal of unpleasantness and profitless arguments, which might be avoided but for the horrible blight that Christian 'faith' puts on the intellect of anyone who professes it. It is horrible to think of people's minds being warped in this way. I really must stop now: I *do* hope I shall see you in England next month: perhaps the 'Mass of Life' has only been transferred to a later date? It *is* a pity the performance on the 7th is off.

[86] Anthony M. Ludovici (1882–1971), English author and translator of six volumes of Nietzsche's philosophy.

[87] Thomas Henry Huxley (1825–95), English biologist, a powerful advocate of the principle of agnosticism.

[88] Charles Robert Darwin (1809–82), English naturalist who first established the theory of evolution.

[89] Evelyn Heseltine (1850–1930). This wealthy uncle had built a church at Great Warley, Essex, in memory of Heseltine's father, Arnold Heseltine.

I will write again soon, when I have more time, a less mangy letter than the present one, I hope.

Much love from yours affectionately
Philip Heseltine

P.S. By the way, could you let me know the date of the concert of your works that was given in London in 1899?[90] I should very much like, while I am in Oxford, to go to the Bodleian Library (where all old papers are kept) and read the contemporary notices of it.

37
Frederick Delius to Philip Heseltine

Grez sur Loing
(S & M)
14 Dec 1912

My dear Heseltine

We returned here day before yesterday, having been 4 weeks absent—Berlin, Frankfort—Wiesbaden & Cologne. I cannot tell you how glad I am to be back here again—I received your interesting letter in Wiesbaden & postponed answering until I was quietly at home again—The 'Mass' was postponed because Felix von Kraus[91] could not sing on Dec 7th   I know of no English Baritone who could sing the part of Zarathustra impressively—I hope it will be given early in the year—On Jan 20th it will be given in Munich. 'Life's dance' was given in Berlin on Nov 15th at the Philharmonie—Oskar Fried—wonderfully well—I want to work now so am afraid I shall not be in England before the 'Mass' is given. Should you hear 'Midsummer song' tell me how it sounds —I have never heard it & dont know if it comes off—It was very kind of you to make the transcription of Life's dance' for Gardiner   I, myself, prefer a transcription with everything in it—altho' for publishing purposes I believe the

---

[90] This was a concert of his own works which Delius organized on 30 May 1899 in St James's Hall, London. *Over the Hills and Far Away* (first English performance), *Légende*, two movements from the incidental music for *Folkeraadet* (first English performance), 5 Danish songs (first performance), *The Dance Goes On* (an early version of *Lebenstanz*) (first performance), *Mitternachtslied* (first performance), extracts from *Koanga* (first English performance). The conductor was Alfred Hertz.

[91] Felix von Kraus: Austrian baritone who made his name at Bayreuth in 1899 and later taught at the Royal Academy of Music in Munich.

Editors prefer the boiled down one—A musician, of course, wants everything so that he can form an idea of the work—One need not agree with all Nietzsche says—I dont—But read *him*—& dont read books about him—as you get no real idea of the man—He often contradicts himself—But that is just what makes his work so human & Life itself is full of contradictions of all sorts—He is not pedantic & not theoretical, Like all other Philosophers—he erects no system whatever & looks at Life itself straight between the eyes—I hate war just as much as you do & so does Nietzsche—He means, of course, the war of Life—war against frauds—Lies—Religious Dogmas, & everything which tends to paralize the individual & his development—I have not seen your uncle at Marlòtte for quite a long time—It appears he called here just before we arrived—I should have been delighted if you could have spent Christmas with me here & hope that you will have, at least, a Merry one with your uncle—The next time you have holidays come over here & stay with us—Should you be able to come for this Christmas instead of going to your uncle we shall both be delighted & have a real good time—You can leave London in the morning & be here for dinner—With love

yours affectionately
Frederick Delius

My new Music drama 'Fennimore' will be performed at the beginning of next season at Cologne or Frankfort—

38
Philip Heseltine to Frederick Delius

16.12.12.   *Cefn-Bryntalch*
                              Abermule
                              Montgomeryshire

Dear Mr Delius

I heard the 'Midsummer Song' in Windsor last Monday, and was only too thankful that you were not present, as the performance would have made you *writhe*!! It was even worse than I had expected. Parratt is a hopelessly bad conductor at the best of times, and well known to be out of sympathy with any modern music: he beat something which looked more like four in a bar than two in a bar, though what he actually meant to beat was not clear! The choir was sadly deficient in numbers, and, being accustomed chiefly to Palestrina and antique madrigals, obviously failed to grasp the music. I believe they call Stanford and Parry 'modern'! However, a striking testimony to the outstanding value of your part-song, as music, was afforded by the fact that, presented as it was under such adverse conditions, it was more appreciated by the audience than any other number on the programme! It was the only song that earned an encore, though the encore was not given. Applause, however, continued loudly until Parratt turned to make a speech, and said: 'The only people who will sing that again will be the audience'—a remark, apparently intended to be humorous!

I was very disappointed at not seeing you in London on the 7th, but I hope it will not be long before you are in England again, and I trust that the intended performance of the 'Mass of Life' will not be long deferred. The Edward Mason choir concert (where the 'Midsummer Song' will be done again) comes off in February.

I am having a splendid time here, all alone, with a new pianola which has just arrived. It is an immense and endless joy to me, and is an exceedingly good machine. I am hoping to discover that some of your music has been done for pianola, but I have not yet come across any: if there is none, I shall agitate for some from the Orchestrelle company! I have some very interesting music at present, Moussorgsky, Grieg, MacDowell, Liszt, Chopin and others. The Moussorgsky 'Nuit sur le mont chauve', though scarcely beautiful, is one of the most original pieces of music I have seen for a long while, and is nearly 50 years old! Some of MacDowell's piano pieces I think very beautiful: Carreño[92] has been playing a good deal of his music lately in London, and nearly all the critics disparage it frightfully.

I went to a 'Post-Impressionist' exhibition of pictures in London last week, and was very much surprised at the extraordinary conglomeration of styles that apparently come under that heading. Cézanne,[93] Matisse,[94] all kinds of horrible 'cubists', and weird people who seem to be merely imitating the crudest forms of mediaeval art all jostle one another in the same gallery, and presumably all wish to be in the same class. Can this possibly be right? I have never seen anything more appalling than 'Cubist' pictures, though there was much in the exhibition that I liked very much.

I must stop now for the present.

Hoping both you and Mrs Delius are quite well. Believe me

Yours affectionately
Philip Heseltine

[92] Maria Teresa Carreño (1853–1917), Venezuelan pianist, one of the leading woman pianists of her day.
[93] Paul Cézanne (1839–1906), French painter.   [94] Henri Matisse (1869–1954), French painter.

39
Philip Heseltine to Frederick Delius

18.12.12.   *Cefn-Bryntalch*
                                    Abermule
                                    Montgomeryshire

Dear Mr Delius

Our letters evidently crossed: yours was forwarded on to me from Newbold
Pacey, which place, I am thankful to say, I have left, never to see again! It is
most exceedingly kind of you to ask me to spend Christmas with you: if I were
free, no invitation could possibly have been more welcome to me than yours. I
should have simply loved to come, but, alas, I cannot possibly escape the 'family party' with the religeous uncle. The same people foregather there year after
year (I have had to go every year in succession for the past ten years, in fact,
with one exception, every year I can remember!) and the absence of any person
of this number would cause a most appalling sentimental hullabaloo, especially
so near the date as this. My mother, my small cousin and the friend who spends
his holidays with us are all dragged in, though none of them want to go! The
fact is that the uncle, being very wealthy and very religeous, (one thinks at once
of Jesus and the rich men!) is regarded as the family saint, so that all his wishes
amount to laws in the eyes of the rest of the family!! (Of course, this is a very
'shocking' thing for a nephew to say of his 'elders and betters'!!!!!!) I think even
Uncle Joe adores him, and as a fact, he is quite a pleasant person, though nothing exceptional, though in the capacity of the heavy, religeous uncle I cannot
boast of any great love for him. I have kept, as curiosities, two letters of his,
which were evidently meant to make a great impression on my mind: they cause
vast entertainment to all who read them!! In his last effort he assured me that

'you have my prayers night and morning'!!

Very well-meaning, and I am grateful for his kind thoughts—at least, I should
be, if they were really as valuable as he thinks they are, but you can imagine
the effect this type has on me! A family party is always unharmonious: I hate
most of the people there, and have to pretend to love them! They are all very
religeous, and the chief occupation of most of them is fox-hunting.

It makes me more angry than I can say, when I think that I might have been
having a jolly time with you, and yet have to go and curse my fate among people
whom I never want to see again!! However, I shall remember your invitation

for next time I have holidays, and shall be only too delighted to avail myself of it, if I possibly can. It is *most* kind of you: I thank you a thousand times.

I am afraid I have wearied you with a tedious page of domestic grumbles—I hate this family domesticity and should like to sweep it all into Hell with a stroke if I could, but I cannot keep out of it—just yet, at any rate. It is such an enormous relief to be able to write freely, what is here considered 'wicked'—i.e. to *say* you do not *adore* all those who, by merest accident, happen to be one's relations, though nine people out of ten, I am sure, loathe most of their relations but dare not say so!

I am going to the Musical League concerts in Birmingham next month.

I am reading Nietzsche himself now: at present, I am reading 'The Genealogy of Morals'[95] which I find extraordinarily interesting. I want to wash my mind absolutely clean of all the Christian muck that has stagnated there all these years, and it is a tough job—for me, at any rate, and when one is surrounded by Christians more than half one's time, without a soul with a free mind to speak to, it becomes doubly difficult. But I have lived twice as much since I first started to get clear of its shackles, and a fight—a mental fight of this kind, I love! I quite see now what Nietzsche means in *that* way.

I am sending you a copy of Fiona Macleod's poems, with best wishes for Christmas: if you have them already, return to Joseph Thompson & son, Broad Street, Oxford, and change it for something else. All good wishes to you and Mrs Delius, and many thanks again for your invitation.

Yours affectionately
Philip Heseltine

40
Frederick Delius to Philip Heseltine

[Grez sur Loing
S & M
18 December 1912]

Dear Heseltine—I forgot to tell you that my Concert in London was May 30th 1899. What you wrote about 'Midsummer song' amused me greatly   How can one misinterpret such an easy piece. It is the most harmless thing I ever wrote & dates from a long time ago.

---

[95] Vol. 13 of *The Complete Works of Nietzsche*, trans. Horace B. Samuel (Edinburgh and London, 1913).

It is absolute nonsense to expose a great artist like Cezanne with Cubists etc. Van Gogh Gauguin & Cezanne are great artists & have nothing in common with Cubists or futurists

affectionately
Frederick Delius

Postcard.

41
Frederick Delius to Philip Heseltine

[Grez sur Loing
S & M
26 December 1912]

The books have just arrived—How kind of you to send them to me! I am look-ing forward with great pleasure to reading them—good luck in the coming year

yrs ever Fr Delius

Picture postcard, Grez-sur-Loing. Vue sur le Loing.

1913

DELIUS spent the early weeks of 1913 revising the conclusion of his opera *Fennimore and Gerda*, though regular work was soon halted by various trips away from Grez during the course of the year. In mid-January he travelled to Munich to attend a performance of *A Mass of Life*, whilst in March he was in London, where Beecham presented the second English performance of the *Mass* at Covent Garden. Delius's music now seemed to be gaining popularity in London with Balfour Gardiner including *Lebenstanz* and the Piano Concerto in his series of concerts. Gardiner's role was a very important one as he was, in fact, one of Delius's early champions, promoting his music wherever possible and also assisting in the checking of proofs. However, his greatest contribution was probably the easing of Delius's financial burdens (through the lack of royalties from scores in the hands of German and Austrian publishers) by buying his house at Grez from him and allowing him to live there rent-free for the rest of his life.[1] Heseltine paid a brief visit to Grez in mid-March and in May Delius travelled to Paris to attend performances by the Diaghilev Ballet and then to Jena where *In a Summer Garden* was to be performed at the annual Tonkünstlerfest. After yet another trip to Paris in June, this time to hear Beecham conduct a performance of *Appalachia*, Delius went alone to Norway in early July whilst Jelka returned to Grez to work on her stage designs for *Fennimore and Gerda*. At the end of July she sailed from Holland to Bergen to join him in Norway. On their return to Grez Delius resumed work on the *Requiem*, though there were yet again intervening trips, this time to Leipzig (to hear Nikisch give the first performance of *On Hearing the First Cuckoo in Spring* and *Summer Night on the River* on 23 October) and to Vienna, where he was disappointed by the postponement of an intended first performance of *An Arabesque*. By the end of 1913 he had returned to Grez, where he resumed work on the *Requiem*.

By February Heseltine was having additional coaching in Latin and Greek from another clergyman tutor, the Reverend Hubert Allen in Didbrook, a village at the foot of the Cotswold hills, not far from Cheltenham. It was during his time there that he met Olivia ('Viva') Smith, one of four sisters who lived in the nearby village of Stanway and with whom he was to have an intense love affair during the months that followed. In several letters written during this year we find him turning to Delius for fatherly advice about the problems encoun-

[1] S. Lloyd, *H. Balfour Gardiner* (Cambridge, 1984), 156–7.

tered in this unsatisfactory and, at times, stormy relationship. He managed to pay two visits to France that year: one in March when he spent some time with the Deliuses and his Uncle Joe, and later in September when he met the American poet Alan Seeger and arranged *A Dance Rhapsody* for piano duet. Earlier, in July, the *Musical Times* had accepted his article 'Some Reflections on Modern Musical Criticism'. Having duly passed the Oxford entrance examination, he began his ill-fated year at Christ Church on 10 October. During this unhappy time he neglected his studies, meeting up with Viva Smith and continuing to absorb himself in Delius's music and attending concerts in London whenever possible. A number of important friendships date from this year, especially with the composer Kaikhosru Sorabji and the poet Robert Nichols. The December vacation found him at home in Wales, where he succeeded in escaping the family gathering in Essex, spending Christmas Day with an aunt in Whitney-on-Wye instead. By now angry quarrels with his mother had become a more and more regular feature of his life.

42
Philip Heseltine to Frederick Delius

8. 1. 13.   *Cefn-Bryntalch*
                                   Abermule
                                   Montgomeryshire

Dear Mr Delius

I don't know what you will think of me for plaguing you with so many letters full of trivialities when you are busy with the greatest matters in the world, but you have been so good to me that I think perhaps you will forgive me if I ask your advice before taking or not taking a step which will be of the greatest importance to me: for there is noone to whom I feel I can turn at the present moment, sooner than to you, though I do hope I am not making a nuisance of myself, with my petty affairs. It is this: I simply cannot go on with my present humdrum slavery to Latin and Greek for the next five years, for the sake of a possible post in the Civil Service, where I could vegetate complacently for the rest of my life on a large salary and pension thrown in. To begin with, I have the greatest possible aversion to the work which I should have to do for the next five years—and it involves incessant drudgery, even in vacations: also I believe (though of course I may be quite wrong) that such wholesale immersion in the

'classics' constitutes a real bar to one's development in other ways. I have the
greatest respect for many of the great classical writers, but to study these exclusively is another matter. In addition, I have not the slightest enthusiasm for a
post in the Civil Service and without enthusiasm, noone, I am sure, ever succeeded in a competitive examination. Enthusiasm seems to me to be a factor of
the highest importance for success in any work. There is a passage in Arthur
Symons' introduction to Dowson's poems which rather haunts me though I am
at times a little sceptical as to it's truth. It occurs on page xix and begins: 'For,
there is not a dream which may not come true, if we have the energy which
makes, or chooses our own fate. We can always, in this world, get what we want,
if we will it intensely and persistently enough.' Yet of course the mere *Will*
to Power is a very different thing to having the ability and energy to attain it:
even slaves have a *Will* to Power . . . . There is only one thing I have a burning
enthusiasm for, only one thing I feel I could work for, come what may of adverse
conditions, and that is, vaguely,—Music: I say 'vaguely' because I have absolutely
no confidence in myself, or that I have the smallest ability to do anything in
any specific branch of Music. At the same time, if I could but attain the mean-
est position in the world of Music, I would sooner die like a dog *there* (if need
be), than attain to a comfortable and conventional position in the Civil Service,
or the Stock Exchange. That is exactly how I feel about the matter.

When I was with you in Grez, nearly a year and a half ago, you advised me
to abandon all other pursuits, and to devote myself to music. I was a fool not
to do so at once, I suppose, but at that time my ideas of what I was going to
do were so utterly confused that I had not the courage to take any decisive step.
Do you still advise me to do so? Can I rely upon my enthusiasm—the greatest
I have for anything in the world—for the necessary energy to make something
of my project? Having no definite talent in any particular branch of Music, I
am not particularly hopeful: my chief hope is that if I devote the next five years
seriously to the study of music, instead of wasting my time at Oxford, I may
be able to develop whatever slender ability I may have to some degree of proficiency. This is but a vague and general outline: details are hard to fix upon, and
perhaps unnecessary just at present. If I felt I could ever do anything worthy of
the name of composition, I should have no hesitation whatever. Of course, it
is my greatest hope that by concentrating all my attention and energy on music,
I might, in time, possibly attain even that, but, I frankly admit, I am rather
taken aback by my *present* lack of ability to do anything whatsoever, and by the
consequent lack of confidence in myself . . . Perhaps after all I shall have to resign
myself to the office stool . . But, apart from composition, I would rather do anything in the way of musical work than submit to the life I seem about to enter
upon . . . Perhaps I demand too much from Life, perhaps my castles in the air

will fall with a sudden crash: still, I simply cannot help building them up, even if they are built in vain. . . . At the present moment, what I really have my eyes upon is—do not laugh at me too much!—musical criticism!! With five years general study of music, I think I could do that as well as some of the men whose columns one reads in the press. With this, I also include the writing of books on musical subjects, and as many other musical tasks as I can combine with it. . . . Failing that, I might be able to scrape along by copying orchestral parts, or even make piano transcriptions of orchestral works. I might learn some orchestral instrument, and so get to know the orchestra from the inside—that is, if I could get into an orchestra at all: at least, I could thrash the big drum! Or perhaps, after years of patient study, I might attain to the lofty position of pianist to a cinematograph theatre—I happened to see an advertisement for one yesterday in our little town! However, I do not want to study the piano unless it is absolutely necessary: but I should like to play in an orchestra . . . That is the rough outline of what I might possibly do if I devoted myself entirely to music for the next five years. Any of the courses I have mentioned above I should love to adopt—except perhaps the cinema pianist's job! However, my chief attention must, I think be directed to the requirements of musical criticism . . . . To descend to more sordid details—I have got to make a living out of it somehow. I do not anticipate any very serious opposition from my mother, though there will very likely be a fearful row at first. I have not, of course, breathed a word to her on the subject: I cannot discuss things with her, for, except superficially, we are too far apart in all matters. I shall have to settle upon a more or less definite plan, and then lay it before her: she will not of course, be able to compel me into anything else, much less the Civil Service, for admission to that depends upon very hard work, which I should refuse to do. But I do not really see why she should raise any objection whatever: she may take it quite calmly from the first. But, being under 21 as I am, I cannot break away and strike out for myself. I *must*, somehow, induce my mother to let me spend the next five years in musical education, instead of at Oxford. It certainly will not cost any more. I do not really think there will be any difficulty about this in the end. Only after the five years, I must have some means of supporting myself. In three years time, when I am 21, I shall have an income of £80 a year of my own: all my father's money was left to my mother for her life, so that anything over and above that £80 will have to come from her. But I do not for a moment anticipate any serious opposition . . . . I have not come to this decision rashly, hurriedly or without very serious consideration: to begin a musical career would be the first step towards my highest ambitions: to renounce it for ever would be to bid farewell to the aspirations I have cherished for years:—though perhaps I am a fool, and my ambitions but folly. Please forgive me for inflicting all this nonsense on you, but I cannot help asking your guidance at the present time. I am, so to speak, at a cross-roads: I must make a decision, one way or the other, within the next few days. At the end of next week or the beginning of the week after that, I am supposed to be going to live with *another parson*[2] (!!!!) and read Latin and Greek, Greek and Latin (world without end, Amen!) until I go up to Oxford in October. The whole prospect revolts me: I *must* get out of it somehow, if it is possible: but if not, then I may as well submit quietly. But— . . . it is very difficult.

Even if I have to go to the 'advocatus diaboli' (for such are parsons if ever there were such), I shall undoubtedly run away in order to attend some of the Balfour Gardiner concerts in February and March. The programmes simply make my mouth water, and I rejoice to see that your Piano Concerto is going to be done again.

I went to Birmingham for the Musicians' League concerts and enjoyed them immensely. I did three concerts in two days, and also attended the final rehearsal of the orchestral concert. The London String Quartet played 'Molly on the Shore'[3] splendidly: it is a delicious little work. I did not care for Bantock's[4] huge choral symphony 'Atalanta in Calydon' which was given at the choral concert. The music, apart from the choral effects, struck me as being very trivial and commonplace, having scarcely any affinity to Swinburne's splendid poems, which deserve a far finer musical treatment.

Bantock's harmonic scheme all through the work (except here and there in the last movement) is exceedingly dull, and I do not think the total effect produced justifies the immense and, to judge from the performance, well-nigh insuperable difficulties which must be tackled in rehearsing it. The orchestral concert was the most interesting.[5] Save for one piece of sheer hogwash by a Jew called Keyser, (who has the most revolting face I have ever seen outside the Zoo), the programme was a splendid one. One number, however, stood out above all the rest, for my taste at any rate, namely the three songs with orchestral accompaniment composed and sung by Frederic Austin, which I thought quite lovely. Of the orchestral numbers a delightful overture by Arnold Bax pleased me most. I am extremely fond of his work: it is so poetic, and reflects the spirit and temperament of the Celt most beautifully: in fact, it has a great likeness to the work of some of the modern poets of Ireland, such as W. B. Yeats and George Russell.[6]

[2] The Revd Hugh Bancroft Allen (1856–1950).   [3] A work by Percy Grainger.

[4] Granville Bantock (1868–1946), English composer and conductor; at this time Professor of music at Birmingham University. A great friend of Delius, he gave the first performance of *Brigg Fair* at Liverpool on 18 Jan. 1908.

[5] This programme, given in the Birmingham Town Hall on 3 Jan., included Bax's *Festival Overture*, Prelude to Act IV of *Othello* by H. A. Keyser, and 'Three Songs of Unrest' by Frederic Austin (sung by the composer).

[6] George William Russell (1867–1935), Irish poet and mystic better known as Æ.

I went to see Mr Balfour Gardiner in Birmingham, and I met Arthur Fagge[7] in his rooms, who told me that he had conducted the 'Midsummer Song' several times, and that it was very popular with the London Glee Club.

Is there yet a piano arrangement of the 'Dance Rhapsody'? Several people have asked me about it lately, as it has been done a good many times in London and the provinces during the last few months. It ought to be cut for the pianola: it would be very effective.

I am having great times with the pianola here, and learning a tremendous lot of new music. It is wonderful how very quickly one gets to know an orchestral work quite thoroughly by playing it over and over again on the pianola, with the full score.

If I am ever going to become a musical critic, I think it would be no bad thing if I spent several months doing nothing but making myself absolutely familiar with all the biggest works of 'classical' music by means of the pianola—Brahms, Beethoven, Schumann etc—the symphony writers especially. I have three complete symphonies at present: Brahms no 3 (which I like very much) Schumann no 2 and Elgar no 1. What do you think of this course for a while—the next month or so, for instance!

I hope the performance of the 'Mass of Life' will be fixed for an early date. I am longing to hear it again.

I must stop this epistle: I do hope you do not mind my writing to you like this. I cannot tell you what a help, what a relief it is to be able to turn to you and ask your advice at a time like this.

If you still advise me to devote myself to music, I can assure you that nothing on this earth shall prevent my doing so.

Affectionately yours
Philip Heseltine

---

[7] Arthur Fagge (1864–1943), English organist and choral conductor. He founded the London Choral Society in 1903, giving performances of a vast number of works for chorus and orchestra including revivals of neglected or forgotten as well as performing new works.

43

Frederick Delius to Philip Heseltine

Grez sur Loing
S & M
11/1/1913

My dear Heseltine

Your letter interested me very much indeed—& I may tell you once for all that I take the greatest interest in you & your career, & shall always be only too happy to help you in whatever way I can—You ask me for advice in choosing between the civil service—for which you seem to have no interest whatever —& music, which you love—I will give it you—I think that the most stupid thing one can do is to spend ones life doing something one hates or for which one has no interest—In other words it is a wasted Life—I do not believe in sacrificing the big things of Life to anyone or anything—In your case I do not see why you should sacrifice the most important thing in your life to your mother: you will certainly regret it if you do, later on,—Children always exaggerate the duty they have to their parents—Parents *very seldom* sacrifice anything at all to their children—In your case your mother has certainly not; since she married again—In other words followed her own feelings—&, of course, did entirely right in so doing & I should advise you to do the same—I was entirely in the same position when I was your age & had a considerably harder fight to get what I wanted—I chucked up everything & went to America. One has every chance of succeeding when one does what one loves & I can tell you that I personally have never once regretted the step I took. The greatest pleasure & satisfaction I have experienced in Life has been thro' music—In making it & in hearing it & in living with it—I should advise you to study music,[8] so that you will be able to give lessons in Harmony, Counterpoint & orchestration. You can always become a critic. I think that you are sufficiently gifted to become a composer—Everything depends on your perseverance—etc etc. One never knows how far one can go—I will find out where you can receive the most modern & best musical instruction—Perhaps in Paris—perhaps in Berlin—The opportunities for hearing music are infinitely greater in Berlin—& I have friends there who might be very useful to you—Emerson[9] says in one of his Essays something that resembles the Arthur Symons quotation—

---

[8] Heseltine told Taylor of Delius's letter thus: 'I had a most kind and encouraging letter from Delius about 3 weeks ago: he advised me strongly and unreservedly to devote myself entirely to music, though, of course, my ideas and prospects are as yet very vague.' Heseltine to Taylor, 1 Feb. 1913, BL 54197.

[9] Ralph Waldo Emerson (1803–82), American essayist, poet, and philosopher.

He says something to this purpose—

'A man who works with his Whole soul at anything whatever—will make it a success before he is 50.' I believe this to be perfectly true—Ones talent develops like muscles that you are constantly training—Trust more in hard work than in inspiration—I am getting ready to go to Munich for the 'Mass of Life' 20th Jan—I leave here on the 16th—& shall be back here again on the 22nd— Beecham gives it in Covent Garden in February[10]—Write me again & tell me what you have decided to do. I have already written a song to words by Fiona MaCcleod I-Brasîl[11]—I think it is good—Have you a copy of the 'Mass of Life'? If not I will give you one—

your affectionate friend
Frederick Delius

44
Philip Heseltine to Frederick Delius

28. 1. 13.   Didbrook Vicarage
                                                           Winchcomb
                                                        Gloucestershire

Dear Mr Delius
Your most kind and encouraging letter has remained unanswered too long, I fear, but I have waited this fortnight before writing to you again, in order to get a clearer idea of the course which I shall have to adopt, and my mother's attitude. It is no use mincing matters: my mother is a totally irrational person, so far embedded in Christianity of a certain kind and the thorough conventionalism it breeds that, when confronted by a problem such as I have put before her, she has absolutely no strength to face it, and makes a lamentable display of hesitant moods, being a very impulsive person: she cannot look the matter fairly in the face: she will not even discuss it fairly: her emotions, here as often before, get the better of her reason and sweep it clean away in five minutes when we are having a discussion, so the consequence is that, instead of reasoning the matter coolly and dispassionately, I have been involved in several quite fruitless and very unpleasant arguments, in which I scarcely ever met with anything but

---

[10] The performance was actually postponed until 10 March.
[11] Heseltine had sent a book of poems by Fiona Macleod (pseudonym of William Sharp) to Delius for Christmas.

passionate nonsense in answer to what I had to say, with the result that after a whole fortnight, nothing has been arrived at, and I have come here to pass the time!!

I arrived here last night, but although the man is a parson, he creates a pleasing illusion to the contrary by wearing absolutely rational clothes, and seems, from his ordinary conversation, to be quite a rational being, though I dare say that impression would disappear when professional matters were dealt with! However, I don't think I shall be expected to do any work at Latin etc, or at least very little, and meanwhile, I want to read Schönberg's 'Harmonielehre' right through in German: I imagine I shall derive a good foundation from it for the study of 'harmony' as taught in Conservatoires, and also a good deal more besides, that the ordinary pedants cannot see through!

My present position, however, is extremely unsatisfactory, and I am immensely annoyed at finding my mother so completely unable to face the question properly. Further, I am not so sure of the small private income I mentioned in my last letter: I now find that it is tied up in some way, and can be withheld by my so-called 'guardian' (!) who is the pious uncle that built the church at Warley. Furthermore—one of the most exasperating points—my mother labours under the monstrous conception that Youth (before the arbitrary age of 21— characteristic, that!) is inherently a wicked and depraved period of life, and will certainly perish in one immense debauch, unless kept severely in check either by Christianity, or by uncongenial people appointed for the purpose of imposing absurd restraints—or, in other words, that 'paralysis of the will'!—such people one, of course, always dislikes. My mother insists that, even if I were to go and live abroad, she would see that I were placed in charge of 'good, solid people' (that is her execrable phrase!!)—some pious, Lutheran family, I suppose, from whom one would never for a moment be free . . . . . But it is no good discussing these matters: my mother and I might be inhabitants of different planets for all that we have in common . . . . Apparently, if matters continue to drift as they are now doing, I shall find myself passing into Oxford in five weeks time, and going up there next October! I have repeatedly told my mother I am not going, which I think she realizes, though still hopes I shall change my mind. She has not refused to provide money for a musical education: in a temper, she has consented to do so, but if that mood continued, she would see that I had a Hell of a time!—But, of course, those tempers do not continue. If I am firm enough, she will, reluctantly enough, allow me to go in for music: that is something, but I, for my part, must evolve more definite schemes of life. The Civil Service is definitely 'off'. Of course, it would be *possible* for me to go to Oxford, and to study music at the same time, or afterwards: one could take up English literature or something at Oxford. But that seems to point to a waste of time, and an inevitable lack of concentration on music. Oxford apart, is a really complete musical education possible in England, without spending a certain amount of time abroad? There seem to be a fair number of very good musicians of the present day who have studied entirely in this country—Arnold Bax, for instance, as the most notable—and in my case, I am sure my mother would be far more amenable to my following a musical career, if I could work at it in London.

For my own part, if the instruction is equally good, I should very much like to remain in London, for many reasons: I have a great love for the place, though that is besides the mark, rather, and I could keep in touch with all the musical movements in England, which would, perhaps be useful for critical work later on. In any case, I shall have to come to London eventually. This, of course, is only a suggestion: I should love to go to Berlin, but the pious Lutheran family —!!! What about London first and Berlin later, when the maternal mind will have become tranquillized? The difficulty of the whole matter lies in the fact that I am entirely dependant on my mother until I can earn my own living. And this again prompts me to investigate further how I shall be able to do so later on:—not that this damps my enthusiasm at all, but I have set my mind first and foremost on becoming a critic. However, I have written enough on this subject for the present: your last letter cheered me tremendously: thank you a thousand times for being so kind to me, in interesting yourself in my affairs: it is really too good of you, for I fear my attainments in music will never be worthy of your kindness to me.

Do not trouble to write again if you are busy, though, of course, I always love receiving letters from you: but please understand that I should be the last person in the world to wish to bother you with my little affairs, and although I write at great length and tell you of them, *please* do not let me become a nuisance.

I shall, of course, come up for the 'Mass of Life': (by the way, when is it to be given? I have not seen any advertisement of the performance as yet) I hope to see you then, and if you can spare a little time, I should so like to discuss things with you. I am also going up to one or two of the Balfour Gardiner concerts.

I think if you had not been coming over so soon, I should have come to see you yesterday when I was supposed to be coming here! That would have set the pot a'boiling at home with a vengeance!! But I think peaceable methods are more satisfactory if at all possible.

Is there any kind of musical work, such as transcriptions or anything of that kind, that I could do *now*, at odd times, do you think? I should revel in something of the kind, and if I could get occasional jobs of that order already, it would no doubt be encouraging to those at home! Where could one get such?

I am immensely keen on writing some more articles for musical papers, but unfortunately I have nothing to write about just at present. It is rather appalling to have a burning desire to write something without having anything to say, and I suppose there is no cure for the disease. It is the same with composition: I cannot write a note. Twelve songs, improvised at the piano, make my grand sum total!—That is rather an awful thought. I have heard the phrase 'musical constipation' used in this connection! It sums up the case rather well, I think.

I have read more Nietzsche lately with great interest, though I cannot as yet arouse any enthusiasm for his *constructive* policies. I am so glad you like Fiona Macleod's poetry.

It is very kind of you to offer to give me a copy of the 'Mass of Life', and of course, I should have appreciated a copy given by you immensely, but I have one already, bound up in a large volume with 'Appalachia' and 'Sea-Drift'. Thank you very much, all the same, for the offer.

By the way, have you read Dowson's[12] little book of short stories, called 'Dilemmas'?[13] A new edition has just been published, and I think it is perfectly charming.

This is, I am afraid, a very inadequate letter to thank you for your last to me. I cannot tell you how grateful I am to you for your encouraging advice and sympathy: so you must just 'read between the lines'!

Affectionately yours
Philip Heseltine

45
Frederick Delius to Philip Heseltine

Grez sur Loing
S & M 13/2/1913

My dear Heseltine—

Last Sunday your mother & Mʳ Jones came here to lunch[14]—Of course your mother wanted to consult me about your future etc—Of course she is like most other mothers who have the interests of their children at heart but seem entirely

---

[12] Ernest Christopher Dowson (1867–1900), English poet.

[13] E. C. Dowson, *Dilemmas: Stories and Studies in Sentiment* (London, 1895).

[14] Heseltine had written to Taylor telling him: 'My people are at present in the south of France: they went to lunch with the Deliuses en route!!' Heseltine to Taylor, 17 Feb. 1913, BL 54197.

incapable of being quite natural & rational—I explained to her that the only possible chance of succeeding in Life was to work at something one loved—She seems to think that you do not know your own mind & would change just as suddenly again—I told her that there was no great hurry to *pounce upon a career*. But that I thought all your aptitudes pointed towards the musical profession in some form or other. I think she will consent to anything you seriously put before her—Even if you only intend to write about music it would be wise to go thro' a Conservatory in order to work a year or so at Harmony & Counterpoint as the schools teach it—Only to know what it is. I would also advise you to go to Germany. There is more musical atmosphere there & *England* is so Bourgeois & matter of fact. I told her that should you go to Berlin it would be much wiser to let you live on your own hook & in lodgings instead of with a slow bourgeois family—This, of course, she assented to with some trembling, I surmise. We are never grown up for our mothers—Knowing themselves they at once fear we shall at once fall to the snares of other females—Do not be in a hurry & think over the matter—

Should you decide for the musical profession I would suggest Berlin first & London after so that when you once go to London it may be for good & perhaps to get a position on some paper or weekly or monthly—You write marvellously well, which cannot be said for many of the English critics—Whenever you would like to pay us a visit—just come—Unless Beecham gives the 'Mass' which is doubtful as I hear nothing about it—I shall not come to England—Write me again soon & tell me all about things

yrs affectionately
Frederick Delius

46
Philip Heseltine to Frederick Delius

17. 2. 13.   *DIDBROOK VICARAGE*
                              WINCHCOMBE
                              GLOS.

Dear Mr Delius

Your kind letter reached me on Saturday night—a thousand thanks. It was very good of you to see my mother and to speak about me: she would, of course, be calmer of necessity with you: I find it absolutely hopeless to try and discuss things with her at all. She and I have absolutely nothing whatever in common, and—to you at any rate—I cannot pretend that I am a loving and 'dutiful' (!) son. Now that you have seen the amiable creature she married (and they get on wonderfully well together) you will realize how much she appreciates the imaginative and artistic! I say nothing against my step-father: he is quite a pleasant person in his way, but—well, you will have realized 'his way'. My father was, I understand, excessively pious, fervent in his devotion to the 'grand traditions' of Christianity and the British nation and empire, no doubt! I cannot *live*, so long as I am with these people . . . . . 'distance lends enchantment'. . . . etc, as we have all heard,—a proverb which in this case I find remarkably apt, and, as my mother has frequently said in one of her emotional-hysteric moods, I shall probably regret her absence when she is dead. All these are, doubtless, very dreadful statements: sometimes I am really almost horrified at my own thoughts, though I simply cannot any longer pretend to feel what I really and truly do not and cannot feel—you, at least, can understand this attitude, and would, I am sure, even if it horrified you. My relations with my mother are, however, of a most unsatisfactory kind. If we were openly and avowedly hostile to each other, things would be better. As it is, there is something pathetic—though I cannot by nature pander to pathos—about her fondness for an unworthy son, who has, perforce, to feign an equal affection, which honestly, from his very heart, he does not feel . . . To you alone could I confess this, but, however unpleasant, it is the inevitable truth. The blame must lie upon my nature, not on my lack of conventional protestations to the contrary. From the very fact that she was such a good mother to me in her way, comes the corollary that I am, so far, such a miserable specimen in mine. I never stood upon my own feet, never woke up to life beyond the nursery and my mother's apron-strings until a year or so ago —that is, exceptionally late. I suppose I woke up comparatively suddenly, with a rude shock, so to speak, being quite incapable of standing on my own legs at all—as though all previous foundations had suddenly collapsed. They were thoroughly rotten, I admit: I am never thankful enough to be rid of them: but the unavoidable fact remains that I am, virtually, but three or four years old: my first fifteen years might almost as well never have been lived: and I find this lack of experience and accomplishments of living quite appalling. I struggle hard to develop now, I am trying my very best to live so as to redeem a part at least of the lost years: but I am constantly being dragged back—at least, I always am feeling the drag, though I do think I really am becoming harder and a little stronger at last. At the present moment, I cannot but feel that I am an absolutely useless specimen in every branch of life—only fit, as I am, for a lethal chamber—: hourly, do I curse the name of Jesus with a loathing too bitter for expression: his blasted doctrines are at the bottom of all this kind of thing. But for you, and a very few others—just one or two—I should have slept through life until the last and final sleep. Now, I am just about as fit for Life as one who has only just woken up in the early morning, at the period when one is, perhaps, more inert and incapable of anything than at any other time, is fit to begin the day's work immediately. Though, alas, in my case, it is not quite early morning—so much of that is gone. This mood, however, is very amply out-weighed by a passionate hope that something—perhaps unknown and incon-ceivable to me at the present time—will happen or develop. My strongest joy lies in *expectation*—in looking forward to things, especially if they are unknown, mysterious, romantic, full of possibilities. That is what keeps me going: perhaps it is but a vain illusion, a dream—but it is all I have. I have often felt myself to be a mere *spectator* of the game of Life: this, I know to my sorrow, has led me to a positively morbid self-consciousness and an introspectiveness that almost amounts to insincerity, breeding as it does a kind of *detachment* from real life. Lately I have tried passionately, to plunge into Life, and *live* myself, forgetfully, if possible of this horrible aloofness: I believe I am just beginning to succeed a little, perhaps, though I know only too well that complete success now will be long and difficult, if not impossible, of attainment . . . . Those fifteen years can-not be shaken off: I was formerly lonely, and shunned the healthy animalism of private and public schools, holding aloof, clinging to the atmosphere of home. Now that I can no longer endure *that*—though I have found, in part, a far bet-ter and more congenial atmosphere, though I would not exchange the nature of the typical English public-school animal even for my present unsatisfactory state—I know that I have been too much, too foolishly and fruitlessly alone, and at home now, I am far more lonely than anywhere else. As a result of this I have become morbidly nervous—even down to a physical 'nervous stricture' —which fact is a terrible hindrance to my having free, happy and healthy intercourse with my fellow-creatures—especially strangers, and those of great 'accomplishment' (so-called) in those rather trivial yet, from a social point of view, important things—games, of various kinds, indoor and outdoor, and an easy, natural, unaffected and un-self-conscious manner in general. Though I loathe athleticism, a mild proficiency in the elements of certain of these games is of great use to one, in helping on to opportunities of intercourse with others. Yet all this I would gladly have sacrificed if I could fall back for consolation to dreams which I felt one day I could create into realities. But I have, at this present moment, nothing at all . . . . I said just now, I was three or four years old: in reality I have only just been born. The great fact that Life is before me, to make something of, is all that I have to live on . . . . but surely it is enough to begin upon, with all the bitter, though useful, experience of those other years to look back upon, as upon a nightmare. The fears of my mother as to my relations with females, if 'on my own hook', make me almost break out into bitter laughter. I *feel* as much I *cannot express*—and noone knows how much that is—I had said 'God only knows'—but if he does, if he exists, it is only to laugh at the absurdity of some of his creatures.

(Do you remember the head of the Egyptian goddess in Leigh Spencer's room in Birmingham? It is a marvellously beautiful thing, and the subtle, half-smile of the lips, and the mysterious, far-away effect of the eyes typify my only possible conception of a God that I could reverence.)—I *feel*, as I say, so passionately sometimes, and yet can *never* express myself: sometimes I have a nightmare, in which I experience an intense, an overpowering fear, and struggle with all my strength, literally '*pousser* un cri', yet can, in my dream, find no voice.

You have probably never experienced this dream, as you *can* express yourself. With me the dream has it's exact counterpart with me in waking Life, constantly, every day, and the sensation is *horrible*—even this I cannot express fully.

As for the opposite sex, and my mother's prudish fears,—the situation is truly ironic. I am acutely sensitive to sex, and to all the beauty and romance associated with it, both in Idealism and Reality: but, as a matter of fact, I know practically no females at all:—absolutely none of my own age—for whose mere society I positively hunger—I know this is a morbid symptom, but that is what it has come to with me: (from this I mean that having absolutely no knowledge of women, I simply have nothing at all to say to them when I come across them —if I were to come across them that is, in any more than merely casual intercourse—again the ghastly nightmare of inability to utter!) I have never in my life experienced the 'kiss of passion'—and I am not strong enough—(or is it really—not *unnatural* enough?) not to desire it. Is this but a reaction from Christianity? —I suppose I ought to dance . . . what an almost ludicrous conclusion!

The long and the short of the matter, however, amounts to this—that now, at any rate, I am determined to *live* my life, to drain it's cup to the very dregs, to live each day, each hour, feverishly perhaps just now,—I am absolutely *ravenous* for Life: what I do, matters not so very much, so long as I live. I cannot live, either in 'classical' examination-study, or on the Stock Exchange, or some such place. But these matters, I must discuss with you, 'viva voce'. It is *most* kind of you to ask me to come to Grez: you don't know how much I long to come and see you again and discuss everything with you: if you really do not mind my coming, may I come on the 14ᵗʰ or 15ᵗʰ of March for a few days? Please tell me if this is in any way inconvenient to you, and I will not come, but I should love to come then, at my earliest opportunity, if you could put up with me then . . . . . . I know I am writing you a very horrible letter: the Priest and a fellow-pupil have been spouting out a speech of Cicero all the time, and nearly driving me wild. I have said too much about my wretched little self—please, please do not think that I am absorbed in a mere narrow and ridiculous egoism—but if you only knew what a tremendous relief and comfort it is to me to be able to write down all my thoughts absolutely without reserve to you, the one and only really kind and sympathetic friend I can talk to in this way—though I know it is presumptuous on my part to worry you like this—you would forgive me . . . I can never thank you enough for all your kindness and sympathy . . . .

I am going up to London on Tuesday the 25th for Balfour Gardiner's second concert, to hear the 'Lebenstanz', and staying for Edward Mason's concert on the 27th to hear the 'Midsummer Song': on the 11th of next month I have to go to Oxford for an absurd exam—though in all probability I shall not eventually go up to Oxford at all—. I shall rush up to London for the Gardiner concert on the 11th,15—a particularly fine programme—and on the 15th, I hope I shall be coming over to see you . . . . If you can have me then, it will be most convenient, for my people will have just returned to England from the Riviera, and there will be no chance of my mother wanting to come with me and stay with Uncle Joe!

Do you know, I have never been with you for any length of time without having my mother close at hand, ready to spoil everything. When I was staying at Marlotte, and spent the evening with you just before leaving, she was so angry at what she called my 'rudeness' to my host at Marlotte that she would scarcely speak to me for two days! Of course, Uncle Joe didn't care two straws, so it was entirely due to her ridiculous ideas. Why it should be 'rude' to absent oneself for one evening I never discovered. Again, in Birmingham, she was always frightfully annoyed when I went out for walks with you, instead of sticking with her the whole time . . . . It is one of those things that annoy me beyond all words— that my mother should do her best to despoil me of the few, precious, all too short hours I have spent with you, for the sake of some petty convention that is quite useless, and her own sense of her importance to me—as if I did not spend much too much time at home already!—So you can imagine with what immense joy I look forward to a stay with you at Grez! . . . . . . I am told that Dr H. P. Allen—the man who murdered 'Brigg Fair' at Oxford!—is doing 'Sea-Drift' at Reading this week: but after the splendid Birmingham performance, I could not bring myself to go and hear that murdered too.

I am very sorry to hear that the 'Mass of Life' has been again postponed: Beecham seems to be Strauss-mad just at present: I hope it is only a passing phase. I am longing to hear your Fiona Macleod song:16 I love those poems intensely. Don't you think 'The Immortal Hour' would make rather a good music-drama? 'I-Brasil' is a very lovely poem: the title refers to a very romantic legend

---

15 Originally announced for 11 March, this concert was moved to 18 March.   16 'I-Brasil'.

which always appeals to me very strongly—concerning the lost continent of
Atlantis, supposed to lie submerged with all it's buildings and towns, beneath
the ocean off the West coast of Ireland. It was regarded by the imaginative Irish
poets as a Paradise of the Blessed: and it is a remarkable, and well-authenticated
fact that sometimes, at sunset, a very curious phenomenon appears on the horizon, off the West coast of Ireland—what it actually *is*, noone knows— . . unless
it be one of those 'dreams that are realities' as Fiona Macleod says beautifully
. . . : many people have sworn that they have seen what appeared to be the shores
of an island, with trees, hills, and houses, from which smoke ascended. It is said
also that men have actually sailed out into the Atlantic in the hope of discovering this country, but have always perished in the attempt . . . . . which seems to
be symbolical of something or another . . . . . .

I am really enjoying myself *immensely* here at present: I do very little 'work'
at the classics, of course: if I read Latin or Greek with the Priest, I do writers
who are usually neglected for their so-called 'non-classical style' but they are infinitely more interesting than the stock-in-trade classics. Lately I have discovered
the Satires of Petronius, which are quite splendid. He was a kind of Roman
Oscar Wilde—who lived at the court of Nero—though his treatment of sexual
matters is far more outspoken, more amusing and consequently more healthy
than anything that could be printed in this language. The Priest is a perfectly
delightful person, and thoroughly lives up to the impression given by his garb,
which I described to you before. He was formerly a schoolmaster, and, curiously enough, was a master at the private school Balfour Gardiner went to, and,
further, coached Gardiner privately for a Charterhouse scholarship in 1891. He
has no beliefs or dogmas, and laughs at religeon as much as I do! He says quite
calmly that he never expects anyone who thinks at all to be religeous, but he
considers that a religeon of some sort—however ridiculous—is absolutely necessary to the lower orders of intellect—an almost Nietzschean attitude! He is a
quite splendid person, and I consider myself immensely fortunate in having lighted
upon him. We all call him 'the priest' to his face, and his wife 'priestess'! What
would my mamma say if she knew his religeous views!!! Of course, he keeps
them within the walls of his study, but it is most refreshing to know that he is
only a parson by force of circumstances, and to observe his delicious, and complete lack of conventional piety. My fellow-pupils—three in number—though
not exactly kindred spirits, are quite pleasant to get along with, and really rather
interesting character-studies. To all outward and superficial appearances, they
are conventional in most respects, athletic, though not offensively so: one only
sees their real nature when one talks about women—'eternal feminine'!—: half
our conversation deals with the subject: it is wonderful how it reveals people's
natures, and it makes one loathe English prudery more and more . . . . The

country about here is quite delightful: I ride about a good deal on my motor-bicycle: . . . I have not had such a good time as I am having now for months past, and I look forward to the future with an eagerness and pleasure greater than I have ever experienced before . . . .

Now I really must come to an end: I hope to see you so very soon, so that we shall be able to discuss everything at our leisure. I feel so immensely happy and relieved to have unburdened my mind to you altogether, in this letter. I hope you will pardon it's rather too personal tone and that it has not wearied you past endurance. Do let me know the moment I become a nuisance to you & I will cease.

Yours affectionately
Philip Heseltine

47
Frederick Delius to Philip Heseltine

Grez sur Loing
S & M
21/2/1913

My dear Heseltine

Just a word in haste—I am working hard at the end of 'Niels Lyhne'—your letter interested me enormously—I love so much your frankness & confidence—We will talk it all over at our leisure when you come—We shall be delighted to have you—Write the exact day of arrival—you can travel right thro' to Grez & be here for dinner by taking the first Calais train—Otherwise you can get a train from the Gare du Lyon at 6. pm you must then change at Moret—Should you miss these you can dine in Paris at the Buffet of the Gare du Lyon & get the 9-40 (In the guide 21-40)   I shall then send a conveyance to the station to meet you—the train arrives at 11.20—I am looking forward with great pleasure to your visit—

affectionately yrs
Frederick Delius

P.S. Of course your mother never told me she was afraid of women etc on your account—I only surmise it. *Please buy* for me at Barkers or elsewhere a little tin of *Mercolized Wax—Dearborn L^{td}*.

48

Philip Heseltine to Frederick Delius

4. 3. 13.   *DIDBROOK VICARAGE*
                            WINCHCOMBE
                            GLOS.

Dear Mr Delius

Thank you so much for your last letter: I am looking forward immensely to coming to see you, and hope to arrive on Monday March 17th, by the train which reaches Bourron at 11.20, if that is really not too late for you. As I shall be staying at Eton for the week-end, I am afraid I shall not be able to catch the early Calais train, so I think I shall come by Dieppe, leaving London at 11 a.m., especially as that route is much cheaper—an important consideration.

I was in London last week, and heard with very great pleasure the 'Lebenstanz' and Midsummer Song at the Balfour Gardiner and Edward Mason concerts respectively. The rest of the Balfour Gardiner programme was very interesting, though in some ways disappointing.[17] I did not care for the new Grainger works at all.[18] There were two good things in the Mason programme: Holbrooke's 'Byron' and Gardiner's delightful ballad, 'News from Whydah'.[19]

I am looking forward with very great interest to the concert on March 11th, when your Piano Concerto is being done, together with Frederic Austin's new symphony,[20] which I am told is quite wonderful. There is to be a big Holbrooke concert on the 14th, which I hope to go to.[21]

I am having a quite splendid time here, though my only music-making consists of playing endless comic songs far into the night and early morning at frequent carousals at the house of an old man who is nearly always half drunk, and very jolly altogether!

Au revoir for a few days.

Affectionately yours
Philip Heseltine

---

[17] The Sixth Balfour Gardiner concert took place on 25 Feb. 1913 and included W. H. Bell's *The Shepherd*, Holst's *The Mystic Trumpeter*, three pieces by Grainger, two songs by Quilter, three songs by Poldowski (Irene Regine Wieniawska, Lady Dean Paul), and *Introduction, Mazurka, and Finale* by O'Neill.

[18] The new Grainger works were *Hill-Song* and *Colonial Song*.

[19] Queen's Hall, 27 Feb. 1913. The programme included works by Delius, Grainger, Holst, and others.

[20] Symphony in E major.

[21] Beecham and Holbrooke conducted the Edward Mason Choir and the London Symphony Orchestra in this concert in Queen's Hall on 14 Mar. 1914.

P.S. I have just opened to-day's paper, and find, to my great surprise and delight, that the performance of 'A Mass of Life' is to take place on Monday next.[22] I hope we shall meet there: I am so very pleased it is coming off after all. If I come up early on Monday, should I be let in to the last rehearsal? I shall of course attend the performance as well, but it would be splendid to hear the work through twice.

By the way, as the 'Mass' is coming off after all, shall you be staying in England for some time when you come over for it? If so, perhaps I had better defer my visit to you, or perhaps you would come down to Wales, if you contemplate making a long stay. Please let me know if the date I have fixed for my visit to you is in the slightest degree inconvenient to you, as I expect your plans will be somewhat altered by this rather sudden announcement of the performance.

49
Frederick Delius to Philip Heseltine

[Grez sur Loing
S & M
4 March 1913]

My dear Heseltine

The 'Mass' will be given on the 10th so we are coming over—I arrive on Thursday night 10.45 and stay at 9 Hans Place—S.W. We can then return to Grez *together*—

Affectionately
Frederick Delius

Postcard.

---

[22] 10 Mar. at Covent Garden conducted by Beecham.

50
Philip Heseltine to Frederick Delius

11. 3. 13.   127 High Street
                                                             Oxford

Dear Mr Delius

Just a line to give you my address, in case you are going to stay over Tuesday next to hear the Piano Concerto, at the Balfour Gardiner concert,[23] which, I see, has now been definitely fixed for that date.

If you are going to stay, let me know and I will come to Grez, if convenient to you, on Wednesday instead of Monday. However, if you are not staying, I will come Monday as we arranged. I am here till Friday morning, afterwards at 26 High St, Eton, Bucks. till Monday. Perhaps I shall see you at the Holbrooke concert on Friday?

In great haste before Arithmetic!

Affectionately yours,
Philip Heseltine

51
Jelka Delius to Philip Heseltine

[12 March 1913]

Dear Mr Heseltine. We shall leave on friday [14 March] as we intended and not stay for Gardiners concert, so you will be most welcome on Monday week at Grez. My husband is busy so I write.

Yrs sincerely
Jelka Delius
9 Hans Place

Postcard.

[23] The Eighth (and last) Balfour Gardiner Concert took place on 18 Mar. Besides Delius's Piano Concerto (played by Evelyn Suart), it included Bantock's *Fifine at the Fair*, Bax's *In the Faery Hills*, Austin's Symphony in E, and Gardiner's *Shepherd Fennel's Dance*.

52
Philip Heseltine to Frederick Delius

3. 4. 13.   *DIDBROOK VICARAGE*
                              WINCHCOMBE
                                 GLOS.

Dear Mr Delius

Just a few lines to let you know that I arrived here safely yesterday morning without having experienced the slightest mal-de-mer,[24] and also to thank you and Mrs Delius again immensely for your kindness to me during the most delightful holiday I have ever spent.[25] I cannot tell you how much I enjoyed being with you at Grez, nor how grateful I am to you for enlightening me on many subjects about which I was formerly perplexed, and for clearing up many difficulties that presented themselves to me before: it gives me quite a new and infinitely broader outlook upon things in general.

I will forward the MS of 'In a Summer Garden' in a day or two: I am so glad you are at last going to publish a piano arrangement of it, for I am sure that many people will in this way get to know and love it, since the Elgarian dog-in-the-manger seems bent on preventing them from hearing it performed! I am very much looking forward to trying my hand at transcribing the 'Dance Rhapsody'.

You must not on any account fail to persuade Balfour Gardiner to motor you both down here in May, and to proceed hence to Cefn Bryntalch.

Please give my kind regards and very best thanks again to Mrs Delius, and believe me

Yours affectionately
Philip Heseltine

---

[24] Heseltine told his mother: 'I have no recollection of the voyage, beyond the fact that I embarked at 1.15 a. m. this morning and resumed my slumbers almost immediately. Neptune's realm proved for the occasion but a gentle cradle, though the roar of human egurgitations was occasionally mingled with my dreams.' Heseltine to his mother, 2 Apr. 1913, BL 57960.

[25] Heseltine wrote to Taylor about the visit: 'I returned on Wednesday last from a perfectly delightful visit to France— eight days with Delius and five with my uncle in the next village. I have seldom enjoyed any holiday so much as this fortnight.' Heseltine to Taylor, 7 Apr. 1913, BL 54197.

53

Philip Heseltine to Frederick Delius

5. 4. '13.   Didbrook Vicarage
                                                                Winchcombe
                                                                     Glos.

Dear Mr Delius

I am sending the MS of 'In a Summer Garden' by the same post as this.[26]
I have not been able to play it through again, as there is no piano here, but I
hope there are no serious blunders. I have altered the disposition of notes a
little so as to make it more easy to play, though as I have not the full score by
me, I think there may be some mistakes or omissions in the phrasing and slurs,
and in parts I have been in some doubt as to notation (there being in the score
flats for some instruments and sharps for others) so that an attempt at consist-
ency has sometimes led to a little obscurity (as for example in the 3rd bar before
§§ 16). But I think in the main that it is playable and easy to read.

Affectionately yours,
Philip Heseltine

Postcard.

54

Frederick Delius to Philip Heseltine

[Grez, 24 April 1913]

My dear Boy—Excuse me for not answering your letter & Postcard—I have
been working very hard—I am so glad you enjoyed your stay here—& hope
you will come again—In a summer garden' will be done at the Tonkünstler fest

---

[26] Heseltine wrote to Taylor: 'I have made a new arrangement of "In a Summer Garden" for piano duet (one piano
this time) which he has consented to send to his publisher, and he is going to send me the score of the "Dance Rhapsody"
to transcribe. . . . "In a Summer Garden" is quite one of his most perfect things: of all his works that I have seen, this
and the "Songs of Sunset" appeal to me the most, which is saying a very great deal. It goes very well for piano duet:
nothing whatever is omitted, and it is still quite easy to play.' Heseltine to Taylor, 7 Apr. 1913, BL 54197. A few days
later he told his mother: 'I have just finished the piano transcription of an orchestral work for Delius, and am waiting
for another score to work upon. It is exceedingly good for me being entirely without a piano, for I find, with much
practise, that I am slowly developing the power of hearing with the eye, which of all musical achievements is the one
I most covet.' Heseltine to his mother, 11 Apr. 1913, BL 57960.

held at Jena from June 4th to 8th & I shall then present your transcription to my publisher—

With love—
Frederick Delius

Postcard.

55
Philip Heseltine to Frederick Delius

27. 4. 13.   *DIDBROOK VICARAGE*
                    WINCHCOMBE
                    GLOS.

Dear Mr Delius

Thanks so much for your post-card. I am so glad to hear that 'In a Summer Garden' is to be done at a German festival:[27] I hope it will not be long before it emerges from the disgraceful neglect with which it has hitherto been treated in England. If you have any copies of the 'Dance Rhapsody' yet, I should be so very pleased if you would lend me one for a while, to make a duet arrangement from: I enjoy doing transcriptions tremendously, and I am rather at a loose end just at present. I wish I could get some more work of this description, but I suppose the job is very much sought after, being a thing that anybody can do with a little care and patience.

I suppose you will very soon be coming over to England if you are going to spend the month of May in London. I hope you will motor down here very soon, when you do come over, and continue your journey to Wales the next day. If you can persuade Gardiner to motor you, you will have a lovely ride here from Berkshire, over the Berkshire downs and the Cotswolds. It is 65 miles from Ashampstead to Didbrook, and about 90 from Didbrook to Abermule. The Elchos place at Stanway is at present undergoing repairs so I fear you will not be able to stay the night there, but there is an excellent hotel at Broadway, 6 miles from here, and quite a good one at Winchcombe, 3 miles off. You could put up in the village, but you would be more comfortable at Winchcombe.

I am looking forward immensely to seeing you here, and so is The Priest.

---

[27] The Tonkünstlerfest of the Allgemeine Deutsche Musikverein took place in Jena (4–8 June 1913). *In a Summer Garden* was conducted by Fritz Stein.

I wonder how Cameron is getting on: I heard from Uncle Joe just after I left Marlotte that he met 'Aunt Célie'[28] in the street of Grez, in a very advanced state of inebriety!

I have been looking at some books on Harmony and Counterpoint lately, but it seems necessary to have someone to look over the dreary exercises one has to do and correct them, so I dare say I shall postpone my study of them until I reach Oxford next October: pedants abound there, and it should prove an ideal spot for this kind of 'musical' work!

Having no piano here, I have been practising score-reading, at which I think I am making a little—but only a *very* little—progress. I find it very hard: however, I managed a Berlioz overture tolerably well the other day.

Now, you really *must* come down here with Gardiner very soon: it will be splendid if you can manage it, and Wales will be looking lovely. It is a beautiful motor run from here to Abermule, with excellent roads, and my mother will be *most* pleased to see you all whenever you like to come. I hope my step-father has sent you all the particulars about flats that you want.

Yours affectionately,
Philip Heseltine

56
Frederick Delius to Philip Heseltine

Grez sur Loing
S&M
[28 June 1913]

My dear Heseltine—

It is a long time since I wrote to you but my time has been pretty well filled up & I had little time for correspondence. The Jena Festival went off very well or very badly if one thinks of the miserable quality of the novelties performed—The 'Summer garden' was very well given & seems to have been quite a success. Of course it sounded very light & airy against the background of 'Schwere Musik'. All the pieces were also so fearfully long—Max Reger's

---

[28] Céline Guillet, Joseph Heseltine's wife.

Römische Festgesang was noisy Bier musik. A piece by 'Rude Stephan'[29] was the best—but far too long—Last Sunday 'Appalachia' was played in Paris. Beecham conducted—The Orchestra was 2nd rate & the Chorus awful & Beecham seemed to be entirely out of his water & made nothing of the Orchestra or Chorus— Next Saturday I leave for Norway—sail from Antwerp & go straight up to the mountains—My wife joins me a month later & we then go up to the Lofoten Islands. I am looking forward immensely to the trip—If you care to join me about the middle of July we might have ten days or a fortnights tramp together amongst the finest mountains in the world—Write me here—or Post Restante —Kristiania Norway—which will always find me—I could not come to England as I was hard at work on something new & did not want to break off. Write me soon how you are & what you are doing—

With love
yrs ever
Frederick Delius

57
Philip Heseltine to Frederick Delius

Selfridge & C° L^{td}
Oxford Street
London W
The Reception & Writing Rooms
July 3rd *1913*

Dear Mr Delius

I received your letter at Didbrook just before coming up to London for a little music: it is most exceedingly kind of you to suggest that I should come for a tramp in the Norwegian mountains with you, and I should dearly love to do so: however, at the present time, various circumstances will, I am very sorry to say, prevent my being able to do so, chief amongst them being my financial position, for I have lately made a big splash in buying a new motor—or rather a motor-cycle and side car, for an extra passenger, which necessitated much

---

[29] Rudi Stephan (1887–1915): A promising young German composer, killed in action on the Eastern front and therefore a kind of counterpart to George Butterworth. He was influenced by Strauss, Debussy, and Delius. The piece, his *Music for Orchestra* premiered at the festival on 6 June 1913, established him.

borrowing from my mother, so that just at present any further raising of cash would hardly be possible.[30] Still, even if it were, I am not at all sure whether I could ever face three days on the North Sea! I am the worst sailor imaginable, and the effect that even the shortest sea-passage has on me is so indescribably hideous that I shudder at the thought of a whole week on the sea, which this journey would involve. I only wish I could cure myself of this absurd malady, but, unfortunately, there it is, and I can do nothing! Alas for the bilious!

I have come up from Didbrook on my motor cycle for three days: with the intention of hearing Moussorgsky's two operas, which are being staged at Drury Lane for the first time in England. However, I was so disappointed with the music of 'Khovantchina' which I heard the night before last, that I simply cannot face 'Boris Godounow' after all. 'Khovantchina' is wonderfully interesting as an historical drama, and is quite marvellous in the way of conjuring up the atmosphere of Old Russia—an effect which the music helps very appreciably to create, but in that very fact, to my mind, lies its chief defect. It is too much in the background, too much of a mere commentary, and—too *antique*! Of course, Moussorgsky must have deliberately written 'in modo antico', but, apart from the fact that the music is wonderfully in keeping with the period of the drama, it is terribly tedious. Much of it consists, obviously, in old folk-songs and ancient church music, which is very beautiful, especially when it is sung by such a magnificent chorus as that of this Russian Company: I have never before heard such marvellous choral singing. But, for the rest, I was much disappointed. Moussorgsky's 'modernity' seems to have been frightfully over-rated, and where the likeness between him and Debussy comes in I cannot imagine.

Last night I saw the quite entrancing Russian Ballet—a delicious change after the opera! Balakireff's 'Thamar' is simply too wonderful for words, in every respect. How anyone can compare Moussorgsky with Balakireff and the others I don't know. I met Gardiner on Tuesday night: he seemed very jolly and flourishing as usual. This is only a mangy scrawl: I will write again when I return to Didbrook. Is there any chance of your being in England in September? If so you *must* come to Wales this time!

Thank you again enormously for your most kind invitation, which I am frightfully sorry to have to refuse.

Yours affect^{ly}
Philip Heseltine

---

[30] With a loan from his mother he was able to acquire a new 1913 Premier motor-cycle for £35. In April he wrote to her: 'A million thanks, my dear Mother! It is *most* good of you to consent to my loan proposals: you are really too kind. It is perfectly splendid to be able to get another machine at once: motor-mania possesses me stronger than ever.' Heseltine to his mother, 30 Apr. 1913, BL 57960.

58
Philip Heseltine to Frederick Delius

21ˢᵗ Oct. 1913   Christ Church
                                                                    Oxford

Dear Mʳ Delius
   I am sending the fair copies of the 'Dance Rhapsody' and 'In a Summer Garden'
by the same post as this.[31] I will write fully in a day or so.
   In great haste,

   Yours affectˡʸ
   Philip Heseltine

Postcard.

59
Frederick Delius to Philip Heseltine

[Grez ?October 1913]

Dear Heseltine—Many thanks for your 2 transcriptions I have sent them off
to Germany   Also I received the Musical Times with your article[32] which is
splendid—You write really wonderfully well & say such good things—There
is nothing I disagree with—It sometimes takes 25 years or 50 before an artist
is discovered to be sincere—this word never suffices & it is perhaps well that
it does not

   affectionately, F Delius

Picture postcard, Pont sur le Loing.

---

[31] Heseltine told Taylor: 'I have just finished a piano duet arrangement of the "Dance Rhapsody", and am eagerly awaiting the score of "A Song of the High Hills", a new work for wordless chorus and orchestra, of which I am to make a vocal score. Delius hopes to get it performed at the next Sheffield Festival. I am very anxious to play with you, à quatre mains, the "Dance Rhapsody" and "In a Summer Garden".' Heseltine to Taylor, 5 Oct. 1913, BL 54197.
[32] P. Heseltine, 'Some Reflections on Modern Musical Criticism', *Musical Times* (Oct. 1913), 652–4.

60
Philip Heseltine to Frederick Delius

20th December [1913]   *Cefn-Bryntalch,*
                                        Abermule,
                                        Montgomeryshire.

Dear Mr Delius

I am returning the proof sheets of 'The Song of the High Hills' by this post,
with many apologies for having kept them so long. It is very remiss of me not
to have sent them back long ago, and I sincerely hope you have not been in-
convenienced by their non-arrival. Gardiner brought them to me at Oxford,[33]
in order that I might copy your corrections into his copy of the score, but when
I began to make the piano arrangement, I discovered what appeared to me a
number of misprints still uncorrected, in your copy, so I retained it for further
examination and made out a list of the apparent misprints. Some of them, of
course, may be merely my own mistakes, but some are obvious printer's errors,
and I hope that, in spite of the delay, you will be spared the trouble of going
through the score again. I have not marked these misprints in your score, save
here and there with a query, but I enclose a list of them, so that you may see
for yourself what they are.

I have still got Gardiner's copy of the score, from which I am making a piano
arrangement: I started on a duet arrangement, and did about three quarters
of the work, but I came to the conclusion that a literal transcription, even for
four hands, was altogether too complex and too difficult to make effective, so
I have begun again on a piano solo arrangement which, although it necessarily
involves a good deal of omission, will I think be more effective and give a better general impression of the work than a very full and faithful transcription
for piano duet. But please let me know exactly what you would like done, and
what the publishers want, and I will do my best to arrange the work in any way
you like. If you want the proofs of the orchestral parts corrected, I should only
be too pleased to save you the trouble of doing them yourself, if you think I
am competant to do them for you.

I was very glad to see that your miniature scores are on sale at last, at Breitkopf's
in London: I think they are beautifully got up, for their very low price.

---

[33] Heseltine told Viva Smith: ' . . . on Monday Balfour Gardiner came to tea with me and brought me the proof
sheets of a new orchestral and choral work of Delius, "The Song of the High Hills".' Heseltine to Viva Smith, 20 Nov.
1913, BL 58127.

I am also delighted that your two new orchestral pieces are to be done so soon in England:[34] if you want them arranged for piano, I should be so very pleased if you would send them to me: you could never give me too much of your work to do—I am quite insatiable, especially here, where there is absolutely nothing else to do whatever! Forgive my importunity: I hope my enthusiasm is not becoming a nuisance to you!

This in haste: I am writing you a very long letter—the accumulation of three very full months—which I will post in a day or two.

Yours affectionately
Philip Heseltine

P.S. By the way, did Leuckart accept my piano duet versions of the 'Dance Rhapsody' and 'Summer Garden'?

PAGE	BAR	INSTRUMENT	CORRECTION
5.		Bassoon 3.	𝄡 and *not* 𝄢
7.	4	{ Flute 1.	E♮
		{ Clarinet 1.	F♯
	3 bar	Oboe I	♮ before E
9.		Horns 1. 2.	𝄞
	last	Violas	A♮
11.	3	Bassoon 3.	𝄢
14.	2 (2ⁿᵈ line)	Celesta	F♮
19.		"Cymbals" (not "Cimb")	
16.	5	Cellos.	C and G. *dotted* semibreves
17.	last	Cellos 2.	D♯
	5ᵗʰ	Flute 1.	A♮ minim: *not* dotted minim
24.	6	Bassoons 2.	F♯ 𝅘𝅥𝅮𝅘𝅥𝅮
	6	Clarinet 2.	𝅘𝅥𝅮𝅘𝅥 C♯
25.	4	Violas 2.	G *not* A
34.	6	Tenor solo.	B♭ dotted?
30.	3	Oboe 1.	B♮. ♮ shᵈ be noted.

[34] *On Hearing the First Cuckoo in Spring* and *Summer Night on the River* were played at a concert at Queen's Hall on 20 Jan. 1914 conducted by Willem Mengelberg.

page. 46.	'not hurried'		two words
50.		Cellos.	Tie missing (or if not D♯ sh^d be noted)
		Violas 1.	𝄞 clef

50	Bar 4 after ㊵	Violas 1.	G♯
	next bar but two.	Violins 2.	G♯
	(four bars later, the same)		

61

Frederick Delius to Philip Heseltine

Grez sur Loing
S & M
27 Dec 1913

My dear Heseltine—

I received your letter dated 20th & also a book of poems came this morning which I shall read with the greatest interest & pleasure & thank you most heartily for the gift—the score of the 'Songs of Sunset' has not yet arrived! You say in your letter that you sent it off by the same post—I have a lot of parts here to correct so I hope it will turn up soon—I sent your two arrangements to Hermann Suter[35] in Basel first as he had already looked at all the other arrangements of my works—He wrote back to me that—'Beide Bearbeitungen sind praktisch & gut spielbar[']—He remarks that—Sonder [unclear] weise hat der Bearbeiter einige stellen enharmonisch verändert—Gis dur statt As dur geschrieben was sie unnötig beschwert [Both arrangements are practical and easily playable—Instead the arranger changed some details enharmonically—G major sharp instead of A flat major, which makes them unnecessarily difficult.]—Do you understand? I have sent them now to Leuckart & proposed them both—I had already spoken to him in Jena about them & he had expressed a desire to have arrangements for 2 hands—However I shall try my best—I proposed *150 Marks as fee*. I am looking forward to your long letters & the news about your life at Oxford etc—We have had 8 lovely sunny frosty days, but now it

---

[35] Hermann Suter (1870–1926): Swiss conductor, composer, and teacher who conducted and taught at Zurich until he moved to Basle as musical director in 1902.

has turned bad again & is raining—Do you know what Conductor is doing my 2 small pieces—A friend in Vienna sent me Schönbergs Harmonielehre   I have read some of it & it is by far the most intelligent Harmony I ever read—His theories are *alright* it's his music that is wrong. If you will correct me the parts of my Music Drama I shall be very grateful to you—We have still no servants & are having them down from Norway again—so I hope when we are fixed up you will pay us another visit:—The score of the Song of the high hills has just this moment arrived—many thanks—I shall have heaps of work for you in a week or 2—I hope you will be able to come to Cologne for rehearsals & per-formance—I shall be able to recommend you to my other publishers & have all my things arranged by you—I think 2 hands is the most practical—with 3 systems now & then when it is absolutely necessary—Write me all about your-self & life & outlook & moods—I am working at my requiem—Have just finished the corrections of the 'Arabeske'   The performance in Vienna was postponed until January 26th.[36] Nikisch played the 2 pieces most beautifully—

With love
Your affectionate
Frederick Delius

62
Philip Heseltine to Frederick Delius

28th December 1913   *Cefn-Bryntalch*
                              Abermule
                              Montgomeryshire

My dear Mr Delius

   I have not written to you a real letter for a very long time, and now I feel I have so much to tell you, so much I want to discuss with you, and so much I want to ask your advice about that I fear any attempt to express it will be very inadequate, though I am afraid the letter may wander along to an inordinate length which you will find unutterably tedious. However, I will waste no time over excuses: you have always been so kind and more than sympathetic, more

[36] Delius wrote angrily to Jelka telling her the news: '. . . the Concert is postponed until 26th January—Charmant! to have come all this fearful way [Vienna] for nothing . . . The reason of postponement was rotten orchestral parts of a work by Weigl—Schrecker told me that the parts of Eine Arabeske were almost as bad & he had to send them back again . . .'. Delius to Jelka, 25 Nov. 1913 (Melbourne, Grainger Museum).

than my best friend, that it is a joy and a privilege to me just to feel that I am writing to you, who I know will not misunderstand me, however incoherent my utterances, and even if you never replied or read what I wrote, I should still feel the same sense of immense relief in writing to you when I feel most in need of help and sympathy. Forgive me if I talk overmuch about my puny, insignificant self, but you have helped me so much already, so much more than anyone else could have done, that I cannot but turn to you again now, at a time when certain circumstances of very great significance to me seem to be making a great change in my life . . . . . I cannot express a particle of these things as I would, but I know you will not laugh at my poor attempt to do so, and that you will see through whatever appears, on the surface, to be ridiculous in my expression of them, and understand . . . . . .

The past twelve months have been a very sharply defined period in my life —perhaps the most significant I have yet experienced: and now that the period has been very definitely ended, by certain circumstances which I will explain later on, I find myself surveying it, in retrospect, and wondering at the enormous changes it has brought about in my outlook on Life in general. Let me begin by telling you that, but for your influence, and the wonderfully increased and widened outlook on things that you have given me, I should never have understood, perhaps never experienced, what has happened to me during the past year —almost my first year of *Life*, as contrasted with my previous mere existence: I owe you more than ever, an enormous debt of gratitude, which no words of mine could ever express. Of course, my experiences have deviated but little from those of most people—they are slightly different, as I shall show, from those of most, in certain respects—but to me, they have meant more than anything ever has: you will understand this, since you told me they would, some time ago. When I was last at Grez, I do not think I explained matters at all clearly to you—I see them so differently now and my views have altered very considerably; I was in something of a transition stage then. I remember writing to you, soon after I first went to Didbrook, in the early part of last year, in a restless and passionate mood, telling you that I had never known what Love was: feeling, I suppose, it's intense and vital reality, through what others have expressed of it in their music and their poems, and chafing under my own inexperience: I suppose my love of music has inevitably kindled my own desire and passion:— I was then on the brink of experience, though I did not realize it. I have since wondered whether it was really Herself or my own longing that awakened my Love: the two things may be merely coincident, but I cannot, in spite of the fact that circumstances point to the latter as the real first impulse, believe that to be the truth . . But I wander from my beginning: you, by telling me something of the glories and beauties of Love, and the far-reaching influences of the sexual passion, gave me the courage and impulse to love, and opened up more than a new life for me—for I count my life before as nothing, in comparison with what I now know—even though that be but a little . . . I told you, I think, that I had exceptional opportunities of seeing her,[37] and being with her as often as I liked: also, that she is ten years older than I am—and it seems to me strange that I am never conscious of the fact, and I think she never was: perhaps that was because, in certain respects, she came to be more under my influence— which, such as it was, was derived from yours—than I under her. At the very first, I was not specially attracted to her—in fact, it was some time before I was at all conscious of a possibility that I should love her—though she is reserved, and intimacy was bound to be a matter of considerable time, apart from the restrictions imposed on me by my horribly nervous and retiring disposition. Three months brought about a certain intimacy and mutual sympathy: I suppose my own deeper feelings were held in check by a kind of presupposed certainty that she cared nothing, and suspected little more on my part: I was hardly conscious, save in flights of fancy which I took for dreams remote from reality, of the tremendous flood of passion that was in me, only waiting a sign to be let loose. That sign came, unexpectedly, in June, when I discovered that my presupposed certainty was perfectly fallacious—I say, perfectly, I know not why, for it was even then, a wavering, hesitant sign: but it was an unthought of possibility. . By the middle of July, I knew that we two had fared far beyond the boundaries of mere friendship, and that we had come to an inevitable crisis, a turning point, at which there could be no standing still—it must be either forwards or backwards. But I knew a great deal more that I had learned from her: I knew that it was no longer Love that I wanted, or a woman, but Her, with a burning, passionate desire: I began to understand that, underneath her cloak of reserve, I was beginning to discover the embodiment of a mysterious Something that I had been looking for, half unconsciously, all my life:—that something which pervades my sense of beauty, which is always with me in my solitude, which I see and feel in every sunset, everything that is lovely in nature, and above all in Music. I began to realize that she was absolutely sympathetic and at-one with me in a way noone else had ever been, could ever have been, in a way I should have not believed possible. We kept no secrets from each other, and discussed everything openly and frankly: she gave me a new conception of Love, deeper than I had hitherto dreamt of. At first, I still retained my ideas of a passing love, snatching it's hour of life and joy while it lasted, reaching its consummation, and passing away 'with a sigh, a smile': she had ideals—perhaps we were both

---

[37] Olivia ('Viva') Smith (1884–1962), of Stanway near Didbrook, Gloucestershire. Heseltine met her and became infatuated while cramming with the Revd H. Allen at Didbrook rectory.

a little extreme at first: we both modified a little, but I rather more than she, and subsequently, more still. I began to realize, for the first time, the transcendant and overwhelming beauty of Woman's passion—to know something of what real love meant to a woman, and the *giving* of herself: this was such a new aspect to me, and the beauty of it has grown stronger, of late, in me, in spite of the fact—or, is it because?—it is just that Something that I can never inspire in her, that Something that I can never give her: *there* is the 'mountain and the wood between us', and though I have to suffer by it, I see it all as plainly as she. . . It is a borderland, the edge of a balance—and it was here that unrest and suspense began for me: I knew we were at a crisis: a positive Yes, or a certain No I could have accepted calmly, if I knew it to be true. If she had not cared at all, or if she had loved as I did, all would have been plain. As it was—she held back: and I thought we had come to an end: I knew we could not stand still, as we were: we parted one night . . . . yet why, I wondered, did I see her half-an-hour later crying bitterly, in her garden? Of course, I thought of all the old, obvious things: the innate timidity engendered by the hopeless *British* attitude towards Love and sexual matters, the bitterness of indecision to which it gave rise in women who were in a state of transition twixt the old ideas and new: and it seemed simple. I kept away for five days, till I could stand it no longer, and weakly went back to her—only to receive a strange, fantastic letter which did not seem wholly to understand itself . . . . I didn't, I don't understand it, and later she didn't understand why she wrote it—The whole matter is a frightful tangle, and this letter is becoming increasingly difficult—well-nigh impossible for me, and I expect, more and more incoherent and tedious for you. You see, the affair is frightfully complex, and would take hours to explain: I do so much want to lay it before you, since, although it may appear quite trivial and commonplace, it matters so frightfully much to me, and I am out of my depth, and I feel you would understand it all so much better. I cannot keep it to myself— it has been simply wearing me out for the last few months: I believe the case to be abnormal in some respects—anyway, I am lost in it, and yet it means everything to me. For the past five months, we two have been delving deeper into ourselves, and speculating on all manner of problems: she has been wavering all the time on the brink of the next step farther—we have been standing still for five months, where I thought it impossible to stand still: but if it was not impossible, it has been well-nigh so: and, paradox though it seem, although these months have been golden months such as I had never before dreamed of, yet the indecision, hesitancy, uncertainty of them has been a Hell for me at the same time—I cannot make any of this clear, but perhaps you can guess at what I am trying vainly to convey to you. Five times we thought we had come to an end: and always there was the reaction—there were times when I knew she loved me—. . . and then, just when I thought we were really on some track leading us out of the pathless waste we had lost ourselves upon, there came another swing of the pendulum, back again: but, oh, the time in the meanwhile! . . . . The whole thing has been nearly driving me mad—and then there were complications with Allen, who has proved himself a contemptible, deceitful, lying, slandering hypocrite . . . . The final wrench came at the beginning of this month, and was perfectly frightful (this had nothing to do with anyone but our two selves): it has left me perfectly shattered, but this time I really see that we can't go on in that appalling, wavering manner: if it cannot be forwards, it must be definitely backwards. But I feel it terribly, just because I simply *cannot* understand her: if she didn't care at all, it would be simple . . . or if she cared as I do. . . You see, to me it is everything that she should care quite spontaneously: it would be nothing to me if she merely let herself be taken: she must *give* herself to me, and that, of necessity to *herself*, not because *I* desire it—you understand—that is my strongest condition, and she feels exactly as I do, but cannot . . . . and yet— I am at a loss to know what she would call Love, if it is not that which has influenced her over and over again during the past few months, while she has been with me. Moreover, she has been through not a little that is very unpleasant, on account of me: you know what English village life is, and the beautiful *Christian* delight in anything that savours of a 'scandal' (what a word to apply to these affairs!): Allen, who ought to know better, was the worst offender in this respect: but she never minded that in the least, nor did it ever make any difference to her relations with me . . . . I am afraid this must be boring you dreadfully, but I do so want your advice, as I am simply distracted over what it all means: I simply cannot make it out, but it is a relief to be able to tell you about it, because I know that you will understand it, if only I can make it clear to you—that is the difficulty. With other people, I should feel I were desecrating all that has been so beautiful in our love and intimacy during the last few months, by discussing it, but with you it is so different: I feel I could tell you anything, and that it would be a help, just to tell you. You see, all the usual reasons for dismissing an affair of this kind lightly are of no use to me: I have thought and thought about it till my brain has seemed on fire, I have tried to look at it from every point of view, and in the light of every conceivable objection that might be raised against it on the score of it's being a trivial affair, which, though it seem great at the time, will soon fade into nothingness. I am not one of those that love lightly, and often, and can forget as lightly: moreover, I have not rushed blindly into it: I have looked at it in every mood, and in every light: my feelings have not run away with my reason: indeed, it is one of the curses of my life that in everything, almost, my reason invariably runs away with my feelings, and leaves me cold, critical and cynical, only longing for some burning impulse which would sweep away me and my calculating mind beyond the pale of rationality. So I cannot accept as any consolation the theory that my love for her made me blind to her real nature, and made me see her more wonderful, more beautiful and more wholly sympathetic to myself in every way, than she was in reality . . . . The letter that I referred to just now was, of course, a complete surrender, giving me all that I asked—for the first two pages: then came the fatal reservation, and a great deal about a *secret* relationship being impossible for her. Of course, this would make it appear that the first part was not really sincerely felt, but I know that it *was* passionately sincere at the time. Afterwards, she told me that she must have written the letter when her feelings carried her away beyond what she really meant! There is an unconscious irony about some of her letters, in the matter of this swaying backwards and forwards between a kind of positive and negative pole of emotion that has maddened and tantalized me . . . . I remember your saying to me at Grez that perhaps she wanted to keep me at a safe distance until I could marry her: I satisfied myself that this was not the case with her. Moreover, it is not, as I thought before, and as I think I gave you the impression it was, when I was at Grez, the inherent timidity and cowardice of the traditional English person in sexual matters. You told me that the only thing for such people was to be *taken* by a strong man: it may be in some cases, but here it was out of the question, and I am not the one to do it. To me, it savours too much of mere prostitution: and I have said just now that unless the relation be perfectly mutual and spontaneous, it is nothing to me: to my mind, the physical relation, though intensely necessary, is nothing, intrinsically, but rather a symbol of complete sympathy and unity in everything . . . Of course, this is a somewhat idealized view of what it really is in most cases, but at least it can approximate, however distantly, to the ideal . . . . No, it is not timidity or cowardice with her: it is simply that she says she does not love me: and yet, over and over again, she has lain in my arms and given me such kisses as only real passion could inspire:—one night, when I was staying there in the autumn, we lay together, naked, by the fireside . . . and yet, and yet—what does it all mean? Why is it that, having reached a turning point, we can progress no further and explore together the limitless possibilities that Love opens up for us? She is no more a believer in forced constancy, in the Christian sense, than I am: and still she holds back. In the last letter she wrote me—in answer to a final appeal from me—she explained herself thus—though I confess that the real psychological explanation of her, if there be one, lies too deep for my comprehension. Her words were: 'You think you are working against lack of courage, lack of energy in me . . . but you forget, the great fact that you have against you is that I do not love you. At the right time my love will be active enough—my nature is deep enough (I hope) for me to love greatly: if my love for you was one half what yours is for me, do you think I should hesitate? I should be living with you, and you only, and nothing else in the world would penetrate my consciousness'. . . . of course, that were plain and simple enough, did I not know her as I do, and had I not other letters of hers, which both say and show a totally opposite attitude . . . . . I think you will see that, as things were, it was an impossible position for me: until that barrier were broken down, there could be no further progress: it isn't even as though we were waiting, like those 'engaged' (forgive the word!) with the mutual assurance and confidence that such people have. Outwardly, in the eyes of the world, we were so— 'scandalous', of course! She motored up to London with me in the summer —stayed at the same hotel—in the very next room, in fact . . . . and this was the feeling that pervaded our whole relationship—this feeling that one *must* just get beyond that something, which would give the key to all manner of things undreamed of. It was a perfect agony to me, and I lived only on the hope that, undecided and wavering as she was, Time would bring a change: of course, we discussed it all quite frankly: but it was *fearful*, waiting all the time. Anyway, at the beginning of this month, I made a final appeal, and the answer was the letter I have quoted. And then there remained for me a veritable Scylla and Charybdis—to continue the former relationship, which would now be a thousand times worse, or to leave her altogether—which was just as bad (and has proved to be worse still), though more reasonable. I chose the latter:[38] she was frightfully upset, and I was perfectly ill: that was not quite a month ago, and I have heard nothing since . . . . *Now*, what can I do?—what does it mean? . . I cannot realize, somehow, that she has passed out of my life—at least, I know and feel that she is there, and must remain, even were she to die, the strongest influence I have ever known. Of course, I am still buoyed up by a hope that she may change again, under these new conditions. I know it would be damnably weak of me to go back to her now, on the old terms—though that, I know, is what she would like, since she is frightfully lonely, in a totally unsympathetic environment—but there are times when I feel that I shall not be able to hold out any longer . . . . . Forgive me all this about myself: my letter is running to an appalling length, but I know that you are the only person that can help me now . . . . When I went to Didbrook, I was in a state of complete indecision about my future career, and after I had been there a little while, I became so

---

[38] Heseltine told Taylor of this decision: 'Do you know, you were absolutely right when you told me never to go back to her on any condition whatever . . she wrote to me about a fortnight ago, and, though nothing has happened, it's worse than ever with me . . the whole thing becomes more and more complex . . but details will only weary you, and I don't think I could possibly write them down.' Heseltine to Taylor, 23 Jan. 1914, BL 54197. By the beginning of the year, however, the rift had been healed and Heseltine wrote to Viva: ' . . . oh, it is so glorious to be in touch with you again after all these dreary, weary weeks of thinking and thinking all the time that I'd lost you and that you didn't care a little bit.' Heseltine to Viva Smith, 12 Jan. 1914, BL 58127.

completely absorbed in new experiences and developments on other lines which
were of so much greater moment in my life, that I drifted into Oxford, and
having awoke to find myself there, never cease to wonder what I went there for!
All through this summer and autumn, whenever any thoughts of the future crossed
my mind, I always felt a glorious sense of support and security in the thought
that *She* would be the motive of my existence, would give me something to live
for and work for: and this gave me so much assurance and enthusiasm that I
almost ceased to look at the matter in detail. Now that all that has gone: it is
as though the ground had given way suddenly from beneath my feet: it has left
me without energy, without purpose or enthusiasm for anything, listless and frightfully depressed: and it is just at this time that I feel I have to pull myself together
and decide what I am going to do, for I can see that, for me, Oxford is merely
a waste of time and money, and intensely boring at that. My trouble is that I
have absolutely no confidence whatever in myself, to back me up, to tide me
over reverses, or even to give me a start: and just at present, less than ever. I
believe my mother would consent to my leaving Oxford and devoting myself
to music if I could produce a more definite plan of what I proposed to do afterwards. I have explained to her that exactly what I do depends largely on what
unlooked for opportunities occur during the next year or so, and, more than
anything, on how proficient I become in a branch of learning to which I have
never yet really seriously devoted myself. She only wants to know, in reality, how
I propose to make money by it—for, both from her point of view and mine,
money is an all-important matter, for one simply cannot enjoy oneself without
money, unless one is greatly gifted (as I, alas, am not), and can create wonderful things out of oneself, which completely absorb one and make one oblivious
of the more material things in life. The question is whether, when I had become
fairly proficient, I should be able to get a job as a critic—for I imagine that
there is a good deal of demand for positions of this kind—and whether, by
combining this with other things, such as making transcriptions, etc, I could
ever earn a comfortable income! A friend of my mother's has promised to introduce me to some of the London critics, which will be useful, for obtaining
information, and I am thinking of writing to Robin Legge on the subject, since
he once wrote me some very kind letters, on the subject of a communication
which I sent to the 'Daily Telegraph'. In any case, I think I shall be well away
from Oxford as soon as possible—even if, finally, I have to fall back upon the
stock broker's office! . . . .

I have been pursuing the study of Sex,[39] in which you made me so interested
when I was at Grez, with very great enthusiasm lately: it is quite amazing what

---

[39] Heseltine had also written to Taylor on the subject: 'About the books, try
Love's Coming of Age by Edward Carpenter 3/6
The Intermediate Sex "   "   "   3/6

a wonderful new light it throws on everything: Havelock Ellis[40] and Edward Carpenter[41] I have liked exceedingly. I very much want to read the large work by Ellis, but it is out of print, and, I believe, is not allowed to be read, save under exceptional circumstances, in the British Museum library!![42] Isn't that a thing for Great Britain and the Empire to be proud of!!! Last week, I saw that a large new work had appeared on the subject of 'Artificial Parthenogenesis', by Jacques Loeb:[43] is this the man of whose successful experiments in this line you told me? It is indeed a fascinating subject, and opens up enormous possibilities —anyway for the 'Feminists'—but whatever would Nietzsche have thought about it?! . . Have you ever come across a curious American book by a lady doctor[44] called 'Karezza'?[45] It is based on a so called 'discovery' by one Lugassent, and it appears that there are many books on the subject in America. The book is exceedingly badly written, but I must say that I think it's matter is very sound —though from my lack of experience I am quite incompetant to judge. The theory—which is developed in a very interesting manner, and asserted as having surprisingly beneficial psycho-physiological influences—is that of copulation, without crisis or emission. The author states that:—'During a lengthy period of perfect control, the whole being of each is merged into each other, and an exquisite exaltation experienced. This may be accompanied by a quiet motion, entirely under subordination of the will, so that the thrill of passion for either may not go beyond a pleasurable exchange. Unless procreation is desired, let the final propagative orgasm be entirely avoided. With abundant time and mutual reciprocity, the interchange becomes satisfactory and complete without emission

---

Man and Woman by Havelock Ellis 4/6

(There is also a larger work in 3 vols. "Studies in the Psychology of Sex" (30/=) but it is out of print and I believe very hard to get).

Karezza by A. B. Stockham (an American book, obtainable, I think, from the Times library) contains a remarkable theory, but is so badly written that the thing becomes ludicrous.

Sex and Character by Otto Weininger (10/= English German 6/6)

I have not read this, but it is considered a very good work.

Weininger committed suicide at the age of 23, about 6 years ago.

Love and Lovers by Orme Balfour (3/6)

(not scientific, but contains several remarkable character studies from the sexual point of view, and is wonderfully sanely written)

The great authority on Sexual inversion is Krafft-Ebing: his work is not yet translated into English, I believe.

Of course, the subject is an immense one, and I know very little about it, but all the above books are intensely interesting.' Heseltine to Taylor, 23 Jan. 1914, BL 54197.

[40] Havelock Ellis (1859–1939), English physician, essayist, and editor best known for his studies of human sexual behaviour.

[41] Edward Carpenter (1844–1929), English social reformer.

[42] Heseltine wrote to Taylor: 'I have made enquiries about Havelock Ellis' big work, "Studies in the Psychology of Sex"—forbidden fruit in the British Museum Library!—and have discovered that it is published in America, in 6 volumes at 2 dollars each . . . I have asked Blackwells to advertise, both in England and America, for second hand copies, but if these are not to be had, I think I shall get the lot new, since I understand that this is the most authoritative and exhaustive work that has ever been written on this most fascinating subject.' Heseltine to Taylor, 11 Feb. 1914, BL 54197.

[43] Jacques Loeb (1859–1924), German biologist.   [44] Alice Bunker Stockham (1833–1912), American writer.

[45] A. B. Stockham, *Karezza: Ethics of Marriage* (Chicago, 1896).

or crisis. In the course of an hour the physical tension subsides, the spiritual exaltation increases, and not uncommonly visions of a transcendant life are seen and consciousness of new powers experienced' . . . . . .

Whatever the last line may mean, the theory seems a striking one, obviating, as it does, the need of disturbing elements in the way of preventives. The matter is well worked out, and on the whole, the book is extremely interesting . . . By the way, I read the other day in the 'New Age' a long denunciation of what the writer chooses to call 'Neo-Malthusianism': someone had written a book in favour of it, and this was the review. It denounced all the ordinary methods for the prevention of conception as being injurious to health, and quoted in support of this view the 1904 presidential address to the British Gynaecological Society. Is this British prejudice, or is there some truth in it? Further, can you tell me of any work where I can find a rational account of the diseases incurred by women through prolonged virginity? (By the way, did I tell you that the person with whom this letter is chiefly concerned has already a slight nervous affection of the eyesight for which an oculist has told her the only cure? Further, would the use of the ordinary preventive methods affect this one way or the other, and if so, which way?) The writer of the article in question is himself uncertain as to 'whether the risk to health is greater or not in chastity' . . . .

I sent off to you the other day two volumes of modern English poetry, which I hope you will like: those of AE are very beautiful, and have the Celtic fire and imaginativeness which I know you like. The 'Love Poems'[46] of D. H. Lawrence are very different: I imagine that one must either love them and feel them intensely, or dislike them equally: I should very much like your quite candid opinion of them: they have appealed to me as no poetry has for a long while. I think they are perfectly wonderful, but do tell me quite plainly what you think of them. D. H. Lawrence has also written some very fine novels . . . . .

I saw Gardiner several times last term at Oxford: I went over once to Ashampstead, and was quite charmed with the place and it's surroundings: I had no idea Berkshire was so beautiful. But how can he live there all alone? I am sure he cannot be happy: he seemed very discontented about his music, and seemed restless and worried, fundamentally, for all his geniality and good nature. He seems to spend his time making other people happy, to the neglect of himself, and his own happiness. I wonder if this is really the case.

My article in the Musical Times brought me a long and enthusiastic letter from an interesting person of the name of Dudley Sorabjî-Shapurgî,[47] who lives at St John's Wood! He seems to be a very keen musician, with a hatred

---

[46] D. H. Lawrence, *Love Poems and Others* (London, 1913).

[47] Kaikhosru Shapurji Sorabji (1892–1988): English-born composer, pianist, and writer. Self-taught, he began composing in 1915.

of the classics which exceeds even mine. He is very interesting, since he tells me all about composers of whom I know nothing. His last letter ran to more than twenty pages! He is very enthusiastic about the modern Hungarians, Bela Bartok, and Zoltan Kodaly (whose works you 'edited'!!). He informs me that 'Kodaly is not quite so advanced as Bela Bartok, but of course like him far beyond the modern French or English school'. From what I remember of the pieces I saw at Grez, he is considerably behind any school I have yet come across!—but still, I am glad he likes them! But, for him, Scriabine is the greatest musician that ever lived! He goes into extasies about him for pages on end! I am afraid I must confess to complete ignorance of this composer, save for a few early works. 'Prometheus'[48] seems to be his masterpiece. . . I was in London for ten days at the beginning of the month and went to some interesting concerts: one consisted of the works of Ravel (chamber music and songs);[49] the composer was present and was received with immense enthusiasm by an audience collected by the so-called 'Classical Concert Society'! His music interested me greatly, but did not *move* me in the least. By far the finest music I have heard lately is Vaughan Williams' song-cycle for tenor, accompanied by a string quartet and piano, to six of A. E. Housman's wonderful 'Shropshire Lad' poems.[50] Elwes[51] sang them most beautifully. . . . . When I returned here this time, I found the pianola vanished!! I asked no questions, since it has evidently been removed to spite me, after my affair at Didbrook, which caused a considerable rupture in the family circle: however, it is a very great loss to me, and if I had not got your scores to transcribe, I don't know what I could possibly do here in winter. I am alone at present: even solitude is a thing to be grateful for sometimes! The rest have gone to Essex, to the deadly family party with the religeous uncle; this has become a habit: I have been every Christmas as for the last ten years, but this year I determined to go on strike, doubtless giving great displeasure in the family circle: but I could not face another 'Holy Communion' on a cold and frosty morning (this among the minor things damnable)!

The piano score of the 'Song of the High Hills' is nearly finished, though I find it very difficult, and get along rather slowly. Still I find it immensely interesting doing it. Would you like it written out with the chorus on separate lines (as in the piano score of 'Appalachia'), or shall I transcribe the whole thing together? Also, as it is impossible to work in the quaver accompaniment to the melody beginning on page 7, shall I just transcribe the melody and harmonies

[48] Symphony no. 5, *Prometei—Poema ogyna* (Prometheus—The Poem of Fire) (1909–10).
[49] The programme included Ravel's string quartet in F, and *Introduction and Allegro*. The singer was Rhoda van Glehn and the instrumentalists included the English String Quartet and Gwendolen Mason (harp). *Musical Times* (1914), 118.
[50] *On Wenlock Edge* (1908–9).   [51] Gervase Elwes (1866–1921), English tenor.

for the wind, omitting the violin notes, or would it be better to *suggest* the quaver figure by arranging the harmonies for the left hand as arpeggios in quavers? I am afraid the semiquavers (pp 27–33) will have to be omitted altogether: otherwise, I think I can make a fairly faithful, as well as a playable arrangement. Do send me the other new scores to do, if you have not already arranged for anyone else to do them: also the parts of the 'Song of the High Hills', if you would like me to correct them. Are you coming over for the performance of your new work in January?

Heavens! what a letter I have inflicted upon you! I ought to have split up all this into several letters distributed over a period of several months—if, indeed, I have any right to inflict it upon you at all. But before—I have always been intending to write to you, over and over again, and then events moved, and points of view shifted with such kaleidoscopic rapidity that I could never survey the matter as a whole in the same light one day as the day before or the day after. As it is, I have only given a very muddled and incoherent account, but I do hope you will forgive me, and that you will tell me at once if I am boring you and presuming too much upon your kindness to me in talking so much about my stupid self. Indeed, I should not dare to write thus to you at all, did I not know that you would tell me quite frankly when you had had enough of me.

And now I really must stop! So with my very best wishes, both to you and Mʳˢ Delius, for a very happy and prosperous New Year, I remain

Ever yours affectionately
Philip Heseltine

1914

1914 began well for Delius. There were promises of performances of his operas in Frankfurt and Cologne as well as performances of his orchestral works in Germany and England. Mengelberg conducted the first British performances of *On Hearing the First Cuckoo in Spring* and *Summer Night on the River* at Queen's Hall on 20 January and Henry Wood conducted *A Dance Rhapsody* on 14 February.[1] The Deliuses, however, were not present on either of these occasions as they had travelled to Germany to hear excellent performances of the *Mass of Life* at Wiesbaden (16 February) and again in Frankfurt a week later. Heseltine visited Grez at the end of March and stayed for a while assisting Delius with proof-reading *Fennimore and Gerda* and translating the words of *An Arabesque* into English. On 21 June Delius went to London where he was to attend yet more performances of his music conducted by Beecham. In England he stayed with various friends, including Beecham, Balfour Gardiner, and Norman O'Neill, and was generally fêted and lionized. He returned to Grez on 10 July. Whilst Delius was working on his *Requiem* at Grez war broke out and, anxious about the situation in Europe, the Deliuses decided to leave Grez in early September. After spending a week at Orleans they changed their minds and returned home. However, as Beecham had offered them accommodation in Watford, they eventually moved to England in November.

For Heseltine 1914 was a year of turmoil. His relationship with Viva Smith was proving a stormy one and he was desperately unhappy at Oxford. It was a career in music he really wanted to pursue but he lacked confidence in his musical abilities and his mother was adamant that he stay at Oxford to prepare for a career in the Civil Service. In March Gardiner introduced him to Ernest Newman and his thoughts moved in the direction of becoming a music critic. His stay at Grez with the Deliuses in March provided a welcome break and he began contemplating writing a short book on Delius and his music. He returned to Oxford at the end of April and, though still depressed at the prospect of studying there, was encouraged by Balfour Gardiner's positive reaction to some of the songs he had composed. The declaration of war, however, decided his immediate fate and he managed to convince his mother that, because of the ensuing financial scare, it would be cheaper for him to live in London rather

---

[1] Heseltine and Balfour Gardiner were present, and Heseltine wrote: 'Henry Wood did the Delius "Dance Rhapsody" disgracefully badly', adding that Wood 'has no ideas whatever, where D. is concerned'. Heseltine to Viva Smith, 14 Feb. 1914, BL 58127.

than Oxford. By October he was installed in London and had registered at London University to study English Language and Literature, Psychology, and Philosophy.

63

Frederick Delius to Philip Heseltine

Grez sur Loing
S & M
2 Jan 14

My dear Philip—I need not tell you that your long letter interested me in the highest degree—I thank you for the confidence you bestow upon me in writing me so thoroughly & frankly all about your life, thoughts & doings—It is a letter from a real & loving friend—I shall be just as sincere & frank with you—Not everyone falls really in love—only few men & few women are capable of a great & real passion—But in my opinion it is of enormous importance for an artist to have had a great passion—It is that which gives that extraordinary depth of emotion to his work—2 never love each other at the same time or scarcely ever—The woman when she sees she is the object of a great passion often gets inspired by the lover to something almost equivalent—The man either loves or does not. When he does not—he takes & enjoys & that is all—Women are never blind when they love. Men nearly always—Your friend knew you loved her a good deal sooner than you did—Women are very much wilier in these things than men think. Men always take women to be so innocent, in these things, forgetting that they spend most of their life thinking about them—Men think, on the whole, little about them—& when they do think it is mostly in a purely sexual way—When love awakens in them it mostly awakens in an astonished child who will innocently fall in to the most obvious trap or be led on to anything by the most commonplace guile—I have had a very similar experience to you—I was madly, passionately in love when I was 21, & with evidently a very similar sort of woman—She was, however, not ten years older than me—but just my own age—My opinion of your friend is the following—She does not love you but is flattered at being the object of such a great passion & wants to make it last as long as possible—Most women have the idea when they do not love—that as soon as they let the man obtain what he wants—or satisfy his desire—His love will stop & the whole thing will be over—The only possible

way of bringing her to the point is the one you have taken—to see her no more—
If she wants you *she* will come to you & then you might enjoy the one thing
that is absolutely necessary between a man & a woman before they can be true
friends. I am afraid your friend is cold—all you tell me about her lying naked
with you before the fire points to a very self-possessed & cold nature—quite
impossible in France & Germany—Only possible in England & America—It
is very cruel—If she meant well by you she ought not to exasperate your senses
when she does not intend to satisfy them—Indeed if she had real tenderness
for you she would behave quite differently—It is unhealthy & enervating & no
wonder you feel depressed & in an unsatisfactory state of mind—The whole
affair is much simpler than you imagine—You see everything now thro' those
wonderful eyes of love—such wonderful colors & it really does not matter a bit
who you do love, or wether she is worthy or not of your passion—for me the
important point is that you are *capable* of a great passion; that sets a mark on
you which elevates you greatly in my eyes. She is of course afraid of getting a
child like all women who are not in love are—This touches, of course, on the
old question of convention & Society which I will not touch on here—
Everybody must settle that for himself—You have done well in fleeing & getting out of that atmosphere for the present. I had just as bad a time of it as you
& almost identical. She would not give herself. Probably what occured to me
will happen also to you—7 or (or) 8 years after she came to me of her own
accord—but I was no more in love with her & then she became madly in love
with me—but all in vain—I had another dear & charming friend who had given
herself to me without compunction & I had learned to appreciate what a fine
& real woman was—Love is a thing one must snatch at & hold & keep & enjoy
as long as it lasts—for *it does not last*—but friendship does & that very often
follows on love & gives place to something more lasting & gentler & more sure
& healthier. A man who is in love can never be brutal & take a woman by
force—Only a man who is not in love can do that—But the sort of woman
you speak of is destined either to never get a man—or be forced by a man she
does not even like—or get married to a perfectly indifferent person who can
support her in a so called respectable way. When she writes to you that at the
right time her love will be active enough it really means that she is incapable
of a love sufficiently great to become active. If a woman has not loved before
27, or 30 I very much doubt whether she ever will—Now to another subject—
To become a music critic is to become nothing at all—The only possible attrac-
tion in music is to be a musician   You could write criticisms when you felt like
it & also do something else—I could, of course, help you in several ways &
should do so as soon as you wanted it—But *critic* is no career—Do not be in
a hurry. Go into an office if it must be & gain time & money that way—You

would be able to make a little money making piano arrangements etc. but what is that? mere drudgery—To start with: work at any subject you fancy to get into a calmer state of mind: It will not be lost. Harmony, Counterpoint or anything that attracts you—Write to me as often as you feel like it—I will always give you my advice which you can take for what it is worth—but it might be of help to you. I have so much more experience—The world will presently be obliged to adopt methods to prevent over population & also the procreation of children by diseased people—A good syringe never hurt anyone & is used by every clean woman on the continent   Cundums are not as healthy for the woman— I have already heard of 'Karezza' but do not agree with any of those methods— That sort of thing might be all very well for the woman but for the man it would be very unhealthy & would shatter his nerves ultimately—The one real natural & healthy way to enjoy a woman is the natural one—with emission —& even this not to be abused especially when one is doing brainwork— Prolonged virginity for women is always very bad—they simply dry up & often become entirely sterile at a comparatively early age—30. 35. There are many works on this subject: I do not interest myself enough in it to read them— They are mostly medical—Kraft Ebing[2] & Havelock Ellis I believe also write on this subject   Christianity might be entirely condemned by its *morals* alone —Ignoring sex & the very source of life & Bringing forth generations of onanizing men & women: both becoming hysterical & impotent & disatisfied— The womans question in England & America especially is one of enormous importance. The suffragettes are nearly all menless women   Sex is at the bottom of it all & they will ultimately carry the day & perhaps change entirely & revolutionize sexual life—In Germany & the North (Scandinavia) girls are beginning to live entirely free & enjoy men whilst they are quite young & before they get married—they want to live   Very few people now really believe in any life hereafter & they want to, at least, get something out of this one—The next ten years will see enormous changes—I received only *one* volume of 'Love poems' by D. H. Lawrence—I do hope the other volume has not been lost— When did you send it off?—I have not had time to read the poems yet as I am working hard just now & scarcely read at all—I thank you heartily for the poems & am looking forward to them. How foolish of your mother to take the pianola away—Well! Well! parents still seem to be the same—but abroad there is a decided change taking place—much more so than in England—In your piano score of the Song of the high hills, the chorus must of course be on separate lines—When necessary also use 3 systems (lines) instead of only 2 for the piano— Why is it impossible to work in the quaver accompaniment to the melody on

---

[2] Richard Krafft-Ebing (1840–1902), German neuropsychiatrist, best known for his work in sexual psychopathology.

Page 7. Put it on a 3rd line perhaps—you see the effect must be attained some way or other—otherwise one gets a wrong impression of the work—the quavers there are important—I am eagerly awaiting Leuckarts' answer—I should put all the work I possibly can in to your hands, of course, but I have not always the power—as the editor buys the works outright from me & has them arranged by his own man—I can advise him, of course, but he may not always take my advice—We will see now what Leuckart does[3]—I will send you the parts of the 'Song of the high hills' & should be very thankful if you would correct them for me—I am working so successfully just at present that it would be of great help to me—Who is conducting my 2 orchestral pieces at the Philharmonic?

Now, dear boy, write me soon again—your letters always interest me—

your affectionate friend
Frederick Delius

I hope you can read this scribble.

64
Philip Heseltine to Frederick Delius

4th Jany 1914

Cefn-Bryntalch,
Abermule,
Montgomeryshire.

Dear Mr Delius

Our last letters crossed: yours reached me last Monday: thank you so much for it: I am not going to inflict another wearying epistle of tiresome introspection upon you—this is only to say that I have finished the piano score of the 'Song of the High Hills', and am now making a provisional fair copy, which I will send for your inspection in a day or two: if you will mark in pencil where you would like alterations made, I will alter anything you like in the final fair copy.[4]

---

[3] Delius was trying unsuccessfully to interest the publisher Leuckart in Heseltine's piano arrangements of *Brigg Fair* and *A Dance Rhapsody*.

[4] Heseltine wrote somewhat critically to Taylor: 'I have just finished the piano score of the "Song of the High Hills": it is the only work of Delius that has made no definite appeal to me: technically, it is extremely interesting, the orchestration is quite wonderful, and the big chorus in the middle must be tremendously fine, but this, and the last two

I am completely baffled by the last three bars on page 27, and the first three on page 28: a literal transcription of the shifting harmonies for the strings is impossible for 2 hands to play. I am writing it out literally, but do you want it faked so as to be made playable, or shall I leave it as it is? After the first six bars of this movement, I have had to omit the semiquaver figure altogether, since both hands are fully occupied with other matter: otherwise, the whole work has gone fairly easily for 2 hands. I have not written out the choral music separately, but this could, of course, be done afterwards.

I don't think either the 'Summer Garden' or the 'Dance Rhapsody' could possibly be arranged for two hands, without the omission of a great deal of important matter. It is as much as *4* hands can do to play either of them! I think the passage referred to by Herr Suter must be one in the 'Summer Garden' where the harp has chords in A♭ and the strings in G♯.

Your two little orchestral pieces are being done by Mengelberg on the 20th of this month, and Wood[5] is doing the 'Dance Rhapsody' in February. I see in the 'Musical Times' that 'In a Summer Garden' was recently given by Henschel[6] in Edinburgh.

My bookseller has written to say that the Poems by AE are sold out, or reprinting, or something, but I hope they will send your copy before long.

Over the page, I am copying a further list of 'queries', with regard to misprints in the score of the 'Song of the High Hills'.

Goodbye now, for the present. with much love

Yours affectionately
Philip Heseltine. (P.T.O.

PAGE	BAR	INSTRUMENT	CORRECTION
6	3	Flute 2,	last note of triplet B♭?
8	5	Horn 2,	last note but one sh^d be A♮
9	last	Violas	third note of bar, A♮?
21	2	Horn 5,	second note of bar, B♭?
36	1 of 2nd line	Contralto, 1	tie to F♯ (minim) omitted
37	3	Tenor, 1,	last note but one of bar sh^d be F♯

pages are the only parts that really "get there"—on paper, anyway, but I think this is due to the fact that D. relies much more on orchestral colour and effect in this work than he usually does. It will probably seem quite different when I hear it, and the performance will be a very welcome revelation!' Heseltine to Taylor, 4 Jan. 1914, BL 54197.

[5] Sir Henry Wood (1869–1944), English conductor. He was also a great champion of Delius's music, having conducted at least seven world premières—Piano Concerto (final version), Double Concerto, *Idyll*, Dance Rhapsody No. 2, *Eventyr*, *A Song before Sunrise*, *A Song of Summer*—as well as of two orchestrations of *Songs from the Norwegian* and the first English performance of *Sea Drift*.

[6] Sir George Henschel (1850–1934), German-born baritone, pianist, conductor, and composer.

PAGE	BAR	INSTRUMENT	CORRECTION
37	5	Viola	3rd crotchet of bar, C♮?
"	6	(30) is a misprint for (33)	
"	4	Oboe 2	first quaver on second beat sh^d be G?
"	6	Trombone 1	second note of bar sh^d be B♮ and last note G♮ also, why has the A (quaver) two tails? Does the 1st trombone play in unison with the 2nd, 4th and 6th Horns? It looks as if the printers had muddled the whole bar: I cannot make anything of it.
"	6	Trombone 2,	last note but one of the bar, E♭?
"	4	Bassoon 1,	*first* note of the bar. Should bassoon 1 play C? There is no other C in the harmony.
page 48.	bar 2	Horn 1,	minim sh^d be dotted
page 49.	bar 3	Violas,	D sh^d be dotted
page 50.	bar 4	Violas	Treble clef at bar 4, and G♯??
page 39.	bar 2	Violas	Minim D♭?
"	"	English Horn	Minim F♮?
"	6	Horn 5	Does it play in unison with Horn 3, C♯, or should the C♯ be dotted? There should be either a note, dot or rest added.
page 41	bar 10	Horn 2	F♯
p. 43	bar 2	D♯	English Horn: Bassoons 2 last bar but 3 on this page, 3rd note A♮?

65

Philip Heseltine to Frederick Delius

6th Jan. 1914

Cefn-Bryntalch,
Abermule,
Montgomeryshire.

Dear Mr Delius

Our letters again crossed: your most sympathetic and helpful letter arrived yesterday: thank you again and again for your kindness—I can't tell you how much your advice and sympathy helps me and cheers me up. It was more than good of you to write me such a long and wonderful letter, especially when you are hard at work, and I am deeply grateful to you. I will write you another letter in a few days: this is only a brief scrawl, to say that I am sending the piano arrangement of the 'Song of the High Hills' to you by this post. If you have time to play it through, and mark in pencil what you would like altered, and then return it to me, I will make a proper fair copy of the work afterwards. The copy I send you is for Gardiner. I will write out the chorus parts separately in the final fair copy: in the one I have made, I have transcribed chorus and orchestra together, attempting to get a *general impression* of the work on the piano. The quavers on page 7 will, I think, have to be put on a separate line: the pages in the middle where the violins play four-part chords in semiquavers are very difficult: the first six bars are unplayable, I fear, and after that the semiqurs will have to have a separate line. Of course, the whole work is difficult for 2 hands, and in many places unplayable, but I have thought it better to put as much as possible of the score into the arrangement, even at the expense of it's playableness, for I think one gets a better impression that way —through the *eye*, anyway, if not through the ear. But I will alter or modify it in any way you like, if you will tell me what you think of it. The string parts arrived this morning: I will correct them this evening, and return them by to-morrow's post, so that I am now ready for any other proofs you may care to send along.

Of course, I should be very pleased indeed to have my arrangements accepted by Leuckart, even if he paid nothing, since it would be a great help to me after-wards, to have a specimen of my arranging in print, especially an arrangement of one of your works. It is very good of you to say you will let me do your works, but I do hope you are really satisfied with my arrangements of them, because I should hate to feel that I was preventing a better arrangement of them being made.

In great haste: more anon

Yours affectionately
Philip Heseltine

66
Frederick Delius to Philip Heseltine

Grez sur Loing
18ᵗʰ Jan 14

My dear Philip

Let me thank you to begin with for the book of poems which I received a few days ago—I have not read either of the books you sent me yet as I am working hard & not reading at all but am looking forward with great pleasure to them both. It was really so kind of you to send them. All the corrections you sent me 'Song of the High hills were right—It is wonderful how one oversees mistakes—You seem to have an eagle eye! You are doing me a great service by correcting the Score & parts of this work—I will send you more parts as soon as I receive them—Your arrangement of the 'Song of the h. h. is wonderfully good in parts—you seem tho' to have hesitated between putting everything in & eliminating. For Gardiner I would put everything in & then afterwards make a playable 2 hand arrangement[7]—I do not know much about piano arrangements but they must be playable & give a good idea of the work—There is the difficulty I have indicated how the figure on page 7 might be done ④ with the melody—Use 3 lines whenever you like—put the chorus part on separate lines as it is too involved as it is. 3 bars after ㉓ I would use 3 lines—let the left hand play the melody & the right the shifting harmonies—At least that is my suggestion—I know so little about this sort of work   Leuckart wrote to me that he would be willing to publish your two arrangements but could pay nothing for them!! These editors are awful people—I wrote back that you would let him have them for 75 Marks—so I am still awaiting his answer—What do

---

[7] *The Song of the High Hills* was under consideration for a third Gardiner series (of three concerts) in Nov. 1914 that was cancelled because of the outbreak of war. This explains why he had requested Heseltine to make a piano arrangement.

you think? I dont believe much in letting editors have things for nothing   But as a last resort perhaps one might—Especially if you think it would be of use to you—The weather here is lovely hard frost, snow & sun

With best love: in hast—
your affectionate
Frederick Delius

write me soon again

67
Philip Heseltine to Frederick Delius

Feb, 11th 1914   *Christ Church*
                                 Oxford

Dear Mr Delius

   I have postponed answering your last letter far too long—please forgive me . . . First of all, let me try and tell you, as best I can, what a perfect joy it was to me to hear your two pieces for small orchestra at Queen's Hall on January 20th: the first piece is the most exquisite and entirely lovely piece of music I have heard for many a long day—it almost makes me cry, for the sheer beauty of it: I play it often on the piano, and it is continually in my head, a kind of beautiful undercurrent to my thoughts. For me, the deep, quiet sense of glowing happiness, and the mysterious feeling of being at the very heart of Nature, that pervades the piece, is too lovely for words: I only wish I could express to you a tithe of what the music makes me feel: it is simply perfect.[8]

   Lately, things have happened which have made me feel a new being altogether, and given me a deeper joy and a greater realization of life than I have ever known before: your music ministered to this mood in a wonderful manner—it seemed to have a new and intimate message to me, and strangely to express the very

---

[8] Heseltine wrote in similar terms to Taylor: 'The first of the two pieces was almost too beautiful—I simply wanted to cry all the way through: I have never heard anything to approach it in sheer loveliness and depth of feeling . . and the second one was not far behind it.' Heseltine to Taylor, 23 Jan. 1914, BL 54197. He described the *First Cuckoo* to Viva: 'It has a sense of deep, quiet, glowing happiness about it, and a mysterious feeling of rest in the very heart of Nature, as it were, and, strangely and wonderfully, it seems exactly to express the mood and feeling that has awakened in you and me—a deep, tranquil, *looking-forward*, Spring-like feeling of intense, penetrating happiness: it is perfect loveliness in music, and forms a beautiful undercurrent to all my thoughts of You.' Heseltine to Viva Smith, 11 Feb. 1914, BL 58127.

thing that was awakening in me—forgive this confused attempt to express what mere words can never do, but I feel I must try and tell you, however feebly, what a wonderful message your Cuckoo brought me! . . . . Just a week after I received your last letter but one, in Wales, your prophecy came true . . . she wrote, of her own accord, asking me to come back to her, offering me all she had . . . . I had to return to this wretched place just then, but I have been over to see her at Didbrook once or twice, while I have been here, and at last we are in perfect accord and harmony with each other: we are going away together somewhere, as soon as I can get away from this place, which will be about the middle of March. I am leaving here then altogether (at least, I hope so) since I simply cannot stand the depressing, enervating, out-of-date, academical atmosphere of absolute *stagnation*⁹ . . . and, besides, I could never apply myself to the 'classics' again, with any profit—any work would be better than that, and one can at least get paid for one's work elsewhere! I am probably going into an office in London soon after Easter: the work could not be more uncongenial than Latin and Greek, etc, ad nauseam, and I shall have the joy of living in London, and being quit of this fearful 'old-world' atmosphere!¹⁰ . .

I spent a delightful day at Ashampstead yesterday: Gardiner tells me you are coming over for 'Sea-Drift'¹¹ on March 10ᵗʰ: how long are you going to stay in England? I should so love to see you when you come, if we can possibly arrange to meet, on or after the 14ᵗʰ—I fear I shall not be able to come up for the concert, or any day between the 10ᵗʰ and the 14ᵗʰ, as I have a miserable examination on then! I hope to be able to get up to London on the 14ᵗʰ, to hear Scriabine's 'Prometheus'¹²—the work we missed at Birmingham in 1912—but my plans at the end of term rather depend on what She wants to do. In this Christ-ridden country one has to be so horribly careful and secretive on expeditions of this kind! We shall probably end by going abroad somewhere for a week or so: you see, if my mother discovered, by any means, what was happening, I should get no more allowance 'from this time forth and for evermore, Amen'!—and this is

⁹ Heseltine wrote in similar terms to Taylor in April: 'I simply cannot stand Oxford: it has an enervating, depressing influence on me and I am quite sure that I shall never do anything whatever until I can get away from the place.' Heseltine to Taylor, 3 Apr. 1914, BL 54197.
¹⁰ Heseltine told Taylor that: 'I shall probably leave here this term, and go into an office in London, where there seem great possibilities of making money—though this is not quite settled yet, but my step-father highly approves and is doing all he can for me in this direction.' Heseltine to Taylor, 1 Feb. 1914, BL 54197. Heseltine also wrote to his mother: 'Walter [Buckley Jones] has been very kind in looking out for a job for me, but so far I'm afraid very little progress has been made. However, I am quite determined not to be defeated in my attempts, and the appalling alternative possibility of having to spend three years in this fearful place inspires me to the most frantic efforts in this direction.' Heseltine to his mother, 16 Feb. 1914, BL 57961.
¹¹ Charles Kennedy Scott was to conduct *Sea-Drift* in Queen's Hall on 10 Mar. with the Oriana Madrigal Society and the Queen's Hall Orchestra with Thorpe Bates as soloist.
¹² Henry Wood was to conduct a concert in Queen's Hall on 14 Mar. which included Skryabin's *Prometheus* as well as his Piano Concerto in F sharp minor. The composer was to play the piano at this his first appearance in England.

a matter of no little importance to me at the present time. Later on, when I am 21, next year, things will be different—even then it might mean marrying, though I don't care a damn for any rotten little legal ceremony, that means nothing whatever, neither does She. . What a thing it is to live in England! . . .

The Parsee[13] I told you about continues to write me most gushing and enthusiastic letters! In the fourth letter, I was already 'the most sympathetic person he had ever come across', save his mother (to whose apron-strings he appears to be tied!), and by the time the fifth was reached, he was convinced that in a *former incarnation* (!) I must have been closely related to him: 'the law of Karmâ has ordained us to meet in this life. What sort will it be in the higher stages of the Marwantara? Can you imagine?' . . etc, etc!! He concludes with the wonderful phrase, 'Yours quite as much as his own'!!! This to a person he has never seen! It is really great fun, and I encourage him to write more and more, since I find his letters most entertaining, and sometimes really interesting, when he talks about music.[14] . . . . Last week there came to Oxford one Léo Ornstein,[15] who has been aptly described as a 'young ultra-modern composer who out-Schönbergs Schönberg'! I met him one day, and talked to him for a long while —he was very voluble and enthusiastic—(absolutely sincere, though, of course, how far he is unconciously humbugging himself neither he nor anyone else can tell)—and, of course, claimed direct inspiration from Heaven, like Schönberg. He then played several of Schönberg's piano pieces, and followed them up by some of his own compositions. Until I heard this amazing stuff, I always thought Schönberg must have reached the absolute limits of harmonic complexity that it is possible for anyone to reach, without recourse to a new system, with quarter tones, etc: but honestly, without any exaggeration, Ornstein's music is, in this respect, as far beyond Schönberg as Schönberg is beyond Strauss! (By 'beyond', I only mean, of course, beyond in the case of harmonic complexity

[13] Kaikhosru Shapurji Sorabji.
[14] Heseltine told Taylor about Sorabji: 'The blackamore whom you spotted at Ravel's concert was the very man! . . . I shall never dare to visit him now, and I am beginning to fear that, amusing as his correspondence is, I shall soon repent having encouraged it, since I am sure I shall never get rid of him again! He becomes more and more queer, every letter he writes, but it is getting much too personal: I am "the most sympathetic person he has ever met", etc, etc (although he has never *met* me—for that, at least, I am thankful!) Moreover he is convinced that in a former incarnation, I must have been closely related to him!! What funnys these Parsees are!' Heseltine to Taylor, 4 Feb. 1914, BL 54197.
[15] Léo Ornstein, Russian-born composer and pianist (b. 1895) who settled in America in 1907. Heseltine told Taylor of this visit to Oxford: 'Leo Ornstein . . . has regaled us with the strangest of strange musics! . . . He played us . . . his own "Wild Men's Dance", "Impressions of the Thames" and other nameless pieces. Never have I heard anything remotely like them! Technically, they must be, by a very long way, the most difficult pieces in existance. "Sequences" are things abominable to this weird composer! He admits of no system, or form whatever: he claims, like Schönberg, direct inspiration: he is but a medium himself. "What I hear, I write down: when I hear no more I stop", he says. Apparently, his new style all came with a rush one morning, about a year ago! During the last year he appears to have written large quantities of it, but although he is only 20, he has also published a good deal of "ordinary" stuff. The later work is, as yet, in MS. He is not in any sense a follower of Schönberg, whom he thinks too intellectual and formal, because of his "thin" (!!) harmony, and use of definite sequences! He had never heard of Schönberg when he began composing in his present style. . . . These developments of "music"(?) are truly fearful and wonderful: we are all old academics now!!' Heseltine to Taylor, 4 Feb. 1914, BL 54197.

and dissonance, though the latter word has scarcely any meaning and is apt to be used too loosely). Technically, it must be by far the most difficult piano music in existence! Ornstein is a brilliant pianist—of the tub-thumping order—and plays with tremendous fire and enthusiasm: he is going to give a recital of Schönberg and himself in London next April[16]—he has already done so in Paris, I believe. Truly, there are some amazing phenomena in the musical (?) world to-day! . . .

When is your music-drama to be produced in Cologne?[17] I am still quite ready to correct any proofs of parts, etc, that you may care to send me: in fact, I take quite a delight in doing so. About Leuckart, of course I should be delighted to receive any fee for my two transcriptions, but I should be very pleased if he would publish them at all, even without payment, as it would be a great help to me to have something of my arranging published. Is there any chance of his accepting my version of the 'Song of the High Hills'? If so, I will make a fair copy, with the alterations you suggest, but as this is rather a long job, I should like to know, before doing it, what the chances are of it's being accepted. I have made piano versions of the Two small pieces, for my own delight: if these would be of any use to you, I will send them along: also the 'Lebenstanz'. . . .

I do hope I shall be able to see you again before long: I am longing for a talk with you.

With best love,

Your affectionate
Philip Heseltine

68
Frederick Delius to Philip Heseltine

GREZ-SUR-LOING
Seine et Marne
March 11 1914

My dear Philip—

I only returned here last night[18]—We have been away in Germany just 1 month[19]—Heard the 'Mass of Life' at Wiesbaden & Frankfurt—The two Orchestra pieces in Frankfurt & Cologne—& Songs of Sunset in Elberfeld

[16] Ornstein played twice in London during that particular visit to England: 27 Mar. and 7 Apr. 1914.
[17] *Fennimore and Gerda* was due to be produced in Cologne on 10 Oct.
[18] From Frankfurt, Delius had written to tell Hertzka that he would return to Grez on 11 Mar.
[19] Delius had gone to hear the *Mass of Life* in Wiesbaden on 16 and in Frankfurt on 23 Feb.

—It gave me the greatest possible pleasure to hear you liked the 2 pieces so much—I have since written 3 more shortish Orchestra pieces[20]—On my return here I found the whole material of Fennimore awaiting me—Wont you come here & correct it for me? or help me? When do your holidays begin? We brought 2 servants with us back from Germany—I heard Schönbergs Kammer Symphonie[21] in Cologne—it is very dry & unpoetical & entirely intellectual —but did not sound bad at all—At times quite like Strauss in Heldenleben— & sometimes quite interesting—But what sometimes sounds very bad on the piano—sounds quite tame on the Orchestra—I agree with every effort of the young school to do something new—but I disagree with music becoming a merely mathematical, & intellectual art—Be careful Philip!! Be Careful my boy!! you live in a bourgeois world—Take care of yourself & of your friend. Do not travel about with her yet—Come here to me alone—I have lots of things to tell you— Dont break with your family—Come here as soon as you can—Of course you can now stay with us here—

your affectionate
Frederick Delius

69
Frederick Delius to Philip Heseltine

[March 1914]

Dear Heseltine, Do you think that you could bring me over a *bicycle* when you come? Is it asking too much of you? What machine ought I to get? I dont want a too expensive one but a nice light serviceable one—
Perhaps you know

your affectionat
Fr Delius

Fennimore & Gerda will only be given in October—All the material is here—

Postcard.

[20] Delius is probably here referring to his *North Country Sketches*.
[21] *Kammersymphonie*, No.1, Op. 9 for 15 solo instruments (first version, 1906).

70

Philip Heseltine to Frederick Delius

Cranston's Ivanhoe Hotel,
Bloomsbury Street,
London, W.C.,
March 24th 1914

My dear Mr Delius

I feel very wicked for not having answered your kind letter and invitation to Grez, before: I should have simply loved to come, but I fear it is quite impossible at present—for various reasons, financial and otherwise—(the former alone would scarcely hold me back!): I am very sorry indeed to miss a chance of seeing you, as there are a number of things I want so much to discuss with you, but I can see no possible means of coming just now. If I can be of any use in correcting the proofs of 'Fennimore', I should be delighted if you would send them over to me—or any other work I could help by doing. I shall be here till Friday next (when 'In a Summer Garden' is to be played at Queen's Hall):[22] after that, perhaps in Wales, perhaps in Gloucestershire. Anyway, Cefn Bryntalch, Abermule, Montgomeryshire will find me.

I am burning to find some means of escape from the appalling, enervating and depressing atmosphere of Oxford: the place is just one foul pool of stagnation—I simply cannot stand it, and I am getting no good, and any amount of harm, from staying there. Yet *nothing* can I find to do elsewhere: I would do anything to get away from the place, and, if possible, make a little money. But it seems hopeless, and my people suggest nothing. Oxford leads nowhere—and it is fearful to wander on through life, aimless, objectless, and—what is worse—moneyless.

I met Ernest Newman the other day, and sought to discover what it was necessary to do to become a critic: apparently there is nothing to be done, save to study scores, ancient and modern, on one's own account, and write articles, in the hopes of getting them accepted, and thus becoming known well enough to get a permanent engagement with some paper. He considers the ordinary academic musical training of small use, and he strongly advises taking up some other profession to keep the pot boiling till one is ready and able to stand on

---

[22] This was the first London performance of the revised version of *In a Summer Garden*. It was included in a programme in Queen's Hall on 27 Mar. which included the first performance of Vaughan Williams's *A London Symphony* conducted by Geoffrey Toye.

one's feet in the musical world.[23] But as for other professions—this accursed public school, and university 'education' (!!) fits one for *nothing*: at the age of 19, the product of Eton and Oxford is worth a thousand times less than the product of the national board-schools. What, in the devil's name, is to be done? My case, really, is very near akin to that of the 'unjust steward' we used to hear so much about, who could not dig and was ashamed to beg![24]

How more than damnable is this English system of 'education'!

Can you suggest *anything*—no matter what it is—that I could do *now*— or at least, begin studying with a definite view to and prospect of doing in the near future? I simply cannot continue to drift along in my present aimless fashion. Could one get a job in the way of copying or transcribing music, correcting proofs, copying orchestral parts, etc? I don't mind what it is, so long as it gives one occupation.[25]

By the way, will Leuckart publish my transcriptions of the 'Dance Rhapsody' and 'Summer Garden'? It would be a great help to me if he would, and I don't in the least care whether he pays or not, as long as you don't mind.

Forgive this rather pessimistic letter—but you will understand why it is so.

Affectionately yours
Philip Heseltine

[23] Heseltine told his mother: 'Last week I had a talk with Ernest Newman, to whom Gardiner was kind enough to introduce me: he was of the opinion that the only way to become competent as a critic was to know as much music as possible—to hear it and to study it for oneself. The old, theoretical training in (so-called) harmony and counterpoint, etc, was of no use whatever. All one must do is to absorb as much music as possible, and write essays on one's own account, with a view to getting them accepted and thus becoming sufficiently well-known to be able to get a permanent engagement with some paper.' Heseltine to his mother, 25 Mar. 1914, BL 57961.

[24] Luke 16: 1–8.

[25] Heseltine wrote to Taylor: 'Delius and Gardiner are both very strongly against Oxford, which they regard as complete stagnation. [Cecil] Forsyth was very kind, and more encouraging than anyone else I have talked to on the subject: of course he could not (nor could anyone) give one any definite prospects, but he said that, if one devoted oneself to music and lived in touch with musical people, there was every chance of getting something good to do after a year or so, in one branch or another—either criticism, or orchestration (which he said was very useful, as it lead to good things in the way of conducting in theatres, etc), or transcriptions, etc. Delius also suggests studying accompanying, with a view to being engaged in an opera house to teach singers their parts.' Heseltine to Taylor, 3 Apr. 1914, BL 54197.

71
Frederick Delius to Philip Heseltine

GREZ-SUR-LOING
Seine et Marne
25 March 1914

My dear Philip—I hasten to write you a few words in reply to your letter just arrived—Firstly if you can manage to come here for a week or 10 days I should be delighted to pay your expenses & besides correcting the material[26] we might talk things properly over together & take nice walks in so doing. You seem to be in a pretty unsettled state of mind—The career of critic is no career at all— Why dont you try your uncles office to see how you like it? for breathing space —& continue writing your articles at the same time. Leuckart answered me the following—

'So mässig auch das Honarar Ihres Freundes für die vierhändigen Bearbeitungen von 'In a Summer Garden' & 'A Dance Rhapsody' ist so möchte ich diese Werke in diesem Arrangement noch nicht herausgeben, denn es treten noch die nicht unbedeutenden Herstellungs Kosten dazu & die Nachfrage ist leider erfahrungsgemäss sehr gering—' [As moderate as your friend's fee for the four-handed arrangement of 'In a Summer Garden' and 'A Dance Rhapsody' is, I still don't want to publish these works in this arrangement as the not incon- siderable costs add up, and from my experience the demand is unfortunately very small.] Now if you like to do so—write directly to Leuckart & say he can have the arrangements for nothing—Altho' I, personally, am against giving things to publishers for nothing—You can say that I said he would publish them in case you renounced any fee—There is only one way to make money, & that is in business—Write me at once what you decide

Affectionately yours
Frederick Delius

---

[26] Heseltine wrote to Taylor from Grez: 'I am working very hard, correcting the orchestra parts of D.'s new opera "Fennimore and Gerda" which is to be produced in Cologne next October. I have also translated the text of "Arabeske", a new work for chorus and orchestra (just published), for which I hope to get paid by the publishers.' Heseltine to Taylor, 3 Apr. 1914, BL 54197.

72
Frederick Delius to Philip Heseltine

GREZ-SUR-LOING
Seine et Marne
[March 1914]

My dear Philip—

I forgot to ask you to write me at once in case you can come & also to tell me whether you want money sending. In case you come—I also want you to bring two books for me—

A ramble in British Columbia
By *Lees & Clutterbuck*—
with Map & 75 Illustrations 3/6
and also Three in Norway
by the same authors
Map & 59 Illustrations—*cloth* 2/6
both books published by
Longmans, Green & Co
London—

If you can also manage to bring me the bicycle—I should be glad—By having it plumbed I believe one can avoid paying duty. Tell me how much it will cost & I will send you the money—I dont want an expensive machine—If you cannot come I will send you the score & parts over to England—Let me hear from you soon—yours affectionately

Frederick Delius

73

Philip Heseltine to Frederick Delius

Cefn-Bryntalch,   10/4/1914
Abermule,
Montgomeryshire.

My dear Mr Delius

I arrived here yesterday evening, after a journey that would have been very comfortable, but for the Easter holiday crowd, going north from London, which made my train nearly two hours late in arriving.

I can't tell you how much I enjoyed my ten days at Grez, nor can I thank you and Mrs Delius sufficiently for supporting my presence for so long: it was too lovely for words.

My mother is, as yet, far from recovered, and is still in a somewhat languorous condition, usually to be found, dormant, upon a sofa or in a huge arm-chair. This is scarcely propitious for the broaching of my new plans, but I shall fire off my bomb in a day or two, and let you know what effect it has in due course.

I was very grateful for your 20 fr. in London: in fact, I could not possibly have got here without it!—from which you may conclude that buying your books in London was out of the question! However, I will order them from my bookseller in Oxford, who can always obtain anything, new or second-hand.

Again a thousand thanks for all your kindness at Grez, and please give my best thanks also to Mrs Delius. I shall always remember this Spring with great delight, especially when I hear all the delicious fragments of music that floated into the garden from your window woven together into the Dance that will assuredly give to the trade of wool-sorting an immortality even greater than that of the young carpenter we have all been thinking so much about, this sacred day!

Ever yours affectionately
Philip Heseltine

74

Frederick Delius to Philip Heseltine

GREZ-SUR-LOING
Seine et Marne
24 April
1914

Dear Philip—

I am glad you got home alright. You ought to have taken 50 francs instead of 20 as nothing is so annoying as to run short on a journey—I suppose the Orchestral parts will now be about done—please send them in one or 2 packets by parcel post—insured to

Universal Edition
Reichsrat Str 9
Vienna
Austria

Tell me how much the packets cost so that I may refund you—In your translation of the Arabesk[27] there are still 4 or 5 places which will not do—They sound too awkward & too much like a translation—I sent it to Gardiner   He & Bax may be able to help us. I should prefer, of course, having it sung in German —to a weak English translation. Write me what you have decided to do & how things are looking with you—Here it is simply lovely & we have had nothing but sunshine since you left—We both enjoyed your stay immensely & hope you will repeat it. It appears that the Entracte to the Village Romeo & Juliet is done for the pianolo!! Try to get it & tell me what it is like & who has published it. With love. yrs ever

Frederick Delius

[27] Heseltine was hoping that his translation would be published: 'Delius has secured a promise from his niggardly publishers that I shall be paid 40 Mark (£2) for my translation of the text of his new choral work "Arabeske".' Heseltine to Viva Smith, 20 May 1914, BL 58127.

75
Frederick Delius to Philip Heseltine

[Grez-sur Loing
May 1914]

Dear Philip—Gardiner wrote me that he lunched with you in Oxford so I write
there—Universal Edition is clamouring for the score of Fennimore—Please send
it off at once—*Insured*.
Write soon. yrs ever

Frederick Delius

Postcard.

76
Philip Heseltine to Frederick Delius

May 13th 1914   *Christ Church*
                                      Oxford

Dear Mr Delius

I took the score and parts of 'Fennimore' to the post office to-day, but I was
confronted with such a long and grisly list of regulations that must be complied
with before a parcel can be sent, insured, across the channel that I had to return,
defeated, and fill up forms and re-pack the parcel completely. However, it will
go to-morrow morning without fail. I had no idea the publishers were in such
a hurry, or I could have finished off the corrections before. There are very few
mistakes in the wind and brass parts—in fact, scarcely any, except general unclear-
ness in the copyist's handwriting and notation. I hope I have not overlooked a
host of howlers! Inside the score is a paper containing queries anent the score
itself—but these, of course, I cannot deal with.[28]

---

[28] Heseltine wrote to Viva Smith telling her: 'Amongst my other "activities" have been the correcting of the MS
parts of D's opera—a fearful job which had to be done in feverish haste, owing to my usual unfortunate habit of putting
things off! It kept me going at the rate of about 5 hours a day while it lasted—which, luckily was not very long!'
Heseltine to Viva Smith, 20 May 1914, BL 58127.

I am here again, alas, because my mother has been very ill with bronchial pneumonia and general nervous disorder, and my step-father implored me not to do or say anything that might worry or upset her. However, as it is but for one term, I have plenty to occupy myself with. My mother is nearly well again, and I shall be able to settle everything in a month, or so.

I am ordering your books here, and trust they will arrive at Grez safely in the course of a few days. I expect you have read 'Ssanin' by Artzibaschew?[29] A friend of mine is doing an English translation (from a German translation) in which he has asked me to collaborate. I think it is a wonderful book: it has made a great impression on me. By the way, what was the name of the delightful German novel that Mrs Delius was reading aloud to you while I was at Grez?

I have shewn my version of the 'Arabeske' to several people, but noone has suggested any satisfactory emendations, I'm afraid.

I heard some Scriabine the other day—some of the latest piano pieces: it is really wonderful stuff—immensely voluptuous and sensual, and, harmonically, rich and delightful—immeasurably superior in every respect to anything Debussy or Ravel do. It has an intensity and depth of feeling that they never reveal. Never have I heard a more wonderful and beautiful expression of sensuality in music than in the two pieces, 'Désir' and 'Caresse dansée'—though both derive, vaguely, from 'Tristan' . . . I must play them to Gardiner at the earliest opportunity!!

I am *so* much looking forward to your visit to England in June: I hope you have not forgotten that you are coming for a motor-bike tour with me all round the borderland of Wales! I have had some more funny experiences lately that I want to tell you tho' I can't bring myself to write it all down!!

Ever yours affectionately
Philip

[29] *Sanine*, a love novel by the Russian author, Mikhail Petrovich Artsybashev (1878–1927), translated by Percy Pinkerton (London, 1914). Heseltine enthused to Viva Smith about the novel: 'I sent you yesterday . . . "Sanine", a magnificent Russian novel . . . [it] made an immense sensation in Russia: in France, huge editions were exhausted, and in Germany "polizeilich verboten": the English version is slightly more expurgated than the German (which I should not think was expurgated at all!), but it is very good indeed.' Heseltine to Viva Smith, 4 Nov. 1914, BL 58127.

77
Philip Heseltine to Frederick Delius

15ᵗʰ May 1914   Ch. Ch.
                                                                       Oxford

The parcel is safely despatched—insured.
 I have ordered, from my bookseller, the following, for you:—

Louis Becke[30]	'By reef and palm'
Lees and Clutterbuck {	'A ramble in British Columbia' 'Three in Norway'
Joseph Conrad[31] {	'Typhoon' 'Chance'
Grant Watson	'Where bonds are loosed'

(a new novel about life in the South Seas which is said to be excellent)
 I heard from the Mexican poet[32] this morning!! He is now in London.

 Yours affect^{ly}
 P. A. H.

Postcard.

[30] Louis George Becke (1848–1913), English author.
[31] Joseph Conrad (1857–1924), Polish-born writer who became one of the greatest novelists in the English language.
[32] Alan Seeger (1888–1916), an American poet whom Heseltine had met at Uncle Joe's in Marlotte. Heseltine described him as 'a young American vagabond-poetaster . . . interesting, well-read, and, above all, *free* in his outlook on life.' (Heseltine to Viva Smith, 20 Sept. 1913, BL 58127). A promising poet, Seeger was killed in the war in July 1916, a collection of his poems being published in New York the following year.

78

Frederick Delius to Philip Heseltine

[Grez-sur Loing
17 May 1914]

Dear Phil—Please let me know how much you paid for the packet to Germany
& also how much the books cost—shall I send it, or wait until I come in June?
Universal will pay 40 Marks for the translation—we must go carefully thro' it
when I come—as you have altered the meaning in places—

affectionately
F D.

Postcard.

79

Frederick Delius to Philip Heseltine

[Grez-sur Loing]

Dear Phil—A thousand thanks for the books. I have read Where Bonds are Loosed
by Watson—*It is excellent.* I leave tomorrow week—Sunday 21st for London
—& stay with O'Neill. 4 Pembroke Villas—Kensington   Then go out to
Gardiner[33]   We shall no doubt come on to Oxford. Let me know your plans—
Do you know a good & not too dear tailor in London? Buckly Jones gave me
an address but I lost it—

with love—yrs ever
Fr. D.

15/6/14

Postcard.

---

[33] On 21 June Delius went to London to hear performances of his works to be conducted by Beecham. He and Heseltine
stayed a few days with Gardiner at Ashampstead at the end of March after which he went on to stay with Norman
O'Neill and after that with Beecham. Heseltine reported to his mother: 'I was in London for the week-end and came
down here [Ashampstead] on Tuesday: Delius followed on Wednesday. This is a perfectly charming spot, and the house
is quite delightfully arranged, in the cottage style. I am having a splendid time. The country down here is lovely—far
more varied and beautiful than I had imagined possible in Berkshire.' Heseltine to his mother, 26 June 1914, BL 57961.

80
Philip Heseltine to Frederick Delius

July 5th 1914.   *WHITNEY RECTORY*
                                                             HEREFORD

My dear Mr Delius

I am coming up to London on Tuesday—probably by motor-bike: would you be so kind as to send me a postcard to

6 Seymour Street
Portman Square, W.

telling me what time the rehearsal will be—if I may come to it? I am so very much looking forward to the concert.[34]

Yours affectionately
Philip Heseltine

P.S. I shall see the man about your bicycle to-morrow, and will tell you all particulars when we meet.

81
Frederick Delius to Philip Heseltine

TELEPHONE
GERRARD 366

                                                             THE COTTAGE,
                                                             8ᴬ HOBART PLACE,
                                                             S. W.
                                                             [6 July 1914]

Dear Phil—

There is a rehearsal on Tuesday morning 10.30 & Wednesday 10.30 a m— of course—come—

---

[34] An all-Delius concert held at the Duke's Hall, Royal Academy of Music on the 8 July. Included in the programme were *Brigg Fair, Dance Rhapsody, In a Summer Garden, On Hearing the First Cuckoo in Spring, The Walk to the Paradise Garden*, and Danish songs sung by Agnes Nicholls.

Bring me all particulars of Bicycle altho' I may not take it with me—but get it in the autumn, or sent—I have such a lot of new things to talk—you forgot the Arabeske at Gardiners—I brought it in for you—

affectionately
Fr. Delius

82
Philip Heseltine to Frederick Delius

July 10ᵗʰ 1914.   Didbrook
Winchcombe
Glos.

My dear Mʳ Delius

I must write you just a few lines to tell you—however inadequately—what a wonderful and overwhelmingly beautiful experience last Wednesday's concert was for me, and to contribute my tiny share—however futile—to the debt of gratitude the whole world owes you for such superb, such glorious music. No words could do it justice: it is too magnificent: it transcends everything—not only all other music. For me it is the greatest thing in life. Any attempt to express what it means to me in mere words appears weak and ridiculous, but I feel I must tell you, somehow or anyhow, something of what your music makes me feel: please forgive the means of doing so.

I returned from London yesterday on the motor bicycle which I borrowed from my friend[35] here. I shall probably move on to-morrow: I hope to be settled down finally in London, and in the midst of music by the end of August.

Please remember me very kindly to Mʳˢ Delius.

Ever yours most affectionately
Philip Heseltine

[35] Viva Smith.

83
Frederick Delius to Philip Heseltine

Grez sur Loing
(S & M)
30 July—[1914]

My dear Heseltine—

Your letter gave me immense pleasure   It means a great deal to me that you appreciate so greatly what I have done—It was also a great pleasure to me to have seen you a good deal whilst I was in England—I looked out for you after the Concert as I wanted to take you home with me to dinner—I spent the evening purposely all alone—& went into Hyde Park & up to the Marble Arch, where I listened to several discussions—In one *I took part*   It was awfully interesting & you ought to have been there—Have you finished 'An Arabeske'? The editor wants it now—please send it me as *soon as possible*—I do hope War will not break out & knock all Art and Music on the head for years—I am working at my Requiem—Write soon & send the poem—

your affectionate friend
Frederick Delius

84
Philip Heseltine to Frederick Delius

August 1ˢᵗ 1914.   *Cefn-Bryntalch*
                          Abermule
                          Montgomeryshire

My dear Mʳ Delius

I have just received your kind letter: the 'Arabeske' translation shall be despatched to you to-day. I fear it is not very much better than it was when you last read it—the simile about the corpse has defeated me entirely[36]—but I have submitted it to several people, who have not been able to offer any helpful

---

[36] Presumably the line 'Einer Leiche roten Wangen', which Heseltine translated as 'Like the glow of a dead bride's blushes'.

suggestions, and—such as it is now—it is the best I can do. The proof of the vocal score, into which I have copied the words is in rather a mess, but I have no other copy in which to write them. On a sheet of MS paper which I enclose in the proof, you will find some variants of the text: in each case I have written what I consider the best version immediately under the music, but perhaps you will have some emendations to make in the final copy before submitting it to the publisher. If you have any further suggestions to make, please send me a clean copy of the vocal score, and I will write the whole English version in it, clearly so that you can send it direct to the publisher without any further worry.

I am so sorry to have missed an evening with you in London: I would have given anything to have heard you make a speech in Hyde Park! As it was, I had promised to take out to dinner and a theatre, a certain virgin—(medically certified!)—who, after living for five years with an 'impuissant' man, left him—both parties having, naturally, driven each other nearly crazy!—and, upon the annullment of the marriage, was left completely penniless—though the man was well off—and she now ekes out a meagre living as an ill-paid private secretary in London, poor girl. Her nerves are completely wrecked and she is quite unfit for a strenuous life. The man, if you please, has re-married, and is now—nominally, at any rate—a father!! Such is English country life!!!!

I spend nearly all my time here immersed in your music—yet, wherever I am, it is always with me as a beautiful accompaniment to any scene or moment of intense beauty. I hope to begin my little book about it very soon[37]—as soon as I can settle in London, and have access to the British Museum, or some library where I can get material for the introductory sketch of music in this country during the '80's and '90's, prior to your concert in 1899. During the last few days, I have been going through the score of the 'Magic Fountain'[38] very carefully, and making notes thereon. I will return it to you in a few days. All the time I spend over it is tinged with regret that I cannot go immediately and hear it performed somewhere: there is such wonderful music in it: you really ought to reconsider your adverse opinion of it! Meanwhile, I should be very grateful for the loan of a piano score of 'Koanga' (if you have been able to wrest it from Beecham's grasp!), or of 'Irmelin' or any other early work of yours.

I am looking forward to seeing you over here again in the autumn; we must have our day in the East End and our debate-night in Hyde Park then!

Ever yours affectionately
Philip Heseltine

P.S. 'Sanine' is at last announced by an English publisher!—but not in my friend's translation.

---

[37] One of the earliest references to his book on Delius, completed in 1922 and published by John Lane in 1923.
[38] An opera in three acts (1894–5). The work was not performed until a BBC studio broadcast in 1977.

85
Philip Heseltine to Frederick Delius

October 18th 1914   54 Cartwright Gardens
                                                            London, W.C.

My dear Mr Delius

I have just heard from Gardiner that you are still at Grez, so I venture to
break through our long silence with some hope of my letter reaching you. I
am afraid you must have had a very trying time lately in France: I am so very
anxious to hear from you again, and learn what you have been doing, and how
Grez has been affected by this fearful state of affairs. I have heard indirectly that
Joe has fled from Marlotte, but he has not written to me for a long while.

Is not the condition of Europe too frightful for words? To me, it is incon-
ceivable that there should be people who care so little about this wonderful and
beautiful life of ours—which is, at best, all too short for anyone who in the
smallest degree realizes it's possibilities—that they are eager to throw it away,
and both to endure and to inflict unspeakable agony and suffering in doing so.
I have never been able to understand the sentiment of patriotism, the love of
empire: it has always seemed to me so empty and intangible an idea, so impersonal and so supremely unimportant as regards the things which really matter
—which are all the common heritage of humanity, without distinction of race
or nationality. And in spite of the gigantic wave of patriotism that has lately
swept over the whole world, I cannot honestly say that I feel it to be any more
real—or less disastrous, even in it's unreality—than ever I did. It makes one's
position very difficult, since unless one follows the line of least resistance and
becomes a mere hypocrite, one is cut off, in one's sympathies and mental outlook, from at least nine-tenths of one's fellow-beings. Isolation, such as you can
enjoy, is the only escape, but unless one has sufficient wealth of imagination
and creative power within oneself, to absorb one completely, even this becomes
intolerable. One feels oneself to be one of those who, as Dowson says, 'deem
no harvest-joy is worth a dream'[39]—though surely Dowson never pictured such
a grisly harvest of flesh and blood as constitutes the joy of the war-fiends!

But for my 'nervous stricture',[40] which of course renders me 'physically unfit
for service' (thus runs the phrase—the crude mind of the militarist has never

---

[39] E. Dowson, *Autumnal*, stanza 3 (lines 2–3).

[40] The 'nervous stricture' was, in the words of Dr Edwin Ash, a Harley Street doctor who had examined Heseltine,
an 'inability to micturate when mentally excited, and especially in the presence of other people, with the consequence
that he has had occasional prolonged retention'. In the certificate for his exemption from military service Ash added
that Heseltine 'also complained of undue mental fatigue after moderate effort, and inability to carry out consistent

yet dreamed of the mentally unfit!) the general public pressure would probably have driven me to enlist myself: hideous though a soldier's life would be for me, it would be less so than a life marred by the cheap sneers and dismal attempts at wit of the vulgar, blatant and exasperating Jingoes who, at a time like this, carry all before them. Fortunately, in my present condition, I escape both courses: but there must be hundreds of other unfortunate beings who, not having the saving physical blemish, are bullied into a life which is a Hell for them, and at the end of which is the possibility of the great and endless darkness—or worse, a dragging existence with a broken body and a bruised mind—all for an ideal which they have never felt: they have not even the consolation of thinking that it is sweet to suffer for their country's sake! And the conditions of military service must be far worse in Germany—or even in France—than they are here, though there are already rumours of Conscription for this country also . . . .

I have left Oxford for ever! This step was facilitated by the financial panic which is the inevitable concomitant of war.[41] My people, being thoroughly pessimistic, imagine (for no reason whatever) that they will be ruined, so, discovering that it would be cheaper to keep me in London than at Oxford, they welcomed my proposals! And as a matter of fact, I am much better off on the reduced allowance in London than I was at Oxford—which is a most extravagant place, and gives one no return for one's money. I have decided not to concentrate entirely on music for the present: I feel that, in spite of all the years I have spent, ostensibly 'being educated', I know scarcely anything about anything: my interests have outpaced my knowledge completely, and at the present time I feel very keenly the need of a somewhat wider education —as a kind of mental foundation. I have accordingly entered the University of London, as a student of the English Language and Literature, with Philosophy and Psychology as subsidiary subjects, for three years. The London University is a very good place, run on thoroughly sound, modern lines—a complete contrast to Oxford, in every way. One has merely to attend certain lectures there, and for the rest, one is completely free to do what one wants.[42]

---

daily work without distress, having to work in an irregular manner'. On examination Ash had found 'no sign of organic nervous disease', but was satisfied that he was of 'the neurasthenic type, due to an obstinate functional neurosis'. N. Heseltine, *Capriol for Mother* (London, 1992), 119.

[41] He told Taylor that: 'The war had necessitated a certain modification in my plans, the nature and execution of which I have been discussing during the last few days with an Indian friend [Shahid Suhrawardy] . . . who has been staying here. He is a man of real genius—of a quite un-occidental coolness in argument, and much persuasiveness of speech and manner. He ingratiated himself very successfully with my mother and step-father, and has talked to them about my plans far better than I could have done myself, and, although the final tête à tête discussion between my mother and myself has yet to take place, I am quite confident that my connection with Oxford will be finally severed within the next few days, thanks to my friend's mediation and extraordinarily skilful manner of breaking the ice.' Heseltine to Taylor, 7 Sept. 1914, BL 54197.

[42] Heseltine told his mother: 'I am more than glad to have entered the London University: I feel sure I shall really learn something now, and be very happy while doing so. It has been very kind of you to accede to this plan of mine,

In a few weeks I hope to begin lessons in Composition, etc, with Gustav von Holst, whom Gardiner recommends as the best man in London for this purpose:[43] apparently, the Royal College and Royal Academy of Music are so effete and antiquated that it is merely a waste of time to study there.

In music, as in other affairs, I feel very strongly the need of a master, and a thorough course of instruction, in matters of technique. In composition, I am stuck fast: I simply have not the means to express what I want to: it takes me hours to evolve a single bar. During the whole three months of inactivity in Wales, I only managed to do four or five little songs—the making of which could not have occupied more than a week at most. Excepting one week's walking tour in the Lake district with Leigh Spencer (whom you may remember in Birmingham)[44] I was compelled, by lack of funds, to spend nearly the whole of July, August and September with my people in Wales: this was worse than Oxford, I can tell you! I have never been so utterly depressed and 'embougré' [the hell in] in my life: and the climax came when, on the last day but two of my stay—at the very end of September—I discovered the long-lost pianola, covered with sacking, and stowed away in an attic!!!! I was absolutely wild with rage, when I thought of all the blank and bloody days I had been spending there, and then of all that I might have learned and enjoyed from this beautiful instrument that was wasting up in the attic! Noone had ever said a word about it since it's disappearance—(which coincided with mine, over a year ago: I probably told you about it at the time), and my mother thought it was a huge joke when I found out where it was, and was very angry when I told her what I thought of her! It was, forsooth, for those loveable characteristics of the parental mind that prompted such tempers that Moses bade one 'Honour one's father and mother'!! . . . . .

and I hope to have great benefits to show for it at the end of my three years. I propose to do Matric. in January next, and the Intermediate in June: there is more work for these than I had anticipated, for the standard is far higher than at Oxford, and the scheme of subjects far better and more comprehensive. After these, which are merely pass examinations, I shall be able to devote my time wholly to English and Philosophy.' Heseltine to his mother, 7 Oct. 1914, BL 57961.

[43] Gardiner had written to Heseltine: 'So after all you are not going up to Oxford! Congratulations! English literature is a fascinating study, but I think, if there is a chance of your going in for any branch of music whatever, you ought to do some actual work at it. Why not go to von Holst for a while? It would be impossible to find anyone better.' Gardiner to Heseltine, 8 Oct. 1914, photocopy, PWS Archives. In the event Heseltine did not study with Holst.

[44] Heseltine described this trip to Viva Smith: '. . . during my week in Westmoreland, I walked and climbed at least 75 miles, over the mountains, in the genial company of Leigh Spencer. We had a splendid time: we lived in a farmhouse, at the head of the Great Langdale valley, surrounded—almost overhung—by steep, craggy mountains—completely cut off from the world and every jarring element—14 miles from a railway station! We walked six or seven hours every day, whatever the weather (and although we got plenty of sunshine, we returned home wet to the skin every day) and were amply rewarded, not only by magnificent scenery, but also by the most wonderful sense of physical well-being, bringing with it an enormous appetite (which was gratified by the most splendid meals), healthy sleep of ten hours or more every night, and an astounding vigour, and elation of mind.' Heseltine to Viva Smith, 24 Sept. 1914, BL 58127.

I am living in a very jolly part of London—in a quite secluded square, in Bloomsbury, near St Pancras station.[45] The neighbourhood is thoroughly *alive* —which is essential, for my liking—and unrespectable: at night, the streets swarm with whores and hot-potato-men and other curious and entertaining phenomena: and the darkness which the fear of hostile aircraft has enforced upon the city, makes everything doubly mysterious, fascinating and enchanting: for London *is* enchanting at all times and seasons. Music is, of course, at a low ebb: and I fear it will suffer greatly during the next few years: though there will be some consolation for the flood of patriotic filth that will be poured forth, in the fact that those composers who resist the force of the mob's passion will stand out in the greater relief and pre-eminence. Aleister Crowley[46] wrote a fine letter to a newspaper the other day in which he said, 'There is no such thing as patriotic poetry. No self-respecting poet would foul his pen with allusions to petty topical trivialities like the war. The poet's throne is in eternity; clouds and thick darkness are under his feet. He may sing, as Homer, Virgil and many another, the ancient wars of his folk, but he never sways to the passions of his generation. They sway to him'. . . . . I have been to various Promenade Concerts, but as a whole the programmes have been worse than usual, and the audiences— as a result—proportionately larger. It is difficult to escape Walford Davies' 'Solemn Melody'[47] or Gounod's 'Hymne à Sainte Cécile', or some such tosh, which invariably gets encored. Whenever the organ is used, the Britisher applauds: presumably because it reminds him of Church! Wood mangled your two little pieces in the most execrable way: the strings played just anyhow, and the cuckoo came in at the wrong moment nearly every time: as for the rendering of the second piece, one can only imagine that both conductor and orchestra were reading the music for the first time! There was a very striking work by a member of the orchestra, Eugene Goosens,[48] the other night—a big conception, finely wrought and admirably carried out: a type of work one does not often meet nowadays.[49]

For the rest, there has been nothing more exciting than Symphonies by Brahms, Beethoven and Dvorak, Macdowell's Piano Concerto in D minor (twice in a

[45] Heseltine described it to his mother as being 'very convenient . . . and only 10 minutes' walk from University College. I have a good, large and well-furnished "bed-sitter" on the ground-floor, for 17/6 weekly, inclusive of baths, breakfast and electric light. . . . I hope to be able to economise a good deal in this house: I think I shall be able to reduce the entire cost of food, lodging and washing to a margin of 30/= weekly . . . I have 18 lectures a week—of one hour each: the matriculation work is very tedious, but balanced by the interest of the other.' Heseltine to his mother, 14 Oct. 1914, BL 57961.

[46] Aleister Crowley (1875–1947), notorious British occultist.

[47] Walford Davies' *Solemn Melody* had been included in the Promenade Concert programme on 3 Oct. 1914.

[48] Eugene Goossens (1893–1962): English composer and conductor. He was a violinist in Sir Henry Wood's Queen's Hall Orchestra from 1911 to 1915, after which in 1916 he became assistant conductor to Beecham. He subsequently became best known as a conductor, notably in England, the United States, and Australia. He conducted the first night of the English stage première of *Hassan* on 20 Sept. 1923.

[49] Goossens had conducted the Queen's Hall orchestra in a performance of his symphonic poem *Perseus*, at a Promenade concert in Queen's Hall on 13 Oct. 1914.

fortnight, and yours not once in the season!) and 'Tod und Verklärung'. The latter I heard for the first time, and was repelled, but I am grateful to it for causing me to enjoy more than ever the simple, innocent fun of the 'Zampa'[50] overture which followed it! Apart from the music, there is always a good deal of interest to be derived from observation of the crowd at the Proms: and the evenings are not without their humourous incidents. The other night a man fainted and collapsed with a great thud on the floor, exactly in unison with one of the great crashing chords at the end of 'Peer Gynt'![51]

In the absence of Colin Taylor (as 'Private Taylor'!), I have become conductor of a little amateur orchestra in Windsor—1 flute, 1 oboe, 1 clarinet, 1 horn, 2 drums and about 20 strings.[52] I took the first rehearsal last night: never having conducted before in my life, and knowing nothing about either the art of conducting or how the work (Mozart's G minor Symphony) should be played, I was very frightened, but managed to get through an hour and a half's stick-waving without a breakdown: my right arm, however, is dreadfully stiff to-day! It is very good experience for me, and I hope to improve with more practise. There is plenty of good material in the orchestra, to work upon. When I know the scores better, I think I shall be able to do a good deal with them.

If it is possible to get hold of the material of the 'First Cuckoo-note in Spring', without great expense, I want to make them do that; it would be so good for them, after many years' surfeit of Mozart, Haydn and Beethoven.

Is there any chance of your coming over here this winter? *Do* come for a few days if you possibly can: I am longing for some walks in London with you: if you could come in December, it would be great fun, as my term at the University ends about the second week of that month: but at any time, my evenings are free, as a rule.

Some day, I should love to take you to the delightful farmhouse in Westmoreland, where I went with Spencer: the country all round is magnificent, and one is completely cut off from the weary ways of the world beyond.

Do write soon, and give my kindest regards to Mrs Delius.

Ever yours affectionately
Philip Heseltine

---

[50] *Zampa*, an opera (1831) by Ferdinand Hérold (1791–1833).

[51] Grieg's *Peer Gynt* Suite was played at the Promenade Concert in Queen's Hall on 15 Oct.

[52] Heseltine told his mother: 'My orchestral society is not at all good: there is no wind or brass (except four isolated players of various instruments, with no family complete) and the strings intimated to me . . . that they were not accustomed to being pulled up so frequently and made to play passages over and over again, when they made a mess of them the first time. They like to play straight through a thing and then go on to something else: it is perfectly hopeless to expect any kind of refinement or delicacy when they will not take trouble. I explained to them last Saturday that if they do not want to be constantly pulled up at rehearsals, they must take their parts home and practise them, because it is futile to try and get any *interpretation* of a work, till the players know their *notes*—almost by heart, so that they can look at the conductor, and—more important still—play correctly at speed.' Heseltine to his mother, 4 Nov. 1914, BL 57961.

P.S. I have just read all the novels of D. H. Lawrence—three in number: they are, to my mind, simply unrivalled, in depth of insight and beauty of language, by any other contemporary English writer. Shall I send you one?

86
Frederick Delius to Philip Heseltine

GREZ-SUR-LOING
Seine et Marne
[26 October 1914]

My dear Phil—

I was very glad to receive your letter: We have been having very exciting times here—During the German advance there was an ever growing panic here caused, no doubt, by the refugees from Belgium & the North of France streaming thro' Grez—The high road to Nemours was a terrifying sight & we sat for hours watching this terrified stream of humanity pass by in every sort of vehicle possible—We had hundreds every night in Grez & they told terrible tales of german atrocities—On Sept 5th it got too much for us & we also could hear the booming of the canon (Battle of the Marne) so we decided to get out also, so we left for Orleans in a cattle truck with 50 or 60 others. We took 16½ hours to go 75 kilometers & arrived in Orleans at 3-30 in the morning & as there was not a room to be had in the whole town we spent the rest of the night on a bench on the boulevard near the railway station—We had the great luck to get a room at night so we decided to stay there & await further developements—We had a most interesting & exciting time in Orleans watching the soldiers going off to the front & the wounded coming back—trainload after trainload—this was awful—Some of the poor soldiers, carried on stretchers, with one or both legs shot off—As soon as we heard of the great Victory of the allies we quietly returned to Grez & found everything as quiet & peaceful as ever—Your uncle had gone off the same day as we did with his 2 servants en route for Guernsey—At Havre he got a steamer for Cherbourg & had a most fearful passage in a miserable little dirty boat. On arriving in some port or other they were fired on 3 times, it appears, as they had no flag up. I nearly died with laughter when Joe told me of his adventures—We are thinking of going to America until all this is over[53]—I am entirely sick of it   We shall leave about Christmas

---

[53] Delius had been urged by Percy Grainger to move to America.

probably from England—I may come to London a fortnight or 3 weeks before sailing & then I should just love to roam about London with you—I am glad you have not enlisted—I hate & loathe this german militarism & autocracy & hope it may be crushed for ever—but I can get up no enthusiasm whatever for the war. My sympathies are with the maimed & slaughtered on both sides. My North Country sketches are ready & also my 'Requiem'   I shall take them with me to America & perhaps conduct them myself—I shall have to make some money over there in some way or other. Music will be dead in Europe for a year or more & all countries will be ruined—It makes one despair of humanity— Lloyd Osbourne[54] & his wife were here thro' the panic—They were seized with it 24 hours before we were & left for Nantes but they returned a fortnight ago here to Grez & are now on their way to London. We had great fun burying our best wine & silver—I would not have missed this experience for anything. The world has gone mad—Write me another long letter as soon as you can & tell me all you are doing & your experiences

With love—your friend
Frederick Delius

87
Frederick Delius to Philip Heseltine

Grez-sur-Loing

Dear Phil—We are coming to London about the 14th or 15th[55]—A new work of mine will be given at the Philharmonic on the 24th—North Country Sketches[56]—We must wander about London together. We shall first stay 8ª Hobart Place S.W. and afterwards in the Country.[57] With best love—affectionately

Frederick Delius
3 Nov. 1914

Postcard.

[54] Lloyd Osbourne (1868–1947), American author and stepson of Robert Louis Stevenson.

[55] Beecham had suggested that, for the time being, the Deliuses move to England and stay in one of his houses.

[56] This work was, in fact, not performed until 10 May 1915. On 24 Nov. Beecham conducted the Royal Philharmonic Society Concert in Queen's Hall and included *The Dance at the Fair* and *The Walk to the Paradise Garden* instead of the *North Country Sketches*. In that same concert it was hearing May and Beatrice Harrison's playing of the Brahms Double Concerto that inspired Delius to write his own double concerto for them.

[57] At first the Deliuses stayed at Beecham's London home then moved in early December to Grove Mill House, Watford where they stayed until July 1915.

88

Philip Heseltine to Frederick Delius

14th November 1914.   54 Cartwright Gardens
                                                                    W.C.

My dear Mr Delius

I am enormously delighted at the prospect of seeing you here in London so soon. I meant to have written before, but I hope you will get this as soon as you arrive. Please send me a post-card to tell me when you have come and when we can meet. I am free every evening after 6 o'clock, and on Wednesday and Friday afternoons. I should be so pleased if you and Mrs Delius would come and dine with me on the first evening you are free—at the Chinese restaurant, or some amusing little place in Soho, where you will *not* be given English cabbages!! The Chinese place is particularly delightful—to my taste: and we could go for a walk afterwards: London is simply wonderful at nights, without the glare of the arc-lamps and the hideous lighted advertisements: I am sure the Thames has not looked so beautiful for a hundred years or more.

Au revoir—very soon, I hope.

Affectionately yours
Philip Heseltine

89
Frederick Delius to Philip Heseltine

TELEPHONE
GERRARD 366

THE COTTAGE,
8ᴬ HOBART PLACE,
S.W.
[18 November 1914]

Dear Phil—Thanks for your letter come & fetch me here on Saturday afternoon at 2 & we will stroll about together & dine at night—
    In haste—

affectionately
Frederick Delius

90
Philip Heseltine to Frederick Delius

18ᵗʰ Nov. 1914.   54 Cartwright Gardens
                                                               W.C.

My dear Mʳ Delius
    I am *so* glad to hear you are in London at last. I am looking forward ever
so much to seeing you again. On Saturday, however, I have to go to Windsor
at 5 o'clock to conduct the rehearsal of the little orchestra I have undertaken
there, and I have to dine with some people in Eton afterwards. Are you free
any other evening—Sunday for example? The evening is so much the best time
for wandering in London. I do hope we shall be able to arrange to spend some
evening together: I am free every day except Saturday, after 6—usually at 5.
    Is the 'Arabeske' to be played next Tuesday? I have seen a vague announce-
ment of it, but no singer's name.

Affectionately
Philip Heseltine

91
Frederick Delius to Philip Heseltine

TEL: PADD. 4948.

~~56, Seymour Street,~~
~~Portman Square, W.~~
8ᴬ Hobart Place,
S W
[19 November 1914]

Dear Phil—Come on Friday instead as soon as you are free—We are going in the country on Saturday for the weekend—Write me a card what time you will come—

affectionately
Fr Delius

92
Philip Heseltine to Frederick Delius

Nov. 19ᵗʰ [1914]   54 Cartwright Gardens
W.C.

My dear Mʳ Delius

Friday will suit me excellently well: my afternoon lectures are unimportant, so that I shall be free any time after 2 o'clock.

Will you let me know if this is too early for you, and if it is at what time I may call for you? I have made two ineffectual attempts to telephone to you, but on each occasion the exchange has assured me that the number printed on your notepaper (Gerrard-366) *does not exist*!!

Affectionately,
Philip Heseltine

93

Frederick Delius to Philip Heseltine

TELEPHONE
GERRARD 366

THE COTTAGE,
8ᴬ HOBART PLACE,
S.W.
[23 November 1914]

Dear Phil—Enclosed the Belgian composers announcement—Beecham wants to see your article before you publish it as he can give you lots of points—Attack the whole idea of English composers etc—there is no real English music—On Monday the rehearsal is at 2 p m—

 affectionately
 Fr D

H.[olbrooke] has tried every dodge possible in self advertisement—'A wolf in sheep's clothing' would be a good heading.

94

Philip Heseltine to Frederick Delius

[34 Southwold Mansions
Maida Vale
Between 4–7 December 1914]

My dear Mʳ Delius

 My letter about Holbrooke appeared in 'The New Age'[58] last Wednesday—with all references to patrons, etc, carefully omitted!! Out of charity to the Editor, I will suppose that this was due to lack of space! But since further correspondance is bound to follow, I shall have an opportunity of deciding this point in

---

[58] P. Heseltine, 'British v. German music' (*The New Age*, 3 Dec. 1914, no. 1160, v. 16, no. 5, 134–5), a letter attacking the parochial attitude that Holbrooke had shown in an earlier series of articles.

another letter. Do send me those additional 'facts' that you were going to glean from Beecham. Holbrooke's answer to the charge of impersonating a Belgian ought to appear next Wednesday. His excuses are sure to be very funny.[59]

I have just moved to the above address—a small furnished flat—with my friend Shahid Suhrawardy,[60] for six weeks.

When are you coming to London again? Do come and see us here when you come.

Yours affect^ly
Philip Heseltine

95
Frederick Delius to Philip Heseltine

~~TELEPHONE~~
~~GERRARD 366~~

~~THE COTTAGE,~~
8^A ~~HOBART PLACE,~~
~~S.W.~~
Grove Mill House
Watford
[8 December 1914]

My dear Phil—

I have spoken with Beecham about you & he will give you, in future, all his programme work to do   I shall also insist with the Philharmonic that you do the analytical notes for my North Country Sketches to be given in January—We will talk about all this when we meet—you must insist that all your articles are printed in Extenso or not at all—I will get all I can from Beecham re

[59] Heseltine recounted the story to his mother thus: 'That miserable charlatan, Joseph Holbrooke, has seized the opportunity afforded by the present state of affairs to lament loudly and very stupidly in "The New Age" about the neglect of British music—*because* it is British, says J. H. What he really signifies is, "*My* music is neglected: why? Because it is British", the real answer being "because it is poor stuff, and far too dull for anybody to listen to". I have written a very violent attack on the little man, which I hope will be printed next week: the best of "The New Age" is that the more the abusive your contributions are, the better it likes them. Holbrooke is really so contemptible that no abuse were too strong for him. Incidentally, his articles attacked Mr Delius: in return for that, I am going to expose his latest advertizing device, which is to publish a number of his works under the name of "Jean Hanze, *the Belgian composer*"!!!! What do you think of that, for a man who not only calls himself an artist, but is continually whining about British music? . . . I hope to have some fun out of the controversy: Beecham is going to give me a further ammunition of facts about J. H. that need exposing.' Heseltine to his mother, 26 Nov. 1914, BL 57961.

[60] Hasan Shahid Suhrawardy, one of Heseltine's Oxford Indian friends.

Holbrooke for you—but I think you know most of it already—I will come and see you one afternoon if you will tell me when you will be there perhaps next Saturday at about 4—We had a fine concert in Manchester[61] & Beecham gave an address last Friday evening to the Royal College of Music there—It was a Bombshell   He told them all these Colleges of Music were useless & frauds & 3/4 of the 'personel' incompetent—

affectionately
Frederick Delius

You will read an account of it probably in the Standard in a day or 2.
Telephone 493 Watford

96
Philip Heseltine to Frederick Delius

11. 12. 1914   34 Southwold Mansions
                                                        Maida Vale, W.

My dear M[r] Delius

I am sending you a few MS poems by my Oxford friend, Robert Nichols,[62] who has joined the Artillery—of all things!—for the purpose of 'seeing life'! I fear that what he will really see is a speedy death—but he was always dabbling in heroics.

I missed the last train splendidly! Surely it is much more than 2 miles to the Station? It took me ages to get there, although the road seemed quite straight: but I missed the short cut. However there was a huge fire in the waiting room, and I slept there till the small hours.

Do come in here for a meal whenever you would care to, and bring Mrs Delius, to sample her pupil's cookery!

If ever you come here from Watford, get out at Queen's Park station: it is only 10 minutes walk from here.

Yours affect[ly]
Philip Heseltine

---

[61] Whilst in Manchester Delius also attended a Hallé Concert on 3 Dec. which included music from *A Village Romeo and Juliet.*

[62] Robert Nichols (1893–1944), English poet and dramatist who served in France from 1914 to 1916 and eventually found his way to Hollywood writing film-scripts. From 1921 to 1924 he occupied the chair of English Literature at the University of Tokyo. Nichols adapted verses from Walt Whitman for use in Delius's *Idyll.* Nichols' own verses were set by E. J. Moeran in his *Nocturne* (1934), which was dedicated to Delius's memory.

97

Frederick Delius to Philip Heseltine

[8 December 1914]

Dear Heseltine—Will it suit you if I come out to you between 4 & 5 on Thursday—My Telephone No is 493 Watford—I tried to get the New Age today but only found an article by Holbrooke in it—You might come out then here with me to dinner or we might dine in town—

affectionately
Frederick Delius

Grove Mill House
Watford

Postcard.

98

Philip Heseltine to Frederick Delius

22. 12. 1914.   34 Southwold Mansions
                                                            Maida Vale, W.

My dear Mr Delius

I came down to Watford this afternoon on the chance of finding you at home, but was told you were in London.

I wanted to consult you about a certain scheme, which I will here attempt to outline, in writing.

My friend T. W. Earp[63]—(some of whose work you will find in 'Oxford Poetry, 1914') is going to start a little monthly paper, devoted entirely to Music and

---

[63] Thomas Earp (1892–1958) was one of Heseltine's wealthy Oxford friends, later to become the art critic of the *Daily Telegraph.*

Poetry, early in the New Year, and I have undertaken the task of being Musical Editor![64] The paper will be, of course, entirely non-political and non-war, and will simply consist of articles on musical and literary subjects, written from an altogether *free* point of view—together with as much creative work—new poetry, etc—as possible. We do not want to make any tendency or clique unduly prominent in the paper, but, as its title indicates ('The New Hat'), we intend to cry down, in very plain terms indeed, all fogeyish and 'old hat' notions, super-stitions, conventions, traditions, shams, humbugs etc, that are so carefully fos-tered by 'Messieurs les Professeurs', and their disciples.

My friend is paying the cost of publication, and the paper will continue for at least a year—or two—even if noone buys it. We are beginning with a very modest issue of eight double-column pages, so that in any case the financial loss cannot be very great.

A paper of this kind is undoubtedly needed in England, especially now that the War has swamped nearly every paper devoted to art—since they are all run with a view to monetary profit, as ours will not be. 'Poetry and Drama'—an excellent quarterly—has subsided altogether, and, as you know, there has never been a decent paper for music in this country. We hope very much, by plain speaking, to gain the sympathy of many of the rising generation who find—in the ordinary press—that they cannot sincerely voice their opinions without being immediately laughed at by the old fogies in authority.

I am writing to Beecham, to ask if he could possibly write us something rous-ing for the first number[65] (which I hope will appear during January), and if you could also let us have a few words, it would help us splendidly. We shall have to do most of the first number ourselves, but we hope to obtain as many out-side contributions as possible for the succeeding numbers.

Will you please be very kind, and let me know what you think of this scheme, and give me a few suggestions as to how it should be carried out? I am very keen to make the thing an artistic success, and a real influence in the London

[64] Heseltine told his mother: 'I have been given "carte blanche" as contributor of musical articles to a new monthly magazine, devoted to Poetry and Music, from a progressive standpoint—which will appear for the first time early in January. This work—though unpaid until the paper begins to pay—will be excellent practise for me: the paper is pri-vately financed, and its policy will be Perfect frankness and outspoken criticism such as I have always longed for an opportunity of writing.' Heseltine to his mother, 26 Dec. 1914, BL 57961.

[65] Presumably, as a result of Heseltine's request, Beecham suggested an alternative scheme. Heseltine wrote to his mother at the end of December: 'A most outstanding piece of good luck has befallen me! The great opportunity of my life has arrived! It all arose out of "The New Hat". I went down to see Beecham again at Watford last night, and was given the following information: that he was of the opinion that, for many reasons, a paper could not be devoted to Poetry and Music side by side—that a new and revolutionary musical paper was necessary at this juncture of musical life in England, and that a paper of this kind, if successfully organized, would be of the greatest assistance to his great musical and operatic schemes which are maturing. Thereupon, he *offered me the editorship* and complete con-trol of a new musical paper which he himself is going to run, on a large scale, on very advanced and progressive lines— This is the chance of a lifetime for me: in one stroke, I have attained a position better than I had hoped to reach after many years.' Heseltine to his mother, 30 Dec. 1914, BL 57961.

musical world—even if it only serves to stir up the wrath of the Passéistes, and old Academicians!

Affect^ly yours
Philip Heseltine

99
Frederick Delius to Philip Heseltine

~~TELEPHONE~~
~~GERRARD 366~~
493 Watford

~~THE COTTAGE,~~
8^A ~~HOBART PLACE,~~
~~S.W.~~
Grove Mill House
Watford
[23 December 1914]

Dear Phil—What a pity we were in London shopping—You ought to have telephoned first—Come out any day you like—Why did you not come back the other night & sleep here? You must have gone to Watford Station (high Str) which is much farther—I take only half an hour to walk leisurely to Watford Junction—McNaught came out here to interview the other day—I told him he ought to let you write an article in the Musical Times—He wanted Ernest Newman to do so—Place yourself in connection with McNaught & talk about it—I dont want any interview to appear—telephone when you are coming out here & *stay here over night*—Remember me kindly to Mr Suhrowaddy—affectionately

Frederick Delius

1915

IT would be over a year before the Deliuses returned once again to Grez. During his stay at Watford Delius continued working on both the *Requiem* and *An Arabesque*, making some preliminary sketches of *Eventyr*. In February and March he made two trips to Manchester to hear performances of his works. During the first visit he heard *Sea Drift* (at a singing competition which he was judging), as well as the first performance of the Violin Sonata No. 1 (played by Arthur Catterall and R. J. Forbes) and part of *A Village Romeo and Juliet*. During the second visit he heard a performance of the Piano Concerto. This same work, played by Moiseiwitsch, also received a highly successful performance under Beecham in London on 8 February, a concert which Heseltine attended in his new role as a music critic. Delius was also starting work on his Double Concerto for the Harrison sisters and all seemed well until April when his health, which had not given trouble for some time, now necessitated visits for treatment by a physiotherapist. He was advised by his doctor to leave England and on 6 July the Deliuses set off for Bergen, heading for the mountains on the Nordfjord. Unfortunately their visit was dogged by bad weather, and they moved on to Gjeilo where Delius's condition soon improved in the good weather. On 20 November they eventually returned (via Denmark and London) to Grez. They made a short visit in December to the Paris home of their newly acquired friends, the American sculptor and his wife, Henry and Marie Clews, having by then decided to remain in Grez even though the war was still very much in progress.

At the end of 1914 Beecham had offered Heseltine the editorship of a new arts periodical, a venture which ultimately came to nothing and left Heseltine angry and suspicious of Beecham. In February 1915, however, through the influence of Lady Maud Cunard he was offered a position as music critic on the staff of the *Daily Mail*. He consequently abandoned his studies at London University and began a short-lived career on Fleet Street. Besides writing newspaper reviews he also occupied himself with more substantial musical journalism and produced an article, 'Some Notes on Delius and His Music', for the March edition of *The Musical Times*. Heseltine, however, soon found work at the *Daily Mail* unrewarding and extremely frustrating, and once again he became restless. His critical reviews were often suppressed and severely edited if, indeed, any space could be found for them in a newspaper operating under wartime conditions. He consequently resigned in June.

In early April he had spent a brief holiday with two friends in a farmhouse in the Cotswolds, but by May he was utterly depressed and completely lacking in motivation. In August he joined another group of friends (including the painter Adrian Allinson, the writer Jean Rhys, and Eugene Goossens) on a holiday in Gloucestershire, in a bungalow overlooking the Vale of Evesham. Sometime earlier, in the Café Royal, Heseltine had met a beautiful and popular young artists' model, Minnie Lucy Channing ('Puma'), with whom he now became involved in a torrid and ill-fated love affair. Back in London, and still without any prospects of employment, he turned now to the studying and editing of early music in the British Museum, a musical activity which would later establish him as a pioneer in the field.

On 16 November Heseltine met D. H. Lawrence and the two men struck up an immediate friendship, with Lawrence encouraging him to join him and his small party of friends in his planned 'colony of escape' in America. Lawrence also introduced him to Lady Ottoline Morrell and her circle at Garsington. Heseltine visited her for the first time on 29 November. It was here that he met and fell in love with Juliette Baillot[1] (the young Swiss companion to Lady Ottoline's daughter), creating complications both with his relationship with the now pregnant Puma and with Lawrence himself.

100
Philip Heseltine to Frederick Delius

8.1.1915.   34 Southwold Mansions
                                                              Maida Vale, W.

Dear M[r] Delius

I am sorry not to have sent the Piano score of the 'Legende' before: it has been ready since Tuesday, and every morning I have resolved firmly to get up and go to Hobart Place in order to revise it finally with a piano before sending it to you: but, alas, sleep has completely overcome me on each occasion! My afternoons and evenings are all employed with absurd matriculation work —which I fear will prevent me from coming to Watford on Sunday. But I am going to make a desperate effort to rise early to-morrow, and *in any case* I will post you the 'Legende' together with the first two Verlaine[2] songs, which I have orchestrated,[3] and the programme note for 'Paris'.

---

[1] Juliette Baillot (1896–1994) later married Sir Julian Huxley, the eminent biologist.
[2] Paul Verlaine (1844–96), French poet.
[3] Unidentified, possibly 'La lune blanche' (1910) and 'Chanson d'Automne' (1911).

If you will look through the 'Legende'⁴ and the songs and mark in pencil what alterations you would like me to make, I will then revise them, and either write new copies, or alter the others.

As regards the programme note, this is only a tentative effort: one might write many different kinds of notes and say many different kinds of things, though I think the more the music is allowed to speak for itself the better.

However, if you will tell me what kind of note you would like and what you want said, I will write another. I would suggest that when I have written a note that satisfies your requirements, it should be stated that this has been 'authorized' by the composer—which would prevent Kalisch⁵ and C° from saying 'Listen to the birds singing' whenever the flute plays!!

Yours affect^{ly}
Philip Heseltine

I will attempt the scoring of the other songs next week. Please send me any more work you want done: I shall have plenty of time after next week.

101
Frederick Delius to Philip Heseltine

~~TELEPHONE~~
~~GERRARD 366~~

~~THE COTTAGE,~~
8ᴬ ~~HOBART PLACE,~~
~~S.W.~~
Grove Mill House
Watford
[1915]

My dear Phil—

The sentences which we have marked in brackets seem to us to be a little too involved for the ordinary concertgoer. Also Beecham thinks that your antithesis of subjective & objective is in a style of musical writing that is rather out of date: at all events we must be quite modern in these things   The rest of the

---

⁴ *Légende* for violin and orchestra (1895). In 1916 the score for violin and piano was published by Forsyth Bros. while the orchestral version was unpublished at the time.

⁵ Alfred Kalisch (1863–1933), English critic and librettist who contributed to many papers, principally *The Morning Leader* and *The Daily News*.

note we think very good, you might insert something to fill the place of the sentences we sugest you should leave out.

If anything the note is a little on the short side—

Au revoir [illegible] Thursday

affectionately
Frederick Delius

Enclosed the original words I wrote over the score—I also called it '*A night-piece*' 'The song of a great city'

Mysterious city—
city of pleasure
of gay music & dancing,
of painted & beautiful women
wondrous city
unveiling but to those who,
shunning day,
live thro' the night
& return home
to the sound of awakening streets
& the rising dawn.

102
Philip Heseltine to Frederick Delius

9. 1. 1915.   34 Southwold Mansions
                                               Maida Vale W.

Dear Mr Delius

Here are the MSS. I send these by letter post hoping they will reach you this evening.

I shall be able to come to-morrow, after all, but I must leave fairly early in the afternoon. I will bring the score of the 'Legende' with me.

Affect^{ly}
Philip Heseltine

103
Frederick Delius to Philip Heseltine

[January 1915]

Dear Phil—

Novellos write me asking me to send the analytical notes for 'Paris'   Please send them to Novellos Wardour Str

yrs ever
Fr. Delius

Grove Mill House
Watford

Postcard.

104
Philip Heseltine to Frederick Delius

22. 1. 1915   187 Ebury Street, S.W.

Dear Mr Delius

I sent the programme note for 'Paris' to O'Neill, who tells me that he has forwarded it to Novello's, via *Kalisch*, for some reason or other! However, it seemed unnecessary to give Novello's another copy.

Moiseiwitsch[6] did not return the Piano Concerto till last Tuesday: I took it back to him on Wednesday morning, with the corrections written in, and gave him your address, so that he might arrange when he is to play it over to you. I expect you have already heard from him.

I hope 'La lune blanche'[7] was alright.

---

[6] Benno Moiseiwitsch (1890–1963), British pianist of Russian extraction. In 1919 he made a 'hit' in London with Stanford's Second Piano Concerto, and later championed the Delius Concerto, recording it with Constant Lambert.
[7] Song by Delius (1910), a setting of Verlaine.

I have moved into Ebury Street, but have not yet found the kind of rooms I really want.[8]

We shall meet to-morrow, at the Palladium, I expect.

Yours affect[ly]
Philip Heseltine

105
Philip Heseltine to Frederick Delius

187 Ebury Street   1. 2. 1915
S.W.

Dear Mr Delius

Here is the Piano Concerto, together with 'I-Brasîl',[9] which I have taken the liberty of copying, as I cannot be without such a wonderful lovely thing . . . It seems to me that the Piano Concerto requires no 'explanation' whatever in a programme note: there is nothing as it were, *authoritative* to say about it, and I think that speculations and personal opinions about it should be confined to articles and critical notices. I enclose what appears to me to provide all the *necessary* information for the audience, but of course if you would like the note altered or added to in any way, let me know.

Do you think one might add a word of praise for Moiseiwitsch, for having learned the work so quickly, and for playing it in the same week as *three* other concertos?—or should one leave that for a critical report afterwards?[10]

You will be glad to hear that the 'Musical Times' has spared you for yet another month. However, D[r] M[c]Naught has quite surpassed himself in the following paragraph about 'glees':—

---

[8] Heseltine had moved into these new lodgings on 21 Jan. 1915 and described them to Viva Smith: 'This quarter of London (Pimlico) is delightful, and so are my rooms, but—alas!—the wall-paper is pale, shiny green with pink flowers, and the pictures and furniture too unspeakably mid-Victorian to be tolerated for long. Further, I discovered this morning (having moved in only late last night) that the District R[ly] passes directly beneath the house, and produces a minor earthquake every five minutes or so.' Heseltine to Viva Smith, 22 Jan. 1915 (wrongly dated 1914), BL 58127.

[9] 1913, a short song of thirty-four bars, a setting of a poem from an anthology by Fiona Macleod which Heseltine had sent to Delius at Christmas, 1912.

[10] On 8 Feb. 1915 Moiseiwitsch played Delius's Piano Concerto in Queen's Hall with Beecham conducting the London Symphony Orchestra. Heseltine's review of the concert (his first for the *Daily Mail*) included the following sentence: 'Mr. Moiseivitsch's rendering of the piano part last night was as good as taking trouble could make it; the great technical difficulties of the work were all overcome in a masterly manner.' *Daily Mail*, 9 Feb. 1915, 3.

'Take that gem of purest ray serene, Horsley's[11] "By Celia's arbour" (A.T.T.B.) and compare it's linked sweetness long drawn out with an up-to-date modern part-song by some of our young bloods, who it must be feared think in terms of the pianoforte, or perhaps of the orchestra when they are writing for voices, and apparently in terms of the Zoological Gardens when they write for the orchestra.'[12] (!!—loud laughter and applause, I suppose!)

The two quotations at the beginning nearly knock one over, but the idea of '*an* up-to-date modern part-song by *some* of our young bloods' (!!) is too much! The old doctor's ear must be itching for a Sackbut-blast, the anti-asse's Contra-Bray![13]

My mother has returned to Wales, in an excellent temper & very pleased.

Yours ever affect[ly]
Philip Heseltine

P.S. There is no Tempo indication in the score of 'Winter Landscape'.[14]

106
Philip Heseltine to Frederick Delius

16th February [1915]   34 Southwold Mansions
                                                                   Maida Vale
                                                                          W.

Dear M[r] Delius

I have decided to return to my former flat, so my address will be as above for some time.

I presume MacNaught has sent you a proof of my article,[15] as he promised to do.

If you find anything you would like altered, will you please let me know by return of post, since I must return a corrected proof as soon as possible. I have detected three mistakes—'created' for 'creative' in one place, 1889 for 1899, and a large omission at the end of the third column between the words 'new . . . ideas', which makes the sentence nonsensical.

---

[11] William Horsley (1774–1858), English organist and composer.
[12] 'Choral Technique', *Musical Times* (1915), 104b.
[13] A suggested name for the new musical journal had also been *The Anti-Ass*.
[14] No. 2 of the *North Country Sketches*.
[15] P. Heseltine, 'Some Notes on Delius and his Music', *Musical Times* (1915), 137–42.

By the way, I have described the firm of Harmonie as 'now defunct': is this correct?

Yours affect^ly
Philip Heseltine

107

Frederick Delius to Philip Heseltine

Grove Mill House
Watford
[Feb. 1915]

Dear Phil

I have received no proof yet of your article—Tell MacNaught I should like to see it—so would Beecham—Harmonie is not defunct alas! As soon as I go to Watford I will send you the 10 bob you lent me—I expected you in to tea on Monday—I have just written another song words by Thomas Nashe[16] Spring, the sweet Spring. Cuckoo, jug, jug, pee we, to witta woo—[17]

ever affectionately
Frederick Delius

I have just received a *most curious* letter from Holbrooke & will shew it you when next we meet—

---

[16] Thomas Nashe (1567–1601), English writer.
[17] 'Spring, the sweet spring' (Nashe), No. 2 of *Four Old English Lyrics* (1915–16).

108
Frederick Delius to Philip Heseltine

TELEPHONE
GERRARD 366

THE COTTAGE,
8ᴬ HOBART PLACE,
S.W.
Grove Mill House
Watford
[18 February 1915]

Dear Phil—

MacNaught phoned me this morning to asked whether I had received a proof —I said no & told him to send me one—I suppose you sent an copy to Beecham —If you are passing at that old book shop 52 Charing Cross Rd—try & buy me the book of Nauseu's voyage thro' Greenland—He asked me 10/- offer him 8/- If you can get Nauseus voyage to the North Pole also for 8/- buy it also for me. Be careful to inform people of your change of address. Especially Beecham and MacNaught—How about the pianola affair?

affectionately
Frederick Delius

It has been awful weather here yesterday & today—I hope to be able to go into Watford tomorrow—

109

Frederick Delius to Philip Heseltine

~~TELEPHONE~~
~~GERRARD 366~~

~~THE COTTAGE,~~
8ᴬ ~~HOBART PLACE,~~
~~S.W.~~
[22 February 1915]

Dear Phil—

Enclosed the 10 bob for which best thanks—On Tuesday I go with Beecham
to Manchester to judge the Singing competition for 'Sea drift'.

Affectionately
Frederick Delius

110

Philip Heseltine to Frederick Delius

34 Southwold Mansions   March 3ʳᵈ 1915.
Maida Vale, W.

My dear Mʳ Delius

There are no parts of 'Sea-Drift' at the Aldwych Theatre. I bearded the dreadful Donald in his den, and was informed that parts would be hired from Breitkopf
immediately before the date of performance and would be sent to me for correction, on their way to Manchester.

There have suddenly arrived—all at once—my new pianola piano, two dozen
spools of new music, and—my little French girl whom I thought I had lost
for ever! . . . . . . I won't begin to write about her to you, or I should bore you
with innumerable sheets of rapturous imbecilities[18]—I am deliriously happy,

---

[18] Three weeks later Heseltine was writing to Viva Smith: '. . . you have probably been thinking bitterly that pre-
occupation with the little French harlot we discussed together had banished every thought of you from my mind!!—
which is far from being the case, since the damsel in question, though quite attractive *in* bed, proved equally tedious
when out of it: and the appearance of symptoms which could only be those of either (1) inflammation of the urethra

and, now that I have a piano at last, music heightens this glorious mood, which is itself intensified by the right music. Your Spring song is the crowning touch: it makes me very nearly cry for sheer joy. *She* will sing it beautifully, I believe.

Forgive this outburst—but you will understand, even if you laugh.

Ever yours affectionately
Philip Heseltine

P.S. I have heard from MacNaught, who offers to send a paragraph to 60 newspapers.

NB in the 'Oxford Book' a wonderful verse in the middle of one of Ben Jonson's poems: it begins, 'Have you seen but a whyte lilie grow?'—perfect for music.

111
Frederick Delius to Philip Heseltine

Grove Mill House
Watford
Herts
[15 March 1915]

Dear Phil—

I am so glad you like my Spring Song so much—& also that you are so happy about your girl—I never knew she could sing—you must introduce me to her —the 'Seadrift' parts will be wanted in Manchester on the 10th inst so dont forget to correct them—There is rather more work than you think—firstly all the corrections & then the additions—I go to Manchester on the 10th—& come in to Euston at 11.50 leaving here 11.15. If you can meet me at the station at 11.50 we might lunch together—my train for Manchester leaves at 2—

your affectionate
Frederick Delius

or (2) "that most distressing and almost universal complaint", the clap, clinched the matter. . . . Not that either of these complaints is in the least alarming as influenza or a bilious attack, in reality. However, the advent of one or other of them has served as an excellent excuse for choking off a tiresome and rather expensive onhanger!' Heseltine to Olivia Smith, 24 Mar. 1915, BL MS 58127.

112
Frederick Delius to Philip Heseltine

[March 1915]

Dear Phil—Will you kindly get me a dozen sheets of music paper (Song paper) & send them cut at once—You can get them at Augeners   Pay also 1 shilling for me for paper I got before—

yr affectionate
Fr. D.

You should read Newman's notes on 'Seadrift'   I have them here.

Postcard.

113
Philip Heseltine to Frederick Delius

34 Southwold Mansions   March 21st [1915]
Maida Vale, W.

My dear Mr Delius
    Would you care to come down to Wales with me at the end of next week, for a few days? I find I have no concerts to attend after next Friday, for about a fortnight. I shall not go home alone, but if you would like to come, we might have some pleasant walks and bicycle rides, and we need not see much of the family, which is now reduced to my mother, solo. Mrs Delius would find some pleasant subjects to paint, if the prospect of my mamma does not terrify her!
    Let me know.
    I am so glad 'Sea Drift' had such a splendid reception.[19]

Ever yours affectly
Philip Heseltine

---

[19] Performed at a Hallé concert (a Pension Fund concert) on 18 Mar. with Hamilton Harris as soloist.

114
Frederick Delius to Philip Heseltine

[24 March 1915]

Dear Phil—I shall only be able, in a few days, to tell you whether we shall be able to accept your kind invitation to spend a few days with you in Wales. How far is it by train? Your friend wrote me a very nice letter, but I am afraid I shall have to keep the title The March of Spring over meadows, woods & silent moors

  affectionately
  Fr. D

Postcard.

115
Frederick Delius to Philip Heseltine

[26 March 1915]

Dear Phil—
  Come & spend the day with us on Sunday & we will talk things over

  affectionately
  Fr. D.

Postcard.

116

Philip Heseltine to Frederick Delius

Honeywood House,
Oakwood Hill,
Surrey.

Telegrams
Oakwood Hill.

Sunday [28 March 1915]

My dear Mr Delius

Please forgive me for not turning up and sending you no word. I am ever so sorry. I was suddenly called upon yesterday to escort down here a friend[20] who is on the point of a nervous breakdown. He is suffering from acute mental strain and has lately had several lapses of memory, which make it quite unsafe for him to go about alone. It has somewhat disorganized my plans, since I may have to stay here with him a few days. However, if I can get away to-morrow or the next day, as I hope to do, I think of going to a farmhouse on the top of the Cotswolds, near Stow-on-the-Wold, instead of to Wales. The country is far better, the air stronger and one has not the oppressiveness of the 'home' atmosphere.[21]

Could you join me there one day this week? You would love the country. Bring a bicycle and send your luggage by parcel post, and we will have a very jolly open-air time.

The farm is some miles from a station (Adlestrop, G.W.R. 2 hours from London), right out on the Wolds. But it is, I am assured by some friends who have investigated it, very clean and comfortable.

I am so sorry I could not send the music paper, but up to yesterday after-noon, when all shops are shut, I had only just the requisite and necessary[22] amount of cash to feed myself upon, all my surplus stock having been borrowed for the week! The Daily Mail people are becoming impossible. Last week two of my three notices were altogether cut out, for no discernable reason. . My notice

---

[20] Evan Morgan (Lord Tredegar, 1893–1949), a friend from Heseltine's Eton and Oxford days.

[21] Heseltine spent a brief holiday in early April in this farmhouse in the Cotswolds with two friends, the painter Adrian Allinson and another of his Indian friends, A. K. Chanda. Although the setting, some 900 feet above sea-level, overlooking the Avon Valley, the Malvern Hills, and the Forest of Dean, was superb, Heseltine complained to his mother that 'the wind blew hurricanes all the while . . . I have never slept in so cold a bedroom, or on so impossible a bed—One woke every hour or so in the night, either from cold or soreness caused by the bed. Chanda preferred sleeping on the floor, to his!' Heseltine to his mother, 11 Apr. 1915, BL 57958.

[22] cf. Exhortation from Morning and Evening Prayer: 'to ask those things that are requisite and necessary'.

of the Classical Concert Society—which was full of praise, incidentally—was omitted, but space was found for a paragraph recording the doings of a military band on the pier at Felixtowe!! In addition to this, I was made to write a puff paragraph for a quite preposterously idiotic song about knitting socks for soldiers (not even as good as the 'Sister Susie' ditty!).[23] If this kind of thing continues, there is no hope of doing any good for music by means of the Daily Mail, and I am really ashamed to be receiving money for such degrading work. However, some of the sub-editor's conversation may provide amusing matter for subsequent articles in the 'Sackbut' on the utter immorality of the system of musical criticism in this country.

Do come down to Gloucestershire if you possibly can. I am sure you would love the country.

Ever yours affectionately
Philip Heseltine

117
Frederick Delius to Philip Heseltine

Grove Mill House
Watford
Herts
[?2 April 1915]

Dear Heseltine—

How did you get on with Doctor Byres Moir?[24] Tell me what he thought of your friend Evan Morgan—Are you going away for Easter? if not come down here again—Bring also my score of Sea-drift & the 3 Verlaine Songs if you have them which my wife wants & which she says she lent you or Beecham—She wants to sing them & we have no other copy—Also North Country Sketches

---

[23] 'Miss Jessie Pope's "The Knitting Song", dedicated "to our Fireside Forces", which appeared in *The Daily Mail* on 7 January, runs with a pleasant, melodious rhythm, inviting a tune of captivating qualities. Thus Mr. Paul Wentworth, who has now set the words to music, has not failed to supply, and his waltz refrain is conceived in a style well calculated to ensure its popularity.' *Daily Mail*, 25 Mar. 1915, 3.

[24] Dr Byres Moir (1853–1928), House surgeon and Physician to the London Homeopathic Hospital. Heseltine mentioned Moir's name in a letter to Viva Smith: 'I myself am in the lowest depths of depression and utter lifelessness and hopelessness to which I have ever sunk . . . My mind is an utter fog, so that I cannot think or describe or write anything whatever. I shall shortly visit Dr Byres Moir, of Harley Street, at great expense. Have already obtained the cash from a generous mamma, but hav'nt the energy or the initiative to rise up and make an appointment.' Heseltine to Viva Smith, 7 May 1915, BL 58127.

when they are finished—the music club soirée is fixed for April 29th—On the 13th Beecham is doing something out of Koanga at the Philharmonic—[25]

your affectionate
Frederic Delius

118
Philip Heseltine to Frederick Delius

The original of this letter has not survived. This undated excerpt (written probably in April 1915) is quoted in Gray, *Peter Warlock*, 99.

The business of musical criticism for a London daily is really a farce. Would you recommend me to continue doing this? It is quite evident that the cause of music cannot be in the least degree benefited by anyone who writes in such a paper. The people who control it and edit it dare not take the risk of offending anybody (except in political matters) and now even my painfully reserved and non-committal style—which it is exceedingly irksome and degrading to adopt—has been called too violent by the wretched news editor.

I see plainly that I am never going to be allowed to abuse anybody or anything—not even dead composers! My quite mild notice of a pianist who played some Debussy pieces in the most execrably vulgar manner, without either taste or feeling—was suppressed altogether last week. What can one do under such conditions? It is only doing harm to praise what one knows to be bad —and there are already too many critics engaged upon that perfectly hopeless undertaking.

[25] Beecham conducted the final scene from *Koanga* at a Royal Philharmonic Society concert on 13 Apr.

119
Frederick Delius to Philip Heseltine

Grove Mill House
Watford
[8 April 1915]

My dear Phil—

I am glad you have been having such a good time—you must tell me all about Evan Morgan's interview with Byres Moir   I am sure he will cure him   Hold on yet awhile with the D[aily]. M[ail]. I told Lady Cunard about your position & she wrote a long letter to Lord Northcliff telling him to give you a free hand[26]— Otherwise it was no good whatever having a musician there as critic—Probably that will help—Write just as you feel & dont take the slightest notice of their blue pencil—We shall then see what happens & can act accordingly—Lady C. was quite *enchanted* with the playing of Murdoch[27]—She said that she had never heard anyone play Debussy like him!!! C'était un rêve quoi! However dont let that disconcert you—*always* back your own opinion—take no notice whatever of other people's—If you do the hedgings & concessions begin & then you sink into the usual critic tone. I shall be in London on the 12th for a few days & we must go about the docks a bit together—now that the weather is good. Come out here as soon as you can   we can put you up also—I am writing a concerto for Violin, Cello & Orchestra   Heaven only knows what it will turn into—

Ever your affectionate
Frederick Delius

---

[26] Maud Lady Cunard had originally been instrumental in getting Heseltine appointed to *The Daily Mail*: Having set up a meeting with influential *Daily Mail* personnel, Lady Cunard wrote to Heseltine on 3 Feb., begging him not to be 'proud or difficult' at his interview but simply to say 'you can & will', at the same time requesting him to write a review of a performance of the Delius Piano Concerto to be played by Moiseiwitsch with Beecham conducting the London Symphony Orchestra in Queen's Hall on 8 Feb.: 'You *must* make it short but wonderful . . . It is the thin edge of the wedge. If they pay you *tant mieux* if not at first, it does not matter. You must get in.' Lady Cunard to Heseltine, 3 Feb. 1915, Photocopy in PWS Archives.

[27] William Murdoch (1888–1942), Australian pianist; he settled in England in 1905 and made a reputation as a chamber music player, especially in association with Albert Sammons.

120
Jelka Delius to Philip Heseltine

Grove Mill House
Watford
23. 4 [1915]

Dear Phil,

Fred is anxious about his North Country Sketches. He has been awaiting them every day. Did you send them? If not, could you not bring them out as soon as possible, as he has to look through them and have them bound before Wednesday, when he has to give them to Beecham. It would be so nice to see you. We have lunch at 1 and dinner at 7.30   Have you seen Baylis[28]? or Beecham?

Fred is just better after a perfectly horrid bilious attack and sends you his love

always yrs
Jelka Delius

In case you can not come please send the N. C. S. insured, only the Score, of course. The parts are to remain in London.

121
Frederick Delius to Philip Heseltine

[Watford]
Monday [26 April 1915]

Dear Phil—I have not yet received the score of the North Country Sketches Beecham is clamouring for it & I have to have it bound—

In the Biographical Programme for the Festival I see that *my parents* are left out of it this time—

In haste
Fr. D.

---

[28] Donald Baylis, Beecham's assistant from 1910. In 1913 Beecham placed him in full charge of all his musical undertakings.

122
Frederick Delius to Philip Heseltine

[Watford
27 April 1915]

Dear Phil. Music just arrived—We come in tomorrow morning—Come at 4 &
fetch us at Hobart Place—

  affectionately
  Fr. D.

Tuesday

Postcard.

123
Frederick Delius to Philip Heseltine

*TELEPHONE
GERRARD 366*

*THE COTTAGE,
8ᴬ HOBART PLACE
S.W.*
[1 May 1915]

Dear Phil—

  Please bring the parts of the North C. S. here as soon as possible—There
is a change in the strings which you did not note—& I have to deliver them
to Beecham—We are staying here for 3 weeks as I am undergoing a massage
treatment—

  affectionately—
  Fr. D.

124
Frederick Delius to Philip Heseltine

TELEPHONE
GERRARD 366

THE COTTAGE,
8ᴬ HOBART PLACE
S.W.
Sunday [?2 May 1915]

Dear Phil—Come to lunch tomorrow Monday at one—bring the parts & also the analytical note of N.C.S. I have just seen Beecham & he has a lot for you to do—He is editing my new Songs—Sonata & Legend & wants you to get them ready for publication.

In haste—

affectionately—
Frederick Delius

125
Jelka Delius to Philip Heseltine

Watford
29. 6. 15

Dear Phil,

We went to [Dr] Byres Moir today and he wont at all allow Fred to go to the sea, and absolutely advised us to go to Norway. It has entirely upset our plans, and we were looking forward to our sea-life there with you so much. On the other hand, Norway is Fred's land, and it will make him feel well and it is a country 'not at war', which the doctor thinks will be so much better.

We sail next Tuesday Newcastle—Bergen. I am sending you letters about our little cottage so that you can look at it in case you find nothing satisfactory on your side.

I shall send you, as soon as I know it an address in Norway and, please, let us hear from you often—I hope you know and feel that we are very fond of you and have your welfare tremendously at heart. I hope you will have a splendid time in Cornwall and prepare some grand lectures and declame them to the rocks, as I shall not be there to be impressed by them. The Harrisons are coming here on Sunday and then Fred will be able to decide what to do about the Double Concerto.

Anyhow it is a blessing to get into an era of first performances again after these weary years.

Best love,
yrs ever
Jelka Delius

126
Frederick Delius to Philip Heseltine

[Norway, 16 July 1915]

Dear Phil—Here we are in this glorious country   We decided to come here instead of Cornwall—We had a rough crossing over the North Sea—How are you & where—? Send me your address to Post Restante *Molde* Norway   We are travelling slowly about & making our way to the Mountains inland—One does not feel the war here at all—Norway is quite pro-Allies—there are no tourists this year which makes travelling very agreable—

With love from us both, yrs ever
Frederick Delius

Postcard.

127
Frederick Delius to Philip Heseltine

Sandene (Nordfjord)

[?11 August 1915]

Dear Phil—Did you receive our 2 cards addressed c/o Allinson?[29] We left rather suddenly for Norway & have been high up amongst the snow mountains ever since—away from everything. Write me how you are & where you are—I address this to Wales as I fear the other cards did not reach you—If you do not fear the North Sea too much join us here if you can   it is a wonderful country & climate & you would love it—Newcastle to Bergen   We are now in a little place at the Gloppenfjord Nordfjord & shall stay for at least another month

  Ever yours affectionately,
  Frederick Delius

Postcard.

128
Frederick Delius to Philip Heseltine

My dear Phil—Your card came yesterday dated July 21st!! Your letter has not yet arrived   How are you & what are you doing? The weather here is not very good—but now and then heavenly days   I gave the Concerto to the Misses Harrison to become acquainted with it. The transcription can be done later— Beatrice goes to America in September so there was no time to lose—Write to me as soon as possible—With love from us both

  your affectionate
  Frederick Delius

  Aug 22/15

Postcard.

[29] Adrian Allinson (1890–1959), a painter friend of Heseltine's.

129
Philip Heseltine to Frederick Delius

The Bungalow
Crickley Hill
Gloucestershire   August 22nd, 1915

My dear Delius—

There has been never a day in all the past seven weeks on which I have not determined to write to you—and all my intentions have faded away like smoke in a dream, and each succeeding day I have thought—'To-morrow I shall see and say everything more clearly, more concisely', with the result that my letter to you has been deferred and deferred and, so far from my procrastination having the expected effect, my outlook has daily become more confused and trance-like until the difficulty of collecting and writing down myself has been increased to its maximum point. My mind at the present moment is fitly comparable to the blurred humming of the distant peal of bells whose slow, monotonous droning seems to blend with the grey, listless sky and the still trees and the far-off, shadow-like hills in an atmosphere of intolerable dejection and lifelessness on this late summer Sunday evening. Over the wide landscape there hangs a false mood of peace—something seems to have died—or gone out—and there is no peace, but only a weary restlessness. My head feels as though it were filled with a smoky vapour or a poisonous gas which kills all the finer impressions before they can penetrate to me and stifles every thought, every idea before it is born. This is not the mere passing pessimism engendered by an English Sabbath—it is a feeling that has been enveloping me little by little for many months past, and although there are times when I think myself rid of it it always returns after a while more virulent than ever. When I left London early in July it was at its worst—but even these seven weeks in my beloved Gloucestershire have failed utterly to dispel its influence, save at fitful and transitory intervals. It has no definitely apparent cause, and when its power is strongest I have no antidote but must simply wait till it relax its hold. One lives thus perpetually behind a veil. I watch the sun go down behind the hills, flooding the broad valley with a glory of golden light that would in former days have made my whole being vibrate with its beauty—but I wait in vain for that old, ecstatic feeling. The colour and intensity of these pictures have become things external to me—they are no longer reflected in me—I can no longer merge myself in the 'stimmung' of Nature around me—I can only gaze wistfully, from afar, at

her beauteous pageantry—I can no longer take part in it—and so I am debarred
from the greatest—perhaps the only—source of joy, solace and inspiration that
Life offers me. My brain is, at best, merely receptive, and that but rarely and in
small measure—Creative thought or work—or anything remotely approximat-
ing thereto, is entirely impossible, and the chances of their becoming so seem
every day more remote—yet without them existence—for all who desire them
—is void and desolate . . . . Hence those tears . . . .

This letter was broken off over a week ago by a nerve-shattering occurrence
that drove me and my two Indian friends away from Crickley Hill altogether,
and at the moment I feel even less able to write coherently than before! However, I will try to be a little more terse and a little less depressing—for, after all,
it is of no avail to whine and snivel, and I often feel when I write to you that
I am imposing far too much upon your long-suffering tolerance of my weak-
kneed feebleness. Yet, however disgusting one's state of mind may be, one does
feel the need of an emotional safety-valve on occasions—though it is a little cruel
that one should let off this malodorous steam at those friends one loves and
values most of all—Forgive me—I have inflicted this kind of thing on you so
often before, but as time goes on, I feel more and more that you are almost the
only person I can confide in without the very smallest fear of a misunderstanding. And I can say so much more in writing than when I am with you. Often
and often, words simply will not come out of my mouth—and this happens not
only when I am indulging in tedious personal psychologics—It is a fearful feeling, and seems to erect an impassable barrier between oneself and one's most
intimate friends—one doesn't feel it with ordinary acquaintances . . . .
Looking back, I believe I have not written to you at all since that June Sunday
we were together at Watford when Beecham turned up unexpectedly and showed
symptoms of the political agitator he has since become!

Nor, I am ashamed to admit, did I answer the very particularly kind letter
Mrs Delius wrote me a few days later, though it touched and cheered me more
than I can say. I was tremendously disappointed when I heard you were not
going to be with us this summer; if you had been both this letter and the agglom-
erated moods that have prompted it would never have existed. However, you
are greatly to be envied living amongst the mountains that will never re-echo
with the sounds or even the news of war. Here the war-cloud looms over one
like some great sinister bird, poised and ready to pounce upon its hapless prey.
This black influence alone is enough to quench every artistic impulse in all but
the very strongest. It is very hard to escape it,—in London impossible. At the
moment I am in Oxford—Oxford which, in its normal condition, I loathed
and detested, but which now appears as a beautiful haven of peace and quietude.
Of all towns, this is surely the least affected—externally—by the war. This is,

of course, vacation time, but even when all allowance has been made, the difference between the 'atmosphere' of the place as it is now and as it was last year astounds me. Here in this tranquil old street, where, as someone said the other day, even the passing of the baker's cart is an event, one feels as remote from the jarring elements of life as one does in the very heart of the countryside. More so, perhaps, since one's comings and goings are unobserved, whereas in a little village, one cannot fail to arouse rustic curiosity and its invariable concomitant, suspicion. I would gladly live here, with my two Indian friends who are most kind and sympathetic companions, if circumstances permitted—and they may yet do so . . . . My plans are very vague. It took three long letters, separated by intervals of a fortnight, and two reply-paid telegrams to extract from the elusive Thomas any information about the future of the 'Sackbut' and, incidentally, my quarterly allowance. I dislike intensely taking money for nothing done but under the present agreement, I am neither completely free to do my own work, nor am I definitely given anything to occupy myself with, outside of my own studies. The 'Sackbut' is shelved from month to month—it is now postponed till next January at the earliest, and then, if we're all still alive, there'll be still another postponement[30]—and I am given fearful operatic librettos to translate, and requested to 'coach' singers for operatic performances at the Shaftesbury Theatre—neither of which tasks am I competent to perform—and in order to do this I have to remain in London, the one place of all others where the war-fever rages most violently and where its effects oppress and depress one the most. If one had some continuous, all-day occupation, one could live there, but that alone could make life tolerable in such a place at the present moment. The last two months might have been exceedingly profitable for me, as regards work, but for certain psychological accidents which could not be foreseen, but which nevertheless have been useful in providing cautionary experience!! But before leaving Thomas B. I must briefly relate the curious sequel to the Eveline Matthews[31] affair, about which we spoke at Watford. You will remember that

---

[30] In Mar. 1916 this matter was still rankling and Heseltine wrote to Taylor: '. . . I might make Beecham pay a couple of hundred towards publishing some music by threatening legal proceedings on the strength of my three years' "Sackbut" agreement! I must consult a solicitor as to my legal rights in the matter. I think his signed document is binding.' Heseltine to Taylor, 13 Mar. 1916, BL 54197.

[31] Eveline Matthews (1885–?) sang with the Beecham Opera Company. She was married to Leonard Joseph Hall CBE. Heseltine made reference to her in a letter to Viva Smith: 'My desolation at leaving the Cotswolds for London and solitude and the Daily Mail and a cheerless and somewhat filthy flat was considerably mitigated by the presence of your friend, Eveline Matthews, in the cast of the opera which I had to attend at the Shaftesbury Theatre on Friday night. She is an enchanting creature, who seems to have been endowed with all the gifts the gods can bestow upon an operatic artist—a perfectly fascinating presence—which I don't think was altogether due to "make-up"—and an easy, entirely natural manner of acting which was quite charming. Her voice is one of exceptional beauty—not powerful, I should think, but very expressive and of a quality which never blurs or obscures the articulation of the words—and— as if this were not more than one could expect from one person—she must be an exceedingly good musician, for some weeks ago she sang with Beecham in Manchester the Japanese Songs of Stravinsky which, in spite of their extreme brevity, are among the most difficult songs in existence—from the technical point of view. I am longing to meet this

Allinson designed a poster for her concert which was quashed by our friend
B, for motives unknown but not unsuspected by ourselves!—And a very excellent poster it would have been—though it never progressed further than the
proof stage. This, like the hire of the hall, naturally had to be paid for, whether
the concert took place or not; consequently, Allinson, receiving no reply to his
repeated requests for payment (he being very hard up), sent a final note hint-
ing at legal procedure. (The sum of £7.7.0.—half of A's usual poster fee—had
been agreed upon as the price of the drawing, in my presence). This elicited
an insulting letter from the husband of Matthews, which necessitated the placing of the case in the hands of a solicitor. Subsequent details I have discovered
from a mutual friend of mine, A's and the husband's. It appears that the latter
is own brother to the foulest perjurer in the British Empire, to wit, one Hall
who was chief witness in the celebrated MacCormick case in Burma—a typically disgusting Anglo-Indian affair. An English merchant, named MacC. raped
a little girl much below the age of consent, infected her with the clap and refused
to restore her to her unfortunate parents. The affair was exposed by an English
journalist after vain litigation on the part of the parents, whereupon MacC. pro-
secuted the one honest man connected with the case—namely the journalist,
for libel and with the aid of Hall's false-witness and bribed 'interpreters' who,
of course, did not 'interpret' at all, got the poor man locked up. However the
facts are very well-known (thanks to 'Truth' and 'The English Review', which
Anglo-Indian justice is apparently too blind to read) and MacC has had to leave
Burma. This is by the way, but to judge from his letters and those addressed
to Allinson's solicitor (who was in years past Whistler's) the Matthews husband
is not going to be outdone by his brother in the matter of brazen lies. The case
has not yet been heard but it appears that the husband had an interview with
T. B., in the course of which the latter is alleged to have stated that (1) Eveline
Matthews was quite unfit to give a recital, and would have ruined her career by
doing so, and (2) that the programme was drawn up by a musical 'crank' and
would only have appealed to 'cranks'!!!! I leave you to draw your own conclu-
sions from these amusing statements—they provide much food for speculation
—I have not mentioned the matter to T. B. as yet but I expect there will be a
theory, yards long, to support his contention. . . . . I am posting this now, lest
you should read forgetfulness into my silence. That is far from being the case.

wonderful person. When you come up, you must introduce me to her.' Heseltine to Viva Smith, 11 Apr. 1915, BL
58127. Heseltine is here referring to a performance of Puccini's *La Boheme* on 9 Apr. in which Eveline Matthews
played Musetta. In his review he referred to her as having 'a voice of exceptional quality, and by her delightfully natural rendering of a part that had evidently been carefully studied, scored a marked success.' *Daily Mail*, 10 Apr. 1915,
3. A short while later he wrote of her again to Viva Smith: 'I quite fell in love with her in "Boheme" at the Shaftsbury,
but quite apart from her personal considerations, even if she were a hideous hag off the stage, she is such a fine artist
that it would be a perfect joy to see her now and then and make music together. Delius agrees that she is one of the
finest singers in England. I hope she would not be too prudish to come and see me sometimes? How can it be wangled?' Heseltine to Viva Smith, 7 May 1915, BL 58127.

The fact that I don't write often means only that I have too much I want to say, not too little. I have so much to say that I never know where to begin, and thoughts and incidents simply clog up my brain so that it won't work. I have purposely avoided all the Dorsetshire and Gloucestershire incidents, reserving them for another letter which (*really*) will follow this in a very few days. This is just a foreword—the rest will explain the photographs! How I wish I could join you in Norway! I have more than an inclination to throw up all the T. B. money until such time as the 'Sackbut' appears and decamp across the North Sea with my books and music and live on my ten pounds a month till the war cloud passes. I wonder whether this would be possible?[32] I tried to see Dr Byres Moir last week but found him away. Perhaps he is with you in the mountains.

Very much love to you both from your affectionate
Philip Heseltine
August 30th

Present address (which will always find me):—
c/o Apurva Chanda
3 Blackhall Road
Oxford

130
Philip Heseltine to Frederick Delius

'I think I could turn and live with animals, they are so placid and self-contain'd,
I stand and look at them long and long.
They do not sweat and whine about their condition;
They do not lie awake in the dark and weep for their sins,
They do not make me sick discussing their duty to God;
Not one is dissatisfied—not one is demented with the mania of owning things,
Not one kneels to another, nor to his kind that lived thousands of years ago;
Not one is respectable or industrious[33] over the whole earth'.[34]

WALT WHITMAN

---

[32] To his mother he wrote: 'More difficulties with Beecham, and more uncertainty about money. . . . If the Sackbut doesn't materialize, I may go and work with Delius in Norway, where one can live more cheaply.' Heseltine to his mother, 9 Oct. 1915, BL 57961.

[33] 'unhappy' in the original.

[34] Whitman, Walt, *Song of Myself*, 32. Interestingly enough, Elgar's Christmas card for 1929 bore the same quotation.

Letter follows in a day or two. I am very seriously contemplating joining you in Norway, and remaining there for a good while, as I suggested in my last. I have even purchased a Norwegian grammar! What do you think of the scheme?

Best love,
from Phil.

Postcard.

131
Frederick Delius to Philip Heseltine

Dʳ Holm's Hotel
Gjeilo

[12 September 1915]

Dear Phil—Your long & interesting letter & card came here yesterday—We had a lot of rain at Sandene so came up here in the mountains and it is heaven!! Bright sunshine—not a cloud—no wind & the Fjeld is a marvel of colors —from russet to bright golden & scarlet.[35] We shall stay right here as long as this weather lasts & then probably make for Grez. We have decided nothing as yet   I am expecting your other letter—Should you come here come straight thro'. We are 6 hours rail from Bergen—shall answer your letter in a day or two—

your affectionate
Fr. Delius

Postcard.

---

[35] Writing in the same month to Percy Grainger, Delius added: 'We are in the Højfjeld—3000 ft—the fjeld is simply a marvel of colors, russet gold & scarlet & down below where the forest begins the woods are in their brightest autumn tints—This morning I woke up in the middle of a snow landscape. 3 inches of snow on the ground & trees & snowing!' Delius to Grainger, 26 Sept. 1915, Melbourne, Grainger Museum.

132
Frederick Delius to Philip Heseltine

POST ADRESSE:
JUELSMINDE.
TELEGRAM ADRESSE:
SCHOU JUELSMINDE

c/o Einar Schou Esq[36]
PALSGAARD
Juelsminde
Denmark
12 Oct 15

My dear Phil—We arrived here from Norway 3 days ago—& now that I feel rather more settled down I want to write to you & answer your long letter which I got in Norway—the promised 2nd one I have not yet received—you never told me your nerve shattering experience. What has been happening? Since I left England my spirits have been gradually rising & in the highlands of Norway— away from all humans I really got my old self back again—I understand your state of mind entirely as I felt somewhat similarly before leaving England— a certain depression had absolutely taken possession of me—I luckily could forget as long as I was working; But Watford is like an unpleasant dream to me now. You know that all you think & feel interests me at all times & you need not be afraid of being misunderstood by me—It would have been better, I think, if you had come right away to Norway with me—Our plans are rather unsettled —We intend staying in this lovely place a month or perhaps 2 & then either spending the rest of the winter in Kopenhagen or coming back to London via Bergen & going back to Grez—Should we decide to stay in Denmark it might be worth your while to cross to Copenhagen & get out of the depressing atmosphere—As soon as we have decided I will let you know—Did you get the double Concerto from Miss Harrison   Have you seen Beecham? Why has my Sonata not come out yet? Could you not ask Beecham what he intends doing with the works of mine he has acquired? I wrote several times for the Corrections but have received no answer—It seems a great mistake to let so much time slip by before bringing out these works—The North Country Sketches the Sonata

---

[36] Einar Schou, a successful industrialist, a pioneer in the manufacture of margarine. His wife, Elizabeth, had artistic interests and they entertained many musicians at their estate.

the 'Legende' & the 3 songs—Try and see Beecham. I am sure he is giving an Opera Season again at the Shaftesbury Avenue Theatre—Before leaving the highlands we had 3 days & 3 nights of snowstorm & afterwards sharp frost & cloudless sunny weather. It was glorious. 3/4 of a yard of snow on the ground. Norway is truly a lovely country. Here in Denmark everything is autumn colored & we are quite close to the Fjord. Write me at once & tell me everything about yourself & how things are going in general—Do you see anything of Beecham? & Gardiner! We both send you our love—

your affectionate
Frederick Delius

133
Frederick Delius to Philip Heseltine

Dr Holm's Hotel. Gjeilo

[17 October 1915]

Dear Phil

We have decided to stay here a few weeks longer—We read in the paper that a German Submarine had stopped a Norwegian passenger boat & taken off an English passenger!! Miss Harrison 51 Cornwall gardens Gloucester R^d has the score of my double Concerto. If you have time to make a piano score go & fetch it.—I have already written to her about it—Take great care of it as *I have no copy whatever*. Our plans are to stay here another 14 days—then go to Kristiania for a week & then to Kopenhagen for a few weeks returning to Norway for the lovely winter   I liked the photos very much   is one of the man Goosens   What a splendid fellow old Walt [Whitman] was. Thats a quotation taken out of my own heart. Write me at once how you are—what you are doing & your plans

with love from us both
your affectionate friend
Frederick Delius

Postcard.

134
Philip Heseltine to Frederick Delius

34 Southwold Mansions
Maida Vale, W.   Address after Saturday next. (November 20th)
                                            12^A Rossetti Garden Mansions
16th Nov. [1915]   Chelsea, S.W.

My dear Delius,

This evening I met and had a long talk with D. H. Lawrence.[37] He can stand this country no longer and is going to America in a week's time. He wants to go to Florida for the winter, since he is, I am afraid, rather far gone in consumption. I write this hurried note to ask whether it would be possible for him to go and live in your orange grove. He has nowhere definite to go in Florida and is very poor. His last book[38]—a perfectly magnificent work—has just been suppressed by the police for supposed 'immorality' (!!) and the miserable publishers refuse to give him any more of the agreed money for it.

He begged me to write to you at once and ask whether anything could be arranged about living at the grove,[39] but I told him that you probably had very little control over affairs out there now. However, it would be splendid if he could go there. He is such a marvellous man—perhaps the one great literary genius of his generation—at any rate in England.

I hope you had a good journey and found everything all right at Grez. I did *so much* enjoy seeing you in London and only wish you could have stayed a bit longer (though I am sure you were only too glad to get away—I should have been, in your place, also).

Much love to you both. Forgive this hurried scrawl. I will write again very soon.

Affectionately yours
Philip Heseltine

---

[37] Heseltine told Taylor: 'Last week I met D. H. Lawrence, whom I have long venerated as the greatest literary genius of his generation. He has an astounding philosophy of art—diametrically opposed to that of Delius, and, I suppose 99% of the best artists of our time, though one would not infer it from his work. He is against conscious self-expression, introspection and reducing, analytic methods in general. "I believe" he writes to me, "that music too must become now synthetic, metaphysical, giving a musical utterance to the sense of the whole".' Heseltine to Taylor, 25 Nov. 1915, BL 54197.

[38] *The Rainbow* (1915).

[39] Lawrence wrote to Robert Nichols: 'Did I tell you also that I asked Heseltine to write to Delius about the Florida estate? I want us all to go and live there for a while. You must get well enough, and we will all go to Florida for a year or two.' Heseltine to Nichols, 18 Nov. 1915, Yale University. To Lady Ottoline Morrell Lawrence wrote: 'I am waiting now to hear from Delius, through Heseltine, about *his* place in Florida. That is nearer to Jacksonville. If there is nothing for us from Delius, we will go to Fort Myers.' Lawrence to Lady Ottoline Morrell, 22 Nov. 1915, Stanford University.

135
Frederick Delius to Philip Heseltine

GREZ-SUR-LOING
Seine et Marne
24 Nov 1915

My dear Phil

We arrived here last Saturday after a long & tedious journey—I received your letter—California is a far better climate than Florida—My orange grove has been left to itself for 20 years & is no doubt only a wilderness of gigantic weeds & plants—The house will also have tumbled down—Even if the house had been habitable I should not have advised Lawrence to live in it—The place is 5 miles from any house or store. Life is frightfully expensive on account of the isolated situation—One lives entirely off tinned food & a servant costs 1 dollar 50 cents a day. In the south of California—there are nice little towns—The climate is devine & living far less expensive—I should have loved to be of use to Lawrence whose work I admire—but to let him go to Florida would be sending him to disaster—I am so happy to be back here again in our own house & amongst our own things—& the food is all so good—What a pity you did not come to Pagani's after the Concert—I should so much like to have seen you again. Send me my score as soon as possible—*Insured* & let May Harrison[40] have the piano score of which she will have a copy made—We shall not leave Grez now until the war is over: travelling is really too difficult—Write to me soon & tell me how things are going with you—How about Surawadj's[41] servant? With love from us both

your affectionate
Frederick Delius

We have found an awfully good french servant who cooks splendidly

[40] May Harrison (1891–1959): violinist sister of Beatrice, the cellist. Delius's Double Concerto was written for, and dedicated to, them. Heseltine had made a piano score of the work (see R. Threlfall, *Frederick Delius: A Supplementary Catalogue* (London, 1986), 96).
[41] Hasan Shahid Suhrawardy.

136
Philip Heseltine to Frederick Delius

Telegrams—Garsington   *Garsington Manor*
                                                                             Oxford

Stations $\Big\{$ *Oxford 6 miles*
                    Wheatley 3 miles

December 15th [1915]

                                                    (address 13 Rossetti Mansions)
                                                                Chelsea S.W.)

My dear Delius,

I sent off to you on Monday, by insured post, the score of the Double Concerto, and copies of Goossen's first String Quartet[42] and a song by an entirely
unknown man, George Whitaker.[43] I know nothing better in young English music
than these two works, and I shall await your verdict on them with very great
interest. Goossens appears to me, more and more, a man of astounding genius.
It is a tragedy that he is compelled by want of a few paltry pounds a year to
remain in this country, where all is apathy and stagnation, as far as music is
concerned—where, save among personal friends who would applaud anything,
there is not even a semblance of enthusiasm—no discrimination and no selective appreciation. Delius is complacently coupled with Elgar (though, of course,
it is 'Elgar—and Delius'!), and Goossens is 'one of our promising young composers'—a mere private in the ranks of an army officered by Edwin Evans[44]
and Alfred Kalisch and commanded by Sir Hubert Parry[45] and Percy Pitt[46] and
others of the same calibre. And, as far as I can see, music is no worse off than
the other arts. I am afraid Goossens does not realize the full extent of his own
powers. His genius pushes through to the surface in all he touches—but what
tremendous strength it must have, to be able to flower in West Kensington!
. . . . As for George Whitaker, I know very little of him, but I suspect him of
being a poor, half-starved north country teacher of music. It is horrible to think

---

[42] String Quartet No. 1 in C (1916).

[43] Little is known about Whitaker except for the fact that, besides being a composer, he was also a violinist and led
the second violins in the orchestra which recorded Heseltine's *Serenade for Strings* in Jan. 1927 (*The Gramophone*, 4/9
(Feb. 1927), 390). Heseltine printed a song of his, 'Thou wilt not goe and leave me heir' in the Aug. 1920 *Sackbut*.

[44] Edwin Evans (1874–1945), English critic and writer on music.

[45] Sir Charles Hubert Hastings Parry (1848–1918), English composer, teacher, and writer. Principal of the Royal
College of Music, 1894–1918.

[46] Percy Pitt (1870–1932), English conductor and composer.

of—and the irony with which Fate deals out the petty cash makes one despair of the future of music, in this land at any rate. To think that the bank-clerk, and the man who scrapes dung from the roadway are accounted of more value than the creative artist—to think of all the glorious creations that poverty strangles in the womb—and, (for me the bitterest and most galling thought), to think of the splendid talents of the two men I have mentioned—let alone countless others—stifled by the lack of the very same opportunities which I myself have and can put to no good use . . . . all this is an appalling, heart-rending nightmare of a reality. For myself, I feel that I am—and have been for years past —rolling downhill with increasing rapidity into a black, slimy cesspool of stagnation. . . . . and with every day the difficulty of pulling up and reversing becomes more apparent. A big effort is needed—and lately my eyes have been opened to a clear and terrifying vision of this necessity, and I am filled with devastating fears lest it be already too late to do so. Four years ago you warned me of all this, and I was not ripe for understanding it and paid no heed. Now I am determined to follow not only your advice but your example too; casting all cautious fears to the winds, I am going away, to the uttermost parts of the earth, to *live*. Does this sound wild and vain? I don't much care if it does, nor if I perish in the attempt. This living death I can endure no longer.

Here have I been for years, lamenting the barrenness of my life, waiting for my seed to flower in a desert soil—worse than fool that I am. I have never yet lived at all—and that is why I am going away—to Florida, Tahiti, anywhere —to have at least a year or two of real life to try and make something out of. The scheme originated with the writer I mentioned in my last letter, who is keen that a small group of enthusiasts should detach themselves from harassing surroundings and endeavour for a while to till the soil of their natures in a congenial atmosphere. There are some half-dozen confederates already, but innumerable difficulties beset the path. However, I myself have at last obtained from my late doctor (now a colonel) a certificate of my unfitness for military service, so the passport difficulty will be considerably lessened for me. Of course, all prospect of money-making vanishes—but my £3 a week remains fairly stedfast—that is to say, if my mother proves amenable, and now I am of age she cannot cut me off on any account.

Now do write, when you have time, and tell me more about Florida, and about Tahiti—which I myself favour personally, though the others are inclined to the west coast of Florida—Fort Myers way. Is the orange-grove entirely impossible? Couldn't we by any means rejuvenate it with the aid of niggers? . . . As a preliminary, we are going to a farmhouse in Berkshire (quite near B. G.) for January and February. God only knows ('and he won't split') as to whether we shall ever get any further! . . . This all sounds utterly wild—an irresponsible adventure, unthinkable to the cautious. But, good God, one must plunge, even if one never comes up again . . .

—I am in a state of flux—my mind is a whirlpool of alternating excitement and depression—I am also on the brink of another, more personal affair which may be big—it almost frightens me with joy at times . . . But enough—I am getting a little mad. Please write soon.

I like the Concerto very much, though I have not yet got a conception of it as a whole, so that it seems fragmentary at present. The second subject is a perfect joy, and the scoring is too lovely. The piano score is ready, in a fair copy which can be printed from as soon as you want to publish it. In Berkshire, I hope to do my book on your work. If you have any more suggestions or information for it, please send them along.

Much love to you both from your ever affectionate

Φ

I am convinced that the writer in question is about the greatest man in England at the present time. He is far greater than his books—which he himself accounts as nothing in comparison with what he wants to do. Certainly he and his views are entirely opposed to the spirit of his published works. More of him anon.

137
Frederick Delius to Philip Heseltine

GREZ-SUR-LOING
Seine et Marne
21/12/15

Dear Phil—

Your letter interested me in the highest degree. All you say about music in England is entirely true; it is just the same with the other arts—but, of course, music is nearer to our hearts. I, of course, have been aware of this for many years & I have no hopes that it will ever become better, but when I work I forget everything &, as you know, I only write for myself—Every artist ought to have just enough to live on—The real tragedy begins when he is obliged to earn his living: for the more he concentrates upon the earning the worse his art seems to become—The greater the artist the greater the tragedy & the greater the difficulty of being understood—The great artist has not only an entirely uncomprehensive public—but he has all the mediocrities of art against him or when not against him, absorbing the attention of the public as soi-disant great geniuses—Then again he has the charlatan at his elbow & the officially not understood original genius—who has cribbed certain peculiarities of an individual & works them up logically into a system so that he also adds to the confusion in the brains of the otherwise well disposed public & as a rule passes off as the real thing—I wont talk of critics since they really dont alter things one way or the other—They simply dont count except to 'embêter l'artiste'—Embêter him with their condemnation or embêter him with their praise—I am most eager to see Goossens quartet & also the song of Whitaker   I shall write as soon as I have made myself thoroughly acquainted with them—My dear Phil—I would not advise you to go to America or to Tahiti except for *adventure* & to get out of a groove—You are only 21. I went to Florida at your age & had not yet become a musician—Dont get despondent & desperate—The conditions of art in America are far worse than in England—If you dont feel sufficiently gifted to become a composer why not become a powerful writer—not a critic—but a writer on artistic things—on music. Why not, with your pen, try to help on Goossens & Whitaker & try to persuade the public at least to try & understand them—It would be a great work to discover the gifted musicians & help them out into the light so that they dont become mouldy—If you went to Tahiti I am afraid you would stay there for good & gradually lull yourself to sleep under the coco palms & in the arms of the lovely 'Waheenees' (Vahinés)[47]   Very few Europeans who go out there ever come back again—You must have a real fight with life before you give it up & there is some satisfaction to be got out of surmounting difficulties—By force to overcome the bourgeois! To lift oneself by degrees over the mob & feel ones powers—Dont let yourself be crushed by masses of inferiority & phrases of catchwords—Dear old pal! you are on the brink of being in love again—a phrase in your letter seems to tell me so—I have been in love twice myself—the 2nd time by far intenser than the first—in fact it gave the direction to my life—Perhaps you will get your direction that way —You are very much like I used to be—very much—If you can—come over to me here in Grez & stay with me awhile & we can talk it over together—I suppose the authorities will allow you to take your Xmas holidays in France— In any case I want to see you before you go out on adventures & mind, that is the only thing to go out on—to tramp the highroads of the world & sail the great seas—to hear languages one doesn't understand & see strange customs & not always come home to five o clock tea—to sleep with a revolver under

---

[47] Women of Central Polynesia.

ones pillow—I have done it for months—All that is splendid & colors ones life
—If I were not such a music scribbler I would come with you—I simply love
travel & adventure & the country in which I found it the least was England—
old Roast Beef, Yorkshire pudding England—I remember when I was only 7
trying to find it by running away from home over the moors—Write me soon
again or, better, come & spend Xmas with me

  your affectionate friend
  Frederick Delius

Please leave the copy of the Concerto with Miss Harrison —51 Cornwall gardens, Gloucester R^d & ask her to have it copied—Many thanks for doing it[48]

138
Frederick Delius to Philip Heseltine

[Grez-sur-Loing
December 1915]

Dear Phil—
  How about the Sonata? Have you corrected the proofs? On no account allow
it to be printed before you have corrected it—After you have done it send the
proofs over to me if possible—I am anxious about it   Write at once—

  Yrs ever
  Fr. Delius

Postcard.

[48] Heseltine was also busy correcting proofs of the Violin Sonata which Delius had recently composed.

139
Frederick Delius to Philip Heseltinc

Dear Phil—

I have not received the Concerto. When did you send it off? I am rather anxious about it. with love

Frederick Delius

Dec 27/15
Grez-sur-Loing
(S&M)

How about the Sonata proofs?

Postcard.

1916

FILLED with renewed enthusiasm and energy, Delius had been composing ever since his return to Grez at the end of the previous year. The beginning of 1916 found him working on the conclusion of the *Requiem* and by late April he had also completed two movements of a string quartet, beginning work on another movement in May. He also began composing a second *Dance Rhapsody* in early June before making a series of visits during the ensuing months to the Clews in Paris. Between trips he carried on composing, beginning work on a concerto for violin after a visit to the Clews in late September. All in all, 1916 was to prove a happy and productive year.

At the beginning of 1916 Heseltine joined the Lawrences, who had moved to Cornwall at the end of 1915. He was soon followed by Puma on 2 February. His idea was to publish and promote Lawrence's books but, for reasons unknown, the friendship turned sour and Heseltine and Puma returned to London in March. Soon after his return he met Cecil Gray in the Café Royal and the two men soon became close friends, sharing a studio in Battersea. Their subsequent meeting with the Anglo-Dutch composer Bernard van Dieren in June had a profound effect on both men, particularly on Heseltine, who immediately became a disciple and an ardent promoter of his music. His own compositional technique was influenced by the music of van Dieren with whom he studied briefly. There was another highly significant event that year. In November an article by Heseltine on Goossens's chamber music was published in a journal, *The Music Student*, and for the first time he used the pseudonym 'Peter Warlock', to conceal his identity from the editor.

Heseltine and Puma were married in December 1916. It proved a disastrous marriage and a step that Heseltine soon regretted. A son, Nigel, had been born in July that year but Heseltine seems to have shown little interest in the boy, who was looked after by Heseltine's mother at Cefn Bryntalch.

140
Philip Heseltine to Frederick Delius

January 1ˢᵗ 1916.   c/o D. H. Lawrence
                                                         Porthcothan
                                                          Sᵗ Merryn
                                                           Cornwall

My dear Delius,

This is just to give you my new address—on the north coast of Cornwall[1]—
my best greetings to you both for the new year—and to reassure you about the
score of the Concerto. I made enquiries at the Chelsea post-office, and was told
that owing to the Christmas pressure, a parcel might easily take three weeks or
more to reach France—Insured parcels scarcely ever go astray. However, if the
worst occurred, I could probably rescore the work for you, since in my piano
copy I have made very careful notes on the instrumentation, including all the
entries of instruments, and in the rough copy the whole score (condensed to
four staves) is written out.

I sent off the day before yesterday two songs of my own for you.[2] I will write
you a long letter in a day or two. I have only just reached here after an all-night
journey. The sun shines and a gale is making the sea tremendous.

affectˡʸ yours
PH

Postcard.

---

[1] Heseltine described the setting to his mother: 'Our house—a big old farm—is on a hill a quarter of a mile from
the sea overlooking Porthcothan Bay. The surrounding country, though not really high, gives one a sense of vast expanse
and openness, and the skylines are wonderful. On the headland a mile away a red light revolves and flashes all night,
like a great heart throbbing.' Heseltine to his mother, 3 Jan. 1916, BL 57961.
[2] These were probably early versions of songs later destined to find their way into the song-cycle *The Curlew*.

141
Philip Heseltine to Frederick Delius

c/o D. H. Lawrence
Porthcothan
St Merryn
Padstow
Cornwall.

January 6th [1916]

My dear good friend—Your last wonderful letter was a real inspiration. How splendid it is to have a friend such as you to encourage one's faltering steps on the threshold of life! I cannot express to you all that it means to me, but I think you know. I have made five or six abortive attempts to write to you in reply, but during these first days in a new environment I feel completely at a loss, mentally, and cannot write one coherent page. So you must pardon an apparent reticence, an apparent lack of enthusiasm and vitality, which I think and hope is only temporary and superficial. The past months have been full of anxieties and small nagging worries, each petty in itself individually, but en masse powerful and wearing to one's nervous vitality. At the moment I am completely exhausted, as though I had been dragged, insensible, out of the sea. And although I trust that with 1915 I have put behind me for ever a great deal of foolish and harmful stock-in-trade with which my life was encumbered, I have not yet gained enough positive energy to set out on the forward track again. Like the man out of whom Jesus cast seven devils, I feel 'swept and garnished'[3] but empty, awaiting the arrival of the soul's new tenants—(which in the case instanced were, I believe, seven more devils worse than the first!![4] However, one can but hope for the angels!)

At any rate, this is the beginning of a fresh start. Here on this stormy coast the winds blow through and through one from mid-Atlantic, and the waves surge and thunder and break right over the cliffs, and the spray falls on one's face with a chill, cleansing moisture. It is a wild, open country of vast expanses, giving a great sense of freedom and openness. The morning and evening twilights are incredibly beautiful—Yesterday, as I was walking home, into the sunset, I was

---

[3] cf. 'Empty, swept, and garnished.' Matt. 12: 44.

[4] cf. 'Then goeth he, and taketh with himself seven other spirits more wicked than himself, and they enter in and dwell there: and the last state of that man is worse than the first.' Matt. 12: 45.

haunted all the while by the Dance from the North Country Sketches, which seems most perfectly to express the Stimmung of Cornwall . . . .

I asked Lawrence to write to you a few days ago, to give you his exposition of our plans.[5] However, I don't want to identify myself with him in anything beyond his broad desire for an ampler and fuller life—a real life as distinct from the mere mouldy-vegetable existence which is all that is possible here. He is a very great artist, but hard and autocratic in his views and outlook, and his artistic canons I find utterly and entirely unsympathetic to my nature. He seems to be too metaphysical, too anxious to be comprehensive in a detached way and to care too little for purely personal, analytical and introspective art. His views are somewhat at variance with his own achievements. But he is, nevertheless, an arresting figure, a great and attractive personality, and his passion for a new, clean, untrammelled life is very splendid.

There has been a characteristically English muddle over the Violin Sonata. The proofs instead of being sent to me were sent to Beecham, and—as he is now in Italy—of course, are quite lost for the time being!

There are many other things I should like to talk to you about, but I feel too unclear to broach any of them at present. A few days will, I hope, bring both clarity and developments.

I wish so much that I could have come over to you at Grez this New Year. But it appears to be quite impossible to get a passport. I suppose there's no chance of seeing you over here for some while?

Much love to you both.

Ever yours affectionately
Philip Heseltine

P.S. I am working at the Delius-biography! I think it will work out well.[6]

Could you send me some time a copy of the text of the 'Requiem', and, if possible, the score also, though that is not yet done, I think.

When it is, I will make the Piano Score and thus familiarize myself with it.

Enclosed is a delightful dance-tune from a 16th century lute-book which I heard sung as a carol this Christmas.[7]

---

[5] No letter from D. H. Lawrence to Delius has been found.

[6] Although the biography of Delius was mentioned as early as 1914, Heseltine took a long time to complete it and it was not published until 1923.

[7] Heseltine had begun transcribing early music towards the end of 1915: 'Meanwhile, I am delving deep into the origins of keyboard music, and receiving daily delights and surprises from the works of Byrd, Gibbons, Tomkins, Farnaby and many another astonishing composer who preceded J. S. Bach by more than a century. I am also scoring from the old part-books in the British Museum a quantity of early 17th century chamber music, which is exceedingly interesting from an aesthetic as well as an antiquarian point of view—a fact entirely ignored by most of the old fogeys who have taken the trouble to do this in years past.' Heseltine to Taylor, 12 Nov. 1915, BL 54197.

142
Frederick Delius to Philip Heseltine

GREZ-SUR-LOING
Seine et Marne
Jan 22 1916

Dear Phil—

Just a few words to tell you how much I like Goossens quartet: it is the best thing I have seen coming from an English pen & full of emotion—Tell Goossens that I will get it published for him as soon as the war is over—Your Song the 'Curlew'[8] is lovely & gave me the greatest pleasure.—Turn to music, dear boy. *There* is where you will find the only real satisfaction—Work hard at composition—There is real emotion in your song. *The most essential* quality for a composer—Whitaker's song I like also—altho' it is, at times, a little preciéuse & *cherché*. Is he young? If so, *it is very promising*. I am hard at work on the end of my 'Requiem' I should love to shew it you—Cannot you come & stay with me here for a fortnight? & bring the biography you are writing with you—Say in March or April when the weather gets nice & springy—How are your other plans developing—I cannot understand Lawrence wanting to give up writing —What on earth for?—Surely not for planting potatoes or tobacco. Just fancy neglecting the gifts one has—those most precious & rare & mysterious things coming from one knows not where, nor why. My most earnest advice to you is to turn to musical composition at once & for good—Voilà—Please send the piano score of the double Concerto to Miss May Harrison, 51 Cornwall Gardens, Gloucester R^d. Kensington—Write me soon again

In haste—your affectionate
Frederick Delius

P. S.
The little dance tune is charming

P. P S
Get the proofs of the Sonata from Forsythes[9]—
Other proofs if the first have gone astray—

---

[8] 'He Reproves the Curlew' (1915). This setting of a poem by Yeats was later incorporated into *The Curlew* song-cycle.
[9] Forsyth Brothers, publishers. Originally founded in Manchester for the sale of pianos in 1857, the firm began engraving music in 1872. The following year they opened a London publishing business in Oxford Circus, becoming a limited company in 1901.

143
Philip Heseltine to Frederick Delius

February 11th 1916.   c/o D. H. Lawrence
                                                        PORTCOTHAN
                                                        ST MERRYN
                                                        NORTH CORNWALL

My dear Delius. Your splendid and encouraging letter cheered me immensely
—It is hard to have faith in the progress of oneself when one's forward movement is so slow that is almost imperceptible. Yet there is always the little smoul-
dering fire of confident hope at the bottom of one's heart and a letter like yours
makes it leap into joyous flame. Oh, but this country is black and horrible
—although, for me, things are tolerably easy. How right you have been to abjure
humanity from your earliest days! But it is no good lamenting over one's fellow-
creatures—the more one thinks of them, the more sick one feels . . . . . . so to
other topics.

I am indeed glad that I was not mistaken, in my estimate of Goossens: he is
a genius—a real one—who will do great things. I only wish it were possible to
help him along—but the English apathy towards music has now crystallised into
complete disregard. The Britisher cares less for his composers than for his lunatics
and criminals, who are at least clothed, fed and housed—and what more can
one want? Poor Lawrence—certainly the greatest writer we have[10]—is in the same
box—He cannot make a bare hundred-a-year with all his fine work! Of course
he never really means to give up writing, but the treatment he has received in
this country has driven him to a most gloomy and pessimistic outlook on things
in general. It is bad enough when an unknown writer is allowed to starve, but
when a country neglects its acknowledged men of mark, one surely has just
cause for despair. I am sending you a little philosophical work of his that has
been privately printed in a small magazine—a wretched form for such splendid
writing.

I am very interested in Whitaker. His music appeals to me very strongly—
I have written him a long letter, asking for more details about himself and his
work, but although he has promised to write and send more MSS, nothing has
as yet been forthcoming.

---

[10] Heseltine wrote in similar terms to Viva Smith: 'I am sure you, for one, realise that Lawrence is a man of transcendant genius . . . [he] is now so poor that he can barely live in comfort—and his health is far from robust—: beyond
the next few months he has no prospects, as far as money goes, whatever!' Heseltine to Viva Smith, 16 Feb. 1916, BL
58127.

This Cornish coast is strange and sinister—one feels that there is nothing superfluous in the country (save the inhabitants, of course!)—it has been stripped
down to its bare essentials. One could not deceive oneself in a place of this nature.
The winds seem to search out one's very heart—and if one is weak and failing,
it is no good pretending to oneself—Christianwise—that weakness is strength!
There is a wealth of sombre colour in the landscape. The bare branches of the
trees and hedgerows have all a kind of winter coat of a reddish tint which they
put on to protect themselves from the excess of salt in the damp air. At this
time of year, this dull red is the predominant hue—it is emphasized by the red-
ness of the soil which is just now being ploughed up. And at sunset (on clear
evenings one sees the sun sink right into the sea) everything becomes burning
red—even the grass seems to have a lair of red over the green. On the greyest,
dullest days, a faint bluish-red comes filtering through the cloud-masses. All the
roads, for some curious reason, are cut very deep down in the rock, below the
field level—and on the rock, at the level of the field, grows the high hedge of
evergreen Tamarisk[11]—so that one is always overshadowed. On the uplands,
there are scarcely any shrubs or trees—the hedges are replaced by stone-walls,
built in an intricate and very beautiful herring-bone pattern. It is all stark and
elemental, rather cheerless and repelling, if one wanted to assimilate it, identify
oneself with it, but for a while invigorating, cleansing—essentially a country
for deliberation at a turning-point rather than settled work—at least I find it so.

While this war lasts, one feels that 'sauve qui peut' is the only safe rule of
life—if one does not want to throw one's life away. It is so difficult to keep one's
head above water at all. But if one can weather *this* storm . . . !

I have found my Vrenchen[12]—I hinted this in my letter from Garsington,
but even now I can't write about it. I have not seen her since Garsington, where
she lives, but she has written me long, wonderful letters—and I am more sure
of her than I have ever been of anyone. She is Swiss—but very different from
the generation Keller[13] wrote of . . . .

Meanwhile, I am still worried to death by the little model[14] I took away in
the summer, in sheer desperation of loneliness. I never really liked her, but she
has been staying with me a good deal during the winter, because she had no
home and little money, and, as I told you in London, she is going to have a
child. Fortunately, I had a legacy of £100 the other day which I can draw upon

---

[11] A graceful evergreen shrub or small tree with slender, feathery branches and minute scale-like leaves.

[12] Juliette Baillot. Vrenchen is the leading female character in Delius's opera *A Village Romeo and Juliet*.

[13] Gottfried Keller (1819–90), Swiss narrative writer of the realistic school. Delius's opera *A Village Romeo and Juliet*
was based on *Romeo und Julia auf dem Dorfe*, from *Die Leute von Seldwyla*, a collection of short stories (1856).

[14] Minnie Lucy ('Puma') Channing (1894–1943), an artists' model whom Heseltine had met in the Café Royal.
With black hair and olive complexion she was of striking, almost classical Mediterranean beauty. Heseltine married
her on 22 Dec. 1916, a son having been born on 3 July that year.

to supply her needs, but I have no idea what is to become of the child. She cannot possibly afford to keep it, and I have far too little liking for her to want to help her afterwards. As it is, I reproach myself for having been too Christian, too weakly compassionate towards her.[15]

I have just read 'Niels Lyhne'[16]—it is quite wonderful—the more so for the period at which it was written. But it seems to me surprising that Denmark has not progressed more rapidly of late years, seeing that it was so far advanced in the seventies.

I would really love to come to Grez—I can't tell you how much of a relief it would be, after two years uninterrupted in this foul country. But I fear it would be quite impossible to obtain a passport, as I am of 'military age', although physically unfit for military service. Perhaps when Conscription is in force it may be easier, but I am very doubtful. I should be enormously interested in the 'Requiem'—I suppose it would be too risky to send it over?

Your first experience with English publishers does not promise to be very happy. Forsyth and C° do not answer my letters at all! So I fear I can give you no news of the Violin Sonata.

This is a scrappy, jerky letter—but I feel entirely disjointed and incoherent at the present time. My nerves are getting worse and worse—I am going up to London soon and I shall go and visit a doctor, since nervous unrest is making my life wellnigh intolerable—It is fogging my mind, too, and my concentration dwindles daily.

Much love to you both—write soon again.

Yours ever affectionately—
Philip Heseltine

[15] In 1918 Jelka Delius reported: 'Little Philip Heseltine has made such a terrible mess of his life he's gone and married a model who got a baby, which he thinks is his—If he *liked* the girl—but he doesn't—there he is in a small flat a-quarrelling with her—pitiful—He looks so pale and miserable that I think he takes drugs.' Jelka Delius to Marie Clews, London, 20 Dec. 1918, Delius Trust Archive.

[16] Delius's opera *Fennimore and Gerda* was based on this novel (1880) by Jens Peter Jacobsen (1847–85), Danish novelist and poet. Heseltine enthused over the book to Viva Smith as well: 'I am sending you . . . "Niels Lyhne" translated, very indifferently, from the Danish of Jens Peter Jacobsen, a great writer very far ahead of his time. Delius considers the book one of the greatest novels ever written, and has set to music a dramatised version of it.' Heseltine to Viva Smith, 16 Feb. 1916, BL 58127.

1. The younger Delius

2. Philip Heseltine

3. Jelka Delius in the garden at Grez, July 1932

4. Delius's house at Grez

Grez sur Loing
S&M
18 Dec 1911

Dear Mr Taylor
Many thanks for
your kind note &
the music —
his talent seems
to me to have
remarkable musical

5. Letter from Delius to Colin Taylor (18th December 1911), (Colin Taylor Collection, University of Cape Town Library)

Intelligence & also to be very gifted —
I like him very much & find his enthusiasm
very refreshing — I hope I shall
have the pleasure of meeting you
when I next come to England

I remain
sincerely yours

Frederick Delius

6. Reproduction of Heseltine's transcription of 'The Song of the High Hills'

7. Uncle Joe Heseltine

8. Sir Thomas Beecham

9. Olivia ('Viva') Smith

10. Minnie Lucy Channing ('Puma')

11. Eugene Goossens, 'Puma', Philip, and Hassan Suhrawardy (1915)

12. Frederick and Jelka Delius

13. Philip and Fred and Jelka Delius at the 1929 Delius Festival

14. Beecham and Eric Fenby at Delius's funeral

144
Philip Heseltine to Frederick Delius

13 Rossetti Mansions
Chelsea, S.W.

March 1ˢᵗ 1916.

My very dear friend—Here is the tentative prospectus of a despairing project
I have set on foot in order to discover whether there are any left in this country to whom life and its expression mean more than the lust for death and
destruction. I fear that our small voice will be altogether drowned in the roar
of the storm: one can but do one's small best to rescue from oblivion the things
one values most. More and more I am convinced that Lawrence is one of the
greatest writers we have had for generations; and yet only fifty pounds stand
between him and starvation at the present moment! 'The Rainbow', a superb
piece of writing and intricate psychology, was accorded (thanks to the *Purity
League*!!) a treatment from which thousands of books of the filth-for-filth's-sake
order are exempt—as witness the windows of the 'Hygienic Rubber-goods
stores' in Leicester Square and the Charing Cross Road! So one is driven to utter
despair[17] . . . . What has happened to your Three Elizabethan Songs? If I get a

---

[17] Heseltine wrote to Viva Smith about the scheme in great detail: 'I am getting a circular printed . . . we suggest
that the only resort is private publication by subscription. Those who agree with our attitude—and there must, after
all, be a large number—must come together and form a nucleus—those who love the truth must support it. So we
invite subscriptions for such books or musical works as would be either rejected by publishers or overlooked when
thrown into the public trough along with the hogwash this country devours as literature and music. We shall have no
capital—save perhaps a few pounds for the printing of our circulars. When enough subscriptions have been promised
to pay the bare cost of publication, we shall print each book and send it to those who want it. Any profit that may be
made will go to the author, or towards the printing of another book. But the object of the scheme is *not* money-
making, but the mere desire that fine works should be accessible to those who desire them. . . . The first book will be
a reprint of "The Rainbow", unexpurgated, from the original MS. This, of course, cannot be publicly advertised or
offered for sale in the booksellers' shops in this fair and righteous country, but for £120 an edition of 1000 copies can
be printed. The price will be 7/6, post free. Afterwards, will follow a sequel to "The Rainbow" and a philosophical
work "Goats and Compasses" (a veritable soul-bomb, a dum-dum that will explode inside the soul!) by Lawrence, and
a novel by Middleton Murry—this as a preliminary announcement. Of course we shall discover new writers hitherto
entirely submerged. Above all, there will be no committee—since committees are only the public on a small scale. The
scheme is anonymous, an impersonal project for the propagation of fine, living works of art. Lawrence will select the
books and I the music—but no names are associated with the scheme except mine, and that only of necessity, in my
capacity as Secretary, since someone must receive the subscriptions and despatch the circulars and manage the actual
affairs. If you can distribute some circulars, I will send over a consignment next week—say 50: you could easily dis-
criminate 50 possible sympathisers. Attached to the circular is a form, to be signed and sent to me at Cefn Bryntalch
(the only stable address I have at present), by which the signer *undertakes* to subscribe for one or more of the works
offered. No money need be sent until it is asked for, i.e. until enough promises have been received to enable us to start
printing. . . . Do be interested and try and help—I see a rosy vision of a large house in London *full* of wonderful books
and music, stacked up ceiling high, waiting to be despatched to enthusiasts all over the world!' Heseltine to Viva Smith,
16 Feb. 1916, BL 58127.

good number of applications for music, why not let them head the list? They would bring us good luck, and, after the bare cost of printing is paid, you get *all* the proceeds derived from their sale—e.g. (approximately, in this case) you would get a clear 2/= on every copy after the first 75. . . . . After many fruitless enquiries, I find Forsyth has actually begun to print the Sonata, but I cannot discover how far he has got or when the proofs will be ready. This first experience of an English publisher cannot be causing you much joy!! Shall I send you the piano score of the Double Concerto when May Harrison returns it, or shall I keep it till you want it published? . .

I will finish later on: there is so much to tell you.

Much love to you both.

Yours ever affectionately
Philip H.

P.S. It is rumoured that you and Tommy B. have had a row—this being the reason why no work of yours is performed nowadays!

I am not surprised! Poor Bax was let down at the Philharmonic over his 'Spring Fire', which was postponed 'owing to exceptional difficulty and insufficient time for rehearsal'.[18] I agree with the critic who wrote, 'The work being three years old, one would have thought that the exceptional difficulty might have been discovered before.' The work has been postponed successively at Norwich and at the Gardiner concerts (since the latter never came off). As Beecham still, by law, owes me £150 a year if I choose to extract it, he ought to subscribe fairly liberally to our scheme!

The final prospectus read as follows:

THE RAINBOW BOOKS AND MUSIC

Either there exists a sufficient number of people to buy books because of their reverence for truth, or else books must die. In its books lies a nation's vision; and where there is no vision the people perish.

The present system of production depends entirely upon the popular esteem: and this means gradual degradation. Inevitably, more and more, the published books are dragged down to the level of the lowest reader.

It is monstrous that the herd should lord it over the uttered word. The swine has only to grunt disapprobation, and the very angels of heaven will be compelled to silence.

---

[18] *Spring Fire* (1913, an unpublished orchestral work based on Swinburne's 'Atalanta in Calydon'). It was to have had its first performance at the 1914 Norwich Festival, but the performance and the Festival were cancelled at the outbreak of the war. Heseltine here refers to a performance scheduled at a Royal Philharmonic Society concert in Queen's Hall in Feb. 1916 which was subsequently cancelled on account of insufficient rehearsal time. It was not heard in Bax's lifetime and had to wait until Dec. 1970 for a performance.

It is time that enough people of courage and passionate soul should rise up to form a nucleus of the living truth; since there must be those among us who care more for the truth than for any advantage.

For this purpose it is proposed to attempt to issue privately such books and musical works as are found living and clear in truth; such books as would either be rejected by the publisher, or else overlooked when flung into the trough before the public.

This method of private printing and circulation would also unseal those sources of truth and beauty which are now sterile in the heart, and real works would again be produced.

It is proposed to print first 'The Rainbow,' the novel by Mr D. H. Lawrence, which has been so unjustly suppressed. If sufficient money is forthcoming, a second book will be announced; either Mr Lawrence's philosophical work, 'Goats and Compasses,' or a new book by some other writer.

All who wish to support the scheme should sign the accompanying form and send it at once to the Secretary,

PHILIP HESELTINE,
   Cefn Bryntalch,
     Abermule,
       Montgomeryshire.

145
Frederick Delius to Philip Heseltine

Grez-sur-Loing
(S&M)
15th March 16

My dear Phil—

I received your two letters & the opuscule of Lawrence & should have answered before but I have been, & am, very hard at work & in good form. I have heard nothing of the proofs of my 'Sonata'   could you not go & see Forsythe & make them send me the proofs & manuscript—There is no truth whatever in the rumour that Beecham & I have had a row—I have never had a row with B since I know him—The sketch of the double Concerto you had is now quite ready & finished   I have made a few changes which can easily be made in your piano score—my 'Requiem' is also quite finished in the complete full score.

Dear Phil, dont get despondent—Things have always been thus—especially in England—The most disinterested country in the world as regards good art of every description: Nobody cares for art: especially the good things—Sport tops everything & in a way, perhaps, it is alright as long as it keeps the nation physically fit. You have chosen a very bad time to bring out a new Artistic scheme —& I am afraid you will not have much success—*Nobody*, just now, interests themselves in such things—Until this war is thoroughly over I would not advise you to start it—In itself an excellent idea it will be strangled in the bud by the war interest. You should have had my 3 songs but Beecham is also editing them —God knows when? Your description of the country in Cornwall gave me a desire to go there once; it is probably rather like Brittany   The weather here is heavenly & I am happily at work so excuse a brief letter, dear friend; I of course, subscribe to Lawrences 'Rainbow' & am very curious—I think he is best in his shorter stories about sex which I admire very much—The pamphlet you sent me I dont like at all. Why all this symbolism—There is no need for it nowadays & then Nietzsche says all that so much better & in such a wonderfully pithy & clear language in 'The Will to Power'   read it & get Lawrence to read it. L. is not yet far enough away from Good & Evil—Dont bother about crowds. Develop your own individuallity, old pal, for you have *have one*, believe me, climb on to the mountain plateaus & get a good view of the vallies & the humans crawling about. With love—ever your friend

Frederick Delius

I love receiving your letters so write me again
What about conscription? Gardiner, Allinson etc
all friends—Goosens
give me news

146
Philip Heseltine to Frederick Delius

14 Whiteheads Grove
Chelsea, S.W.

April 22nd 1916.

My dear friend—After a long, long period of storm and stress, I have at last attained to something approaching peace of mind and have settled down, I hope for a long spell, in a tiny studio attic from which I can gaze, over the roofs of

South Kensington, at the sun setting behind those architectural glories of which we sturdy Britishers are so justly proud, to wit the Natural History Museum, the Vict. and Alb. Mus. and the ultra-phallic Imperial Institute (the Royal College of Music though adjacent, is happily invisible)!!—A garret of one's own—however bare—is so vastly preferable to any 'furnished flat' or 'apartments' that I am full of regret that I never hit upon this place before. It is very light and cheerful, being on the top floor of an old house surrounded with lovely trees just bursting their green buds, limes and a rare species called Shumack[19] of which I never heard before; it is said to have long, drooping fern-like foliage. My 'flat' consists of a bedroom, facing east for the morning sun, the studio—with a submerged bath beneath the floor—and beyond, down two steps, a wee kitchen with a gas stove and oven, and water laid on—two windows and a skylight facing north-west. The house is discreet and pleasant, quite un-English or at least un-Londonish with its queer-shaped rooms, full of nooks and crannies and secret cupboards, its casement windows and innumerable, gorgeous cats who dine with me daily. My furniture is scanty but sufficient; for decoration two 'Allinsons', a Tibetan devil, a west-African carving,[20] and rows of books; my piano, I suppose, will follow me here—as it is, my mother to whom I sub-let the last flat, has gone away and—either by accident or malice aforethought—locked the flat up, so that I can neither have access to my piano or have it conveyed here! I hope this is not one of her little 'jokes' of which the burying of the Pianola in Wales was so 'humorous' an example . . . . As for my personal affairs the narration of them would be so complicated—and painful also, to both of us, I expect—that nothing short of a novel (which I hope some day to write) would convey any sense of them to you. I hate bare, fragmentary outlines of things that are full of subtle and vital details, for they invariably lead to misjudgements and misconceptions. I always wait before writing to you—on whom so much has to be inflicted—for events, material and psychological, to assume some kind of recognizable perspective: but one might as well wait for a river to run by before trying to cross it. So scrappets must suffice. . . .

One still wastes much energy resisting and resisting, saying No to the sausage-machine which gulps down human individuals at one end and disgorges at the other a conglomerate mass of units organised for human destruction—though this vortex is an influence rather than an actuality, something intangible—one feels it in the streets, in the strangers who pass one by, but one cannot lay hands on it—all the while one must σκιαμαχεῖν—be fighting a shadow. There was

---

[19] Sumac, sumach or shumac, any of the shrubs or small trees of the genus *Rhus*, especially *Rhus Coriana* indigenous in southern Europe, which is the chief source of the material used in tanning.

[20] These details were later incorporated by Lawrence into his novel *Women in Love*, where in Halliday's flat 'there were several negro statues, wood-carvings from West Africa, strange and disturbing'. D. H. Lawrence, *Women in Love* (London, 1988), 63.

♯ never any real chance of my being 'taken for a soldier';[21] indeed, as soon as conscription was proclaimed, I put in an appeal before the Local Tribunal (comprised of fishmongers, greengrocers, vetinary surgeons, V.C.'s and the like), 7/8 of which was devoted to an impassioned denunciation of the compulsory measure and 1/8 to my physical disabilities and ill-health. The latter brought an immediate summons to appear before the military doctor—who was very old and very sagacious (for a wonder, and by a miracle of good fortune, since lunatics and cripples have been passed for general service with H.M. forces, while many of those who have appealed on grounds of ill-health have not even been accorded the privilege of an examination)—and in a few days I received by post a certificate of complete and absolute exemption from any form of service enjoined by the Military Service Act . . . . The passing of this Bill has shown, to those who have eyes to see beyond the immediate present, *who* are the real heroes of this war—the real advance-guard of our age, who, far more than any blood-stained warrior in Flanders or Mesopotamia, are liberating Humanity and earning the immortal fame so glibly promised to every vagrant who dons the khaki armlet emblazoned with a blood-hued crown—symbol of attestation which my good friend Sorabjî has aptly termed 'the scarlet badge of infamy on its appropriately dung-coloured background'. These are the men who in the face of the ramping and roaring Military, in the face of the hideous passions and prejudices of an inflamed and infuriated multitude, in the face of a possibility of a dog's death and burial beneath clods of 'Serve him right, the coward', are resolutely refusing to have anything whatever to do with the military machine, and the grisly progress of materialism backed up by false gods and foul ideals for the sake of which it has been set in motion. The old, glorious, resolute, pioneering spirit that has given us all the freedom of thought we have already attained is not yet dead; and it is well—for it has now before it the task of slaying the most gigantic and hideous monster of superstition that has ever made this poor world its prey. It is beginning nobly—for as yet the fight is a matter of ones and twos against millions—but all great movements have had just such small, almost insignificant beginnings . . . even Christianity, to name one. Never has the contrast between the modern Christian, with his snivelling hypocrisy and compromise with everything he pretends to abhor, and the fine spirit manifested by Jesus and his early followers been so glaringly exposed as by the attitude of this 'Christian' country towards the so-called Conscientious Objectors. If ever there were true Christians—(in the best sense of that unsavoury word)—in spirit if not in name—these are they; for the professing Christian of this 20th century is a veritable emetic, and, were Jesus to come to London to-day, his soi-disant

[21] Heseltine starts each new page with an additional sharp in the margin until there is an enharmonic change to flats (in brackets), then he reduces the flats, one at a time—hence the reference to B flat major in the last paragraph.

worshippers would have him instantly arrested, under the Defence of the Realm
Act, for making statements prejudicial to recruiting in H.M. forces . . . In justice to Asquith[22] and the few fair-minded ministers whose honesty has survived
the war-fever, one must add that in the Military Service Act there is a clause
providing that those who have a Conscientious Objection to combatant service
may, at the discretion of the Local Tribunal, be exempted therefrom, on condition that they undertake some other work calculated to assist the workings of
the military machine—or, in certain cases, they may be granted complete and
absolute exemption from all military duties. But oh, the hypocrisy of it! How
characteristic of England to proffer benefits with one hand (the hand which the
world sees) and withdraw them with the other (which the world cannot and
99% of the English *will* not see)! What is the procedure by which this generous
Act of Parliament is administered at the Local Tribunal, comprised of sensitive,
intellectual and understanding fishmongers, vetinary surgeons, V.C's etc, who,
though they would reduce all things to the level of Reason, are ignorant of the
most elementary laws of logic and reasoning (or in some cases know only too
well what fallacies will best floor the untutored mind), and contemptuous of
anything that is *felt* and cannot be expressed in terms of their mulish nationality? The greatest tragedies are those of the inarticulate who *know* within themselves too well to *feel* refuted by any specious argument, but are incapable of
interpreting or expressing their intuition and flounder hopelessly before a windy
storm of words from their opponents. Here is an almost verbatim report from
among the many I have made on behalf of the No-Conscription Fellowship.
Apart from its psychological interest, it deserves to be incorporated in a future
text-book on Logic as a 'norrible example'.

The case of one Tugwell, a tailor's cutter and fitter. The town-clerk reads a
statement by the applicant in which the latter protests that he cannot take the
military oath which would bind him to the performance of duties entirely out
of keeping with the spirit of his religion. (Remember, if you please, that this is
a man of limited intelligence and little education, utterly inarticulate: and that
the Chairman of the horde of fishmongers, vetinary surgeons, V.C's, etc, is nothing less than a 'Lord Justice'!)

Tugwell is then summoned—a frail, worn little man for whom life, outside
the domestic and sartorial circle in which he is accustomed to revolve, seems
altogether too bewildering.

CHAIRMAN 'Well, what are your objections?'

TUGWELL 'I'm against war, on conscientious grounds and I've been against
it all my life long.'

[22] Herbert Henry Asquith, 1st Earl of Oxford and Asquith, Prime Minister of Great Britain from 1908 to 1916.

CHAIRMAN   (with unruffled complacence) '*Well, so are most of us, but since the country is at war,* what is your objection to helping it?'

✝♯✝ [Oh, the foul humbug and hypocrisy of it all! The country, forsooth, '*is at war*' automatically, spontaneously—it has not been willed or even given permission to be so by anyone at all!!!!]

TUGWELL   'War to me is murder.'

CH.   'You'd rather let the enemy do what they liked?'

T.   'They're not enemies of mine.'

CH.   'Don't say enemies, then, say Germans.'

T.   'I should mind. I'd do my utmost to prevent them. But my 'ands are clean of 'uman blood and I intend to keep 'em so.'

CH.   'Do you object to serving in the R.A.M.C?'

T.   'I should only be making wounded men fit to fight again.'

CH.   'But the man might never be fit to fight again.'

T.   (after a pause) 'No, I'm against war altogether.'

Mʳ Salisbury. (a member of the Tribunal; with a loathsome smirk of self-satisfaction at having hit upon a 'clever' remark) 'I'm afraid, my Lord, that this is a question they have not sufficiently rehearsed.'

T.   'If I help the wounded, I am only releasing someone else for the firing-line.'

CH.   'That you don't know for certain.'

General Sartorius,[23] V. C. (a member of the Tribunal) 'He harps on these phrases without knowing what they mean.'

CH.   'No, I think I understand what he means.'

The Military Representative. 'Would you defend yourself if you were attacked?'

T.   'If anybody attacked me, I should lose my head.'

THE M.R.   'What religion do you belong to.'

T.   'None. I believe in 'Umanity. That's my religion.'

✝♯✝✝ THE M.R.   'Have you always held these views?'

T.   'I've been against war all my life.'

General Sartorius, V.C. 'We have all been against war all our lives.' (!!!!)

CH.   'All right; we'll let you know our decision.' (Exit T.)

---

[23] Major-General Euston Henry Sartorius (1844–1925), who served in the Afghan War and Egyptian Campaign of 1882. He was awarded the VC in 1896.

Then follows an invariable ritual, performed over every 'conscientious' case; there is no discussion, no attempt to ascertain whether the applicant is sincere or not. The Chairman glances round the table at his colleagues with a supercilious smile and eyebrows raised in question, with the words:—

'Non-combatant service?'

Assent is nodded, and the applicant, whose object was not so much to avoid actual conflict with the enemy as to protest, by his willingness to submit to any penalties that might be inflicted upon him, against the whole civilization (so-called) which compels one group of men to organize themselves for the efficient destruction of another, is drafted into some 'clearing-up-the-mess' branch of the army, whose spirit is precisely the same as that of the fighting units in the trenches; and, in refusing to accept this alternative service, becomes automatically a 'deserter'; whereupon the law hands him over to the military authorities, which is equivalent to thrusting him into a den of lions . . . Whether to laugh or cry at such a case? I scarcely know. One aspect gives me the sort of hopeless terror one feels in shouting to black rocks in solitude. One might as well try theology on a cat as reason with a body of men who seem so utterly incapable of grasping the main, fundamental issue, who persistantly piddle round unessential details. It is pitiful that their victims should have such splendid courage to stand up for a great principle without knowing why they do so; in fact when questioned, they make so lamentable a show and assign their conduct to such poor reasons that their opponents, whom even angels could not convince, become suspicious of their sincerity. Their action is so supremely right, their arguments so painfully wrong and inadequate. Although, mind you, I have heard cases of Christians, conducted admirably, the Tribunal being thoroughly refuted in all its arguments, the applicant exclaiming triumphantly:— 'I put my trust in God. Though he slay me, yet will I trust in him, and I refuse to set at naught his laws for the laws of man.' Yet the ritual of the procedure is unaltered—the supercilious smile, the raised eyebrows, the question whose answer is taken for granted. (I am speaking of the Chelsea Tribunal which is, as these bodies go, very mild and lenient. Many Tribunals refuse even alternative service, and no London Tribunal has granted absolute exemption to any applicant on conscientious grounds—and I don't suppose any provincial one has either—though there may be one or two isolated instances. But what are these compared with the numbers of innocent creatures who have been told by brazen recruiting serjeants:— 'You must attest (i.e. take the military oath) before you can put in an appeal on any ground', and when they go to appeal they learn the true fact that, having attested 'voluntarily', (!) appeal is not allowed. And you should see the numbers of little tradesmen exempted, as being indispensable, of 'national importance'—

while musicians and artists are despatched with rogues, vagabonds and crossing-sweepers to the front. Allinson, I am sorry to say, is one of the sufferers. (Apart from his deep-rooted objection to War—this is hardly the term, for like most of us he is *beyond* war, in the sense of *Jenseits von Gut und Böse*—he has been certified as physically unfit by two specialists, though the military doctor passed him as fit!) Among other things, he said to the tribunal, 'My work is creation, therefore I cannot become an agent of destruction'. You should have seen their blank expressions! What percentage of persons, in this machine-made age of materialism, understands by Creation anything save the event recorded in the first chapter of Genesis? The Tribunal asked Allinson . . . '*Have you ever killed a flea?*'

But I would forgive the honest fire-eaters (German *and* English) their blatant appetites, for they at least say openly what they are and what they want. It is the Christian Militarist (oh, oxymoron indeed!!) at which one's gorge rises. I can conceive no more damnable or utterly filthy kind of humbug than the thing that cries 'War for Jesus Christ's sake'. ('Humbuggery' is my more picturesque word for his attitude!) Not only do they attack those who, they well know, exhibit the best of the spirit of Jesus to a degree they themselves would not dare approach, but they do so with all their pulpit security, knowing that their opponents (in this case) could not possibly get a fair and unprejudiced hearing at the present time before any such large or heterogeneous audience as they themselves can address any Sunday . . . There is a certain 'parsoon' by name the Rev. A. W. Gough,[24] vicar of Brompton, an obscure parish church which he has filled, even so as to necessitate extension of the building, by his peculiar histrionic talents; and every Sunday, for years of my childhood, when we lived in his parish, he was inflicted upon me by my mamma. He, among numerous others, has been lately lifting up his sweet voice against the Conscientious Objectors whom he refers to as 'egotistical decadents', 'neurotic curiosities' and the like. So, having some personal acquaintance with the gentleman, I could not refrain from addressing to him a long letter of protest which, if possible, I hope to get printed in some Socialist organ, as an open letter to the Judas-like ministers of the Church at large. 'I observe', I began, 'that in the true Christian spirit of "hit-him-again-he-has-no-friends" you have taken up the cudgels against those brave men whose conscience bids them "resist not evil but overcome evil with good",[25] whatever penalties a Christian country may inflict upon them for attempting to do so. I am not a Christian, nor am I personally affected by the Military Service Act but I cannot refrain from expressing my disgust at this Jingo Jesus,

---

[24] The Revd Alfred William Gough (1862–1931), vicar of Brompton from 1899 until his death.
[25] cf. Rom. 12: 21.

this fetish of Mars cynically veiled in the garment of the Prince of Peace,[26] that you and your fellow-ministers have set up for public worship' . . . etc, etc—

Oh, these Christians!! They hurl 'Coward' at the bravest amongst us, with the rabble who know no better. But this war has revealed the greatest coward in the world to be the Christian church and its ministers who are ashamed of the simple, plainspoken, pacifist teaching of their Master! . . But enough of this. I will send you the whole letter if I can get it printed, together with the Christian replies!

I heard, to my sorrow, the other day that poor old Gardiner has succumbed to the sausage-machine and donned shit-coloured raiment, though in what capacity I cannot say. I have heard nothing from him for months. But it is very sad; he has always oscillated, first one way then another—and this is a fatal step, for it may finally give the victory to the hard, paternal side of him which has always been at war with the gentle, refined, artistic side he inherits from his mother. It is really tragic when those go under who neither desired war, nor in their more real selves, acquiesced in war as a possible reality. They are just swept away in the blind flux of the age. But I never regret the death of a real, true British sportsman, for it is they who are directly responsible for all this. The War-Fiend is quite as much the English Public-School Spirit as the Jingoism of Bernhardi.

Did I tell you in my last letter about the amazing Piano Concerto[27] written by Sorabjî, my Anglo-Hispano-Indian friend? I believe I did so I will not weary you with repetition. Last week Goossens (happily exempt, like myself) gave a chamber concert of his own works. The Aeolian Hall was fuller and more enthusiastic than I have seen it since the war began. To hear a representative selection of Goossens' work in one concert was indeed an artistic revelation.[28] Most heartily do I endorse your verdict that his is the finest music England has yet produced—and although he will no doubt be submerged for years, as you were, beneath the tide of mediocrity, yet one day the tide will ebb and leave at least two figures standing firm amid the wrack . . We had the Phantasy-Quartet

---

[26] cf. Isai. 9: 6.

[27] Concerto [no. 1] pour piano et grand orchestre Op. 3 (1915–16) 'a Monsieur Philip Heseltine: / en témoignage d'amitié / K. S.' Heseltine described the work to Taylor as 'a soul-shattering Piano Concerto, in a style *evolved* from late Scriabin & Ravel with a dash of Stravinsky (post-Petrouchkan period), but not ape-ishly imitative of any of them. He claims perfect mental auditory powers, for all the complexity of his harmonic scheme. If it's true, he is a psychological phenomenon of the most astounding order—for a year ago he had no thought or even desire of composing anything at all. Even the piano passages were evolved without any reference to an instrument!!' Heseltine to Taylor, 13 Mar. 1916, BL 54197. In July 1916 Sorabji wrote to Heseltine: 'I suppose I had better make a fresh 2 piano 4 hand version, as the one you have does not correspond with the full score as I have told you.' Sorabji to Heseltine, 6 Jul. 1916, BL 57963. No piano reduction of the work has, however, been found.

[28] The programme consisted of the Phantasy Quartet Op. 12 (1915), the Suite for Violin, Flute and Harp, Op. 6 (1914), *Deux proses lyriques*, Op. 8 (1916), Two Songs Op. 9 (1914), Suite for Piano, Flute and Cello Op. 5, Four Sketches (1912, later withdrawn), and Two Sketches for String Quartet Op. 15 (1916) (1. *By the Tarn* 2. *Jack o' Lantern*). Heseltine to Taylor, 20 May 1916, BL 54197.

I sent you, a delicious Suite for the difficult combination of Flute, Violin and Harp, two groups of songs, the longer Quartet in which his three colleagues of the 'Philharmonic Quartet' are mirrored and two most exquisite sketches for String Quartet, which are the most perfect and wholly satisfying pieces I have ever heard for that combination. The first, 'By the Tarn' is a lovely portrayal of moorland solitude—the strange, half-heard, intermittant note of a gentle wind in the distance croons with a gentle rise and fall beneath a serene melody that sings of wide, heathery uplands and spacious skys and great slow-rolling clouds. This, like the Phantasy Quartet and many other pieces by Goossens, is very perfectly complete and rounded off in its form which together with the dynamic range, may be well symbolized by the sign < >. The second piece, 'Jack o Lantern' is a fantastic, will-o'the-wispy scherzo, wonderfully and humorously suggestive of the quixotic moods of vain endeavour and exuberance run riot—but it is rather a sardonic commentary on these moods than a presentation of them. Not the least amazing thing about Goossens is the careless rapidity with which he can produce perfectly finished works. These two pieces, for example, were thrown off in a week, and the Phantasy Quartet in little more time than it would take the average composer to make a fair copy of his work. And this seems to show that, once the mood or emotion is felt, it is at once translated into terms of music in his sub-conscious self, whence for the purpose of its 'composition' (i.e. writing down) it need only be fished up. All his music seems to come so straight through—there is never any sign of technical limitation—which I think is marvellous seeing that Goossens is only 22 and the work of most men of that age is only, as a rule, squeezed out of them with much pain and labour, and when it *has* come out, it generally has the appearance of having passed through some sub-conscious custom-house where it has been rudely handled by the paws of something hard and rigid, something *official*—only that gets through which has, in some form or other, been through before: the best, that is the newest and most vital things, get held up as suspicious. But for Goossens, as for Sorabjî, technique does not seem to exist, as a thing separate from expression; what they have to express they can express to perfection. And of how small a handful of musicians can this be said! . . . .

Christ's hat! what a length I've run to! I expect before you reach these lines you will have given up reading in despair. This letter is like 'the great Alberto's' tree (which I saw again the other day!) which was always being given 'a little more wat*er*' and forthwith shooting up another yard into the air! Do you remember it? However, the curtain shall soon descend—for the time being—and I will end happily in the key of E flat!

What my immediate prospects are I know not—save that I hope to work more steadily and with more apparent result than hitherto, in my new surroundings.

But my mamma, having made some startling discoveries about certain things in my life which I have never attempted to keep secret, is only giving me my meagre allowance very grudgingly, and I feel that at any moment it might cease! My mother is always rediscovering things one has told her quite plainly months before! She is really too impossible. Nothing can persuade her that any art is anything more than amusement, and she cannot see why I should not 'keep music and literature for hobbies' and apply myself to the serious business of life in an office where I should be 'useful' and 'earn an honourable livelihood'! She and my father lived lavishly for years in the Savoy Hotel,[29] and yet she grudges me a paltry £10 a month. Fortunately, my entire expenses here, including the very modest rent, don't exceed 25/- a week—but one day Beecham will either have to start the 'Sackbut' or pay me £300 with which I can start it myself; for the contract is still legally binding and this year I have heard nothing at all from him!

The 'Rainbow' scheme fulfilled your prophecy and died the death. I got about 30 replies to 600 circulars. But I will gladly lend you my copy of 'The Rainbow' if you are keen to see it. My sojourn with Lawrence did me a lot of good, but not at all in the way I had anticipated. Lawrence is a fine artist and a hard, though horribly distorted, thinker. But personal relationship with him is impossible—he acts as a subtle and deadly poison. The affair by which I found him out is far too long to enter upon here—I will tell you about it one day, and we shall laugh together over it. The man really must be a bit mad, though his behaviour nearly landed me in a fearful fix—indeed, it was calculated to do so. However, when I wrote and denounced him to his face, all he could say was:— 'I request that you do not talk about me in London'—so he evidently had a very bad attack of guilty conscience. So I replied with a page of prophetic reviews of a future book 'D. H. Lawrence, a Critical Study by P.H.,' of which the 'Times' will say:— 'Reveals the distorted soul of this unhappy genius in all its naked horror', and the 'Spectator' will gloat over 'A monster of obscenity tracked down to its secret lair'; 'John Bull' alliterates with 'Personified perversity pitilessly portrayed', while the 'Christian Herald' is 'grateful to the author for his scathing indictment of the immorality of the present generation. The book is a veritable sermon and should be in the hands of every Sunday-school teacher'—etc, etc. Lawrence was quite comically perturbed at the prospect of my 'revelations'. He has practically no friends left. The last one to drop off before me was an Armenian[30] who published in the 'New Age' directly after the quarrel a most scathing and amusing satire on a 'brilliant young author, whose work

---

[29] Heseltine was born there on 30 Oct. 1894.
[30] Dikran Kouyoumdjian (Michael Arlen, 1895–1956), Bulgarian-born, Armenian author. He became a British citizen in 1922 and later moved to the USA.

was too good to be published' discovering his sub-conscious self in the middle of the night!! . . .

I have found in Gilbert Cannan[31] a writer who, though lacking Lawrence's sense of the beauty of words and enchanting power of creating atmosphere, has a far more subtle psychological sense and a much firmer and saner grip on life as a whole—in other words a sense of proportion which is a sense of the ironic humour of the greater part of life. I have requested that my copy of 'Round the Corner'[32]—his finest work which, to me, is quite amazing—be sent to you—it is at present lent to a friend in France. When you have read it will you please hand it over to Uncle Joe? Most of my books do a round and end up with a very dear friend in Ceylon[33]—where, apparently, Nat Gould[34] and Louis Tracy[35] are the only purchasable authors!

I suppose you will not cross the 'Kanal' again just yet? You must not on my account risk the fate of Señor Granados, composer of 'Goyescas' who went down on the Sussex,[36] though it would be great to see you over here again. If by any chance you do come (to risk modulating into B flat major, I must write on the back!) remember that the warmest of warm welcomes always awaits you in a certain garret 5 minutes walk down a straight road from South Kensington station. You will know the house by the green caravan in which dwells the Hausmeister, a pleasant person who smells atrocious, though he is a successful painter and has written books on metaphysics and mesmerism! Very much love to you both and all good wishes; and may the first cuckoo of this spring bring you inspiration as lovely as he brought you four springs ago. This, I think, is the best wish of all!

ever yours most affectionately
Philip Heseltine

[31] Gilbert Cannan (1884–1955), novelist and dramatist, educated at Cambridge, called to the bar (1908), dramatic critic on the *London Star* (1908–10).

[32] G. Cannan, *Round the Corner: Being the Life and Death of Francis Christopher Folyat* (London, 1913).

[33] Nigel Bannerman (1892–?), one of Warlock's boyhood friends. As early as 1903 Warlock and he spent holidays together. Bannerman went to Malvern College (1906–9) from where he was expelled. After studying at Heidelberg University he went to Ceylon as a tea-planter.

[34] Nathaniel ('Nat') Gould (1857–1919), English journalist and novelist. He wrote some 130 novels, all concerned with horse-racing.

[35] Louis Tracy (1863–1928), English author.

[36] Enrique Granados (1867–1916), the Spanish composer-pianist, and his wife were drowned when the liner *Sussex* was torpedoed by a German U-boat in the English Channel between Folkestone and Dieppe.

147
Frederick Delius to Philip Heseltine

GREZ-SUR-LOING
Seine et Marne
25th April [1916]

My dear Phil—

Miss Harrison wrote me she had sent you the copy of the Concerto by mistake instead of your own copy which she sent to me—I have returned it to her so that now she has both—Many thanks for having done the piano score for me—*It is very well done* & very playable—Get the piano scores from Miss Harrison & make the alterations (quite a lot) in your own score returning the copy to Miss H. I am now writing a string quartett—2 movements finished. I heard the cuckoo for the first time day before yesterday & the swallows also have returned 3 or 4 days ago so the weather will now become warm & lovely, I hope; Today it is heavenly. How are you getting on & what are you doing? are you composing? write me soon—We are having visions of Gardiner in Kaki, walking up and down under a railway bridge with a gun over his soldier[37] & whistling Tiperary.[38] When will 'The Rainbow' appear? I should like to have it. I gave my circular to Brooks[39] who also will get it—I hope he wont go off on the symbolical line—I hope also that you have begun the discovery of yourself & developement   I feel sure you will accomplish beautiful things—What a pity you cannot come over here to me for a bit. The war, in my opinion, will be over within six months.—Give me some news. What are all the friends doing? The musicians must be having a pretty bad time of it—

We both send you our love—

your affectionate friend
Frederick Delius

---

[37] 'shoulder'.

[38] 'It's a long way to Tipperary' (Harry Williams and Jack Judge), popular chorus (1908) sung by soldiers in the First World War. In Jan. 1916 compulsory military service was introduced for single men and Gardiner was forced to enlist. In March he was sent to Hazeley Down Camp at Winchester. He was later (May) appointed a deputy assistant censor, first in Calais and Boulogne and finally in London.

[39] Alden Brooks, American author and for a time a neighbour of the Deliuses at Grez.

148
Philip Heseltine to Frederick Delius

14 Whiteheads Grove
Chelsea, S. W.

May 8ᵗʰ 1916.

My dear Delius—

Our letters crossed—You must have got my lengthy scrawl just after posting your last.

I am enormously pleased and interested to hear that you are doing a String Quartet. It is very exciting news—but alas, our two best London quartets have now perforce disbanded, and their re-uniting is only a possibility one scarcely dare anticipate. Now we see the true worth of all the parrot-cries about British artists! They get sent off to the war sooner than the little grocers and other 'indispensables'—and afterwards (if there ever is an afterwards) back will come the tide of Kapellmeister and other 'enemies'.

My last letter to Messʳˢ Forsyth and C° elicited the following gem of intelligence for a reply:— 'I have sent your letter on to Mʳ Forsyth who will see Sir Thomas Beecham at the end of the week and communicate with you about the Delius Sonata'!

I have nearly finished a new piano score of the Concerto.[40] The alterations were too numerous to write into the old copy and there were some improvements to be made in the piano part. Miss Harrison guards the score so jealously that it took a great deal of coaxing to induce her to surrender it to me at all!

Poor Allinson is in a sad plight, awaiting the hideous destiny that may pounce any day upon him. Of HBG [Balfour Gardiner] I have no further news —so I don't know whether he is a mere private or a gaudy 'ossifer'. I heard one of his most sentimental piano pieces being tried over in the pianola shop the other day and felt quite moved! I'm afraid he must suffer very much in his present predicament.

Beecham is giving 'grand opera' in Manchester—but the majority of the works to be performed, whilst having great artistic pretentions, possess less merit and far less sincerity than musical comedies that do not pretend to be works of art at all. This is a great humbug—one of the many frauds imposed upon us by generations of 'professional musicians'—I have begun a little work

---

[40] Double Concerto for Violin and Cello (1915).

(which will not, I fear, see the light of publicity for a long while) whose text is:— 'The greatest enemy of music is the musical profession.'[41] And really, one cannot but marvel at the 'law' which arrests harmless palmists and fortune-tellers as frauds imposing upon a credulous public and allows the Professors of Composition to be not only loose but accredited!

Of recent events in the world I dare not speak, for the torrents of impotent rage that would be unloosed! . . . So I will subside for the moment.

Very much love to you both, in your almost incredible I-Brasîl[42] of peace—

Ever yours affectionately
Philip Heseltine

I am dying to see the 'Requiem' but I suppose you will not trust it to the post? I could translate it and make the reduction for you.

149
Frederick Delius to Philip Heseltine

[Grez-sur-Loing
1916]

Dear Phil—I have just received the parcel   many thanks—How about the corrections of the Sonata at Forsyths? Write soon

affectionately,
Frederick Delius

Just received your songs also   Am going to play them & will write you about them   Send me the address of Nichols.

Picture postcard, Les borns du Loing.

---

[41] 'So none greater enemies to their own profession than musicians', Dedication, Robert Jones's *First Book of Songs and Ayres* (London, 1600).

[42] I-Brasil was the name given to the Celtic Isles of the blessed whose haven was attained, not by death, but through the ultimate victory of spirit over flesh. Heseltine described the Scilly Isles as being 'like a mysterious gateway leading to a mysterious, unknown faeryland of impossible dreams come true—like Hy-Brasil the old Celts used to see shining far out in the western sea at sunset'. Heseltine to Phyl Crocker, 19 Apr. 1917, BL 57794.

150
Frederick Delius to Philip Heseltine

GREZ-SUR-LOING
Seine et Marne
11 May 1916

My dear Phil—

I read & reread your long letter which interested me most tremendously
—It shews me that the 'Christian world' is gradually revealing itself to you as
it revealed itself to me,—when I was about your age & went to Florida,—in all
its colossal hyprocrisy, brutality, & materialism & you can understand my enthusiasm when I suddenly opened Nietzsche for the first time—with his readjust-
ment of values & his wonderful & daring frankness & courage. His attack on
Christianity & the whole existing state of things—It absorbed me so much that
after reading most of his works—some again & again—I came to the conclusion that *I* was not a philosopher but a musician & would have to restrict my
powers to one of these two—Philosopher is a rotten word—Reformer would
be better—Nietzsche was not a philosopher either—but a gigantic reformer, an
enthusiast & poet—Perhaps the experiences you are now going thro' will give
you your direction in Life—mould you to your own capacities—Lead your enthusiastic honest & sympathising nature into certain channels by necessity & the
force of great events—As you know I chose solitude & music & nature—I have
never been in love with humanity—For me—humanity is a dung heap upon
which certain flowers grow & flourish—These flowers are all that is left & all
that are remembered thro' time—*Individuals*. After several thousand years we
look back upon a few names of Individuals—This war is the outcome of the
grossest materialism, prepared by all nations—but certainly let loose upon us
by 'Prussianism' in an endeavour to '*bag the lot*'—I thoroughly understand the
nations who dont want to be bagged. We had to leave Grez in a hurry because
the same German hordes were sweeping over France & we never expected to
see our home again except as smoking ruins—I can tell you we were pretty glad
when the battle of the Marne took place & the germans had to get out quick
& we could again return to our peaceful & productive life. No one in England
has felt invasion yet & all that it means—the story of 'Tugwell' is, of course,
touching & he is surely a little Jesus, but it would go sore with England if they
were all like him—Of course, I object to all the hypocrisy just like you & to
the attitude of the 'pillars of Society' playing 'le beau role'   Emetic is the word
—but they always are an emetic, on every occasion of importance, & I have

fled them—the whole system is so rotten & wrong & so complicated that only the greatest Cataclysm will put things again right or in a normal & natural state. Shall we ever see it?!! Everybody is being swallowed up in the machine which they have made themselves, or at least, tolerated—Valuable & promising individuals disappearing in the same slaughter with rotten useless ones. It is natures little way when she cleanses herself—as in an earthquake or volcano eruption —Now man has forged a machine which he cannot control anymore & it is anihilating the clever, dirty, vicious, brave, stupid, enthusiastic, ferocious, gentle, dreaming, idiotic, humble little ruffian. In the meantime I have written music —Two movements of the String quartet are entirely finished & I am working on the 3rd—How kind of you, dear friend, to do the piano score over again— When I looked at the Concerto again many things did not please me & I am sure I have improved the work. I would send you the 'Requiem' but dare not just yet: as soon as the boats can go in safety I will send it. Do send me 'The Rainbow'   I am awaiting the book of Cannan with great interest—You never said anything about the piano Concerto of Sorabjî—You are right when you say that professional musicians are the real enemies of music—they all have a little string to pull & are, all trying to make the world believe they are idealists & working for the benefit of Humanity—Hypocrites again: Christianism in another form—Oh! for the honesty of the brothel! Remember me to all my friends & Allinson & Goosens. In the garden the birds are singing lovely. The Laburnum & lilacs are in full bloom & every morning, early, the call of the cuckoo is wafted unto me, in bed, thro' the open window—What a pity you are not with me here! Write again soon to your

most affectionate
Frederick Delius

151
Frederick Delius to Philip Heseltine

GREZ-SUR-LOING
Seine et Marne
11 June 1916

My dear Phil—
   I received your song safely & am glad to see you are working at your music —The 'Curlew' is my favorite of the 3 altho there are beautiful things in all 3—I wish you were here so that I might point out little things which strike me

as unnecessary & which could be easily avoided—I find No. 3 less spontaneous—
I have finished my String quartett—& am now writing a 'dance'[43]—which I
think is going to be good. How sweet of you to take the trouble to do another
piano score of the Concerto for Cello & Violin—Miss Harrison wrote me that
she has had it copied. You must be nice & snug up in your new little flat; the
description is delightful & it must be quite charming—I hope it will not be
long before I visit you there—Keep pegging away at your work. Our garden
here is simply lovely. We have done it all ourselves this year & it has never looked
as well—I mow with a scythe every afternoon & am now quite an Expert at it.
The book 'Round the Corner' arrived here safely & we have started reading it.
It sounds very good indeed up to the present—Your uncle Joe has turned out
an awful old fraud—Just fancy,! whilst we were in England, he spread the report
about Bourron & Marlotte, that we had been interned in a concentration camp
in England & many other idiotic but treacherous reports about us—What do
you say to that? He also said that I had thro my influence prevented you from
enlisting—I had such confidence in him that I had written to him to go to my
house in Grez & get me a certain book—It appears he searched the house like
a detective & went thro everything—this as a friend mind you, & told people
he found nothing really suspicious—Of course, I do not want to see any more
of him—His excuse may be perhaps that he is a fearful moral coward & has a
most tremendous respect for all conventions & he wants to give himself a certain importance with the social & conventional people who I have always fought
very shy of: in fact I wont associate with that crowd here & so he found a ready
public—But his falseness raises my gorge—How about the Rainbow—Brooks, next
door, wants his copy as soon as it appears—or has the thing come to nothing
altogether—Gardiner wrote me a long letter from Calais where he is employed
reading soldiers letters 7 hours a day—Sundays included—He enlisted as an ordinary Tommy & had a very hard time of it drilling in a camp (Hazely Down) He
was lodged in a sort of Hut with 37 others—fearful discomfort—He got so confused at last that he could not understand what people were saying to him. However he has been promoted to Sub Lieut now & has an easier time of it. Write
me soon again, your letters are always so welcome & send me all you compose—
I will, if you like, send you back a comment on the things I do not like—

Believe me ever
your loving friend
Frederick Delius

How about Nichols—
I have still a few books of his with me here—
Have you his address?

[43] This is probably a reference to *A Dance Rhapsody* No. 2.

152
Philip Heseltine to Frederick Delius

2 Anhalt Studios
Battersea, S. W.   October 11th 1916.

My dear Delius

Another long silence! And I have just recollected with alarm that since I moved from Chelsea some months ago you have not even had my address. Forgive my negligence. This time I have great news for you, so I will confine myself to the one important topic.

I have found an enthusiast[44] whose tastes and aims in music are almost identical with my own—*and* he has money! So we are going to set about the regeneration of music in this benighted country in real earnest![45] Quite definitely, next March, we shall take a small theatre and give a four weeks season of opera and concerts, with a definite artistic policy and no compromise with the mob. Preparations are already being made, and I have an important proposition to lay before you concerning the 'Village Romeo and Juliet', which I have always longed to see staged in a manner that shall allow the full significance of the work to be clearly perceived, and not buried beneath a mass of stage properties and theatrical misconceptions.

I will try and explain in a few words the general principles which we have arrived at for our guidance in presenting musical dramas. Needless to say, they are diametrically opposed to those of Thomas Beecham, whose productions, as well as the choice of works, are becoming more and more inferior and artistically valueless. Your opinion in this matter will be of enormous value to us, more especially since the 'Village Romeo' is a work which has been presented in the traditional manner, and you will be able to judge whether it would gain or lose by being given in the way I suggest. Please forgive me if this statement of my own views appears a little dogmatic; but I am so tremendously interested in this problem which appears to me to be of vital importance and to open up,

[44] Cecil Gray (1895–1951), composer and music critic. He was a close friend and eventually the first biographer of Heseltine. They had met in the Café Royal in late spring (1916) and were soon sharing a studio in Battersea.

[45] Heseltine also told Taylor of the schemes whereby he and Gray hoped to bring about a 'regeneration of music in England', which included the launching of a musical journal and a subscription scheme for cutting modern works for pianola. They also hoped to secure a large studio where weekly free concerts of all the best contemporary music would be given and where new works by aspiring, young composers could be auditioned. There would also be very simple and non-technical lectures on music, 'addressed to those who have been gulled by financially-interested pedants into believing that music is an esoteric mystery which they cannot hope to understand without invoking the aid (*and* paying exorbitant fees) of the said pedants.' Finally each year they would publish an anthology of songs or short pieces, 'representative of the real tendencies of *to-day*, by young composers who have never before appeared in print'. Heseltine to Taylor, 5 June, 1916, BL 54197.

if satisfactorily solved, so many possibilities for future development, that I cannot help advocating it with a great deal of enthusiasm.

I am firmly convinced that the 'realistic' type of opera is dead, utterly dead:
further than this, I believe that the realistic manner of presenting opera is also
dead. Opera is essentially a *conventional* form (conventional, in the purely artistic sense of the word); it is therefore as futile to attempt to make it represent
real life as it is for a painter to make his pictures merely represent Nature photo-
graphically. Even the ordinary spoken drama is not used aright if it merely portrays the external aspects of real life. And to opera, where the text is sung, this
principle applies with still greater force.

In the drama of the present-day, whether it be spoken or sung, the *action*
must tend more and more to take place *within* the characters of the piece—in
a word, it must be psychological and not physical. Representation and realism
(in the theatrical sense) must be replaced by suggestion and symbolism: where
music drama is concerned the idea seems so self-evident that it is astounding
that so few modern composers have grasped it. Perhaps this arises from the fact
that most musicians are, alas, pure musicians—that is to say they know nothing
about anything but music, and even where music is concerned they have not
got as far as realizing its true function or its connection with life.

In the pure drama, these principles have already been put into practise—
in productions, by men like Granville Barker,[46] William Poel,[47] and Gordon Craig[48]
and in actual creative work by Maeterlinck, Fiona Macleod, W. B. Yeats and
the Russians, Andreev[49] and Evreinov,[50] though these latter seem more intent
on returning to the old idea of allegorical dramas, so prevalent in the middle
ages, by personifying attributes and qualities, than on making a drama of individuals and of character study . . .

Now to come to the 'Village Romeo and Juliet'. Your work has always seemed
to me to be immeasurably greater than Keller's story by reason of its greater
universality—that is to say, its symbolical qualities. It is so much more important than the mere story it is woven around; in fact the story—the 'plot', in the
theatrical sense, scarcely matters at all; *and this should be realised*. What you have
achieved in this work—and it is a great and unique achievement—is a drama
in which the various emotions, brought into play by various contingencies and
circumstances, are the real protagonists. But they are not *personified*, in the old
allegorical, 'morality' style. They are far too subtle. They are presented, typified,

[46] Harley Granville-Barker (1877–1946), English actor and director, one of the outstanding figures of the progressive theatre at the beginning of the 20th c.
[47] William Poel (1852–1934), English actor and director.
[48] Gordon Craig (1872–1966), English scene designer and theorist, son of Ellen Terry.
[49] Leonid Nikolaivich Andreyev (1871–1919), Russian dramatist.
[50] Nikolai Nikolaivich Evreinov (1879–1953), Russian dramatist, an exponent of Symbolism.

in certain individuals who appear on the stage. But it is not these individuals that really absorb us. The work grips one, entrances one and carries one away because these individuals are so shadowy, so unrealistic that they become symbols of the pure emotion they are feeling—so that one can project oneself into them and feel with them. The attendant physical circumstances are nothing; the fact of the two fathers quarrelling over a piece of land belonging to a certain Black Fiddler is unimportant. But what is real and vital and magnificent is the way you have expressed for us the conflict of love and hate, and blind fatality—the poignancy of love thwarted by circumstance, and the tragedy of materialism. The fact that the suicide of the lovers might easily have been averted does not really matter; nor does it prevent the last scene from being one of the most supreme things in all tragedy. But, of course, if the work is presented realistically, as a drama of facts, it falls flat—from what I have heard of the Beecham production, I should imagine it to have been an entirely 'naturalistic' affair—as though one should hold up a landscape of Cézanne in a gold frame at the Royal Academy and expect people to appraise it with all the other colour-photographs hanging round it! Naturally, everyone accused it of being 'undramatic'—and I do not believe even Beecham himself realized that it was never intended to be dramatic in the stagey sense of the word. Now there are certain very real difficulties to be encountered in its production. First of all, it is too subtle and intimate a work for a large theatre; moreover, it is questionable whether the symbolic-suggestive method of production is yet far enough advanced to be able to stand the cold, aloofness of a large theatre. (This is very difficult to explain!) But then there is the question of the orchestra; in a small theatre, where alone the right 'atmosphere' can be obtained, there is no accomodation for 70 or 80 players. And the scene at the Fair becomes an impossibility. But I believe the work would gain more than it would lose, even if one had to omit the Fair scene and dispense with the orchestra entirely, using two pianos instead. This proposition may fill you with horror, but I must lay it before you, because I believe that, however barbarous it may appear at first sight, it would enable the essential significance of the work to be brought to light, and this a Beecham production could never do, however beautifully the music might be played. But the decision rests, of course, entirely with you.

I propose to have no scenery—i.e. no set pieces: only plain curtains—possibly a suggestive back-cloth or two—nothing more—costumes of extreme simplicity. Perhaps, in the old Chinese fashion, one might have the stage-directions read out or thrown upon a screen before the commencement of each scene. In any case, the stage must be free from disturbing elements—the curtains or back-cloth beautiful but entirely free from any elaboration. The interest must be centered entirely in the play and the music; and as regards the setting, *the*

imagination of the spectators must take an active part (this is, as far as I remember, Maeterlinck's[51] idea, but it is a very important one, and seems to tend to
break down the sharp division between stage and auditorium which so often
prevents the audience from being entirely caught up and absorbed in the piece
that is played). And one can set their imagination working by the simplest clues,
the plainest suggestion. . . . . .

I have made certain alterations in the text of the 'Village Romeo'—no notes
have been altered, but I have brought the English version in some cases nearer
to the German, and have emended certain phrases that seemed a little stilted
and unnatural. For example, in the vocal score p. 47 the words 'Wahrhaftig, wir
sind Bettler bald' are, I think, better rendered by 'Yes, truly, we shall soon be
beggars' than by the printed version. Moreover, the former is an exact metrical
equivalent of the music. Again, on p. 198, to take an example at random, the
juxtaposition of 'love' and 'hate' is inverted by the printed translation! But these
are minor points. In the first scene, I should like Sali and Vreli to be played by
children actually not more than twelve years of age. They have very little to sing
and their parts could either be spoken, or sung by the actual Sali and Vreli behind
the scenes. Otherwise it is very difficult to mark the transition in age, between
the first and second scenes. We can get Eveline Matthews to sing Vreli. Sali,
however, presents some difficulty; Arthur Jordan[52] is, vocally, an ideal person
but he is most unpleasant to look upon and ponderous withal (though not as
bad as Mullings!).[53]

For a piano rendition, pages 57–60 would have to be omitted, and, for the
reasons given above, the Fair scene and the various mentions of the Fair that
occur at p. 127 and thereabouts (i.e. p. 128, section ㊽ to p. 133). Perhaps someone might come before the curtain and recite in a poem the significance of
the Fair Scene, and how the hostile gossiping crowd make life impossible for
delicate and sensitive souls. Now what do you think of the idea? . . . . 'Niels Lyhne'
might also be given in this way; as far as I recollect, you have scored it for a
smaller orchestra than the 'Village Romeo'? And what about 'Irmelin'? Or have
you resolved to keep it, nun-like, cloistered from the world?

Ordinarily, we shall have an orchestra of 25 performers—12 strings, flute
and piccolo, clarinet and bass clarinet, oboe and English horn, 2 bassoons, 2
horns, 2 cornets and percussion. There will be a chorus of 16—but all these,
both players and singers, will be first-rate soloists: unless our performances can
surpass any that have hitherto been given, they will not be given at all.

[51] Maurice Maeterlinck (1862–1949), Belgian poet and dramatist.
[52] Arthur Jordan (1886–?), English tenor; he studied under Rutland Boughton and sang leading parts at the Glastonbury
Festivals and with the British National Opera Company (Siegfried in the *Ring*).
[53] Frank Mullings (1881–1953), English tenor, member of the Beecham Company from 1916 to 1921.

There will be no reliance upon 'tradition', the entire musical and dramatic direction will be in the hands of Cecil Gray (my friend, mentioned above), Bernard van Dieren[54] and myself. Van Dieren is an altogether epoch-making personality —a composer beside whom all the little Debussys, Ravels, Stravinskys and Scriabins pale into insignificance. And, as you know I do not consider any of those writers by any means bad, you will have some idea of the great regard I have for this man's work. Very few people have ever seen it—and even he has scarcely ever heard a note of it. I met him, quite by chance, with Epstein,[55] the sculptor. He is always ill—his life is one long torment—and he may die any day, or linger on for a year or so, But he bears it all with magnificent courage, and works with feverish energy night and day to get as much of the music that is in him written down before he collapses altogether. It is terribly tragic, more especially since his work is not merely good, but absolutely epoch-making. We shall perform two long symphonic works of his, for 17 solo instruments—amazingly beautiful and wonderful creations—a string quartet and an opera, if it can be finished in time. There is a great dearth of suitable modern works. The world is apparently so pleased with Puccini—Mascagni—Charpentier[56] and C° that the idea of psychological opera has never taken root. Some tentative efforts have been made—by Rebikov[57] and Gustav von Holst—for example, but although their conceptions are good, the music is extremely bad. Rutland Boughton[58] seems to have a glimmering perception of the *idea*, but when he actually writes a work, it is nothing but worn-out Wagnerism of the most horrible kind, worse, I should imagine, than that of the generation of Bungerts and Kistlers. But Lady Dean Paul[59] is engaged on a work of the kind we want, and from what I have seen of her work, I expect it will be a great deal better than anything any other British composer could turn out. I also have sketched out a little mimodrama (very short—about 15 minutes)—very intense and very grisly—a sort of prolonged strain. No one speaks, scarcely anyone moves: the atmosphere is charged with emotion, but nothing *happens* in the theatrical sense. This is the 'text' (such as it is), written by one John Rodker.[60] It is called 'Twilight'.

[54] Bernard van Dieren (1887–1936): Dutch-born composer who moved to England in 1909. Heseltine had been introduced to him by the sculptor Jacob Epstein and had been completely bowled over by his music. Van Dieren's influence resulted in Heseltine's music becoming more contrapuntal in style. At this time Heseltine was trying to get van Dieren's 'Chinese' Symphony published.

[55] Jacob Epstein (1880–1959), American-born, British sculptor whom Heseltine had met in the Café Royal. He knew Delius, probably through the agency of Heseltine, describing him in his autobiography as 'argumentative, cranky and bad-tempered . . . we had many a set-to.' (Carley, *Letters*, ii. 206.)

[56] Gustave Charpentier (1860–1956), French composer, pupil of Massenet.

[57] Vladimir Rebikov (1866–1920), Russian composer; composed operas and 'psychological dramas'.

[58] Rutland Boughton (1878–1960), English composer; inspired by Wagner's theories, he attempted to create an English equivalent of Bayreuth at Glastonbury with a series of 'choral dramas' based on the Arthurian legends.

[59] Poldowski (Lady Dean Paul, born Irene Regine Wieniawska, 1880–1932), Polish composer, English by marriage.

[60] John Rodker (1894–1955), English poet.

'Columbine, Harlequin and Pierrot sit relaxed in armchairs in a wide, white
    room.
Columbine sits swinging her legs.
It grows gradually darker.
They sit as though waiting.
Creepers swing against the window.
It grows darker.
They sit as though waiting.
It grows darker.
Only the windows and the white linen of Pierrot and Columbine can now
    be seen.
Harlequin a faint blur.
It grows darker.
Pierrot and Columbine show faintly. The easy-chairs are rocks of shadow.
They sit as though waiting.
The creepers grow larger and swing against the windows.
It grows darker . . . .
The moon rises.
They sit as though waiting.
It is quite dark.
Columbine shudders, rises and walks quickly to Pierrot.
When she is close she turns from him suddenly and walks rapidly back to
    her chair . .

Harlequin leaps across the room, then seats himself and stares intently out
    of the window.
The moon gradually fills the room and it becomes lighter.
Pierrot has let his head fall on his knees.
Columbine sits relaxed swinging her legs . . .
Harlequin stares intently out of the window.'

The other stage works we propose to do are all very old and very lovely:
— Monteverde's 'Orfeo', Purcell's 'Dido and Aeneas', Pergolesi's 'La Serva
Padrona', Mozart's 'Schauspieldirektor' (with—this is a dead secret—the theatrical
manager and the comic actor made up respectively as Beecham and Baylis!!)
and Gluck's 'Orfeo'. No 'transition-period' or 19th Century music—It deserves
a rest. There will be a concert of Bach's orchestral Suites and Concertos, and
several concerts of modern music, both chamber and orchestral, at which I should
like to do as much of you as is practicable with the limited orchestral resources
at our disposal. The 'First Cuckoo', 'Summer Night' and 'Winter Landscape'
will all sound lovely. But I wish you could write a new work for small orchestra,

for those three pieces are not enough. While we have a chance of giving good works, and only good works, we ought to give plenty of them and alas, there are so few. (I used to disagree with your judgment of the modern French school of composers, but I have at last perceived its essential shallowness. How right you have always been!) *Do* write some more pieces for small orchestra this winter: it would be so lovely to do them. I have always longed to conduct your work, and now at last an opportunity presents itself. I hope I shall be able to do it something like justice; it has certainly meant more to me than any other music (or art of any kind) and I would like so much to convey to others a little of what it has given to me.

If you can think of any other works we might do, please tell me. No modern French (except Ladmirault[61] who is a Celt) or Russian, no 'British' music except two little pieces by Grainger and a quartet by Goossens: but heaps of the splendid old English madrigals (which, by the way, were intended for 12 or 14 voices and not for the large, unwieldy choirs by which one always hears them sung), old English virginal music, etc—and some Rameau, Aliessandro Scarlatti and other early people. But the operatic side of the scheme is really the most important. (If one could only slay the fetish of 'grandeur' in connection with opera, one would remove half the difficulties in connection with it in one stroke.) I do hope you will approve, and let us do the 'Village Romeo'—The question of performing fees can be arranged with the Board of Trade here. I don't think it would be practicable to 'reduce' the score for small orchestra; but if you can let me have the full score, I will make a very full arrangement for two pianos which will, I think, give quite a satisfactory version of the music. I wish we could have a big orchestra, but it is impossible, firstly on account of the smallness of the theatre we require, and secondly because we have not *unlimited* funds— though, I am glad to say, we have more than enough to meet all expenses even if there are no returns. I see your Quartet is announced for a first performance on November 17th.[62] Are you coming over? I *do* hope so: it seems ages since I last saw you—it is, in fact, nearly a whole year. How I wish I could visit you at Grez again! But I suppose it is still almost impossible to travel in France except on military business.

Do come over next month: I long to talk to you again: there is so much to tell you.

Much love to you both from yours ever most affectionately
Philip Heseltine

[61] Paul Ladmirault (1877–1944), French composer whose music Heseltine enthusiastically championed and who held Heseltine's compositions in high regard.
[62] Aeolian Hall, London by the London String Quartet (leader, Albert Sammons). This was the original three-movement version.

P.S. Have you, by any chance, got a copy of Schönberg's 'Pierrot Lunaire' you could lend me? It was published by Universal Edition just before the war, and I am most anxious to see it.

Gray bids me add that if you have any recent Schönberg full scores that you want to dispose of, he would be very glad to buy them from you.

153

Frederick Delius to Philip Heseltine

GREZ-SUR-LOING
Seine et Marne
15 Oct 1916

My dear Phil—

I was so glad to receive your news; not having heard from you for so long I was beginning to think you had been 'conscripted.' Your enthusiasm is always so refreshing—Now to your idea of regenerating music in England, especially the musical drama—I entirely agree that realism on the stage is nonsense & that all the scenery necessary is an 'impressionistic' painted curtain at the back with the fewest accesories possible—Even furniture ought mostly to be painted—but one requires a real artist to have thoroughly understood the Drama & then to paint the scene after his own conception. In Germany this has been already tried with success   The Village Romeo was performed like this for the first time & the scenic part was a great success: The theatre was awful & no music could be heard in it—The orchestra therefore—*the chief thing*—dropped into the 3rd plane. They gave the Fair quite simply with a painted curtain—it cannot be left out as it is so important—& the walk thro' the fields & woods to the 'Paradise Garden' would have no contrast. I entirely agree with all your ideas about the music drama—they are also mine & all my works are written in this spirit. I have not much hope for English music or music Drama in the near future for the following reasons—the English have very little imagination & therefore are very hard to appeal to—I have experienced the press & public acclaiming Electra as one of the greatest masterpieces of the world—a work which has already died a natural death—which it deserved—& the Village Romeo was declared undramatic. It is one of the most dramatic & emotional works ever written & in years to come will be constantly played everywhere—Beecham's production was from a scenic point of view perfectly mediocre & insufficient—He used old Covent

Garden scenery—now a scene out of the Gotterdämmerung again one out of some other opera. The singers were nearly all bad & insufficient & none of them could act. I know no English singer who can act or who is capable or willing to show any emotion on the stage & mind, dear Phil, this is going to be one of your great stumbling blocks—the English are an unemotional race & wallow only in the worst & most obvious sentimentality. I quite agree that the Village R ought to be given in a small theatre but there must be an orchestra of at least 60. The piano Idea does not smile to me—My orchestra is too all important & almost the whole action on the stage is indicated in the Orchestra—To tell you the truth I have no desire to have any more of my dramatic works given in England for some years—*There is no public*— mark my words—Even if there were—I dont think that anything ought to be undertaken before the war is over & the people have calmed down a bit. In itself the idea is excellent & your friend Gray unique with his enthusiasm to pay for such a highly artistic under-taking—*Wait a bit*—prepare—gather works—look out for singers & teach them to act & then open up in a small theatre a highly artistic & original repertoire —you may form gradually a public—but dont open before March 1918. I believe in the english youth under 25 or 30. After this age he is hopeless. The war will have changed much—people will have suffered—many will have realized the *rot*—that has been going on—the hollowness of patriotism & jingoism & all the other isms—Politicians & diplomats & experts of all kinds have been making & continue to make such fools of themselves that the wiser folk will, perhaps, look for a little truth in art & the artists—& perhaps find some satis-faction in that rare event—*A really artistic & emotional performance*. I should like to come over for the quartet—but everything is so difficult—It takes 10 days or more to get your passport in order & the journey across the channel is dangerous—I should just love to talk with you about all these things & help you if I am able—At the beginning of a London Season 1915 I went to see 'Deidre of the Sorrows' by that remarkable writer Synge[63]—It was an artistic affair—a good ensemble & a remarkable play—The theatre was not half full —quite a small theatre. Nobody cares!—The Russian ballet, because it was new —sensational, very artistic & tremendously boomed—& fashionable, drew full houses—otherwise only a low style of entertainment succeeds in London— Barker no doubt endeavoured to do something—but did he succeed? could he exist? & then it was not music drama. You see you must be able to keep at it, in order to form a public—one season is not enough—it must be followed up by another season equally good & for this purpose you only ought to begin such an undertaking at a favorable moment—Why not begin by a series of concerts

---

[63] John Millington Synge (1871–1909), Irish poetic dramatist.

in a small hall with a small orchestra—giving only rare & excellent works—
Some of which you have named. The Mimo drama you sketched for me would
only have an effect with 3 great artists—Which at present do not exist in England & It might turn out simply ridiculous   Nijinski,[64] Karsavina[65] & Fokine[66]
might do it—I have written another Elizabethan Song. 'It was a lover & his
Lass' from 12th night—I am writing a Violin Concerto now—When you start
your Scheme you must absolutely make it a success or it will again fizzle
into nothing like all artistic attempts in London—including Beecham's & that
makes the public more & more sceptical—Practise conducting—if possible, take
an engagement at any theatre simply to get a little routine—even if you have
to conduct musical comedy—What you write of Van Dieren interests me
exceedingly—cannot you send me something? Can I not help him in some way?
Does he want a publisher? I am going to publish with Schirmer now. Is Van
Dieren a dutchman? Write soon again   We both send you our love

your affectionate friend
Frederick Delius

154
Philip Heseltine to Frederick Delius

2 Anhalt Studios
Battersea, S.W.   October 28th 1916.

My dear Delius
    I am afraid your pessimism is, in the main, justified, with regard to this coun-
try and music. But I think one must definitely fight it, by flinging good things
in the face of the public, and not be scared off by any number of defeats.
    Gray is determined to give a season in the Spring at all costs, and we are
counting very much on the 'Village Romeo', as it is absolutely the only modern work which exemplifies the theories of music-drama we want to propagate.
    It is no good waiting, I am sure, for this reason: at the present moment, there
is a great deal of interest in music which lacks direction and purpose, in this
country. There is a large body waiting to be led in any direction anyone is strong

---

[64] Vaslav Fomich Nijinsky (1889–1950), Russian dancer and choreographer.
[65] Tamara Platonovna Karsavina (1885–1978), Russian-British dancer and ballet-mistress. She joined the Diaghilev
Company in 1909.
[66] Mikhail Mikhailovich Fokine (1880–1940), Russian dancer and choreographer.

enough to point out to them. The public is now in a plastic state (not, of course, the herd, but the few who really care) and can be moulded into what shape one wills; there has never been such an opportunity; music has never been—and I hope never will be again—in such a condition of utter stagnation. But it will soon begin to move again, and it is surely better to make one's effort to direct its course before others begin to move it in an opposite direction!

For the 'Village Romeo' performances, our orchestra could be increased to 45, arranged thus:—

2 Flutes	4 Horns	6 First Violins
2 Oboes	2 Trumpets	5 Second Violins
1 English Horn	1 Timpani	4 Violas
2 Clarinets	1 Percussion	4 Cellos
1 Bass Clarinet	1 Harp	2 Double Basses
2 Bassoons	3 Trombones	
1 Contrabassoon	Tuba	

The two piano idea, was of course absurd; but I fear one cannot possibly increase the orchestra any further. I have borrowed a full score of the work from Chester's, and I do not think the music would lose so much as one might expect from the reduction in the number of instruments. One will have to be very careful in order to preserve a balance between strings and wind—and the Fair Scene still presents a problem which seems insoluble (but see below): yet, in spite of these real drawbacks, I feel we could catch more of the essential spirit of the work by our methods than any production save the most lavish, expensive and, in every sense, artistic that even Germany could offer.

As regards singers, I think we could get Eveline Mathews and Robert Maitland[67] for Vrenchen and the Fiddler. For the other parts I have in mind Arthur Jordan (Sali) Mostyn Bell (Marti), David Evans (Manz) [by the way, who was the Manchester baritone who did 'Sea-Drift' so well? He would, I should imagine, be excellent for this part] Marguerite Nielka (the Slim Girl) and Bertram Binyon (Hornist).

Since writing the above I have looked through the Fair Scene carefully and decided that it could really be done quite effectively with the means at our disposal. Now *do* please think over the matter: if only you would come over for the Quartet performance, we could discuss it and I am sure I could convince you, and even make you enthusiastic over our plans for the performance.

We have secured an admirable stage manager, and a special feature will be made of the lighting, which will be, as far as possible, diffused from *above* the stage.

[67] The baritone Robert Maitland had played the role of the Dark Fiddler in Beecham's 1910 production of *A Village Romeo and Juliet*.

The work *must* be done; it is too wonderfully lovely to be allowed to remain in quasi-oblivion for the next ten years—and if Beecham revives it, he will do it far more harm than good.

We are only doing five works, which must all be, of course, first rate; and I want ever so much to include this which is, for me, the most perfect music-drama in existence. Besides, if you withdraw it, it cannot possibly be replaced by anything—it is unique: there is absolutely nothing till one gets down to the level of 'Pelleas et Melisande'—a big drop indeed!!

Please forgive a rather breathless letter—I am fearfully busy with the preliminary preparations for the opera already—selecting and engaging singers, and all the other thousand and one things one has to do at such times. I will continue this in a day or two (it has already been broken off once)—but, best of all, do you make it unnecessary, and come over—London is lovely at this time of the year.

Ever yours affectionately
Philip Heseltine

155
Frederick Delius to Philip Heseltine

GREZ-SUR-LOING
Seine et Marne
Nov 6th 1916

My dear Phil,

I want to lay before you, very precisely, my point of view with regard to artistic &, especially, operatic enterprise in England—I am so fond of you & admire your whole attitude so much that I wish you to thoroughly understand my attitude towards artistic undertakings in England—I know of no artistic(tic) musical dramatic undertaking that has *ever come off* in England. The great success of the Russian Ballet was, firstly, it was boomed by a fashionable clique —2[ndly] no Englishman had anything whatever to do with it—bar financing— It came to London entirely ready to ring up the curtain. Every other enterprise has been a failure & often a miserable failure—Where there has been enthusiasm amongst the promoters there has been amateurism & inexperience & inefficiency which has just as thoroughly ruined the whole affair—Electra came to London from Berlin—with singers scenery & stage managers—a finished work.

The attempt to mount the Village Romeo with English singers, Chorus & stage manager was a miserable failure—inefficiency & inexperience bursting out from every crack—The only good point was the splendid english Orchestra & Beecham conducting. Beecham however knew nothing about the stage & how the singers ought to behave & therefore the whole was a failure—Now here you come & want to mount the Village Romeo once more & under worse auspices —Firstly—an inadequate orchestra   2nd singers who are an unknown quantity I know of *no English* singer who can act—& certainly of no 2 singers who could act Sali & Vrenchen—Especially thro the love scenes—A love scene between 2 English singers is a farce which only one who know what a love scene ought to be can appreciate—The English singer is by far too self possessed, he & she is afraid to show emotion & especially passion—you should have only seen Mr Hyde—Sali & Ruth Vincent[68]—Vrenchen—kissing each other!! & when at the end in the great love scene on the Hay boat they ought to possess each other whilst the boat gradually sinks they were both reclining gracefully side by side on the hay—as if they were out for a boating tour on the Thames at Maidenhead—Mr Hyde pulling a left hand oar—you tell me Mr Gray, you & Mr Van Dieren will entirely control the music & dramatic direction—Tell me which of you 3 has any experience whatever?—Every gesture of the actors in my work must be controlled & ordered by the Conductor—for my music is conceived in that spirit—Only thus can the whole be made comprehensible to the public—an old actor stage manager will be no good whatever—for he will make the singers act from the stage & not from the music—Dont you see, dear Phil, that you are all going towards disaster with the best intentions possible & that is what seems to me so hopeless in our own country—With no experience whatever you are going to undertake one [of] the most difficult of tasks & you want to begin at once with one of the most difficult works—Why at least dont you give the 'Village Romeo' in your 2nd season—It is the Dardanelles—& Mesopotamia over again—I again advise you to begin in quite a small way— in order to gain experience—. The Russian ballet did this—it began in a barn in the slums of Petrograd with old cast off costumes & gradually acquired the wonderful perfection which we have all admired—Tell Gray he has the oppor- tunity of doing quite a *unique thing* & it would be a terrible mistake to spoil the whole affair by a too ambitious opening—Feel your way & whilst you are so doing you will gradually be acquiring valuable experience—My whole heart goes out towards your undertaking & for this reason I write as I have done— It would be better & less harmful for the future of art in England not to begin

---

[68] Ruth Vincent (1878–1955), English soprano. During the 1910–11 Covent Garden season she sang leading roles with the Beecham Opera Company.

this undertaking than to do it badly & fail—there have been *too many* such failures in England & already the public only really believe in what comes from
abroad—[69]

your affectionate friend
Frederick Delius

156
Philip Heseltine to Frederick Delius

2 Anhalt Studios
Battersea, S.W.   November 27th 1916.

My dear Delius—

I entirely agree with all your strictures about English singers, but I do not
think there is sufficient ground for an a priori argument against any attempt
one may make to improve them. The idea of the régisseur-conductor having
the whole production in his own hands is entirely new to this country: English singers are still under the impression that, so great is their individuality,
that any manager will be glad of the assistance of their own ideas. They have
never yet been properly subordinated to the ensemble. The conductor and the
producer must control, in collaboration, every gesture just as much as every
inflexion of the voice. And so long as one has sufficiently definite ideas about
the rendering of the work, the singers can learn the interpretation just as well
as they can learn the mere words and notes of their part—provided, that is, that
one catches them young enough.

I have suggested to Gray that the 'Village Romeo' might be prepared and put
into rehearsal, and then you could come and decide whether the production
was good enough for public performance. But, of course, if you would rather
we did not touch the work, we will leave it altogether; although its omission
will immeasurably lessen the interest of our repertoire. There are *no* modern
works for the stage whatsoever. Ravel, Dukas, Stravinsky and C°—they are
all triflers, technicians, dry bones round which the next generation may con-
struct flesh and blood: but, oh God, when one considers 'modern music' in the
abstract . . . !

---

[69] The scheme was eventually abandoned and Gray's trustees insisted that it be postponed until after the war.

Now I fear I have some bad news for you—though you may have had a little of it administered already in a sugar-coated pill from someone else.

The performance of your String Quartet last Friday week would have confirmed your darkest doubts as to the musical understanding of English players. It is, of course, always difficult to speak of the rendering of a work with which one is not already familiar. But I think I probably understand your work well enough to be able at any time to perceive the real you peeping out from the adumbrations of unintelligent performers.

To begin without any reference to the actual music, the first movement, headed 'with animation' was accorded a monotonous, spiritless, rhythmless performance, about as far removed from animation as any performance could be —while in the lovely 'Late Swallows' section, nothing was audible except the persistant four-note figure which is quite obviously a background. One heard snatches of beautiful melody for a second or two from the other instruments, and then everything was blurred again. The whole rendering resembled nothing so much as an unintelligent pianola-performance where, by reason of the mechanism, every note comes out with equal strength and only the top part is really heard! It was horrible to hear such beautiful music smothered—for I know there was great beauty there. As far as I could appraise the work itself, I thought it really finer than the Double Concerto—There is a wonderful remoteness about the first two movements—a rather wistful yet tranquil retrospect of things long, very long past—and all through the work you seem to be very aloof, almost a disembodied spirit contemplating itself. Is this a very false and fantastic interpretation—or has the performance blinded even me to the music's meaning?

In any case, I hope you will very speedily come over and give the L.S.Q. party a little sound advice before they give any more unintelligible renderings of your work.

I hope, perhaps, we may be able to give a performance of it during our season.

Plans are maturing and various people are becoming interested and enthusiastic—Bernard Shaw, for one, has already helped us very considerably. The theatre is the problem: the only suitable one, as regards size, is the Kingsway and that is occupied with 'Révue'!

The theatre in London is in an almost more filthy condition than music— the only performances one can see at all are the Shakespearean shows at the 'Old Vic'—which is an antiquated old place in a slum on the south of the river, near Waterloo. And these, although there is no attempt to break away from the 19th century traditional style, are in their own way quite admirable. Last week I saw a really moving presentation of 'Richard the Second', and during the next month 'A Comedy of Errors' and 'The Two Gentlemen of Verona' will be presented.

Do send me a copy of your new Shakespeare song[70] if you have one.

Ever yours affectionately
Philip Heseltine

---

[70] 'It was a lover and his lass' (1916).

1917

THE beginning of 1917 saw Delius still hard at work and by the end of January he returned to the sketches of *Eventyr*. Most of the winter was, in fact, spent at Grez though there were one or two excursions to Paris, including a brief sojourn with the Clews. In late June, however, Delius's health took an unexpected turn for the worse and, almost unable to walk, he visited a spa in Normandy in July. His condition soon showed signs of improvement and, by the end of the month, he was walking once again. In August he and Jelka holidayed in Brittany and by the end of 1917 his health was considerably better. But the weather in December was excruciatingly cold and this, coupled with Delius's precarious state of health and the ever-present uncertainties presented by the war, made the Deliuses now consider the possibility of relocating in England for a while.

Heseltine and Cecil Gray, now caught under the spell of van Dieren's music, decided to organize a concert of his works in the Wigmore Hall on 20 February. It proved, however, to be a disastrous occasion and was loudly condemned by all the London music critics. In early April Heseltine decided to return to Cornwall with the intention of escaping from London and rewriting his first sketches of the proposed book on Delius. Outwardly he and Lawrence resumed cordial, if cool, relations, though at the time he was unaware that he and Puma were being included as two rather unpleasant characters in *Women in Love*, the novel which Lawrence was then writing. By June Heseltine was temporarily back in London once again trying to promote van Dieren's music. His stay there was, however, brief and within a month he suddenly returned to Cornwall. Heseltine's anxieties about military conscription had now become a reality and, ignoring a summons to appear for yet another medical examination, he and Puma fled to Ireland in August.

157
Frederick Delius to Philip Heseltine

GREZ-SUR-LOING
Seine et Marne
10 Feb 1917

My dear Phil—

I have been very busy on a new orchestral work[1] & therefore postponed answering your letter until now. You can understand, I am sure, my timidity & scepticism vis a vis your new undertaking—I have had such a lot of disappointments in that direction & do not want the Village Romeo to be given again except under the very best & most favorable auspices. You see, you, yourself recognise that the regisseur conductor is absolutely necessary—I only know of 2 in Europe & none in England—Where are you going to find the conductor with the artistic instinct & the necessary experience of the drama & stage? I have seen many conductors at work & have noticed how helpless they are before the stage & the singers: they feel, themselves, their inabillity to suggest or shew the right gesture or expression & therefore leave them alone or leave it to the old actor regisseur who is lurking on every opera stage with his old clichés— Write me all about how the scheme is progressing & how far you are—Bernard Shaw can, of course, be of great help—but only from a dramatic standpoint— Musically he is a nul—Mozart & Strauss are his musicians quite naturally also —the two clever ones—the facile composers—without any emotion—In fact just like Shaw himself—At all events Shaw is the clearest thinker in England & independent & courageous & can be of immense use to you & I love his humor & sarcasm—I had to smile at your description of the string quartet performance —I have always had my doubts about S [Albert Sammons] as a musician—you were very keen on him in London at the time my Sonata was being played— What you say about the quartet is quite right—The figure which you noticed so persistently is marked—ppp sotto voce   The melody & harmony ought to be heard most. However all my works have been very difficult to accoucher— My Violin Concerto is quite finished   The weather here has been heavenly for the last month—Hard frost up to 22° Centigrade & Sun—not a cloud—I have been working wonderfully & taking long walks—I have no desire to be on the

---

[1] *Eventyr*. Jelka had written to Marie Clews in January: 'Fred is writing a wonderful new Orchestra-piece and hard at work.' Jelka to Marie Clews, 20 Jan. 1917, Carley, *Letters*, ii. 176.

sea just now especially since the submarine campaign 'in extremis' has been threatened—My Violin Sonata is not yet out—Isn't it incredible—I have not yet received the proofs—How will you get young singers! now that every man is enlisted? your affectionate

Frederick Delius

158
Philip Heseltine to Frederick Delius

Trewey Down
Newmill
Penzance—Cornwall.   Sunday—May 13th [1917]

My dear friend—This horrid silence of mine must have seemed very strange to you, all these months. Forgive me—The fact is—unpleasant though it be to have to admit it—at the beginning of March I found myself on the verge of utter collapse, physically and mentally. Material and psychological difficulties combined with other things to produce a kind of climax, a decisive point at which it became imperative to break right away from old paths and choose a new direction—or rather, to pull oneself out of the mud and regain the path one had slipped away from.[2] The English capital, which our countrymen like to call the hub of the universe, is really a great cesspool—more especially where any kind of art is concerned: if one lives in it continuously for a year or so, one sinks deeper and deeper into the mire until one reaches such a pitch of blasphemy that one begins positively to enjoy one's wallowing. Then comes a horrible moment when the truth of one's position rises up against one—and then there's nothing to be done except to clear out of all the muck, or else sell one's soul to Satan for ever and a day! There seems to be a fatality about our generation—I mean the generation born at the tail-end of the old century: those of us who are not killed off sur le champ de bataille are marked down for a big dose of death and

---

[2] He wrote similarly to Viva Smith on the same day: 'I left London in early March, on the verge of a complete collapse—Various forces, seen and unseen, material and psychological, combined with circumstances to bring about a crisis—(a spiritual crisis, not dependant on *facts*)—that there was no evading. There are moments when one has either to admit defeat and turn back on oneself, or else go forward into the dark, seeking a new path—in other words one must die completely in the old self, in the sure and certain hope of resurrection. And so, just in time, I managed to get out of the mud which had almost swallowed me up, *just* managed to evade the whirlpool of sheer madness which had almost sucked me down—and then came here.' Heseltine to Viva Smith, 13 May 1917, BL 58127.

corruption in an other than material form. In ten years time the survivors amongst us will be as rare as first-folio Shakespeares! However, providence is kind to some of us, in letting us have our dole of death in the form of an inoculation, with the 'sure and certain hope of resurrection'[3] to follow. The whole of the past year has been a nightmare for me—chiefly through my own imbecility—but it has also been a good cautionary experience. But now—in this wonderful country—this wild end of England which is not England at all—I feel a real regeneration, I feel the Spring in me as well as around me: this is a real new beginning—but only a beginning. You were quite right—though I hardly appreciated the truth of your words at the time—when you wrote last winter that we—Gray and I—were as yet unripe for a big enterprise. I have now thoroughly understood how immature, how really *uneducated* one is—in every sense of the word—and, most important of all, how necessary it is to *be*, fully, before attempting to *do*. For one can only create out of the fullness of being—of this I am sure: it is no good building on the patterns of the past—which is all that the musicians of the present day are doing—not one of them has any real individual *being*. You have always been so very right in your estimate of them: and now I know what patience you must have exercised in tolerating my absurdly exaggerated and ill-founded opinion of the value of present-day artists! Really, when I consider what myself and my opinions have been during the last four years I am quite overcome with shame and confusion. You have been so good and so tolerant, and all the while so right!

The collapse of the opera season, through the withdrawal of the promised funds owing to 'war economy' was a very bitter disappointment. But the scheme was a good one in outline and no harm will be done by allowing time to mature its details. And, really, there are so few operas that are worth performing at all! When one tries to think out a reasonable artistic basis for the musical drama, one finds that no works yet exist which can possibly be said to conform to its canons—except, perhaps, a few very old works which do so by accident—and the 'Village Romeo'. The spectacle of Beecham lavishing his hundreds of thousands on performing 'Louise'[4] and 'Cavalleria'[5] up and down the country makes one despair of arousing any interest in serious musical art for the next fifty years. This, forsooth, is 'pioneering work'—'breaking new ground'! 'The public owes an immense debt of gratitude to Sir Thomas', we read almost daily in the newspapers. For what? Not for introducing the works of Frederick Delius into England—oh, dear no, they've forgotten all about that by now. But rather for providing shows which combine in one theatre what Herbert Tree[6] and Carl

[3] *Book of Common Prayer*, Burial of the Dead.   [4] An opera by Gustave Charpentier.
[5] *Cavalleria Rusticana*, opera by Pietro Mascagni.
[6] Sir Herbert Beerbohm Tree (1853–1917), one of the most successful actor-managers of his time.

Rosa[7] in their respective spheres have been doing for the last twenty years and more. And just think of what *might* have been done for a tithe of what has been spent on these ridiculous marionette-exhibitions! Even if Beecham gave us Wagner and Mozart every night, he would be achieving far less and spending far more than if he were to build a model of the Fortune playhouse and give us Shakespeare and Ben Jonson, Webster[8] and Marlowe,[9] Dekker[10] and Heywood[11] and a host of other dramatists of an age of whose riches the English public is still totally unaware. It is so ridiculous to specialize in matters of art—to give people opera, which is one of the least developed and most imperfect of all art-forms before they are even superficially acquainted with a *dramatic* form which once reached a state of perfection rarely attained by any of the arts. I hate this modern differentiation—this rigid separation of one art from another, of form from form and medium from medium. If only people would begin to think about the function and nature of art, apart from its various manifestations, there would be some hope of finding a little real understanding and appreciation in the place of senseless jesting and complacent ignorance.

We gave an orchestral concert of van Dieren's works late in February—and this only served to show us the utter futility and hopelessness of presenting any new art to the English public without first wrapping it up in the sugar-coating of the past—or, perhaps, of the present, which is much more dead than the past.[12] Van Dieren, of course, is not an end in himself: he is only the first adventurer in a new country which will be tilled by others. But compared with his contemporaries—the little Ravels and Stravinskys, and oh, what sickening swarms of them there are!—he is a giant and a prophet. The comparative, relative, 'good-*considering*' method of appraising a composer is, I know, a bad one, but for the present generation of 'music-lovers' (!!) one has to adopt it. I won't even enter into the details of the pitiful press-controversy that took place over van Dieren. It may amuse you to read some of it when you come over to England. Our programme-commentary, in which we pointed out very plainly the utterly foul condition into which music has sunk during the last two decades really aroused as much wrath as the music itself! But it was good to stir up the foully complacent cesspool of musical London for once in a way: and it was very good to give all the newspaper-men an opportunity of eclipsing even their own pro-verbial imbecility . . . But enough of music, for the time being. We must discuss these topics when we meet: that will be much better. Also, the little book about

[7] Carl Rosa (1842–89) who founded the touring Carl Rosa Opera Company in 1875.
[8] John Webster (*c*.1578–*c*.1632), English dramatist.   [9] Christopher Marlowe (1564–93), English dramatist.
[10] Thomas Dekker (?1570–1632), English dramatist.   [11] John Heywood (?1497–?1580), English dramatist.
[12] Two of van Dieren's works (*Overture* and *Diaphony*) were played at this disastrous concert in the Wigmore Hall on 20 Feb. 1917. Heseltine's sensational advance publicity and Gray's controversial programme notes succeeded in antagonizing the London music critics, who to a man condemned van Dieren's music.

your works which I partially wrote last year, I am re-writing (since a great deal of it was very crude and stupid) and expanding into an examination of the condition of music in general at the present day. I hope to have it quite ready by the autumn—and it will be mostly done before you come over in the summer. Do come soon. I have not as yet been troubled again by the military but one never knows what may happen from day to day. You must come and stay down here: the country is quite marvellous. My little cottage is on one of the highest points of the moor on the little neck of land that runs down to the Land's End—midway between the two seas, north and south, and one can see them both from the cottage, since they are only seven miles apart at this point. For miles around there is nothing but wide, solitary moorland, with little grey stone farms dotted about here and there. My cottage stands quite alone, half a mile away from the nearest farm. The effect of living in wide open spaces is quite miraculous; I feel a new being! From Zennor hill, two miles away, you can see 70 miles of the north coast, from Trevose Head to the Scilly Isles, which gleam in the distance like some impossible Hy-Brasîl! To the south there's the long length of the Lizard Head, and St Michael's Mount, and inland, mile upon mile of rugged, open country. The hills are not very high, but they rise from the sea with steep, rock-strewn slopes: on many of them are to be found marvellous Druidic remains—huge boulders piled up—God knows how!—one on another, immense cromlechs and 'logan stones' of enormous size, poised so that they rock at a finger's touch! The cliffs on the coast are marvellous too, very high and sinister, of black granite—but the sea, at this time of year, is calm and of a quite Mediterraneany blue. The other day I saw a lovely seal gambolling about in a deep pool! And there are birds innumerable—all day long a chorus of larks rings out over the moor, and cuckoos call and answer one another from far and near, all with different pitch and different intervals—sometimes one hears two at once, in harmony:—

cuckoo!

cuckoo!

(I actually heard that one day!)

Gray has taken a big, lonely house about three miles away in a very wild spot, almost on the cliffs.[13] He is going to live there permanently and is mov-

---

[13] Gray himself wrote: '. . . I was entranced by the magical beauty of Cornwall. My house at Bosigran Castle, near Gurnard's Head, stood on the highest summit of the chain of cliffs that stretches unbroken between St Ives and Land's End, facing out over the Atlantic with no land between it and the New World.' C. Gray, *Musical Chairs* (London, 1948), 115.

ing all his belongings from London. We are keeping on the London studio between us, but I shall also stay on in this part of the world as long as I can. So you *must* come over and stay with us—there will be heaps of room for both of you—and even if Gray and I are swept away, there will still be the house and, I hope by then, a housekeeper, waiting for you. So *do* come very soon— there is already a foretaste of summer in the air. Much love to both of you.

Ever y^{rs} most affectionately
Philip

I am longing to see your latest works—the Requiem, the new orchestral work,[14] etc. Do bring them with you.

159
Frederick Delius to Philip Heseltine

GREZ-SUR-LOING
Seine et Marne
May 27/ 17

My dear Phil—

I was so glad to receive your letter & learn that you are still in the land of the living—We have been in Grez all the winter & I have done a lot of work —It is a great thing to be able to isolate ones self completely: altho' not very practical—I was relieved to hear that your opera scheme is still 'in petto'[15]— the idea is excellent & perhaps when the war is over I shall come over & join you & Gray in trying to present something really artistically excellent to the English public—It is no good whatever coming with anything half mature & imperfect—But to attain perfection one wants a lot of experience & must work hard & a long time in training entirely new young artists who have not already been spoiled by the old 'clichés'. Why do you not attach yourself to some theatre—as orchestra conductor? so that you may attain some experience of the 'métier'? It does not matter much what you conduct. Or go into a theatre & help to mount a play & see how things are done—I mean the B.B.C. The weakness of the whole English nation is 'amateurism' & inefficiency & old methods—The race has crystallised—Look how they are running the war!—

---

[14] *Eventyr* (Once upon a time).   [15] A private intention, undisclosed.

they never seem to wake up to realities & altho' the world is out for killing
at any price—they are shouting for 'fair play' & 'keep the rules'   They cannot
adapt themselves to new circumstances—Even less than here—altho it is bad
enough & crystallised enough here—As you know I believe in 'Individualism'
to the utmost—I dont believe in Committees or societies of people—One man
is always stronger than 2 or 4. & as the number increases *he* becomes weaker—
Our whole epoch suffers from socialism & collectivism & all the other 'isms'
weakening of course—*The Man*—the war is diddling along like this because there
is no *man*. The nations now would hale with enthusiasm *a man. a genius* & he
would be able to remould the world—Our rotten epoch of false Christianity &
altruism has failed to breed a 10th part of a man—It has only bred a *politician*—
Don't think that the public is any more rotten now than it ever has been—It
was always rotten & there never has been an artistic epoch—they will follow
the genius always—only—the rotters have blinded them for the real thing &
they only realise the genius when he is no more. The chief thing is for you to
develope your own personality to its utmost. Never mind if you make mistakes
—We have all made the most stupendous blunders—But keep your soul intact
—By soul I mean your real bed rock self—that what you really are & not the
trimmings or the adopted. Because a thing is new it is not necessarily good or
bad—Dont be misled by 'jargons' & 'mannerisms'. There is really only one quality for great music & that is 'emotion'—Look with what ease hundreds of young
composers are quietly expressing themselves in the so-called 'new idiom'. Otherwise the wrong note system—Hundreds of painters are seeing in Cubes—But
it all means nothing more than a fashion—& merely intellectual when at its
best.[16] You must be living in a lovely spot   I should love to come & stay with
you—but how to get across the channel dry! Your description of the country
in Cornwall tempts me mightily—I should just delight in such scenery. I have
always loved the far, wide, distance—When I come over I shall bring my new
works with me. A cello Sonata—Violin Concerto—'Requiem' Dance Rhapsody
no II My new ballad 'Once upon a time' for orchestra & two small a capella
choruses To be sung on a summer night on the water—which I am dedicating
to the Oriona Society (Kennedy Scott)   They have no words—Our garden is

---

[16] Delius had made some interesting observations to Grainger in 1915. It would seem from Heseltine's later writing about intellect and inspiration that he was somewhat influenced by Delius's views on the subject: '*My firm belief
is* that when the Intellect outweighs the Instinct in all art—*especially music* 'then the trouble begins'   As long as the
instinct has the upper hand everything sounds *right & rare*. That is why the discords of primitive savage music sound
so strange & wonderful—& right & as soon as the intellect gets hold of the idea and *systematises* it—it *sounds wrong
& is wrong* & is not rare—since it runs around like the measles & one finds every Tom, Dick, Harry & Louisa doing
it—& especially every little Jew musician who sees his opportunity in the new fad or the rising stocks & shares of art
in other words—I admit that one man can come along & see everything in Cubes—He may have something the matter with the lense of his eyes, but I dont admit that several thousand at once see everything in Cubes—otherwise than
thro their intellect which has less to do with art than one likes to think.' Delius to Grainger, 26 Sept. 1915, Melbourne,
Grainger Museum.

lovely & we shall have lots of fruit—Are you going to keep your cottage on? For we should both love to visit you there if we can get across—It takes 10 days to get a pass & you have to have some very good excuse for going—I am very much interested in your book on me & am looking forward to reading—Have you got the pianoforte score of the 'Magic Fountain'—I think I lent it to you— Dont send it however. Keep it until we meet. We both send you our love & hope to meet you soon—

Ever your affectionate—
Frederick Delius

I have rewritten my string quartet & added a scherzo—I heard it in Paris— there was a little too much double stopping—I think it is now good—

1918

THE beginning of 1918 did not bode well for Delius. By the end of January he was in a Paris sanatorium for the treatment of a nervous condition, though he was able to return to Grez by the end of March. Feeling much better, he resumed writing once again. The summer was spent at Biarritz (where they arrived on 5 June), where Delius was able to relax in the baths and in the sea. He also carried on with his composing. The only blot on the year was the fact that French soldiers had been billeted in the house at Grez and had left it in a disgraceful condition as well as stealing some of its contents. The Deliuses thus decided to move to London where they first stayed in Henry Wood's house in St John's Wood for September and then moved the next month to a furnished apartment in Belsize Park. Even though Wood had performed the first *Dance Rhapsody* at a Promenade concert in September, there was little in London that proved cheering. They would, however, remain there until the middle of the following year.

Early in 1918 Heseltine spent almost two months on a desolate island off the west coast of Ireland where he proceeded to study the Irish language. By April he was back in Dublin where he met the poet W. B. Yeats and began planning a lecture which he was to give in the Abbey Theatre on 12 May. It was entitled 'What Music Is' and was illustrated with folk-song, piano solos, and duets. During his time in Dublin he gradually became involved in a circle of occult practice, particularly in the field of automatic writing, which possibly had an effect on his creative genius. Letters written to his friends at this stage tell much of his ideas on composing and inspiration presumably formulated from these occult experiences. He also pursued his interest in early music in the library of Trinity College, Dublin. In August he was suddenly inspired to compose ten songs in a fortnight, among which are some of his finest compositions—the songs that made him, in fact. Messages allegedly received from supernatural sources convinced him that van Dieren was dying and in August he returned to London. Angry with the publisher Winthrop Rogers for having rejected some of van Dieren's piano pieces, he submitted his newly composed songs to Rogers under the pseudonym Peter Warlock. Much to his delight and amusement they were accepted for publication. He also spent some more time studying early music in the British Museum.

160
Philip Heseltine to Frederick Delius

May 15th 1918.

My dear friend—

You will have thought this long years' silence very strange—some day I will explain it altogether. At present I can only tell you that I have passed through a year of dark and critical vicissitudes, metamorphoses of various kinds, follies and their consequences, from which I am only now fully extricating myself—and something, perhaps shame of my own stupidity, has kept me from writing to you about these things—for you are never long out of my thoughts and I have time and again begun a letter to you and continued it at great length only to destroy it. But for years my letters to you have been too full of petty personal complaints—for all the world as though you were some old father-confessor priest in an ecclesiastical rabbit-hutch! Now however the skies are clearer, and I am no longer tempted to dilate upon the mere circumstances that have lately hedged me round—after all, one is always *free* the moment one ceases to *imagine* one's difficulties! . . . .

I suppose, in view of the rigidity of the censorship, it is still necessary to act upon the old Greek adage ΕΥΦΗΜΕΙΤΕ which, though literally meaning only 'Speak words of good omen' resulted in enjoining complete silence, owing to the immense difficulty of complying with it! Nowadays one never knows what innocently-intended remark may not get one's letter consigned to the official waste-paper basket and one's name to the official black list!—so it will be best perhaps to stick to music altogether in this correspondance.

In your last letter—almost exactly a year ago—I remember you detailed a long list of new compositions—and I envied, as I do still, the tranquillity of mind that enabled you to work on steadily amid the turmoil of the world, producing even more prolifically than in the old days of calm and quiet. How I long to know these new works! I have neither heard nor seen any work of yours since the String Quartet was raped by that lecherous party of players in London—the Cello Sonata, Violin Concerto, Dance Rhapsody, 'Once upon a Time', the Requiem and the wordless choruses—all these will be new to me. And I suppose there's no chance of my seeing them for some time to come. I feel that I shall like 'Once upon a Time' best—the title sets one dreaming, and all your loveliest music comes from the once-upon-a-time mood, I think! I have not been in London for nearly a year, and have heard no music whatsoever

—a great blessing, when one considers the utter poverty of nearly all the music one hears to-day. Most modern art is what Blake called 'A pretence of Art to destroy Art'—for where there is *no*, art the great man, when he comes, will be reverenced: it is only where there is abundance of *bad* art that he is despised and rejected.[1] For this reason I mistrust all this frenzied awakening of so-called artistic interests in the world at present: the first principles of art have been lost sight of, and the herd is fantastically chasing something of whose very nature it is entirely ignorant. . . . I have not written much music during the past year— a few small works which are, I know, immeasurably better than the very paltry productions I have sent you from time to time—but I am still only in a very experimental stage, and do not expect to do anything of any real significance for another seven years. If I cannot come forward before the world with something I *know* to be better than anything of any of my contemporaries, I will not come forward at all—and, good heavens, one has'nt much to eclipse, anyway! At present there's only Bernard Van Dieren who can even share the name of Composer with you: Béla Bartok has done some very fine small works (tho' you wouldn't think so to judge from those fearful Roumanian Dances!),[2] but I have seen nothing of his that is less than ten years old. I hope the war has left him unscathed—he might become a very great man. But who else is there? Goossens has gone to Hell, intoxicated with professional success, Schönberg still shows a cold, white light, but he will never escape from the toils of his self-imposed originality—I cannot think of a single name that does not seem to belong to a barrel-organ-grinder or his performing monkey rather than to a composer. Van Dieren, however, is a man of miraculous genius for whose music my love and enthusiasm grows by what it feeds on.[3] It would be well worth your while to journey to England only to see this wonderful man and his works: he is still so ill that it seems impossible to predict whether he will live another year or another day. He has long passed the stage at which a normal man would have died—and this baffles the doctors: his will to live is all that he has to rely on, and he is working feverishly day and night whenever he has strength enough to hold a pen . . . .

It is wonderful how much more clearly one can think about music when one is right away from it than one possibly can do when in the whirl of a concert-season. I have done a great deal of work at the philosophy and history of music while I have been in this country. The wilderness is the best place for meditation—and I have spent a considerable time in the most desolate and solitary region of the West coast. I believe it is so necessary to be sure of one's

---

[1] cf. Isai. 53: 2.   [2] *6 Rumanian Folk Dances* for piano (1915), transcribed for orchestra in 1917.
[3] A repeat of an earlier misquote from *Hamlet*. See letter of 17 Jan. 1912.

first general principles before proceeding to formulate any ideas about particular examples in art that I have spent most of my time lately in attacking the most comprehensive question of all, in music—namely *What Music is*—in all its aspects: and I really feel I have arrived at results which—at any rate as a beginning of new discoveries—are of some value. Last Sunday evening I made my first public appearance and gave a lecture at the Abbey Theatre, taking simply 'What Music is' as my title. It was certainly of a startling and revolutionary nature, but it was listened to with attention and even enthusiasm by an audience of nearly five hundred, which was encouraging for a first attempt.[4]

Well, I must end this rambling epistle. Do write to me all about yourself when you feel inclined: I have missed your letters all this while, and I shall look forward to them the more eagerly after so long a silence.

Very much love to you both, and all good wishes from Φ.

74 Lower Leeson Street, Dublin

161
Frederick Delius to Philip Heseltine

Grez-sur-Loing
(S & M)
May 19th [1918]

My dear Phil—

I need not say how welcome your letter was: I was beginning to have serious misgivings about you & was splitting my brains to imagine what could be the matter! It would interest me enormously to hear all about your experiences & troubles; as I can assure you that there is no one who takes such an interest in

---

[4] On 12 May Heseltine delivered this illustrated lecture at Dublin's famous Abbey Theatre. During the three-quarters of an hour lecture there was much youthful criticism of the music profession, as well as an attempt to expose what was wrong in current musical life—providing all the answers. The theatre was practically filled, and dramatic, coloured lighting effects were used throughout—the auditorium itself being in complete darkness. The musical illustrations consisted of a group of piano duets by Paul Ladmirault, three piano pieces by Bartók, and four arrangements of Dutch melodies by van Dieren played by Heseltine himself. Two singers, an Irish-speaking one and an Indian, sang some traditional songs, Heseltine hoping thus to demonstrate what he believed to be a striking similarity. The Indian singer was evidently superb and a great success, the Irishwoman nervous and not so good, but the comparison had proved interesting. The discussion at the end of the lecture, which Heseltine had hoped would be controversial, 'fizzled out' poorly: 'There was no indignation—only a few fatuous and harmless questions. I think and hope that the "intellectuals" (who are more hopelessly clique-y and static here than in England even) were hurt and insulted by various remarks in the lecture.' Heseltine to Taylor, 14 May 1918, BL 54197.

you or is as fond of you as I am. So you have been in the wilderness—a wonderful place—& the only place to find oneself after a prolonged sojourn in Towns
—one gathers such a lot of dross that it ultimately smothers one's real self. I
was also in the Wilderness in Florida & have since never been able to live long
in a crowd. I was immensely glad to hear that you are writing music & also
that you had lectured in Dublin—What you say about art is so true—where
there is no art whatever, there is a chance for an original artist & none where
there are crowds of mediocre thrusters—This general interest in Art is deadly—
Example America. In England it is no really so bad as there is *very little* interest in Art—But the 'Cenach' & artistic cliques flourish—the Villon Societies &
Rabelais Societies & Brahms Societies & Beethoven Societies etc, etc—What
you say of Van Dieren interests me enormously—Cannot you send me something? I should love to help a man of such genius, if it were possible[5]—I heard
the other day in Paris a young lady, Miss Deacon, speak about him—she met
him at the sculptor Epsteins. What a misfortune to be so ill—poor fellow. You
know my opinion on Contemporary music. For me 'music' is very simple—it
is the expression of a poetic & emotional nature—Most musicians by the time
they are able to express themselves manage to get rid of most of their poetry
& all their emotion—The dross of Technic has killed it or they seize upon one
little original streak & it forthwith develops into an intolerable mannerism
—Debussy & Ravel[6]—I am seriously thinking of going to New York in the
autumn to have my new works produced & then go to California until the war
is finished. Will you come with me?—seriously—You might lecture on Music
—you will find a better public than in London—I want also the 'Requiem' produced—I dont think I have ever done better than this—I have dedicated it
to 'all the young artists fallen in the War'   Do write soon & tell me all your
troubles & dont keep your friend again so long without news—We both send
you our love

ever yours affectionately
Frederick Delius

On back of envelope, in Heseltine's handwriting: 'We are the vagrants of the world
and need no ceremony to be friends (Po Chü-i)'

    [5] Heseltine told Gray: '[Delius] is very interested in the Maestro and keen to help him in every way possible: he
will of course visit him in London.' Heseltine to Gray, 19 July 1918, BL 57794.
    [6] Delius had written in similar terms to C. W. Orr the year before: 'You see "cleverness" counts for very little in
my opinion—the french composers are all far too clever   when young your technique ought to develope with your
ideas—Debussy wrote his best things before 30 & got gradually more superficial & uninteresting—The same with
Ravel who is even cleverer than Debussy but even more flimsy & superficial—But their chief idea is to startle & be
brilliant . . . But without Debussy Ravel would not exist.' Delius to Orr, 10 Apr. 1917, Carley, *Letters*, ii. 178–9.

162
Philip Heseltine to Frederick Delius

June 19th 1918.

My dear friend—It was a very great joy to me to receive a letter from you again: there is nothing in the world I prize so much as your sympathy and interest and kind thoughts for me—without the help of which, I need hardly repeat, I should never have emerged as far as I have out of the Cimmerian darkness which for most of our race constitutes Life! How gladly would I confide everything about myself to you if we could but meet again for a short while! But these personal difficulties, these psychological complexities are so difficult to set down on paper with any degree of coherence and intelligibility: and although I think I may thank heaven that I have at last managed to extricate myself from the particular network of complications to which I referred, I am still too near to the old circumstances to be able to write about them with that complete detachment which alone could frame them into a consistent narrative. And, as I said in my last letter, I think it is better to confine oneself in one's correspondence at present to matters musical—or at least to things remote from the filthiness of the world at large. I should dearly love to come with you to America—indeed, were it possible for me to do so, there is nothing that would be at once more delightful and beneficial also to me than to make this trip, but alas, I fear it would be impossible for me to obtain a passport despite the fact that I am completely useless for any military purposes. The atmosphere of these islands becomes more and more stifling and putrescent to anyone who cares for art above all things. To get away altogether, to be with you, to be able to hear and study your new works and to be able to carry on my own work, writing and lecturing, in surroundings which gave it a chance of having some influence—this would indeed be joy and a new impulse of life to me. Oh, what a curse has fallen on the world—and when will it be removed? . . . .

Now about van Dieren. It is very good and kind of you to offer to help him and I do think that, with your influence and reputation, a word of praise from you would work wonders with publishers and conductors in America—and elsewhere too. You, at any rate, could not fail to recognize the transcendant genius of the man—and I can assure you that your appreciation of his work would in itself more than outweigh all the misunderstandings and bitter calumnies to which it has given rise in other quarters. I cannot write of van Dieren or his work without what may seem to you—unacquainted as yet with either—a certain amount of enthusiastic exaggeration. However, I feel less inclined to tone down my words when I reflect on all the stupid and spiteful and ignorant and altogether disgusting things that have been said of him by his enemies. It is not that one resents hostile criticism—far from it: indeed one respects it when it is pointed and well-informed. But the kind of hatred that van Dieren arouses among musicians (and I think you too have had some experience of this kind) is chiefly prompted by the realization, which not even the most obtuse of them can escape, that here is a man who does not belong to their level at all, one who neither in his person nor in his work has ever had anything to do with what one may call their trade-union—in short, an *individual*, the traditional enemy of all herds: and contemporary music, such as it is, is purely a matter of herds and cliques—look at the modern Frenchmen, Debussy, Ravel, Roussel,[7] Séverac[8] and a score of others without any individuation whatever, a regular little mutual-admiration-society: and in England the same thing is repeated, even more feebly. Van Dieren's music is indeed that bunch of fine grapes which the fox could'nt reach!—and, good Lord, what a stinking lot of foxes the world of music contains! It is the musical profession that is always the greatest enemy of music—chiefly because, in listening to music, they cannot view it as pure utterance, pure expression: they regard as real the purely verbal, and so—in cases of true expression—non-existant, differentiation between the thing expressed and the mode of expression: with the result that instead of giving their attention to *what* is being expressed, they concentrate always upon the manner—the '*how*' —and thus is perpetuated the dismal superstition that technique, as a separate entity, exists as a thing apart from expression. It is this fallacy that lies at the root of all the rottenness of modern music. It is responsible for the prevailing view of music as mere sound-for-sound's-sake—a kind of aural counterpart of sweet scents: and it is to this fallacy also that one must attribute the fact that certain sounds have come to be regarded as 'beautiful' and 'ugly' *in themselves*, quite without reference to their context or to what they are used to express: and so we have arrived—so far as the musical trades-unions are concerned—at a kind of static musical diction which one may fitly compare with the formal 'poetic diction' of the eighteenth century—a tyranny which was only destroyed after a long and bitter struggle by Wordsworth, Coleridge, Keats and the rest. To us of to-day it seems incredible that the general appreciation of these poets was impeded by an obstacle of so ludicrous a nature. But it has always been so—in poetry, in music, in painting: almost every great manifestation in art has had to be forced upon the public, like a disagreeable medicine, against their will—I say 'their' will, but what will of their own have they? They have surrendered it long ago to the hypnotic influence of the 'recognized profession' . . . .

---

[7] Albert Roussel (1869–1937), French composer.
[8] Joseph Marie Déodat de Sévérac (1873–1921), French composer.

Some weeks ago a string quartet was collected in London for the purpose of reading through van Dieren's string quartet and three songs with quartet accompaniment, at van Dieren's house. Of this performance the composer—whose sense of humour long illness and suffering has in no way impaired, as you will see— wrote me such an inimitable account that I must copy it for you in his own words, not only for its own intrinsic comedy, but also because in the graphic and penetrating portrayal of this one scene, you have a perfect epitome of the way in which new works of art are invariably received in England—if they are at all above the 'art-level' of the herd . . .[9]

Extract from van Dieren's narrative:— . . . . 'M[r] Murray Davey[10] had been invited to sing the part. He turned up but apparently did not understand that he was expected to sing (he was not invited for his all-round intelligence)! He was rather drunk and talked more than the whole company together. When I asked him to sing, he started off on a long story about his opinions concerning my music which apparently begins always quite beautifully but then goes off into most incomprehensible chaos so that M[r] M. D. cannot do anything but take his head in his hands and shake it in despair. As if this were not enough he gratuitously made loud criticisms after each piece played—the Villon music[11] for instance was much too dissonant and far too sad—the Baudelaire[12] was entirely out of harmony with the spirit of the poem (I discovered since that this gent has composed the work himself for string quartet, piano and Murray Davey!) and so on. I did not reciprocate his somewhat misconceived position as a guest on false pretentions by abusing mine as host, and therefore politely ignored as much of his effusions as I could and slightly argued some points in the most academic manner. He then made use of a short interval to address every one of the musicians and ask for support or otherwise. Beckwith and Jeremy of course had to admit that they too did not understand a note of it all (oh yes, so simple one cannot be, but . . .): the ladies of course had great opinions of me and Goossens performed again his special miracle of agreeing with everybody and disagreeing with everybody's opponents. That this and other judgments were considered ones was amply proved by the following monologue delivered, after the musicians had departed, to the stupefied ladies, during my momentary absence, by this hirsute bass and faithfully recorded by my better half[13] . . . .

M[r] M. D. "*of Covent Garden and the Grand Opera Paris and London Concerts etc etc*" (very drunk and highly conscious of his irresistible charms) rambles

[9] Heseltine wrote a similar account to Taylor on 13 June 1918.

[10] Murray Davey was an English bass who had sung both at Covent Garden and the Paris Opera.

[11] Ballade, *Dame du ciel, regente terrienne*, for voice and string quartet, words by François Villon (1917).

[12] Recueillement, *Sois sage, ô ma Doleur*, for voice and string quartet, words by Charles Baudelaire (1917).

[13] Van Dieren's wife, Frida.

off:— "First I thought, on reading it through, que cette song était most beautiful, but comme je désirai to sing it and as I savais not play it sur le piano
I took it to my friend Poldowsky—Lady Dean Paul you know! Now she is a
composer elle même and she knows *everything* about modern harmonies, pour
être sur, she writes them herself. She played it through and moi, je listened
avec attention. When it was over nous nous regardons et je say: 'Irene, what
do *you* think of it?' and she answered, 'Murray, I don't understand', and moi,
je reponds 'Irene, neither do I'—'*But*', she said: '*Murray let us try it again!*'
(most magnanimous! [note of victim]) and she played it again and I said:
'Irene, I am just as far as I was' and she answered 'Murray, so am I'—and
mesdames je vous jure que nous avons, un whole afternoon, essayé de jouer
et comprendre this music and neither Lady Dean Paul—Poldowsky—*a modern composer herself you know!*—nor I—M. D. of C. G. and the G.O.P. and
L.C. etc etc—could make anything of it, and nous avions to give it up dans
parfait despair. The fact is that these harmonies . . . . etc . . . . etc . . . . etc".
Here the maestro enters and offers M. D. of the etc etc a sixpenny cigar . . . .
In the meantime I had had the consolation of listening to Eugène Goossens
J^{nr} who, on the stairs and at the front door—without witnesses!!—paid me
the warmest and vaguest compliments accompanied by his silent gestures of
a somewhat enigmatical character and his marvellous mimicry of significant
looks into a hypothetical distance. Also he asked me to dispose of him at any
time for similar performances. They have however not yet taken place . . . .'
                    (Here the narrative breaks off into other matters.)

I think, as a matter of fact, that this incomparable pair of composers, Murray
and Irene, really made a more honest attempt to understand the music than
most of their English colleagues would have been capable of: but see how, with
the best *will* in the world and the best intentions, they are both quite stultified
by the self-satisfied thought that they, of course, 'know *everything* about modern
harmonies, peu être sur', and that what they *don't* know isn't worth knowing
and is consequently all wrong—as though there were a morality of 'right' and
'wrong' in music, as though there were a fixed and *known* standard of judgment, as though all truly-*created* art were not, by its very nature, essentially of
the *Un*known! It was not in any such spirit that the oracles of ancient Greece
were received! This obsession with technique, with the mere surface of music,
not only obscures the vital significance of the music but causes the work to appear
only as a conglomeration of parts without the *unity* which is an essential of all
great art—and realization of which is essential to all true *understanding* of art.
Suppose one were to take a work of yours and, stopping at every note, one
should make a vertical analysis of every chord—what frightful complexity, what

chaos, what mathematical puzzles would appear to this microscopic view—this dissection which would blind one not only to the spirit of the music but even to the proportions of what one may call its body! There is no more real complexity—in a creative sense—in the mental act of thinking a progression of chords than in thinking a succession of single notes: you would not stop to analyze the chords any more than you would think of the mathematical vibratory relations between the notes of a melody. And in the case of van Dieren, it is for him as simple and as spontaneous an act to think a combination of melodic lines as to think a single melody—though a horizontal analysis of his work would reveal the same complexity and chaos as the other microscopic view. There is an utterance of Mozart somewhere to the effect that on occasions he conceived *instantaneously*, in a flash of vision, a whole symphony in all its parts and proportions and detail, in a flash of vision that seemed to transcend all sense of time. After such conception, the composition of the work would be only a matter of *unrolling* the vision (so to speak) into terms of time. I have frequently come across similar remarks that point to this same amazing clarity of initial conception—and I should be very interested to know whether you ever experience anything of the kind. I think this kind of evidence of the *inner* processes of creation—as distinct from the outer methods which are classed as technique—is extremely valuable to the psychology of music—as psychology is the only *science* by which any essential part of music can be elucidated. I think van Dieren has at times these 'conceptions-in-a-*mathematical-point*-of-time'—if you can understand that rather clumsy phrase. I remember seeing on his desk one day a small sheet of paper on which were a few small pencil jottings of notes: and I was astonished and somewhat incredulous when he told me that the whole work to which they referred (the second string quartet—a long work in four movements which would occupy 3/4 hour in performance) was *already composed* in all its detail—that this paper contained all the preliminary sketches that were necessary and that it only remained to write out the work in full score. I think I can understand now the literal truth of this astonishing statement—though I am if anything *more* astonished than ever at the possibility of such miraculous clarity of conception. The evidence of the later works themselves certainly corroborates this view of their creation. There is a certainty, an inevitability, an unalterableness about them which I think could hardly fail to strike even an unsympathetic listener. They have too a strength of construction that seems to have resulted not so much from a conscious process of thought as from an inherent architecture of the mind which quite unconsciously moulds and forms every thought and every idea that passes through the mind. I do not mean to imply that the creation of music is a merely mental process—far from it—but inasmuch as the creative impulse or intuition makes use of the mind in expressing itself, so the very logic and structure of the mind itself infallibly impresses itself upon the utterance. . . . It is at least an ironical circumstance, and one that tragically lights up the absolutely fundamental errors of contemporary judgments, that music conceived so clearly and precisely that it can be written down by the composer in his bed, straight into a fair copy score, as though he were actually copying from a mental score, should be considered 'abstruse' and 'laboured' and 'calculated' by soi-disant composers who must needs sit and sweat and travail at the piano for hours before they can squeeze a single bar of music out of themselves! They would do well to ponder the words of Flaubert[14]—a 'technician' indeed to those who prefer to concentrate on matters of technique—who wrote:— 'Si votre conception est faible, jamais vous n'écrirez d'une façon forte—le style n'est qu'une manière de penser' and 'Si vous saviez précisément ce que vous voulez dire, vous le diriez bien'. . . .

I am having a copy made of the full score of van Dieren's symphony for soli, chorus and orchestra, based on Chinese poems[15]—his biggest and hitherto, I think, his finest work, of which a good performance would have an absolutely overwhelming emotional effect. Alas, that its composer will, I fear, not live to hear it. It is a work full of that poignant, reflective emotion which the Chinese poets knew so well how to express and which by the very reticence of their expression seems to gain in intensity and sharpness till it becomes almost unbearable. This is the most profoundly moving music that I have known since the 'Songs of Sunset', which I think it might very appropriately companion in a concert-programme. The score shall be sent to you as soon as it is ready: it will give you a fairly complete view of van Dieren's work, and you would be rendering him a very great service if you would take it with you to America. I am so anxious for you to become acquainted with this music for I am sure you have only to know it in order to love it and to realize, as alas so few, so very few will realize till many years after his death, that in van Dieren has appeared one of the greatest composers of all time. I hope too that he will be still alive when you come to England again—but his life hangs by a thread which the mere relaxation of his almost superhuman power of will would snap at any time. There is absolutely no hope of his recovery—indeed he has long passed the stage at which death would have occurred in an ordinary person. The length of his days now depends entirely upon this amazing power of will and his desire to leave as much work behind him as he can.

I cannot but feel that the fact of his music having been to me and to one other (Cecil Gray)—and as yet to us alone—so great a revelation and so deep

[14] Gustave Flaubert (1821–80), French novelist.

[15] Symphony [No. 1] for five solo voices, chorus, and orchestra, based on Chinese poems translated into German by Hans Bethge.

a source of joy and beauty, lays upon us both an obligation, which is at the same time a privilege, to exert ourselves as much as possible on his behalf, in mere common gratitude, while he yet lives—for there is no one else to whom he could entrust the care of his works after his death.—But for our chance meeting with him two years ago, he would never have heard any of his works performed, and he would probably have died without a word of appreciation or sympathy from anyone. And we, after all, can do so little for him—without money, without influence, and the condition of the world being what it is: I become exasperated at my own impotence in this direction, and it is heart-breaking to see whatever small efforts one *can* make to spread the knowledge of music that, to oneself, is so full of profound and vital significance, met with apathy and misunderstanding and bewilderment, if not with actual hostility, on *every* side. . . . I hope I hav'nt bored you by writing so much about this man and his work, but I feel so strongly the necessity for action on his behalf —since there is no one else to help him in any way—and you are one of the very, very few who could really understand and appreciate him—more than I do myself, maybe.

Well, I had better bring this long scroll to an end now. I should very dearly love too see the Requiem and your other new works—more especially as I am absolutely starved of music at present: but I suppose it is no good suggesting the sending of any of them through the post—though I believe the mail ser-vices are now as safe as anything, thanks to the convoys of destroyers and aero-planes that accompany every boat. Still, if you feel inclined to send anything I need hardly say what tremendous joy it would give me—it seems, and indeed it *is*, years since I heard anything of yours. And I should greatly like to do any transcriptions or piano scores or other arrangements of them that you may want. How I wish we could meet again and talk! I have so much, ever so much to tell you and discuss with you, so much that, try as I will, *will* not come out in a mere letter.

My love and all good wishes to you both.

Ever yours affectionately
Philip Heseltine

28 Upper Fitzwilliam Street
Dublin.

P.S. I wish you would write me, sometime when you feel inclined, some account of those inner processes of creation, to which I have referred, as they appear to you. As you know I have been working a great deal lately to try and arrive at a more clear idea of the psychology of composition[16]—we know all about the secondary processes of mere technique, but the primary stages—which are purely internal—are still wrapped in obscurity. Your words on the subject would give me the most valuable help since you would speak from real experience while I who am not a composer at all can only make surmises based on my examination and understanding of the works of others.

163
Frederick Delius to Philip Heseltine

4 Rue Gardague
Biarritz
(Basses Pyrenees)
[3 July 1918]

My dear Phil—

Your long & interesting letter was sent on to me here where we have been since June 5th.[17] Our house has been commandeered & is full of officers—Grez is now in the War Zone. After spending a few weeks here we shall probably go to London—All what you wrote me of Van Dieren makes me wish to get there as quick as possible—So that he, himself, may make me acquainted with his music & that I may yet be able to help him. I will certainly do all in my power both in England & America for this unfortunate genius—God help a genius without money & influence anywhere, but most of all in England—I again got a whiff of the London musical atmosphere on reading Van Dieren's description of the 'Audition' at his own house—almost the same scene has been enacted by myself in bygone years—I know, also, what it is to pass, for years, as a sort of musical idiot & be patronised by 4th class musicians & dilettants interested in young modern composers—You ask me about the mental processes of my own work. I dont believe in the possibility of conceiving an entire work in all its details instantaniously—Especially one in several movements—I, myself, am entirely

---

[16] For some time Heseltine had been fascinated by the process of composition and the respective roles of technical skill and inspiration. In his letters to Gray and Taylor he constantly reiterates his belief that mere technical equipment is not enough—the composer is the vessel into which a higher force pours the finished product—that is, provided the recipient is open to this flow. As he summed it up: '. . . all art that is of any real value, must be the *overflow*, and not merely the *fullness*, of life. Music is the voice of the God in man.' Heseltine to Taylor, 31 Oct. 1917, BL 54197.

[17] Heseltine wrote to Cecil Gray: 'A letter from Delius arrived this morning. Grez having passed into the war-zone, his home has been commandeered for the use of the soldiery, and he is at present in the south—address, 4 Rue Gardague, Biarritz, Basses-Pyrenées.' Heseltine to Gray, 19 July 1918, BL 57794. Gray later wrote of his impressions of Delius and his music in his autobiography *Musical Chairs*.

at a loss to explain how I compose—I know only that at first I conceive a work suddenly—thro' a feeling—the work appears to me instantaniously as a whole, but as a feeling—The working out of the whole work in detail is then easy as long as I have the feeling—the emotion—it becomes difficult as the emotion becomes less keen; sometimes I am obliged to put the work aside for months— sometimes years—& take it up again, having almost, or entirely, forgotten it, in order to bring back my first feeling. You see the two most conventional people in Europe are the English & the French because they have the oldest culture— Italians, of course, have simply lived off Rome—until the Renaissance—& have been paralysed ever since—The french have never got over the eighteenth cen- tury in many forms of art—& look at their architecture today—An old race seems to have greater difficulty in inventing new things or adapting themselves to new conditions. You see an individual or genius is always dangerous—The bourgeois feels it instinctively—He feels that an individual is going to alter his tastes & habits—& the individual does alter them—that is why the new has such a lot of enemies, especially in old countries—America is a better coun- try for a genius than either France or England or Italy—In America they have no very old preconceived ideas & welcome something new even if they dont understand it—It, at least, amuses them—They dont get angry & abuse you. England had music, before Handel came over & gave them the Oratorio—this formed their taste for generations. Then came Beethoven, & Mendelsohn—& then Wagner came along & had a devil of a time,—then he formed their taste. In the meantime England had been turning out—Sterndal Bennets[18]—Fields[19], Stanfords, Barnbys,[20] Mackenzies[21] & Elgars—Not one of whom has any very real personality & all based on one of the greater composers from abroad—France the same—& Beethoven is to this day the most popular composer in France— The french are quicker witted, however, & cleverer than we are—Debussy came along & formed a precieux school—He himself by far the most gifted of the lot—But not profound or capable of any great developement & so he fizzled out, into a manneristic composer & chef d'ecole   The head of a clique of clever musicians who have nothing to say or very little—but try to impress one by very suggestive & picturesque titles—Debussy the most gifted encountered also the most opposition—In England we have again the french equivalents—always very much weaker & slower—You know who I mean—the Scotts etc—The people here in Biarritz are a terrible crowd of nouveaux riches—& as soon as I have finished my briscous baths we shall clear out—Women in short dresses &

[18] Sir William Sterndale Bennet[t] (1816–73), English composer, pianist, and teacher.
[19] John Field (1782–1837), Irish composer.
[20] Sir Joseph Barnby (1838–96), English composer, conductor, and organist.
[21] Sir Alexander Mackenzie (1847–1935), Scottish composer, violinist, conductor, and teacher. Principal of Royal Academy of Music, 1888–1924.

silk stockings, very much powdered & rouged walking in 3ˢ & 4ˢ with 1 immaculately dressed man along the esplanade—Where have the intellectuals hidden themselves? They seem to have disappeared until the end of the war—I am thirsting for music & shall endeavour to have all my new works given this winter—How long shall you stay in Ireland? cannot we meet in London? I should love to have long talks with you & hear about all your experiences since we last met. I could also shew you my new works—I am looking forward to Van Dieren's Symphonie, & can assure you that when I believe in anything I am capable of putting forward considerable energy & persuasive powers—Especially when it is someone elses work—Write me at once, whether we shall meet in London—I will write you again as soon as we have decided when we shall go. This is the noisiest & loudest place in the world—I am trying to work & thro' the open window I hear a blanchisseuse singing at the top of her voice—a parrot is shouting Go away & Papa—& a trumpet is playing variations on Gounod's Faust.

 With love from us both—ever your affectionate
 Fr. Delius

On back of envelope, in Heseltine's handwriting, signed 'Talisman. Φ Kernow / 2/8/18':

164
Frederick Delius to Philip Heseltine

4 Rue Gardague
Biarritz (Basses Pyrenees)
[13 July 1918]

Dear Phil—As we intend going to Cornwall after a week in London please let me know where you where when you wrote me from there to Grez. It sounded so beautiful. Where is Gray? I should love the far & wide outlook & cliffs, moors

& sea—Perhaps you will join me there. I am just finishing my new work—The 'Poem of Life & Love' for Orchestra—

Ever affectionately
Frederick Delius

Do not fail to send me Van Dieren's address.

Postcard.

165
Philip Heseltine to Frederick Delius

[Dublin]
22/7/1918.

My dear friend—You could not find a more wonderful district anywhere in England than the little corner of Cornwall I wrote to you about. There is real inspiration in the place—something more than the ordinary joy one feels in wild and beautiful surroundings. Nature seems more alive there—it is as though the air were full of joyous spirits. This particular tract of country is quite different even from the rest of Cornwall. It is a kind of peninsular, and includes the coast-line from St Ives on the north coast, round the Land's End to Penzance on the south. The peninsular is only seven miles across from sea to sea: where my cottage stood, on the moors, you could see both seas, north and south. Gray is still living in the house I found for him, between the cliffs and the sea. I am sure he would be greatly delighted if you went and stayed with him. I have written to him about your visit and asked him to communicate with you direct.[22] There is plenty of room in his house, and you could not find a more enchanting spot to stay in. But I don't know much about his domestic arrangements: a while ago he had to get rid of his housekeeper and he may not yet have secured another. However, this difficulty might be overcome by the temporary importation of one from London. You would find life very simple and primitive there, and you

---

[22] Heseltine wrote to Gray: 'In a few days [Delius] proposes coming over to England, and he asks about you and wants to know whether last year's invitation to the house on the cliffs is still open. In any case, he will go down to Cornwall for a while, after spending a week in London. I hope you will re-invite him to Bosigran: you will love him. If you have no servant, a temporary one might be imported. But please write direct to Delius as soon as possible.' Heseltine to Gray, 19 July 1918, BL 57794.

might be very uncomfortable, but the surroundings would compensate you for a great deal! I hope this visit will be possible: I am very fond of Gray—he is a remarkable and gifted person who is developing very slowly and is forced, for lack of congenial companionship, into an almost unbroken solitude which I think is not wholly good for him—I mean that he has too much of it, and really needs more sympathetic understanding and guidance. You would be a godsend to him at the present moment. His address is Bosigran, Pendeen, Cornwall. The village I stayed in was called Zennor. There is a good inn[23] there but it is very small and would certainly be occupied during August and September. If you don't stay with Gray, go to the Land's End Hotel—a magnificent place that stands right on the edge of the last cliff of England. You would be very comfortable there. To reach it, you take the train to Penzance and proceed by motor-bus: for Bosigran, too, the station is Penzance. I can thoroughly recommend the Land's End Hotel; but you should spend some time at Bosigran too, for in many ways the country is even finer there than at Land's End. I have never in my life been so fascinated by any country as by this bit of Cornwall: in retrospect it seems a veritable paradise. Nothing would give me greater joy than to join you there and go for long walks with you over the moors: but it is absolutely impossible —for reasons van Dieren will explain to you. Alas! it torments me to think how lovely it would be, and what miserable things prevent one from realizing this dream! . . . Van Dieren lives at 35A Sr George's Road, Abbey Road, West Hampstead, N.W.6. You get there by the bus to Kilburn station. I am so very glad you are coming over soon so that you will be able to meet him, for I fear he cannot live very much longer. He is a dear and wonderful man, a fascinating personality—you will delight in him as much as in his music. I am myself copying the full score of the Symphony on Chinese lyrics for you: I have sent the first half of it to Balfour Gardiner in Wales,[24] as there seems to be some chance that he might sandwich it, in his forthcoming private orchestral concert, between the masterpieces of Austin and von Holst!—not the whole symphony, of course, but a short interlude out of it. I have not much hope that Gardiner will do this from motives of genuine appreciation—his tastes are curiously limited—but he may be moved thereto by a certain feeling of curiosity![25] I have had a great controversy with him lately over the British composers—quite uselessly, since all his ideas are absolutely fixed and rigid, and he persistently

---

[23] The Tinner's Arms.

[24] Heseltine wrote to Gray: 'Some days ago I despatched my copy of the first half of the Chinese Symphony (full score) to Balfour Gardiner, as it seems possible that his curiosity may prompt him to squeeze the Interlude into his forthcoming private orchestral concert, between the eclipsing masterpieces of Arnold Bax and Gustav von Holst. I have lately expended a great deal of ink and energy on H. B. G. but to little purpose. He is a very singular bird and it is highly diverting to make him flap his wings—but, as I say, of little actual use.' Heseltine to Gray, 19 July 1918, BL 57794.

[25] Gardiner wrote bluntly to Heseltine about the *Chinese* Symphony: 'On my first two attempts to read van Dieren's Symphony, I suffered acute mental distress. . . . he uses combinations that I cannot imagine I shall ever bring myself to tolerate.' Gardiner to Heseltine 12 Aug. 1918, photocopy in PWS Archives.

misrepresents nearly everything one says, and flies into the hugest rages over points that he has himself imagined into one's remarks! A singular bird indeed, especially when a-flapping of his wings!! But a very dear person too . . . . I feel that you will be a real deus ex machina for van Dieren in England: it is very good to think that at last he will be comforted by a little recognition—he has waited so long for it and so patiently, never seeking it for himself. It is terrible to think of the possibility—the extreme probability, I am afraid—of his dying without even hearing many of his works . . . .

As for myself, I cannot tell whether we shall meet in England or not: but I think you know me well enough to understand that it will not be through lack of effort on my part if we do not. You can imagine how hungry I am for a long long talk with you after three long years. But there are considerable difficulties in the way of travelling and, quite literally, if I were to set out with the strongest will in the world to see you, I might still never reach my destination. It exasperates and maddens me that one's life is circumscribed with so many petty and idiotic restrictions in these evil times. For ten years now all my best strength and energy has been dissipated by the mere effort required, in these islands, to keep the flood of national bilge-water from surging in upon me and engulfing me completely: and when one bungs up one hole, it begins at once pouring in from another quite unexpected quarter. Just now, when I am bursting with fresh schemes and enthusiasms after my long sojourn in the wilderness (for artistically the whole of this island is a wilderness), there is no outlet for them or for any activity on my part. However, you may be sure that if it is anywhere within the bounds of physical possibility I shall come and see you at all costs: and I am longing for a sight of your new works too—there are so many now that I know nothing of. The past three years have been a real nightmare to me—not perhaps unbroken by flashes of light which, added together, do no doubt mean real progress, yet for their very brilliance the general gloom has only seemed afterwards to deepen and grow more intense. I have sunk to the very lowest depths, stuck fast in the mire and only lately realized, when on the very point of being wholly submerged, the supreme necessity of getting out of it even if I left my own skin behind—of throwing over the whole wretched past at all costs: and this, thank heaven, I think I have now succeeded in doing once and for all, though perhaps the costs are not all paid yet. Still, I believe in Destiny: one *does* what one *does* because one *is* what one *is*—and it is often necessary for the general plan of one's existence that one should have the most apparently absurd and profitless experiences. I have long ceased to imagine that anything one does has any connection with praise or blame, intrinsically, save in the minds of fools. You may hear all kinds of unpleasant things about me in England—but I know you are too good a friend to listen to these things before you have heard the whole truth from myself—for nobody else knows the whole truth: I have my sojourn in the wilderness to thank for the impulse that finally extricated me from the morass—and no two experiences in the wilderness are the same . . . How one grumbles and moans over circumstances and yet how little they really matter! After such a little while one is roaring with laughter over things that one formerly wept about. If only one has the courage to make no compromises and to be ready at any moment to chuck anything and everything that becomes a nuisance overboard—then not much harm can happen to one. And it is surprising, after a little practise at clearing the decks, what strength and dexterity one acquires in the art of throwing overboard one's lumber—people, things, ideas, superstitions, fears, fetishes—the whole cargo: lastly perhaps the old creaking ship itself! Then one develops wings! But enough of this: and by the powers of Kether, Chokmah, Binah, Gedulah, Geburah, Tiphereth, Netzach, Hod, Jesod and Malkuth,[26] I swear that it will not be my fault if we are not talking face to face, if not pacing the moors together, before many weeks have passed . . . .

Let me know at once when you come to England and where you stay.

Au revoir, my dear friend. Much love to you both.

Yours ever affectionately
Phil

This is a wretched letter—I shall write again soon about many things that at present I feel too confused to touch upon. I *must*, by hook or by crook, somehow manage to come to America with you and bring off that lecture tour. One might begin, even in England, if only the accursed politicians would cease pissing upon each other—for that is what the war has come to now, when you reduce the situation to its lowest terms!

166
Frederick Delius to Philip Heseltine

[Grez-sur-Loing
August 1918]

Dear Phil. your letter just received—We shall be in London between the 25th & 30 inst. We are packing up in Grez—arrived 2 days ago. What you write about poor Van D & the eminent English composer is really too funny. It is

[26] Heseltine is here referring to the main work of Kabbalah (the developed forms of Jewish mysticism and theosophy), the *Sefer ha-Zohar* (Book of Splendour) which appeared in the 1280s. The names referred to are the ten Sefirot, aspects of the higher soul, the divine life overflowing into the entire creation.

difficult from such a slight piece to say much—But one certainly cannot talk of Harmonic faults—For modern musicians that is rather tame to say the least of it—the piece is simple & childlike—as you say 'a reminiscence of childhood' One or 2 little harmonic turns reveal individuality & taste—The melodic line is as clear as cristal—Address in London 4 Elsworthy R^d NW. I have hired [Henry] Wood's house for a month

ever affectionately
Fr. D.

Postcard.

167
Philip Heseltine to Frederick Delius

[Ireland]
Wednesday August 28th 1918.

My dear friend

I wonder whether you have arrived in London yet? I am getting ever so impatient to see you and I would certainly have crossed over already but for the fact that there are, as I told you before, considerable difficulties in my way.

At present I am living in a state of the utmost anxiety. Ten days ago I had a most alarming letter from van Dieren: he has lately become much worse and I greatly fear that the end is very close at hand. I wrote to Gray who was in Cornwall, begging him to go to London so that someone should be at hand to render any assistance to van D. that might be necessary.[27] I also asked him to find some friend with whom I could stay for a week or so in security, in order that I might have sufficient time to do a few things on behalf of van D. (who is in very unfortunate financial difficulties) before running any risk of further molestation from the conscription authorities—who now pounce on all alike, fit and unfit. For that reason it is necessary to avoid such places as hotels, as you can see. However, Gray has not written to me, either about van Dieren's condition, nor about the other matter—so that I am left in considerable suspense and anxiety—more especially as I had made all my plans for coming away

---

[27] Heseltine wrote to Gray on 16 Aug.: 'I feel certain the Master is dying. My worst fears have been renewed and confirmed by a terribly distressing letter which I received from him last evening. His heart has given way . . . I think it would be wise if you went to London immediately. I am sure the climax has come and there is much that must needs be done.' Heseltine to Gray, 16 Aug. 1918, BL 57794.

from here—where already my position is somewhat precarious. I conclude from this silence of Gray's that he has stupidly taken offence at some references I made in a recent letter to him on the subject of a very disastrous liaison he has contracted with a woman[28] much older than himself and from which, as I can tell from his letters alone, he is unconsciously suffering a great deal. It is the usual nasty English story—intellectual vampirism—though of course all vampirism is the same in its ultimate origins! However, the wretched man is evidently too much infatuated to heed the warning of a friend: but it is very irritating to me that he should select this rather trying moment for his child-ish fit of sulking! As a result—what I want to ask you, though I do so with con-siderable reluctance as I hate to trouble you, is whether you could give me a bed at Elsworthy Road for a week or so if I come over at once?

As regards van Dieren, his condition is really so serious that my anxiety increases with each day that my visit to him is postponed—for there is so much that must be settled and discussed with him—quite apart from such material assis-tance as I might be able to render him in one way or another. (I cannot make the whole of this matter clear in a letter: it is long and complex and far more significant than I can even hint at here—I will explain it when we meet). And I *must* see you while you are over in England: there are ever so many plans and projects I want to talk over with you—and I want to make a thorough study of your new works too—and then I might be able to finish off my little book on your life and works: it would be well if its issue coincided with your visit and the performances of your latest achievements. For all this, one needs a brief period of tranquillity, free from risks. After that—when everything is done for the time being, let come what may—I am indifferent.

It is hard for me to make the exact difficulty of my position quite clear to you but you will, I think, understand it to some extent: and I will explain it fully when we meet.

If, then, you can possibly without great inconvenience let me have a bed in your house for a brief while at this rather critical moment, I shall be ever-lastingly grateful to you. If not, then I must try and make other arrangements —though I have already tried my utmost in other directions, or I would not —I can assure you—inflict this nuisance on you.

Will you please let me know about this as soon as ever you can, for I feel that there is danger in every day's delay?

With much love to you both
Ever yours affectionately
Φ.

---

[28] Hilda Doolittle ('H. D.') (1886–1961), American poet and novelist.

168
Philip Heseltine to Frederick Delius

12/12/18.   35 Warrington Crescent, W. 9.
                                         (Telephone: Paddington 3484)

My dear Delius

After all I forgot to give you the list of works I suggested the other evening.

The *Beethoven 'Namensfeier-Ouverture'* (op 115) is a capital work, very well worth reviving.

Of *Berlioz* there is the fine *Funeral March for Hamlet* (in 'Tristia') which is never heard, and the wonderful penultimate movement from 'Romeo and Juliet' entitled *'Roméo au Tombeau'* in the score. This movement and the Queen Mab scherzo both occur in part IV of the Symphony and might well be played together. Schubert's 7th Symphony and Liszt's Faust Symphony you have already thought of. Then there is *Liszt's Todtentanz* for piano and orchestra; *Schumann's Overture, Scherzo and Finale* is quite a good work, and *Brahms' 3rd and 4th Symphonies* in F and E minor, should be heard more frequently.

Marschner's[29] *Overture to 'Der Vampyr'* is an excellent example of the early Romantic school: the whole opera, indeed, is so good of its kind that I cannot imagine why it is now entirely unknown.

There is, of course, no lack of earlier music that is most unjustly neglected, but when one gets back beyond the 19th century, there is no longer any need for the full orchestra. Two rather out-of-the-way 19th century pieces suggest themselves to me at random: *Meyerbeer's* March from the 4th act of '*L'Africaine*' and *Henry Hugo Pierson's*[30] interesting '*Romeo and Juliet*' Overture.

Handel, of course, comes off very well with a big orchestra—His *Overture to the Occasional Oratorio* is a fine, massive piece of work.

Rameau, too, should not be forgotten.

I hope to have my pianola-piano here next week: you must then both come round one evening and hear some music, including Van Dieren's Six pieces.

Ever yours affectionately
Philip Heseltine

[29] Heinrich August Marschner (1795–1861), German composer and conductor. His opera *Der Vampyr* was composed in 1828.
[30] Hugo Henry Pierson (1815–73), English composer and teacher.

169
Frederick Delius to Philip Heseltine

44 Belsize Park Gardens
NW 3

Monday [30 December 1918]

My dear Phil—We were so sorry to miss you on Saturday   How kind of you
to give us such nice presents   The book looks extremely interesting. Come &
spend an evening with us soon. Any evening except Thursday, as on that night
we are going to a labor Meeting at the Albert Hall—It may be interesting   Would
Wednesday suit you. come at 7 or earlier   Bring the Requiem if you can &
the other music—Virginals & Magic Fountain—Warmest Christmas greetings
& thanks from us both—

ever affectionately
Frederick Delius

1919

THE Deliuses stayed in London until June 1919. There were several performances of Delius's works during that time: the first performances of *Eventyr* (11 January, Queen's Hall) and the Violin Concerto (30 January), both of which were enthusiastically acclaimed. Heseltine, however, had reservations about the former work, writing critically about it to his former piano teacher, Colin Taylor. Considering his earlier total obsession with Delius's music, this reaction is the somewhat surprising beginning of a disenchantment which gradually becomes more marked during the course of the next ten years. The revised version of the String Quartet was also given on 1 February. Despite all this success it seems that Delius did little composing during this period and in the months that followed. After a week in Sussex in early June, the Deliuses departed on Heseltine's advice for Sennen in Cornwall, but the weather was bad and after six weeks they decided to travel to Norway. They spent time first in the Valdres region and then moved on to Christiania. In late September they travelled to Frankfurt, where they were to attend the première of *Fennimore and Gerda*. After a successful season of the opera they returned once again to Grez on 25 October. In mid-November they journeyed to London again, this time for Beecham's production of *A Village Romeo and Juliet*, which was eventually postponed until the following year. By the end of the year they were back in Grez.

Early in 1919 Heseltine began planning the publication of a musical journal to be called *The Sackbut*, an idea which had been mentioned as early as December 1914. These plans, however, came to nothing, even though a prospectus was produced. On 13 May Heseltine delivered a paper entitled 'The Modern Spirit in Music' to the Musical Association, and in July he became involved in a heated controversy with Leigh Henry in the columns of the *Musical Times* over the music of Stravinsky. Later in the year, in autumn, Winthrop Rogers published his recently composed songs, but it was only in November that Rogers eventually discovered the true identity of Peter Warlock. By the end of the year Heseltine was in the midst of another feud, this time with the music critic Ernest Newman, whom he accused of being unwilling to espouse the cause of new composers such as van Dieren and Sorabji.

170
Jelka Delius to Philip Heseltine

44 Belsize P. Gs
10/1/19

Dear Phil,

Your letter and the delightful book of plays came just as Fred had to rush off to a string-rehearsal of his 'Eventyr'[1] and so he wants me to thank you very heartily.

Fred is most interested in the East-end concerts and would love to go on Sunday.[2] Won't you come to tea (afternoon) there is a man from the north coming at 4. We might then go on to the concert from here. Please bring your wife if she cares to come.

Wood came yesterday and certainly has studied the new score most carefully; he seems to enjoy it, so I hope he will do it *well*! Anyhow it is a blessing to get into an era of first performances again after these weary years.

Best love
Yrs ever
Jelka Delius

---

[1] The first performance of *Eventyr* took place on 11 Jan. in a concert in Queen's Hall conducted by Henry Wood. A critical Heseltine wrote to Taylor: 'Not so very long ago I should have laughed if anyone had suggested that in 1919 I should go to a concert and be enchanted, overwhelmed by a Beethoven Symphony after the first performance of a new Delius work had left me cold and disappointed!' Heseltine to Taylor, 14 Jan. 1919, BL 54197.

[2] Heseltine had also told Taylor about these concerts: 'Do you know the South Place Sunday concerts? This strange "ethical" chapel is, musically, the brightest spot in London. I took Delius there last Sunday and he was delighted with the keen intentness with which the crowded audience listened to the music. He says it is the only intelligent musical audience he has seen in London. I hope it may be possible to arrange a Delius evening there before long. Every Sunday there is a good chamber concert, and though some of the "standard classical" works may be a little dull, nothing that is worse than dull is ever included in the programme—which, I think, is a great deal more than can be said of any other concert society in England.' Heseltine to Taylor, 14 Jan. 1919, BL 54197.

171
Philip Heseltine on behalf of Frederick Delius

April 30th 1919.   44 Belsize Park Gardens
                                                                London N.W.3

Dear Sir

I wish to make a formal charge, against some person or persons unknown, of forcible entry and theft committed in my house at Grez-sur-Loing Seine-et-Marne during my absence.[3]

The military authorities commandeered our house for the use of officers in June 1918 and it has been occupied by them since that date. I returned there last August with my wife, but for reasons connected with my work it became necessary for me to leave home for London soon afterwards. In view of the fact that officers were still billeted upon us, we collected all our possessions of value into certain rooms which we locked up and in addition made doubly secure with padlocks. These rooms contained our pianos, our books, our works of art, old furniture, pictures and drawings of great value, *all our houselinen, antique china, glass, porcelain, copper and brass utensils, trunks, valises, etc. etc.*[4]

Now we hear that someone has forcibly entered these rooms, breaking both lock and padlock, and has stolen many articles of considerable value.* I cannot give an exact and detailed list of what is missing until I return myself to Grez-sur-Loing, but I am told that most of my bed- and table-linen has disappeared, together with a number of *copper, brass and aluminium* ~~kitchen~~ utensils. Several cupboards and chests that were in these rooms locked up have been forcibly opened, and one drawer in a chest of drawers has been found completely empty. Besides this, another door leading to my wife's painting studio has been broken.

In view of these facts, I trust that you will take the necessary steps to prosecute those responsible for the theft and damage, and that in the meanwhile you will see to it that the doors are repaired and the locks *sealed up* until I return

---

[3] Delius had written to the Clews about the damage done to their home at Grez by the occupying French officers: 'We thought we lived in a fairy dell called Grez & we returned to a filthy barrack—All transformed by a few filthy humans & evidently reflecting the real state of their souls. . . . Luckily we had locked up our most valuable things in my study & the summer bedroom—But they opened several locked cupboards & took things taking care to lock the cupboard again . . . I wont go into details—The house was *filthy & is so still*—We cannot clean it.' Delius to the Clews, 21 Aug. 1918, Delius Trust Archive. Jelka told Marie Clews that: 'I must go and make lists of all that is missing. I am afraid all our houselinen and copper and aluminium kitchen things are gone.' Jelka to Marie Clews, Carley, *Letters*, ii. 217.

[4] The italicized words are in Jelka's handwriting.

home, when I shall be able to furnish you with a complete list of the articles that are missing.

Yours faithfully

* at the time of the theft 3 officers were living in the house

172
Frederick Delius to Philip Heseltine

44 Belsize Park Gardens—
[26 May 1919]

Dear Phil—Please bring the Requiem back as I have to show it to Volkert[5] & we are leaving the flat on Saturday. I hope the 'Text' was in the full score—

Fr. Delius

Postcard.

173
Jelka Delius to Philip Heseltine

Dear Phil; we are here: British Empire Hotel 28 De Vere Gardens Kensington.
It was so kind of you to send the letters. How the owners of our flat can have got that address into their heads is indeed a mystery to me and strangest of all that Gray's brother was there. We are here till Saturday morning and should love to see you. We are generally in at about 1 and seven if you can ring us up. No answer from Zennor. We are *so* unsettled in our plans. Must tell you all about it. If we could only go to some nice place nearer town!

always yours
Jelka Delius

10. 6. 1919

Postcard.

[5] Charles G. J. Volkert (1854–1929), German-born music publisher who became the London manager of Schott & Co. in 1881, being also associated with Augener. A naturalized British citizen, he furthered the cause of British music, publishing the works of Elgar, Grainger, Ireland, O'Neill, and Scott.

174
Jelka Delius to Philip Heseltine

Treeve Lodge   Sennen   Cornwall
19th June 1919

Dear Phil, Here we are here and we love the place. I dont know whether you ever got my card, written after receiving the letters from Knareshurst. We returned to London for a few days and had hoped to see you there. We stayed at the British Empire Hot. De Vere Gardens. Norway seemed quite exhorbitantly dear, also the actual journey, so we had to give it up for the moment. Besides it is said to be packed full. So we came here on the 14th straight to the Lands End.—The air and Landscape are grand. The Hotel rather disappointed us; we were lucky enough tho' to find very nice rooms in Sennen a little more inland and quite near the 'Cove' a sandy bathing beach. But we are right at the top and it is very bracing. Fred got a Piano from Penzance; our only trouble is that this place is let for August, as indeed everything else, also Penzance and St Ives (but they are not nice anyhow after this.) We do not know *what* to do for August; we shall go prospecting around in a dingle tomorrow to have a try near St Just etc. Do let us hear how you are getting on and whether the great T. B. gave any signs, and whether you came into your money and are starting the Sackbut? We never quite unravelled the mystery of the letters going to Surrey. Mrs Russell Kelly said we had laid that address on the telefone—which of course we had *not* done. There was one very important letter and I am very grateful to Grays brother—Really an extraordinary piece of luck.

I love the square Church towers here, and the little stonehouses, and the little walls and the blue sea is beautiful of course. We are eating wonderful fish and crabs and lobsters and our lady cooks most excellently for us. Fred sends you his love. He brought your little score here. Shall we send it?

With all good wishes from us both yrs affl^{ly},
Jelka Delius

175

Frederick Delius to Philip Heseltine

Treeve Lodge
Sennen Cornwall
[July 1919]

Dear Phil—Enclosed I send you a letter just received from a certain Dr
Eaglefield Hull[6] which might inspire you for an article in the Sackbut. Mind I
have never met this person, nor even heard of him or his Society & this is the
way he approaches me. Is one to wonder that all musical & artistic enterprises
fail in England when such people are at the head of things. I have been now
10 months in England & have never been approached on this subject—I want
nothing from any British Music Society—if they want anything from me they
have a strange way of doing things—

Personally I think British music has had more than a fair chance & has
been performed much too much—If they continue the concerts will eventually
be entirely empty—English music continues to be dull—They gave a Concert
of English Music in Paris last April & took care to leave my name out of the
program—Why? The real Britishers were all there. This is all very amusing &
of course I dont claim to be a British composer   Nor do letters like the enclosed
make me feel any more inclined to have anything to do with a British music
scheme—the Musical League cured me forever of that—It is delightful here, fresh
& bracing—but cold—Are you getting on with the Sackbut?

Love from us both
ever affectionately
Frederick Delius

---

[6] Arthur Eaglefield Hull (1876–1928), an organist and writer on music; founder of the British Music Society
in 1918.

176
Philip Heseltine to Frederick Delius

July 13th 1919.   35 Warrington Crescent W.9.

My dear friend

I ought to have written to you ages ago, but I have been for several weeks in a horrible state of inanition, with the result that things get put off from day to day until days grow into weeks and weeks into months.

I am so glad you like Cornwall: I felt sure you would find the Land's End district congenial and stimulating to work in, and I hope you have found a comfortable habitation for the rest of the summer. Perhaps when the weather gets colder you will migrate to the Scillies, whose climate is the mildest to be found anywhere in the British Isles.

What a scandalous communication that was from Eaglefield Hull! I also had one (*before* you, please note!!!!) and replied suitably. How could you fail to be impressed by a society to which Messrs Albert Sammons[7] and Waldo Warner[8] had already accorded their illustrious patronage?!!!! But in a country where a man like Cyril Scott[9] can be acclaimed as 'musician, *poet* and *philosopher*' (!!) and my noble lord Berners[10] hailed with profound respect as an 'advanced' composer, all things are possible and nothing need surprise one.

Newman has written two magnificent articles in the Observer, last Sunday and to-day, about the imbecilities of Goossens, Berners and C°. 'There is' he writes 'not one of us who could not do this sort of thing at any odd minute of the day with as much ease as lighting a cigarette. There is no idea, not even an ironical or a nonsensical idea at the back of it: it is within the scope of anyone who cares to take a piece of ruled paper and fill it with music that has every chord but the common chord and every interval but a lucid one.'

These modern French and Russian composers, with their little English satellites, are always insisting upon the quality of wit and irony in their music, which is supposed to have taken the place of what is commonly called emotion. But they cannot or will not face the fact that they have never even approached the wit and irony of two of the most emotional composers that have ever lived

---

[7] Albert Sammons (1886–1957), English violinist, first violin of the London String Quartet (1908–17); he gave the first performance of Delius's violin concerto, which was dedicated to him.
[8] Waldo Warner (1874–1945), the violist of the London String Quartet.
[9] Cyril Scott (1879–1970), English composer, poet, and pianist.
[10] Lord Berners (Gerald Hugh Tyrwhitt-Wilson) (1883–1950), English composer, painter, author, and diplomat.

—Liszt and Berlioz. What is Stravinsky's wildest extravagance when one compares it with such masterpieces of irony and grisly humour as the Todtentanz, the Mephistopheles movement in the Faust Symphony and the last two movements of the Symphonie Fantastique? I should think that the present is on the whole the most decadent and fatuous epoch in musical history.

'The Sackbut', I am afraid, will never materialize. I have not yet been paid the full amount of my legacy, and as Beecham has not condescended to pay any attention to the communications of my solicitors and his own, the case against him has had to be put down on the list of cases waiting to be heard in the courts and will not, I am told, come on before next October, So that unless a deus ex machina in the shape of a musical millionaire turns up to save the situation, the undertaking will not be financially possible. The same fate overtakes all my enterprises—lack of funds, for which no earthly amount of good intentions can make up. I have written to Beecham several times about the score of the 'North Country Sketches' but of course no reply has been vouchsafed. I also called at the Albany but found that he had given up his flat there three months ago. I have not been able to discover his present address, so that I can only communicate with him c/o his solicitors, Ernest Simmons and C° 199 Piccadilly, W.1. But if you will give me what is called a 'power of attorney' (which you could effect without returning to London), I could sue him through my solicitor for recovery of the score; or you could make a deed, assigning the manuscript to me (for purposes of the case), since it is still legally your property, Beecham not having fulfilled his contract to you in connection with it. I wish you would do this: I have asked my solicitor about it and he tells me that you could certainly obtain the score in this way without being yourself involved in any litigation—and moreover the additional charge against Beecham would materially assist my own case. But apart from that, the little upstart ought to be taught that he cannot treat people as if they were dogs—least of all, yourself.

What happened about the Requiem? I took the MS to Augener's just before Whitsuntide, but have heard nothing from them about it.

And did you ever receive the photographs from Coburn[11]—for I never heard any more about them either.

Nothing much is happening here—though I suppose the city will become absolutely unbearable next week-end with the 'peace celebrations'.

---

[11] Alvin Langdon Coburn (1882–?), American photographer. Heseltine first mentioned him in 1916 in a letter to Taylor, having discovered that Coburn was also a pianola enthusiast: 'I visited the ringleader of this band at his charming house in Hammersmith Mall, on the river, and was staggered, both by his enthusiasm and the splendid accomplishments it has led to. He is an American, by profession a photographer . . . He is also a painter of very advanced ideas . . . He has a library of 800 pianola rolls, of the best.' Heseltine to Taylor, 20 Apr. 1916, BL 54197. He would later write an article, 'The Pianola as a Means of Personal Expression', for *The Sackbut*, 1/2 (June 1920), 57–9.

The sudden disappearance of Mme Lopokova,[12] the dancer, has caused a mild sensation. She is said to have eloped with a Russian general! I wonder if you saw 'La Boutique Fantasque'[13] before you went away. It is a most delightful production (barring the décor by Dérain[14] which is hideous) with the most delicious music by Rossini, who I never dreamed could have written so well.

Very much love to you both

Ever yours affectionately
Philip Heseltine

177
Frederick Delius to Philip Heseltine

Treeve Lodge Sennen
Cornwall

July 17th. 1919

My dear Phil—

We have again been obliged to alter our plans: my wife has now to go to Grez to make a list of the things stolen by the french officers for the Conseil de Guerre; I shall stay on here for a few days longer—Jelka leaves on Monday & I on the Monday following.[15] Jelka will join me in London on her return from Grez & then we shall either go to Germany (if we can) or to Norway for a few weeks for Mountain air. I like it very much here but the sea has been too cold for us yet to bathe. The air is bracing & invigorating. I am sorry about the 'Sackbut' your circular made such a good impression everywhere. You would have done better if you had followed my advice & waited until you had the funds—Dont begin to think, dear Phil, that luck is against you because the real reason is that you do not push your ideas to their materialisation with sufficient energy & 'Suite dans les idées'. You would succeed at anything you take up if you would concentrate on it & not diffuse your energies on so many things. (I am not booming Pelmanism !!!)[16] Stick to one thing just for fun for 2 or 3 years

---

[12] Lydia Vasilievna Lopokova (1891–1981), Russian-British dancer and actress. She joined the Diaghilev Company in 1910.

[13] Music arranged by Ottorino Respighi (1918); produced Alhambra Theatre, London, 5 June 1919.

[14] André Dérain (1880–1954), French painter and designer.   [15] Delius left Cornwall on 28 July.

[16] The system taught by the Pelman Institute (founded in 1899 by Charles Louis Pelman) for the scientific Development of Mind, Memory, and Personality in London, and used attributively to designate the system of memory training taught by this Institute.

& see if I am not right. I think you are admirably gifted as a writer—you would succeed either as a writer on music or as a composer if you *stick to one* & push it thro' regardless of everything. I vouch that you would have the most influential & powerful paper in London if you started one & stuck to it. Why not get Newman to join you   I read his articles & they were splendid. Altho' I cannot understand why anyone gives such importance to what a russian ballet master & a few french miniaturist composers think about English music & composers. Ravel is the only one who has any talent whatever & he has absolutely no emotion & they have established for themselves entirely false values which they want everyone to accept. Stravinsky at his best is a musical acrobat. I shall write you before arriving in London so that we may meet. Volkert has not written me yet about the Requiem   If he does not take it, I know Leuckart will—or the Universal. We both send you much love.

Ever yours affectionately
Frederick Delius

Dont think I want to preach at you but I am so fond of you that I would like to see you become something & assert yourself as I know how gifted you are & what possibilities are in you. It annoys me to see fools succeeding all around us

178
Frederick Delius to Philip Heseltine

[?Treeve Lodge
Sennen
Cornwall
July, 1919]

Dear Phil—I shall try & get back the score of N. C. Sketches some other way I dont want to take such measures against him. He used to be a good friend & has been very kind. I am coming up to town on Monday week the 28th. Shall write you again my address—

Yours
Fr. Delius

Postcard.

179
Frederick Delius to Philip Heseltine

[24 July 1919]

Dear Phil. Could you get me a single room for Monday night in some good hotel. I arrive at Paddington at 5. Perhaps near Charing + or Victoria & if not there then where you can get one. There are a lot of Hotels near Bedford & Russel squares—I shall be several days in London: meet me if you can.

yrs ever
Fr. Delius

Treeve Lodge
Sennen.
Telegraph not later than Saturday morning

Postcard.

180
Frederick Delius to Philip Heseltine

address
Fosheim—Saeter. Valders
[10 August 1919]

Here we are after very rough voyage.[17] Dont forget to take the score of Requiem to Volkert. give him also this address so that he may forward all letters *at once.* We shall be at Fosheim for 2 or 3 weeks. I lunched with Beecham Monday last!!! at Lady C[unard]

Love from us both. Fr Delius

Picture postcard, Norge, Stalheim Hotel, Naerödalen.

---

[17] Heseltine told Taylor that: 'Delius has gone to Norway and from there will travel to Germany later on. His opera "Fennimore" . . . is to be produced for the first time in Frankfort-am-Main in November. There's no art-chauvinism nonsense there at any rate.' Heseltine to Taylor, 23 Aug. 1919, BL MS 54197.

181
Frederick Delius to Philip Heseltine

Fosheim Saeter. Valders
[13 August 1919]

Dear Phil. Dont forget to ask Sammons about the faulty Violin part of the Concerto then look at it carefully & take it to Volkert. It is heavenly here. we are 3000 ft up with a magnificent view. Did you take the full score of the Requiem to Volkert? with love from us both

> ever affectionately
> Fr Delius

Postcard.

182
Philip Heseltine to Frederick Delius

September 8ᵗʰ 1919.   35 Warrington Crescent
W.9.

My dear friend—I took the piano score of the 'Requiem', with the corrected translation, back to Volkert last week for him to despatch to you. I hope you got it safely. The full score he still has (as I think I told you in the card I sent to Bergen, if you received it).

I have also been looking through my piano copy of the 'Song of the High Hills' which needs a few corrections. Is there a proof or MS of the full score in England, with which I could revise it? Because, in view of the forthcoming performances,[18] Leuckart will want to issue an edition with piano and he may just as well take the one I have already done as get someone else to do another.

---

[18] The first performance of *Song of the High Hills* took place in London at Queen's Hall on 26 Feb. 1920 at a Royal Philharmonic Society concert with the Philharmonic Choir conducted by Albert Coates.

I got Sammons' copy of the Concerto and made such corrections as were necessary: but one or two points are still doubtful. At figure ③ where tempo changes to 4/4 he has A flat where C is printed: it does'nt make much difference, but the next edition may just as well be quite correct.

A more important change seems to have been made at the close of the accompanied cadenza, where the full score and printed copy have one bar of 7/4. In Sammons' copy this becomes an 8/4 bar, thus—(the notes marked + being omitted from the printed version)

He has also a large number of Ritenutos and crescendos and decrescendos which are not in the full score. Are these to be written in also?

I hope you are having a fine time in Norway, and that the mountain air has blown away all your unpleasant memories of England and its British music societies!

There is a chance of my getting the post of regular music critic on a new literary paper—which I shall welcome. And Fox-Strangways[19] has commissioned me to write several articles for his new musical quarterly (to be issued first in January next) beginning with one about you. Otherwise there is little inducement for me to stay here—life becomes blanker, emptier and more sickening every day.

Someone who is supposed to have met you in Cornwall has started a rumour that you are writing another Piano Concerto. Is there any foundation for it? And what about the 'Village Romeo'—is it to be done here this winter?[20]

My love to you both—How I wish I could join you for the première of 'Fennimore'![21] My thoughts are with you and all my good wishes. You must let me know your address when you leave Norway so that I can write to you often.

Yours always affect[ly]
Phil

[19] A. H. Fox Strangways (1859–1948), music critic of *The Times*, established a new quarterly journal, *Music and Letters*.

[20] This was due to have taken place in London in Nov. 1919 but, because of the unsatisfactory preparations, it was postponed until Mar. 1920.

[21] The first performance of *Fennimore and Gerda* took place in Frankfurt on 21 Oct. 1919.

183
Frederick Delius to Philip Heseltine

ANNE KURES HOTEL
VOKSENKOLLEN
PR. KRISTIANIA

DEN 17 Sept [1919]

My dear Phil—Many thanks for your letter & the 2 corrections   The first one (3) ought to be A flat. C. double notes

The 2ᵈ one is right in the printed copy. 7/4—Sammons is wrong. Leave it out all the ritenutos etc. That ought to be left as it is.

We have had a lovely time up in the Mountains & now we are at a lovely place right above Kristiania with a heavenly view: On Saturday we leave for Francfort via Copenhagen & Hamburg. My address there is c/o Dʳ Heinz Simon.[22] 3 Untermainkai Francfort ᵃ/m—In Vienna they are doing The Mass of Life, Appalachia & The Arabesque this winter. It appears life is again becoming normal in Germany—Beecham intends giving The Village Romeo in Nov. Dec. so he says. The première of Fennimore is Oct 18. I shall write you all about it. I dont know whether Leuckart will print a piano score of the Song of the high hills—shall let you know when I have seen him. I have received the piano score of the Requiem which is very good & plain. I shall offer it to Leuckart or Universal Edition   Keep your spirits up & write me soon. The Crescendos & decrescendos you can put in—Good luck to you! & much love from us both

Ever yours affectionately
Frederick Delius

---

[22] Heinrich Simon (1880–1941), Editor of the *Frankfurter Zeitung* and a close friend of the Deliuses. He printed a long review of *Fennimore and Gerda* in his newspaper. A Jewish refugee from Nazi Germany, he was later murdered in America.

184
Frederick Delius to Philip Heseltine

Dear Phil, Fred dictates:

Be a good chap and buy me 2 Colgate shaving sticks at Selfridges 1/4 a piece and send them to Frankfort per post   My address is c/o Dr. Heinrich Simon UntermainKai 3

I come to London right after the first performance and will then refund you. W. Rothenstein[23] wrote to me; he wants to do a drawing for the Music-paper you are writing the article for. I'll pose for him on my return to London. We are on the point of leaving for Frankfort.

Aff^ly yours
Fr Delius

Love from J. D.
[Voksenkollen]
19. 9. 1919

Postcard, in Jelka's hand.

185
Philip Heseltine to Frederick Delius

September 20th 1919.   35 Warrington Crescent W.9.

My dear Friend

Last week 'Brigg Fair' was given at the Promenade Concerts.[24] I went, expecting to hear it murdered: what actually took place was the best performance of it that I have ever heard. It is very seldom that Wood reveals new beauties in a work that is so familiar to me as this, but I can honestly say that it never sounded

---

[23] Sir William Rothenstein (1872–1945), English artist known for his portrait drawings of his contemporaries. He did a drawing of Delius in 1919. (See R. Threlfall, 'Delius as They Saw Him: A Further Attempt at an Iconography', *Delius Society Journal*, 83 (1984), 5–18.)

[24] Queen's Hall, 11 Sept. 1919.

so lovely as on this occasion. His reading is now (whatever it may have been in the past) infinitely more subtle and sensitive than Beecham's: he has evidently taken a great deal of trouble, not only in rehearsing the work with the orchestra, but in studying the score himself. One big mistake (the only big mistake) he made, as they all seem to do—namely taking page 27 (theme in trumpets and trombones 4/4 'with solemnity') twice too fast and accellerating on page 28 (theme in violins, horns and clarinets 'maestoso') to three or four times faster then the most elastic conception of 'Slow' would permit.

I remember writing to you on this very point after hearing the work for the first time in 1911 under Kes in Coblenz and you replied, as I thought you would, that this section 'cannot be taken too slow'. Would it not be a good plan, in view of this general misconception, for you to fix a metronome rate for this passage? If you will do this, I will publish it in an article as the official tempo. I have not a metronome by me, but I see you have marked the first statement of the theme in the oboe (page 7) ♩. = 66. It occurs to me that the right tempo for the slow section on page 28 would be ♪ = 66—beating eight quavers to the bar—or thereabouts. One's only regret on hearing 'Brigg Fair' is that so much beauty passes by so rapidly and never recurs again: it leaves a sense of longing—but perhaps that is just the secret of its charm.

At the same concert we had the Liszt A major Concerto[25] which I hadn't heard for years, and I was thrilled to intoxication by it: what superb energy, what fire and passion and tenderness—and what a synthesis of contrasted emotions! It has the quality of a divine improvisation.

I have tried all over in London to obtain a copy of this work but without success. If you could procure a copy of it for me in Germany (it is issued in Eulenburg's kleine Partituren-Ausgabe at 3 M^k) I should be immensely grateful. I have read through the score in the British Museum but it is a work one likes to possess. I am trying to collect the complete works of Liszt—he is such a magnificent old fellow.

Fox-Strangways' musical quarterly, which I mentioned in my last letter, will appear on December 15th. He wants a musical supplement for each issue, and as Mrs Gordon Woodhouse[26] is contributing an article on clavichords to the first number,[27] I suggested that you might be willing to let him have your little piece for the harpsichord as his first supplement. It will be copied and photographed by the zinc-block process, and you will of course retain full copyright of it. What do you think of the proposal? He has asked me for an article on your works, and Rothenstein (or should I say Rutherstone) wants to make

[25] The soloist was the Belgian pianist Arthur de Greef (1862–1940).
[26] Violet Gordon Woodhouse (1872–1948), a pioneer recorder and broadcaster on the harpsichord.
[27] V. G. Woodhouse, 'Old Keyed Instruments and their Music', *Music and Letters*, 6/1 (Jan. 1920), 45–51.

a drawing of you, when next you are here, for a series of musicians which he has promised Fox-Strangways. I do'nt know what you will say to that—but still, there is the plan.

I am eager to hear from you about the rehearsals of 'Fennimore'. You must let me know all about the production and also, if possible, send me the press-cuttings after the performance so that I may write about it here. There will probably be no English musical correspondents present and it would be a shame if the production were to pass unnoticed by the London press.

My love and all good wishes to you both.

Always yours affectionately
Philip Heseltine

P.S. A friend of mine came to see me the other day who did not know your works at all. I played him the 'First Cuckoo in Spring' and he became so enthusiastic that he insisted on hearing the 'Village Romeo'—not merely sections of it, but the whole work, right through from the first bar to the last. And now he is clamouring to hear it again.

186
Philip Heseltine to Frederick Delius

September 26th 1919.   35 Warrington Crescent W.9.

Dear Friend

Two days before receiving your last letter I posted to you a long communication about the tempi of 'Brigg Fair' and other matters to Fosheim Saeter. If it is not forwarded to you, please let me know and I will write again on the same subjects as there were one or two important things in it.

Amongst other things I asked whether Fox Strangways might have your harpsichord piece as a supplement to the first number of his new quarterly which appears in December—you, of course, retaining the right to re-publish it elsewhere later on. I suggested this as Mrs Gordon Woodhouse has an article on old instruments in the same issue and the piece is so beautiful that one would like to see it become widely known. (Will you please let me know by October 10th whether you would like it to appear in this journal?)

If 'Fennimore' is published already, will you please send me a copy so that I may write a full account of it in some London paper.[28] A few press cuttings of the première would also be welcome.

If you go to Vienna and see Herzka,[29] you would be doing a very kind action if you would mention to him those six piano pieces of Van Dieren which I played you and which, whether one likes them or not, are certainly serious and interesting works which deserve to be known and studied. They were actually accepted for publication by Universal-Edition seven years ago, on the recommendation of Busoni, but they never appeared on account of a disgraceful intrigue engineered by Godowsky[30] who threatened to withdraw some of his own obviously more saleable manuscripts if these pieces were taken. No need to ask why —Van Dieren was at that time a critic!!!! If you feel inclined to put in a word for them, I will send you over a copy of the MS. It might be well to mention that they have been cut for the pianola and that copies of the rolls can be supplied.

Van Dieren went across to Holland last Monday, in a desperate condition of ill-health, hoping as a last resort that the doctor who operated on him some years ago might be able to do him some good.

Much love and all good wishes for 'Fennimore'

Yours ever affectionately
Philip Heseltine

187
Philip Heseltine to Frederick Delius

September 27th 1919.   35 Warrington Crescent W.9.

Dear Friend

Your card came last night and I am sending you the shaving sticks but with little hope of their reaching you quickly owing to the railway strike which started this morning. I have just seen in the Daily Telegraph this morning an

[28] An article on *Fennimore and Gerda* by Heseltine, entitled 'Delius's New Opera', appeared in the Apr. 1920 *Musical Times*, 237–40.

[29] Emil Hertzka (1869–1932), Austro-Hungarian music publisher; in charge of Universal Edition from 1907.

[30] Leopold Godowsky (1870–1938), American pianist and composer of Polish birth, who taught piano in Vienna from 1909 to 1914.

announcement that your Requiem is to be produced by Albert Coates[31] and the London Symphony Orchestra on March 8th 1920 at Queens Hall. I sincerely hope that you will insist upon his revising his programme in order that your work may be heard to the best possible advantage—for as the programme now stands, the Requiem comes in the middle and at the end is Scriabin's 'Prometheus' which is not only a detestable and, in parts, absolutely ridiculous work from a musical point of view, but is also, in spirit, a flat contradiction of the basic idea of your Requiem: it is a disgusting compound of erotomania and pseudo-mystical religiosity, and should certainly never be permitted to figure in any scheme which includes a work of yours—or indeed of any other decent composer.

If you could without trouble procure me an Eulenburg kleine-Partitur of Liszt's A major Piano Concerto (no 2)—3 M[k]—I should be most grateful: and if Universal C[o] will pay me anything for the translation and Klavier-auszug of the Requiem, I wonder whether it could be arranged that I should receive certain scores which I want, to the value of the sum agreed upon, since the rate of exchange is at present such that I should lose heavily if I were paid in actual money. I am told that £1 is equivalent to 70 or 80 M[k].

Always yours affectionately
Philip Heseltine

188
Jelka Delius to Philip Heseltine

7. Oct. 1919

UntermainKai 3
p.a. Hrrn Dr Simon
Francfort/a M

Dearest Phil, I write for Fred who is hurrying over [h]is toilet to get to the rehearsal at 10 a.m. Let me first answer your questions.

He never received your letter to F. Saeter re Brigg Fair etc, so please write again here. He agrees to F. Strangways publishing the Harpsichord piece, but

---

[31] Albert Coates (1882–1951), English conductor and composer. He studied in Leipzig and conducted in Germany, Russia, and at Covent Garden. On his arrival in England he immediately took up Bax, Delius, Holst, and Vaughan Williams. He was appointed to the music staff of the English Opera by Beecham in May 1919. He conducted the premières of Delius's *Requiem* and *The Song of the High Hills*. *North Country Sketches* is dedicated to Coates.

of course it must not be reprinted and he reserves all rights. I am writing to Hertzka to send you a P. Sc. of Fennimore at once. H. is coming here of course, so Fr. will certainly speak to him of v. Dierens pieces and do his best to get them published. The Tischers[32] and the Jagenbergs are also coming, also Strecker of Schotts, v. Klenau etc. I cannot tell you how lovely it is to be in this musical atmosphere—they are rehearsing every morning and splendidly. Brecher[33] sits on the stage with his score and Lippay the 2d conductor—very musical also from Vienna plays it on a piano   the singers sing and act and the regisseur teaches them every movement, every nuance of expression, according to the music. Quite a young regisseur—splendid. They take every short scene and when it at last goes well repeat it, to learn it quite safely. The work, I think is too beautiful and so entirely new in every way, freed from everything of the old conventions. Brecher and Lippay love it. the latter young, hungry thin and emaciated plays it with real love and looks like a mediaval ascetic monck or Saint at the piano —they all know *all* Freds works. It really is another world here. Yesterday at the Schauspielhaus, under the same direction as the opera they gave a Shaw evening with the killingly amusing farce Die grosse Catharina[34] and Blanco Posnel's awakening. Full house and enthusiasm. Not a *bit of* hatred for the British. You can speak english anywhere. As Fennimore plays only 1½ hours they will give an orchestral work probably Appalachia first with Chorus unseen—and make a Delius evening of it. They love the Libretto and have seen at once that it must be acted entirely in a new way—only expression of the Stimmung and 'Seelische Vorgänge'   No throwing about of arms

Food conditions are very difficult yet and most people very thin and wan, rings round the eyes, some children so wretched that it *hurts* one to see them. Prices enormous. The scenery is being painted quite new in spite of the difficulty with stuffs and materials. I *do* wish you could be here.

Now another thing. We have now used up all our resources and these wretched people do not settle up with Germany and we cannot get at a penny of our money. So we are trying to raise a small loan in London. With german money of course one could not live over in France and England. Anyhow under these conditions Fred thinks he would like best to go direct to Grez from here and stay there till he goes to London for the Song of the High Hills in Febr. Now we have 2 trunks full of all our warm clothes and things in London which we greatly need in Grez. Should perchance any reliable friend of yours go over to

---

[32] Gerhard Tischer (1877–1959), German music publisher and editor. From 1909 he was head of the publishing firm of Tischer and Jagenberg, Cologne, which he founded.

[33] Gustav Brecher (1879–1940), German conductor, composer, and writer on music. He conducted the first performance of *Fennimore and Gerda*.

[34] *The Great Catherine* (George Bernard Shaw, 1913).

France in the near future and would be willing to take them across it would be a real blessing for us. I would have fetched them myself but have to clean and prepare and keep house at Grez, and it is all important for Fred to get to his work again whilst he feels happy and thrilled and angeregt. We know that if we send these trunks they will kick about for weeks, be opened without anybodys presence and all that is useful in them will be stolen. If we were not so hard up I would ask you to bring them and pay your trip across. We should love to have you at Grez for a few days—but I suppose that is out of the question. Should however—by chance—anybody go, do send us a wire and I'll send the keys and receipt of Barkers. If you go to Mrs Woodhouse perhaps you might ask her if she knows anyone. I do not know, whether Cooks would undertake to bring them or send them in a *guaranteed safe* way. Fred has no warm overcoat, not even his dark blue suit, no evening suit no shirts—all is in these trunks, so they really *must not* be lost, otherwise we are entirely busted. You see, when I came back from France it was Bank Holiday. Fred had taken the Norway tickets and we had to leave without anything. Of course Fred or I could easily go to Paris and take the trunks from the person who brought them. All this worries Fred so. How they *do* drag on with those financial settlements! One gets quite desperate at last and I *know* that if Fred could work quietly at Grez he would forget it all. So be an angel and find out what we had best do.

I must run off to the rehearsal now and look at the Scene painting. Poor van Dieren. We'll do all we can! And I hope his dutch physician will help him

Good bye—Your old affectionate friend
Jelka Delius

189
Philip Heseltine to Frederick Delius

October 7th 1919.   35 Warrington Crescent W.9.

My dear friend
    I sent off the shaving soap you asked for some days ago, but owing to the railway strike which only finished yesterday, I very much doubt whether you received the packet. There has been such congestion in the post offices and I believe all parcels for abroad were simply laid on one side.

I write this to tell you that last Friday I met Allinson who told me that he was actually at work upon scenery for the 'Village Romeo', having received a definite commission from Beecham to execute the designs: moreover, to my utter astonishment, he assured me that your sanction had been obtained!!

I feel quite sure that this cannot be true, as you have so often told me that you will not allow the work to be given except with Jelka's designs. If this is another trick of Beecham's, I hope you will get this warning in time to prevent any further steps being taken in this direction.

I feel so anxious about the success of your lovely work—so much depends on this second production, and it could be made one of the most beautiful pieces ever put upon the stage, if the task were only approached with real sympathy and understanding.

Let me hear all about 'Fennimore' at the earliest opportunity—I am reading Jacobsen's novel again, so as to be quite familiar with the story. It is really wonderful.

On Saturday next—mirabile dictu—we are to hear the Symphonie Fantastique at Queen's Hall! I feel most elated at the prospect of hearing this glorious work once again.

Much love to you both and all good wishes for Fennimore's success.

Always yours affectionately
Philip Heseltine

P.S. Don't bother about the Eulenburg partituren: I think they will be shortly imported again.

P.S. I have lately been making a study of Spontini[35]—a curiously interesting figure in music—and would very much like to know what has become of his last work 'Agnes von Hohenstaufen' [1829] which he considered by far his best achievement and which Berlioz praised very highly—but I can discover nothing about it, and it does not seem to have been printed—which is extraordinary. If you have an opportunity, would you be so kind as to ask Brecher who is the great authority on operatic matters, if it has ever been revived or published in Germany?

---

[35] Gasparo Luigi Pacifico Spontini (1774–1851), Italian operatic composer.

190

Philip Heseltine to Jelka Delius

October 15th 1919.   35 Warrington Crescent W.9.

My dear Jelka

I have only this morning received your letter dated October 7th. If you had told me earlier what you wanted done with the trunks I could have arranged for them to be taken as far as Paris by the Orrs[36] who left last Thursday. However I know someone who is going to Switzerland and will presumably pass through Paris: I will ask him about it. If in the meanwhile you will send me the keys and receipt I am sure I can find someone to take them. I am not quite sure when my friend proposes to go to Switzerland, otherwise I would send you a wire at once: but I will find out as soon as possible.

My letter to Fosheim Saeter was about a performance of 'Brigg Fair' which was given at the Promenade Concerts five weeks ago. On the whole Wood gave the most sensitive and poetical interpretation of this work that I have ever heard—very much better than Beecham's! It is so very seldom that old 'Timber' achieves anything in the way of interpretation that it is quite a pleasure to be able to record the fact. Well as I know the music, this performance revealed fresh beauties and made the work sound all-of-a-piece—which is always difficult with the variation form. Wood had evidently taken a great deal of trouble, not only in rehearsing the orchestra but in assimilating the score himself. One glaring mistake he made, though: and as it is a mistake that is, to my knowledge, almost invariably made, I thought it might be as well to tell you about it.

When I first heard the work in Coblenz, under Willem Kes, in 1911, the same thing occurred—it is in connection with the tempo of page 27 of the full score, which I thought much too fast. I wrote to Fred about it on that occasion (it was the time when he heard a 'telepathic' performance of 'Brigg Fair' at Grez!) and he replied that the passage in question 'cannot be taken too slow'. I think most conductors are led astray by the notation. A slight rallentando takes place on page 26 and at the end of the page the time changes from 3/4 to 4/4— but *actually*, I should say, changes from 3/4 to <u>4/2</u>—that is to say that ♪ of the 4/4 on page 27 is equivalent to ♩ of the 3/4 on page 26—the movement being, relatively, twice as slow. At least that is my conception of the tempo, and I do not see how the direction 'With solemnity' can be carried out if the pace is any

---

[36] C. W. Orr (1893–1976), English song-writer.

quicker than that, for the syncopated chords for the strings lose all their weight and dignity if it is hurried: this remark, of course, applies even more forcibly to page 28 where the syncopated chords are more heavily scored. I have not a metronome by me, but as the opening section ('with easy movement' page 7) where the tune is first stated by the oboe is marked ♩. = 66, it seems to me that ♪ = 66, beating *eight* quavers to the bar, would be about right for page 26. If Fred will think over this passage with a metronome and give me his marking, I will communicate it to Wood, or get it published somewhere as the official tempo: for it is a pity that performances otherwise excellent should be marred by this curious misunderstanding.

I was very much struck on this occasion by the *richness* of the music: so much is happening all the time, one wants to linger over a bar here, a progression there. And I began to wonder whether one of the secrets of the wistful charm that pervades so much of Fred's music is not just this evanescence of beautiful things, things which appear for a moment, give one a glimpse of something perfectly lovely and then vanish, only to make way for another new glimpse. Until one knows the works inside out one never feels one has the music within one's grasp (and even when one does know them there are always surprises in store)—there is always a sense of beauty beyond one's reach. I think the wealth of purely harmonic colour accounts for this to a great extent: it gives a peculiar kind of *depth* (in a dimensional sense). Listening to music, whether harmony or polyphony prevail, we are always most conscious of the *flow* and horizontal-ness of it, so to speak: and where the interest is centred on a single melody we grasp it far more quickly and more completely than when the line is broken by the kaleidoscopic colouring of changing harmonies, when the two dimensions are equally important and not in any conventional sense inevitably interdepend-ant on each other.

Last Saturday we had the usual indifferent performance of the 'Dance Rhapsody'.[37] I have never yet heard this work played satisfactorily, and Wood might well leave it alone. On the same day he gave an adequate, if somewhat unimaginative performance of the Symphonie Fantastique—What a work that is! The Marche au Supplice gave me a feeling of positively physical terror: I have never experienced anything like it in listening to music. Berlioz had the power of the black magicians, and used it, in this work.

I am so pleased to hear of all the excellent preparations for 'Fennimore'— I hope it will be a great success. What a contrast to the Beecham methods! By this time I expect you will have received the shaving soap (what a testimonial for Colgate! *Famous composer writes from Norway to England for American soap*

---

[37] At a concert conducted by Henry Wood in Queen's Hall on 11 Oct. 1919.

to be sent to Germany and afterwards taken to France!!) together with the news of the sinister conspiracy of Messrs Brown Bread and Pills against the hapless Sali and Vrenchen!

Well, no more now: I shall think of you on Saturday evening. Do send me news and press cuttings as soon as possible.

Much love to you both

Ever yours affectionately
Philip Heseltine

P.S. The works of Warlock are announced immediately underneath the Elizabethan songs of F. D.—a happy augury for his first appearance in public!

191
Frederick Delius to Philip Heseltine

Grez-sur-Loing
(S & M)—Oct 27
[19]19

My dear Phil—

We arrived here day before yesterday—The performance in Francfort was very good—Singers excellent & the regisseur the best I ever knew. I had 9 Orchestral rehearsals—No trouble or expense was spared   I am satisfied with the work & it is certainly a step in a new direction—perhaps the only direction where 'Singspiel' has any future—There are no tedious moments.—The drama plays wonderfully well & is clear to the public—Almost every word is heard. Brecher was not as good as I had thought—but gradually got into the spirit of the whole—I send you a criticism of Paul Becker[38]—It has now to be translated—Hertzka of the Universal offers 2000 Kronen—it is not much translated into £ sterling but if you leave it in Vienna it will go up—Hertzka will supply you with any music you desire—also for the 70 Mark he still owes you—Life in Vienna is cheaper than anywhere else in Europe. It would be the place to go to. The opera is excellent: & the Concerts excellent & numerous. There is absolutely no feeling against the English in Germany or Austria & Hertzka has any amount of translating

[38] Paul Bekker (1882–1937); German musician and writer on music. He was a music critic of the *Frankfurter Zeitung* from 1911 to 1923.

work for you to do, which would be sufficient to keep you. I spoke to H. very warmly of Van Dieren & his piano pieces—tell Van D. to send them at once. I am sure he will take them after what I told him. I know nothing of The Village R. performance in London but have written to Beecham. My wife has not yet made sketches.[39] Try & see what Allinson is doing. I told H. to send you the piano score of Fennimore: it is only provisoire—& there are many mistakes, also bars missing. Write as soon as you get this & tell me about the trunks. With love from us both—

    ever affectionately
    Frederick Delius

The Universal Edition is also going to publish my new works. North Country Sketches, Dance Rhapsody—etc. etc. Please send North Country sketches to me here—Insured as I want to revise it.

192
Frederick Delius to Philip Heseltine

[Grez-sur-Loing
(S & M)
October 1919

I am so glad Wood gave such a good performance of Brigg Fair—What you say about the Tempo at the End is quite right   it ought not to be taken fast—I have no metronome here unfortunately or I would send you the exact tempo. It is, however, so evident that I dont understand why they take it fast. Send me the article you are writing about me & also the Harpsichord piece[40]—the Requiem will be published by Schott or by Universal. I am just in 'pourparlirs'.

    ever yrs
    F. Delius

Postcard.

---

[39] In fact the designs for Beecham's 1920 production were made by Adrian Allinson. Six of his scene designs are in the possession of Bradford Grammar School.

[40] *Dance for Harpsichord.*

193
Philip Heseltine to Frederick Delius

October 31ˢᵗ 1919.   35 Warrington Crescent W.9.

My dear Friend

I am so very pleased to hear of the success of 'Fennimore'. I was a little afraid
that there might be an anti-English element in the audience and I feel greatly
relieved to know that 'Fennimore' did not evoke the same kind of salvo as
'Folkeraadet'![41] Let us hope that the work will go the round of the German opera-
houses and, perhaps in twenty years time even reach this melodious country.

I am eagerly awaiting the arrival of the piano score from Vienna: Of course
I shall be delighted to translate the work and I am enormously grateful to you
for mentioning me to Herzka—and for your very kind recommendation of Van
Dieren. I have just despatched the piano pieces with a letter to Herzka, and
think Busoni is writing to him also. There is no doubt that, even from a com-
mercial point of view alone, he would be doing very well to publish these—
and the string quartets. The 'Village Romeo' is to have two performances at
Covent Garden, the first on November 26ᵗʰ and the second on December 5ᵗʰ.
There are also to be Sunday concerts during the season, so that you could get
Beecham to play one or two of your new orchestral works. A pianist of the name
of Tyrer[42] is giving four orchestral concerts with Hamilton Harty[43] and the London
Symphony orchestra. At the second, on December 10ᵗʰ, 'Paris' is to be performed,
and at the fourth, on February 24ᵗʰ, he is playing your piano concerto, as well
as the Liszt A major. The Violin Concerto is down on the Philharmonic programme for January 29ᵗʰ and the 'Song of the High Hills' on February 26ᵗʰ,
while the 'Requiem' is announced for March 8ᵗʰ, under Coates who is, on the
whole, the best conductor we have here.

I expect you will be in London again in less than three weeks, for the 'Village
Romeo'. Do you want your trunks and the 'North Country Sketches' sent over
at once or shall I keep them till you come?

My friend who was going to Switzerland has now abandoned the idea, as,
being a Russian, there are all kinds of fantastic difficulties in the way, not of his

[41] Incidental music to the play by Gunnar Heiberg (1897). The play was a satire on Norwegian parliamentary government and the political tension existing between Norway and Sweden at that time. On the opening night there was
a student riot as a result of Heiberg's heavy satire and Delius's use of the Norwegian national anthem in a minor key
as a funeral march for the Parliamentarians in the fourth act.
[42] Alexander Tyrer (1891–1962), pianist and conductor. He made his debut in Queen's Hall in 1919.
[43] Sir Hamilton Harty (1879–1941), Irish conductor; conductor of the Hallé orchestra, 1920–33.

going but of his coming back. There is still a stupid 'alien' panic here with regard to Russians. The trunks would be perfectly safe if they were sent insured under the supervision of Messrs Cook. If you want them sent off at once, send me a telegram and I will see to their despatch.

By the way, Beecham announces the 'Village Romeo' as being '*a revised version*' and in a newspaper interview the other day he said that *a new scene had been added* to the work which would greatly increase its dramatic interest.[44] What on earth can this mean? I begin to be very much alarmed at the prospect of what you will find happening when you attend the first rehearsal, more especially as I recall a conversation which I had with Beecham some years ago during which he remarked airily, 'Of course, when I give the work again I shall rewrite all the voice parts'!! Though nowadays he would more probably employ Eugene Goossens to rewrite them, as he employed him to add obbligato parts for the cor anglais and bass clarinet in two numbers of 'The Messiah'!

I have heard nothing more about my case against B: it seems to be still on the waiting list. I should like nothing better than to go to Vienna this very winter but of course I can't leave till this case is favourably settled. But I have asked Herzka in the meanwhile to send me any translations or piano scores he wants made, and as you say the money can wait for me in Vienna. I have just revised my 2-hand piano arrangement of the 'First Cuckoo'. Do you know if Tischer is thinking of publishing a piano version?

Well, no more at present: we shall meet again very soon. I cannot tell you how excitedly I am looking forward to the 'Village Romeo' performances.

Much love to both of you from

Your ever affectionate
Philip Heseltine

P.S. The harpsichord piece is to appear in the first number (December 15th), the article and the drawing in the second—March 15th.

P.P.S. Muriel Foster[45] is singing three songs by Peter Warlock at her recital next week! I feel very glad that I did not put my own name to them.

[44] Stephen Lloyd suggests that most likely it was the raising of (or keeping up) the curtain during *The Walk* and showing the two lovers 'to stop the audience talking'. (See Sir Thomas Beecham, *A Mingled Chime* (London, 1944), 88–9.)
[45] Muriel Foster (1877–1937), English contralto.

194
Jelka Delius to Philip Heseltine

3. Nov. 1919   Grez

Dearest Phil,

Just received your letter and of course we must come to London to see it through. Fred says the extra scene is his own idea. It takes place during the last entracte when you see the lovers on their way to the Paradiesgärtchen. Probably the 'revising' is mere advertisement, however Fred will see to all that and has already written to Beecham about it.[46]

The great difficulty is, of course, where are we to live? Could you order us a doublebedded room in a central heated *warm* hotel. I am afraid it is very full in London, so you must see about it at once   We'll arrive on the 12th or 13th.

If there is a lift it can be high up. Ask for prices, please! If only you knew of someone (a private person) who could let us have one or 2 rooms and we could eat in Restaurants?

Of course keep the trunk keys and we'll take back our trunks ourselves.

It is awfully nice of you to keep us posted about these things. We should not have known, but for you.

We are looking forward greatly to you and Fr will tell you all about what he arranged with Hertzka. And you must get going at once on Fennimore translation.

Possibly we could stay in a little flat of one of your friends who was absent? Maybe you'll be able to find something!

Aff^ly yours
I am only the pen for Fred
Jelka

---

[46] Jelka wrote to Marie Clews later: '. . . we were summoned to London as Beecham intended giving the Village Romeo and Juliet—and Fred thought it necessary to be on the spot, and actually postponed the performance—it was all too hurried and they could not get the music over in time—so it was a good thing we went . . . Freds Village Romeo will now be done at Covent Garden in February.' Jelka to Marie Clews, 5 Dec. 1919, Carley, *Letters*, ii. 223.

195
Philip Heseltine to Frederick Delius

November 11ᵗʰ 1919.   35 Warrington Crescent
                                                                          W.9.

My dear Friend

London is fearfully full at present, on account of the big motor show at Olympia
and other things that are on for the time being. I tried hotel after hotel without finding any accommodation whatever: all the large ones are absolutely full
up for the whole month, especially those whose prices are reasonable.

At last, as I have just telegraphed to you, I found you a room with two beds
and a gas fire at the Tour Eiffel in Percy Street, off Oxford Street, which I engaged
for you from Thursday next, the 13ᵗʰ, as you requested. It is the best I can do,
as I know no one with a private house where you could go to—all my friends
live in rooms or in flats. The Tour Eiffel is not large but I know the proprietors
well (the owner has only recently emerged from internment: his mother used
to be the prima ballerina at the Vienna opera) and I am sure they will do their
very best to make you comfortable. You may remember having dinner with me
at their restaurant on your return from Cornwall.

If you will send me a telegram I will meet you at the station when you arrive
and conduct you there.

The opera season is, I think, doing well as regards the size of audiences that
attend the performances but the taste of the London public is inscrutable. I
went to 'Prince Igor' last Tuesday—a marvellous production—gorgeous scenery
—vast crowds on the stage—a good chorus—one or two fair singers and several quite capable actors—above all Coates with *everybody*—chorus, principals
and orchestra—*absolutely* at his command, giving a first-rate account of this really
admirable score. Yet, in spite of extensive cuts, the audience showed obvious
signs of restlessness during the last act and scarcely gave the singers a single recall
when the curtain fell at 11.45.

Yet three nights later a larger audience was enraptured by an indifferent
(and that word is hardly strong enough) performance of 'Tristan' which began
at 7.30 and ended two minutes before midnight, after which a demonstration
of approval for Mullings & Cᵒ lasting for quite five minutes took place.

Personally I must confess I am more and more bored by the first two acts of
'Tristan' every time I hear them. For me the work is (historical considerations
apart) only interesting as the fore-runner of the 'Village Romeo'.

I have also seen 'Falstaff'—the title role magnificently played, in true Shake-
sperean manner, by Ranalow[47]—the women poor—orchestra (under Goossens)
drowning all the singers at every opportunity. But what a miraculous work—
surely the best comic opera since Mozart![48]

Well, till Thursday then!

Much love—

Ever affectionately
Phil

Great success and long flattering reviews for 'Warlock'!!!

196
Frederick Delius to Philip Heseltine

Grez-sur-Loing
(S & M)
6 December 1919

My dear Phil.

We had a terribly rough passage & were both frightfully ill, however we
arrived safely here on Sunday noon. Thanks for the letter you sent on. I send
you to-day a periodical published in Vienna with an article on me.[49] it might
be useful to you; after perusal send it on to Albert Coates 23 Sumner Place
South Kensington—Why Marx drags in Macdowell[50] I cannot understand. I
dont remember ever having heard any of his music—Fennimore continues to
run in Frankfort & has been acquired by Copenhagen. You said something once
at Belsize Park Gardens, when we were playing thro your arrangement of 'A
Song before Sunrise' of there being a mistake in my full score—I have carefully
revised & find none—before printing compare your arrangement with the score
to be quite sure. I see from an advertisement in 'Anbruch' that the entire course
at the 'Academie für Musik' (Conservatorium) costs *Kronen 1000* —or £2-10.0.

---

[47] Frederick Ranalow (1873–1953), Irish baritone.

[48] For a further amusing and lengthy discussion of these performances see the letter from Heseltine to van Dieren,
14 Nov. 1919, BL 65187 (L. Foreman, *From Parry to Britten: British Composers in Letters (1900–1945)* (London, 1987)),
111–13.

[49] Presumably the detailed review of *Fennimore and Gerda* by the German musician and writer on music Paul Bekker
(1882–1937), which appeared in *Musikblätter der Anbruch*, 1/2 (Nov. 1919), 60–3.

[50] Edward MacDowell (1861–1908), American composer and pianist.

per year. I advise you strongly to go there as soon as you have some money in Vienna. Let me hear how things are going on & take care of yourself—With love from us both

> ever affectionately
> Frederick Delius

Ask Coates to return the Anbruch to you. I hope you sent the Requiem to Hertzka Karls Platz 6 Vienna. Send me Fennimore with your translation as soon as completed.

197
Philip Heseltine to Frederick Delius

December 7th 1919.   35 Warrington Crescent W.9.

My dear Friend

So far my copy of 'Fennimore' has not arrived from Vienna. The English translation, however, is quite finished, though there are still a few rough places which I shall improve when I go over it again and write it in a fair copy. I have pencilled in my version in the copy you gave me and I shall send you this copy in a day or two (as soon as I have finished an article I am writing about the work) in order that you may be able to approve of it and tell me anything you don't like in it before my copy arrives: for when that comes, I shall write in the translation in ink, (as well as translating all the stage-directions) and send it direct to Herzka.

I have tried to keep as near as possible to colloquial English speech, but in the more impassioned moments it seems to me necessary to substitute 'thou' and 'thine' for 'you' and 'yours'. What do you think? I won't say anything more about the work now except to congratulate you most heartily on having made a big step forward towards the solution of the biggest problem connected with opera—that of fusing the demands of dramatic propriety and those of purely musical logic into a perfectly harmonious whole. The music of each picture is so wonderfully complete and self-contained, closely-knit and symphonically worked and yet at every point it is absolutely appropriate to the course of the action. It must be sheer joy to see on the stage. The fourth picture appeals to me particularly: the way in which you have expressed that strange and rather terrible mood is simply miraculous.

Best love to you both.

Ever yours affectionately
Philip Heseltine

198
Frederick Delius to Philip Heseltine

[Grez-sur-Loing
(S & M)
?26 December 1919]

Dear Phil—Send me the translation of Fennimore as soon as possible as they are waiting for it in V. I dont think that 'Thou' is very good—but cannot judge before seeing the places. Did you not receive the copy of Fennimore from Hertzka? We send you our heartiest good wishes for the new year. Many thanks for the lovely cards you sent us. Write soon—

ever affectionately
Fr. Delius

Postcard.

1920

BECAUSE much of his money was tied up in Germany, Delius's financial position had now become somewhat precarious and was a cause of constant concern. On 18 February he travelled to London to attend the first performances of his Double Concerto (21 February) and the *Song of the High Hills* (26 February). After staying for a while with Norman O'Neill, he then spent a few days with Balfour Gardiner at his home at Ashampstead in Berkshire before returning to London in mid-March to attend rehearsals of Beecham's second production of *A Village Romeo and Juliet*, which opened at Covent Garden on 19 March. He returned to Grez on 22 March, where he soon began work on a new choral piece that later became *Songs of Farewell*. In July he received a request to compose the incidental music for James Elroy Flecker's play *Hassan*, which was to be produced in London. By now he was finding it more and more difficult to write and Jelka was writing many of his letters for him. When Heseltine came to spend some time at Grez in August, he agreed to make a neat score from Delius's pencil drafts which would be sent on to him in England. In September a holiday at Hendaye on the Spanish border was terminated because of bad weather and the Deliuses returned to Grez towards the end of the month, where work on *Hassan* was resumed. After spending a few days in Paris in early October, Delius moved to Frankfurt on 15 November, where he was joined by Jelka at the end of the month. They were to remain there until March of the following year.

Early in 1920 Heseltine contributed a number of articles and reviews to a new journal edited by Fox Strangways, *Music and Letters*, as well as writing on Delius's opera *Fennimore and Gerda* for the April *Musical Times*. In April Winthrop Rogers invited him to become the editor of a new journal called *The Sackbut*. In the agreement with Rogers, Heseltine was to receive £50 an issue, an amount which was, in fact, never paid to him. Between May 1920 and March 1921 nine issues appeared, many of which contained material of a highly controversial nature. In August the publisher John Lane offered Heseltine £25 for his proposed book on Delius, and he spent about ten days at Grez that month collecting material. During his absence he left Gray to edit *The Sackbut*. On his return on 26 August Rogers withdrew his financial backing for the journal and Heseltine decided to act as sole proprietor and editor. On 6 October Gerald Cooper sang the original version of *The Curlew* (5 songs) in a concert described by Heseltine as 'a dismal affair'. There were also two *Sackbut* concerts (18 October and 2

November) which included works by Purcell, Sorabji, Delius, and Ladmirault. Two more concerts were planned but were cancelled because of financial problems. On 2 December Heseltine went to France, leaving Gray to edit *The Sackbut* once again.

199
Frederick Delius to Philip Heseltine

[Grez-sur-Loing
?6 January 1920]

Dear Phil—I am awaiting the piano score of Fennimore with your translation![1] Is it ready? Have you sent the piano score of the Requiem to Hertzka? He wants it badly in order to get the material ready—Send it at once registered—also Fennimore to me here—We intend coming to London on the 15th or 16th February. Try & get us a nice double bedded room in a heated & comfortable Hotel with lift—

Ever affectionately
Fr. Delius

Perhaps an hotel near Victoria station or Charing cross—

Postcard.

200
Philip Heseltine to Frederick Delius

January 11th 1920.   35 Warrington Crescent W.9.

My dear friend—I am sending you the 'Fennimore' score with translation but this is only a rough, provisional copy: the one you asked Universal to send me has never arrived. I wrote to Hertzka about it when I sent off the Requiem

---

[1] 1925, Universal Edition 6308. For further details see Threlfall, *Delius: A Supplementary Catalogue*, 30.

several weeks ago, telling him the translation was done and that I was waiting for my score into which I would write a fair copy of the English text. To this letter I have had no reply. But I am very glad to be able to tell you that, thanks to your kind words of recommendation, he is publishing Van Dieren's piano pieces[2] and will doubtless take up his other works later on.

Van D. is still in a nursing home at the Hague but he is recovering rapidly. The operation not only saved his life but has put him in the way of regaining a state of health he had never dared to hope for.

Much love to you both.

Ever yours affectionately

Φ

P.S. Have you found the Papus book yet?[3] I should so much like to see it.

201

Philip Heseltine to Frederick Delius

	Cefn-Bryntalch,
Sunday.	*Abermule,*
8/2/1920.	*Montgomeryshire.*

My dear Friend,

I have revised my translation of 'Fennimore' very carefully and enclose a copy for your inspection.

I shall send the piano score, with the revised text and all the stage directions written in, by registered post to-morrow. I do hope you will find it improved. It is so difficult to translate the short simple sentences that mean very definitely one thing and one only without disturbing either the sense or the musical accentuation. Your declamation is so amazingly accurate that even a slight alteration in the order of words is often enough to make a phrase that is perfectly plain and simple in the German sound strained and unnatural in English. However I sincerely hope I have left no howlers this time. If you find any more bad places

---

² Universal Edition published van Dieren's *Skizzen* [6 *Esquisses*; 6 *Sketches*]: Op 4a [1911] in 1921.

³ A reference to the notable French physician and occultist, Dr Gérard Encausse ('Papus', 1865–1916). Delius had collaborated with him to produce a booklet entitled *Anatomie et Physiologie de l'orchestre* (1894) which explored 'the mystical properties and characteristics of the orchestra'. It was an attempt on Encausse's part, assisted by Delius, 'to find a new Orchestral system' (Carley, *Letters*, i. 70 and 102).

perhaps we can go over the score together when you are in London and I will do my best to mend them. It often happens in translating to music that one may puzzle one's brain for hours over a single sentence without result and then, when one has laid it aside for a few days, one suddenly lights upon a happy phrase that just fits the music.

On page 68 I am very much in doubt for a line or two. What can one say for 'Gesunden'? It is so very emphatic, being thrice repeated, that the mot juste is indispensable. I am also doubtful about the various titles—Prokurator and Kanzleirat—but you can no doubt tell me exactly what these signify.

As regards the tempo indications, you have some in German and some in Italian. Do you want English added or would it not be simpler to translate them all into their universally-understood Italian equivalents?

The newspapers are again announcing a 'completely revised and largely rewritten' version of the Village Romeo, the Daily Telegraph even going so far as to add that this 'rewritten' version had lately been produced in Frankfort!

I am sending a strong letter of protest to the editor.

It is wonderful here—lovely mild days with an atmosphere so clear that one can see for miles in every direction. All the spring flowers are coming out ahead of their time, and the lingering evening twilights are made more beautiful and mysterious by the fluting of innumerable owls in the woods.

You ought to come down for a few days later on. I shall be in London at the end of this month again. My case against T. B. (after a *whole year* of delay) is actually fixed for this month—though there will probably be no case but, following the usual precedent, a cheque on the latest possible day!

Much love to you both.

Ever yours affectionately
Philip Heseltine

202
Frederick Delius to Philip Heseltine

[Grez-sur-Loing
February 1920]

Dear Phil—translation just received. it looks infinitely better but have not yet received the piano score—I arrive in London on the 18th at 8 p.m. Victoria & shall stay with O'Neill. 4 Pembroke Villas. Kensington. Let me know as soon as you arrive—Ever affectionately

Fr. D.

Legges article is too funny! 'Entirely rewritten' !!!

Picture postcard, Grez-sur-Loing, Le Pont.

203
Frederick Delius to Philip Heseltine

TEL. 3069
WESTERN.

4, PEMBROKE VILLAS,
KENSINGTON, W.
[2 March 1920]

Dear Phil—Where are you? Come here as soon as possible as I want to give you the score of Fennimore—Phone—

ever affectionately
Frederick Delius

204
Frederick Delius to Philip Heseltine

Tuesday

> Ashampstead Green
> Pangbourne
> Berks
> [9 March 1920]

Dear Phil—I am staying here until Monday next & then I shall stay the night at the O'Neills in order to pack my trunk—As I leave for Paris on the following Sunday perhaps it would be wiser to go to some hotel near Victoria—Kilburn is rather far—

I spent a delightful afternoon yesterday in Oxford—

affectionately
Fr. Delius

205
Philip Heseltine to Frederick Delius

March 15ᵗʰ 1920

> 35ᴬ Sᵗ George's Road
> Kilburn N.W.6.

My dear Friend

If after all you have any difficulty in finding a hotel I shall be most pleased if you care to come here for a few nights.

Could you spare the time this week to come and hear my Indian friend's piano sonata? I have heard him play it again several times during the last few days and I become more and more impressed by his quite extraordinary talent. I am sure you would be interested. It is the bigness of his conceptions and the sheer, overwhelming emotional *power* of his music that seem to me so wonderful and so welcome in these attenuated days when composers set out to 'purge themselves of the domestic emotions' and other such miserable things!! (That superb phrase, I have discovered, is the invention of our great and genial compatriot

Mʳ Vaughan Holst—one can but congratulate him on having achieved what he set out to achieve).

When one hears Sorabji, one cannot stop to marvel over his technical mastery of means, nor over his novel and peculiar chord-combinations—though to the analytical mind these things alone would be interesting enough—one is simply swept along by a whirlwind of amazingly significant, evocative sound.

What a joy it is to find a big sweep and surge of emotion in modern music —most of what one hears nowadays inclines one to despair of the future!

Last week I came across the Principal of the Conservatorium of Music in Melbourne, Australia⁴—a very talented composer and an attractive personality —that such a man should be a professor of music bodes well for the colonies —no one with a tenth part of his vitality could hope to become one in England!

He has written several operas, including settings of Synge's 'Deirdre'⁵ and 'Riders to the Sea'.⁶ I have read through the latter and like it very much. In spite of the fact that he has set Synge's play ready-made, so to speak, and practically verbatim, the music has real form and coherence on its own account, and never slavishly underlines the words to the detriment of the purely musical flow and continuity.

Let me know if and when you would like to hear the Indian.

Ever yours affectionately
Philip Heseltine

My article on 'Fennimore' appears in the April Musical Times.⁷ I will send you a copy when it's out.

---

⁴ Fritz Hart (1874–1949). A former Westminster Abbey chorister and later a student at the Royal College of Music, Hart had emigrated to Australia in 1909, eventually becoming the director of the Conservatorium of Music in Melbourne in 1915. He was a prolific composer: his enormous output included amongst other things twenty-two operas and 514 songs, as well as twenty-three unpublished novels.

⁵ *Deirdre of the Sorrows* (Op. 21) [1916]), opera in three acts, libretto adapted from a play by J. M. Synge. An autograph full score is in the Victoria State Library, Melbourne, LaTL 9528/13.

⁶ *Riders to the Sea* (Op. 19) [1915]), opera in one act, libretto adapted from a play by J. M. Synge. An autograph full score is in the Victoria State Library, Melbourne, LaTL 9528/19.

⁷ P. Heseltine, 'Delius's New Opera', *Musical Times* (1920), 237–40.

206
Frederick Delius to Philip Heseltine

Grez 24. 3. 20

Dear Phil, I am very sorry I saw so little of you in London—but of course I was over head and ears in rehearsals, you will understand that. I left early on Sunday and had a lovely passage. On my next visit to London you must arrange for me to hear something of your friend Saradji—it would interest me very much.

Strangways sent me his magazine for Jan. and April with a long dissertation on Vaughan Williams, *the Great English Genius*!!! Get him to send me Febr. and March! Up to now a spirit of dullness pervades these magazines; certainly what Mr Strangways writes is the essence of dulness—I had already judged him at the Concert where you introduced him to me. If he turns out anything interesting *ever*, I shall be a very astonished person.[8] I hope you have sent Fennimore and Gerda off to Vienna. I am now correcting the Double Concerto. As soon as I have finished I shall send it to you and beg you to correct once more, and then hand it on to Augener's.

In haste, Ever your affectionate friend,
Frederick Delius

Love from Jelka—

In Jelka's hand.

---

[8] Heseltine recounted this meeting to van Dieren in amusing terms. Strangways 'in the jocular-schoolmaster-out-of-school-hours manner, with his interminable and pointless conundrums' had evidently asked Delius 'whether the respective lengths of violin bows and cello bows affected the phrasing with regard to the sex of the performer, etc, etc— or something of the sort. After a few minutes Delius smiled benignly and exclaimed: "I don't know what you're talkin' about. You might as well be talkin' *Chinese*"! Whereat the musical critic of London's leading newspaper (who I must add had previously enquired of Delius, with his usual amazing tact, *where his music was published*!) perceptibly blushed through his bronzed and assuredly pachydermatous hide and muttered something about "Mere small-talk, you know: don't *you* ever use small talk?" ' Heseltine to van Dieren, 22 Nov. 1919, BL 65187.

207
Frederick Delius to Philip Heseltine

Grez-sur-Loing
(S & M)
10th April 20

Dear Phil—

Coburn sent me a few photos & 1 very good one of you—Mine are awful —I look as if I had just come back from the grave. The one of you and me is better. Shall I send you your photo or keep it? I should like one of you & will give you one of mine but a better one than Coburns   The article on Elgar in Music & letters by Shaw is worthy of the Pink'un or the tatler. I should very much like to read your article on Fennimore & Gerda—Gr.[ay] wrote to me about it today: Please send it to me—What an article on Vaughan Williams⁹ God! 'We do not classify Matterhorns, we accept them'¹⁰ catches my eye as I peruse it again—& exposes its author, the editor, to ridicule—When you feel like coming over here for a while let me know—your uncle Joe is making tremendous efforts to make it up with us after his absurd & abominable conduct during the war—

Ever affectionately
Frederick Delius

Dont miss the Song of the High Hills on June 3ʳᵈ

---

⁹ A. H. Fox Strangways, 'Ralph Vaughan Williams', *Music and Letters*, 1 (Jan. 1920), 78–86.
¹⁰ The sentence referred to runs thus: 'We come to the *London Symphony* . . . Discussion of the form is apt to be a wearisome business to those who have not the sound of the work ringing in their ears; besides we do not classify Matterhorns, we accept them.' Ibid. 81.

208
Philip Heseltine to Frederick Delius

April 16th 1920.   35^A St George's Road
                                                              Kilburn N.W.6

My dear Friend

Very many thanks for your letters. I hoped to see you again before you left England to tell you—or try and tell you, for words are very inadequate to convey such things—how utterly marvellous the 'Village Romeo' seemed to me. I can honestly say that no music that I have ever heard has ever moved me more profoundly nor given me such a satisfying sense of absolute perfection of expression. Ten years ago it was the piano score of this work that really opened my eyes to what music could mean, but although I have studied it constantly in the meanwhile, the actual hearing of the music was a revelation. I was present at all three performances—the last was the best of all—the four horns at the beginning of the last scene, played in tune for the first time at this performance and produced a perfectly miraculous quality of sound. I was amazed, too, at the manner in which the whole work came off dramatically—it is such a wonderful *whole*, as finely balanced and proportioned as a symphony, unrolling inevitably from the first bar to the last.

I had no idea, from merely reading the libretto, that it would play so marvellously (even with the handicap of bad acting and misconceptions of character) and that it would convey such a sense of cohesion and unity.

The only serious flaw in the performance, musically, seemed to me to be the substitution of a male chorus for the voice of the boatman in the last scene. The A major passage where he enters for the first time is so mysteriously beautiful, one feels that he ought to be heard almost like the voice of a solitary bird crying in the far distance through the night. But the raucous shouting of the male choir robbed the music of all its mystery, and actually conveyed the idea to a friend of mine who did not know the score that the party of vagabonds in the inn were breaking out into a drunken song. But, this defect apart, the work went astonishingly well. Beecham really surpassed himself in conducting it— he seemed to be caught up in the rapture of the music and to be swayed by it, though there were occasional points where one would have liked him to dwell more lovingly upon a bar or a progression that seems to demand the emotional emphasis of an epigram or clinching phrase in a passage of poetry.

However, I will not go on babbling my enthusiasm here, but you shall read, if you care to, much more of it in an article I am writing for the first number of 'The Sackbut' which is in active preparation and will positively appear on May 15ᵗʰ! Winthrop Rogers has taken up the scheme with enthusiasm and I think we shall be able to make a big thing of it.

He took over, when he bought out one of the numerous small firms of which his business is compounded, a very miserable paper called 'The Organist and Choirmaster' which—as it was, by some extraordinary chance, paying its way and making a small profit—he continued to run, rather unwillingly as it was a most uninteresting production. Early this year it occurred to him to re-organize the paper and try and make it into something better and of more general interest, and a few weeks ago he suggested that I should take it over and edit it.

I was against this policy from the first and after many discussions I succeeded at last in persuading him that nothing could be made out of this rotten corpse of a paper and that it would be far better as well as more profitable to start a new paper on quite different lines. Accordingly 'The Sackbut' will absorb 'The Organist' next month, but will start off with the advantages of the 'Organists' existing circulation, subscription list, and organization—the latter including a very able and efficient business and advertisement manageress[11] who has worked with Rogers for years and knows everything about the commercial side of running a paper, a very valuable asset.

It will not take long, I feel sure, to make this the best musical journal in England. Rogers has given me an absolutely free hand in the matter of contributions (save for the fact that a small section of 'organist news' is to be retained at the end amongst the advertisements!), and in no way wishes the paper to be associated in the public's mind with his publishing business. I feel very elated about the project, for it is now on a very much firmer financial basis than it could ever have been if I had started it on my own account, and I am actually getting paid for running it.

I want the first number to be very first-rate, to drop like a bomb into musical and pseudo-musical circles.

As the thing has been announced and advertised before without any tangible result, we are not going to announce it or advertise it at all until the first number is actually ready. Then we shall distribute gratis, instead of circulars, a large number of specimen copies, to encourage the timorous and unbelieving among our potential subscribers, and to prove the actual existence of this long-threatened but almost legendary monster.

---

[11] Miss May Voules.

If you could write me a letter which could be printed in the first number, saying a few words about the need for a good musical journal in England and about the general condition of music here, it would be a tremendous help and I should be immensely grateful—just a few paragraphs in a quite informal way: your approval and commendation means so much and would give us such a good send-off.

I should love to come and spend a few days with you at Grez and perhaps later on I shall be able to, but just now I am, as you can understand, kept very busy getting everything ready for publication on the 15th of next month.

I have written to Coburn asking if I too may have copies of the photographs: I would love to have a really good one of you. In an old copy of 'Die Musik' (1903) with an account of a Tonkünstler-Fest at Basle I discovered a most amazing portrait of you which I had never seen before—but I can't believe you ever resembled it!

Very much love to you both—I hope Jelka has quite recovered from her sciatica. She must have been distressed to miss the 'Village Romeo'—

Ever yours affectionately
Philip Heseltine

209
Frederick Delius to Philip Heseltine

Grez-sur-Loing
(S & M)

19th April 20

Dear Phil—your letter gave me great pleasure & I am astonished that you see so clearly what I tried to do when I wrote the 'Village Romeo'   In 'Fennimore' I think I have realised it still more—when you hear the performance you will, yourself, become much more conscious of this—As far as I can see (I have only seen 2 or 3 criticisms) no one in London realises what I am driving at & they have constantly the old music drama as their model before their eyes—the only possible future the 'Singspiel' has, is in the direction that I have indicated in the Village Romeo & still more in Fennimore & Gerda. Do send me the article on The Sackbut—Of course, you can put me down as a subscriber—Please write at once what sort of a letter you would like—just jot down about what you would like me to say & I will add something if I find it necessary. I am delighted about The Sackbut & I am sure you are just the man to edit such a paper. I am so glad Winthrop Rogers has had the wit & intelligence & perspicacity to seize hold of this most excellent occasion. There is really no first rate, unbiassed musical periodical in England—They all have some clique to support or some other iron to grind—or they are under the ban of the modern french or Russian schools   They are all prejudiced & have, none of them, a personality sufficiently big, fine, perspicacious & intelligent enough on their staff to keep their ideas unhampered by fads & fashions of the moment—Even those that mean well & begin well very soon lose the clearness of vision in muddy controversy, of old or new fads—& then goes the only thing worth anything as regards musical writings—Enthusiasm   your Fennimore article is also excellent—We can always put you up here when you want to come—Love from us both

ever affectionately
Frederick Delius

210
Frederick Delius to Philip Heseltine

Grez-sur-Loing
(S & M)
April 29th 1920

Dear Phil—I hope you got the photos which I sent you a few days ago. Let me know, as soon as possible, about what sort of a letter you would like me to write. I would, of course, not like you to publish my last letter—It must be much more to the point—It seems to me that your first appeal to the public whilst I was in London was not at all bad—The chief features of the Sackbut ought to be Independence & real criticism—the old cliché of fault finding as a sub-terfuge for ones impotence & incapacity ought *never* to figure in your paper— Only then will it become a real live paper & only then will it be read by the real music lovers & enthusiasts. You have now a wonderful opportunity; I hope you will grasp it—I am sure there is a wonderful field open to you waiting to be cultivated—What is wanting in England & what is wanting in British music is idealism & enthusiasm. Up to now when the british composer is sin-cere he is generally dull & when he tries to be original he nearly always adopts the latest foreign mode—nearly always belated—25 years ago it was german; now it is french or Russian—Their outlook must change entirely & they must cultivate their own personalities with untiring effort & enthusiasm before anything really great will make its appearance—No amount of advertising or booming will make British music any more interesting—The individual alone can accomplish the miracle—ever affectionately

Frederick Delius

211
Philip Heseltine to Frederick Delius

The Sackbut
18 Berners Street
London,
W.1

Telephone   *Subscription:*
Museum 3721   *One Year, 6/-*
                                                                      Post Free.

3/5/1920

My dear Friend

Thank you immensely for the lovely photograph of you which arrived some days ago. It is quite the best I have ever seen of you—the photographer must be a real artist: he has caught a beautiful and characteristic expression of you and at the same time has made an admirable composition of the whole picture. The hands too are particularly fine.

On second thoughts it will perhaps be better if you could write a short article about music in general or about the condition of music in England for 'The Sackbut'. It would not, perhaps, look well to print anything specifically *about* the 'Sackbut' or about the need for it before the first number has actually appeared—especially as I am writing about the 'Village Romeo' in the first number. If you like the first number when you see it a word of appreciation in the second would be more than welcome—or better still a short article in the style of your letters which are always admirably terse and telling and to the point.

Later on I should very much like to include some pages of your autobiography. An account of your life in America and of the influence of your surroundings in Florida upon your musical development would be of very great interest to everyone. Perhaps if I might come over and spend a few days with you at Grez later on, you could dictate a few autobiographical chapters to me—or we might write them together.

I hope and believe the paper will eventually meet with success. At first there may be difficulties. The old 'Organist' connection will prove rather an incubus for the first month or so, but I hope that the circulation will increase so rapidly that there will soon be no need to consider it any longer. The first number has been rather a rush, but it is not so bad considering the brief space of time at one's disposal. Above all one wants (in addition to sound knowledge, sound judgment and enthusiasm) *brilliance*—a literary style with a generous ration of 'nutmeg and ginger, cinnamon and cloves'[12] in it, if the general public are to read one: and it is the general public, not musicians, whom one depends on for one's success in a venture of this kind. Above all things the paper must be *readable* —without this, the finest and most intelligent criticism is useless. I shall send your copy of the first number as soon as it appears—next Saturday week, that is to say.

Much love to you both and again *very* many thanks for the photographs.

Ever yours affectionately
Philip Heseltine

212
Frederick Delius to Philip Heseltine

Grez-sur-Loing
Seine & Marne
20. 5. 1920

Dear Phil,

Please send me as soon as you can as recent a Baedeker of Spain, as you can find in the Charing Cross Rd. and please tell me how much you pay for it and I will send it you per return. We are thinking of spending next winter there.

---

[12] A quotation from *Of all the brave birds*, a glee by N. Freeman, the chorus of which runs:

> 'Nose, nose, nose,
> And who gave thee that jolly red nose?
> Cinnamon and ginger, nutmeg and cloves
> And they gave me this jolly red nose.'

I received the Sackbut which I think a splendid number and an excellent begin-ning. Your article on the Village Romeo is awfully good and will go far to make the Public comprehend what I am driving at.

Your foreword also is *very* good, as is also Grays article on musical criticism.

We shall be delighted to have you here any time you can come over. we can do an article together. Dont forget to hear the Song of the High Hills again as I think the performance will be a better one and I shd like to know how it went.

I hear there was a good article about the Village Romeo in the Spectator.[13] Could you get that for me as the Universal wants so much to have them. I am sending also my Sackbut. Thanks for the lovely Postcard the other day. Yrs are always so artistic. With love from us both Ever aff[ly]

Frederick Delius

Excuse this impossible ink—J. D.

In Jelka's hand.

213
Jelka Delius to Philip Heseltine

Dear Phil, Fred has made a mistake; the article he wants you to send is in the '*New Statesman*'.[14] They are doing Fred's Arabesque at the Welsh Festival at Newport 28th May. Cyril Jenkins[15] will conduct it, I think. We're awfully nervous what they are going to make of it.

Best love from us both
Jelka

22. 5. 1920

Postcard.

[13] The article was, in fact, in *The New Statesman* and not *The Spectator*, as Jelka correctly informed Heseltine on 22 May.

[14] W. J. Turner, 'The Village Romeo and Juliet', *New Statesman* (Mar. 1920), 739–40. In the article the opera is described as having 'a strange dreamy quality which is no doubt partly what appealed to Mr Delius, for it certainly stimulated him to write his finest music. . . . it would be difficult to overpraise the music. The reticence and briefness of the love-passages between Sali and Vrenchen are extraordinarily refreshing, and in sensitiveness of outline and in harmonic colouring the music of modern Italian opera with its crude and blatant emotionalism will not bear compar-ison with it. . . . I know of no happier setting of any modern opera. *The Village Romeo and Juliet* may not become a very popular work, but is an opera that will wear better than three-fourths of the operas that are popular today, although it will always depend more than most on the way it is produced.'

[15] Cyril Jenkins (1889–1978), a prolific Welsh composer, a pupil of Stanford. In 1922 he became Director of Music to the London County Council. Arthur Sims, in fact, conducted the work.

214
Philip Heseltine to Frederick Delius

The Sackbut
18 Berners Street
London,
W.1

Telephone   *Subscription:*
Museum 3721   *One Year, 6/-*
Post Free.

[May or June 1920]

35ᴬ Sᵗ George's Road. N.W.6.

My dear Friend—I'm so glad you like the first number—I hope they will go on improving, gradually throwing off the organ-incubus as new subscribers increase.

I will get you a Baedeker, also the New Statesman article, if there are any copies left at the office, but weekly papers are apt to sell out in these days. I tried to get another Musical Times (with the Fennimore article) to send to Hertzka but the issue was sold out. I shall send you also an excellent article on Fennimore which appeared in the 'Music Student' last month. I am making definite arrangements with John Lane and Cᵒ to publish a book about you in their 'Living Masters of Music' series. They seem very pleased with the idea.

The other day I suggested to the British Museum library authorities that many of your scores were lacking and that they ought to be procured at once: to which they replied that they had ordered a number of them from Universal-Edition but had neither received them nor any reply. This is not the first example I have heard of lately of people who want your works but find them difficult or impossible to obtain.

The 'Arabeske' is being done at Newport on Friday. I would certainly have gone to hear it but for the fact that at the moment I am very hard up and have not enough for my train fare! The money adjudged to me in my case against Beecham has not yet been paid! He keeps on trembling on the brink of bankruptcy and then getting another and yet another month in which to clear off his debts which still, I am told, amount to tens of thousands.

As soon as I get this, I should love to come over to Grez and we can prepare 'biographical material' for the book: the rest is practically all written, though I shall of course re-write the whole thing and touch it up.

I hope Beecham's executors wo'nt dally till you have gone away to Spain! Whenever my solicitor rings them up they promise faithfully to pay 'in a day or two' but devil a payment have they made up to the present.[16]

Much love to you both.

Ever yours affectionately
Philip Heseltine

P.S. Who was the Manchester singer who did 'Sea-Drift' so well, and did he ever get the engagements he was promised on the strength of it? I should like to draw attention to him in 'The Sackbut'.

215
Jelka Delius to Philip Heseltine

Grez 14. 6. 20

Dear Phil, Fred is in Paris to-day and he wants me to write to you that he will have to go to London for about a week on the 1ˢᵗ of July to see about our claim, which can not be established without him, it appears. He has to sign it before somebody. He is so afraid of not getting room in any hotel. Could he perhaps stay with you in St George's Rd if the Van Dierens are not yet back?

He has not been so very well lately and this constant anxiety about the money makes him so nervous, I should love him to be in a place where he can rest a bit. If he is in an hotel he rushes about all day. I would go with him, but the journey is so frightfully expensive and I also think it much easier for 1 person to get lodged. Please write a p.c. at once and do not mention anything about his not being very strong; as he hates me to say so. But I cant help it, I get so anxious about him—

I am sure if once the claim and all that were satisfactorily settled he would be quite a different being.

You understand, dont you?

Affˡʸ your old friend
Jelka

---

[16] Heseltine wrote to his mother in April: 'I have not received my money from Beecham! It appears to be still possible for him to delay on the strength of his promise. I sincerely hope I shall not be obliged to institute proceedings all over again to compel him to keep his promise.' Heseltine to his mother, 28 Apr. 1920, BL 57961.

216
Philip Heseltine to Frederick Delius

The Sackbut
18 Berners Street
London, W.1

Telephone: *Subscription:*
Museum 3721   *One Year, 6/-*
                                                                        Post Free.
                                                          17ᵗʰ June 1920

Dear Friend

Here is the Baedeker—not a very new one but the best I can get second-hand. 10/=—the new ones are now 16/=. I am getting a definite contract from Lane for your book in 'Living Masters of Music' series this week, and I hope very much to be able to come over soon and discuss it with you, but T. B. has not yet paid and is, I hear, now nearer to complete bankruptcy than ever.

Much love—

Ever affectionately
Philip Heseltine

Am sending N° 2 of the Sackbut.

217
Jelka Delius to Philip Heseltine

Grez 19. 6. 20

My dear Phil,

I wrote to you a few days ago, asking you if Fred could stay with you for a few days at St George's Rd. But now his lawyer has written that his presence in London is not necessary, he will be allowed to sign his claim in Paris before the consul. We both wish you could come over *now* and stay with us and get all the details and material for the Delius Biography. Fred intends going to the sea, either Brittany or Normandy for July and 1ˢᵗ half of August. Of course, if he knew you were coming he could postpone it a little. Surely that little bit that T. B. owes you is but a corn of sand in the sea of his debts. Is there no way of worming it out of his lawyers? We should love to have you here a bit. If you cannot come now, it must be latter half of August.

The Sackbut has not arrived yet, nor the Baedeker   Fred is in Paris to-day but he will send you a cheque for the book at once.

Best love from us both
Jelka

How is van Dieren?

218
Frederick Delius to Philip Heseltine

Grez-sur-Loing
(S & M)
22 June 20

My dear Phil—Many thanks for the Baedeker   Enclosed 10/—Your leader in the Sackbut is *very good*—If you keep up to this mark you are bound to succeed —It is also very courageous & very true   It was well you showed the different attitudes of Newman & Busoni towards unknown work—Try & get at all abuses which are so many in the musical world of England—you will become respected by all earnest musicians & feared by all 'arrivists' critics & humbugs.

I wish you could come over here for a few days—or come with me to Brittany —I would gladly pay your expenses if I had my money—but, I fear, it will take some months yet before I touch anything. I shall be in Grez until the 8th or 10th of July & then go to St Malo or Roscof.

With love from us both

ever affectionately
Frederick Delius

Many thanks for the songs   My little sweet darling is charming & so is 'There is a lady sweet & kind'—'When the rye' is also good—'Mourne no more' I like the least—

219
Philip Heseltine to Frederick Delius

The Sackbut
18 Berners Street
London,
W.1

Telephone
Museum 3721

Subscription:
One Year, 6/-
Post Free.

June 24th 1920.

My dear Friend

Very many thanks for the 10/= which arrived safely this morning, and for your kind words about my article in 'The Sackbut', which cheered and encouraged me very much indeed. It would be a very great help to me if you would write and tell me which of the many abuses and anomalies of English musical life you consider the most heinous and most worthy of attack at the earliest possible moment. I feel sure than an offensive policy is the right one, so long as one balances one's attacks with constructive articles and sound original ideas.

I should love to come over to Grez at once but I simply hav'nt got the train-fare. If I can possibly manage it, I will come and spend a few days at St Malo with you, or at Grez, if you return there in August.

Much love to you both

Ever affectionately
Philip Heseltine

220
Frederick Delius to Philip Heseltine

Grez-sur-Loing
(S & M)
29 June
20

My dear Phil—

I am leaving for Paramé or Roscof in Brittany about July 11ᵗʰ—I hope you will be able to join me there later or if not come & stay with us here in September for a couple of weeks. One of the abuses in the English music world is the 'first performance craze'—There are many others which I will indicate to you when I have a little leisure—You ought also to have a column in the Sackbut of enquiries—for instance—We should like to know why so & so etc—Let us say, as an example—'We should like to know why none of the works of Delius were included in the Programms of the so called British Music Festival.' Here we have the clique abuse again—You ought also to have a sort of review of the musical criticisms on a new important work—Especially to draw attention to anything especially inane or idiotic—Ernest Newman could be held up to great advantage every now & then—Some of his articles are really nothing but words—a sort of writing Diarrhoea—Such a review would at once make the critics more careful—It would perhaps raise the standard—What are more useless or idiotic than Kalisch's notices in the Daily News! Newman wrote an especially stupid notice on my 'Double Concerto' as time will show—There is no Concerto where the solo instruments blend so well with the Orchestra or where there are fewer unnecessary passages—Write soon again

Ever affectionately
Frederick Delius

P.S. I've not read or heard a thing about that Welsh Festival and should like so much to know how the Arabesk went?[17]

Postscript in Jelka's hand.

---

[17] *An Arabesque* was conducted by Arthur Sims at the Welsh Musical Festival at Newport on 28 May.

221
Philip Heseltine to Frederick Delius

The Sackbut
18 Berners Street
London,
W.1

Telephone   *Subscription:*
Museum 3721   *One Year, 6/-*
                                                                      Post Free.

Tuesday. [July or August 1920]

My dear Friend

Very reluctantly I have put the piss-pot away out of sight and Pussy no longer copulates. I have added a very cryptic *editor's footnote* about the Martyr's Memorial tradition at Oxford which will indicate that 'bowler hat' (which I have substituted as the spire-decoration) is more or less of a euphemism.[18]

I have changed fecal matter to 'dung' ('manure' if you like) and left the quotation which, *being in French*, won't matter at all. Remember the respectable American 'Musical Quarterly' referred to a *pot de nuit* last month!

I assure you this last reference won't do any harm whatever, but if you are still anxious about it let me know at once and I'll strike it out in the proofs—which are not yet to hand or I'd send you one.

But *please* let it stand—it is such an excellent comparison!

In great haste—

Affectionately
Φ.

P.S. Many thanks for forwarding letters and the MS sketches which arrived safely last week.

---

[18] These are all references to the article 'At the Cross-Roads' which Delius wrote for *The Sackbut*, 1/5 (Sept. 1920), 205–8.

222
Frederick Delius to Philip Heseltine

Grez-sur-Loing
(S & M)
14/7/20

My dear Phil—I have decided to stay here until I go to Spain in September. Brittany was so overfull I could get in nowhere—Now come here when you like & stay as long as you like—The weather is lovely & the garden full of fruit —I am receiving the visit of a M[r] Basil Dean[19] of the St Martin's Theatre to morrow—He wants to shew me a play!! Who is he?—M[r] Dent's song[20] in the Sackbut rather amuses me—He has taken the sherzo of my quartett as his motiv!—Have you heard anything of the 'Arabesque' performance? Who conducted etc.?—When you come I advise you to go via Southampton—they have large & comfortable boats & one can go to bed—you arrive in Paris at noon & can take the 5.45 train to Bourron (Gare de Lyon) arriving in time for dinner.

Ever affectionately
Frederick Delius

223
Philip Heseltine to Frederick Delius

The Sackbut   *Telephone:*
18 Berners Street   *Museum 3721*
London,
W.1   July 25th 1920

Dear Friend

All being well, I hope to be able to come over and see you in about a week or ten days from now—if that would suit you?

[19] Basil Dean (1888–1978), English critic, dramatist, and theatre director. From 1919 onwards he was active in the London theatre, both as manager (with Alec Rea as ReandeaN until 1926) and as director. He was a pioneer of stage lighting.
[20] Edward Dent, 'The Piper', *The Sackbut* (May 1920), 23–6.

I must first prepare the August 'Sackbut', and also see about moving my things into some new rooms I am taking. After that I shall be free for a while.

Much love to you both.

Ever affectionately
Philip Heseltine

Postcard.

224
Frederick Delius to Philip Heseltine

Grez-sur-Loing
(S & M)
27/ 7/ 20

My dear Phil—We shall both be delighted to have you. let me know a couple of days before your arrival   If you come by Southampton-Havre you can catch the 5.45 pm train to Bourron—(P. L. M. station & be in time for dinner in Grez—The Sackbut is splendid—better & better—if you keep on like this it will be the best periodical in England & the whole of the young lot will support it—Someone sent me Newman's article in the Sunday times—about you—Excellent! fancy consecrating a whole article to excusing himself—Tell Gray how much I appreciate his article[21]   It is first-rate & quite too much for Newman —I did not know that Gray had such excellently sound ideas & could express them so well—I feel altogether something very fresh about the Sackbut—the 'new Spirit'—It will blow away very soon all those very musty mists hanging over *all the London critics*   They will begin to be careful—

I felt that even Newman is beginning to fear the Sackbut—or let us say to become uneasy—For the last 15 years he has been spouting musical platitudes to admiring readers—Do you know where I can buy a violin—A friend of mine in South America wants one—Cheap—a good tone is the only essential.

With love
Frederick Delius

[21] C. Gray, 'The Task of Criticism', *The Sackbut*, 1/1 (May 1920), 9–13.

225
Philip Heseltine to Frederick Delius

The Sackbut   *Telephone:*
18 Berners Street   *Museum 3721*
London,
W.1   *August 1ˢᵗ 1920*

Dear Friend

After all I find I have too much to do just at the moment, preparing the August 'Sackbut', but I hope to come across next Sunday or Monday at the very latest. I am so much looking forward to seeing you. Thanks ever so much for your kind words about the paper.

Ever affectionately
Φ.

Postcard.

226
Jelka Delius to Philip Heseltine

[Grez]

Dear Phil—We are looking forward immensely to your visit—Could you bring about 1/2 Lb of Carrowy seeds[22] (not obtainable in France) and some Ceylon tea, a pound if you can

Do not forget to ask for your Passport visa *aller* et *retour* as otherwise you have to start all formalities again for the journey back.

Best love from us both. The most luscious plums are awaiting you here.

Affly J. D.

Wednesday 4. 8. 20

Postcard.

---

[22] Caraway seed, the aromatic, pungent fruit of the caraway used in cooking.

227
Philip Heseltine to Frederick Delius

The Sackbut
18 Berners Street
London,
W.1

Telephone
Museum 3721

Subscription:
One Year, 6/-
Post Free

August 11ᵗʰ 1920.

My dear Friend

All being well, I shall come over on Saturday. I hope to reach you by the evening but I'm not sure of the trains out of Paris. I ca'nt face the long sea-passage by Southampton. However, I am going to make enquiries at Cook's to-day about the routes and will send you a telegram.

I have been horribly delayed by one thing after another—including the move into my new rooms in Cheyne Walk—the best street in London, for my taste.[23] The August 'Sackbut' has been rather a difficult number but I am glad to say it has turned out extremely well and will be quite the best so far.

I will find out about a violin for your friend. There are several good places in Wardour Street. Winthrop Rogers plays the violin and would no doubt go and select a good instrument.

Much love to you both—how nice it will be to see you again in your own home!

Ever affectionately
Philip Heseltine

---

[23] He described his new lodgings to his mother: 'I believe I have at last found a habitation—in Cheyne Walk, the one street in London where I feel most happy. . . . I shall feel infinitely better once I get settled in a place of my own after such a long period of changing about from one place to another. Besides, I shall be able to have a pussy cat in Cheyne Walk, and that makes all the difference to one's happiness!' Heseltine to his mother, 22 July 1920, BL 57961.

228
Philip Heseltine to Frederick Delius

The Sackbut
18 Berners Street
London,
W.1

Telephone   Subscription:
Museum 3721   One Year, 6/-
                                                                          Post Free.
                                              122 Cheyne Walk, Chelsea S.W. 10.

Friday 27th August. [1920]

My dear Friend

I called at St Martin's Theatre yesterday but did not succeed in seeing anyone. This morning, however, I encountered Dean's manager who told me that a letter settling the whole matter was posted on Tuesday: so that is all right. I am so tremendously pleased, as the play is so good and a run at a London theatre will enable thousands of people to become acquainted with your work who might otherwise never hear a note of it.

I wonder whether Dean said anything about the conductor in his letter? Do let me know if he did: I am fearfully excited over the project. I have always longed for a chance to conduct a performance of some work of yours, but never dreamed that it would come.[24]

John Lane has written with a definite offer of £25 for a book of 25,000 words about you, materials for illustrations to be provided by me. This is better than I expected and I shall accept it and get to work at once.[25] As regards the illustrations, I suggest one of the Frankfort photographs, the early photograph taken at Bradford with your mother (which I find I brought away in the MS book of autobiography) and—if they can be procured—photographs of the outside of the house at Grez taken diagonally from the street and showing the church

---

[24] Heseltine had written to Gray: 'At present negotiations are on foot with a London theatre-manager for incidental music for a very admirable new play for next January. If it comes off (i.e. if the manager accedes to D's somewhat elevated terms) D. has promised to get me the conductorship for the run—as far as it is in his power to do so, at least. This would mean a very pleasant little orchestra which might (given the shekels) be turned to very good account in Sackbut concerts.' Heseltine to Gray, 21 Aug. 1920, BL 57794–57803.

[25] Heseltine told his mother that: 'John Lane has finally offered £25 for my book on Delius—which is more than I hoped for from this notorious skinflint.' Heseltine to his mother, 31 Aug. 1920, BL 57961.

tower, and of your room, showing the piano and the Gauguin.[26] These, I think, will fulfil all the conventional publisher's requirements.

I shall call and see Volkert this afternoon. Rogers is not in town at present but I will see him as soon as he returns and suggest that he hold himself in readiness to produce the 'Hassan' music simultaneously with the production of the play, giving you the same royalty as for the songs—i.e. 33 1/3%. Send me over your pencil sketches as you do them and I will make the score and any additional copies you want. Your part-songs are being sent off to-day: it appears that a former parcel of them was despatched at the time of publication but evidently never arrived. I am sending at the same time my first set of 'little Peterisms' which you said you had'nt seen. Rogers has apparently become very alarmed at the expenses of 'The Sackbut' and now proposes not to pay either me or the business manageress any more salary till the paper begins to make a profit! As far as I am concerned, I am indifferent so long as the paper is carried on on the present lines: I know it is doing good work and whether I make money out of it or not affects me very little. But the 'business' lady is, of course, furious and wants me to stand by her and insist on a salary; she also works in the advertisement business for other publishers and she assures me that the paper has made such a good start that even if Rogers dropped it altogether she could get a certain other publisher to continue to finance it. However, I don't want to contemplate the possibility of any such change. But this lady, in her righteous indignation, has opened my eyes somewhat as to Rogers' financial methods; his respectability, it seems, is not altogether a guarantee against a certain slipperiness. He proposes *when the Sackbut does pay a profit*—if ever!—to keep <u>50%</u> himself, dividing the other half between me and the manageress! As it is, for the amount I write, I get paid less than any other contributor—to say nothing of having to do all the editorial work, correspondence etc myself. However, the work itself is, I feel sure, good and useful, and money is—if one has enough of one's own to keep body and soul together—quite a secondary consideration. Still I think the old man is rather mean. I was amazed when he launched out on a new paper at all—but he is a business man and he cannot have imagined that a new paper can be started with no initial outlay. One is bound to lose

---

[26] A reference to the painting *Nevermore* (oil on canvas, 60.3 × 116.2 cm.) by Paul Gauguin (1848–1903), which hung in the music-room at Grez. The work is a free adaptation of Manet's *Olympia*, which Gauguin had copied before going to Tahiti in 1891. It attempts to suggest the superstitious dread of the Tahitian woman who lies alone in the foreground. In a letter to his friend Daniel de Monfreid in Paris in 1897 describing this work, Gauguin wrote: 'With a simple nude I wished to suggest a certain long-gone barbaric luxury. It is all drowned in colours which are deliberately sombre and melancholy . . . for its title "Nevermore", not exactly the raven from Edgar Poe, but the bird of the devil which keeps watch. It's badly painted . . . never mind, I think that it's a good canvas.' A. Bowness, *Gauguin* (London, 1991), 23. Delius had bought it for 500 francs in 1898 but was forced to sell it during a financial crisis in 1920. It now hangs in the Courtauld Institute Galleries in London. Jelka Delius made a copy of it which was hung at Grez.

money, not only for 3 months but for 6, a year even, over any artistic enterprise in this country. . . .

The journey to London took *27 hours* this time. We remained at
Southampton an hour in the harbour and another hour in the station. In Paris
I met a friend at the Café de la Rotonde (what an incredible place—in these
days!—to have survived the war!) and very nearly remained there. . . Paris is
infinitely more alive than this wretched place.

I enjoyed my ten days at Grez so very much and wish it could have been
longer[27]—but as it is I don't know how I am going to get through all I have to
do in the next three or four weeks—besides having to face interminable inter-
views with old Rogers over this Sackbut business. And he never stops talking!

Well, good-bye for the moment—and may 'Hassan' grow and prosper—I am
longing for the first instalment of sketches: that lovely serenade still floats in
my mind.

Much love and very, very many thanks to both of you for all your kindness
during my most delightful stay with you.

Ever yours most affectionately
Philip Heseltine

P.S. Of your songs I find that about 150 of each have been disposed of—which
means about 100 actually *sold*.

229
Frederick Delius to Philip Heseltine

Grez 29. 8. 1920

Dear Phil,

Your letter just received. I received Deans letter accepting my conditions the
day after you left. Enclosed I send you a letter I received from him this morning concerning the conducting

I think we shall get at in the end all the same, namely in this way:

---

[27] Heseltine had been to Grez to collect some information for his book on Delius. He wrote to Gray: 'I have extracted
a great deal of interestin' biographical material from mine host, and also examined a number of early scores which
reveal an extraordinary mastery of conventional technique and here and there a bar or two of the later harmonic idiosyn-
crasies interspersed. He has written very much more than I ever suspected: his list of works from 1885 to 1893 is quite
formidably long.' Heseltine to Gray, 21 Aug. 1920, BL 57794–57803.

I am writing to Dean to-day and am suggesting that you shall attend all the rehearsals, that you will conduct the chorus behind the scenes free of charge and that you conduct the performances when the other man has a day off or is in any way prevented. In this way we shall gradually get there. In a couple of days I shall send you the first and 2ᵈ acts Pencil sketches. Please write big and wide apart so that the conductor can conduct from your score.[28]

The prelude to the 1st act I shall finish when I have done the 5 acts. It is awfully kind of you to make me this score, dear Phil; you are saving me an enormous amount of trouble.

I'm glad you've arranged with J. Lane. I shall send you a number of photos of the house and garden—the more the better. People always love illustrations. I think you also ought to have the little one with the stick. We'll get Mrs Brooks to do one of the study with piano.

There is not a publisher that isn't 'slippery' to say the least of it. Stick to the Sackbut and I shall speak to Rogers when I come to London. Please also try and find out how many Cello Sonatas have been sold. As soon as I get my money I shall be able to help you ought if you run short. Jelka reminds me that we borrowed 10 frs from you which I enclose—excuse! We loved your visit and hope you will soon come again. Dont forget about the furnished appartment. It will be for about the 1st December.

With love from us both
Frederick Delius

Dear Phil,
I have at last found leisure to read the latest Sackbut and have enjoyed it immensely. Love from Jelka

In Jelka's hand.

---

[28] See Threlfall, *Delius: A Supplementary Catalogue*, 32, for details of this MS.

230
Philip Heseltine to Frederick Delius

The Sackbut
18 Berners Street
London,
W.1

Telephone   *Subscription:*
Museum 3721   *One Year, 6/-*
                                                          Post Free

August 31ˢᵗ 1920

My dear Friend

Thank you so much for your letter and the 10 franc note which arrived this morning. I am sorry about the conducting but I feared all along that there would be a permanent conductor attached to the theatre, fixed and immutable as the rock of ages. The only drawback to my becoming conductor of the chorus (and there's probably one of those, too, waiting to bob up as soon as one mentions the subject!) is that it would necessitate my giving up all my concert reporting, and I dont know whether I can really afford that. It would, of course, have been well worth while to give it up in order to take over the whole musical direction of the piece since, payment or no payment, I would far rather be a conductor than a critic; but as it is, it would involve the almost complete absence of any concert or opera notices in 'The Sackbut', for Lorenz²⁹ is not often free in the evenings and Gray is too erratic to be depended upon for definite concert work. In addition to this, Dent³⁰ who is shortly going to Germany for several months, is doing his best to get me installed in his place as musical critic to 'Truth', a weekly publication³¹ which pays tolerably well; and if they will have me, I do not think—in view of Rogers' sudden withdrawal of my meagre 'Sackbut' salary—that I ought to refuse this offer, especially as it will enable me to address a wider circle of readers than I can get at through a purely musical

---

²⁹ Robert Lorenz (1891–1945), an amateur musician, writer on music, and broadcaster. He was clearly a typical member of the Heseltine circle. On several occasions at Queen's Hall he raised his strong and resonant voice in protest against some work of which he disapproved. He would wait until the applause had died down and then give tongue with startling effect, declaring that he had as much right to express his opinion as the rest of the audience had to express theirs.

³⁰ Edward Dent (1876–1957), a lecturer at Cambridge University and later to become Professor of Music there.

³¹ *Truth*, a weekly paper which devoted a column to musical comment and criticism. It carried the high-flown quotation 'Cultores Veritatis Fraudis Inimici' (Cicero) on the first page. Heseltine was not appointed to the staff of this paper.

paper: and, of course, the more papers I can gain admission to, the more chance our anti-humbuggery campaign has of making a big effect on the musical public. Dent has also offered me the 'London Mercury' music pages; this is a literary quarterly, edited by J. C. Squire.[32] However, it is possible that by December something may be arranged so that I can do both critic and chorus-masters jobs. Besides, Dent may be back before the play is actually produced.

A letter from Gardiner, which I enclose, pursued me to Grez and back here again. He thinks Leuckart's demands exorbitant. They wanted £7:10:0. for the mere permission to use the Philharmonic Choir's parts of the 'Song of the High Hills'. I saw Volkert and he tells me that the Genossenschaft and the Performing Right Society will be re-amalgamated within a few weeks, that Goodwin and Tabb cannot possibly collect your performing fees and that your best course will be to send in your resignation to the Performing Right Society which will automatically collect your fees here as soon as relations are established again with the Genossenschaft. You cannot now be a member of both societies, though during the war it was permissible for a British member of the German society to transfer his membership to the British society—which is apparently what happened in your case.

If you are not too frightfully busy with 'Hassan', would you be very kind and write in the phrasing in the enclosed Purcell quartet? I should be most grateful if you could find time to do this as I want to perform this piece at the first 'Sackbut' concert in October and not being a string player I find the technicalities of correct string quartet phrasing extremely difficult. Please forgive me for troubling you with this but I know no string players here and I dont want to leave the work to the tender mercies of the performers as it stands, as they are not, I think, overburdened with intelligence.

I think it is still a bit early for the furnished flat if you dont want it till December. If it were vacant now, the owners would of course want to let it at once; and they don't usually put it on the house-agents books until the time it does fall vacant—or thereabouts. But I will keep my eyes open and make enquiries.

Much love and every good wish to you both.

Ever yours most affectionately
Philip Heseltine

[32] Sir John C. Squire (1884–1958), the editor of the *London Mercury* and a friend of Heseltine's. Heseltine set his poem *Mr Belloc's Fancy* to music.

231
Frederick Delius to Philip Heseltine

Grez sur Loing
Seine et M.
31. 8. 1920

Dear Phil,

I have thought rather a lot about my article in the Sackbut and I come to the Conclusion that I shall only weaken the effect of my article by having in it those 2 or 3 rather risky similes. This article is too serious that I should leave myself open to attacks which will surely be made on these points   It is not quite dignified enough. For the Jerry on the Cathedral I should like to find some other Simile; Perhaps the Jester's cap and bells?[33]

Take away *copulating* perhaps you can put caterwauling cats?[34] Take out the fecal matter and chocolate and ce n'est pas de las [unclear] entirely; you will probably find another Simile: You see they would try (Evans and C°) to discredit me just on these points. I absolutely do not want to have weak points— I know my english public—Send me the proofs or answer as soon as you can. I shall be from tomorrow til Saturday in Paris 13 Rue Alger Hotel Oxford and Cambridge.

I hope you got our registered and other letters we sent on. Dont forget the Violin and get a good Violinist to try it.

Ever aff[ly]
Frederick Delius

What had Gardiner to say
P.S. Tell Rogers to send me on the contract of those partsongs as he promised to do.

In Jelka's hand.

---

[33] In the final version of Delius's article the relevant sentence ran: '. . . sticks a bowler-hat on the top of the spire . . .'. In a footnote to the article Heseltine added 'To anyone acquainted with the "Martyr's memorial" tradition, this will seem a euphemism'. F. Delius, 'At the Cross-Roads', *The Sackbut*, 1/5 (Sept. 1920), 205–8.

[34] In the final version of Delius's article the phrase 'cries of cats' was eventually substituted.

232
Jelka Delius to Philip Heseltine

[Grez]
10. 9. 20

Dear Phil, I sent Fred your letter about the Sackb. article today to Hendaye where I am to join him on Saturday. So if not yet posted send proofs straight there. But I was under instruction to leave out the chocolate synonym altogether; and think it is really better. People who do not know him personally would get a wrong idea. The spoken word is so different from cold print

In haste to catch post affly Jelka

address Hendaye (Basses Pyr[enées])
Hotel de la Plage

Postcard.

233
Frederick Delius to Philip Heseltine

Hotel de la Plage
(Basses Pyrenées) Hendaye
11/9/20

My dear Phil—I received your two letters—one enclosing the string quartet which I will return you a few days—I am not acquainted with Purcel's music—but will do my best—

I am afraid the 'Chocolat' must come out as well—I can easily bring it in in another article—but I want first to feel the pulse of the public & it is no use shocking them to start with—Send me the proofs here to above address—I am having a lovely time sea bathing on a sunny beach—Hassan does not come off until March *earliest*   When you make the copy of the score please write out all bars marked idem in full it avoids confusion & mistakes.

Jelka joins me here for 2 or 3 weeks on Tuesday

Ever yours affectionately
Frederick Delius

Rogers made out my account on the basis of 4^d in 2/. 2^d in the shilling whereas I had arranged with him for 4^d in the shilling—He seems to resemble the rest of them   I am writing about it.

234
Frederick Delius to Philip Heseltine

Hotel Imatz
Hendaye
(Basses Pyrenées)

[12 September 1920]

Dear Phil. I am down here for a few weeks—I hope you got my letter altering the Jerry & copulating & chocolat!! It is better not to risk spoiling a good cause for a few jokes

Ever affectionately
Fr. Delius

Postcard.

235
Jelka Delius to Philip Heseltine

Dear Phil, To-day is the 22nd and we are awfully disappointed not to have received the Sackbut yet??

affly yours
Jelka

Hotel Imatz
Hendaye (Basses Pyr[enées])
22. 9. 1920

Postcard.

236
Frederick Delius to Philip Heseltine

Grez sur-Loing
S et M.
30/9/20

My dear Phil—I sent you the 5ᵗʰ act of Hassan   did you get it—Thanks for your letter—what a nuisance about Rogers & the Sackbut—Stick to it if you possibly can as it will pay in the end & the worst part has been done—namely starting a new paper successfully—As soon as I get my money I can also help— Can't Gray help now? I hope you sent the proofs of the Requiem back to Vienna as it is in a hurry. Write me all about the Concert.

With love from us both

ever affectionately
Frederick Delius

P.S.
Why unearth old Gesualdo Venosa?[35]

---

[35] Don Carlo Gesualdo (c. 1560–1613), Italian composer and lutenist. Heseltine and Cecil Gray later wrote a book on him: *Carlo Gesualdo: Musician and Murderer* (London, 1926).

Or any old mouldy composer?
Let him rest in his grave,
Why these madrigals save?
Enough rotten music we know Sir.

237
Frederick Delius to Philip Heseltine

Grez sur Loing
Seine et Marne
30. Sept 1920

My dear Phil,

We received 1 Sackbut of Sept. and one of August   Send me another copy if possible. This number is again splendid   If there is any fee forthcoming for my article please keep it yourself.

I want now to buy that Violin. Have you looked about? 20 to 40 £.

It must be a violin with a strong carrying sound. It need not be ancient. I will send you the money as soon as you let me know that you have purchased one.

Get any good violinist of the Queens Hall or so to try it.

I was first at Hotel Imatz, then I changed for la Plage, and there found it so bad that I returned to Imatz. We came back here as the weather broke up entirely. I am working at Hassan and shall send you some more MS in a few days. If W. Rogers wishes to publish the music he can but I want 4^d in the shilling and not 2^d.

With love from us both Ever your affectionate
Frederick Delius

Heavenly warm weather here—Oh treacherous south!

In Jelka's hand.

238
Frederick Delius to Philip Heseltine

Grez sur Loing
S et M
3. 10. 20

Dear Phil. I send you to-day the correction of the Requiem. Please look it thro' carefully as quickly as possible and then send it to U. Ed. Vienna. I have corrected it, but of course you must recorrect it yourself. There are a few places I should like changed in the words.

Pg 9 'We are even as a day'. I put 2 quavers, but would it not be better to put 'e'en as a day[']? Decide yourself and correct it.

Pg 12 I have put 'again no more' instead of 'no more again'.

Pg 26. I do not think it quite gives the meaning in english. Gods and idols would be better; it means that the highway of life produces the beautiful (the Gods) as well as the absurd (Götzen). Please change it.

Page 27 I do not like 'remembrance more['']. I should prefer: nor have they (for the triplet) any *part* (on the d) in the ways and doings. Please put it in if you think it all right, for the triplet we should then have 2 notes only.

Pg 33 I have put 'her love she gave'. 'She gave herself' seemed to me too direct

Pge 46 'and swollen with rain the mountain torrents are over flowing' gives quite a wrong picture. It is *midsummer* and the sun has ripened the harvest. I suggest: 'and silvery brooks are ever chattering round their borders.' Please put it.

Also the last line

'*And then new Springtime*' I do not like much. If you can find something better or more sonorous vocals please put it. *Springtime* of course must remain *and then new* is not very good.

I have put my manuscript of the 3ᵈ Act Hassan in for you to copy if you will be so kind.

Gray's article is excellent again, but I think it a pity that he ends with that Depussy foot—and un-Ravel pun   It takes off the dignity of the whole. Stop him doing that. Scholes[36]—what a reply! He does not seem to mind publishing

---

[36] Percy Scholes (1877–1958), English music critic, organist, teacher, and lexicographer.

to the world that he has no discernment whatever. What a milksop. Send anything else about it! Please!

With love from us both Ever yours afft^ly
Fr. Delius

In Jelka's hand.

239
Frederick Delius to Philip Heseltine

16th Oct. [1920]
Grez-sur-Loing
(S & M)

My dear Phil,

I received to day another letter from my friend saying that the violin must
have a *big carrying tone*—It must not be a gritty instrument   Nothing for
amateurs. He is a concert player   Dont be in a hurry but get a professional
fiddler to try it. No doubt one will be able to take it on a 2 or 3 months trial.[37]
Did you get the Requiem proofs & the manuscript of Hassan? How are things
going with you & the Sackbut? I shall send you some more manuscript in a
few days

Ever affectionately
Frederick Delius

[37] On 24 Oct. Heseltine wrote to Anthony Bernard: 'I wonder if your friend Mangeot would be very kind and help
Delius in the matter of purchasing a violin.' Letter in the possession of Mary Bernard.

240
Jelka Delius to Philip Heseltine

Grez s/Loing
17. 10. 1920

Dear Phil,

Fred begs you to kindly find out Howard Jones's[38] address and to forward the enclosed to him.

What are the prospects in London, I mean, about the coal strike. How is the outlook for the private people   Would one get sufficient coal? We shall either spend the winter months at the Riviera or in London, and if we could only be warm and comfortable I think London would be much nicer. Little Orr who of course wants Fred to go down there gave such a lugubrious account of the prospects in London, that Fred at once decided for the Riviera, and wrote to some agencies. I think in a few days from now you will probably know what is going to happen and then *do let us know* so that we can decide. Dont you think for the English future of Fred's music London would be infinitely preferable.

He is playing something *so lovely* out of Hassan whilst I am writing.

It has been summer, warm till now, but to-day it rains most dismally.

Best love from Fred
affly yours
Jelka

Out of the treacherous D. Mail one gets no idea what is going on.

241
Philip Heseltine to Frederick Delius

Saturday Oct 23rd 1920.   122 Cheyne Walk, Chelsea S.W.10.

My dear Friend—Forgive me for not answering your letters before. I have been very hard worked and so much worried these last few days that I hardly know where I am. The second instalment of 'Hassan' MSS and proofs of the

---

[38] Evlyn Howard-Jones (1877–1951), English pianist who was later to become a close friend of the Deliuses. He taught piano in London and excelled in the playing of Delius's small-scale piano works. He was also founder and first conductor of a group of instrumentalists later to become the New Symphony Orchestra.

'Requiem' arrived safely and will be attended to this week. I am turning over the matter of the violin to a player named Mangeot[39] who no doubt will be able to select a suitable instrument. I myself unfortunately know nothing about violins nor how to set about purchasing one.

The Sackbut is in imminent danger. Rogers is a damned old milksop if ever there was one and has behaved so preposterously that I have been compelled to refuse to edit the paper any more under his proprietorship. His idea is that all controversy is vulgar and injurious to a paper (!!) and that however virulently anyone attacks you or your paper, you must never reply! (much less ever attack anyone yourself!) Of course this sort of thing would be intolerable, as much to one's contributors as to oneself—even if it were not the worst possible policy from a journalistic point of view. My article 'Ille Reporter' (June number)[40] has had the direct result of getting an 'advisory board' of well-known musicians set up to examine the MSS of unknown composers and report upon those suitable for publication or performance. Of course E. Newman has been very much riled at this, and without replying to my finishing blow delivered in August, started abusing me and Sorabji all over again in another paper, just as though one had never answered his ridiculous Sunday Times attacks. Following this comes a paragraph in the S. Times directly calculated to prejudice the public against the Sackbut concerts *before the event*.[41]

Now because I reply to these attacks in the October Sackbut,[42] Rogers goes quite mad, *tries to suppress the issue* of the paper and writes a letter to E. Newman expressing his regret that The Sackbut should ever have attacked that venerable personage!!![43] The whole business is thoroughly Tibetan, and I have been—and am still—at my wit's end, seeing solicitors and running round wildly after various people who might be able to help me financially to smash Rogers and continue the Sackbut—which has begun to do very well indeed—no thanks to Rogers for same! Of course he can, as publisher, continue with another editor (and an

[39] André Mangeot (1883–1970), Belgian-born violinist, leader of the International String Quartet.

[40] In this article 'Ille Reporter' (*The Sackbut*, 1/2 (June 1920), 53–6) Heseltine had discussed the function of a music critic, at the same time making reference to the Newman–Sorabji controversy. He told his mother 'my article *Ille Reporter* has had the direct result of prompting the British Music Society to establish what is called an "advisory board" to examine the manuscripts of unknown composers and report on those worthy of publication and performance. This Newman has had reluctantly to admit—and it has, of course, made him very wild since *Ille Reporter* was a direct attack upon himself.' Heseltine to his mother, 11 Oct. 1920, BL 57961.

[41] Heseltine told his mother: '. . . hence [Newman's] attempt on Sunday to prejudice the public against the Sackbut concerts in a particularly underhand way. However, he is not quite clever enough or else I am not quite such a fool as he takes me for: I at once sent off the article to Mr Emmet who tells me the paragraph in question is clearly actionable as malicious libel, so unless a profuse apology is forthcoming next Sunday (i.e. the day before the first concert), the Sackbut will proceed against the Sunday Times for damages. *Criticism before the event* is a principle which cannot be tolerated in any country where the most elementary notion of justice and fair play prevail.' Heseltine to his mother, 11 Oct. 1920, BL 57961.

[42] 'Contingencies', *The Sackbut*, 1/6 (Oct. 1920), 274–82.

[43] Rogers wrote to Heseltine: 'I have so far as possible, recalled the present edition of "The Sackbut" . . . I also feel that I must write to Mr Newman and apologise on my own behalf, and tell him that I strongly disapprove of the whole controversy—I am sure it has done "The Sackbut" harm.' Rogers to Heseltine, 19 Oct. 1920, BL 57964.

entirely new set of contributors, for not one of mine will help him), in which case I want to start a rival concern as the New Sackbut, or some such thing, and effectually smash his milk-and-water production. The business and advertisement manageress—an extremely competent person—is entirely on my side and will not work for Rogers any more if I go[44]—but will, on the other hand, assist me gratis. Personally I dont think Rogers can possibly continue—but he will of course try and get his old debts paid by the new concern—which he wo'nt succeed in doing, though.

I have secured a guarantee of £200 already but that is'nt enough for a new enterprise[45]—though if Rogers collapses, as I feel sure he will under legal pressure—it will do to carry on with for a few months.

Isn't it wretched—just when we were doing so well?

I'll write again in a day or so when my solicitor has had a go at Rogers, and will let you know what is to happen and how the land lies.

I hope you'll tell Rogers what a fool he is when next you see or write to him!! After this I certainly wo'nt offer him 'Hassan'. No doubt Augener will take it up as soon as I have a piano score ready. I hope you got your royalties all right in spite of his apparently characteristic attempt to swindle you out of 2^d in the shilling!

Much love to you both.

Ever affectionately yours
Philip Heseltine

Please excuse this wretched, idiotic letter—I am weary and very depressed and seem incapable of coherent expression. Will tell you about the concert in my next.

---

[44] Although she stayed with Heseltine during *The Sackbut*'s short existence; Robert Beckhard, however, reported May Voules as saying: 'I thought Warlock was quite mad. He had no sense of responsibilities. Gray warned me about his unreliability. We often stayed up until 4 am getting out an issue.' R. Beckhard, 'Notes from an American on a 1950s Warlock Odyssey', in D. Cox and J. Bishop (comps. and eds.), *Peter Warlock: A Centenary Celebration* (London, 1994), 202.

[45] Heseltine wrote to his mother: 'Evan Morgan [Lord Tredegar] has volunteered to buy Rogers out on my behalf if I can find the funds for continuing to issue the paper—so now I think success is assured.' Heseltine to his mother, 7 Nov. 1920, BL 57961. The next year he wrote to her again on the subject: 'The Sackbut . . . during the last two months has been in a state of inanition owing to the non-payment of the promised £200 from Evan Morgan.' Heseltine to his mother, 15 Mar. 1921, ibid.

242
Jelka Delius to Philip Heseltine

HOTEL OXFORD & CAMBRIDGE   PARIS
13, Rue d'Alger

Paris, le 15. 11 *1920*

Dear Phil

The Universal-Edition has written to Fred that the Piano Score Correction of the Requiem has not arrived yet and they are waiting for it anxiously. Fred hopes you have sent it off!!!!

I fear you have had a bad time over the Sackbut and we should love to hear that you have been able to manage, and that you have brought out the next number. We are here in Paris. Fred is leaving day after to-morrow for Francfort, where our friends have found us rooms. If we like it we shall stay a few months otherwise we'll come to London. Fearful Passport struggles of course. I am going a week later and shall be in Grez till then. Fred has not received any of the Hassan music back yet. As soon as he is settled in Francfort he will send you his address. And I am to send you the Prelude to the 1st act from Grez.

The Riviera seems horribly full and fancy-prices—besides we are looking forward immensely to all the good music, theatres and friends over there. I am glad to get away from all those household-duties.

Let us hear how the Sackbut fares. Hertzka is in London and negotiating with old Winthr Rog for a continental Ed. of the Delius Songs. I do not know his London address but old R. would of course. This in case you would like to see him. Best love from us both

always yrs
Jelka

243
Philip Heseltine to Frederick Delius

20.11.20.   122 Cheyne Walk
                                                   Chelsea S.W.10.

My dear Friend

The proofs of the *Requiem* went back to Vienna some time ago. They will no doubt have arrived safely by now as the packet was registered.

I saw Hertzka when he was in London, and liked him very much. He was very interested in the *Sackbut* and promised to send me all the new Universal publications of importance. He also took away several MSS of Van Dieren, including the 2ⁿᵈ String Quartet.[46] As publisher of Delius, Schönberg, Béla Bartòk and Van Dieren, he has now secured *all* the living composers of the first rank!

The *Sackbut* very, very nearly collapsed, but after long, complicated and extremely wearying negotiations I managed to buy it from Rogers and to scrape together enough capital to carry it on for another year at least—by which time there is a good chance of its being self-supporting if we make a great effort to make it known all over the world and to secure good contributors.

The November issue will be very late, owing to the fact that an agreement as to ownership was only reached last Thursday. However, better late than never and by next Thursday the new number will be on sale. The concert scheme, though, will have to be abandoned. One loses too much money over concerts in these days.

I hear from Hertzka and from Adila d'Aranyi[47] who has just returned from Budapest that poor Bartòk is in very difficult circumstances and scarcely able to keep body and soul together. He is compelled to spend all his days teaching and has no time nor energy for composition any more. This is a great shame, for he is one of the finest creative minds in the musical world to-day. I have lately made a careful examination of all his published works and my love and admiration for his music increases with each new work I come across.

The November number of the Sackbut is largely devoted to him.[48] Adila d'Aranyi is most anxious that he should come to England next year and give

---

[46] Van Dieren's 2nd String Quartet (Op. 9, 1917) was eventually published by Oxford University Press in 1928.

[47] Adila d'Aranyi (Fachiri) (1889–1962), Hungarian violinist; great-niece of Joseph Joachim and elder sister of the violinist Jelly d'Aranyi.

[48] For the November edition of *The Sackbut* (Vol. 1, no. 7), 309–12, Cecil Gray had written an article on Bartòk for which Heseltine copied out four pages of musical examples.

some concerts—and if a small sum of money could be guaranteed (say £100) he would gladly come: and it would be a very great help to him to take back to Hungary a little English money which would, of course, translate into an immense number of Kröner. Hertzka says that Schönberg has been in a similar plight. It is dreadful to think of the very few men of real genius in music at the present day being so harassed by mundane cares of this sort while tenth-rate vulgarian upstarts like Gustav Holst are acclaimed as great composers and imbeciles like Stravinsky crowned as veritable gods.

Dont stay in Frankfort too long but come over to London and help in the fight for good music and the recognition of true genius among composers!

Much love.

Ever affectionately yours
Philip Heseltine

244
Frederick Delius to Philip Heseltine

1. Dec. 1920

Carlton Hotel
Francfort a/M
Germany

Dear Phil,

We are now both here, and very comfortably lodged and we find it very agreable.

How is Hassan getting on? And how about the Violin. If your friend has not found anything suitable by now please let me know and we'll try and get one here.

Jelka told me that you met Hertzka and got on so well with him and that you have finally succeeded in assuring the existence of the Sackbut for another year—

I am very glad of this and I would thought it a great pity to have stopped it. I wrote to old Rogers about it but have not yet received an answer!!!

I hope you will send us the November number here. You never wrote me about your concert and Sorabji's sonata

Please let me hear a little how things are developing in London.

Hertzka's firm is the biggest publishing firm in the world now. Do go and hear the Harrisons play my double concerto on the 12th of Dec. Sunday afternoon and evening, and tell me how it went.[49]

How was van Dierens Quartett?

Ever affectionately
Frederick Delius

In Jelka's hand, signed by Delius.

245
Jelka Delius to Philip Heseltine

Dear Phil   Fred is so disappointed not to have heard from you. He'd love to know how the Sackbut fares and how things are getting on in London. Also he wants to go on with his composition of Hassan, but for that he requires the copies of the MSS. we sent you. Would you please do all you can to send them soon and *registered* of course. We have found a delightful little flat on the river which is most beautifull with all the churches in the misty distance. There are no end of Beethoven Concerts now.—Should you have a few earlier Sackbuts over, do send them and we will get the Frankfurter ztg interested. Also Simon would love to see the Harpsicord-piece, if you could send us a number with it in.—affly love from us both

Jelka

Carlton Hotel till after Xmas
13. 12. 1920

Postcard.

[49] Henry Wood conducted the Queen's Hall Orchestra on 12 Dec. in a programme which included Delius's concerto for violin and cello played by Beatrice and May Harrison. Beatrice played three cello solos (Bach, Saint-Saëns, and Kreisler) for good measure.

246
Frederick Delius to Philip Heseltine

91 Schaumainkai
Frankfurt a/M
26th Dec 20

My dear Phil—It is a long time since I heard from you & I hope that things are going well with you—I received the November Sackbut & was very glad to see an article on Bartok by Gray—You never let me know how the concerts went[50]—Van Dierens' quartet—my songs—Sorabji's Sonata etc—When you have a little leisure sit down & let me have a little news—I hear nothing about English affairs here—Did you hear the Harrisons play my double Concerto at the Sunday Concerts Dec 12th? When can I have the copy of Hassan—I should like to work on it here as soon as possible—Life here is very agreable Lots of music & operas & excellent plays at the Schauspielhaus—They are playing again a good deal of my music in Germany—amongst other things—the Violin Concerto—on Febr 21 & 22nd The Mass of Life at Elberfeld—Next tuesday 5 of my new Tischer Songs here—Life for us is cheap & we have hired a lovely appartment on the Main & feel very comfortable—the food in Restaurants is excellent—Prices for German's terribly dear—We shall stay here until we come to London—Did you hear Sammons & Felix Salmond[51] play the double? Write soon—A happy & lucky new year to you my boy—ever affectionately
Frederick Delius

---

[50] Two *Sackbut Concerts* had been organized for 18 Oct. and 2 Nov.
[51] Felix Salmond (1888–1952): English cellist. He played in the London String Quartet and also gave the first performance of the Elgar Cello Concerto in 1919.

1921

DURING the months remaining to them in Frankfurt the Deliuses were able to attend a goodly number of operas and concerts, including performances of Delius's own works. In about the middle of March they moved on to London where they rented an apartment in Swiss Cottage; here Delius commenced work on his Cello Concerto, which would occupy him until the end of May. The Deliuses left for Norway on 17 June where they had a relaxing holiday in Lesjaskog, in the valley of Gudbrandsdal, and it was here, on the mountainside above the village, that they had a small chalet built which commanded a spectacular view across the valley. During the course of their return journey (they left Norway on 24 August), they spent a further few days in London before returning to Grez on 2 September. During October Delius worked on the proofs of both *Hassan* and the Double Concerto. His last visit away from Grez that year was a week-long trip to his home city of Bradford to hear a performance of *Sea Drift*.

1921 was to prove a busy and eventful year for Heseltine. After editing the March edition of *The Sackbut* he travelled with a friend, Gerald Cooper, via Marseilles and Algiers, to Biskra, spending three days in the Sahara (24–6 March), travelling by train to Tunis, and then by sea to Naples. After a few days in both Rome and Vienna, he went to Budapest via Venice. There he stayed with Bartók and met Kodaly, returning to London via Vienna and Munich towards the end of April. On 28 May he left England once again, this time for France, where he spent a few weeks in Brittany. By July he was stranded in Paris almost penniless and, on returning to London, found that in his absence he had been relieved of the editorship of *The Sackbut* and publication had been taken over by Curwen. In the autumn Heseltine moved back to Cefn Bryntalch, where he was to stay until mid-1924. Lawrence's novel *Women in Love* appeared and Heseltine threatened legal action, but the matter was settled out of court. Besides composing an ever-increasing number of songs, Heseltine was also working on Delius transcriptions for Universal Edition and also transcribing a large number of Elizabethan lute songs.

247
Frederick Delius to Philip Heseltine

Jan 7. 21   91 Schaumainkai
                                                      Frankfurt ª/M

My dear Phil—I received your letter 2 or 3 days ago & the score of Hassan yesterday—Many thanks for the copy which saved me a lot of tedious work & strain on my eyes—I have not received the December Sackbut—To what address did you send it? I should very much like to have it—If you possibly can, hold out with the Sackbut—No one wants anything at first, but they will begin to want it—Try & hold out until I can help you with money—which I hope wont be long. Dont go to Paris for a long stay[1] it will entirely unfit you for any more work in London—Especially the Life in Montparnasse which is very agreable but which also breeds endless ratés. I never quite approved of the Sackbut Concerts—The Sackbut is quite sufficient & will absorb all your energy to run it successfully—The start is excellent, but you must keep at it & not give way if success does not come at once—you must make it a success & now that you are rid of Rogers you are no longer hampered—Gray is a valuable asset—You ought, of course, to review new works & first performances— naturally in a different way than the daily press. We shall probably come to London in March & hire a flat or small furnished house. I shall have to be in London most of this year—I should like a piano score with vocal part of Hassan & as soon as I have finished it I will send you the complete score—
    With love from us both

    ever affectionately
    Frederick Delius

P.S
One ought to be able to read in the Sackbut what is going on in the musical world—

---

[1] Heseltine had suddenly gone to France in Dec., leaving Gray to edit *The Sackbut*. He returned early in Jan. 1921.

248
Jelka Delius to Philip Heseltine

Dear Phil, Fred wants me to tell you that he has not received the Sackbut of December—and would love to have it. Also he has not seen the Programmes of the Philh. concerts and O'N[eill]. does not send them. *Could you* send them? You see he does not even know what they are doing of his, and at what dates? Besides he would like to know what they are doing altogether. Do not bother about a Violin any more, as he has just bought one. We are very comfortable here, we heard D'Albert² last night; he played a lovely Ballad by Grieg—but has gone off a bit upon the whole. We also heard the 2nd Mahler Symphony.
    Best love from us both

Always yʳˢ
J. Delius

20. 1. 21
Frankfurt ᵃ/ M
Schaumainkai 91

Postcard.

249
Jelka Delius to Philip Heseltine

Schaumainkai 91

21. 1. 1921

Dear Phil
    Fred who is working hard asks me to write and ask you to show the music of Hassan to *no-one*. I enclose the letter Dean sent Fred to-day—and you will understand.

---

² Eugene d'Albert (1864–1932), Scottish-born pianist and composer of Anglo-French parentage, German by adoption. He studied under Liszt and succeeded Joachim as director of the Berlin Hochschule für Musik in 1907.

I do hope you'll send us as much musical news from England as possible and also the last Sackbut—We hear nothing—not an english newspaper to be had in the place.

How are you?

In haste with both our love
Jelka D.

250
Basil Dean to Frederick Delius

Ltd
REANDEAN

GENERAL OFFICES:
ST. MARTIN'S THEATRE,
WEST STREET, W.C.2.
DATE 18th January, 1921

Frederick Delius Esq.
Carlton Hotel,
Frankfurt, A/M.

My dear Mr. Delius,

I have been hoping to hear from you for some days. My next production, which is a play by H. G. Wells[3] and St. John Ervine,[4] is approaching completion. So soon as that is over I want to come over to France to go into the question of 'HASSAN' pretty carefully with you. So I hope you will let me know when you are likely to be back at Grez.

A rumour came to my ears the other day that some of the music for 'HASSAN' was already in London for copying purposes. As this information was brought to me by the Musical Director of another management, (who declared he had seen some of it himself!!) I was naturally astonished. Of course I do not place any credence in idle rumours, but I think I ought to say that I should be deeply hurt if I were not to be given the first opportunity of seeing

---

[3] H. G. Wells (1866–1946), English novelist, journalist, sociologist, and popular historian. The play was *The Wonderful Visit*, a dramatization of a Wells novel.

[4] St John Greer Ervine (1883–1971), Irish dramatist and critic who settled in England. He was dramatic critic for a number of newspapers, including *The Observer*, and wrote a number of light drawing-room comedies for the London stage.

the work in connection with one of my own productions. As a matter of fact, it probably would be best for you to hold all the music until we have had our discussions then it can all come over to be copied at the same time.

Warmest regards to yourself and your wife,

Yours sincerely,
Basil Dean

Typed letter.

251
Frederick Delius to Philip Heseltine

91 Schaumainkai
Frankfurt ᵃ/M
[14 February 1921]

Dear Phil—What has become of *you*? I have never seen the December number of the Sackbut in which you published my souvenirs of Strindberg[5]—I should at least like to read it!! I have written several times for it without result. Are you ill? On the 15th March there is a concert of my works here[6]—then we go back to Grez for a fortnight & then to London—Write at once

Ever affectionately
Fr. Delius

Postcard.

---

[5] F. Delius, 'Recollections of Strindberg', *The Sackbut*, 1/8 (Dec. 1920), 353–4.
[6] A concert of Delius's chamber music for an audience of invited guests was being organized by Heinrich Simon.

252
Philip Heseltine to Frederick Delius

Cie G^{le} A bord
Transatlantique

16^e Mars 1921
Marseilles

My dear Friend,

I was so sorry not to be able to see you on Sunday, but I felt so wretchedly upset and bilious that I stayed in bed—which was I think just as well, seeing that all arrangements were made for setting out on this trip on Tuesday morning and it would have been a great nuisance if I had had to postpone our departure. As it is I feel much better and am greatly looking forward to the voyage across the Mediterranean which looks quite perfect on this golden sunny morning, under a cloudless sky.

I hope you have received the March Sackbut by this time. The April number is quite ready and will come out punctually on the 15th of next month. But I may be back by that time. However, in case I am not, would you or Jelka be so very kind as to read through the translation of an article by Busoni which I want to go into the April number?[7] It is the article which appeared in the *Anbruch* devoted to his works and it is being translated by Brian Lunn[8] (who once came to see you with me at Hobart Place). He is a very good German scholar but there may be certain purely musical phrases with which he is not acquainted and which you could just alter on his manuscript.

The Musical Times has asked me for an article on your choral works which I shall write when we get to Biskra.[9]

I can't tell you how much I enjoyed 'Appalachia'[10]—I do hope that your presence in London will stimulate more frequent performances of this and other things.

---

[7] In the event there was no Apr. edition of *The Sackbut*. The article referred to appeared in the July 1921 edition (edited by Heseltine's replacement, Ursula Greville) under the title 'A Schönberg Matinee'. A letter from Heseltine appeared in the Sept. edition pointing out that this article should have been acknowledged as 'a leaf from Busoni's Diary' reprinted from *Musikblätter der Anbruch*. 'Correspondence', *The Sackbut*, 2/3 (Sept. 1921), 35.

[8] Brian Lunn (1893–?), one of Heseltine's Oxford friends. There are several references to Heseltine in his autobiographical book, *Switchback* (London, 1948).

[9] No such article ever appeared.

[10] This performance of *Appalachia* took place in Queen's Hall on 10 Mar. with Albert Coates conducting the Royal Philharmonic Society Orchestra and Philharmonic Choir.

Are you choosing any of the performers for 'Hassan'? I know an excellent tenor who is very enthusiastic about your songs and would be very good for the serenade to Yasmin.

I shall write to you from the various places we visit.

With much love to you both.

Ever affectionately
Philip Heseltine

253
Philip Heseltine to Frederick Delius

March 28th 1921   Biskra

My dear Friend

I should have written to you before, but the heat and the general effect of this climate is such that one has very little energy for doing anything at all, even thinking. I suppose one benefits physically, but in other respects one feels rather dead. We have just returned from a three days expedition in the desert, on horse-back, with two camels to carry the tents and provisions. The effects of light and colour in this country are wonderful, especially in the evening about sunset; but there is a certain deadness about it that robs it—for me at any rate—of any emotional suggestiveness. And I found while riding in the Sahara that when-ever I travelled in my mind to some other place, the vision seemed more intense and real than my own surroundings: the desert has a strange tendency to vanish suddenly and give place to whatever rises up in one's imagination.

The Arabs on the whole are a degenerate, depressing crew—ill-clad and evil-smelling, persistent beggars and inveterate swindlers. Most of the wares exhib-ited for sale here look as though they had been imported from Manchester. And as for the women, Leicester Square or the lowest pub in Limehouse has nothing so incredibly revolting to show as the 'Ouled-Naïls' or dancing-girls who sit on the pavement in the evening and try to lure the unwary traveller into some stinking Café Maure where, as a preliminary to other things, the tedious Danse du Ventre is performed to the strains of a hideously strident tin-oboe and various kinds of tom-tom. For glamour and poetical suggestiveness give me the barrell-organ or the automatic piano! Only a Bantock or a Holst could find them in the street of the 'old nails'.[11]

We leave here to-morrow for Tunis and cross thence to Naples by sea. From there we make a wild rush up to Budapest where we shall be able to visit Béla Bartók.[12] We shall arrive there about April 7th and stay five or six days. If you should want me to do anything for you there, a letter addressed c/o Béla Bartók, I. Gyopar utca 2, Budapest would find me.

On the way home we shall spend a few days in Vienna (where I hope to see Hertzka)[13] and Munich, arriving back in London about April 20th—possibly a little later, but in any case before the end of the month.

I hope you have succeeded in finding a nice comfortable flat and that everything is going well with you. I look forward to seeing you again in a month's time, when I hope to have lots of news, as well as some new music to show you from Budapest. I understand that the other Hungarian composers, Zoltan Kodaly[14] and Ladislas Laitha,[15] as well as Bartók, have been writing very interesting things during the last few years.

It is possible that my generous host, Gerald Cooper,[16] may help Bartók to come to London and give some concerts. I hope so at any rate.

With much love to you both,

Ever yours affectionately
Philip Heseltine

[11] A reference to Gustav Holst's oriental suite for orchestra, *Beni Mora* (1910); the third movement is subtitled 'In the Street of the Ouled Naïls'.
[12] Heseltine had told his mother: 'I am looking forward most of all to Budapest and the interesting people I shall meet . . . If it turns out as good as I expect, and things can be arranged as I should like them to be, I might return there later in the year for a prolonged stay, to study composition with Béla Bartók, which would do me a world of good.' Heseltine to his mother, 4 Apr. 1921, BL 57961.
[13] Heseltine also told his mother: 'I shall visit Dr Hertzka, the director of the largest music publishing house in Europe—"Universal Edition"—whom I hope to interest in certain old English compositions of 300 years ago that still remain in manuscripts.' Heseltine to his mother, 27 Mar. 1921, BL 57961.
[14] Zoltán Kodály (1882–1967), Hungarian composer and teacher.
[15] Laszlo Lajtha (1892–1963), Hungarian composer, writer, and folk-music expert.
[16] Gerald Cooper (1892–1947): English singer and musicologist who was also one of Heseltine's friends. He was appointed secretary of the Royal Philharmonic Society in 1928. 'A budding London concert entrepreneur', he was described by Heseltine as being 'fabulously rich'. M. Gillies, *Bartók in Britain: A Guided Tour* (Oxford, 1989), 122.

254

Frederick Delius to Philip Heseltine

6.4.1921

21 Lancaster Rd
Hampstead N.W. 3

My dear Phil,

Many Thanks for your two nice letters which interested me very much. I know what the near Orient is. I was at Tangiers once and just as disgusted as you with all this picturesqueness got up for the stupid Europeans.

I have finished Hassan and am now just waiting for you to do me the Piano score. I am at present working at a Violincello-Concerto. We have a nice little flat very near where we were before in Hampstead, only smaller and nearer Swiss Cottage.[17] Broadwoods have put me a beautiful piano in.

The rehearsals of Hassan begin in August and it is to be produced in September.

Please give my kindest regards to Bartok and to Hertzka. I hope you'll thoroughly enjoy the rest of your trip.

Ever aff[ly] yours
Frederick Delius

In Jelka's hand.

255

Philip Heseltine to Frederick Delius

Budapest—April 21st 1921

My dear Friend

Many thanks for your letter which I found awaiting me at Bartók's. I am glad to hear you have found a nice flat and are feeling happy and comfortable.

---

[17] Lancaster Road is now Grove Road. This apartment was not far from where the Deliuses had stayed in Belsize Park Gardens.

We are having a most delightful though all too short stay in Budapest. Everybody is most kind and hospitable and Bartók is quite one of the most lovable personalities I have ever met. I have seen a good deal of him and of Zoltan Kodály and they have played me many of their works which have proved in the highest degree interesting.

Bartók is the biggest figure in Hungarian music by a long way—and the most comprehensive. Kodály seems to be developing chiefly in the direction of melody and rhythm, rather to the exclusion of harmony—save that which is implied by the melodic lines. Laszlo Lajtha, on the other hand, relies almost exclusively upon a very rich and complicated harmonic texture. Kodály has written an extraordinarily fine Sonata in three movements for the cello unaccompanied.[18] I would not have believed it possible for any modern composer to maintain such a high level of interest throughout a long work for a solo instrument, without ever for a moment being reminiscent of Bach or any other of the older composers. The work is to be published by Universal-Edition and ought to become very popular with 'cellists since, apart from its musical merits, it contains passages which, from the point of view of technique, are absolutely original and new. He has also a Duo in three movements for violin and cello—which contains an Adagio of wonderfully impassioned beauty; a string trio, a new string quartet, and two magnificent songs for baritone and orchestra which I am bringing back to London in the hope of getting them performed at the Promenade Concerts.[19]

Both Bartók and Kodály have suffered very severely, I am sad to say, from lack of food and fire during the last few years—and political disturbances have not made their lives any easier. Music seems to be very much bound up with politics—although the musicians are not by any means actively concerned with politics—and the present Christian-Socialist government does not seem to be at all favourably disposed towards new music—or new art of any kind.

At the opera here one gets an eternal round of Carmen, Evangelimann,[20] Die Jüdin[21] and even things like Meyerbeer's Nordstern![22] What a contrast to Vienna! The opera there is superb—Strauss conducts—and such an orchestra! There is nothing in England to approach it. The performance of 'Tristan' there was a perfect revelation to me. I heard it as though it were a new work altogether.

In Vienna I found, to my extreme delight and astonishment our old friend Shahid Suhrawardy who has been missing for the last five years! Everyone had quite given him up for dead, so you can imagine how pleased I was to see his

[18] Sonata for Unaccompanied Cello, Op. 8 (1915).

[19] The works referred to are the Duo for Violin and Cello, Op. 7 (1914), String Trio (1904), String Quartet No. 2 (1916–18), and Two Songs for Baritone and Orchestra (Ferenc Kölesey; Endre Ady) (1912; 1913–16).

[20] Der Evangelimann, opera (1895) by the Austrian composer Wilhelm Keinzl (1857–1941).

[21] La Juive, opera (1835) by Jacques Halévy (1799–1862).

[22] L'Etoile du Nord (1854), opera by Giacomo Meyerbeer (1791–1864).

name on a bill of the Moscow Art Theatre C⁰· (who are giving a season in Vienna), with whom he has been for some months ago acting in the capacity of régisseur. He hopes to come to England this summer for a much-needed rest, and proposes to write a book about his three years in Russia—which should prove most interesting as he seems to have known everybody and seen everything— which is much more than the casual visitor or journalist has ever been allowed to do.

I shall be back about May 1ˢᵗ and will then come and see you and tell you all the news.

Bartók and Kodály send you their very best wishes and would like to know more of your later works which have not yet penetrated to Budapest.

Much love to both of you.

Ever yours affectionately
Philip Heseltine

256
Jelka Delius to Philip Heseltine

Dear Phil, Fred says he begs you to make a complete Piano Score with everything in, the entries etc—as it has to serve for the 'Régie'. We shd so much like you to come up to supper one evening. Please name your own day.

Always yours
J. Delius

21 Lancaster Rd
N.W. 3
11. 5. 1921

Postcard.

257

Jelka Delius to Philip Heseltine

Tuesday [17 May 1921]

Dear Phil, will you come and sup with us ~~thursday~~ to-morrow, (wednesday) evening 7.30? Please wire or write if you can not come—

Always yours
Jelka Delius

21 Lancaster Rd N.W. 3

Postcard.

258

Frederick Delius to Philip Heseltine

[21 Lancaster Rd
Hampstead N.W.3]

Dear Phil, I hope you are getting on rapidly with the Hassan Piano score. I am due to deliver it and must also at once have a copy made to send to Vienna for publication. Try to meet me in Clark's[23] concert on friday and we'll arrange for another evening. I was so sorry yesterday—want to have a good chat with you

Always Yours
Fr. Delius

19. 5. 1921

Postcard, in Jelka's hand, signed by Delius.

---

[23] Edward Clark (1888–1962), English conductor and administrator, connected with the BBC in various capacities from 1923 to 1936. He was especially interested in contemporary music and was responsible for the first performances and broadcasts of important works. As Musical Director of BBC Newcastle, between 1924 and 1926, Clark conducted several first broadcast performances of Delius's works, including *Légende*, *In a Summer Garden*, and *North Country Sketches*.

259
Philip Heseltine to Frederick Delius

Tuesday [27 May 1921]   122 Cheyne Walk S.W.10.

My dear Friend

You are quite right—things have been just about as wrong as they possibly could be. For the past few weeks my existence has been such a nightmare that only my increasing belief in and fear of the something after death could have stopped me from putting an end to it altogether.[24] But you need have no anxiety about the piano score of Hassan. It will be ready in plenty of time to be copied and delivered by June 17th. I am going away to-morrow for a short while,[25] and hope to be able to deliver the complete MS to you by the 4th or 5th June. Please forgive the delay and my silence but I have been nearly demented during the past days.

Ever affectionately yours
Philip

[24] This mood persisted and in July Heseltine told his mother: 'I am sick and weary of wandering about, having no home and no certainties in life. I would, if necessary, abandon music altogether and take up something fixed and definite that brought in money steadily—if I were any good at anything else or could find anything else that I could take up. . . . I want to settle down and feel secure in a material sense—I have too little confidence in myself to resign myself to music and poverty for the rest of my days—though for myself alone, it would be no bad thing.' Heseltine to his mother, 25 July 1921, BL 57961.

[25] Heseltine was about to travel to France. He wrote to his mother from Camaret a few days later: 'I left London last week—it was getting altogether too much for me. I found I was spending too much time and energy over things that didn't really matter and my work was suffering in consequence . . . I shall probably remain here for some time as I have a great deal to do and the conditions for working are ideal. There is even a piano—of a sort.' Heseltine to his mother, 31 May 1921, BL 57961.

260
Philip Heseltine to Frederick Delius

June 1ˢᵗ 1921.

Hotel Moderne
Camaret
(Finistère)

My dear Friend

I have finished one fair copy of the piano score of *Hassan* and propose to make the other copy myself as I am desperately hard up and whoever is going to pay for it may just as well pay me as a copyist in London. I shall send off both copies to you on Saturday next at the latest, and the full score as well.

I think the work as a whole represents you at your very best and I am sure it will have a huge success. Some passages—notably the little 'Street of Felicity' motif, Hassan's Serenade to Yasmin, the wordless chorus, the Prelude to the third act, the Prelude to Act V with the entrancing horn theme, and the final chorus are among the loveliest things you have ever written, and I rejoice to think that they will be brought before a larger number of people than could ever be mustered in a mere concert hall for a single performance. Anyone who didn't previously know your works could not have a better introduction to them. *Hassan* is, to my mind, a sort of quintessence of Delius!

This is a lovely little village on the west coast—very like Cornwall and quite un-French. Lovely cliff scenery, splendid air and absolute peace and quiet—an ideal spot for work. I feel ever so much better already.[26]

Much love to both of you, and I hope you will thoroughly enjoy your trip to Norway.

Ever affectionately yours
Philip Heseltine

[26] In June Heseltine wrote to Gray: 'I have been staying here on the Breton—quasi-Cornish—coast for some weeks, working very hard—and really, for a change, getting on quite well—and drinking practically nothing. In fact I haven't been anything but strictly sober since the afternoon I left Paris when, staggering towards the Gare Montparnasse with a bag in one hand and a bottle of Calvados in the other, I fell prone before a tram-car and but for timely assistance might easily have missed more than my train. . . . To-morrow I am going down the coast to Quimper (nothing sexual about it) and thence to Carnac, the mystical centre of the Celtic world.' Heseltine to Gray, 21 June 1921, BL 57794.

261
Frederick Delius to Philip Heseltine

21 Lancaster Rd
Hampstead N.W.3

Wednesday [8 June 1921]

Dear Phil—The piano scores just received: I have not looked thro' them yet—
I shall send one off to Vienna at once—Many thanks—I wrote to Hertzka some
time ago to send you £5. I shall ascertain what the price of copying is here &
send you the money. There has to be also a copy of the full score—Can you
also undertake it?—I shall see to it that you get the highest possible fee.

Rean Dean pays this & I see him to morrow. Should you want money *at
once*. telegraph & I will send you some before leaving England—I surmise you
still have the full score as I have not received it—

I am glad you like the music. I have just finished my cello Concerto which
is good—a pity you can't join us in Norway. or can you? Keep up your spirits
my boy. ever your friend

Frederick Delius

I heard 'le Sacre du Printemps'[27] last night—an Anti-musical pretentious row—

262
Philip Heseltine to Frederick Delius

June 9ᵗʰ 1921.   Hotel Moderne
                                                              Camaret
                                                            (Finistère)

My dear Friend
    I am sending off the full score of *Hassan* to-day, together with a fair copy of
a song (4 sheets). Will you please give this latter to Orr when you see him.

    Affectionately
    Philip Heseltine

Picture postcard, Camaret-sur-Mer.

---

[27] Eugene Goossens conducted this, the first English concert performance of *Le Sacre*, in Queen's Hall, 7 June 1921.

263
Frederick Delius to Philip Heseltine

Mølmen
Lesjaskog
Gudbrandsdalen

Aug 6th/21

My dear Phil—I have been so lazy enjoying the wonderful scenery & air up here that I had not the energy to answer your letter before—Hassan arrived safely & is being printed in Vienna—I hope you received £5 from Hertzka—The piano score seems playable & well done—altho' you know I am a bad judge as I am no pianist—one or 2 passages I altered. As soon as I return I will go over it with you—I left the full score of the Cello Concerto with Beatrice Harrison for her to practice—May [Harrison] was going to try to make a piano score so that she might accompany Beatrice. No doubt a proper one will have to be made later. We will go over the North Country Sketches on my return—I shall be in London on the 26th inst & stay until the 30th—31st & then leave for Grez where we intend staying until Hassan calls me to London—I do not quite remember the passage of which you write. I am glad the Sackbut is not quite defunct— In order to make it pay you must in a certain measure appeal to the public taste. It must not be too dry or learned—you ought to have a review of the concerts & tell the public what is going on in the musical world—Bartok's article[28] is good but dry & prejudiced—to say that the 'sacre du printemps' is based on the real russian folk music is 'bunkum'   I have now heard it 3 times & it becomes duller more monotonous & brutally noisy every time one hears it   Eternal repetition of one entirely uninteresting phrase—I heard before leaving England quite a lot of the younger English composers—Bliss, Goossens & Co. Not one of them has any real personality—a sort of mixture of everything we have been hearing imported from Paris & Petrograd. More cheek than anything else—I am longing to get back to work again in Grez—I heard the Oriana choir[29] do my 2 a capella chorusses—'to be sung of a summernight on the water' *you must hear them*—to realize what one can do with a good chorus—We both send you our love—We intend building a little house upon the mountain for the next

---

[28] B. Bartók, 'The Relation of Folk Song to the Development of Art Music of our Time', *The Sackbut*, 2/2 (June 1921), 5–11.

[29] The Oriana Madrigal Society was founded by Charles Kennedy Scott in 1904. A hand-picked group, it was noted for the excellence of its performances of both old and new music. Beecham was a founder member, singing bass at its first public concert in 1905.

summer as we expect our money shortly—so you will be able to spend a summer with us here.

Ever affectionately
Frederick Delius

264
Frederick Delius to Philip Heseltine

Grez-sur-Loing
(S & M)

29 Sept 21

My dear Phil—I wrote to you several times to the address in Fleet Str which you told me would always find you. 10 days ago I wrote to ask you to send me the score of Hassan, as Rean Dean has my score & there are a few obscure passages in your piano score—please send at once & I will send you the score & piano score back as soon as corrected. The piano score is excellent—alter anything you think will improve—What has happened with the Sackbut? tell me all about it—If you can, come over & stay with us here for a while. the weather is heavenly & we have lots of fruit—In haste

Ever affectionately
Frederick Delius

P.S. If you could come at once we could go over the whole Hassan together. We found far the best route for Grez is Newhaven Dieppe, leaving Victoria at 8.15 p.m. Paris 6 a.m. Leaving gare de Lyon about 9. a.m. (Good café au lait breakfast at Gare de Lyon.

Postscript in Jelka's hand.

265
Frederick Delius to Philip Heseltine

Oct 14/21

Grez-sur-Loing
(S & M)

My dear Phil—I was very glad to hear from you & learn the truth about the Sackbut: I could not make out what had happened to the last 2 numbers.[30] I sent you yesterday the proofs of Hassan—There are several places which I cannot make out—not having the score—Please verify from the score in your possession. Try & come over here soon & we will go over things together. I will pay your return fare of course

I am very keen to see your piano version of the High Hills & Summer Garden[31]—Bring them when you come—I dont know when Hassan will be produced but I dont think before Christmas. I am also very glad that you left London & are quietly working in the Country having, no doubt, the same lovely weather as we are here—Since we returned on Sept 2 up til now unbroken Sunshine. We have several good photos for your biography—a very good one of my study. The 2nd Dance Rhapsody—'Eventyr' etc are locked up in Augener's safe & God knows when they will see the light—They are so terribly slow—I have only just corrected the proofs of the Double Concerto. When you go thro' London go & speak to Volkert about them & hurry them up. What you say about the Celtic element in my music is perfectly true. I have a latent streak some where deep down in my being which flames up every now and again—Probably atavistic from my Northern forebears—I know nothing whatever of Hebridean music & I believe never to have heard any. I have lost half of the poem of Life & Love & dont know whether I shall be able to complete this work. The lost part is just the new part & the best. I ought to be over in Bradford for October 26th Musical Festival where they are giving Sea-drift but I have not the courage to go. I have a pencil sketch of the Cello

[30] Heseltine wrote to Taylor about the fate of *The Sackbut*: 'The unhappy Sackbut, having expired for lack of funds, was put up for sale and I was thoroughly swindled and otherwise disgracefully treated by Mr Curwen who gave the poor old paper to his slut-like mistress [Ursula Greville] for a new toy. . . Mr C. added insult to injury by at first insisting that I should continue to edit the paper for him and then, without even communicating with me or telling me even that he proposed to resume publication on a certain date, he raked about among the MS articles I had collected, published a new number on his own account and then quietly appointed his whore as editor in my place—swindling me over the purchase money and refusing to pay the contributors to the number made up of MSS appropriated from me.' Heseltine to Taylor, 17 Oct. 1921, BL 54197.
[31] For details of the MS of this arrangement see Threlfall, *Delius: A Supplementary Catalogue*, 83.

Concerto which I will send you—it is, however, not complete. Come as soon as you can—

Love from us both—

ever affectionately
Frederick Delius

They are bringing out a newer edition of the 'Village Romeo.' bring your copy with you. with mistakes

266
Frederick Delius to Philip Heseltine

Dear Phil, On your way through London please go to Goodwin & Tabb and get from them the full score of Koanga and one corrected copy of the Village Romeo Piano Score. As soon as you have decided if and when you can come here let me know and I will send you a cheque for the journey. I *may* be obliged to go to the Bradford Festival on the 25th and 26th inst. and in that case we could travel back together   You could then study my cello Concerto here from my pencil sketch.

With love from us both

yrs affly
Fr. Delius

Grez s/Loing
S. et M.
15. Oct. 1921

Postcard, in Jelka's hand.

267

Philip Heseltine to Frederick Delius

Cefn-Bryntalch,
Abermule,
Montgomeryshire.

18.10.21.

My dear Friend,

I received your letter and card by the same post this morning and hearing of your intention to visit Bradford for the festival I hasten to add my entreaties to those of the municipality—in the hope that after due hommage has been paid to you in the north you will come and spend a few days with me here. I should be *so* pleased to see you here, and so would my people.[32]

Now do make up your mind and come! The country is looking quite lovely and the woods in their autumn dress are enchanting. I am sure you would enjoy a glimpse of wild Wales—and we have an aged but still very serviceable car which would enable you to see something of the fine hill scenery without fatigue.

I have looked up all the trains for you, both from London to Bradford and from Bradford to Abermule, so if you keep this letter in your pocket you can't go wrong. I am very glad that Bradford has at last become sensible of the honour you conferred on it by causing the stork that brought you into the world to alight on one of its chimneys—and I hope you will have a royal welcome.

Augener's have lately brought out a piano duet version of 'Eventyr' arranged by B. J. Dale.[33] I had a written contract from them for the arranging of this work and had been waiting in vain for months for them to send me the score. However I made up for the loss by extracting £10 out of Volkert for my arrangement of the 'North Country Sketches'. I shall write to him at once and ask for the loan of the MS score of the 2nd Dance Rhapsody.

My copy of the 'Village Romeo' is fully corrected and contains suggested re-translations of certain passages in the text. The 'Mass of Life' badly needs re-translation also. Wm Wallace's[34] version—printed in the programme of the

---

[32] Heseltine wrote to Gray two days later: 'Delius is probably coming here for a few days after the Bradford festival. I suppose it's no use inviting you—though if the family go away for Christmas as they doubtless will, we might have a good time a deux.' Heseltine to Gray, 20 Oct. 1921, BL 57794.

[33] Benjamin J. Dale (1885–1943), composer and educationalist. His compositions include a piano sonata (1902), cantatas, and several works for viola.

[34] William Wallace (1860–1940), Scottish composer and writer on music.

Covent Garden performance—reads better than Bernhoff's[35] but doesn't fit the music.

Hoping *very* much that you will come here on your way back from Bradford.

Ever affectionately yours
Philip Heseltine

TRAINS:—

	a.m.	p.m.	p.m.
London to Bradford (from King's Cross)	10.10	1.30	5.40
arrives at Bradford:	2.30	5.45	9.56

Bradford to Abermule:Bradford (Exchange sta^n: Lancashire and Yorkshire R^y) depart *9.40 a.m.*
Change at Halifax. Arrive Manchester (Victoria sta^n) *10.41*. Leave Manchester (London Road st^n) *11.50*—and there is a through carriage to the Cumbrian main line, to Welshpool (*arr. 3.0*) where I will meet you.

268
Frederick Delius to Philip Heseltine

Bradford Liberal Club,
Bradford,
Yorks.
12 Oak Avenue
Bradford

[26 October 1921]

Dear Phil—Many thanks for your kind invitation but I am afraid I cannot come—I only leave here on Friday & have to be in London for the 30th. & on the 31st leave for Grez. I do wish you could come to us—

Did you receive the proofs of Hassan—Thank your mother for her kind letter & invitation—

In haste

ever affectionately
Frederick Delius

[35] John Bernhoff, who was Harmonie's translator, made the original English translation of *A Mass of Life.*

269
Philip Heseltine to Frederick Delius

31 October 1921   *Cefn-Bryntalch*

I was so disappointed that you couldn't come and spend a few days here after Bradford. The weather has been perfect and I have never seen so glorious a riot of autumnal colours as we have in our woods and on the hillsides this year.

I would love to come over and see you and it is most kind of you to offer to pay the fare—but at present I feel that I daren't stop working and leave Wales.[36] I have been travelling about so much this year that things have got very much in arrears—and for one thing I am determined to get this book about you finally completed this year; it has been already too long hanging about halfdone.

And I am also, with great difficulty and still greater diffidence, starting composition again—an orchestral piece this time. I don't know what will come of it, but I am driven ahead, in this as in other work of a less interesting but more remunerative kind, by a fearful feeling of having to use every hour to make up for lost time. Perhaps it is good for one, in a way; but I know that if I left Wales and stopped working even for a couple of weeks, as I inevitably should if I went away, I should find it very difficult to begin again.

The whereabouts of the original of this letter is not known. Part of it is quoted in Gray's Peter Warlock *(p. 241).*

---

[36] The next month Heseltine wrote to Gray telling him that 'In these admirable and tranquil surroundings I can work more quietly and steadily than I have ever been able to before . . . I have had a number of Delius piano scores to do lately, and several others to revise, make fair copies of and prepare for printing—and this has taken up most of my time, even though I work on an average six or seven hours a day. The "North Country Sketches" (piano duet) and "Hassan" (piano solo) have already reached the proof stage. Since I have been here I have arranged the "Song of the High Hills" and "In a Summer Garden" for piano solo, and both the Dance Rhapsodies (the second a surprisingly feeble production) for piano duet . . . I have also re-translated the "Village Romeo" for a new edition.' Heseltine to Gray, 19 Nov. 1921, BL 57794.

270
Frederick Delius to Philip Heseltine

[Grez]

Dear Phil, I think you are very wise to stick to your work and live in the country. When later you feel you want a change come over! *I have not* received the corrections of Hassan back from you. How is that? I thought you had sent it straight to U. E. I do hope it is not lost? I have any amount of most urgent corrections to do Requiem Cello-Concerto Scores and therefore could not visit you. When you do come bring the biography and all your piano arrangements which I am very keen to see. We have Photos for you.

Yrs ever
Fr. D.

3. 11. 1921

Postcard, in Jelka's hand.

271
Jelka Delius to Philip Heseltine

[Grez-sur-Loing]

Dear Phil, Please send your copy of the Village Romeo, which is correct, as quickly as you can. Fred has to correct it for the new edition.

We've just had 3 dark days of steady rain, but the lovely autumn leaves are all on the trees still and it is quite warm.

I have had the Kitchen painted a most amazing combination of blues, and it looks lovely.

Ever affly
J. Delius

4. 11. 1921

Postcard.

272
Frederick Delius to Philip Heseltine

Dear Phil, I have not received Hassan. What shall I do? Is your reduction in it? Hertzka wants it back in a hurry. Write at once to Hertzka for another proof and correct it yourself as I have nothing to correct it by. I've received a proof of the North Country Sk. I see quite a number of mistakes, but no doubt you have corrected them in your proof. When I've done I'll send you my corrections and then you must send your proof to Augener's as I have no document here to correct by. It looks awfully well done and I am very pleased with your arrangement. As regards annotation employ always the easiest way of expression avoiding as many double flats and sharps as possible. With love

F. D.

Grez, 19. 11. 1921

Postcard, in Jelka's hand.

273
Philip Heseltine to Frederick Delius

22.11.1921   Cefn Bryntalch, Abermule, Wales.

Dear Friend—I have filled up several forms and the postal authorities are now making inquiries about the parcel which contained the Hassan proofs and the MS as well. It was insured and I have the receipt of posting. The day before I sent off this parcel to you I despatched the MSS of three piano scores and other things in an insured parcel to Hertzka and although it is more than five weeks ago I have had no acknowledgment of the parcel from him. I wrote to him again last week and mentioned the loss of the Hassan proofs in my letter. I sent you my copy of the Village Romeo by registered post last Friday. Please return it to me when you have finished with it as it is an old friend—I have had it more than eleven years! Much love to you both—

Φ.

Picture postcard, Shoebill (Baloeiceps Rex).

274
Jelka Delius to Philip Heseltine

[Grez-sur-Loing]

Dear Phil,

Your Village Romeo Piano Score *has not arrived.* Today the U. Ed. is again clamouring for the corrected piano score as there are absolutely no copies left. What are we to do? It seems extraordinary that 2 music parcels have been lost in so short a time. Hassan has never come back? Are you quite sure you addressed right; there are 3 or 4 other Grez in France. Please make a big research at the post. Let us hear at once please. It is terribly cold here but has been summer all the time but to-day all is white and grey. Affly yrs

Jelka Delius

28. 11. 1921

Postcard.

275
Frederick Delius to Philip Heseltine

Grez—2. 12. 21

Dear Phil   I have receive neither Hassan nor the Village Romeo What *can have* happened? I am very anxious for the Village Romeo at once   they are entreating me to hurry with it.

I send you the corrections back

On Nr 3 there is something wrong in the 3rd bar. I advise you strongly to get the full score and revise it thoroughly; there must be quite a number of mistakes—it is impossible to correct a 4 handed arrangement without documents.

I asked Hertzka to send you another proof of Hassan as I have absolutely nothing here to correct it with. You have all my sketches. I dont suppose I shall be in London before March 23ᵈ for the Requiem, but maybe you will give us the pleasure of your visit before then. The winter landscape of Grez is more beautiful than the summer.

I hope you are well. Please remember me kindly to your mother and father-in-law.

I hope you are well and working successfully.

Ever affectionately
Frederick Delius

In Jelka's hand.

276
Frederick Delius to Philip Heseltine

Dear Phil, The Village Romeo arrived to-day. The trouble was you sent it by parcels post, which is absolutely rotten in France, unsafe and incredibly long We had sent some books and they took 10 weeks also we have to fetch it at Bourron and pay 'impôt sur le chiffre d'àffaires' 3.90 for this. Always send: *printed matter, registered*—Was Hassan also Parcels Post? We have not received it. Best love from us both

Fr. Delius

Grez 7. 12. 1921

Postcard, in Jelka's hand.

277
Frederick Delius to Philip Heseltine

[Grez, 11 December 1921]

Dear Phil—Please send me *Hassan* by registered post—I must see it before it is published—you never sent me the original sketch of my full score—
We at last received the Village Romeo.

Ever affectionately
Frederick Delius

Postcard.

278
Philip Heseltine to Frederick Delius

Cefn-Bryntalch,
Abermule,
Montgomeryshire.

December 16th 1921.

My dear Friend,

I asked Gray to go to Augener's and look at the full score of the 'North Country Sketches' in order to save Augener's the time and trouble that would be involved in posting me the whole MS score for the sake of one bar.

He tells me that the violin part in the bar in question is exactly as I have transcribed it, and that in one of the other parts there is a C natural on the third beat which makes matters worse. As it stands, the bar sounds wrong; but it is a perfectly correct transcription from the score.

The C♮ is arrived at by 3^{rds} moving chromatically downwards, thus:—

But it seems to me that the chord on the third beat should be

in which C♯ is very definitely out of place. And the F♯—G (quavers) in octaves in the violin and harp parts don't agree with it at all.

Gray has kept the two sheets of proofs which contain this bar, so will you—to save time—write direct to him (34 Great Ormond Street, London, W.C.1) and tell him what to alter.

It seems to me that the C♮ must go out and the violin part be altered in respect of two or three notes—unless the chord on the 3rd beat is really

(equivalent to A♭)

in which case the doubling of the theme in the lower octave

ought to go out, in the piano version, as it makes the chord too thick and pre-vents the essential C♮ from sounding clearly.

It seems fated that the appearance of these pieces in print should be delayed by accidents of one kind and another!

I am sending the proofs and sketches of 'Hassan' by a friend who leaves here to-day, to be posted (registered) in London, so you will no doubt receive them safely in a few days.

Much love to you both—

Ever affectionately
Philip Heseltine

1922

EARLY in 1922 the signs of Delius's deteriorating condition became more acute as weakness began setting into his limbs. Eventually it was decided that he should go to Wiesbaden for a course of treatment and the Deliuses left Grez in early February. He was instructed to take a complete rest though he was, at any rate, too ill to carry on composing or correcting proofs. In March he wrote to Heseltine asking him to help with correcting the proofs of the Cello Concerto. He was beginning to show some signs of improvement by mid-April and managed to work at the proofs of the *Requiem*. In May the Deliuses were able to travel to Frankfurt to hear a performance of this work on 1 May. In the middle of May they left Wiesbaden for Wildbad where Delius was to take yet another cure and by the end of June he could report that he was feeling better. On further medical advice he left on 22 June for a holiday in Norway. Installed in their little chalet they were nevertheless worried about their finances, which were being eroded by continuing high medical expenses. Although he was still walking with a stick, he felt his condition was improving and so the Deliuses returned to Grez on 14 September, travelling by way of Oslo, Hamburg, and Cologne. Two months were spent at home before they left Grez once again for Frankfurt for the winter.

Life for Heseltine was fairly uneventful in Wales. In February he composed more songs and completed his book on Delius though it would not be published until 1923. He wrote controversial letters to the *Musical Times* and a two-part article, *Musik in England*, was published in the *Musikblätter der Anbruch*. In June he completed the final version of his masterpiece *The Curlew*, whilst the months of July and August were occupied with the group of songs *Lilligay*. In October he was in London briefly supervising the publication the first of his many transcriptions of early music, whilst in December the first performance of the revised version of *The Curlew* was given by Philip Wilson. He was also busy arranging the publication of *Saudades* and *Lilligay*. Christmas was spent at Cefn Bryntalch with the poet Arthur Symons as a house guest.

279
Frederick Delius to Philip Heseltine

[Grez 19 January 1922]

Dear Phil—I sent you 'Song before Sunrise'   there is one mistake I believe, please
veryfy. The arrangement is excellent. I am working at a sonata. Violin & piano
—When are you coming? Fennimore will be given in Cologne at Easter. The
Requiem in Frankfort 23rd April—Ever affectionately

Frederick Delius

Postcard.

280
Philip Heseltine to Frederick Delius

Cefn-Bryntalch,
Abermule,
Montgomeryshire.

January 27th 1922.

My dear Friend,
   I have been working assiduously at the book and have already exceeded the
25,000 words required by the publisher. However, as no definite limit was fixed
to the length of the book, I shall add another four or five thousand. The whole
thing will be finished next week and then as soon as my very untidy manuscript
has been typed it will be ready for your inspection. There are four sections: a
short introduction, a biography, an essay on the relation between music and words
with special reference to opera, and a detailed examination (though not, I need
hardly say, an analysis in the programme-annotation style) of various works. At
the end comes a complete list of your compositions with dates, where first performed, where published etc, etc. For illustrations, I think we cannot do better
than reproduce the Frankfort photograph which appears on the latest Universal
circular—it was also in the Musical Times accompanying my article in 1915.

Then there is that delightful 1884 photograph which I have; and we ought to include a picture of Grez from across the river, an interior showing the Gauguin if possible, and a page of facsimile score. In Max Chop's[1] pamphlet there is a page of 'Appalachia' very well reproduced—but it is unlikely that the plate still exists, and that particular page is not a specially good example of your style. Incidentally, is the quotation of the old song '*Farewell Manchester*' quite an accident??!! (3rd bar, Horns 4 and 6 Bassoon 2) It's a most appropriate coincidence, anyway! In the piano score it looks more prominent and almost might be intentional. Passages for quotation are always difficult to select; torn from their context many lovely pages lose half their significance and beauty. If however I had to say which was the most perfect page you ever wrote, taken as a page apart from its context, I think I should decide on that miraculously lovely variation in the first Dance Rhapsody where the solo violin soars above the other strings with the melody in augmentation. So if you have the MS score of the work, I think this page would do very well . . . though having made this decision, half a dozen other pages at once suggest themselves—'Und sie sahen sich und blickten auf die grüne Wiese' [And they gazed at each other and gazed upon the verdant meadow] from the Mass, the end of the Entr'acte in the Village Romeo, 'O rising stars' in Sea Drift, etc. But we can discuss these matters later on. I should love to come over and see you, but the return journey from here costs no less than £8 via Southampton and Havre and at the moment I haven't even enough money to get to London. Living here, I get fed and provided with everything that is necessary—including a very liberal allowance of most excellent beer!—but I don't get any money except what I manage to make from writing articles and occasional songs—and that is a very meagre amount. For the book I am to get £25 from Lane, but of course the MS must be delivered ready for printing before I get it. So that's how the matter stands!

I suppose you will be coming over to England for the performance of the Requiem which is announced for some date towards the end of March, the 26th I think. Cecil Gray is going to Frankfort for the production of Bartók's opera on April 1st. When is the Fennimore performance in Cologne? If it is early in April he ought to stay and hear it.

We have at last got back our regular water-supply, but it is only since Christmas that the springs have been normal again on the high ground. We have had a week's deep snow—a fall of seven inches froze and lingered for several days but it has all gone now and to-day is mild and spring-like. I feel ever so much better here than in any city and I have never been able to work so

---

[1] Max Chop (1862–1929), German writer on music, critic, and composer. Besides writing a number of articles on Delius, he was the author of the first book on the composer: *Frederick Delius* (Berlin, 1907).

whole-heartedly before. There is great joy in turning out stuff regularly even though one knows that it is very bad! However, I am trying to cease to care about that; excessive self-criticism leads to complete sterility which is a most horrible condition.

I have just finished a work for chorus and orchestra.[2] I find great difficulty in scoring *Tutti's*—to get the right balance in sequences of large shifting chords, for example.

I shall not, of course, send the book to Lane until I have discussed various points with you. The biography needs a certain amount of gingering up which you will no doubt be able to do when you read it.

The more I study the Mass, Sea-Drift and the Village Romeo, the more firmly convinced I become that these are among the very greatest achievements in all music. I do not think Bach or Beethoven ever did anything more sublime than the end of the Mass: the whole work is so wonderfully constructed that the stupendous effect of the last section, to which all that has gone before seems to have led, is indeed overwhelming. These three works seem to me to stand out pre-eminently—even from among the many other beautiful things you have done: especially the Mass and Sea Drift which come as near to perfection as human nature can ever come. I fear it is impossible to do anything like justice to these wonderful creations in an essay.

Much love to you both—and very many happy returns of your birthday!—

Ever affectionately yours
Philip Heseltine

---

[2] Heseltine also wrote to Taylor saying: 'Since I last wrote to you I have finally completed my book on Delius . . . and a short work for chorus and orchestra.' Heseltine to Taylor, 7 Feb. 1922, BL 54197. This latter work, however, did not survive. The mention of 'sequences of large shifting chords' suggests something rather Delian. In 1925 he wrote yet another similar letter to Taylor: 'I've just finished a largish work for chorus and orchestra, but I don't like it much.' Heseltine to Taylor, 15 Feb. 1925, BL 54197. All this suggests a growing frustration at his having followed too closely in Delius's wake.

281
Jelka Delius to Philip Heseltine

HOTEL QUISISANA

WIESBADEN.

9.2.1922

Dearest Phil,

Fred had suddenly such a great weakness in the legs that we decided to come here at once to do the Wiesbaden cure. At present he is not allowed to walk at all and has to be rolled about in a bath chair. I am awfully glad we came, for it is most comfortable here and most attractive looking in the snow He has had his first bath to-day and seemed to enjoy it very much. Your letter came just before our departure and gave us great pleasure, Fred was as delighted with your appreciation of his works. I am sure you love and understand it better than anyone could. It was so good to hear that you have written the biography. We are very keen to see it. I did a very nice little photo of Fred standing at his piano, but could not get the Gauguin on; then I did 2 more one with the Gauguin and one with the garden window behind   They may be failures; I shall have them developed here and send you copies. We have not got the garden from across the river, but we can do it when we are back.

Re manuscripts   Fred says he has never heard 'Farewell Manchester' and would like to see it. All the manuscripts are in the hands of the Universal Edition. He must have got those of Leuckarts too with the works, but it seems to Fred that the one from the Village Romeo or the heavenly one you mention from the Mass of Life would be more all round appropriate   I am not sure whether Fred will be able to go to England for the Requiem 23^d of March; his cure is absolutely the most important thing now. Fennimore is to be given at once after easter in Cologne, and the Requiem and Seadrift in Francfort on the 21st of April[3]   Perhaps you could come over here then and bring the biography with you? We shall get into touch with the people here and get exact dates and let you know. Also we shall see our plans more clearly in a week or so, when we see how this agrees with Fred.

We were so happy to hear that you are working away like that in the country—and your principal is *quite right*: Turn out a lot of stuff and not be sterile by over-criticism. Fred says: Just go ahead! If the Chorus is rather highly pitched and forte you want a strong orchestra against it.

---

[3] This performance, in fact, never materialized.

The people are skating here and look awfully nice in the late afternoon sun. Those bright coloured woollen jumpers give marvellous colourspots to it all—like jewels.

Happily the railway strike seems over now—and we shall be able to communicate with our friends.

Fancy, when I handed in my passport the man in the german consulate in Paris said: Delius, ja diese wunderschöne Musik, die hab ich oft in Berlin in der Philharmonie gehört; Herrlich! I was pushed on with the crowd and this man still called from afar to hear more about Delius!!! How german!

Best love and affectionate greetings from us both

Yrs always
Jelka Delius

In BL 57962.

282
Frederick Delius to Philip Heseltine

Hotel Quisisana
Wiesbaden

25.2.1922

My dear Phil, Fred dictates:

I have just received from Augener's the full score, parts and Piano Score of the Song before Sunrise—to correct. I send it all to you hoping that you will render me the great service to correct them all. I am far from well and am undergoing a very severe treatment, tiresome and fatiguing—am not allowed to walk at all or to use my hands much and so am quite unable to do the thing myself.

I am afraid I shall not be able to come over to London for the performance of the Requiem,[4] but hope you will be there, at the rehearsals too and report me about it all. Anyhow do not tell anyone I am not coming, as it would make them prepare the performance less well.

I have just heard from Hertzka that they are thinking of doing the Village Romeo here at Wiesbaden next season. The Francfort performance of the

---

[4] Albert Coates was to conduct the première of the *Requiem* at a Royal Philharmonic Society concert in Queen's Hall with the Philharmonic Choir on 23 Mar. The soloists were Amy Evans and Norman Williams.

Requiem is fixed for April 21st and the Darmstadt theatre now has the Score of Hassan and they are most likely to do it also at about Easter.

When is Gray coming to Francfort? Do tell him to come and see us here. We are sending you the other photos with the Gauguin behind. If you think they could be enlarged I might send you the films. Or should we try and have it done here. Or perhaps there is a proceeding to print them for the book straight from the film?

Let us hear from you soon to cheer us up a bit—Up to now we have not heard anything especially interesting here—and the place is full of very loud and boysterous Dutch. Dutch everywhere.

How are you getting on?

Best love from us both

Ever aff^{ly} yours
Frederick Delius

In Jelka's hand. In BL 57962.

283
Philip Heseltine to Frederick Delius

Cefn-Bryntalch,
Abermule,
Montgomeryshire.

March 5th 1922

My dear Friend,

I am so sorry to hear of your illness—what is it? I imagine it must be connected with your old sciatica which was troubling you when you were in London three years ago. I do hope the cure is doing you good and that you will soon be about again. It is indeed horrible to be so suddenly stricken down and unable to move.

I should have written before in answer to your first letter from Wiesbaden but I had to go to London a fortnight ago and I was kept fearfully busy while I was there. Your second letter with the photographs I found waiting for me here when I returned last Thursday; also the proofs of the score and parts of the 'Song before Sunrise' which I will gladly correct for you. The MS, however, is not with them; I do not anticipate any serious mistakes in so short and simple a work but it might be necessary to consult the MS to verify small points. Have you got it or have Augener's?

The photographs are very nice indeed as they are, but I don't think they are sharp enough to stand enlargement and reproduction. Photographs intended for reproduction ought to be focussed with the very greatest accuracy, otherwise all the outlines appear indistinct in the enlargement.

I am rather afraid I shall not be able to get up to London again this month, to hear the Requiem. I am still in none too affluent a condition financially and in London, especially on a short visit, one always spends more money than one intends to. My recent fortnight rather depleted the supply of funds. I had intended to postpone my visit until later so that I might be there for the 23rd, but circumstances arose which necessitated my going up to see my lawyer and I was specially asked to transcribe from the old tablature notation an entirely unknown book of Elizabethan songs for a singer who wants to sing them at a recital in a few weeks' time; so I couldn't put it off any longer. I don't get an allowance now from my people and although that doesn't matter while I am here, it makes a visit to London seem more expensive than ever.

Béla Bartók is coming to England next week. He is giving a concert in London with Jelly d'Aranyi.[5] Later on he is coming to spend a few days with me here, and will give a concert at the University of Wales in Aberystwyth.[6]

This month's 'Musical Times' publishes an interview with Lionel Tertis[7] in the course of which occurs the following:—

'At present the limited prospects of a viola work are such that he considers it almost philanthropy for an eminent composer to write one. He has had definite promises, so far unfulfilled, from Delius, Ravel and Glazounov, and he tells me that if one of them would keep his word, it would advance the viola twenty-five years in a night.'[8]

Augener's are bringing out ten more songs of mine—or rather of 'Peter Warlock's'. The first three will be out next month and are all drinking songs,

[5] Jelly d'Aranyi (1895–1966), Hungarian-born violinist and sister of Adila Fachiri. She and Bartók gave two concerts in London in Mar. 1922—a private recital at 18 Hyde Park Terrace, the residence of the Hungarian chargé d'affaires, on 14 Mar. and a public one in the Aeolian Hall on 24 Mar. Both programmes included Bartók's first violin sonata, which was dedicated to Jelly d'Aranyi.

[6] This took place on 16 Mar. as part of the series of weekly concerts organized by the music department of the local University College of Wales. Returning to London after the concert, Bartók broke his journey on 17 Mar. to spend a short time with Heseltine and his family at Cefn Bryntalch.

[7] Lionel Tertis (1876–1975), English violist. He arranged the Double Concerto for violin and viola, the *Caprice and Elegy* for viola and piano, Violin Sonatas Nos. 2 and 3 for viola and piano, and the Serenade from *Hassan* for viola and piano. He described his visit to Grez in his autobiography, *My Viola and I* (London, 1974).

[8] E. Evans, 'British Players and Singers III. Lionel Tertis', *Musical Times* (1922), 157–9.

one about rum and two about beer![9] The last has a XV century text with the refrain:—

> 'But bring us in good ale, and bring us in good ale
> For Our Blessed Lady's sake bring us in good ale,'!![10]

I have discovered in Philip Wilson[11] a really admirable and intelligent singer. I wish you could hear him. There's no scope for him in England apparently and as he has no money he will probably have to go to South Africa[12] or Canada soon and get a teaching post at some college there. His speciality is XVI century English songs, but he is very enthusiastic about modern things and is keen and quick to learn anything, however difficult. He came down here for a few days and we did a lot of work together.

Much love to both of you and heartiest wishes for a very speedy recovery.

Ever affectionately yours
Philip Heseltine

284
Philip Heseltine to Frederick Delius

Cefn-Bryntalch,
Abermule,
Montgomeryshire.

March 20th 1922

My dear Friend

I have corrected the proofs of the Song before Sunrise but as there are a few ambiguities in the MS (such as—whether both clarinets play certain passages, or only one, and the exact position of *arco* after a *pizz*) I return it to you so that these small points may be corrected. I am sorry to trouble you but it would be a pity if mistakes were to remain in the score.

---

[9] 'Captain Stratton's Fancy' [rum] and 'Mr Belloc's Fancy' [beer].

[10] 'Good Ale' (words anon., 15th c.), Augener, 1922.

[11] Philip Wilson (1886–1924), English singer. He visited Heseltine at Cefn Bryntalch, bringing with him copies of a number of Elizabethan lute songs in tablature. Wilson had been professor of singing at the State Conservatory in Sydney from 1915 to 1920 and, on his return to England in 1920, gave a number of recitals at the Wigmore Hall.

[12] On 15 Feb. Heseltine had written to Taylor in Cape Town: 'At the present moment [Wilson] is staying here with me and is learning half a dozen new songs of mine which I have just finished. I couldn't want anyone better or keener to work with. If you can find an opening for him, I feel sure he would be a very valuable asset in the musical life of Cape Town.' Heseltine to Taylor, 15 Feb. 1922, BL 54197.

If I can possibly raise enough money I shall come to Frankfort at the end of April.[13] The prospect of seeing you again and hearing the Requiem,[14] Sea-Drift and Fennimore as well as Bartók's opera and ballet, new violin sonata and quartet which are all to be given there in April is really most alluring. Bartók is in England at present and came here for a couple of days on his way back from Aberystwyth where he gave a concert at the University. His last book of piano pieces—Improvisations on Hungarian folk-songs[15]—is really wonderful; the most vital and stimulating music I have heard for a long time.

Please let me know the exact date of the Fennimore performance. The Requiem and Sea Drift are, I think, on April 21st. Bartók's concert is on the 24th and the opera and ballet on the 30th.

I do hope you are getting better with the cure and the baths.

Ever so much love to you both

Affectionately yours
Philip Heseltine

285
Frederick Delius to Philip Heseltine

Villa Mon Repos Wiesbaden
Frankfurterstr 6

28. 3. 1922

My dear Phil,

Many thanks for your letter. I return you the M.S. of the Song before Sunrise. I had corrected all the questionable points in the proof Augener's sent me. Did not you see that proof? I also send you the proofs of my 'Cello Concerto, which you desired to see. Would you be an angel, dear Phil and correct carefully for me as I am as yet quite unable to do it myself, as I cannot write. If there are any doubtful places please mark them and send it back here—I shall be most grateful for you for this great service.

[13] A few days later Heseltine wrote to Gray: 'After all, I feel very much inclined to go to Frankfort next month if I can raise the money or get some newspaper to commission an article on the performances. Have you definitely made up your mind not to go? There will be performances of Fennimore, Sea-Drift, Requiem and possibly Hassan (the latter at Darmstadt) as well as the Bartók operas and a concert at which one of the string quartets will be given. I must see F. D. soon as he seems to be undergoing treatment at Wiesbaden.' Heseltine to Gray, 25 Mar. 1922, BL 57794.
[14] The performance of the *Requiem*, conducted by Oskar von Pander, took place on 1 May.
[15] B. Bartók, 8 pieces, Op. 20 (1920).

The Requiem will be in Francfort on the 21st of April. They are not doing Seadrift, two new works was too much for them. There is a question in Cologne whether they will not first do the Village Romeo and Fennimore only later, but nothing is settled yet.[16] There is also a question of doing the Mass of Life in Berlin. We shall let you know as soon as we hear anything definite. Balfour Gardiner just writes me that he would love to go and see me at Wiesbaden but cannot bear to travel without a companion, and Bax and Austin cant go. I shall write him at once and suggest he should invite you. If only we had received our money we should *of course* have invited you ourselves—but we are still signing papers before consuls and getting nothing. It would be so delightful if you came! Can't you write also yourself to Balfour?

I am dedicating the Song before Sunrise to you and have written it on the M.S., but if you have the proof please put it on, otherwise inform Augener's.

I enclose you two criticisms of the Requiem, daily Mail and Observ.   it is *only*, I think, in England, that 2 such utterly incapables could be Musical Critics on a paper. The tone of the Daily Mail is simply scandalous!

With love ever affectionately
Frederick Delius

In Jelka's hand.

286
Jelka Delius to Philip Heseltine

15. 4. 1922

Dear Phil, We have heard from the Conductor Oscar von Pander[17] that the Requiem Concert in Francfort will take place on May 1st. Last rehearsal April 30th 10 a.m. Earlier rehearsal Thursday or friday before. If we have no set-back we shall go there and I *do* wish you could be there. I'm so sorry my plans with B[alfour]. G[ardiner]. entirely failed. We have just received the Anbruch[18] with

---

[16] Otto Klemperer (1885–1973), the conductor at Cologne, had visited Delius early in March, proposing that *A Village Romeo and Juliet* be performed later in the year in place of *Fennimore and Gerda*.

[17] Oskar von Pander (1883–1968), German conductor and composer. He was conductor of the Rühl Choral Society in Frankfurt.

[18] In Feb. and Mar. 1922 a two-part article by Heseltine entitled 'Musik in England' appeared in *Musikblätter der Anbruch*, a periodical published by Universal Edition. Originally one long article, the publishers divided it into two parts. Part I was entitled 'Rückblick' and Part II 'Frederick Delius'. An English translation by Evelin Gerhardi of the article was printed in 'The Published Writings of Philip Heseltine on Delius', *Delius Society Journal*, No. 94 (Autumn 1987), 21–2.

your beautiful little essay on Delius! We had a most delightful visit from Lloyd and Ethel Osbourne. They are the dearest friends imaginable, and I want you to know them so much   they are settling down in London   should you be in town just go and see them Almonds Hotel, Clifford str until they find a flat. They will love to see you and tell you all about Fred. He is at last a *little better*, but it is deadly slow here. Is Cecil Gray coming? We dare not stir from here for some time yet. Heard Mahler's Lied von der Erde *deadly slow*. He is frightfully revered here. Do you know violinist Ernest Whitfield. He has been playing Fr's Violin Concerto in Vienna & Berlin. Best love from both   Affly

   Jelka

Frankfurter str 6
[Wiesbaden]

Postcard.

287
Frederick Delius to Philip Heseltine

Dear Phil, I sent you 2 days ago the proofs of my Cello Concerto which I corrected myself as there were really too many mistakes. As soon as you have looked at it please send it by post, registered, to Univ. Edition Vienna Karlsplatz 6. We are off to Francfort to-morrow for the rehearsals and performance of the Requiem to-morrow and I am *awfully* sorry that you cannot join us. Thank you so much for your nice letters—It was a pity Balfour did not bring you along! We are off to Wildbad to take the baths there on May 15th. We both send you our love. Write soon again

   Ever affectionately
   Yrs F.D.

Frankfurter Str 6
Wiesbaden 27.4.22

Postcard, in Jelka's hand. In BL 57962.

288
Jelka Delius to Philip Heseltine

Wildbad Würtemberg
Hotel zur Post   21.5.1922

Dear Phil, I have just received a letter from Hertzka clamouring for the 'Cello-Concerto, which he is in *immediate need of.* Please send it off at once registered *by post.* We are here since a few days and much happier here than at Wiesbaden. It is a cosy little place a narrow deep valley with a little river rushing through—it is in the black forest. There are only Germans here, the baths seem splendid; they come straight out of the earth into ones baths through a system of holes in the bottom of the bath, so that they have their natural temperature, which is a delicious tingling, live warmth. We both take them and expect to be entirely rejuvenated. We are to stay here till end of June. The Requiem was too beautiful! The Chorus was very good but the orchestra only medium and the conductor not 1st rate. Yet he gave a 'stimmungvolle Auffuhrung, and the work was most enthusiastically received. After the publ. rehearsal the people simply would not go away, and crowded all around Fred's seat—who of course could not go up to the platform. The work made a deep impression—and nobody bothered about the words being anti-christian like Mr Scholes!! Write soon, my patient loves your letters. Affly yours

Jelka

21.5.1922

Postcard, in Jelka's hand. In BL 57962.

289
Philip Heseltine to Frederick Delius

Cefn-Bryntalch
Abermule
Montgomeryshire

May 22nd 1922.

My dear Friend,

    I ought to have written to you sooner about the Cello Concerto which I have enjoyed most tremendously. I think it is the best work you have done for years —anyway since the Violin Concerto. It is brimful of beauty, mellow and golden like evening sunlight in late summer. The slow movement is a perfect miracle and will sound most lovely; I have never seen a score of such amazing subtlety in the treatment of every instrument—they all *sing* all the while. I look forward with the keenest delight to hearing the work. I have made a piano score and sent it to Hans Kindler[19] (Van Dieren's brother-in-law) who is the finest cellist I ever heard; I hope he will play it in America—for you could not find a better performer anywhere. Have Universal people had a piano score made by one of their own people—I see one is advertised in their advance lists—or shall I send them mine when Kindler returns it? Hertzka accepted my versions of 'In a Summer Garden' (solo) and the first 'Dance Rhapsody' (duet) but they do not appear to have been engraved yet.

    You had better ask for a second proof of the score of the Concerto, embodying the corrections, before it is printed, as in addition to the misprints you marked I found nearly fifty more—mostly obvious ones—clefs omitted or accidentals, etc, but there are one or two doubtful points which need your attention. First, there is no indication of the tempo for the first subject of the first movement, either on its first appearance or at the reprise after the slow movement. The first five bars are the same in both cases except for one note in the flute, which is B the first time and A the second. (Score page 6, bar 1 and page 37, bar 5). Is this intentional? Page 23 (fifth bar of principal theme, slow movement). Score reads

[19] Hans Kindler (1892–1929), principal cellist of the Philadelphia Orchestra, 1914–21. He took up conducting, founding the National Symphony Orchestra in Washington, DC in 1931, where he remained as its conductor till 1948.

for the cello. Should not the E♮ be F?—so as to conform to the repetition of the melody later on? E♮ sounds queer. Page 48, 1ˢᵗ bar; surely D for the trombones, not E? Page 55, last bar does not add up to four beats. Crotchet rest should presumably be minim. And at the very end, the last phrase for English Horn should surely read

(actual sound) The score marks no sharp. I have sent the proofs straight back to Vienna.

In your last letter—written just before you went to Frankfort for the 'Requiem'—you said you were going to Wildbad for a new treatment, but you didn't give any address, so I must send a letter to the last address in Wiesbaden. I did not send the MS of Hart's opera[20] for fear it should go astray and not be forwarded, but if you would like to see it I will post it to you as soon as I hear for certain where you are.

I wonder if you met Bartók in Frankfort and heard his opera when it was performed there.

The 'Daily Telegraph' came out with a very laudatory, if somewhat belated, review of my arrangement of the 'North Country Sketches' the other day. After a paragraph about piano duets in general and orchestral transcriptions in particular, they wrote that this piano score 'is a good second-best to the full score itself. We have never seen any work of the kind more thoroughly and sensibly done . . . This is the perfection of editing.'

This pleased me rather because it supports the view which I think you hold also, that a piano transcription is first and foremost a guide to the orchestral score and only quite secondarily a piano piece (unless it is simply a pianists' free fantasia, and this only a Liszt or a Busoni can do with justification to another composer's work).

What cannot easily be played can always be left out in performance, but it is still heard with the mind's ear—but if, as most arrangers do, one sacrifice vital

---

[20] Heseltine was here referring to an opera, *Riders to the Sea*, Op. 19 (1915) by Fritz Hart. 'I sincerely hope you did remember to send off the copy of "Riders to the Sea" . . . for I shall be seeing Delius in a few weeks' time, and in April he is going to Germany to supervise another production of "Fennimore and Gerda" and he would then be able to show the work to the conductors of the Frankfort and Cologne opera houses as well as to Dʳ Hertzka of the Universal-Edition. . . . I do not doubt for a moment that "Riders to the Sea" will be recognized by Delius as well as by the Germans as a work of first-rate quality—personally I consider it the best opera I know by any living composer except Delius . . . Whatever you care to send me a copy of, I will show Delius who has more influence with the Universal directors than any other Englishman—and he, I am sure, will do his very best for you.' Heseltine to Fritz Hart, 7 Feb. 1922, State Library Victoria, Melbourne, MS 9528.

notes for the sake of 'Spielbarkeit', one simply gives a false impression of the whole passage.

Spring is very late here this year, and the fruit blossoms—though lovelier than I have ever seen them—vanish away almost as soon as they appear. The oaks are only just out and the ash trees are yet in bud.

I hope to hear, in your next letter, that the baths have done you lots of good and that you are getting about again as usual.

With best love to you both,

Ever affectionately yours
Philip Heseltine

290
Frederick Delius to Philip Heseltine

25.5.1922
Hotel zur Post
Wildbad
Schwarzwald

Fred dictates

Dear Phil, Your letter was forwarded to us here where we have been for the last 10 days. It is a lovely place and wonderful baths, much nicer than Wiesbaden and the food in the Hotel absolutely 1st class. Altho' the first few baths make one rather weaker I am now beginning to pick up gradually, and I hope the improvement will continue. I am so glad you like the Cello Concerto. It was one of my happy inspirations I believe and I wrote it in one go, without any break. I wrote at once to Hertzka and advised him to take your piano-score. I quite agree with the Daily Tel. about the North Country Sketches and I think all of your Piano Scores are excellent. Several of the corrections you mention in your letter I thought I had corrected, but I have asked Hertzka to forward me another Proof so that I can look it thro' again, when all these corrections are made. Hertzka is in a great hurry to have the Piano Score, I think you *best have it sent to him at once*, so that he does not go and get another one made.

At the end of June we are going to Norway to our hut which will just be completed to spend the summer. We should love to have you with us. We could then talk about the Biography. I am sure you would love it up there and we should love to have you. It will cost you nothing except the journey. You would have to go, shortest route Newcastle—Kristiania and from there per rail to Lesjaskog, where our hut lies about 3/4 of an hour from the station up the hill. Should I in the meantime get my money at last from the publ. [unclear] I would gladly pay your journey. Otherwise *do try* to raise the funds somehow.

I shall get a piano for the hut and we are having our good pre-war tyrolese cook with us. I think you will be thoroughly happy up there and so shall we with you.

With love from us both

Ever affly
Frederick Delius

In Jelka's hand, signed by Delius in pencil. In BL 57962.

291
Frederick Delius to Philip Heseltine

Dear Phil, Hertzka writes he has not yet received the proofs of the Cello Concerto please send it off as quick as you can and also your piano-score. I am very keen to see your arrangement of the Summer-Garden, bring it to Norway—I shall have a Piano. Also bring Hart's opera, he wrote us a very nice letter to which I shall shortly reply. The cure takes up all our time here, but it is doing me a lot of good. We leave here on the 22 and Hamburg on the 24th for Kristiania 26th, where we stay at Victoria Hotel, probably 2 days. Do let us know *here* whether you will be able to come to Norway, which we *do so hope* you will. Bring warm things and a good travelling rug, thick boots. Jelka has been in Grez and sent off things to Norway from there. We are looking forward to Norway immensely, and to get away from all cures and doctors, that alone will make us well, I am sure. Write at once, please   We have to make all sorts of arrangements

Affectionately yrs
Fr. and Jelka Delius

Wildbad
Hotel zur Post
Wurttemberg
11.6.1922

Postcard. In BL 57962.

292
Philip Heseltine to Frederick Delius

Cefn Bryntalch,
Abermule,
Montgomeryshire.

June 17th 1922.

My dear Friend

It is most awfully kind of you to invite me to come and stay with you in Norway and I should enjoy it immensely, being with you in such lovely surroundings: but I fear it is quite impossible. I have practically no money and what little I do get is very quickly absorbed by the barest necessities—music and manuscript paper, a few books and a few pints of beer; train fares—even as far as London—are quite out of the question.

Life on these lines becomes a bit monotonous at times, but it has its advantages—one is driven, whether one will or no, to keep on working continually and it is certainly a great satisfaction to get stuff done month after month, even though it is pretty bad stuff. I have just re-written my song-cycle 'The Curlew', for tenor voice, flute, English horn and string quartet. This has no connection (save for the two opening bars) with the earlier setting of the same poem which you saw some years ago; the present work dates from two years ago when it was murdered at a London concert by some of the most incompetent performers ever let loose in England—which is saying a good deal.[21] Now, however, it is to be properly produced by others in London next autumn[22] and I think I have made it very considerably better. The poems—by W. B. Yeats—are very beautiful.

The proofs of the Cello Concerto were sent back to Hertzka by registered post on May 31st. As soon as I heard from you that he would take up my piano arrangement, I wrote to Hans Kindler asking him to send the MS straight to Vienna. So doubtless both copies are there by this time. Hertzka also has the

---

[21] Four of the songs later to be incorporated in *The Curlew* had been sung by Gerald Cooper at a recital in the Mortimer Hall on 6 Oct. 1920. Heseltine had not been particularly happy with Cooper's performance, telling his mother that it had been 'a dismal affair'. Cooper's voice, 'never very thrilling, was in very bad form and most of the instrumentalists were simply incompetent. There were passages in my songs that sounded just like Pussy at midnight.' Heseltine to his mother, 11 Oct. 1920, BL 57961.

[22] *The Curlew* was performed in Nov. and again on 31 Jan. 1923. Heseltine reported to Taylor: 'My "Curlew" cycle was performed on November 23rd—and for the first time in my life I really feel pleased with something I have written. [Philip] Wilson buggered up the voice part completely but the instrumentalists were fine. It is going to be given again in January—with another singer, John Goss, who will do it far better.' Heseltine to Taylor, 7 Dec. 1922, BL 54197.

MS of my piano solo version of the 'Summer Garden' and piano duet version of the first 'Dance Rhapsody' but although he wrote saying he would publish both, he has so far not done so. Has 'Hassan' (vocal score) appeared yet? I never received a copy. And I am still bombarding the post office for compensation for the loss of the MS vocal score and first set of proofs.

Orr has sent me four very excellent songs[23]—settings of poems from Housman's 'Shropshire Lad'. He is really gifted and appears to have a very good technique as well. It is a pity his bad health ties him down to so much hotel life which must be most uncongenial for serious work.

Augener's have just brought out my drinking song[24] to which the rector (or, as one might more appropriately say, the rectum!) of this parish objected on the score of the poet's association of the Blessed Virgin Mary with Good Ale! I pointed out, however, that the 15th century, when the poem was written, was a much more pious age than the present and clearly what was good enough for an age when people were grilled for blasphemy is quite good enough for our day.

I wrote to Gardiner and invited him to pay us a visit but he replied that he was too full of engagements! I wish I could write a 'Shepherd Fennel'[25] and get out of this pecuniary quagmire!!

Well, I hope you will have a splendid time and come back completely rejuvenated! With much love to you both and again ever so many thanks for your invitation which I am truly sorry to have to refuse.

Ever yours affectionately
Philip Heseltine

293
Jelka Delius to Philip Heseltine

Avsender Delius
Lesjaskog
Gudbrandsdalen

Dear Phil, Have you ever received from Fred or from Leuckart the Nietzsche songs and one danish song to translate? They are lost and Leuckart says you have got them. Please a p.c. After our long pilgrimage we have at last arrived

---

[23] These included the settings, 'When the lad for longing sighs', ' 'Tis time I think by Wenlock Town', and 'Loveliest of Trees'.
[24] 'Good Ale', setting of an anonymous 15th-c. poem, published 1922.
[25] *Shepherd Fennel's Dance* (after Hardy), a highly successful piece composed by Balfour Gardiner in 1910.

here and our lovely little hut is standing on the Hillside all spick and span. To-morrow the piano is to be taken up the steep hill, a terrible task, the kitchen stove, our beds and then we'll take up Fred in great triumph. It is so lovely up there, the view so changeable and really exquisite. It breaks my heart to think you are not coming. Perhaps you will find means yet. You would love it, I know. Fred got over the journey all right and Senta[26] the german maid is such a splendid help and so amusing and nice and pretty, I feel she is going to make us most comfortable—And what a blessing it will be to be alone and not in hotels with crowds of strangers *at last*. Our address is Lesjaskog Gudbrandsdalen
   Norway.

Please send a line about the songs and messages from Fred.

   Affly Jelka—

2.7.1922

Postcard. In BL 57962.

294
Philip Heseltine to Frederick Delius

Cefn-Bryntalch
Abermule
Montgomeryshire

July 17th 1922

My dear Friend,
   I am so awfully sorry about those proofs—When I received your card I hunted everywhere for them without success; then it occurred to me that they might possibly be amongst a lot of music I left with a friend in London. So I wrote and asked him to search, and there they were! It is dreadful of me to have over-looked them. I had them with me in Brittany last year and spent some time in vain endeavours to produce some sort of English version—but Nietzsche's verse, difficult at all times but much more so when one has both to rhyme and keep to the accents of music—proved too much for me and I had to abandon the task. I quite thought I had written to you to that effect and returned the proofs at the same time. Do please forgive me.

---

[26] Senta Mössmer.

I have just corrected the proofs of my piano duet arrangement of the second Dance Rhapsody which I returned to Augener's requesting them to send a final proof to you, as I thought you might wish to see it before it appeared.

The Nietzsche songs, together with Hart's opera, have been sent off to-day to you by registered post—insured this time for £15!

I am so glad to hear that you are happy and comfortable at last, and I hope that the good air and mountain walks will restore you to perfect health again before the summer is out.

With heaps of love to you both

Ever affectionately yours
Philip Heseltine

295
Jelka Delius to Philip Heseltine

3.8.1922

Lesjaskog
Gudbrandsdalen

My dear Phil,

I forget whether I already told you that Dr Heinrich Simon of Francfort had been asked by the Munich Publisher, Piper to write a *short* biography/monograph of Delius.[27] This is to be brought out for Fred's 60th birthday on the 29th Jan 23 and they want to get up a Delius-Concert for that date in Francfort. So Simon is rather in a hurry about writing it. He asked me to put down some reminiscences for him, but perhaps you would be kind enough to send him some things we had written down and gave you? Can you put your hands on them? Simon came to Wildbad to see us just before our departure. He asked very kindly about you, and said that if ever you came to Francfort he could put you up at his house in all simplicity. He also sent us a copy of a Drama he has written and which has been performed at that very enterprising modern theatre at Darmstadt, of which Hartnung[28] is the Director, and where Hassan will be brought out in the autumn. He would like you to translate it if you feel that way inclined.

---

[27] This publication never appeared.

[28] Gustav Ludwig Hartnung (1887–1946), German theatre director. *Hassan* was premièred in Darmstadt in June 1923. The English production followed.

He thinks your translation of the Requiem so awfully good, in fact some of the papers thought it had been translated from the English into German.

It is very probable that we shall spend part of the winter at Francfort and it would be so nice if you could come there too and stay with Simon.

How are you getting on with your biography? Could it not also be ready for Xmas or thereabouts and make rather a boom? It is of course a much more important thing than Simon's, and I think it would be so splendid if it came out, and it would certainly help people to appreciate Delius's Music.

Fred received Hart's opera and the Nietzsche songs but there was no second Dance Rhapsody arrangement with it; but Augeners sent one and Fred corrected it and we played it. It is charming and very playable. Dont you think all these arrangements could be put on the Pianola? I am sure they would sound awfully well. What steps has one to do for that?

Fred wants to know whether you borrowed the Piano Score and full score of Koanga from Goodwin and Tabb's? You had said you wanted it for the biography. Has the U.E. already sent you the Piano Score of the Cello Concerto for correction? We want it pushed thro' as quickly as possible.

Did we tell you that the Village Romeo will be done in Cologne before Fennimore, this season?

We have had very uncertain weather lately and often the clouds have quite enveloped us. If only it would be fine again! This place is so lovely and the house a great success. I do hope you can come up with us next year! Fred is improving all the time, but slowly; and he does need sunny weather. We are reading O'Brien's[29] very interesting book 'Mystic Isles of the South Seas.[30]

Fred sends you all his love

Ever aff[ly] yours
Jelka

In BL 57962.

---

[29] Frederick O'Brien (1869–1932), American journalist and author of travel books.
[30] F. O'Brien, *Mystic Isles of the South Seas* (1921).

296
Jelka Delius to Philip Heseltine

22.8.1922
Lesjaskog

Dear Phil, I have had another urgent letter from Dr Simon, so please, if you have not yet sent the typographed biography send it first to him direct, with instructions to forward it ~~here~~ to us at Grez. We shall leave here on the 7th Sept and go via Hamburg & Cologne straight to Grez, where we shall be with the Osbourne's till late autumn. We have just corrected the piano score of the Cello Concerto and sent it back to Hertzka. It was very carelessly engraved. How I wish I could hear it.

Simon's address is Untermainkai 3, Francfurt.

Fred is very much improved in health and strength; altho lately we have had abominable weather. I almost think the profile photo would be best, the large one. The Gauguin is sold but we have a large photo at Grez, I can also find you the Dance Rh. M.S as soon as I get back, and also get good photos of the house and garden done. I have also the photo of the bust by Riccardi. ?Did you see the bust? It was bought by Duveen[31] and presented to the Tate Gallery.[32] I'll send you all that at once from Grez. The Gauguin is sold to a man at Manchester.[33] affly

    yrs J. Delius

Postcard. In BL 57962.

---

[31] Joseph Duveen, 1st Baron of Millbank (1869–1939), international British art dealer. He was knighted in 1919 for his services to British art, made a baronet in 1926, and raised to the peerage in 1933.

[32] There is no record of such a presentation to the Tate Gallery.

[33] The painting had been sent to London in 1920 and was finally bought by Samuel Courtauld, an industrialist and art-lover. It now hangs in the Courtauld Galleries in London.

297
Philip Heseltine to Jelka Delius

Cefn-Bryntalch,
Abermule,
Montgomeryshire.

August 28th 1922

My dear Jelka,

I sent the whole manuscript of my book to a typist over a fortnight ago, but it has not yet been returned. So I am sending Dr Simon the book of autobiographical notes you lent me and an article from the Boston Evening Transcript of 1909[34] which contains quite a lot of biographical details. My own notes were taken from Fred's dictation and would be quite unintelligible to anyone else.

I think perhaps I ought not in any case to show my book to another writer before it is published, as it was definitely commissioned by John Lane and of course the disposal of all translation rights, etc, belongs to him. However, when the typescript arrives, I will make a list of the principal facts and dates and send that to Dr Simon, so as to save you the trouble of preparing fresh notes. When I was in Vienna, Hertzka seemed anxious to bring out a book on Delius music and said he would approach Lane for the translation rights when my book appeared.

I have not had any proofs of the piano score of the Cello Concerto. It is a pity Fred should have had the bother of a carelessly engraved first proof. They ought to have sent these to me and sent only the second proofs to Fred for final revision.

If you could send me the score of the Dance Rhapsody from Grez, I can photograph it here with a big camera. I have seen a photograph of the Riccardi bust[35] —but one would have to get permission to reproduce it. I was not much impressed by the photograph, but perhaps it did not do justice to the work.

No. I never had the score of 'Koanga' from Goodwin and Tabb; in fact, I was under the impression that Beecham had swallowed it up and could not be induced to disgorge it.

---

[34] E. B. Hill, 'An Isolated Figure among New Composers', *Boston Evening Transcript*, 24 Nov. 1909.

[35] Jelka had written to Marie Clews the previous year saying: 'Lady C.[unard] had a young sculptor (Secessionist from Rome called Riccardi) and she got him to make a bust of Fred. It was really awfully fine and full of character and I am very curious to see it again in plaster or bronze on our way thro' London.' Jelka Delius to Marie Clews, 31 July 1921, Delius Trust Archive. This bust of Delius by Eleuterio Riccardi is now housed in the Cartwright Gallery, Bradford.

Does Fred regard it as a mature work? I have not dealt with any of the unpublished music in my book, as there is so very little space (Lane only asked for 25,000 words and as it is, it exceeds 35,000) and I have rather concentrated upon the really great works—Village Romeo, Mass of Life, Fennimore, Sea Drift etc.

There is one difficult point which has troubled me a great deal—and that is the question of definite criticism. After a lot of consideration, and consultation with others who know and love Fred's music, I came to the conclusion that a book consisting wholly of praise would, in these days, be so suspect of propaganda and partizanship that it would really do more harm than good. And as I am known in London as a rather exacting critic, I am afraid that if I omitted to mention any points that appear to me to be weak in Delius music, I should merely be accused of writing in favour of my friends—and this would I feel sure detract from the weight of all that I have written in praise and appreciation. So I have tried to be absolutely impartial and to apply to the consideration of this music exactly the same standards of criticism that I should apply to anyone else's. I am sure that this is the only way in which one can be taken seriously when one writes about one's friends; and after all, no artist ever lived whose work was all of a piece, all equally perfect. Such an art would be almost inhuman—so I think it is much better to face the fact at once and not try and pretend that a phenomenon has occurred which everyone knows never does occur.

It may be—I am rather inclined to think it is—the very perfection and greatness of most of Fred's work which makes the minor weaknesses of some of the other work more apparent than they would be elsewhere. Even the minor work of a genius is often better than the masterpieces of men of mere talent but by comparison with the best work of genius it is apt to seem even less good than it is.

I am so glad to hear than Fred is so much better. Let us hope that he will be quite his old self again in time to celebrate his diamond jubilee next year! Ever so much love to you both from

Phil

Hertzka has never brought out my piano arrangements of 'In a Summer Garden' and the 1st Dance Rhapsody. Now the 2nd Dance Rhapsody will be out before the first! Could you not hurry him up a little?

298
Jelka Delius to Philip Heseltine

Lesjaskog 2. 9. 1922

My dear Phil

I received your letter of the 28th last night and hasten to say, that naturally you must write your book like a real criticism and not only praise—that
would quite take the flower and flavour from it, and make it like those odious
panegyrics written for the Publishers of the Music. Please write all just as you
feel, says Fred.

I shall be so glad if you send some biogr. notes to Simon, as he is in a hurry
to write his thing and I have no documents here, and also no tranquillity or
leisure for such work, as all these months I have been busy *only* for Fred, to
read to him, to help correcting, correspondence, in fact to keep him from depression etc. in this lonely place! I am grieved that I had quite given up my piano
playing. I have now to stumble to it again with the greatest difficulty and out
of sheer devotion so as to help him, as he has such difficulty about using his
hands. Ah! if only you had been able to come here! We expect Balfour G. to-
night and we leave on the 7th and hope to be in Grez on the 14th.

Should I suggest to Hertzka to apply for the rights of translation of your book?
Also I wrote about it to Pierre Garanger a very gifted young frenchman, great
admirer of Fred, a writer, and very artistic alround and he wrote that he would
love to translate your book into french. Please let me know what should be done
about it? How would it pan out practically?

I'll also write and ask Hertzka about your arrangements of In a Summer
Garden and the 1st Dance Rhapsody. But when you write again please tell me
about the Pianola for all these arrangements? Which ones would suit? Should
I approach Augeners?

The Philharm are going to do the Song of the High Hills on Dec. 6th and
we shall try to go to London[36] for that and from there on to Francfort.

We have just received 'Hassan the Piano Score. It plays awfully well—and I
do hope it will be a success!

Best love from Fred!

your affectionate friend
Jelka Delius

---

[36] This performance, conducted by Albert Coates, took place on 7 Dec. 1922 in Queen's Hall.

299
Philip Heseltine to Frederick Delius

Cefn-Bryntalch,
Abermule,
Montgomeryshire.

November 28ᵗʰ 1922

My dear Friend

I was very sorry you could not come over to England this month, but I expect you would have found the journey rather trying and London rather uncomfortable. It is good to hear that you are installed in cosy quarters in Frankfort and that 'Hassan' is at last to be produced on the stage. The play was very well received everywhere on its publication this autumn, so it ought to have a good success when it is performed in London. Let us hope Dean will not delay much longer. Douglas Goldring,[37] who has just published a biography of Flecker,[38] tells me that Dean is anxious to produce it but has lost a lot of money lately over unsuccessful pieces.

Is the piano score published yet? I have never received a copy, nor have I had a copy of the Cello Concerto, although I see it is already in the Universal Catalogue. (What a pity, by the way, that Hertzka has allowed that rotten swindler Curwen to take his English agency!) I also see announced an arrangement for 2 pianos of the 'Dance Rhapsody' (no 1). A year ago Hertzka accepted from me a version of this work for 4 hands (*1* piano) together with a 2-hand arrangement of the 'Summer Garden' but I have heard nothing more of either of them.

I have not received any of the photographs back from Lane yet. I called there about a month ago, but he had not yet decided which he would use. However I've written to him again, asking also for a definite date when we may expect the book to be ready.

I am sorry the Osbornes felt hurt about their invitation. The fact is I was away at the time and a telegram came for me to Wilson's address asking me to go to a concert with them; so Wilson (who had been with me when I called for the photographs) replied by telephone at once, saying I could not go.

It's just as well you didn't hear the 'Curlew' last Thursday. The instrumentalists were admirable (especially when one considers the inadequacy of two

---

[37] Douglas Goldring (1887–1960), novelist, playwright, and editor.
[38] D. Goldring, *James Elroy Flecker: An Appreciation with Some Biographical Notes* (London, 1922).

rehearsals of 1½ hours for a work that takes 20 minutes to play straight through) but Wilson, who had been studying the thing for months, made an awful hash of it. However I was very glad to hear the work and to know I had not made any bad miscalculations as to what it would sound like. It encourages me to go on and I hope to write a lot this winter.

The first volume of 'English Ayres: 1598–1612' will be out this week and the second before the end of the year. Enoch's are an enterprising firm and I am sure will make these songs go. What a contrast to the average English publisher who keeps MSS in his safe for a year or two quite contentedly! The first volume of 21 songs with a long preface has been engraved and made ready for publication within a month.

With much love to you both and hoping your recovery proceeds apace,

Ever affectionately yours
Philip Heseltine

300
Frederick Delius to Philip Heseltine

Grez-sur-Loing
(S & M)
20th /12/ 22

My dear Phil
Why do you double the bass in the enclosed few bars? I have scratched out in pencil—The questionable bar runs as enclosed bar. I send the correction to you for approval—Send on to Cecil Gray

Wishing you all sorts of good luck for the coming year—I am in haste

ever affectionately
Frederick Delius

1923

DURING January and March there were several performances of Delius's music in Frankfurt. Also early that January Percy Grainger came to stay in Frankfurt until summer, visiting and playing for Delius on numerous occasions. On 29 January Delius celebrated what was thought to be his 60th birthday. It was only later when Heseltine checked at Somerset House that the birth year was found to be 1862. For this occasion, however, Heseltine had especially composed a *Serenade* for string orchestra. April found the Deliuses for over two months in Bad Oeynhausen, near Hanover, where Delius had gone for yet more treatment. He made good progress and was much cheered to hear that *Hassan* (premièred in Germany in June) was to be produced in London that September. Leaving the spa on 21 June the Deliuses travelled to Lesjaskog where they arrived on 29 July and where, assisted by Grainger, Delius continued composing some additional music requested by Basil Dean for the London production of *Hassan*. Percy Grainger assisted him in this task. On account of bad weather they left Norway in mid-August arriving back in Grez (via Christiania and Antwerp) on 21 August. Although Delius was feeling unwell, he and Jelka travelled to London to attended the final rehearsals and opening performance of *Hassan* which had a long and highly successful run. On his return to France Delius bought a car and began composing again, this time a sonata for violin. There were a number of visitors to Grez including, at various times, Thomas Beecham and Lady Cunard, Heseltine, and Cecil Gray. Delius's condition began to show signs of slight improvement and he and Jelka were driven down to Rapallo by their chauffeur that December, staying with the Clews at their Château de la Napoule en route.

By and large 1923 was another rather uneventful year for Heseltine. By spring his transcriptions of early music began to appear in print and in August he had completed three carols for the Bach Choir, composed at the suggestion of Vaughan Williams. He also carried on with his journalistic work and between July and September he produced a number of articles for the *Weekly Westminster Gazette*. In August he stayed with Victor Neuburg at Steyning before travelling to Paris with Gerald Cooper that same month to consult some MSS at the Conservatoire. In September he spent some time in Essex with Judith Wood, calling himself Peter Wood on this occasion. His book on Delius appeared at last that summer, much to the delight of the older composer. Heseltine was also delighted to discover himself portrayed as one of the characters in Aldous Huxley's amusing novel *Antic Hay* published that same year. In November he and Gray paid a short visit to Grez and on 19 December the *Three Carols* were given their first performance at a Bach Choir concert conducted by Vaughan Williams.

301
Philip Heseltine to Frederick Delius

Cefn-Bryntalch,
Abermule,
Montgomeryshire.

January 22nd 1923.

My dear Friend,

Here's to congratulate you most heartily on your diamond jubilee and to wish you many more years of good health and happiness! May you enter like Verdi upon a second youth and go on writing glorious works for another quarter-century![1]

I send this to the last address you gave me, in Frankfort, but I was wondering whether the disturbed condition of Germany[2] has perhaps made life too uncomfortable there. However, you'll be staying for Hassan and the concerts I expect[3]—unless those too go by the board in the general disruption—though I daresay, as usual, the English newspapers have exaggerated and distorted the facts of the matter to a large extent, to suit their own political views.

I've been here two months working steadily all the while—except for the Christmas week when Arthur Symons was staying here and we went out for long walks every day. The first volume of the 'English Ayres: 1598–1612' has appeared and is having a very good success—I feel it is quite an event in the history of English music to have Elizabethan songs encored at the ballad concerts—and this is what happened when Wilson sang a group of them a week or two ago. The second volume is printed already and will be out in a few days

[1] At the time of the actual birthday (29 Jan.) the Deliuses were in Frankfurt, surrounded by numerous friends. On the day itself Delius was given a surprise chamber concert at the home of his close friend, Dr Heinrich Simon, proprietor of the *Frankfurter Zeitung*. Percy Grainger and Alexander Lippay, conductor of the Frankfurt Opera, played Heseltine's birthday gift, the *Serenade*, through to Delius.

[2] The occupation of the Ruhr by French troops in Jan. 1923 had led to what was virtually a state of undeclared war between the French and the Germans in the Rhineland.

[3] *Hassan* was due to be performed in Darmstadt on 15 Mar. but was eventually postponed until June. On 1 Mar. a concert of works including the *North Country Sketches*, the Cello Concerto, and the *Song of the High Hills* was given in Frankfurt.

now—and two other volumes are being printed in Vienna. Next week I am going to London for a few days, to do some more transcriptions in the British Museum and look after the rehearsals for the second performance of 'The Curlew' which takes place (with a different and much better singer) on the 31ˢᵗ at one of Lady Dean Paul's (Poldowski) chamber-music concerts.[4] But I shan't stay long —I find solitude and the country most necessary accompaniments to any sort of good work—at present at any rate.

The enclosed cutting may amuse you—it came out of the social gossip column of the Evening News! I can't imagine who could have written it. The 'jagged edge' remark is almost as good as the description of van Dieren in the Daily Sketch as 'all futurist and funny'.

Much love to you both, and again very many happy returns of the day and all good wishes for the future.

Ever affectionately yours
Philip Heseltine

Enclosed Press Cutting:

'Peter Warlock'
The name Peter Warlock has a habit of occurring fairly frequently on London concert programmes nowadays, and people may be heard wondering, after some pointedly original song, 'Who is Mr. Warlock?'

The name, of course, is rather too good to be true. There is neither a warlock nor a witch in the current London telephone directory!

The musician who has chosen this rather sinister *nom de guerre* is Mr. Philip Heseltine. His works are not heard at Saturday afternoon ballad concerts or other haunts of easy music, for he is one of the adventurous young men, and his art has a somewhat jagged edge.

The Oriana Choir, however, fear nothing—witness the success with which they sang his strange 'Corpus Christi Carol' last night. Mr. Heseltine belongs to a circle of young musicians who chiefly revere Mr. Frederick Delius (composer of the opera 'The Village Romeo and Juliet') and also are impressed by Schönberg and by the rather fierce modern Hungarian school. He has reduced several of Mr. Delius's works to piano score, and was the founder of an esoteric little review, the *Sackbut*.

In Heseltine's handwriting: Evening News. 21.xii.1922.

---

[4] This was the fifth of the *Concerts Intimes* held at 12 noon on 31 Jan. 1923 at the Hyde Park Hotel. John Goss was the soloist in *The Curlew* with the Charles Woodhouse string quartet and Leon Goossens (cor anglais).

302
Frederick Delius to Philip Heseltine

26. 2. 1923

Domplatz 12
Francfort o/M

Fred dictates:

My dear Phil,

Forgive me for not answering your kind letter of congratulations and acknowledging your charming serenade,[5] which I received early in the morning on my birthday to my greatest surprise and pleasure   I like it very much indeed. it is a very delicate composition of a fine harmonist. Composition is your true vocation and I cannot tell you how happy I am that you are now following it and have left the Polemic of the Sackbut behind you.

Percy Grainger and Alexander Lippay[6] played me the Serenade several times from the Score and they all liked it.—Just at present I am in the midst of rehearsals and very busy indeed as the Delius-Concert is to take place on March 1ˢᵗ with the following programme. North Country Sketches—Cello Concerto and Song of the High Hills. Barjansky[7] played me the Concerto at the house yesterday; and he is wonderfully good; a Russian; he played it with great success in Vienna on Jan. 31ˢᵗ. I shall write you again and tell you all about the concert when I have a little time. I had an awful lot of parts to correct, also those of Hassan. The 1ˢᵗ perf. takes place on March 15ᵗʰ at Darmstadt.

Life is extremely agreable here in spite of the Chaos of the Ruhr.—I think Europe is at its last gasp and does not seem to react to anything anymore.[8]

---

[5] In Dec. 1922 Heseltine told Taylor: 'I'm writing a Serenade for strings in three movements now—which I think is going well.' Only one movement was eventually completed and there is no evidence that Heseltine actually began work on either of the two other movements. The work bears the dedication 'To Frederick Delius on his sixtieth birthday'. Heseltine to Taylor, 19 Dec. 1922, BL 54197.

[6] Alexander Lippay was conductor at the Frankfurt Opera and a good friend of Delius. He eventually left Germany to conduct in the Philippines.

[7] Alexandre Barjansky (1883–1961), Russian cellist who was a fine interpreter of Delius's music. He gave the first performance of Delius's Cello Concerto in Vienna on 31 Jan.

[8] At the end of Jan. Delius had written to Sydney Schiff about the conditions in Europe: 'Things are getting worse and worse here every day and it is inconceivable to me how the middle classes and the "Intelligentia" live. As to the lower classes they are completely demoralized. They are convinced of the uselessness of saving their money and eat and especially drink up everything as fast as they get it. Prices are soaring up. The cheapest meat is Mks 2000 per Lb; Butter 5000 —a loaf 1000, Milk 1500 a liter, but hardly obtainable at all. I fear it can only end in rioting and bolchevism. Since the Ruhr-occupation it has got ever so much worse and there is a fanatical hatred against the French. The passive attitude of England and America seems incredible to anybody living here; for in the coming catastrophe, which is inevitable England will go down with the rest. Englands policy seems extraordinarily short-sighted. Of course our European civilization is at its last gasp, but I believe that the United States may rise out of the ruins.' Delius to Schiff, 30 Jan. 1923, BL 52917.

Give my kindest regards to your mother and thank her for her kind birthday wishes.

Percy Grainger had 2 orchestral rehearsals of his Warriors,[9] a very strong, vital and rhythmic piece, dedicated to me—very interesting indeed. Lippay conducted —by far Graingers greatest thing. He is indeed a wonderfully gifted musician and a most lovable personality.[10]

Ever affectionately yours
Frederick Delius

In Jelka's hand.

303
Philip Heseltine to Frederick Delius

May 4th 1923   125 Cheyne Walk
                                                            Chelsea, S.W.10.

My dear Friend

I had just written you a letter to your old address in Frankfort when Jelka's card from Bad Oeynhausen was forwarded to me. But I expect the other letter has been sent on to you by this time so I won't recapitulate.

The Delius book is not out yet; in fact I only received the first proofs yesterday. There are very few printer's errors, so that I shall probably get the page proofs next week and then the printing and binding can go ahead. The book ought to be on the market about the middle of June.

I hear that, thanks to the letter you so kindly wrote on my behalf to Basil Dean two years ago, there is quite a good chance of my being engaged to conduct the London production of 'Hassan'. I need hardly say what a tremendous joy it would be to me to do this, especially as, having so to speak watched the music grow and seen it in every stage of its evolution, I feel a particularly intimate affection and love for the work which I should dearly like to try and convey to people in performance.

---

[9] *The Warriors* (1913–16) for large orchestra, including three or more pianos, an enormous section of tuned percussion instruments, and offstage brass. It is dedicated 'in admiration and affection to Frederick Delius'.

[10] Grainger had been invited to Frankfurt (from Holland where he was staying) to help train the chorus for a concert of Delius's music scheduled for 1 Mar. and conducted by Paul von Klenau.

It seems fairly certain that 'Hassan' will be put on in the autumn—and, to judge by its initial success, the Kapek play 'R.U.R.'[11] ought to go a long way towards re-establishing the fortunes of the Reandean company.

I rejoice to hear that you are well enough to take your usual summer holiday in Norway and I hope it will do you no end of good, so that we may see you completely restored to health when you come over in the autumn.[12]

Bartók is in London again for a couple of concerts.[13] It is very good to see what great progress he is making in the regard of the English public—and it must be very encouraging for him after all the hard years of poverty and neglect. He is indeed a true genius, and a most lovable personality.

With much love to you both

Ever affectionately yours
Philip Heseltine

304
Philip Heseltine to Frederick Delius

May 14th 1923   125 Cheyne Walk
                                                   London S.W.10.

My dear Friend

I am writing two copies of this letter as I am not sure whether you are in Germany or in Norway and I am anxious that you may get it quickly.

A great friend of mine E. J. Moeran[14] (pronounced Móran) has gone to Norway for the wedding of a friend of his, and if his money lasts out he wants to stay there a bit and take a trip up to the North Cape. He is a very good composer and a great admirer of your work and would very much like to come and see you if you are in Norway and have no objection. According to his plans when he left, his trip would finish up at Bergen about the 28th of this month; so would

---

[11] *R.U.R.* (*Rossum's Universal Robots*) was a play by the Czech playwright, Karel Capek (1890–1938), which opened in London on 5 May at St Martin's Theatre with Basil Rathbone in the cast.

[12] Delius had written to Henry Clews: 'I am still pretty weak on the legs and am taking the baths at Oeynhausen near Hanover. After 6 or 7 weeks here we go to Norway for the summer to our little Châlet in the mountains.' Delius to Clews, 10 Apr. 1923, Delius Trust Archive.

[13] Although Bartók would play in at least seven concerts in London in late 1923, his recitals during his earlier visit in May were given in the provinces.

[14] E. J. Moeran (1894–1950), English composer of Irish descent. He and Heseltine would later share a cottage in Eynsford from 1925 to 1928.

you be so kind as to send him a line Post Restante, Bergen, to tell him whether you will be at Leskajog[15] at the end of the month and whether he may come and spend a day or two with you? I am sure you would like him—he is a most interesting and many-sided man.

I see that 'Hassan' is now quite definitely announced for the autumn and Basil Gill is mentioned as likely to be cast for the title role. I feel very excited at the prospect of getting the conductorship which does not seem nearly so remote as it did two years ago. It would be the finest opportunity I've ever had to establish myself in the music world here and I should dearly love the work, as you know,

I believe Edward Clark is also after the post, as he came and asked me for your address the other day.

With much love and all good wishes

Ever affectionately yours
Philip Heseltine

305
Frederick Delius to Philip Heseltine

Italia
21. 12. 1923

Villa Raggio[16]
San Ambrogio
Rapallo

Dear Phil, We just arrived here at this lovely place after a very long and tiring but really beautiful trip in the car.[17] We were very well driven by our young french chauffeur, but the days are so short it took us 8 days to get to Rapallo. We stayed nearly a week at La Napoule with the Clews' our american friends. It was perfectly lovely, right on the sea in an old fortress chateau, the sea beating against the foundations all around. The weather was warm like in May and the snow mountains high above the blue mountains too beautiful in the bay of Cannes.

---

[15] The Deliuses stayed in Lesjaskog from 29 June until about mid-August.

[16] The Deliuses had rented a house belonging to the theatre designer Edward Gordon Craig (1872–1966).

[17] 'We have decided to always keep Grez as headquarters and have bought a little Motorcar which *does* make living here delightful.' Jelka Delius to Marie Clews, 27 Oct. 1923, Carley, *Letters*, ii. 283.

I received the contract from Hawkes but should very much like to know something about this firm before signing. Are they a new firm? A big firm? Honest? Have they a good reputation? You know how dreadfully I have been cheated already. What, for instance, would happen, if this firm went bankrupt? One has no control over publishers, so one must try to get hold of really honest ones.

I have immediately written again to Hertzka to send you the £10 at once and hope you will receive it.

I told the Copyright Society to forbid any cuts to be made in my records[18] but I am very grateful to you for telling me about the Dance Rhapsody. I am writing to them again about it.

From the Oxford Press I have not heard yet, neither have I received a contract or the money.

We have only just arrived and are very busy starting our house-keeping and getting eatables. We do not know Italian so it is quite a job to get going

We both wish you a very happy Xmas and New year.

Kindest regards to your mother if you spend Xmas with her

Ever affly
Frederick Delius

In Jelka's hand.

---

[18] 'The music for Hassan is being recorded by the Gramophone Co and Fr. has become a member for the Copyright protect. Soc.' Jelka Delius to Grainger, 14 Oct. 1923, Carley, *Letters*, ii. 283. The recording of nine numbers from *Hassan* by His Majesty's Theatre Chorus and Orchestra conducted by Percy Fletcher (G-C1134/5) was withdrawn.

1924

EVEN though life proved to be very isolated at Rapallo, Delius received visits from Balfour Gardiner, Arnold Bax, and Max Beerbohm. Having found an old Broadwood piano, he also did some composing, but at the end of February a visiting German specialist advised him to go to Kassel for yet another course of treatment. The Deliuses left Rapallo on 16 March, first staying for five weeks at La Napoule near to the Clews. By the end of April they had returned to Grez and were in Kassel by mid-May. The sanatorium was not, however, to their liking and they soon moved to a hotel. By the end of June Delius's condition seemed to be showing some signs of improvement. On 12 August they were back in Grez once more and, with slightly improved eyesight, Delius began composing again. As the time in Kassel had been so beneficial they returned there in mid-November, but now Delius's condition began to deteriorate again. He was having trouble with his left eye and by the end of the year was generally growing weaker.

For the first few months of 1924 Heseltine was still living in Wales. His song-cycle *Lillygay* had been published in January and he was continuing with his transcriptions of early music. In May he broke a leg in a fall whilst capering at Montgomery Castle and by June had decided to return once again to live in London. *The Curlew* was performed at the International Music Festival in Salzburg and Heseltine now began his association with Oxford University Press, where Hubert Foss had recently been put in charge of the music department. In July he holidayed in Poole in Dorset and by autumn had almost completed his work on the book on Gesualdo which he and Gray were jointly writing. At the end of the year he rescored *The Old Codger* (a send-up of the Franck symphony) for the Savoy Orpheans and on 5 December presented a BBC radio programme on early English vocal and keyboard music. Christmas was spent on holiday at Palma de Mallorca on Majorca.

306
Frederick Delius to Philip Heseltine

Dear Phil, We hear from Augeners that they have sent you various proof scores of mine for correction. Needless to say I never instructed them to do so. If you have any of these scores kindly return them to Augener's so that they can send them to me for correction. The quartet & 2ᵈ Dance Rhapsody score were amongst them. Could you tell me which is the best gramophone to get for orchestral music and can also the records of other Societies be used in it? I should like to purchase one and have it at Grez.

We have had heavenly weather and for the last fortnight have spent our time on the terrace from noon to almost sunset bathed in delicious sunshine.[1] The view from our terrace is so lovely, the sunsets so beautiful; that we have been out but rarely in the car—there is no place to go, except round the coast, which is no special fun.[2] We shall be here till March 15ᵗʰ and then probably stay in Cannes or Nice a while.

Affectionate greetings from us both Fr D.

Am writing again to Hertzka about S. Garden etc.
[Rapallo]
9. 1. 1924

Postcard, in Jelka's hand.

[1] A few days later Jelka told Balfour Gardiner: 'The weather is heavenly now and we are sitting in the sun on our verandah.' Jelka Delius to Gardiner, 14 Jan. 1924, Carley, *Letters*, ii. 285.
[2] The Deliuses had motored down to Rapallo via Lyon, Avignon, the Provence, and along the coast from Cap Fréjus on, staying with the Clews at La Napoule near Cannes en route.

307
Frederick Delius to Philip Heseltine

23. 3. 1924

'Les Brisants'
La Napoule
Alpes Mar.
France

Fred dictates:

My dear Phil

We left Rapallo on the 16th in the car and spent the night in San Remo. From there we went next day to La Napoule lunching at Mentone where we met Orr in the street who looked very well. We are now in a Villa in La Napoule where we intend to stay till the end of April. Then we go to Cassel in Germany, where there is a wonderfully good doctor who cures my sort of trouble. We shall probably spend a month or 6 weeks in his Sanatorium. This doctor came from Cassel to see me in Rapallo and spent a week with us, examining my case and beginning preliminaries for his cure.[3]

Which is the best Gramophone, as I want to get one; but of course, I want absolutely the best. Have you heard all my things, Hassan, Brigg Fair, the cuckoo and how do they sound?

Schiff seems awfully anxious to arrange concerts of my works in London. I should so much like the Mass of Life, Songs of Sunset, the Arabesk and the Requiem to be done again. Schiff takes great interest in this and can evidently command a good deal of backing and would like to see you again and talk things over. What have you got against him? He seems to like you very much and always asks so kindly after you. I should so much like the few friends I have in London to be in harmony with one another.

Please write me here soon and tell me what you are doing and what is going on.

---

[3] Jelka had written from Rapallo telling Grainger more about this doctor: 'Now I must tell you about a german doctor in Cassel, of whom I heard and who is alleged to treat all Lähmungen Geh-Störungen [lameness] etc so successfully. I wrote to him describing Freds whole state and antecedents. He wrote back rather hopefully; As it is too cold for us to go to Germany at once we have arranged for him to come here [Rapallo] to see Fred, begin the treatment and tell us exactly what to do. He has greatly bettered and almost cured resembling cases. . . . The Doctor is coming in a day or 2 and going to stay with us and it will be a great thing really to hear all about this new cure and be fixed what we have to do.' Jelka Delius to Grainger, 24 Feb. 1924, Melbourne, Grainger Museum.

I enclose a cheque for £5-0-0 which, I surmise will be useful to balance your budget.

With love from Jelka

Ever aff[ly]
Fr. Delius

In Jelka's hand.

308
Frederick Delius to Philip Heseltine

18-9-24

Grez-sur-Loing.
S. et M.

Dear Phil.

I was very glad to hear from you again.

We returned here a fortnight ago[4]—from Cassel, where I underwent a 3 months' treatment, with a wonderfully clever Doctor. His treatment (mostly electrical) has really done me good; altho' I can walk a little alone for five or ten minutes, I walk mostly on Jelka's arm, when I can go for twenty or twenty five minutes. I am also beginning to write again.[5] The whole trouble has been nervous, caused by the tremendous strain & anxiety of the War.

Many thanks dear Phil for the Score of the 'Curlew', which I only received on my return to Grez; it having been forwarded here from La Napoule. I think it is a very delicate piece of Music, but I think—if I may make a criticism—that you have spun it out a little too much—It seems to me that your Song 'The Curlew' was more concise, & therefore more effective; but, on no account must you get disheartened about your Music, Keep hard at work, & you will eventually do something fine & great.

[4] In fact the Deliuses had already been home for five weeks when this letter was written.

[5] Jelka wrote to Marie Clews in October: 'Certainly Fred is *much* better in every way, can walk better, eat better, play the piano better looks so much better. Yet he has not quite got his balance yet and that is what ought to be obtained. His eyes are ever so much better. He does not wear his glasses any more and uses weaker glasses for reading than he has used for 5 years. We had several visits from friends, who saw him last in London last autumn and find him wonderfully improved.' Jelka Delius to Marie Clews, 6 Oct. 1924, Carley, *Letters*, ii. 294.

The Philharmonic are giving 'The Mass of Life' on 2ᵈ April, & of course—
we shall come over—I *do hope* they will engage a really good & impressive singer,
for the Baritone-part.[6]

Won't you come over here & stay with us a week or two—We should so much
like to see you.

Remember me kindly to Agustus John[7] when you see him.

Ever your affectionate
Frederick Delius

Letter in an unknown hand, signed in pencil by Delius.

309
Frederick Delius to Philip Heseltine

Grez 22. 10. 1924

My dear Phil,

I was very glad to get your letter   I will look again at the piece for string
orchestra and let you know about it in a day or two. If you could let me know
exact date and time of the Delius concert at Newcastle I could probably hear
it here on the schoolmaster's Radio. This would give me great pleasure.

As regards John Goss's[8] choice why sing my oldest songs like Abendstim-
mung and Verborgne Liebe. Let him choose from the following songs: Verlaine:
Les Sanglots songs (5 Gesänge Tischer Le ciel est pardessus le toit (Tischer) Autumn,
Irmelin, So sweet is shee, Daffodils, The nightingale has a Lyre of Gold—Henley,
Spring Song Jakobsen (both in 5 gesänge) and of course I-Brazil. If he has not
got these 5 Gesänge (the group containing I-Brazil) he could borrow them from
Mrs Howard-Jones.

I thank you very much for your two part Songs of which I think the Dirge[9]
is the best   Please tell me how it sounded, as there are one or two places where

---

[6] Conducted by Paul von Klenau with Kennedy Scott's Philharmonic Choir.

[7] Augustus John (1878–1961): English painter who was a friend of Heseltine's. He would have met Delius during one of the composer's visits to London; a few years later he made pencil drawings of Delius during his final visit to London in 1929.

[8] John Goss (1894–1953), English baritone.

[9] This was probably 'All the Flowers of the Spring' (1923), one of Heseltine's settings of *Three Dirges of Webster*. Heseltine also sent a copy of the piece to Balfour Gardiner who thanked him, saying: 'This is music I can live with for days, in great content. Nowadays I am so starved of musical delights that whenever they come I am endlessly grate-ful to the author of them.' Gardiner to Heseltine, 13 Aug. 1924, photocopy, PWS Archives.

you employ unnecessarily harsh chords. they seem to me too 'voulu' and not instinctive enough.

In a week or 10 days we are off to Cassel again to continue my treatment and I will write you from there. Seadrift will be done at Cassel this Season, Songs of Sunset at Hagen, The Mass of Life at Vienna, Prague, Berlin, Wiesbaden.

With Love from us both

Yrs ever affectionately
Frederick Delius

In Jelka's hand.

310
Philip Heseltine to Frederick Delius

October 24th 1924.   6^A Bury Street
                                                          Chelsea S.W.3.

Dear Friend—Many thanks for your letter—I will give Goss your message— but I still consider that 'Abendstimmung' is quite one of your most beautiful songs. If you are listening in to wireless concerts you can hear my 'Serenade' on Sunday next about 9.10 p.m. from London (2 LO. 365 Metres) and 'Brigg Fair' by the Hallé Orchestra, under Harty, (also from London) Thursday next, about 8.30 p.m.

Ever affectionately
Philip Heseltine

Postcard.

1925

STILL in Kassel at the beginning of 1925, Delius was by now virtually an invalid, having lost most of the use of his arms and legs as well as being almost blind, although his mind was still unaffected. By February he was in a badly depressed state, medical expenses and the resulting financial worries being foremost in his mind. Despite all this he did, however, manage to hear performances of his works in Kassel (*Sea Drift*) and Wiesbaden (the *Mass*). There were also a number of visitors to Kassel, including Balfour Gardiner, Charles Kennedy Scott, and Gerald Cooper, who presented Delius with the Royal Philharmonic Society's Gold Medal. At the end of May the Deliuses returned to Grez and from now on they were away from home less and less. Heseltine visited them at Grez in July together with E. J. Moeran, and on 26 July the cellist Alexandre Barjansky and his wife came to stay for the summer. Other visitors at that time included the pianist Howard-Jones, Grainger, and Gardiner, who entertained Delius with performances of his music. The other comfort to Delius at this time was the wireless and gramophone, and he was thus able to listen to much music, including the early recordings of his works. Gardiner and Kennedy Scott visited the Deliuses during the Christmas holidays and once again were able to play the piano for him.

In January Heseltine moved to a cottage in Eynsford in Kent together with his mistress, Barbara Peache, Moeran, and a general factotum, the Maori Hal Collins. He was to stay there for some three years and it is from this period that much of the Warlock 'legend' originates. Visitors to the Eynsford cottage included Arnold Bax, Constant Lambert, Lord Berners, and the young William Walton. In April Heseltine informed Delius that he intended writing another book about him, this time concentrating on his music instead of his life. The book, however, never appeared, more than likely because of the change in Heseltine's attitude in the coming years towards Delius and his music. After a visit (with Moeran) to Delius at Grez in July Heseltine settled down to some hard work, completing his books on Gesualdo and *The English Ayre*. He continued to devote much energy to the editing of early music and in December he spent time editing at the Bodleian Library in Oxford.

311
Jelka Delius to Philip Heseltine

Schlosshotel
Wilhelmshöhe
bei Cassel
14. 2. 25

Dear Phil,

I have not had leisure to answer your kind P.C. sooner. We have had such a bad time. Fred has been so very poorly suffering from entire loss of appetite and an unquenchable thirst. Of course this made him extremely weak. We came up here a fortnight ago to have the purer and more bracing air; and he certainly is getting a little better and eating a little now. We keep him as much as possible in the air and sunshine, the weather is lovely and almost springlike. It would be very nice if you could send your serenade. Fred has naturally been very depressed about his health and especially as he wants ever so much to go to London for the Mass of Life on April 2^d. At the time we had written about John Goss for the Mass of L; but they had already engaged Heming;[1] Austin chose him. Do you know anything about him? I never see him mentioned anywhere? Did you hear Beecham conducting 'Paris' by heart? We are having a very lonely time here —the only event was the performance of Seadrift here at Cassel the other day. The work sounded so beautiful and in spite of a sort of partial strike of the Orchestra the performance was good, the Chorus excellent and the Baritone very musical and with fine earnest voice. It did Fred good to hear it. On Febr 23 and 24th the Mass of Life is to be done at Vienna, on March 16th at Wiesbaden[2] and on March 26th at Berlin.

I wanted to ask your advice, dear Phil. We have such a lot of trouble about certain royalties. When Hassan was recorded Fred was advised to become a member of the Mech. Copyright Prot. Society. They paid him only till the end of 1923. Then the Society amalgamated with the present Society and he gave

---

[1] Percy Heming (1883–1956), English baritone. He was the principal baritone with the British National Opera Company from 1922.

[2] The performance was conducted by Carl Schuricht, a champion of Delius's music in Germany. Jelka wrote to Grainger: 'It was an excellent performance and really Fred enjoyed it ever so much; and the whole thing—the atmosphere of music—quite took him out of himself. . . . Fred was a touching figure, sitting in the middle of the hall in his bath-chair, listening so intently. The applause was wonderful—no clapping at all between the sections—and at the end by a sudden impulse of reverence the whole audience rose and turned toward Delius and bowed to him and then only the enthusiastic applause began.' Jelka Delius to Grainger, 23 Mar. 1925, Melbourne, Grainger Museum.

his signature to the new one. They however only payed the 3ᵈ quarter of 1924, telling us that we should shortly receive the 1ˢᵗ half year 1924 from the accountants of the old Society. But we never received anything (it was just the half year when Hassan was running)   Now Gardiner advised Fred to become a member of the Society of Authors and to let them collect all his fees. But I see that they keep 5% of the profits for doing so.

You who are young and practical, do you think it is advisable to do so, or what should we do? There is also the Anglo French, who published the 3 little preludes. They sent us the Royalties and instead of 9ᵈ a copy had given only 3ᵈ. Fred's contract stipulates that he gets 25% of the price published on the music (3/- a copy). We have written to them of course ever so often, and after promising last summer to rectify their mistake they have not yet done so and leave all letters unanswered.

The Society of Authors would, I suppose see to it that Fred got paid.

The Violin Sonata II and the little piano pieces[3] are recorded now by the Columbia and there will be more and more of these fees to be collected. Owing to Fred's illness we have a lot of expense. We have an excellent trained nurse now—and really we must not be diddled out of all these profits. In short: Would you consider it to be the best plan to become a member of the Society of Authors? Or is there another more practical way of managing these things?

We were delighted with your card and your peaceful looking little village of Eynsford. If you have leisure, please write Fred one of your nice letters; it would give him great pleasure and I welcome all things that keep up his interest in the world of music—he gets so depressed. I do wish we could go to London for the Mass of Life! But for that he would have to make a lot of progress again. It is a terrible, desperate struggle to fight this disease

I hope you are working happily, dear Phil,

yrs ever affectionately
Jelka

---

[3] Violin Sonata II, played by Albert Sammons and E. Howard-Jones (Columbia, C-D1500-1). Piano pieces (*Mazurka*, *Waltz for a Little Girl*, *Toccata*) (American Columbia 2098M and Columbia, C5444) and *Preludes* played by E. Howard-Jones (American Columbia, AmC 2095M).

312
Philip Heseltine to Frederick and Jelka Delius

March 13ᵗʰ 1925   Eynsford
                                                                        Kent.

My dear Fred and Jelka

I should have answered your letter long before this, but I was waiting for the score of the 'Serenade' which the publishers promised would be ready weeks ago, but with the usual dilatoriness of publishers, they have delayed and delayed, and it is not yet ready.

I was very sorry to hear that you were not so well as you had been, but perhaps during the last month you have taken a turn for the better. Anyway, we should all be overjoyed to see you if you were well enough to come over for the performance of the 'Mass of Life' next month.

It is very good to see that this great work seems at last to be coming into its own. Let us hope that after the various performances this spring it will be recognized as a work that must never again be shelved for ten years. I am looking forward immensely to hearing it in London, but it is a little alarming to hear that Klenau[4] has sent Kennedy Scott[5] what the latter describes as 'impossibly slow' metronomic indications.

When one remembers how Goossens and Harrison between them made the Cello concerto ten minutes too long by their 'impossibly slow' tempi, one hopes very devoutly that this mistake will not be repeated with the 'Mass'.

As regards the collection of royalties, I do not know of any society other than the Society of Authors who will undertake this job. One is always liable to be swindled under the royalty system unless one spends half one's time investigating matters and keeping the publishers up to the mark. Literary men are much better off in this respect, as there are several very competent agents who will handle all their affairs—but I do not think they also act for composers. It is particularly difficult for an English agent to check returns of works published abroad, especially with the variation in selling price of the same work in different countries.

[4] Paul von Klenau (1883–1946), Danish composer and conductor and a great supporter of Delius's cause. He was also the brother-in-law of Heinrich Simon.
[5] Charles Kennedy Scott (1876–1965), English choral conductor and teacher; founder of the Oriana Madrigal Society in 1904 and the Philharmonic Choir in 1919.

You will be glad to hear that Van Dieren seems at last to be getting a little recognition. The Oxford University Press is publishing immediately a dozen of his best songs, and giving a concert at which they will be introduced by John Goss. A motet for unaccompanied chorus[6] will be produced at Westminster Cathedral at the end of this month, and the British Music Society are going to perform the wonderful Quartet for 2 violins, viola and double-bass in a few weeks' time.[7]

Do let me hear you are progressing and whether there is any hope of seeing you on April 3rd.

With much love to you both.

Ever affectionately yours
Philip Heseltine

313
Frederick and Jelka Delius to Philip Heseltine

Schlosshotel
Wilhelmshöhe
19. 3. 25 bei Cassel

Dear Phil,

We received your kind letter last night on our return from Wiesbaden, where we had attended a beautiful performance of the Mass of Life. It really did Fred good and quite uplifted him. It had *tremendous* success and the public was incredibly enthusiastic.

Klenau is in London already and Fred would welcome it very much if you got into touch with him. His address is 8 Kidderpore Gardens Hampstead N.W. It would then be easy, or at least possible for you to suggest certain tempi to him   In Wiesbaden the first Chorus went off with a superb brio great enthusiastic animation and so on. It would be such a terrible pity if after all these years the work were not brought out in its full splendour—for it *is so beautiful*. On the other hand I heard that the Vienna performance was very fine and made 'einen gewaltigen Eindruck' [an enormous impression]. Klenau is a fine

---

[6] Possibly one of two settings of 'Ave Maria' (Op. 10).   [7] String Quartet No. 4 (Op. 16; Dec. 1923).

musician; he loves the work. He is a refined nice man (no little jew[8] like Dr
S[imon]) and you will like him. It is very sad that Fred cannot be in London—
but the journey would be impossible in his present state, especially as he would
have to return right here to continue his treatment. It was on that account that
I arranged the journey to Wiesbaden, so that he should at least hear the work.
It is also being done at Hagen and Barmen next season, and very probably here
in Cassel and Duisburg and Dortmund.

We were delighted to hear about Van Dieren; please give him all kind messages from us. Since I wrote last the Anglo-French have paid up, The Oxford
U. P. wrote again about the small orch. piece and I am keeping it in mind; but
Fred cannot look it throu' now on account of his eyes, but I do hope, and I
feel he is on the way to get better now. He was so animated at Wiesbaden.

With the Mech. Cop. Soc. we are still in trouble. I do hope they did not go
bankrupt just when Hassan was running—it looks like it. Please send us news
about the Mass of Life rehearsals. Fred is thinking of it so much.

Ever affly your friends
Frederick & Jelka

314
Philip Heseltine to Frederick and Jelka Delius

March 28th 1925   Eynsford
                                                                                                                  Kent.

My dear Fred and Jelka

I went last Wednesday to a choral rehearsal of the 'Mass of Life' and I can
only say that I am astonished both at the excellence of the choir—even in the
highest and most exacting passages—and at the fire and vigour and real understanding displayed by Klenau who is evidently a quite first-rate man. Neither
at Elberfeld in 1911 nor in London in 1913 was there any choral singing anywhere near the level of what I heard on Wednesday, and if orchestra and soloists

[8] Delius and his wife seemed often to show anti-Semitic tendencies, typical at the time. For example Jelka wrote to
Marie Clews: 'It is a pity that all these theatre people in Germany are Jews and they resent these wonderful true revelations.' Jelka to Marie Clews, 31 Aug. 1925, Delius Trust Archive. In 1924 Jelka had written to Grainger: 'Delius
has no jewish blood at all, not a drop; no jewish relatives . . . Delius says: Please deny this of the jewish origine wherever you can; altho I have no antipathy to the Jews. Music indeed would be in a very bad way without them. They
have done *a lot* for Delius' Music. Here again Haym, Buths, Beecham are *not jews*, no more are *you*. F. D.   Lippay
also not a jew.' Jelka Delius to Grainger, 24 Feb. 1924, Melbourne, Grainger Museum.

are as good the performance ought to be as nearly perfect as is humanly possible. It is a pity though, that nos 2 and 5 from the second part are to be omitted —the solo 'Süsse Leier' is so wonderfully beautiful—and there is no occasion for any omissions on the score of length.⁹ (Klenau's tempi, by the way, are all admirable: it was evidently quite a false report that I heard).

The baritone soloist has been changed: the present man Roy Henderson,¹⁰ I have never even heard of. What a pity, when Heming dropped out, that they did not secure John Goss!

A week or so ago I heard your second violin sonata beautifully played by Sammons and Murdoch, and so great was the applause that the whole work had to be played a second time.

At the same concert five amazingly lovely songs by Van Dieren were given for the first time by John Goss. They were, of course, greeted by all the newspaper-men with a shower of abuse and derision—but perhaps that is a good sign, when one considers the mentality of these miserable creatures. Is there any other country in the world where such idiots would be allowed to comment publicly on any subject whatever, least of all music?

My 'Serenade' is still hung up in the press. It is to be performed on April 5ᵗʰ (broadcasted) at Newcastle-on-Tyne, under Edward Clark.

I will write again after I have heard the full rehearsal of the 'Mass' and tell you all about it.

With much love to you both and all good wishes

Ever affectionately yours
Philip Heseltine

⁹ This cut had been sanctioned by Delius himself, who had written to Universal Edition: 'I think the work might be too long without any cuts at all, have therefore asked Klenau to omit "Süsse Leier" & maybe something else in London'; Delius to Universal Edition, 20 Mar. 1925, Universal Edition Archives; Carley, *Letters*, ii. 299.
¹⁰ Roy Henderson (b. 1899), Scottish-born baritone, professor of singing at the RAM 1940–74. Début Queen's Hall, 1925. He was a last-minute replacement as baritone soloist in this performance of *A Mass of Life* under Klenau and was to sing the work on many future occasions.

315
Philip Heseltine to Frederick and Jelka Delius

April 6th 1925   Eynsford
                                                                              Kent.

My dear Fred and Jelka

The 'Mass' was performed wonderfully well and made a very deep impression.[11] Klenau was admirable, both at rehearsals and at the performance. The choir was so good that I felt I was hearing these marvellous choruses for the first time, so much did the singing reveal that had not been clearly brought out at previous performances. The opening chorus of each part of the 'Mass' and the two dance-songs were given with amazing vigour and abandonment (though the first dance-song was taken much too slow—far slower than at the rehearsal I wrote to you about)—I shall never forget the terrific outburst at the words 'Werdet hart' (here Klenau holds back the beat a fraction of a second with excellent effect), and at the other end of the dynamic scale we had some of the most thrilling pianissimos I have ever heard—notably at 'Heisser Mittag' and at the close of certain numbers. The young baritone Henderson—so young-looking that it seemed absurd for him to impersonate Zarathustra—has a fine voice, very rich in tone, sings in tune and without portamento (rare virtue) and with apparent intelligence (though Klenau tells me he had to teach him the whole interpretation of the part), but his voice was not powerful enough to be heard through the orchestra—at any rate from where I was sitting, in the centre of the gallery, and at times he seemed (to quote 'Sea-Drift') to be 'singing uselessly all the night'! His first solo was taken very much too slow (whether through his fault or Klenau's I don't know) so that it lost all its lightness and gaiety. I still think Goss would have interpreted the part much better, although in some respects, as a mere voice, Henderson may be the better singer. The 1st oboe and bass oboe were poor and the tympani too insistent in some of the choruses —otherwise the orchestra was excellent. Klenau is certainly a great conductor. Soprano and tenor soloists moderately good, but the contralto appalling—every bit as bad as Clara Butt in style, and horribly out of tune, with perpetual portamento. Her rendering of the 'Jenseits von gut und böse' [Far beyond good and evil] passage was too frightful for words. She is evidently incapable of any

[11] The performance on 2 Apr. took place in Queen's Hall with Paul Klenau conducting the Royal Philharmonic Society Orchestra and the Philharmonic Choir. The soloists were Miriam Licette, Astra Desmond, Walter Widdop, and Roy Henderson.

thing above the ballad-concert style. Still, the performance as a whole was far better than one expected, and I feel sure this marvellously beautiful work has at last come in to its own. I do so wish you could have been present—but there will no doubt be another performance before long, and then I hope you will be able to be present.

I am preparing a little book—rather in the nature of a very detailed analytical programme—about certain of your works, giving—as I could not give in the other book—detailed technical accounts of each work, with plenty of musical examples, and above all, exact metronome indications for each movement and change of tempo.[12] As soon as it is finished I shall send it to you, and if you will be so good as to read through it, checking the tempi and altering anything that may be wrong, the book can then be published as an authoritative interpretation of your work—and in view of the absurd mistakes that are so often made by performers, I think that such a book is really needed. I think Foss[13] of the Oxford Press will be glad to publish it, and it could also be issued in German.[14]

Well, I must stop now as the post is going. I hope so much to hear better news of your health before long. The spring ought to cheer you up and put new life into you.

With very much love and all good wishes to both of you.

Ever affectionately yours
Philip Heseltine

[12] Heseltine had evidently asked Gardiner for some suggested metronome markings for Delius's works. In Aug. and Sept. Gardiner sent him two letters with a number of detailed tempo markings 'for your book'. Gardiner to Heseltine, 26 Aug. and 3 Sept. 1925, photocopies in PWS Archives.

[13] Hubert Foss (1899–1953), English pianist and editor; joined the staff of Oxford University Press in 1921, becoming head of the music department on its foundation in 1923.

[14] Though there was a good deal of correspondence about this book, it never materialized. Heseltine also wrote to Taylor about it: 'I have three small books in commission for the Oxford Press—one on the English Ayres of Elizabeth—James I. (completed) and two more or less technical studies, in the nature of analytical notes with musical examples, on Delius and Liszt (in preparation).' Heseltine to Taylor, 25 June 1925, BL 54197.

316
Philip Heseltine to Jelka Delius

April 29th 1925   Eynsford
                                                            Kent.

My dear Jelka

I have now secured a definite commission from the Oxford University Press for the book about which I told you in my last letter   They want it for publication in the early autumn, so I am getting ahead with it as fast as possible and hope to have a rough draft ready within two or three weeks. When this is completed, I should like so very much to bring it over myself so that I could read it to Fred and—if we can get a piano—let him check the metronome tempi which I am suggesting for each movement. There will be very detailed descriptions of about fifteen works, with many music-type examples, and full indications of tempi etc, for the use of students and conductors—and I am very anxious that the book shall be absolutely authentic: that is to say, that it shall embody as far as possible Fred's own wishes as regards the performance of his works. If it achieves as much as that, it will, I hope, be of considerable use to future generations—for it is not often that a composer has left us very precise indications of how he wished his music to be played.

I hope Fred is getting on well and keeping cheerful.

Much love to both of you. I'm so much looking forward to seeing you again.

Ever affectionately yours
Philip Heseltine

317
Frederick Delius to Philip Heseltine

30.4.1925

Schlosshotel
Wilhelmshöhe
bei Cassel.

Fred dictates:

Dear Phil,

Your letters giving me so much news about the rehearsals and performance of the Mass gave me the greatest pleasure. From all sides I hear it was a wonderful performance and I *was* sorry that I could not be present, but it would have been impossible in my present state of health.

The book you tell me of, which you are preparing seems to me to be an excellent idea and I hope you will be able to bring it out soon. We shall go back to Grez in about a fortnight or 3 weeks and I shall be able to look at it there.

Balfour Gardiner and Kennedy Scott paid me a very pleasant visit here.[15]

The Royal Philharmonic Society is presenting me with its Beethoven Gold-Medal and Gerald Cooper will come this week to hand it to me personally.—

3.5.25. We could not finish this letter the other day, and now your last letter has arrived. We shall be delighted if you come to Grez as soon as we are there, which will be so delightful and we can go thro' all the indications and tempi. It is a splendid thing you have written this little book, it will prove most useful. We are only waiting for permission from the french authorities for a german male nurse we have engaged—to enter France—and we are most eager to get back.

We expect Austin's visit here in a few days and are looking forward to seeing him—it is so monotonous here. I have seen a very excellent eye specialist and he thinks, as Jelka always did, that the whole trouble comes from my

---

[15] Gardiner wrote to Heseltine about Delius after his visit: '. . . he is very frail, owing to his long illness, & that being so, his power of resistance might prove unequal to any fresh strain. Exposure & fatigue during a long railway journey, a serious illness of Jelka's, or any other similar occurrence, might be fatal. None of these things, however, is likely to occur. He is wonderfully well looked after, Jelka is strong, & the return to Grez will be a great stimulus to him. He certainly seems to respond readily to all such influences as the visits of friends, talk about music & so on; such things do him more good than medical treatment. Fred Austin has just gone over to see him in Cassel: then comes his return to Grez: after that, in August, Percy Grainger & I will pay him a visit: if you yourself would go to see him in June or July, I feel sure it will do him good.' Gardiner to Heseltine, 5 May 1925, photocopy in PWS Archives.

general weakness and cerebral anemia and I hope we shall be able to better that in Grez.

As soon as our departure is fixed we'll let you know.[16]

With best love, dear Phil,

yours affectionately
Frederick & Jelka—

In Jelka's hand.

318
Philip Heseltine to Jelka Delius

July 20th [1925]   Eynsford
                                                                        Kent.

My dear Jelka

I am so sorry that after all, it became impossible to return to Grez to see you again. Our funds were horribly depleted by the exorbitant charges of the Hotel Chevillon, some money that we were expecting in Paris never turned up, so I had no alternative but to return home on Friday.

I hope we did not tire or worry Fred too much while we were at Grez. When he is talking, he is so much his old self that one is apt to forget his condition and how quickly he may become fatigued. It was perhaps a mistake to try and get from him such very detailed indications as to the tempi of his works; but from our conversations generally I was able to gather a great deal of useful information. Perhaps when Grainger is with you, he might play you three or four passages I am still a little doubtful about, and take down approximate metronomic indications; but in a general way I am quite clear about the works and feel sure that I can write about them in a manner which will prevent conductors from making such gross blunders as they have made too often in the past.

This afternoon I shall go carefully through the gramophone catalogues and will order a selection of bagpipe records, Hebridean folk-songs, sea-shanties etc. to be sent you. And if you will write that letter about 'Brigg Fair' I will take it personally to the recording manager of the gramophone company and have a talk to him. Will you please also ask Fred if I may write a letter to the press,

---

[16] The Deliuses probably left Wilhelmshöhe for Grez at the end of May or early in June.

pointing out, for the benefit of those who may hear him for the first time by means of the gramophone, that he considers this record to be a complete travesty of his work?

If you will send me the MSS of the piece for string orchestra, the Henley song, and anything else he may wish to publish, I will take them to Hawkes or to the Oxford Press and get the best terms I can. It occurs to me that if one of these firms were offered the 'Norwegian Suite', they would probably be able to procure it from Beecham more easily than any private individual could do.

Sir Herbert Barker[17] has just retired, but he has announced his intention of treating a few private patients in the course of his travels on the continent. I have written to Augustus John asking him to write to Barker and see what can be done.

Slivinski[18] is reorganizing his business in Paris and getting in more capital. He is coming over here this week in the hope of doing a deal with the Oxford Press. The shop is a very beautiful one and is visited by all kinds of artists, and as it provides unique opportunities for displaying music, it would be so good to have all Fred's works on view there—especially as it is quite impossible at present to procure any of them in Paris unless they are ordered from Vienna. Will you write and urge Hertzka to send copies along?

Much love to you both and all good wishes.

Ever affectionately yours
Philip Heseltine

319
Philip Heseltine to Jelka Delius

July 24th 1925   Eynsford
                                                                            Kent.

My dear Jelka

Yesterday I was in London and ordered for you three records[19] of shanties, folk-songs etc. by John Goss (including a beautiful setting of 'Saeterjentens Söndag'

---

[17] Sir Herbert Atkinson Barker (1869–1950), a specialist in manipulative surgery rendering unnecessary many cutting operations and orthopaedic appliances.

[18] Jan Sliwinski (1884–1950), Polish singer, librettist, and musical organizer.

[19] Details of these ten-inch 78 rpm records, together with a lengthy review, appeared in the *Gramophone* magazine, June 1925:

for unaccompanied voices, by Moeran); three records of Irish bagpipes which are excellent, and one of three English folk-dances—including 'Heddon of Fawsley' which I know is an old favourite of Fred's—played by Mrs Gordon Woodhouse. There are practically no other records of British folk-songs yet published; there is a set of records of folk-dances collected by Cecil Sharp,[20] played by a military band, but although the tunes are very good, the records are rather monotonous, being made to dance to, so that the tune has to be repeated over and over again. There are no Spanish records in stock in London, but I have ordered three records of national songs sung to the guitar to be sent you from Spain (they may take five or six weeks to reach you, I am told); if you like these, I can obtain plenty more.

The people in the shop tell me that 'Brigg Fair' sells very well—so it is probably doing a great deal of harm. Do let me have a letter of protest to take to the manager of the company.

I went yesterday to Schott's to try and get copies of the full scores of Grainger's Strathspey and Reels, and 'Green Bushes' as I think I could get these works performed by the Radio orchestra in London. They assured me that there was no score and parts of 'Green Bushes', and that the Strathspey was only published in vocal score (although I saw the full score with my own eyes at Grez!) It seems as though music-publishers really wished to put every obstacle in the way of getting modern works performed and known.

I have just got a little job as musical critic to the 'Wireless League Gazette', a new weekly paper which starts next month.[21]

Love to you both and all good wishes.

Ever affectionately
Philip Heseltine

Songs from the Week-end Book (Nonesuch Press), John Goss (baritone) with male quartet and pianoforte accompaniment played by Hubert J. Foss. 10 in., 3s each.

B.1999 *Shenandoah* with (a) *Rio Grande* and (b) *Billy Boy*. Sea shanties arranged by R. R. Terry.

B.2016 (a) *Hey Ho, to the Greenwood* (William Byrd), (b) *Lillibulero* (Old English song arranged Reginald Paul), with *Aye Waukin' Oh* (Scottish song), arranged W. Augustus Barrett.

B.2017 (a) *O good ale, thou art my darling* (Old English song), arranged Peter Warlock; (b) *Sinner, please doan let this harves' pass* (Negro Spiritual), arranged H. T. Burleigh, with *O sweet fa's the eve* (Norwegian folk tune), arranged E. J. Moeran.

B.2018 (a) *And when I die*; (b) *The last long mile* (Army marching songs), arranged Hubert J. Foss, with (a) *Can't you dance the polka?* (sea shanty), arranged E. J. Moeran; (b) *A-Roving* (sea shanty), arranged Cecil J. Sharp.

[20] Cecil Sharp (1859–1924), English folk-song and folk-dance collector and editor.

[21] Only one issue of the *Wireless League Gazette* appeared (15 Aug. 1925). In an article, entitled simply 'Music', Heseltine expounded one of his favourite theories, namely that the musical profession was the greatest enemy to music.

320
Jelka Delius to Philip Heseltine

FREDERICK DELIUS
Grez-sur-Loing
S. et M.
27. 7. 1925

Dear Phil

Your letter from the 24th crossed my card. I am sorry you got the records so quickly because of the 33 1/3 % discount. Could you ask for it now? If possible, please do so. The records you have chosen are very fine. But Fred does not care to have spanish National songs with guitar. He wants 2 or 3 records of *real spanish Malaguenas* with the real accompaniment, voice guitars, a sort of tam-tam, also murmured voices accompanying—a very strange moorish effect. If that does not exist, it had better be left. Or catalogue to be sent first.

Fred does not care to write to the Press about 'Brigg Fair' and he does not care about writing to the Manager. (I think he ought to do the latter and will try to get him to dictate it in a favourable moment.[)]

I must tell Grainger about his scores at Schott's. It is incredible. the Barjansky's were here yesterday. Barjansky would love to play Fred's Cello Concerto & Sonata and also the Double Concerto in London. He would love to play them for the Gramophone and Wireless. I only tell you this, should there be an opening.

I am writing to Universal about Slivinsky. Slivinsky had been very nice to Barjansky and I am so grateful to him.

Please let me know as soon as you hear about Sir H. Barker.

The Barjansky's thought Fred looking *remarkably* much better than end of May, when they saw him at Wilhelmshöhe.

I think you can do a lot of good as critic on this Wireless paper.

I must stop and go on reading to Fred. With love from us both always

aff^ly

Jelka

The thing with Tischer & Jagenberg and Hawkes is entirely off. As soon as possible I will send you the things that are to be published and follow your advice about Norwegian Suite; perhaps you could talk to Voigt[22] about the matter?

---

[22] 'The firm of Winthrop Rogers has been acquired by Hawkes of Denman Street, Piccadilly Circus; the manager is an American, E. R. Voigt, a very intelligent and progressive person who is keen on getting good things to publish. He might be useful to you.' Heseltine to Taylor, 25 June 1925, BL 54197.

321
Philip Heseltine to Jelka Delius

August 4th 1925   Eynsford
Kent.

My dear Jelka

I have received the enclosed letter from Goodwin and Tabb. It seems that the full score of the Norwegian Suite must still be in the possession of Beecham, so I am writing to Voigt to ask him whether he has any means of getting hold of Beecham or some representative of his who might be able to lay hands on the MS.

Anthony Bernard,[23] to whom I spoke about the small piece for strings, would very much like to produce it this autumn with his London Chamber Orchestra. I am sure he would do it very well.

The bill for the records has not yet come in, owing to the fact that the prices of the Spanish records are subject to fluctuation of exchange. I doubt if it would be possible for me to obtain a discount, but possibly you might if you wrote yourself. I think Fred will enjoy the Spanish records. Those that I heard some years ago were extremely interesting.

Augustus John has written to Sir Herbert Barker and hopes to be able to persuade him to make a journey to Grez.

Much love to you both.

Ever affectionately yours
Philip Heseltine

---

[23] Anthony Bernard (1891–1963), English conductor, composer, and pianist.

322
Jelka Delius to Philip Heseltine

FREDERICK DELIUS
Grez-sur-Loing
S. et M.
16. 8. 1925

Dear Phil, I've been fearfully busy. Thanks for all your kind letters and all you did. I did not think it was a case for Sir H. Barker after what he said. Yet I wrote and thanked him and gave him further particulars of Fred's state and receiving no answer, I suppose it really *is* no case for him.[24] I wish you would thank Augustus John for his kindness in enquiring. 200 guineas and 1 class fare there and back is pretty stiff! Percy G. has heard so much about osteopathy in U. S. but thinks it is understood that anything with the spinal chord would require *greatest* precaution.

After being very bad Fred is now rallying under the enjoyment of the beautiful music. He enjoys it wonderfully and Barjansky and the 2 pianos are going all the time.

If ever John Goss is in Paris tell him to come and sing to Fred. Howard-Jones came for a few days before Balfour and Percy, and played a lot too. If you want any tempi please write at once. Percy only stays till end of the month latest.

The records arrived safely and are quite amusing. Fred likes Shenandoah best and of the Bagpipes Lanigans Ball Jig etc. There was no bill. To whom am I to apply about payment?

It is delightful to hear Goss's voice. Howard-Jones is very keen on producing a lot of Fred's songs with Goss; he plays those difficult piano parts delightfully for Spring the sweet spring; a real pianist is what is needed.

Graingers Green bushes are not out yet but coming out quite soon. You had better write and get into touch with him whilst he is here; he will be touring in U. S. and Australia and difficult to reach for quick answers. I must stop now

Affly yours as ever
Jelka

---

[24] Delius's eyesight had deteriorated, as Jelka told Marie Clews: '. . . I thought that all the world knew of Fred's sad state: *he can not see at all*. We have passed a terrible winter in Cassel, trying to save his eyes and seeing them get worse and worse, trying all specialists etc, at last we came back here [Grez] end of May and since then his general state is *slightly* improved, but not his eyes. He therefore cannot walk at all.' Jelka to Marie Clews, 31 Aug. 1925, Delius Trust Archive.

The Barjansky's are stopping here at the Pension Corby and very contented. Only when *you* come next time you must stop with us.

Percy has made a 2 piano arrangement of the Song of High Hills. Could you not send yours for 2 hands[25] for him to play thro? We could return it at once?

They are all so devoted to Fred and it is a great consolation to me that he has all you friends!

323
Jelka Delius to Philip Heseltine

Dear Phil, We have had quite a music season with Grainger, Balfour G. and Barjansky. Only Barj. is here now   Gr. played your arrangements to Fred and they think they are excellent, as good as they can be for *2 hands*. Fred gave many useful indications for tempi etc. and enjoyed himself vastly. Our neighbour Brooks has a fine wireless now. Should there be anything of special interest, please let us know and we can get Fred to hear it there. We should love to hear John Goss singing too, but especially orchestral concerts.

The Mass of Life will be done at Hagen, Barmen, Wiesbaden and Francfort.

Am I to send your manuscripts to you or Slivinsky?

The spanish records have not come yet.

Love from us both
J. D.

5. 9. 1925

Postcard.

---

[25] Heseltine had arranged Delius's *The Song of the High Hills* for piano solo in late 1913 or early 1914.

324
Philip Heseltine to Jelka Delius

September 11ᵗʰ 1925   Eynsford
                                                                            Kent.

Dear Jelka

I enclose the bill for the gramophone records which came a little while ago.
I don't know whether it includes the Spanish records or not. These, I was told,
would take at least six weeks to reach you.

I also send two letters from Robert Nichols; I think Fred would like to hear
his account of the reception of the 'Dance Rhapsody' at Hollywood. Please let
me know if you would like me to act on the suggestion in the second letter and
communicate with Dʳ Head.²⁶

The wireless programme of my compositions is timed for 8 o'clock next
Thursday evening (tune in either to London or Daventry, whichever you get
best from Grez). The 'Serenade' comes first, then a group of songs.

Much love to you both.

Ever affectionately
Philip Heseltine

²⁶ Dr (Sir) Henry Head (1861–1940), a leading and distinguished English neurologist. Robert Nichols remembered
him as 'a conversationalist who could talk with knowledge in the course of an evening on the influence of reasoning
on Goethe and Mozart, apprehension in listeners to symphonic music, looping the loop, co-ordination in a golfer,
Ninon de Lenclos, Conrad, religious ecstasy, and social customs in Melanesia'. *Lancet*, 2 (1940), 534.

325
Jelka Delius to Philip Heseltine

FREDERICK DELIUS
Grez-sur-Loing
S. et M.
13. 9. 1925

Dear Phil

Thanks to your card[27] we all *actually* heard the Gloucester Concert.[28] Unfortunately just during the 'Cuckoo in Spring' the fearful Radio-Paris playing a sort of polka was distinctly audible and often drowned the cuckoo. Brooks was so nervous screwing the machine constantly. The songs were better heard—roaring applause, so that Daffodils were repeated, which gladdened my heart. Fred enjoyed listening very much, and stayed on to hear all the newspaper-news beautifully clear from London.[29] On Thursday we'll go again to hear *your* concert.

It seems as if Fred were decidedly—if ever so little—better. He has put on a *little* flesh, his cheeks less emaciated and his appetite not *quite* so poor.

Did I tell you that I wrote to Explain the case to Sir H. Barker, he then wrote me a little letter saying it was no case for him and recommending another doctor Clement Jeffry (also Park Lane). Howard-Jones promised me to find out

---

[27] This postcard has not survived.

[28] This concert took place in the Shire Hall, Gloucester, on 11 Sept. at 8.00 p.m. with Herbert Brewer, the organist of Gloucester Cathedral, conducting a portion of the London Symphony Orchestra. The Delius content of the programme consisted of 'On Hearing the First Cuckoo in Spring' and 'To Daffodils' and 'Spring, the Sweet Spring' sung by Muriel Brunskill. A report in the *Gloucester Citizen* (12 Sept. 1925) ran as follows: 'Broadcasting of the last concert on Friday night of the Three Choirs Festival was carried out successfully and the effect was such that the great army of listeners-in and auditors by means of loud speakers were delighted at the magnificent programme. So faithful was the reproduction at one period that the baton of Dr A. Herbert Brewer was distinctly heard to give the starting tap upon the music stand.'

[29] Jelka told Percy Grainger: 'Yesterday Heseltine had written that the Gloucester Festival concert would be broadcast. They were doing "On hearing the first cuckoo" and 2 Elizabethan songs "To Daffodils" and "Spring the sweet spring" of Freds. Also a Song of Roger Quilter (very charming and well sung) [Quilter's 'Spring is at the door' and 'Song of the Blackbird']. So the Bruder drove Fred to the Brooks' to hear it.

'We *actually heard it*, only unfortunately a polka of Radio-Paris (about the same Wave length) was well audible at the same time, especially during soft parts. Still it was a miracle to be in Gloucester and hear the applause etc. The songs we heard better only hardly a note of the piano part. The voice comes out best. After the songs there was enormous applause, so much so, that "Daffodils" was repeated—the only encore of the evening! It was really enjoyable to hear—as if one were there, how Fred is beloved of the public in England—and that: a provincial public!! Reed conducted the cuckoo and took it too slow. On the 17th there will be a London programme of Phil Heseltines works. The Serenade dedicated to Fred, another smaller orch. piece and Songs sung by John Goss. We must go to hear that too. Brooks was too nervous, he will do better when he does not change his screws all the time.' There seems to have been some confusion in the Deliuses' minds as to who actually conducted the 'Cuckoo'. It was in fact Herbert Brewer, not W. H. Reed, who was the conductor. Jelka to Grainger, 12 Sept. 1925, Melbourne, Grainger Museum.

more about this man. Meanwhile if you could speak to this Dr Head—perhaps
on the Phone, please do so and ask him if anything can be undertaken for Fred's
eyes   He astonished us the other day by seeing a movement, when Barjansky
took up a match-box and since has said that occasionally when we move he sees
a shadow going by. He had previously said for weeks that he saw nothing but
a light glare. This same glare also at night. The slightest improvement would
indicate to me that there may be hope? I wrote to the Paris Eye-doctor and he
told me to give him 12 pills during 12 days and then stop 12 days. I see that
they are Arsenic pills, and they may have a revivifying affect. But can anything
else be done? I greatly fear an electric treatment, as during the electric treatment in Cassel his eyes got worse constantly. From what R. Nichols said in 1918
I thought his doctor was more for such nervous disorders where suggestion or
Psycho-Analysis helps; but I should love to know. Fred received a delightful letter from R. N. yesterday too, but yours is even more enthusiastic and beautiful. On April 25ᵗʰ or May 3ᵈ 1926 Percy Grainger is going to conduct the Song
of the High Hills at Los Angeles and I hope after this performance it will be
well received!! I am *so* glad you sent your letter of R. N. It was a great joy for
Fred. Shall I keep it?[30]

By the way, was it Reed[31] who conducted the Cuckoo at Gloucester   He took
it to slowly.

Now another question: Fred is willing to publish the little piece for Strings,
and I think Hawkes would be the most satisfactory firm. What do you think?

Also Augeners have written to *me* that they would be very glad to sell or cede
all Fred's works to any firm in England or Continent who would pay them their
outlay, about 1200 £. Fred has had quite big sums in advance on his royalties,
so that if that is taken into account it might be not a bad bargain for an *enterprising* firm of publishers. Augeners do *absolutely nothing*, and of course the things
are never played. They could be put on Gramophone and Pianola—a lot could
be done to have them played on the continent etc. In Germany they are practically unknown. When I spoke with Voigt at Cassel he said they could not undertake works for America. I thought that perhaps they might purchase these works
for Gr. Britain & Dominions and Schirmer's might take them over for America.
This is a beautiful plan, but as I already failed to bring about the affair with

[30] Jelka wrote to Grainger: 'Fred and I are delighted about your conducting the S. of the H. Hs at Los Angeles!
Especially as to-day Robert Nichols, the poet, who is in California wrote such a delightful letter, telling all about the
performance of the Dance Rhapsody in a natural Amphitheatre [Hollywood Bowl] in the Californian hills before a
huge audience of 25000. He said the work sounded incredibly beautiful in those surroundings and made a very great
impression on the audience (conducted by Wood) and they "caught on to it" immediately, and that the Californian
coast is demanding more Delius.' Jelka to Grainger, 12 Sept. 1925, Melbourne, Grainger Museum.
[31] William Henry Reed (1876–1942), English violinist, conductor, and composer. He was leader of the London
Symphony Orchestra from 1912 to 1935 and was particularly associated with the Three Choirs Festival, being also a
great friend of Elgar. He had led the orchestra and played solo items in this programme broadcast from Gloucester.

Tischer and J. I cannot very well propose it and I should be very grateful if you would 'tâter le terrain' and see what could be done. If we could make a profitable arrangement the works would soon pay, I think. I have asked Augeners for a detailed statement, and they promised to send it during the next fortnight. We could do very well with a few more royalties and use the money to buy a good pianola etc. to give Fred pleasure. I know several people who want to play the Violin Conc. in Germany and Vienna and Barjansky is tremendously keen on playing the Double.

Please, dear Phil, see what you can do. I am making a copy of the piece for strings to send you.

There is also the Verlaine song

'Avant que tu ne t'en ailles

Pâle étoile du matin'

ready for publication. Voigt wanted to publish that with other Verlaine Songs belonging to T. and J; but of course their conditions were impossible.

Fred prefers the royalty-system, I do not think he would sell the Augener works outright.

Percy Grainger is on very excellent terms with Schirmer and could possibly negotiate with them.

I am sending a cheque to Imhoff for the records. The worst is the duty 25% and 12% taxe de Luxe on the top of that!! It is ridiculous.

Please forgive the length of this letter—I have been writing in a hurry, just as the thoughts came.

Affly your old
Jelka

As yet Brooks can not hear Newcastle. Is there no remedy when a wrong place of about the same wavelength persists in coming through? He has a set of 4 lamps and *ought* to hear Newcastle

J. D.
Love from Fred

326
Philip Heseltine to Jelka Delius

September 21ˢᵗ 1925   Eynsford
                                                                 Kent

My dear Jelka

Of course I will gladly do anything I can to help you in your negotiations
with the London publishers. As soon as I receive the manuscript of the piece
for strings I will take it to Voigt, of Hawkes', and discuss the matters you mentioned in your letter. I suppose I should ask for the string piece (which, by the
way, will sell much better if it is given a title) the same royalty terms as for the
violin sonata.

I hope the concert on Thursday night came through all right. I was in the
room with the performers where all sound seems very dead, so I could not tell
how it sounded to those listening at a distance. As far as interpretations went,
Goss and the admirable pianist who accompanied him, Reginald Paul,[32] rendered
the songs almost faultlessly—I have never before heard my piano parts properly
played. The 'Serenade' was taken a trifle too slowly, but otherwise not badly
played. The other orchestral piece 'An old song'[33] was almost unrecognizable—
the wind players were *frightfully* bad; they missed their entries, omitted whole
phrases and played dozens of wrong notes. The *old song* itself (oboe solo) was
completely distorted, owing to the oboe, whose part is in 3/4 time, mistaking
the conductor's *two* beats in a bar (*two* dotted crotchets in a bar, for 6/8 time)
for two crotchet beats of 3/4—the result was chaos.

Much love to you both,

Ever affectionately
Philip Heseltine

Moeran has just finished a Symphony, commissioned by the Hallé orchestra.[34]
It will be produced in Manchester next March.

---

[32] Reginald William Paul (1894–?), English pianist.
[33] *An Old Song*, for small orchestra, composed by Heseltine in 1917.
[34] Moeran's Symphony in G minor. The work was, in fact, rewritten, completed in 1937 and given its first performance in Jan. 1938 by Leslie Heward at a Royal Philharmonic Society concert.

327
Jelka Delius to Philip Heseltine

FREDERICK DELIUS
Grez-sur-Loing
S. et M.
14. 10. 1925

My dear Phil

I have all the time been delayed from writing to you. We heard the Serenade *fairly* well, too softly, but yet Fred had those things on his ears and says he heard very well and thought it a delightful delicate and very harmonious piece. Your second piece and the songs we only heard broken off snatches of, unfortunately.

Since then Brooks has been away and it was impossible to hear Van Dieren's concert, which Fred and I were so keen about. It was a great pity. Please let us know, when anything more is done, as Brooks has returned. Fred is *very eager* to hear things and it is unfortunate that it never comes off properly at Brooks's. It discourages me from getting a Radio for ourselves. If I only knew whether all these interruptions and impossibilies to catch the right wave are *habitual* in all Radios? I should love to hear John Goss sing Fred's songs and Fred too would love it. Brooks has never caught Newcastle yet.

Strange to say the Copyr. protc. Soc. has written about recording 'Twilight Fancies' and 'Venevil' *published by Breitkopf and Härtel.* (sic.) I wonder whether Chester goes on selling these songs?

We have written of course that they are published by T. and J. Unfortunately Fred cannot make up his mind now to publish the little string orch. piece, as he does not quite like the end and in his present state sees no prospect of altering it himself. We expect Balfour G. and H. Jones beginning of Nov for a few days; I will get them to play it to him again and try to arrange it.

I have just subscribed at Mudies circ. Libr.[35] Should you know of interesting new books, please send titles. They have everything. I found no reference to the performance of the S[ong]. of H[igh]. H[ills]. in the Morning Post.[36] Is it possible that they left it out at the last moment? We were very disappointed. I saw that during the Concert of the 9th Symphony Coates was ill and only revived for the final Chorus. Send a p.c. please! Love from us both

affly
Jelka

---

[35] Mudie's Select Library, 30–34 New Oxford Street, London W.C. 1.
[36] 10 Oct. 1925, Leeds Triennial Festival, conducted by Albert Coates.

328
Jelka Delius to Philip Heseltine

Many thanks for your kind wishes and all best greetings to you.

B. Gardiner and Kennedy Scott are spending Xmas with us. Fred is gradually improving a little

Love from us both
Jelka

25. 12. 1925

Picture postcard, Grez-sur-Loing—L'Eglise L. C.

1926

ALTHOUGH Delius's condition seemed not to be worsening, the Deliuses remained at Grez throughout 1926. Their solitude was much cheered by the radio and gramophone and by occasional visits from friends such as Bax, the Howard-Joneses, and the Barjanskys in the spring. Other visitors included old friends, the conductor Fritz Cassirer and the painter Edward Munch, who came to Grez in the late autumn. Apart from this, life followed a pattern of predictable routine which would more or less continue for Delius's remaining years.

Early in January Heseltine was in Oxford completing yet more transcriptions of early Elizabethan songs. For the rest of the year he busied himself with his numerous activities: he composed a number of original songs, carried on with his editing, wrote an anonymous miniature essay on Moeran for Chester's in June, as well as composing the *Capriol Suite* in October. In September his books on Gesualdo and the English Ayre were published and in the winter he collaborated with Jack Lindsay, producing two books for the Fanfrolico Press.

329
Jelka Delius to Philip Heseltine

FREDERICK DELIUS
Grez-sur-Loing
S. et M.
14. 1. 1926

Dear Phil,

Enclosed a little letter dictated by Fred. I too must thank you all—The feeling that you love his works—you all who really understand makes him so happy—We did not hear a word of the performance—it must have been good, to be so impressive.

The Mass of Life has just been given in Hagen, without any cut and has made a wonderfully great impression.

Fancy, the University of Oxford wanted to make Fred Doct. of Music Honor. causa. but as he is unable to go to Oxford for the Ceremony it cannot be done.

Being a woman I feel proud of this honour and I cannot understand such peculiar rules—And surely—exceptions *could* be made?

Especially as they have waited all too long to confer this title—and *now* he is unable to attend.

They will hold another meeting tomorrow and discuss it.

Please give my best love to the Van Dieren's and Gray. We should love to see them all again.

Ever affly yours
Jelka D.

Did you hear the Cello Conc. with Bernard's orchestra? How did it sound?

330
Jelka Delius to Philip Heseltine

FREDERICK DELIUS
Grez-sur-Loing
S. et M.
24. 2. 1926

Dear Phil,

Fred was very pleased that you wrote so courageously in the D. T. about his records.

They are just about to record the Cello Sonata with B. Harrison and Howard Jones,[1] and with their new improved method. We wrote them H.M.V. a short while ago that really Brigg Fair and the Cuckoo in Sp.[2] were very unsatisfactory, explaining about the tempi etc—cuts, and to-day they wrote promising to *re*-record it all[3]—and I am sure they are greatly chastened after your article.

There is a scheme afloat to do the Mass of Life with Klenau and the Philharmonic choir in Paris. A Delius enthusiast in Paris is giving and garanteeing all in Paris. But the bringing over of the Choir which costs, as Klenau says 600 £ is not provided. *How* Klenau—or *whether at all* he can raise this sum in England is the great question. He of course is very keen to conduct in Paris

---

[1] The Cello Sonata was in fact recorded by Beatrice Harrison with Harold Craxton, not Evlyn Howard-Jones, in Feb. and Mar. 1926 and issued on HMV D1103/4.

[2] Recorded in 1922 with the Royal Albert Hall Orchestra conducted by Eugene Goossens and issued on D799/800.

[3] *On Hearing the First Cuckoo in Spring* and *A Song before Sunrise* were recorded by the Aeolian Orchestra, possibly conducted by Stanley Chapple, and issued on Vocalion KO5181.

under these auspices and thinks that a few Londoners who have money could easily send the choir over—but it seems very problematic.[4] I suppose you will hear Eventyr to-morrow, let us hear how it went etc. please![5]

It is a pity that the Vocalion Cuckoo is so fast—otherwise that and the Song before Sunrise are delightful. How fresh and charming the latter is too! I had never heard it on the orch.

I received a letter for Moeran the other day c/o Delius. I thought he perhaps intended coming here but as nothing has been heard, perhaps it is a mistake. If you see him tell him please. Our love to Gray

Yrs
Ever affly
Jelka D.

331
Frederick Delius to Philip Heseltine

FREDERICK DELIUS
Grez-sur-Loing
S. et M.
14. 3. 1926

Fred dictates:

Dear friends,
Your warm and sympathetic telegram came like a streak of sunshine and gave me the greatest pleasure.
Your appreciation of my Song of the High Hills deeply moved me.[6]

Ever your affectionate friend
Frederick Delius

Dear Phil, Kindly communicate my thanks to the others F. D.

In Jelka's hand.

---

[4] This scheme did not, however, materialize. Jelka had written to Grainger on 8 Dec. 1925: 'A french friend of ours has offered 25000 frs if we can organize a Delius-Concert in Paris. It will be a most difficult thing, especially as Fred wants the Mass of Life with the Philharmonic Choir and Klenau conducting. I have written to Klenau, who is most willing.' Jelka to Grainger, 8 Dec. 1925, Melbourne, Grainger Museum.

[5] Paul Klenau was to conduct the work at a concert of the Royal Philharmonic Society at Queen's Hall on 25 Feb.

[6] Charles Kennedy Scott conducted the London Symphony Orchestra and his Philharmonic Choir in a performance of the *Song of the High Hills* in Queen's Hall on 11 Mar. 1926.

332
Jelka Delius to Philip Heseltine

FREDERICK DELIUS
Grez-sur-Loing
S. et M.
[July 1926]

Dear Phil. I was delighted to hear from you and the little pamphlet[7] with your good photo gave us great pleasure. Fred said: I am doubly glad Phil is getting on so well, as I always encouraged him to keep to his music. I wish we could have heard the concert with Goss. We have a very good Radio now at last   Yet it is not easy to get English towns, except Daventry, London Cardiff, Bournemouth; the latter by no means always. But I get Munich, Francfort, Barcelona—But just now programmes are abject. We keep the Radio-Times.

Fred is really quite a lot cheerier and better, tho' his eyes do not change much. But his general status and food assimilation are much improved and he is much more his old self. It would be jolly if you could come. Balfour G. is coming on Aug 16th for 8 or ten days. You had better come after that—or if more convenient, *before*. Please stay with us if you come alone.

We have gramophone records of the Cello Sonata Harrison-Craxton[8] and 'Daffodils' Columbia, the latter sung by Brunskill[9] (a contralto-dragoon!)! Twilight Fancies (Princessin) and Venevil have also been done by H.M.V. Could you perhaps go and hear it somewhere? If it is no better than Daffodils it is no pleasure for Fred to hear it. Fr. has dictated a few bars twice the other day and I *do so* hope he will go on with it. The difficulties are so great as he cannot see what he has written, I mean: dictated. But I can play it to him. *It could be done* and it would be so good, and he would think about music again. Barjansky is in Grez again. Best love from us both—dear friend

Ever aff^ly
Jelka.

---

[7] [E. J. Moeran], 'Peter Warlock' (Chester, 1926). This pamphlet was published anonymously.
[8] Harold Craxton (1885–1971), English pianist who taught at the Royal Academy of Music from 1919 to 1960.
[9] Muriel Brunskill (1900–80), English contralto who sang with the British National Opera Company.

333
Jelka Delius to Philip Heseltine

FREDERICK DELIUS
Grez-sur-Loing
S. et M.
8. 9. 1926

My dear Phil.

When are you coming? We had the H. Jones's, O'Neill and Balf G. and Barjansky. But they have all left now.

I read in the papers that the B.B.C. are planning 12 big concerts at the Albert Hall. We have a very good wireless set now and *I do hope* they will do some of Fred's things. It seems all to be the Elgar-clique and official celebrity-conductors. Yet Coates ought to be made to do something. Are you in the know? I wish you could push in Fred's direction a bit   It would do him so much good to hear some of his bigger works again. He needs stimulus. After the guests were gone (they made much music for him) he was at first very tired but now his eyes are really a bit better. He must not be allowed to stagnate and 'Le absents ont toujours tort.' They give mighty little of his music in England now.

We are having lovely weather hot summer still and the garden is charming just now. And Fred really is a good bit better than when you saw him last year.

I hear Moeran lives with you. It was so kind of him to send his record, which very much interested Fred and we also listened to his Quartette[10] on the Wireless. If I only had a little more leisure I would have written him about it.

Please give him all this message and come and see us!

Yrs affectionately
Jelka Delius

We saw your photo and article in the D. Tel. (we are proud of you). Barjansky and 3 Americans played him, Delius, his Quartette in the Garden, where it sounded quite lovely. The London String Quart. never understood it.

---

[10] E. J. Moeran, String Quartet in A Minor (1921).

334
Frederick Delius to Philip Heseltine

I heard your Serenade on the Radio this evening and am charmed with its musical sensibility and coloured atmosphere![11]

Please keep me posted as you know how interested I am in what you do. When are you coming to see me again?

Ever affectionately
Frederick Delius

Grez 19. 10. 1926

Picture postcard, Grez-sur-Loing, L'Eglise, in Jelka's hand.

335
Jelka Delius to Philip Heseltine

FREDERICK DELIUS
Grez-sur-Loing
S. et M.
13. 12. 1926

Dear Phil,

I posted your letters back yesterday, with much regret, because we had quite looked forward to seeing you, when they came.

Please do not fail to come when you come to France again and stop with us a few days.

We are so pleased the score of the Norwegian Suite has been recovered; Fred would be very glad if you would start negotiations with Hawkes. We think it best to give it him for England and Dominions and to another publisher for Central Europe. We spoke about this with Mr Voigt re Jagenbergs Publications.

---

[11] Heseltine told his mother: 'My "Serenade", dedicated to Delius, was broadcast a few weeks ago and D. dictated a very kind letter of appreciation to me, having heard it on his set at Grez. It is being broadcast again from London next Wednesday afternoon.' Heseltine to his mother, 5 Nov. 1926, BL 57961.

There is hardly any gain for him on continental sales and when he gives it in Commission in Germany we have to halve with the german firm, which takes away all profit. Fred would like to publish it on a royalty of 25%, just like the Violin Sonata II.

But Fred is worried about the work, having not seen it for so long. And he would be very glad if you could go thro it, best here with him and revise it for him, as of course we are quite helpless now. Fred cannot read the score and I cannot play it to him. So if you came and, having perused it before could get from him essential advice it might work out very well.

Please let me hear! I see from the papers how well you are getting on, which is splendid.

Best love from us both
aff^{ly} yours
Jelka

Yesterday a letter came for Moeran. I am keeping it here until further instructions.

1927

ONCE again it was the visits of old friends in 1927 which cheered the ailing Delius. Early in the year Beatrice Harrison came to Grez with her mother and sister Margaret and played to him. Later in the winter Beecham made several visits, bringing with him on one occasion a London-based doctor. But for the Deliuses it was largely a lonely and depressing time made bearable by the loan of a pianola and rolls, as well as music heard on the radio. Further visits from Nadia Boulanger, Gardiner, and Grainger in late summer, as well as Oskar Fried, were also much appreciated. Gardiner and Frederic Austin came to spend Christmas in Grez, which was celebrated together with Delius's neighbour, Alden Brooks and family. Heseltine, however, was not one of the visitors. In fact, by this time the friendship (particularly on Heseltine's side) seems to have cooled off considerably and only two letters from this year survive. In the second of the two Jelka, writing on Delius's behalf, makes a valiant attempt to heal whatever had caused this drifting apart.

1927, spent mainly in Eynsford, was a fruitful year for Heseltine. Besides a considerable amount of original composition, he continued his work both editing and writing. On 3 January there was a recording session for the National Gramophone Society in which John Barbirolli conducted his *Serenade* for strings, the record being released in April. His friendship with the poet Bruce Blunt dates from round about this time and in February there is a reference to the two men being fined for being drunk and disorderly in Cadogan Street. On 22 February Heseltine went to Cambridge for three days to work on Dowland's lute music in the library there. Social life in Eynsford continued and among the visitors to Eynsford that March were Constant Lambert and Lord Berners. In October there was also an excursion to nearby Wrotham for the ceremonial unveiling of a sign painted by Hal Collins. On 24 December Heseltine's beautiful carol 'Bethlehem Down' was printed in *The Daily Telegraph*.

336
Jelka Delius to Philip Heseltine

FREDERICK DELIUS
Grez-sur-Loing
S. et M.
9. 1. 1927

My dear Phil, Many thanks for your good letter—the only thing I regret is to see the typewriter has now taken the place of your unique and much loved handwriting!

Enclosed cheque will perhaps make it possible for you to come over and see us for a few days which would give Fred much pleasure (and me as well.) In principle we quite agree to the proposals of Hawkes. But we wish to let him have the Norwegian Suite only for British Isles and Dominions and we could therefore give the work to a continental Publishers as well

The 2ᵈ Violin Sonata, which Hawkes has been so ably handling in England is practically unobtainable in Central Europe. A friend of mine has had endless trouble and over a month's delay trying to procure it in Munich. The same trouble is again and again reported to me about Augener's works in Germany. If as is the case of certain works an english Publisher gives the rights for Central Europe to, say Univ. Edition, the result is that Fred barely gets 10% instead of 25%, the profits all having to be divided between the 2 firms. I do wish we could get Fred to publish the last Henley song with Orchestra and the little piece for strings; I think, when you come you will be able to carry them off with his consent. There is also his last Verlaine Song of which he spoke once to Mr Voigt and which he would like to publish. It seems absurd that Hawkes cannot see his way to an agreement with Tischer and J. about Fred's songs. Would perhaps any of the other publishers do so? As it is they are practically unobtainable in London and look what an opportunity there would be now with all this Broadcasting etc. I Brasil, Les Violons de l'automne and the other Verlaine songs the Henley Nightingale etc. are all lost in Cologne. Life's Dance is never heard and the 2 short pieces constantly pirated.

You will have heard that the B.B.C. are giving a 1 hour concert of Delius Music as his birthday Celebration on Jan. 30ᵗʰ. Percy Pitt in charge!!!¹ The family

---

¹ In March Jelka told Grainger: 'I suppose you have heard about the B.B.C. Concert given in the London Studio for Fred's birthday End of Jan. Geoffrey Toye conducted Brigg fair, Violin-Concerto, Summer Garden, 1ˢᵗ Dance Rhapsody. (Sammons fiddled) It was quite good upon the whole, Summer garden better than the other 2 works; we heard really quite well, and they addressed a little speech to Fred, which seemed so personal and extraordinary; he enjoyed it all.' Jelka Delius to Grainger, 30 Mar. 1927, Melbourne, Grainger Museum.

Harrison came here to play to Fred—and played beautifully too.[2] Pitt hints that in March or later a more important Delius Concert is to be given;[3] perhaps we might have the Song of the H. H. and Seadrift? I suppose it would be one of the National Concerts.

We heard your Serenade again the other night, and it was charming; so glad it is recorded.

Paul Klenau has written a very interesting article 'The approach to Delius' in the January number of 'The Music Teacher.'[4]

Please come whenever you can fit it in, just let us know.

Best love from Fred

yrs ever aff[ly]
Jelka Delius

Fred certainly is stronger and better in many ways.

337
Jelka Delius to Philip Heseltine

25. 9. 1927

FREDERICK DELIUS
Grez-sur-Loing
S. et M.

My dear Phil, We are so disappointed that you did not come! Could you not spend a week or a fortnight with us now? Fred would so much love to have you.

We always play your Serenade on our gramophone; it is charming and Fred likes it very much.[5]

---

[2] Jelka told Grainger: 'The Harrisons came here to play to Fred and played really beautifully. Beatrice plays his Concerto splendidly now and the younger sister Margaret the Violin Concerto with great style and purity. Fred was delighted with their playing.' Jelka Delius to Percy Grainger, ibid.

[3] Delius's Violin Concerto was played by Albert Sammons at Queen's Hall on 24 Feb. 1927 with Frank Bridge conducting the Royal Philharmonic Society. Jelka wrote to Grainger: 'The Philharmonic did Fred's Violin Concerto; but it appears Frank Bridge conducted—and not well at all.' Jelka Delius to Grainger, ibid.

[4] P. Klenau, 'The Approach to Delius', *Music Teacher* (Jan. 1927), 19–21.

[5] On 3 Jan. 1927 Heseltine's *Serenade* was recorded by the National Gramophonic Society for sale to its subscribing members. This was the Society's first venture into orchestral recording and Heseltine's violinist friend André Mangeot, the leader of the International String Quartet, formed a chamber orchestra of fourteen string players especially for the occasion. Mangeot invited John Barbirolli to conduct and Heseltine attended a rehearsal to approve the tempo, about which there had evidently been some doubt. It was released in Apr. on a 12″, 80 rpm record (NGS75).

We sent you a little money for the journey, but should you be hard up, please tell me frankly.

Love from Fred

yrs ever
affl^y
Jelka D.

1928

THE same quiet routine continued through 1928 for the Deliuses, with life at Grez brightened from time to time with occasional broadcast performances of Delius's works. In Spring there was a visit from a doctor from Cassel who examined Delius and prescribed further treatment. In June Delius received a letter from the young Eric Fenby, then 22, offering to come to Grez to act as amanuensis. His offer was accepted and Fenby duly arrived on 10 October. After a difficult start, he soon began to assist Delius in the completion by dictation of several compositions. Other visitors that year included Barjansky, Gardiner, and May Harrison. Christmas visitors were the Howard-Joneses and the year ended on a brighter note with Delius in more enthusiastic spirits.

At this time Heseltine was still living in Eynsford, continuing with the composition of songs and part-songs as well as editing early music. In February a recording of 'Captain Stratton's Fancy' sung by Peter Dawson (accompanied by Gerald Moore) was issued and the following month Heseltine scored *Capriol Suite* for full orchestra. In April he travelled by motor-bike to stay with Bruce Blunt at Beauworth in Hampshire. In the following month he slipped on the wet platform at Eynsford station, breaking his ankle. During the time he was forced to spend in bed he made a piano score of Gray's opera, *Deirdre*. By autumn, however, he was once again in dire financial straits and, reluctantly forced to give up the cottage in Eynsford, he returned once more to Cefn Bryntalch. By November he had moved to London once again and December found him working on an anthology of drinking poetry, *Merry-go-Down*. Heseltine seems by now to have turned his back completely on Delius and the only surviving letter from 1928 shows the Deliuses once again trying to re-establish contact.

338
Frederick Delius to Philip Heseltine

Dear Phil,

It is an age since I heard anything from you. Where are you & what are you doing? Are you working? You know all this interests me very much.

What has become of my Norwegian Suite.[1] I have tried in vain to get information from Hawkes.

My health is a little better and I am enjoying the sunshine in the garden.[2]

You know, there is always room for you here when you feel inclined to come & see me.

Ever affly yours
Frederick Delius

[Grez]
27. 5. 1928

In Jelka's hand.

---

[1] From incidental music to *Folkeraadet.*

[2] In May Jelka wrote to Grainger telling him of Delius's improved condition: 'We have had a weeks visit from Dr Heermann from Cassel and he has tested and observed Fred most carefully. His general impression was very good as regards looks appetite, well-being, digestion. He has a marvellous way of Diagnosis and he is convinced that Fred's eyes are not blind but the optic nerve is not nourished with blood, as it should be. . . . The treatment we are doing seems to make Fred more active, more inclined to dictate letters, less sleepy; he also sleeps more quietly at night.' Jelka Delius to Percy Grainger, 11 May 1928, Melbourne, Grainger Museum.

1929

1929 proved to be a year of recognition and honour for Delius. On 21 April the Order of the Companion of Honour was conferred on him and plans were also afoot for a festival of his music to be held in London later in the year. In the first half of the year there were many visitors to Grez, including Barjansky, Gardiner, Roger Quilter, Edward Dent, and Anthony Bernard, as well as Heseltine himself. Delius was also beginning to work again and with Fenby's assistance that summer completed *Cynara* and *A Late Lark*, which were to be performed at the Festival in October. Percy Grainger and his recent bride Ella also visited in June as did Gardiner, the Howard-Joneses, and Norman O'Neill. Now there was much correspondence over the forthcoming Festival which Beecham and Heseltine were busy arranging. Fenby left Grez on 7 September for a holiday, a new male nurse was engaged, and a doctor from Paris pronounced Delius fit to travel to England. The Deliuses arrived in London on 9 October, staying at the Langham Hotel near to Queen's Hall, where most of the concerts were to be held. The Festival was a triumph for all concerned and Delius returned to Grez in early November soon after the final concert. After all this excitement the rest of the year seemed particularly quiet as the Deliuses found themselves alone at Christmas time.

Heseltine was at the Hambledon cricket ground on New Year's Day 1929 for the famous mid-winter's match between the Hampshire Eskimos and Invalids, for which he had written the song 'The Cricketers of Hambledon'. Although invited by Robert Nichols to holiday as his guest in Majorca, Heseltine reluctantly had to decline as he was desperately looking for work in London. This came in the form of an invitation by Beecham to assist in the organization of the Delius Festival he was planning. Despite the fact that Heseltine had seemingly cut his ties with Delius and all but rejected his old friend's music (early that year he had written harshly to Taylor on the subject[1]), he accepted the offer and in May visited Grez to look through some of Delius's early works in an attempt to find something new for the Festival. By July he was installed in the offices of Beecham's Imperial League of Opera planning a new magazine

---

[1] 'Delius, I think, wears very badly. His utter lack of any sense of construction, coupled with the consistent thickness of texture and unrelieved sweetness of harmony (even at moments where sweetness is the most inappropriate thing in the world) get on one's nerves, and make one long for the clean lines, harmonic purity and formal balance of the Elizabethans and of Mozart—or else the stimulating harshness and dissonance of Bartók, and the Stravinsky of *Le Sacre du Printemps* . . .'. Heseltine to Taylor, 19 Jan. 1929, BL 54197.

called MILO and on 29 August conducted his *Capriol Suite* at a Promenade concert. After the highly successful festival, for which he wrote the programme notes, Heseltine took a brief holiday to stay with Bruce Blunt at Bramdean in Hampshire. The two men combined to produce yet another Christmas collaboration, this time 'The Frostbound Wood'.

339
Frederick and Jelka Delius to Philip Heseltine

GREZ-SUR-LOING (S & M)
[station] BOURRON
[?2 February 1929]

My dear Phil, Your article about Delius was a delightful surprise in the Radio Times yesterday.[2] It is so simply and comprehensively said, and, I am sure, will do a lot of good.

We are looking forward *so much* to Beecham's concerts   I have got a new set for Fred as with our old one it was impossible to eliminate the Eiffel Tower.

Balfour G will have told you that we have a young musician here and that Fred is trying with his help to complete his last orchestral work and also to make an orchestral Suite of the Hassan Music.

Young Fenby[3] is very sensitive and adaptive, but, of course, it is very difficult for Fred to control [unclear—possibly 'f. ex.'—'for example'] his orchestration.

Fred says he would be delighted if at any time you had leisure to come over here—were it but for a few days—to look at what he has been doing. Needless to say Fred would be glad to pay your journey. And anyhow Fred would be delighted to see you again, and so should I, you know that, dear Phil, don't you?

With much love your affectionate old friends
Frederick & Jelka Delius

P.S. I heard that John Goss was to sing Seadrift at the Schola Cantorum N. Y. U.S.A. We should love to hear how it went.

In Jelka's hand.

---

[2] P. Warlock, 'The Yorkshire Genius of Friday's Concert', *Radio Times*, 22 (1 Feb. 1929), 259 and 273.
[3] Eric Fenby (1906–97), English organist, composer, and teacher. At the age of 22 he went to Grez to act as Delius's amanuensis.

340
Jelka Delius to Philip Heseltine

GREZ-SUR-LOING (S & M)
[station] BOURRON
12. 5. 1929

My dear Phil,

I must write again to-day, firstly to thank you for the delightful book you so kindly sent to Fred, and which he is looking forward to with the greatest pleasure. It is just what he likes to read.

Fenby received your letter and the Van Dieren score last night[4]   he was so pleased and will write himself about the Van D. As you wrote to him about the Henley song for voice and orch., we made another search for it as it had inexplicably been lost. To-day we actually found it. It is really quite completed in pencil. So Eric has gone to work on it at once to make a piano score and play it to Fred.[5]

I think Fred, if he approves of this, would not object to its being included in the Festival, but he will not hear of the other old works at present. We have all the unfinished things, a whole packet of Cynara Sketches and Fenby is very eager to play them to Fred as well as Sommer i Gurre, which is finished.

We will look at everything and report to you again; I am so happy to have your interest and help; so is Fenby. He was greatly touched and delighted with your letter and Score.

How is Van Dieren? I do hope he is getting better, as he used to do when warm weather returns.

With love from us all

yrs ever affly
Jelka Delius

---

[4] Heseltine had written to Fenby saying: 'I was extremely pleased to find in you one more addition to the increasing number of enthusiastic admirers of the works of Van Dieren. I send you a score of his latest string quartet, in the hope that you will enjoy it no less than n° 3. It is a wonderful work.' Heseltine to Fenby, 8 May 1929, in the collection of Robert Beckhard.

[5] Heseltine had written to Fenby: ' " The late lark" (Henley) ought certainly to have its first hearing at the festival . . . If you would be so kind as to give me any news of these things, it would be most helpful—provided, of course, that my suggestion is acceptable at all.' Heseltine to Fenby, 8 May 1929, ibid.

341
Jelka Delius to Philip Heseltine

GREZ-SUR-LOING (S & M)
[station] BOURRON
[May 1929]

My dear Phil, It was so delightful to hear from you yesterday so promptly about the recording of the N.C.S.'s and the little string piece.[6] I hope they will send us test-records as soon as possible, as Fred is very keen to hear it. It is a great pleasure to him that you have such a high opinion of the N.C.S. as he evidently knew it was one of his best works, and yet it was hardly ever played.

Further I think it is splendid that you are to to help Beecham plan the Delius Festival. I read Fred your letter; as you foresaw he was not very much for performing the early pieces. At least not yet, while there are several things he has never heard yet, and which he considers among his best things, notably the Arabesk, Songs of Sunset (not heard in England since 1912 or 13.) the A capella chorusses. When Beecham unfolds his plans to you you will see what a lot of works he has already.—I, myself, however am inclined to think like you, that there may be much that is lovely, young, fresh in those early works and I will keep your idea in mind and speak to him when a favourable moment presents itself.

For instance, *I* think that if he could hear the Norwegian Suite he might decide to have it published or possibly to make some alterations. At least then one could decide.

One must be very careful. I was so annoyed at all the stupid things Newman told us last night about the Delius Music on the wireless. Among other things he said, that Delius never had a gift of adapting words to music. This, he said, was in part because Delius was really not english at all, but quite international. Moreover, he said that in Seadrift, for example, as in other works he composed the words in German, thinking of probable German performances and then the thing had to be translated back to the english words laboriously. Not a word of

---

[6] *North Country Sketches* and *Air and Dance* conducted by Anthony Bernard were recorded on 7 May 1929. Heseltine wrote to Fenby: 'The "North Country Sketches" and "Air and dance" were brilliantly played in the recording studio yesterday. Bernard's handling of the orchestra was quite masterly.' (Heseltine to Fenby, 8 May 1929.) The records were evidently not released because of the poor quality of the orchestra assembled for the recording. *The Gramophone Shop Encyclopedia of Recorded Music* (New York, 1936), 130, gives the following information: 'Once announced as recorded by the London Chamber Orch. conducted by Anthony Bernard for British Brunswick, but never released'.

truth in that, and God knows I had to exert all my powers to give an adequate german rendering fitting in with the music; and how I tried to render in the german some of the colour and emotion of the english words! You will remember that the same thing was said about the Village Romeo. Here, of course, it was in a way easier to get the german, as I had Keller's novel as a guide. But Fred wrote the whole libretto in English. What can be more english in feeling than Brigg Fair, North Country, in fact, most of his works? Fred's idiom is english, his language is English. Apart from the exceptionally beautiful Zarathustra, german poetry has never appealed to him, as you know. No german poem could have appealed to him like Seadrift and Dowson did. In the case of the Arabesk and Fennimore, of course, the german resembled the danish more and he had *me* as a translator and was sure I would try to retain the whole flavour. I write all this because when occasion comes you might put these erroneous notions right.

I think these Music Critics do all that *can* be done to hinder the listeners from understanding Delius, when they *could* and *should* help them; in fact they seem rather annoyed that so many people insist on liking his music.

When next you come to France, and you could stay here a few days, I should so much love you to go thro that M.S. Music. Please give my love to your friend Barbara;[7] I am afraid she must have bored herself here; had I but known that she was *your great friend* I should have taken her to my heart at once. Well that is for another time.[8]

Please let us hear developments with Beecham. Fred must go to England for the Festival. I think it can be done, if all goes well.

Love to Bernard[9] and blessings for his fine conducting.

Ever aff[ly]
Jelka

[7] Barbara Peache (1900–?), who Heseltine had first met at a party in Chelsea in the early 1920s. She lived with him through the Eynsford period until his death, eventually moving to Malta in her later years. Described by Eric Fenby as 'a very quiet, attractive girl, quite different from Phil's usual types' (Carley, *Letters*, ii. 351), she was small and trim with bronze hair, sharp, green eyes, and a sharp chin. Heseltine had visited Delius around end-April/beginning of May. In later life she spoke of the 'bad influence of Delius' on Heseltine. Information from a letter to the author from Robert Beckhard, 5 Mar. 1993.

[8] Heseltine related this visit in his last letter to Taylor: 'I was over at Delius's home at Grez-sur-Loing lately. The old fellow gets no worse, though he gets no better either, and is naturally very weak. Going through a pile of his old pencil sketches, I came across an almost-completed full score of a song for baritone and orchestra—a setting of Dowson's "Cynara"—planned on very big lines, and containing some excellent music. I knew he had once attempted this poem, but had no idea he had got so far with it. He had completely forgotten it—it is more than twenty years old—but it was copied out and played to him, and he managed to dictate the last few bars of the music. This—sung by John Goss—will be one of the few novelties of the festival. The others are a charming light piece for string orchestra, "Air and Dance", composed in 1915, which will probably win more immediate popularity than anything Delius has written; and a setting for voice and orchestra of Henley's "Late Lark", which was the last work Delius was able to complete with his own hand.' Heseltine to Taylor, 6 Aug. 1929, Eton Music School.

[9] Anthony Bernard.

342
Jelka Delius to Philip Heseltine

Dear Phil, I have lost Anthony Bernards address. Please tell him that Fred wants so very much to hear his records of N. C. Sketches and Seadrift as soon as possible; he is to get Decca or Brunswick to send them, please.

Have you started negotiations with the Publishers for Fred? Please let us hear as soon as you can.

Affly yrs
Jelka D.

[Grez-sur-Loing]
14. 6. 1929

When you write please send me Bernards address
P.S. Universal Edition Karlplatz 6 Vienna asks for news about the Delius Festival as soon as possible, to give it preliminary publicity. Please write to them. J. D.

Postcard.

343
Philip Heseltine to Jelka Delius

78, Denbigh Street,
PIMLICO, S. W. 1.

June 21st, 1929.

My dear Jelka,

I saw Beecham again today, and the programmes of the Festival were definitely fixed. I enclose a copy. Of the works omitted, Song of the High Hills, and Paris and Cello Concerto have all been heard in London this year, and Brigg Fair, Dance Rhapsody no. 1. and Double Concerto are being played at the Promenade Concerts in the autumn. Beecham wishes to make a special feature of the songs, both with piano and orchestra. He proposes to perform twenty or twenty-five of these, and would very much like to see the score of the Maud cycle, as it was composed in the same year as the Shelley songs which he so much admires. Would you be so kind as to send this and Cynara to me as soon as you possibly can? I am particularly anxious to have Cynara, for several reasons. First, because I could see from the sketches that it is one of Delius's most beautiful songs: secondly, because it is a novelty, and a first performance always gives additional interest to a programme: thirdly, because the poem—undoubtedly the best that Dowson ever wrote—is very popular in England and has never been set to music before: fourthly, because it will be sung by John Goss, who is an exceptionally intelligent singer, and has a great love and understanding of Delius's music. It was a very bitter disappointment to him when sudden illness prevented him from singing Sea Drift at the Schola Cantorum in New York last year, and he will very deeply appreciate the privelege of singing two new Delius works at the Festival. If Fred does not feel well enough to finish the score, I would gladly do it for him and send it back for his approval; but there is really so little to be done to it that I am sure Fenby will manage to complete it without any difficulty. As there will be a chorus at this concert, the choral parts can be retained as in the original sketch, if Fred so wishes. Personally, I think it would be more effective as a solo, the poem being of so intimate and personal a character—especially as it no longer forms part of a larger choral work. But anyway, do please do your best to persuade Fred to let this admirable work be sent over.

I have made enquiries about the gramophone records, and find, to my astonishment, that Sea Drift is being actually issued to the public on July 1st. The test records had already been sent to the factory when I called, but the staff assured me that they were very well satisfied with them. The orchestral pieces have been put back for re-recording, owing to mechanical defects in the first set of records.

Anthony Bernard seems inclined to adopt a very dog-in-the-mangerish attitude about the Air and Dance. He seems to think that, because Fred gave him the score for a first performance, he therefore has the right to keep the piece for his own exclusive use for an unlimited period of time. Because he will have no opportunity of performing it himself until November, he has told Beecham that he will not give him the score for use at the Festival—which seems to me an utterly unjustifiable attitude. The Festival programmes are designed to be representative of all that is best in Delius's work; this is the only piece for strings alone that he has ever written, and, by common consent of all who have heard it, one of his best short works, and as there are only four pieces in all that are available for performance at the Chamber Concert in the Aeolian Hall, the omission of this piece would make a serious gap in the programme for October 23rd. I am sure Fred would not wish his work to be witheld from the programme for such a petty personal reason; so it would be best if you would write to Bernard and say that Fred wishes this work to be given at the Festival. I have made a copy of the score myself, which I will give to Beecham as soon as I hear definitely from you that Fred did not intend the work to be kept for Bernard's exclusive use.

I took all the other manuscripts—Norwegian Suite, A late lark, Wine Roses, and the new Verlaine song—to Beecham on my return to England, but now that the programmes are made up, I will get them back from him, and take them round, together with the Air and Dance, to the various publishers, and see what offers I can get for them.

Much love to you both and kindest regards to Fenby.

Ever yours affectionately
Philip Heseltine

Bernard's address is 19 Ladbroke Grove, London, W.11.

Typed letter.

344
Jelka Delius to Philip Heseltine

FREDERICK DELIUS
Grez-sur-Loing
S. et M.
25. 6. 29

Dear Phil,

We were very pleased this morning to get your letter and to see the programmes, which we all think are most beautifully chosen and arranged. Fred only said at once: 'I do wish they had included "the Song of the H. H's." ['] He has also written that to Beecham.

Cynara is almost finished and without Chorus. Fred said he had first planned it with Chorus but afterwards dropped the idea. There was a little delay on account of music paper which failed to arrive. I am sure John Goss will sing it beautifully. Fred has worked with Fenby at the score of Cynara and seems to think it quite perfect now. I can see that he loves it himself and is happy about it. I will send it off as soon as possible to you or Beecham.

Unfortunately I cannot fulfil your wish regarding 'Maud' Fred will not hear of sending it. I will do my best at a favourable moment again; but he seems adamant.

Now to Bernard. His attitude is despicable. You know that there was no question of his having the first concert performance: He did not even keep his promise to send a test record *at once*, which Fred wanted to hear so much before deciding about publication. Fred has dictated a very terse letter to Bernard in which he says that he allowed him to record the work, as he wanted to hear it but that he has naturally accorded the performance of all new works to Beecham, who has undertaken so great a scheme of Delius Concerts.

As you have a copy you can hand it to Beecham. I told you already, when you were here last, that it certainly shd be included in the Festival—it is just what was wanted.

Fred wrote to Beecham to-day and enclosed a copy of his letter to Bernard (this in case you wanted to see it.) It is certainly absolutely definite.

Please tell John Goss that if he is in Paris any time this summer he would give Fred great pleasure by singing these things to him here. Fred has not heard either Cynara or the Arabeske. Howard-Jones or Fenby will be here and can accompany him.

Percy Grainger is here just now and playing a lot for Fred.[10]

With love from us both

Ever affly
Jelka

Keep us posted always, please! We are always thinking of the Festival.

Surely the Brunswick-Decca people ought to send Fred a record of Seadrift.[11]

345
Philip Heseltine to Jelka Delius

July 4th. 1929.

15 Gloucester Street
London. S.W.1
(*N.B.* Change of address)

My dear Jelka,

There have been slight changes in the Festival programmes. The first concert, at Queen's Hall, on October 12th. is being backed to some extent by the

---

[10] Percy Grainger and his wife Ella (whom he had married in Aug. the previous year) visited the Deliuses in June 1929.

[11] *Sea Drift* was recorded on 29 May 1929 with Roy Henderson and the New English Symphony Orchestra and Choir conducted by Anthony Bernard, and issued by Decca on S1010-2.

Columbia Company, and they want the programme to include works that have been, or are likely to be, recorded for them by Beecham. On this occasion Brigg Fair, Sea Drift, A late lark, Dance Rhapsody no. 2., In a summer garden, and the closing scene from Village Romeo will be given. The B.B.C. concert on Oct. 18th. at Queen's Hall will consist of Eventyr, Arabeske, Piano Concerto, Cynara, and Appalachia. Instead of the Central Hall concert on Oct. 26th., there will be a concert at Queen's Hall on the 24th. under the auspices of the Philharmonic Society, with North Country Sketches, Violin Concerto, Songs of Sunset, the fjord scene from Fennimore, and the whole of Gerda. Beecham considered the question of including Song of the High Hills very carefully, but came to the conclusion that it was not possible to add another long work to the programmes, especially since the Song of the H. H. has lately been given by the Philharmonic Choir and will be given again during the winter at one of Malcolm Sargent's[12] concerts.

Beecham is at present ill in bed with tonsillitis, but as soon as he has re-covered, the full programmes, with the names of the singers and a list of all the songs he has selected for the chamber concerts will be published.

I am delighted to hear that Fred has been able to finish Cynara to his satis-faction. I thought when I looked through the MS. that it would prove to be a very good song. Please send the score to me here *as soon as possible*, as John Goss is keen to get to work on it at once. He will be in Paris during the summer, and will be delighted to come out to Grez and sing to Fred. You will find him a very sympathetic and charming personality.

I am only waiting for the MS. of Cynara and I will then take all the new works to the publishers and see which one offers the best terms. I think the popularity of the Air and Dance would be greatly increased if it were published also as a piece for violin and piano. I have made an arrangement of it in this form, and I am sure it would come off very well. It is not suitable for a piano arrangement—the piano copy which I have, by the way, is very inaccurate.

I will write again as soon as the final details of the programmes have been settled.

Much love to you both.

Ever affectionately yours
Philip Heseltine

Typed letter.

---

[12] Sir Malcolm Sargent (1895–1967), English conductor. The concerts referred to are almost certainly the Courtauld–Sargent concerts that began in the winter of 1929–30 and continued in the 1931–2 season, during which he conducted the first performance of *Songs of Farewell*. These concerts were financed by Mrs Samuel Courtauld.

346
Frederick Delius to Philip Heseltine

FREDERICK DELIUS
Grez-sur-Loing
S. et M.
6. 7. 1929

Dear Phil,

I send you to-day the Full Score and Piano Score of Cynara

I have gone through it very carefully and marked it dynamically.

Is John Goss really the man to sing it and also the Arabesk? From what I have heard through the Radio of his singing it is not very expressive and the voice rather beery   These two works require very delicate interpretation. Would not Roy Henderson be better? He sang the Mass of Life so expressively and also Seadrift. (I heard the latter on the Radio.) It seems a pity that he is not singing at all in the Festival. Please see Beecham at once about this. Why get D. Noble[13] for Seadrift, who is not specially good, after what I have heard?

Please write me as soon as possible about this.

Have you got the 'Air & Dance' score back from Bernard and is that affair settled? How about the parts of Cynara? Will you correct them carefully when they are done or will you send them here for Fenby to correct.

I should like very much to see your arrangement of 'Air & Dance.' I shall have several violinists here who can play it to me.

Which scene do you call the Fjord scene in Fennimore and Gerda.

I was delighted to hear of the collaboration of Columbia and the Philharmonic in the festival!

Ever affly yours
Frederick Delius

In Jelka's hand.

---

[13] Dennis Noble (1889–1966), English baritone.

347
Jelka Delius to Philip Heseltine

Grez 7. 7. 29

Dear Phil,

I add a few words to Fred's letter. I notice that Fred has declamed *Cynara* throughout, and on looking at the music it seems to me that it is always so expressively put that way that it would be a pity to change it. I suppose such a licence is permitted?

We did not like to say anything to Fred about it and possibly delay the sending off again.

Should Beecham think it absolutely necessary to change it, Eric could do it and get Fred's approval. But I must say, I hope they will leave it as it is.

The Graingers were here for over a week and that rather delayed the finishing of Cynara.

Now we expect the Howard Jones's but they will not stay at the house.

We are so delighted that those scenes from Fennimore are included in the Festival.

Much love. dear Phil

Your old
Jelka Delius

348
Philip Heseltine to Jelka Delius

July 8th. 1929.

15 Gloucester Street
Pimlico. S.W.1.

My dear Jelka

Very many thanks for the copies of Cynara which arrived this morning. It is an exceedingly beautiful work, and I am sure it will be a big success at the Festival.

I heard the Sea Drift records to-day and was agreeably surprised. There are bad patches here and there, but on the whole the recording is much better than

I had expected. Bernard's tempi are rather odd in certain sections—the opening is surely about twice too slow?

Beecham is much better, and I shall be seeing him again on Wednesday. We hope to send the preliminary prospectus of the festival to the printers this week.

Ever yours affectionately
Philip Heseltine

Typed letter.

349
Philip Heseltine to Frederick Delius

July 11th. 1929

15 Gloucester Street
Pimlico. S.W.1

My dear Fred,

Many thanks for your letter. I am delighted with Cynara; it gives the singer a fine opportunity for dramatic expression, and I am sure it will be greatly liked by the public. There are all too few songs for voice and orchestra constructed on big lines; such songs as Cynara and A Late Lark will afford a welcome change from the eternal operatic excerpts, in intelligent singers' repertoires.

The soloists for the Festival are all engaged, and the preliminary prospectus is in the printer's hands already. You need have no anxiety about the choice of singers. Beecham says that Dennis Noble gave the best rendering of Sea Drift he ever heard, at Leeds last autumn.[14] He has recorded the work with Noble, for the Columbia Company, and as it will be given at the concert which the Columbia Company are backing, it must naturally be sung by their man. Henderson has a good voice, but in the concert hall he cannot always hold his own against the orchestra. In the Mass of Life he was often inaudible. When you hear him on the gramophone or the Radio, you must remember that he is standing close to the microphone, which makes a big difference.

In my opinion, you could not have a more expressive and intelligent singer for your works than John Goss. He has studied your songs for many years and sings them with real understanding and feeling. It is hardly fair to judge a voice

---

[14] Beecham had conducted the London Symphony Orchestra and Leeds choir in a performance of *Sea Drift* at the Leeds Festival in Oct. 1928. Dennis Noble was the baritone soloist. Beecham recorded the work with Noble, the Manchester Beecham Opera Chorus, and the London Symphony Orchestra at the Portman Rooms, London, on 11 Nov. 1928, but it was not issued.

from radio transmission alone. Besides, when Goss broadcasts, he generally sings sea-shanties and other popular stuff, in which a 'beery' quality is by no means out of place. But I can assure you that the effect is quite deliberate on his part, and not due to any defect in his voice.

I have the original score of the Air and Dance in my possession, and have made a copy for Beecham. I am sending you the arrangement I made for violin and piano. Will you please ask Fenby to write in the bowing and phrasing as you want them, and return it to me as soon as possible, so that I may write the phrasing etc. into the full score? As soon as I get the MS. back, I will get busy with the publishers.

Your Violin Concerto is to be played at the Proms. (by Orrea Pernel) on August 15th.[15] and the Cello concerto (B. Harrison) on Aug. 29th.,[16] on which occasion I am making my first (and probably last) public appearance as a conductor, with my Capriol suite.

Ever affectionately yours
Philip Heseltine

Typed letter.

350
Philip Heseltine to Jelka Delius

THE
IMPERIAL LEAGUE OF OPERA
FOUNDER—SIR THOMAS BEECHAM BART.
MONTHLY REVIEW

Head Office:
90, Regent Street,
London, W.1

August 6th 1929

My dear Jelka,

Many thanks for the photographs, four of which I handed to the Press Association last week, with an interview, for general circulation. They are very striking and impressive, giving the head a fine sculptural quality.

---

[15] Henry Wood conducted this performance at a Promenade Concert in Queen's Hall.
[16] On this occasion Beatrice Harrison played the Cello Concerto with Wood conducting.

I have not yet received the scores and material of the songs which Fenby promised in his last letter, nor the violin and piano version of the 'Air and Dance'. It is important that this work should be available in print by mid-October, and time is getting short. How have Hawkes' done with the Violin Sonata on the continent? It has had a great success here and they must have advertized it well. They are, I think, the only possible English publishers for this work. If you are not satisfied with their handling of the Sonata, the 'Air and Dance' had better go to Universal. The egregiously incompetent Mr Voigt has left the firm.

Beecham has asked me to edit a monthly musical journal in connection with the League of Opera,[17] and we are publishing the first number on September 2nd. Though primarily intended to make propaganda for the League, it will contain articles of general interest to lovers of music.

I shall make a special Delius feature in the October number.[18]

Much love to you all.

Ever affectionately
Philip Heseltine

P.S. Will you please let me have Grainger's address if he is still in England?

351
Jelka Delius to Philip Heseltine

FREDERICK DELIUS
Grez-sur-Loing
S. & M.
Aug. 8. 29

Dear Phil,

Just received your letter and was delighted to hear about the Monthly Review under your editorship.

We sent the Songs: Scores and piano version to Beecham as he seemed a little offended (according to H. Jones) that we sent Cynara first to you. But we sent

<hr/>

[17] *MILO—The Official Organ of the Imperial League of Opera.* Three issues appeared, Oct., Nov., and Christmas 1929.

[18] See *MILO*, 1/1 (1929), 28.

the orchestral parts straight to you 15, Gloucester Str and you will have received them by now, I hope.

As to the Violin arrangement of Air and Dance Fred got Mrs H. J. to play it and he thinks it makes quite a pretty little piece and that it is *well done*. Hawkes did very well with Sonata II in England, but the sales in Germany are nil. Nobody can find out how to get it and the royalty is reduced to almost nothing for us. If U. Ed. published it one could do as with the 5 pieces; give it to Curwen for England with the same royalty payable to Fred. If Hawkes take it he ought to make a similar arrangement with a german publisher, so that Fred has his profits.

I will return Air & Dance Violin arrangement to-night if the H. J.'s return in time for the post; they are on a motor trip.

9. 8. I have posted Air & Dance early this morning. Fred wishes me to repeat that he is quite willing to give Air and Dance to Hawkes but only for England and Dominions and he himself will either give it to U. E. or Hawkes must make an arrangement with a german firm for the European continent, so that Fred gets his royalties undiminished.

I hope you will send some material about the Festival to U. Ed. and Tischer as soon as possible, so that they can advertise it in their publications.

If you have an english article they will have it translated. The Frankfurter Zeitung ought also to be informed at once.

I must post this at once, as I am sure to be called away again.

Yrs ever affly with Fred's love
Jelka

352
Jelka Delius to Philip Heseltine

Dear Phil, We hear everybody has received Prospectus for Festival. We have not seen it yet. Please send a few to send to distant friends, and make propaganda.

Fred says you could simply get the works published for England, dominions and leave Fred free to publish them in Germany for the other countries? How would that pan out.

Your friend came, Praga, a little while ago and brought measurements and tilted our Gr. Soundbox better. It plays much better now. We greatly enjoyed

Bernards Seadrift on our own Gram. We first heard it thro wireless, which was rather bad.

Please keep us posted as to encourage Fred to envisage the journey

Much love from us both
J. D.

[Grez]
14. 8. 1929

Postcard.

353
Jelka Delius to Thomas Beecham

Grez 14. 8. 29[19]

Dear Thomas,

Fred received your delightful letter and it quite relieved him of his anxieties about the singers and he is greatly looking forward to seeing you on your way back.

It is all too wonderful about the Festival and I can not tell you how much it means to us—and then your delightful and generous invitation to stay so comfortably at the Langham!

And then all those glorious Gramophone records the Columbia is bringing out!

Then there is your great idea about the Delius-Edition!!

Fred has no works published on a profit sharing scheme. They all belong to the publishers and Fred has a royalty, varying for every work. But quite a number of works he has sold outright and so gets no royalty! They are chiefly the ones Leuckart had bought, and which Univ. Edition bought up. They are: 'Dance Rhapsody 1' 'Paris', 'Songs of sunset', 'In a Summer Garden', 'Brigg Fair', 'Song of the High Hills'.

Cuckoo, Summernight and the Songs at Tischer & Jagenbergs are all on a Royalty system; so are the works at Augener's.

---

[19] This letter was given (presumably by Beecham) to Heseltine, who makes reference to it in the letter to Jelka Delius dated 25 Sept. 1925.

It will be a difficult thing to arrange and we must talk it over. How glorious to see you so soon!

I have written about the Arabesk on a separate sheet and will rush it all to the post.

Our hearts are ever with you!

Ever affectionately
Jelka Delius

I hope the glorious mountain air has made you quite well again—

14. 8. 29

I received your letter about the Arabesk yesterday. Do you remember how we discussed the poem in 1914 at Grove Mill House? At that time you made certain alterations in Heseltine's translation. I send you to-day a copy into which you wrote the amended words. These were put into the orchestral score later on, and also in the later piano scores; only the poem printed on the title page is wrong.

Fred composed the poem to the german words, translated from the Danish by myself. The german lends itself extremely well, and almost always the same words can be found; corpse is 'Lig' in Danish, 'Leiche' in german, poetic germanic words! Corpse, of course is latin and horrid and must be circumscribed. In german and scandanavian Fairy tales the dead girl, beautiful with her red cheeks lies in a glass coffin—so this image is familiar.

It is of course frightfully difficult to find quite adequate words that will fit to the music. But in case you should like to try I have written you down the Danish words with always the exact english word underneath.

This is one of the finest Scandinavian poems and to me it does not seem obscure. Think of the endless scandinavian winter and the marvellous all too short summer.

It is a lover's rhapsodic recital of his love. *First* he describes the so typically northern summer-feeling—Pan—the sensual love, destructive, unreasonable under the spell of a short moment of bliss only.

2^d *section*

The flower coming into bloom in its almost unnatural colour and beauty symbolizes the exhaltation of that *one moment*

3^d *section*

Then he describes the girl he loved, how she seemed so calm, deep, pure, but how a wonderfull spell, an almost withering, poisonous fascination emanated from her and how she drank to eternal faithfulness with all her lovers: with himself, with the one who is dead already and with the one who is at her feet now;

how she wielded her power over them, so that they gladly drank to her out of
the poisonous lilies dazzling chalice (their undoing)

This is also typical of the Scandinavian woman.

last section   Then all is past. Winterstorms—the red berries, last vestige of
the mad summertime drop one by one into the snow.

Ever yrs
Jelka D.

En Arabesk

An Arabesque

Har du faret vild i dunkle Skove?
Hast thou driven wild in dark forests?
Kender du Pan?
Knowst thou Pan

Jeg har følt ham,
I have felt him

Ikke i dunkle Skove,
Not in dark forests

Medens alt tiende talte,
While all (generally) silent talked

Nej! den Pan har jeg aldrig Kendt,
No! *that* Pan have I never known,

Men Kærlighedens Pan har jeg fölt,
But Love's Pan have I felt

Da tav alt talende
Then (was) silent all (that is) speaking

———

I solvarme Egne
In Sun-warm meadow

Vokser en saëlsom Urt,
Grows a strange herb!

Kun i dybeste Tavshed,
Only in deepest stillness,

Under tusende Solstraalers Brand
Under thousands Sun rays Blaze

Aabner den sin Blomst
Opens it its blossom

I et flygtigt Sekund
In a fleeting second

Den ser ud som en gal Mands Øje,
It looks like a mad Man's eye,

Som et Ligs röde Kinder:
Like a corpse's red cheeks:

Den har jeg set
This (plant) have I seen

I min Kærlighet.
In my Love.

———

Hun var som Jasminens södt duftende Sne,
She was like Jasmin's sweet-scented snow.

Valmueblod randt i hendes Aarer,
Red Poppy-blood ran in her veins

De Kolde, marmorhvide Haënder
The cold marble-white hands

Hvilede i hendes Skød
rested in her lap

Som Vandliljer i den dybe Sö,
Like Waterlilies in the deep lake.

Hendes Ord faldt blödt
Her words fell softly

Som Äbleblomstens Blade
like Appleblossom's leaves

Paa det dugvaade Graës;
on the dew-wet Grass;

Men der var Timer,
But there were hours

Hvor de snoede sig Kolde og Klare
Where they curled themselves cold and clear

Som Vandets stigende Straale
Like water's rising jets.

Der var Suk i hendes Latter,
There was sobbing in her Laughter

Jubel i hendes Graad;
Jubilation in her weeping

For hende maatte alt böje sig—
before her must all bow (themselves)

Kun twende turde trodse hende
Only twain dared defy her,

Hendes egne Øjne.
Her own eyes

————

Af den giftige Liljes,
(Out) of the poisonous lilies

Blaëndende Kalk
dazzling chalice

Drak hun mig til,
drank she me to (to me),

Ham, der er död
(To) Him, who is dead

Og ham, der nu Knaeler ved hendes Fod.
and (to) him who now Kneels at her foot.

Med os alle drak hun
With us all drank she

— Og da var Blikket hende lydigt —
— And then was (her) look (to) her obedient —

Löftets Baeger om usvigelig Troskab
(or The Vow's) Troth's cup/tankard/goblet to unending trueness/
    faithfulness/fidelity

Af den giftige Liljes
from the poisonous lilies

Blaendende kalk
Dazzling chalice.

Alt er forbi!
All is past!

Paa den snedaekte Slette
On the snow covered plain

I den brune Skov
In the brown forest

Vokser en enlig Tjørn.
Grows a lonely thornbush

Vindene eje dens Løv
(the) Winds own its leaves;

Et for et,
one for one

Et for et,
one for/by one

Drypper den de blodröde Bær
Drops it the bloodred berries

Ned i den hvide Sne,
down into the white snow,

De glödende Bær
The glowing berries

I den Kolde Sne. —
In the cold snow

Kjender du Pan?
Knowest thou Pan?

354
Philip Heseltine to Jelka Delius

THE
IMPERIAL LEAGUE OF OPERA
FOUNDER—SIR THOMAS BEECHAM BART.
MONTHLY REVIEW

Head Office:
90, Regent Street,
London, W.1

August 21st 1929

My dear Jelka,

I received the parts of the Danish songs safely, and all the material is now stored here in the Beecham library which is in charge of an excellent librarian, Henry Gibson,[20] who has a detailed catalogue of everything in the place. The 'Norwegian Suite' will not, after all, be played at the Festival, but if you will send over the parts, I could easily arrange a performance by the B.B.C. orchestra so that Fred could hear the work. The three Verlaine songs—'Il pleure', 'Le ciel est par-dessus le toit', and 'La lune blanche'[21]—will be sung by Kate Winter, with orchestra, at the Promenade Concert on September 5th. I have overhauled the parts carefully, and corrected a number of mistakes.

The songs finally selected for the Festival are as follows:—

Dora Labbette[22] (soprano):—	The Nightingale (Welhaven)
	Wiegenlied (Ibsen)
	Abendstimmung
	Vogelweise
	La lune blanche
	Avant que tu ne t'en ailles
Heddle Nash[23] (tenor):—	Irmelin
	Three Shelley Songs
John Armstrong (tenor):—	Daffodils
	The Nightingale (Henley)
	Spring (Nashe)
	Il pleure dans mon coeur

[20] Henry Gibson (1882–1954) was Beecham's music secretary from 1927 to 1932.
[21] For details of the orchestrated version see Threlfall, *Delius: A Supplementary Catalogue*, 64.
[22] Dora Labbette (1898–1984), English soprano who later sang under the name of Lisa Perli.
[23] Heddle Nash (1894–1961), English tenor.

John Goss (baritone):—
- Venevil
- Spielleute
- Silken shoes
- Autumn (Jacobsen)
- Hy-Brasil
- So sweet is she

Olga Haley (mezzo-soprano):—
- Homeward Journey
- Secret Love
- Le ciel est par-dessus le toit
- Let springtime come
- The violet
- Seraglio garden
- Black roses
- Autumn (Verlaine)

Goss and Haley sing at the first chamber concert, and some of their songs will be accompanied by the orchestra. 'Cynara' will be given at the Queen's Hall concert on October 18th.

A new and enterprising man has, I hear, taken Voigt's place in the Hawkes-Rogers firm; I hope to see him to-morrow about the 'Air and Dance'. I do not think there would be any advantage in publishing the Henley and Dowson songs in England. They are not suitable for singing with piano accompaniment, and we have too few orchestras to make it worth a publisher's while to issue songs in full score. The U.E. has a much better market for such things. Will you translate the texts yourself, or leave Hertzka to find his own translator? I hope you will be able to find time to do it yourself, as your German versions always suit Fred's music so admirably. I do not think there is any need to hurry on the publication of these two large songs, but the 'Air and Dance' should certainly be on sale in time for the Festival.

Will you please send me the address of the Frankfurter-Zeitung offices: also Grainger's address in England? And can you tell me of anyone who could give me some reminiscences of Fred's early years in Yorkshire?

The Festival is already arousing great interest and I have a large daily correspondence on the subject. Next week we are having posters displayed outside the Queen's Hall, with full programmes and a list of the performers, in order to attract the attention of the Promenade concert audiences.

Love to you all,

Ever affectionately yours
Philip Heseltine

355
Jelka Delius to Philip Heseltine

Grez 23. 8. 29

Dear Phil, Your letter gave us great pleasure and I am so delighted that you are installed now at the League of Opera and also so intimately connected with the Delius Festival.

I hasten to answer all questions. Fred would be very glad to hear the Norwegian Suite and I will send you the parts

The 3 Verlaine songs* that Kate Winter sings. Fred says: Who has orchestrated them? He does not remember having done so.[24]

Fred had written to Beecham the other day that he would prefer 3 of the songs *not* sung. They are *Nightingale*—Welhaven (the first song he ever wrote) *Spielleute   Verborgene Liebe*. Of course these are not very good and he dislikes them. But if it upsets Beechams plans, let them be sung. Only in that case they must be retranslated, as the english words are so terrible. Fenby and I are trying to do it.

Wiegenlied and Abendstimmung and Venevil we have also much improved, especially Venevil and Fred would very much like them to be sung in the new version. Fenby will make copies of the words and send them.

The Shelley Songs. They are of course to be sung in English. Armstrong the other day sang Queen of my heart on the B.B.C. and a notice said that this song was composed to a *german version* of Shelley's song. We immediately sent a wire about such an absurd idea to the BBC, and I took the occasion to write to Newman about the Seadrift being composed in German, which is of course preposterous. I think I had told you about his saying that on the B.B.C.   I think these mistakes may have arisen thro' the publishers entirely against Fred's will printing translations above english words (for use in Germany).

Air and Dance   Please negotiate with Hawkes about it. We will see about Cynara and Henley work after the Festival. Certainly I want to translate them myself; but for that I need time as I can only do it well when I know words and melody by heart and then at night on walks try all sorts of words till I get it to declame right.

---

[24] It would seem that Heseltine himself did. See Threlfall's *Supplementary Catalogue*, 56 and 64. At least two of these orchestral versions were first performed in Jan. 1915 at the Grafton Gallery, Beecham conducting.

Frankfurter Zeitung
  Redaktion
    Frankfurt a/M
is sufficient.

Percy Grainger
  Lilla Vran
    Pevensey Bay
        (Sussex)
only until Sept 1ˢᵗ, then

White Plains N.Y.
  47 Cromwell Place U.S.A.

Percy G. has written a very nice article for the American Press
  'Delius reaps his Harvest'.
(meaning the Festival and recognition.)
  We can not think of anybody for reminiscences. Fred says: For God's sake, dont let him ask my sisters, they will only tell lies.
  There is a Mrs Astley Roberts
  [10 Seaside Road]   née Edith Salmond
  Baddlesmere Eastbourne
who knew him well when a child in Bradford. By making a clever question-naire she might tell things. They were very musical and Fred loved them and went there on sundays to make music and hear them sing. Try her.
  I think the first programmes you sent me excellent and I could distribute some more.
  Those of to-day have not the programmes, which people want to know.
  So long for to-day dear Phil

Love from us both!
Jelka

*Many thanks for correcting the parts
  Some Americans told me yesterday that the Festival is well announced in the U.S.A. Press!

356
Philip Heseltine to Jelka Delius

THE
IMPERIAL LEAGUE OF OPERA
FOUNDER—SIR THOMAS BEECHAM BART.
MONTHLY REVIEW

Head Office:
90, Regent Street,
London, W.1

August 26ᵗʰ 1929

My dear Jelka,

I have to-day collected from Goodwin and Tabb and brought to this address the complete orchestral material, chorus parts and soloists' copies of 'Koanga': but there is no full score and no complete piano score—only the solo singers' individual parts in voice-and-piano transcription.[25]

Are you *quite certain* that the full score is not at Grez? There is no trace of its ever having been at Goodwin and Tabb's (where the rest of the material has lain for ten years), it is not at Curwen's with the other Delius (Universal) material, and it is not here in the Beecham library, nor in the operatic section of the old Beecham library which was sold to the B.N.O.C.

You have, I think, a complete piano score of the opera at Grez—at least, I sent one that I borrowed back to Grez several years ago. If you have this, would you be so kind as to send it over here, together with the material of the 'Norwegian Suite' (the score of which is now in the hands of the B.B.C.)? Beecham wants to see 'Koanga' again, and the B.B.C. will certainly play the 'Norwegian Suite', and might very possibly broadcast an act of 'Koanga', if the piano score were available.

It is a pity next Thursday's Prom. will not be broadcast—Fred will miss the 'cello concerto, in addition to missing the violin concerto a fortnight ago. But Thursday week's programme—with the Verlaine songs—will probably be transmitted.

On Thursday the big posters of the Festival will be ready for display at Queen's Hall, and I have arranged with B.B.C. to insert a leaflet dealing with the Festival in the Prom. programmes one night each week.

---

[25] Heseltine had discovered the parts of *Koanga* as Jelka told Grainger: 'Heseltine discovered the Orch parts at Goodwin & Tabb's last summer . . .'. Jelka Delius to Grainger, 23 Apr. 1930, Melbourne, Grainger Museum.

Beecham is still abroad and, I am afraid, in very poor health.

Will you ask Fred how he wants the opening of the 'Air and Dance' phrased —that is to say, are the notes to be completely detached, using an up and a down bow for each pair, or should they be phrased in pairs, thus:—

or played with *two movements of the bow in the same direction,*

I hoped that Mrs Howard Jones[26] would have marked the violin part with phrasing according to Fred's wishes, but there are very few marks of any kind. Much love to all.

Ever affectionately
Philip Heseltine

357
Jelka Delius to Philip Heseltine

Grez 30. 8. 29

My dear Phil,

That was indeed good news that you have found the orchestral and choral parts of Koanga and we *so greatly* appreciate all the trouble you have taken to unearth it. As to the score it is not here, there was only one orch. Score and that was given to Beecham. I remember all this material lying in 8.^A Hobart Place in the Spring 1915, there were even the german books of words.

Is there a possibility, do you think, of the score and piano score having remained there when Beecham left rather suddenly spring 1915? It might have been put

---

[26] Mrs Howard-Jones was the violinist, Grace Thynne.

on a loft or in cellar, as it was evidently not taken to G. & Tabb's or to the Aldwych.

We have enquired at G. & T's many times and corresponded with Laurence there about the lost works and they never said that they had some of Koanga; so it might be possible that they have the orch. score too. We have a (seemingly) complete piano score here; written on it is 'Prompter's copy'. Fred wants you to keep in mind that certain changes were made for the Elberfeld performance. They made the action clearer and the thing more pithy. There is also an aria, which he composed for the 2^d act at Elberfeld 1904. He said yesterday I think that Aria was very good. All these new bits have no english words. In fact the copy we have here has only german words.

Monday 2. 9. Here I was interrupted. Our new 'Bruder' has arrived and I was busy all the time. Our old one is leaving to-morrow. Fenby is going to Scarboro' on holiday on friday.

We have had no news from Beecham who had planned to pay us a flying visit here these days. I am very sorry to hear that he is not well. With such colossal work in front of him, too!

About 'Koanga' Fred wants me to say that he wishes to revise it—but of course there is no time before the Festival, so you can talk it over in London.

Fred says the opening of Air & Dance is to be played like your 2^d model, that is to say, with 2 movements of the bow in the same direction. May Harrison has offered to help phrase anything of Delius's. She has a great feeling for all that and would do it much better than Mrs H. J. You could easily get hold of her.

The H. Jones's have left yesterday and you will see them in London. I sent you the song translations a few days ago and I hope you have received them. Affection and haste

Jelka

A Miss Florence C. Schute   Green Gables Cottage   Falsgrave Park, Scarboro' has written to Fred. She is a girlhood friend of his and might have reminiscences. J. D.

358
Philip Heseltine to Jelka Delius

THE
IMPERIAL LEAGUE OF OPERA
FOUNDER—SIR THOMAS BEECHAM BART.
MONTHLY REVIEW

Head Office:
90, Regent Street,
London, W.1

September 1ˢᵗ 1929.

My dear Jelka,

Many thanks for your letter and the new translations of certain songs. Beecham will no doubt drop those songs Fred does not wish to have performed, though I think 'The Nightingale' is very charming. As regards the Verlaine songs, to be performed next Thursday, Fred will probably remember that I scored them for a performance at the Music Club under Beecham's direction in 1915.[27]

I wrote a long letter to the B.B.C. about the 'German translation' of Shelley, and about Newman's speech, and nothing of the kind will occur again. I am also dealing with Newman in an article. I am seeing Grainger on Wednesday, and will try and get in touch with Mʳˢ Astley Roberts shortly. It would be interesting to know the date of Fred's first visit abroad—that is, the first time he ever set foot in a foreign country. All these small facts are useful as evidence to confute those who try to make him out to be a German.

Did you know that Debussy's first article as a musical critic (in 1901) contained an account of Fred's Seven Danish songs? I wish we could get Fred's impressions of the first Debussy work he heard, but he always seems very vague about this.

Last Thursday's performance of the Cello Concerto was by far the best I have heard—infinitely better, both as regards soloist and orchestra, than the one given by Barbirolli and Barjansky early this year.[28] Balance between 'cello and band was excellent, and Wood curbed the Harrison's usual tendency to drag.

Much against my will, I conducted 'Capriol' (thank heaven one is not also expected to sing one's songs in public!); the orchestra was most sympathetic and

---

[27] For further details regarding the orchestrated version see Threlfall, *Frederick Delius: A Supplementary Catalogue*, 56.
[28] Royal Philharmonic Society concert, Queen's Hall, 17 Jan. 1929.

helpful, and played as well as could be expected under such direction. Anyway, the audience seemed pleased enough and I was recalled four times. But never again![29]

Hawkes has not yet made up his mind about the 'Air and Dance'.
Love to all.

Ever affectionately yours
Philip Heseltine

359
Jelka Delius to Philip Heseltine

FREDERICK DELIUS
Grez-sur-Loing
S. et M.
3.9.1929

Dear Phil,

I am so glad you got thro' so well with your conducting of the Capriol, I am sure you will conduct again too. I am so glad too, that the Cello Concerto went so well.

I will answer your questions:

Fred is not averse now to the 'Nightingale' being sung with the new words. *It is the first song he ever wrote*; that lends it a special interest, also there is that wistful feeling about it that afterwards became so characteristic of his music.

Debussy

Fred did not know and would very much like to hear what Debussy wrote about his Danish Songs. Fred himself was not at that concert. (I was there.) Fred said he really heard nothing of Debussy's before Pelleas, 1ˢᵗ performance, spring 1902 in Paris. He said: 'I liked it, I thought it very good. I noticed a certain similarity in our outlook. Before, I had only heard a piano piece "Pagodes" (1897 played

[29] Heseltine wrote to Taylor about his conducting engagement: 'On the 29ᵗʰ of this month [August] I make my first and last appearance as a conductor, when "Capriol" will be given at the Proms. What a farce this silly "conducted by the composer" fetish is! One feels that one is merely stuck up at the desk to make the audience laugh, as though one were a dancing bear or something.' Heseltine to Taylor, 6 Sept. 1929, BL 54197. Interviewed by the *Evening News* about conducting his own work, he caustically remarked: 'It's absurd. I've never conducted at a concert in my life. Why should I conduct because I'm the composer? Conducting is a highly technical job. Nobody expects me to sing my own songs in public. Why the curious rage for getting composers to conduct their own compositions?' *Evening News*, 17 Dec. 1930.

to Fred by Ravel), which struck me as being much influenced by the Java music and Dancing, which made such a great impression in the Paris exhibition of 1889.' Fred heard 'L'Aprémidi' only *years* later, I think in 1909 in a Prom, in England. I said to Fred 'were you with Ravel, Schmitt and that "bande" at the 1st perf. of Pelleas?' No, he went quite alone. I may mention that we had vaguely discussed the possibility for Fred to write an Opera on the same drama Pelleas, or another Maeterlinck drama. But he was never quite keen on Maeterlinck; whom he even then thought anaemic.

Now Fred's journeys to Germany. He thinks he was 6 or 7 when he first went there with his mother by Cologne to Bielefeld, where everybody called him: 'Der kleine Engländer. After that he went with both parents and 2 sisters when he was about 16 one summer a journey along the Rhine, Francfort etc. then Nurnberg Stuttgart etc. His next big journey was in 1881 when he went to Sweden and Norway. In summer the Delius family always went to Ilkley or Filey. They were so many that they hired a Saloon-car.

We remember now about the Verlaine-Orchestrations. And please send what Debussy wrote.

With love from us both (in sweltering heat)

yrs ever
Jelka D

360
Philip Heseltine to Jelka Delius

*THE
IMPERIAL LEAGUE OF OPERA
FOUNDER—SIR THOMAS BEECHAM BART.
MONTHLY REVIEW*

*Head Office:
90, Regent Street,
London, W.1*

September 6th 1929

My dear Jelka,

Many thanks for your letters. I am interested to hear that 'The Nightingale' is actually Fred's first song; in that case, the catalogue in my book is wrong (as

I suspect it is in some other respects also: we ought to revise this one day), for, according to what Fred told me some years ago, the Hans Andersen song, dated 1885—the MS of which I have deposited for the time in the wonderful Calvocoressi[30] collection of musical MSS—was his earliest surviving piece of music.

What Debussy wrote is not altogether complimentary, nor does it seem, to me, to mean anything as criticism. Still, the opinion of one great composer of another is always interesting. After dealing with a Symphony by Witkovski,[31] he says:—

> 'Je ne vois guère à retenir après cela que des "Poèmes danois" pour chant et orchestre de Fritz Delius: ce sont des chansons très douces, très blanches, de la musique pour bercer les convalescentes dans les quartiers riches. Il y a toujours une note qui se traîne sur un accord; telle, sur un lac, une fleur de nénuphar fatiguée d'être regardée par la lune, ou bien encore, un petit aérostat bloquée par les nuages.
>
> C'était ineffable comme tout, cette musique! Elle fût chantée par Mlle C. Andray-Fairfax avec une voix rêveuse et mélancoliquement distinguée. Mlle A.-F. imagina, pendant que se lamentait la musique, un jeu de comparaison entre le public et le lustre, qui tourna, je dois le dire, tout à la gloire du lustre. Ce jeu charmant semblait défendre la délicatesse des mélodies du bruit barbare des bravos.'[32]

If Fenby is going to Scarborough, perhaps he would be kind enough to see Miss Florence Schute and let me know if she has any interesting reminiscences. I hope to visit Mrs Astley Roberts some time next week.

I have arranged for a number of posters of the Festival to be exhibited in Bradford, where the League has a very enterprising organiser in Mrs Edward Haley.

As tickets for the festival are already being sold, I should like to know as soon as possible how many you would like reserved for yourselves, and in what part of the hall, since it might happen that the particular places you want would be booked by someone else.

I wonder if you heard the Verlaine songs last night: I hope you did not, for the performance was the worst I have heard in Queen's Hall this season. It sounded

[30] Michel Dimitri Calvocoressi (1877–1944), French-born music critic of Greek parentage. He settled in London after a career in Paris as music critic, author, and lecturer on music.

[31] Georges Witkowski (1867–1943), French conductor and composer.

[32] 'After that, the only other thing to catch my attention were some "Poèmes danois" for voice and orchestra by Fritz Delius: these are very sweet songs, very pale, music to lull to sleep convalescent ladies in wealthy neighbourhoods. There is always one note which drags itself over a chord; such as one finds a water-lily on a lake tired of being gazed at by the moon, or rather a little air-balloon eclipsed by the clouds. The music was beyond words, unspeakable! It was sung by Miss C. Andray-Fairfax in a dreamy and sad, refined voice. As the music was wailing on, Miss Andray-Fairfax seemed to be making a comparison between the members of the audience and the chandelier, a game which, I have to say, finished to the glory of the chandelier. This charming diversion seemed to shield the delicacy of these songs from the barbarous noise of the bravos'. *La Revue Blanche* (Paris), 24, no. 188 (1 Apr. 1901), 551.

as though there had been no rehearsal: the wood-wind were coarse in tone and ill-balanced throughout: in the first song, the first clarinet came in a bar too soon and failed to right himself, causing chaos for several bars, and then Woodhouse[33] made a hash of his violin solo at the end. The singer's French accent baffles description! It was a great pity, as these songs are so beautiful, though, I think, of too intimate a character for performance in a large hall by a large orchestra.

Ever affectionately yours
Philip Heseltine

361
Jelka Delius to Philip Heseltine

9. 9. 1929
FREDERICK DELIUS
Grez-sur-Loing
S. et M.

Dear Phil,

Beecham came out here several times and we had a delightful time together. He has left for London today.

As regards the *songs* Fred says, you are probably right and the H[ans]. A[ndersen]. song ['Zwei braune Augen'] was probably the very first one.

Debussy, I think, has a rather absurd way of criticizing; but it is interesting, of course.

Fenby will go and see Miss Schute. He has left today. He says anything you would like him to do you need only write to 12 Mayville Avenue Scarb.

As to the seats, and this is why I write at once, we talked it over with Beecham and he promised to see to it at once. Enough seats have to be kept for him to enable them to form a sort of loge into which he can be wheeled in a very good springy Bath-chair. It should be arranged so that if he is tired before the end of the concert he can be wheeled to the back; how this can be done in view of the steps grading down to the front I do not exactly see. But I suppose it all can be done. Only be sure to remind Beecham to see about it at once. Fred gets terribly nervous about such things.

---

[33] Charles Woodhouse (b. 1879), English violinist. He was Henry Wood's leader in the Queen's Hall Orchestra and led the special orchestra for the first of the 1929 Delius Festival concerts.

We did hear the Verlaine songs, but the orchestra seemed in a jolly mess. Yet Kate Winter was quite good. Fred really thinks them better with piano. The records of Dora Labette are simply glorious.[34] But she has only done one Verlaine song yet: 'Le Ciel' She will do the others too presently.

It is so nice, dear old Phil, that you keep us posted about things. Fred loves it and it tranquillizes him; We also discussed the journey with Beecham and if it is done as he proposes it will be quite feasable.

The Frankfurter Zeitung contained quite a good article about the festival on Sept 7th. It is taken mostly from the notice on the preliminary programme.

With all affectionate messages
Jelka

362
Philip Heseltine to Jelka Delius

THE
IMPERIAL LEAGUE OF OPERA
FOUNDER—SIR THOMAS BEECHAM BART.
MONTHLY REVIEW

Head Office:
90, Regent Street,
London, W.1

September 13th 1929

Dear Jelka,

I enclose 20 more circulars and 20 of a revised leaflet giving the programmes *and* the list of performers.

The booking is going very well—so well for the chamber concerts that Beecham is contemplating an *extra* programme of songs and chamber music. The Aeolian Hall, of course, holds only 500.

---

[34] Dora Labbette's records were made with Beecham accompanying on 24 June and 10 July 1929. 'Cradle Song', 'The Nightingale', and 'Twilight Fancies' were issued on Columbia 2344. In those sessions she also recorded 'Irmelin Rose', 'Le ciel est par-dessus le toit', and 'The Violet', but these were not issued until 1976 in an LP transfer. Delius quite likely received test pressings.

I have reserved seats for you and Fred at the end of the front row of the balcony at the Aeolian Hall, as there is plenty of room there; and Beecham went yesterday to Queen's Hall and selected seats for you.

Much love from
Phil

363
Philip Heseltine to Jelka Delius

THE
IMPERIAL LEAGUE OF OPERA
FOUNDER—SIR THOMAS BEECHAM BART.
MONTHLY REVIEW

Head Office:
90, Regent Street,
London, W.1

September 25th 1929.

My dear Jelka,

An advertisement has arrived here from H.M.V., reproducing a letter from Fred praising their records, for insertion in the magazine and in the programmes.

I think it would be well, in view of Columbia's interest in the Festival and of the fact that Beecham is making so many Delius records for them, if you would send them also a few words of praise for publication in the programmes. This should be done (if you have not already done so) as soon as possible, for time is getting short.

Fenby sent me an excellent early portrait which he had obtained from the lady in Scarborough. If you have any more photographs—either professional or amateur—I should be glad to receive them. So far I have one of (about) 1875, one of 1884, then a gap until 1911 (except for two very poor portraits, one full-face, with a white stock round the neck, and another, a three-quarter length figure, which was reproduced in Max Chop's pamphlet[)]. Have you anything of 1895–1905? A photograph of your portrait of Fred, and of any other pictures of yours, would be very useful for the press. Why not bring some pictures over and exhibit them? I have been through the old lithograph piano score of 'A Village Romeo' with great interest. It is a much better piano arrangement than the published version. I note that 'The Walk to the Paradise Garden' has been almost entirely re-written since this lithographed copy was made. Will you please let me know the exact date when the entr'acte was composed, as this is important for the programme notes? It would also be helpful to know whether 'Eventyr' is based on any particular story of Asbjörnsen:[35] also, the name of any particular story, which I could quote, that embodies the legend of the dead girl in the coffin, in relation to the character described by Jacobsen[36] in 'Arabesk'. I have read the notes you sent to Beecham about the poem, and found them most enlightening.

Hawkes was not keen on taking the 'Air and Dance' on the terms prescribed, and as there is no other English publisher who could handle it satisfactorily both here and abroad, it had better be given to Universal-Edition after the Festival, when it can be published with the additional advantage of all Beecham's markings. He has done an immense amount of work on the scores, making additional marks of expression, bowing, etc, and a new practical edition that should include these markings would be of the utmost value in preserving for posterity the proper interpretation of Delius.

Short tributes to the genius of Delius from twenty or thirty eminent men in various countries would be useful in the press. Perhaps you would be so good as to write to a few conductors and others who are well known in Germany, who would be glad to send short messages of appreciation.

One of Fred's nieces came here yesterday enquiring when Fred would be in England, but knowing Fred's antipathy to his relations, I gave instructions that she should be told nothing.

I am sure the Festival is going to be a big success, both artistically and financially; both the box-offices are pleased with the advance bookings, and are confident of getting full houses.

With much love,

Ever affectionately yours
Philip Heseltine

[35] Peter Christen Asbjörnsen (1812–85), collector of Norwegian folklore.
[36] Jens Peter Jacobsen (1847–85), Danish novelist and poet.

364
Jelka Delius to Philip Heseltine

FREDERICK DELIUS
Grez-sur-Loing
S. et M.
28. 9. 1929

Dear Phil

We are expecting Mr Angus Wilson from Columbia this afternoon and will concoct a letter.[37] It is amusing how H.M.V. come out with their advertisement *now*!!

'Eventyr' is not based on any particular story of Ashbjørnsen; it is a resumé-impression of the book. I remember reading the book in Norwegian to him; the spirit of Asbjörnson is opposed to that in the Arabesk, as A. is not at all erotic; his are rather the old legends still quite alive with lonely peasants, hunters and mountaineers. These people have a naïve belief in the 'Under-jordiske' (the Underearthly ones) Trolls, Heinzelmännchen, hobgoblins; who either help the humans or, if provoked, become very revengeful. A boy alone in a forest would imagine he heard them trotting after him, and get very frightened. At a wedding or Xmas meal a little dish of cream porridge is put on the loft for these underearthly ones, or else they might be offended—they have been known to fetch girls away (even the bride of a wedding) in such cases and dance with them furiously till they fall down unconscious. A hunters luck would depend upon their good or bad will. In the queer noises at night in lonely huts and woods you would imagine you heard the hordes of these mysterious beings galloping along in the distance.

Perhaps this may give you an idea of Ashbjørnson. The dead girl in the Coffin would surely be in Grimm's fairy tales. I think Schneewittchen must be lying in such a coffin of glass, looking lovely and the 7 dwarfs watching her. I will try to find it and write to-morrow.

As to the Photos, what really ought to be done is to get a really artistic photographer to make a Studio portrait of Fred at once on his arrival in London.

---

[37] The Columbia Graphophone Company was only involved in the opening concert of the 1929 Delius Festival; the other orchestral concerts were given under the auspices of the BBC (second and last) and the Royal Philharmonic Society. A typed letter, signed 'Frederick Delius' (doubtless by Jelka), endorsing the Columbia recording of his works as conducted by Beecham was reproduced on the back page of the programme book of the first concert. A similar letter, endorsing Geoffrey Toye's recordings for HMV of works by Delius, was reproduced on the back of the programme for the third concert.

Here I could not get one; and nobody seemed to know one in Paris. But you will be able to find out in London. Elliott & Fry are abominable and they forced Fred to smile and look imbecile in 1923.

I have no photo of my portrait of Fred and no-one here has a good enough Camera to do it. But a little pastel-portrait of Fred by Geo de Monfreid,[38] Gauguins friend from about 1892 to 95 is in London at the O'Neills. It has great charm and the right character, as he was then and the hand on the piano is beautiful. You could get it photographed. But please be very careful as it is pastel. The O'Neills have been keeping it for us and I am going to take it back this time.

I send you a photo of Fred with Dr Haym,[39] probably from, 1903–5 one with Koanga and an early one with mustache, which may be the one you have. But promise dear Phil to restore them to me. I would be miserable if I lost them.

I really can not bring that big portrait over, nearly a yard and a half high.

Fred does not at all care for the idea of getting tributes from german conductors; so you had better cut that out. Anyhow 4 of his principal conductors are dead. Dr Haym, Prof Buths,[40] Fritz Cassirer who brought out the Village Romeo in Berlin and Suter-Basel.

The Entr'acte of the Village R. was composed or changed in 1906 for the Berlin performance   He does not remember who made the first piano Score. The Entr'acte was composed at once after the Mass of Life and just before or in between Songs of Sunset.

A. Wilson was here just now and Fred was very talkative. He also dictated to him the words of appreciation for the Columbia

Fred was particularly pleased about your treatment of his niece!! He said: Ward off all my relations, tell Phil again.

I think it is truly great that Beecham has edited all the works so splendidly. I heard from Hertzka to-day and he is probably going to London for one Concert of the Festival. This would be a very good thing; we could then talk the matter of the Re-Edition over; he also seems to be licking his lips for the new works. Please encourage him to come.[41]

With Barjanskys help I have sent Programmes to all the important german conductors and other important personalities.

[38] Georges-Daniel de Monfreid (1856–1929), French painter, sculptor, and engraver. It was through him that Delius bought Gauguin's painting *Nevermore* in 1898.

[39] Hans Haym (1860–1921), German conductor and composer. He was a very important champion of Delius's music before Beecham, giving the premières of *Appalachia*, *Over the Hills and Far Away*, and *Paris* and other early performances, including *Lebenstanz*, *Songs of Sunset*, and the first (complete) Continental performance of the *Mass of Life*.

[40] Julius Buths (1851–1920), German conductor, composer, and pianist. He conducted the first performance of *Lebenstanz* and other early performances, and was the soloist in the first performance of the Piano Concerto (under Haym).

[41] Hertzka had hoped to come across to London to hear the *Mass of Life* on 1 Nov., but unfortunately was unable to attend on account of illness.

Beecham wrote a splendid letter to me yesterday and it had a most excellent effect on Fred, who was very pessimistic about being able to travel.

I did not quite understand about our seats, and I do not like to bother Beecham, who has all these big rehearsals etc. I suppose I am to sit with Fred, and then the Bruder nurse must be there and also Fenby. Fred particularly wants Fenby near him to make him note down anything he may wish to tell him about the music. I suppose it will be alright and that there are 2 seats behind us?

I must get this off at once, so, Goodbye

Ever Affly
Jelka.

I read to Fred, what I had written to you about Eventyr. He said it was quite perfect and expressed exactly what he had meant. So that is quite alright
J. D.

365
Philip Heseltine to Jelka Delius

*THE
IMPERIAL LEAGUE OF OPERA
FOUNDER—SIR THOMAS BEECHAM BART.
MONTHLY REVIEW*

*Head Office:
90, Regent Street,
London, W.1*

September 28th 1929

My dear Jelka,

The first rehearsal of the Festival takes place to-morrow (Sunday) at Queen's Hall from 10.30–1 and 2.30 to 5. This is only the first of many, and the expenses will be enormous. In order to try and minimise the loss, I have worked out a scheme whereby it will be possible to make a £300 profit from sales and advertisements in the programmes. The only difficulty is to make a large enough number of advertisers come in. Now, if you could let me have a number of short testimonials from Fred, about things he uses and likes, I could offer these to the more hesitating advertisers as an additional bait. I should particularly like one for the E.M.G. gramophone,[42] and for your wireless set and loud speaker: also for any other article Fred has had in regular use, such as a fountain pen, etc.

If you could let me have a few words on the gramophone and wireless *as soon as possible*, it would be a great help, as I want to be able to show as big a profit on the programmes as I can—it is the only department where a loss is not inevitable. But there is not much time, as the first programme must be in the printer's hands on October 7th, and the coaxing of advertisers is often a lengthy business.

Ever affectionately yours
Philip Heseltine

366
Jelka Delius to Philip Heseltine

Dear Phil,

Yes, it is *Sneewittchen* Fairytale N. 53 in Grimm's Kindern Hausmarchen. I am sure there are many others, but it is not easy to find them. Sneewittchen takes refuge with the 7 dwarfs, because a wicked queen, who is jealous of her beauty wants to kill her. The queen comes in disguise & poisons her with an apple. The dwarfs find her dead when they return. But she is so beautiful, and as white as snow, as red as blood and her hair as black as ebony. Her cheeks are red and they can not make up their minds to bury her, so they put her in a glass coffin up on the hillside. Then after many months the prince comes, falls in love with her and eventually brings her to life again

Yrs ever
Jelka

[Grez]
29. 9. 29

Postcard.

---

[42] A typewritten testimonial from Delius concerning his E.M.G. gramophone appeared inside the front cover of the programme for the third concert.

367
Jelka Delius to Philip Heseltine

Grez 30. 9. 29

Dear Phil, Just received your letter and will do what I can.

E.M.G. has already a testimonial from Fred. For safeties sake I write out a new one as well.

Our wireless is a Ducretet Société des Etablissements Ducretet   75 Rue Claude Bernard   Paris.

I do not know them at all; I bought thro' a little wireless man in Fontainebleau; I doubt whether they would care to advertise in England.

The Loudspeaker is American   Western Electric (Great) got it thro' the same man, Robert Gaullier at Fontainebleau. He procured both in Paris.

Fountain pen very old 'Ideal'. Why not tackle Duo-Art. Get Howard Jones at that. You know that they are publishing a Biographic Double Roll of Delius, Howard Jones playing and Beecham to give his name and assistance. It would be quite the thing for them to advertise this as 'shortly to appear'. ~~We have a Ford Motor car, with which in 1923-24 we travelled right to Italy. If this could be of any use, please concoct testimonial yourself in Freds name.~~

Now there are several people who could be tackled: 1. *Sydney Schiff.*[43] H. Jones has already told him he ought to pay for a concert. He answered laughingly, he would like to. Perhaps something could be done with him and H. J. knows him very well. Hurry, as he H. J. will be off to play in Cardiff these days.

Then there is Edgar Simon,[44] the Proprietor of 'Marmite', he came here as an old Schoolfellow of Fred's one day, likes to be important, lives in Grosvenor House, has already spoken to Beecham and might be glad to have his name connected (as a benefactor) with the Festival.

Then there is Frank Stoop 9 Hans Place. He was here yesterday and told us that he has just sold an old dutch picture for 30000£. Very stingy but he might also like to do something in remembrance of his wife who was always so friendly with us and often came to Grez.

All this must of course on no account be asked for in Fred's name.

Thro' Howard Jones we have just bought an Erard Piano   Could he get Erard to advertize? Fred likes the tone-sonority and agreable softness of touch of the Erard. If it were any use please make up a testimonial. I send you several signed sheets for Testimonials, which you can concoct.

---

[43] Sydney Schiff (Stephen Hudson) (1869–1944), English novelist who was also a rich art connoisseur and collector. He was also a friend of Marcel Proust.

[44] Edgar Simon who had been at school with Delius, had visited him at Grez.

We are overrun with the strangest visitors, and now I must rush this to the post. My thoughts were all with you and the big rehearsals yesterday.
In haste,

Jelka

368
Philip Heseltine to Jelka Delius

October 2ⁿᵈ 1929   90 Regent Street
                                                              W.1

My dear Jelka,

Many thanks indeed for the testimonials which will be most useful. This year is the centenary of the invention of the Braille system by which the blind are enabled to read through the sense of touch. I have been approached by the National Institute for the Blind (who have just published a piano score of 'The First Cuckoo' in Braille notation) with a request that Fred should dedicate a work to them. I feel sure he would have no objection to helping them in this way, as they are doing splendid work, and the fact would make a good press paragraph which would benefit both the Institute and the Festival.[45]

The rehearsal was magnificent; the choir sat amongst the orchestra, and for the first time in my life I heard what I have always hoped, in vain, to hear—a chorus and orchestra that sound like one homogeneous body.

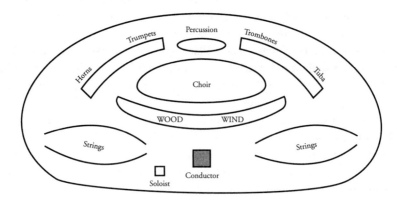

---

[45] A whole page announcement entitled 'Delius and the Blind' appeared for the National Institute for the Blind in the programme of the first concert, announcing the dedication and the first performance four days later of the *Air and Dance*.

John Goss was magnificent in 'Arabesk' and 'Cynara', and also sang 'Sea Drift' as Noble could not come. Beecham was very pleased with him. I am sure you will endorse my own high opinion of his ability when you hear him.

In great haste,

Ever yours
Phil

369
Philip Heseltine to Jelka Delius

*THE
IMPERIAL LEAGUE OF OPERA
FOUNDER—SIR THOMAS BEECHAM BART.
MONTHLY REVIEW*

*Head Office:
90, Regent Street,
London, W.1*

December 5th 1929

My dear Jelka,

We are having a full score of 'Koanga' reconstructed from the orchestral parts, and it would be a great help to the copyist if you would be so kind as to let us have your piano score, as he could then space out his bars, first of all, in relation to the text and voice parts.

I hope you liked Blunt's poem.[46] He had never heard any Delius before October 18th, but was so enchanted that he stayed in London for the rest of the Festival.

I am sending you a copy specially printed on good paper; also, a better pull of Kapp's[47] 'Bantock' caricature.[48]

We have a splendid Christmas number of MILO printing.

Much love and all good wishes to yourself and Fred,

Ever affectionately
Philip Heseltine

[46] Printed in *MILO*; see below. Bruce Blunt (1899–1957), bon viveur, poet, journalist, and writer on wine, gardening, and the turf, was one of Heseltine's closest friends during the last three years of his life. Some of Heseltine's finest settings are of Blunt's poetry.

[47] Edmond Xavier Kapp (1890–1978), English painter, draughtsman, and caricaturist.

[48] *MILO*, 1/1 (Nov. 1929), 6.

DELIUS

The midnight folk, the eerie goblin-kind,
Leap upon drums and dance along the wind,
Pluck at the strings until the darkness fills
With black wings teeming from the tunnelled hills,
And shapes that gibber against the coming of day
Until the day comes, and the gloomy array
Creeps away.

A mood passes and a voice sings
Of passion's hunger and of beauty's thrall
And the faint shades of unremembered things
That fade at last for ever, lonely beyond recall.

Through lands fantastic and lands a-shimmer with heat,
Dark forests and lone plains benumbed with frost
(Icicles glittering over the violins)
The mind has travelled afar—then a paean rings
In praise of the dancing, laughter and strength of Man.

And, all the while, the blind weaver of all these dreams
Listens and dreams.

Slowly a hand falls, the music ends.
From the peopled hall
Call upon call of praise and love
To the ringing roof ascends.
Under a lighted dome
The wanderer comes home:
His country makes amends.

Bruce Blunt

(*MILO, The Official Organ of the Imperial League of Opera*, vol 1, no. 1, November 1929, 7).

370
Jelka Delius to Philip Heseltine

Grez 2. 12. 29

Dear Phil,

I was delighted with Milo. Bantocks portrait is delightful, and so exactly portrays his character, his essence. At least that is how I have always understood him.

Who is the man who made the poem on Delius?

I am greatly looking forward to the next issue with Fred's portrait. Only, Phil, you must not have the back of the page printed. It would be an insult to a great artist like Augustus John and with that thin paper and the print coming thro' it would ruin this most delicate drawing.

I wrote to Beecham the other day about the 'Song of Summer' which we left with him.[49] Fred to whom I told your plans with the Columbia, would like to do something with them; but as Beecham has such far-going plans, he wanted to ask him first.

We are delighted with the Columbia records. Tertis[50] has really played the Sonata II beautifully. Did you hear it?

7. 12. I was interrupted here, as Fred had a few bad days and I had no leisure.

To-day your letter came and I hasten to answer

I am sending the piano Score of Koanga to you to-day. Everything, as it was played in Elberfeld (1904) is in it, as it is the Souffleur's copy, but the english words are not in it and I saw with regret that the 2^d act is not complete. I am going to hunt around for the missing pages and ask Fenby, whether they were missing from the first.

I suppose you have the english words in the copy you found again. All the places that have been altered or added will have to be translated from the german, as principally the aria. But there are numerous small changes. The man 'Honoré' who was spoken of, but never appeared (Palmyre's fiancé) has been eliminated, etc.

---

[49] Although *A Song of Summer* was initially programmed for the sixth of the 1929 Delius Festival concerts, Beecham in fact never conducted the work, of which he had little to say other than calling it an 'ingenious effort of reconstruction'. Its first recording was not until Feb. 1950, for HMV with Barbirolli conducting the Hallé Orchestra.

[50] Tertis recorded his arrangement of Delius's second Violin Sonata for viola on 7 Oct. 1929. It was issued on Columbia L2342/3, coupled with Tertis's arrangement of the Serenade from *Hassan*. The pianist was George Reeves.

Of course all these chorusses must be taken from the original english words. They are not half as good in german; but they insisted that I should make them rhyme and I did as best I could.

Fred suggests that the words be only pencilled into the reconstructed score to start with, as surely all the english words would be better for a bit of fixing up.

There are quite a number of chorus parts, principally from Act I here, should they be needed. Have you got an english book of words? It was typewritten; it might even be here. If you tell me, I can hunt for it. We are naturally *delighted* that this work is being done and anxious to give all assistance we can.

The poem of Blunt is charming, it gave Fred great pleasure too and I have read it to him several times.

There is another Sonnet by a certain 'Brumm' of Manchester, well meant, but more 'pompier' if you know what that means in English. Blunt's has such an original touch.

I have also received a photo of a picture done of Fred sitting in the Queens Hall with the audience behind. I wish you could look at the picture. The photo looks hard, unimaginative, but extraordinarily true in many ways. It is by Proctor[51] and he writes me that it is so much better in the painting. With love from us both

Ever affly
Jelka

Fred has written a letter to the D[aily]. Telegr[aph] about the copyright bill.[52]

---

[51] Ernest Procter (1886–1935), principally a landscape painter and mural decorator. He made several drawings of Delius during the rehearsals of the *Mass of Life* at Queen's Hall on 1 Nov. 1929. The sketch is in the National Portrait Gallery and is reproduced in the *Peter Warlock Newsletter*, no. 42 (Mar. 1989), 7.

[52] Under this new Music Copyright Bill a composer could not charge more than 2*d.* for the perpetual right of public performance of a work. A letter of protest from Elgar also appeared in the *Evening Standard* (17 Dec. 1929). The bill was not passed.

371
Philip Heseltine to Jelka Delius

THE
IMPERIAL LEAGUE OF OPERA
FOUNDER—SIR THOMAS BEECHAM BART.
MONTHLY REVIEW

Head Office:
90, Regent Street,
London, W.1

December 14th 1929

My dear Jelka,

Very many thanks for the 'Koanga' piano score. I am very glad you liked Blunt's poem. He was the large hog-faced man who sat just behind you at two of the Queen's hall concerts. You will find another poem of his in the next 'Radio Times'. He is also an authority on the Turf, and the gastronomic expert of the 'Evening Standard'.

The John drawing will be inserted on a loose sheet of fine paper. John himself is very pleased with the reproduction. I have not yet seen Proctor's picture; it looks very photographic when reproduced.

Much love to you both,

Yours ever affectionately
Philip Heseltine

1930–1931

RECURRING bouts of pain and depression at the beginning of 1930 left Delius unable to work even though Fenby was back again at Grez by the end of January. In March, however, he had recovered sufficiently to be able to compose most of the third violin sonata, which he dedicated to May Harrison, who visited Grez for a fortnight in May. Other visitors included Gardiner in April, who brought with him the young composer Patrick Hadley. Another interesting visitor was a hypnotist, Alex Erskine, who stayed in Grez for two weeks at the beginning of June. For a while Delius seemed to respond to treatment administered under hypnosis. It was after his visit that Delius completed the *Songs of Farewell* with Fenby's assistance. Another work completed at this time was *Caprice and Elegy* for cello and orchestra, written for Beatrice Harrison. Fenby returned to England in October and after his departure Delius's condition seemed once again to deteriorate. The end of the year was a generally depressing time for the Deliuses. There were ongoing problems with the domestic staff and the news of Heseltine's death was a great shock to both Fred and Jelka.

1930 began on a depressing note for Heseltine. With the collapse of the Imperial League of Opera he was again out of work. His wealthy uncle Evelyn died on 28 April and Heseltine attended his funeral at Great Warley on 3 May, discovering later that he had inherited nothing from his uncle's estate. In July he spent a fortnight with Blunt in Bramdean. It was during this time that he composed the song 'The Fox', after a visit to a local pub of the same name. In October he moved to 12A Tite Street together with Barbara Peache. His prospects were gradually becoming bleaker, his inspiration seemed to have dried up, and he was found gassed on the morning of 17 December. At the inquest on 22 December the verdict was death caused by coal-gas poisoning with insufficient evidence to decide whether it was suicide or an accident. There have been countless speculations surrounding Heseltine's death. Eric Fenby is of the opinion that Heseltine found himself in an artistic cul-de-sac (possibly through so much early exposure to the music of Delius) with no other way out,[1] while Denis ApIvor suggested that

---

[1] 'I think he had been influenced too much by the *letter* of Delius's music rather than the spirit. If he had only imitated the artistic integrity, rather than get into this cul-de-sac where he was strangled and couldn't do any more.' E. Fenby, 'Warlock as I knew him', *Composer*, 82 (Summer 1984), 19–23. And again: 'He came to his very tragic end which I don't think had anything to do with women or drinking, but simply because he realised that in following the letter of Delius's art instead of his artistic integrity, he came to an intellectual cul-de-sac. I think that is what drove him: there were circumstances which he told me at the time which confirm me very strongly in that belief.' Id., 'Visitors to Grez', in Lloyd (ed.), *Fenby on Delius*, 115.

faced with the 'drying-up' of his early youthful lyrical impulse, he did not have the technique or the sense of direction to move into new fields and exploit new attitudes towards composition, which would have involved some sort of linguistic extension, some enquiry into what his language had been and why it no longer satisfied him or seemed appropriate.[2]

The Deliuses were shattered by the news of Heseltine's death, telling Fenby that they could think of nothing else. In a letter to Sydney Schiff, Jelka wrote poignantly:

We both feel it very deeply. Such an act gives one a sudden insight into depths of disappointment and suffering—that one cannot bear thinking of, as having been endured by a beloved friend. It is true we were rather separated thro' Phil's latter strange way of living and we lost him bit by bit. But all that is swept away by such a catastrophe. I see constantly the beautiful lovable incredibly intelligent and artistic boy of twenty— and that tragic figure lying in a gas-filled room with his face to the wall in the early morning.[3]

She also wrote a most beautiful, heart-felt letter to Heseltine's mother, part of which appears as the final letter of this volume.

372
Philip Heseltine to Frederick and Jelka Delius

THE
IMPERIAL LEAGUE OF OPERA
FOUNDER—SIR THOMAS BEECHAM BART.
MONTHLY REVIEW

Head Office:
90, Regent Street,
London, W.1

January 2nd 1930

My dear Fred and Jelka,
    I returned from a short holiday in Lincolnshire to find your welcome letter and Christmas present awaiting me, and I should have written sooner to thank

---

[2] D. Aplvor, 'Philip Heseltine: A Psychological Study', *Music Review*, 46 (1985), 126.
[3] Jelka Delius to Sydney Schiff (?Jan. 1931); Carley, *Letters*, ii. 378.

you most heartily for your kind thought, had not an attack of flu laid me low for some days.

Beecham is extremely busy with his plans for the opera season in May. I have spoken to him about the 'Song of Summer', but he has not yet had time to give the work as much attention as he would like to. I am sure the Columbia company would pay very handsomely for the exclusive rights.

Hoping all is well with you both, and with much love and again with very many thanks for your kind present, I am

Ever affectionately yours
Philip Heseltine

373
Jelka Delius to Philip Heseltine

25. 1. 30
[Grez]

Dear Phil,

I wonder whether there are any unsold Milo's with Fred's portrait left?[4] If so I should like very much to buy some, and also some remaining programmes and photos of Beecham and Fred. I enclose a cheque for £1-0-0 as I should like to pay for them. It seems a good occasion as Fenby will be calling at your office on his way thro to Grez and you can give these things to him to bring over.

I wonder how Koanga is getting on.[5] You have not mentioned it again. Fenby, of course, is very willing to do any work on it, which you suggest, or any other work on the Delius music.

I am sure Beecham is tremendously busy with all his conducting and the Opera plans.

---

[4] *Milo*, Christmas 1929 (vol. 1, no. 3) had contained a drawing of Delius by Augustus John.

[5] A reference to the intention of reconstructing the lost score of *Koanga* from the piano score and orchestral parts. The lost score, however, suddenly turned up, as Jelka told Grainger in April: 'The great event is that the big orchestral score of the opera Koanga has been found *at last*, after it has been lost since 1915 when Beecham was in money troubles and really bankrupt and had to evacuate the "Aldwych", where he had it then with its entire material. Heseltine discovered the Orch parts at Goodwin & Tabb's last summer and Hadley got them to make another serious search and they found it . . . Fenby is now to copy and revise the whole thing.' Jelka Delius to Grainger, 23 Apr. 1930, Melbourne, Grainger Museum.

So, if Fenby can take any work off your hands and bring it here it might be good.

Your uncle in Marlotte it appears, is fairly bursting about the Delius Celebrity and has used up all the gum in Seine et Marne sticking news Cuttings about it into Albums—but we have not seen him. It is rather touching.

The BBC people, notably Eckersley[6] has entirely bungled the affair about giving Fred a beautiful Loudspeaker. It was all settled when he suddenly sent us a Radiola 7 lamp set; a huge thing, but not at all as good as our Ducrétet. When he announced this gift I at once tried to make him cancel it as Radiola sets are known to be mediocre. But he insisted I should try it. Of course it is horrid, not selective and no patch on what we have. So I asked him to have it fetched away again. This is a month ago and it is still here and he has not answered me.

I am very much afraid if it stays here much longer they will not take it back. If I knew that he cannot take it back I think I ought to try to sell it before it gets more depreciated. (It is worth about 5000 frs.)

On the other hand I have heard there is a new 12 Guinea Marconi 1930 Loudspeaker that is excellent and I asked Eckersley to give that to Fred instead of the set. No answer. Also I heard that Eckersley was leaving the B.B.C. I also wrote to Filson Young[7] and he answered that he had sent my letter on to Eckersley.

Should you possibly be in touch with any of these B.B.C. people please mention it. I should so much like to know what their intentions are.

Their idea was that an english set was no good for us here, on account of the difficulty in keeping it up. But that would not apply to a Loudspeaker, which needs no such intricate care.

I really think that our set is the best to be had in France. It has 7 lamps. Our loudspeaker is bad in the middle. The hight is *fairly* good and it booms the bass almost too much; if one makes the thing go loud it distorts easily. They say the 1930 Marconi can play as loud or as soft as one wishes, and yet keep balance perfectly.

I hope you are well. Please remember me kindly to all the friends of 90 Regent S^{tr}! Yrs aff^{ly}

Jelka Delius

Fenby need only bring the drawings from Milo, not the printed matter

---

[6] Peter Pendleton Eckersley (1892–1963), chief engineer to the BBC.
[7] Alexander Bell Filson Young (1876–1938), author and adviser on programmes to the BBC from 1926.

374
Jelka Delius to Philip Heseltine

GREZ-SUR-LOING (S & M)
6. 3. 1930

Dear Phil,

I am really sure you have heard that your uncle, old H. in Marlotte is dead. It came very suddenly. His wife has come and I hear she looks as if she could not last very long either. I thought I had better let you know. Mrs Brooks said she looked very vague and dazed, and heaven knows what she will do with his pictures and collections. That terrible Maynard[8] is there all the time and he is a man not to be trusted.

I should love to know how Beecham is. But I am afraid it is no use asking you any questions as you do not answer.

?? Koanga ??

?? My programmes ??

?? Augustus John drawing, out of Milo ??

?

Aff^y in haste
Jelka

Shd you come over stay with us, please, and bring Koanga material along

---

[8] Guy Maynard, American painter who lived in France and who was a friend of Delius. Although Fenby recalled Maynard as being one of the 'rather strange' visitors of Delius's late years, Roger Fry, in 1921, described him as 'a most charming creature who knew Cézanne and Gauguin, and tremendously intelligent about art'. (*Letters of Roger Fry*, ed. D. Sutton (London, 1972), no. 496.)

375
Jelka Delius to Philip Heseltine (Peter Warlock)

[Grez, 12 March 1930]

Dear Peter[9] Fenby brought me the cheque alright, but nobody gave him the Milos and Programmes; also Gibson promised him to send Koanga-Material *at once* and never did so.[10] I have now written to Beecham as it would be the greatest pity to miss this unique occasion of getting it well done, and under Fred's own supervision.

Your uncle only had a bad abcess in a tooth and went to have it treated in a Fontainebleau Clinique They sent him back and blood poisoning had evidently set in as he died a few days after in Marlotte after great suffering and Uremia. The Funeral was quite a sad affair, only his wife, the Brooks' Mathew Smith[11] and a protest[ant]. Clergyman who could not get away from consoling and advising Mrs H. what to do to get over her terrible bereavement He was put in a great tiled tomb for three.—Nobody knows who is to be the third. Mrs H. as 2ᵈ looked gloomily into the tomb in the pouring rain—You know we wrote and wired and wrote again to Gibson ever so many times—and never an answer.

Yrs ever
J. D.—

Postcard.

---

[9] This is the first time that either of the Deliuses addressed Heseltine as 'Peter Warlock' in a letter.

[10] Gibson was supposed to have sent the surviving orchestral material of *Koanga* to Grez.

[11] Sir Matthew Smith (1879–1959), Halifax-born, English artist who settled at Grez in 1912 and divided his time between London and Paris. He made England his permanent home in 1940.

376
Edith Buckley Jones to Jelka Delius

Jan 3ʳᵈ 31

Cefn Bryntalch
Abermule
Montgomeryshire

Dear Mʳˢ Delius

I have long felt I wished to answer your most & kind sympathetic letter on the death of my own dear Phil, but somehow, I just felt I could not, & even now, I cannot believe the awful tragedy has really happened & that my dear boy has gone, with all his wonderful talents silenced for ever, & it seems all so needless he was all the world to me, & I feel quite heartbroken. I know you & Mʳ Delius sorrow with me, as he loved Mʳ Delius & his wonderful music. I do hope he is keeping well & that this terrible blow did not make him worse. Phil was buried in the same grave as his father at Godalming Surrey & many of his good friends came there but the time was so short it was not possible to let them know, otherwise many more would have been there. I cannot believe that it is of Phil I am writing it seems as if it must be an evil dream. Forgive an incoherant letter from Phil's most sorrowing Mother

   Edith Buckley Jones

Grainger Museum, University of Melbourne.

377
Jelka Delius to Edith Buckley Jones

January 1931

I am thinking of you and all you must have lived through since the great sorrow came—constantly—It is a terrible loss to us. It is a sort of consolation to me that he was really happy last year in the activity about the Delius festival, where he really was, next to Beecham, the *soul* of the thing. He wrote to me constantly then about the progress of his activities. I have kept all his letters and cherish them all the more now.

We shall always love dear Phil as the best of friends, ever helpful, ever supremely intelligent and understanding and lovable, and we shall sorrow for him and miss him with you.

Tomlinson, *Warlock and Delius*, 28.

Appendix 1

Heseltine's arrangements and translations of works by Delius

KEY: A = Augener; BH = Boosey & Hawkes; BL = British Library (*Brigg Fair* is part of Add. MS 54391); DT = Delius Trust; LS = National Library of Scotland; O = Oxford University Press; UE = Universal-Edition; PO = privately owned. MS 57966; all the Augener transcriptions are in Add.

DELIUS compositions and dates	HESELTINE arrangements, translations etc.	Published[a]		MS
Air and Dance for string orchestra (c.1915)	Score copied for Beecham (May 1929); also arranged for violin and piano			DT (now BL) untraced
Arabesk (An Arabesque) for baritone solo, chorus and orchestra (1911)	Text translated into English (Mar. 1914)	UE	1920	PO
Avant que tu ne t'en ailles. Song with piano (1919)	Copied			DT
Brigg Fair: an English Rhapsody for orchestra (1907)	Arranged for two pianos (May 1911)	Thames	1996	BL
Concerto for violin and orchestra (1916)	Reduced for violin and piano (1919)	A	1919	BL
Concerto for violin, violoncello, and orchestra (1915–16)	Reduced for violin, violoncello, and piano (Nov. 1915) (2 copies)	A	1920	BL & DT
Concerto for violoncello and orchestra (1921)	Reduced for violoncello and piano (July 1923)	UE	1923	DT (now BL)
Cynara for baritone solo and orchestra (1906–7)	Reduced for baritone solo and piano (Oct. 1929)	BH	1931	DT (now BL)

Work	Details	Publisher	Year	Location
Dance Rhapsody (No. 1) for orchestra (1908)	Arranged possibly four times: for two pianos (1912–13); piano solo (1913); military band (1912); and piano duet (1921). Only the last version survives.	—		DT
Dance Rhapsody No. 2 for orchestra (1916)	Arranged for piano duet (Nov. 1921)	A	1922	BL
Fennimore and Gerda. Opera (1908–10)	Text translated into English (Mar. 1919)	UE	1921	PO
Hassan: or the Golden Journey to Samarkand; incidental music (1920–3)	Vocal score (first version) (Nov. 1921)	UE	1923	?
	Vocal score (second version) (Sept. 1923)	UE	1924	DT (now BL)
	Full score partly in PH hand			
I-Brasil. Song with piano (1913)	Arranged for voice and orchestra	—		DT
	Copied (2 copies)			DT & BL
In a Summer Garden: Fantasy for orchestra (1908)	Arranged at least three times: for two pianos (Dec 1911);	Thames	1982	DT
	piano solo (1913 and ?1921);			PO
	piano duet (late 1912–early 1913)	—		
Late Lark (A) for tenor solo and orchestra (1925)	Reduced for tenor solo and piano (May 1929) (2 copies)	—		LS & DT
Life's Dance (tone-poem for orchestra) (1912)	Arranged for piano solo (Oct 1912)	—		PO
Mass of Life (A) for soloists, chorus, and orchestra (1904–5)	Translation revised for the programme of the 6th concert of the Delius Festival: 1 Nov. 1929	—		—
North Country Sketches for orchestra (1913–14)	Arranged for piano duet (Nov 1921)	A	1922	BL

DELIUS compositions and dates	HESELTINE arrangements, translations etc.	Published[a]	MS
On Hearing the First Cuckoo in Spring (1912) No 1 of Two Pieces for Small Orchestra	Arranged for piano duet (late 1913–early 1914); a piano solo version from the same time. Arranged for brass band (?1928)	O 1931; Thames 1982; O 1976	DT; PO
Requiem for soloists, chorus and orchestra (1914–16)	Reduced for soloists, chorus & piano; text translated into English (Jan. 1919)	UE 1921–2	?
Slumber Song. Song with piano (1888); No. 1 of Five Songs from the Norwegian	Copied		PO
Sonata No. 1 for violin and piano (1905–15)	Copied for printers (1915)		DT (now BL)
Song Before Sunrise (A) for small orchestra (1918)	Arranged for piano duet (1921)	A 1922	BL
Song of the High Hills (A) for chorus and orchestra (1911–12)	Arranged for piano solo (late 1913–early 1914)	—	DT
Songs paraphrased for the programmes of the 2nd and 4th concerts of the Delius Festival: 16 and 23 Oct. 1929: Five Songs from the Norwegian (1888) No 3. Am schönsten Sommerabend war's (Summer Eve) No 4. Sehnsucht (Longing) No 5. Beim Sonnenuntergang (Sunset) Seven Songs from the Norwegian (1889–90) No 2. Heimkehr (The Homeward Way)			—

Work	Arrangement / Notes	MS	Published
No 4. Klein Venevil (Sweet Venevil)			
No 5. Spielmann (The Minstrel)			
No 6. Verborg'ne Liebe (Love Concealed)			
No 7. Eine Vogelweise (The Bird's Story)			
Seven Danish Songs (1897), No. 5 Irmelin			
Two Songs (1900), No. 1 Das Veilchen (The Violet)			
So Sweet is She. Song with piano (1915) No. 2 of Four Old English Lyrics	Arranged for voice and small orchestra (Oct. 1926);	PO	
	Copied (2 copies)	DT & BL	
Spring, the Sweet Spring. Song with piano (1915)	Copied with suggested instrumentation	PO	
No. 3 of Four Old English Lyrics	Two further copies	DT & BL	
Summer Night on the River (1911); No. 2 of Two Pieces for Small Orchestra	Arranged for piano duet		O 1931
To Daffodils. Song with piano (1915) No. 4 of Four Old English Lyrics	Copied	DT	
3 Verlaine Songs	Arranged for voice and orchestra (?1915)	DT	—
Il pleure dans mon coeur (1895)			
Le ciel est, pardessus le toit (1895)			
La lune blanche (1910)			
Village Romeo and Juliet (A). Opera (1900–1)	Excerpts arranged for two pianos were planned in Oct. 1910; the English text was revised in Nov. 1921		UE 1921

ª Where the date of the actual arrangement is not known, the date of the relevant correspondence is given. The Published column gives the original publisher and date of the editions incorporating Heseltine's work, while the MS column gives the location of autograph manuscripts.

Appendix 2
Delius Festival: October–November 1929
(Six Concerts)

Artistic Director and Conductor-in-Chief: Sir Thomas Beecham, Bart.

12 October at Queen's Hall

Orchestra of the Columbia Graphophone Company led by Charles Woodhouse
Brigg Fair (1907)
A Late Lark (First performance) (Heddle Nash) (1925, completed 1929)
Dance Rhapsody No. 2 (1916)
Sea Drift (1903) (Dennis Noble, The London Select Choir)
In a Summer Garden (1908)
A Village Romeo and Juliet (1900–1) (excerpts sung by Pauline Maunder, Heddle Nash, and The London Select Choir)

16 October at Aeolian Hall

Orchestra led by Charles Woodhouse
A Song Before Sunrise (1918)
Seven Songs: for voice and piano (Olga Haley acc. by Evlyn Howard-Jones)
  'Heimkehr' (1889)
  'Verborg'ne Liebe' (1890)
  'Beim Sonnenuntergang' (1888)
  'Sehnsucht' (1888)
  'Le ciel est, par-dessus le toit' (1895)
  'In the Seraglio Garden' (1897)
  'Eine Vogelweise' (1889)
Sonata for Violoncello and Piano (1916) (Beatrice Harrison and Evlyn Howard-Jones)
Summer Night on the River (1911)
Air and Dance (First public performance) (1915)
Six Songs for voice and piano (John Goss acc. by Evlyn Howard-Jones)
  'Black Roses' (1901)
  'Chanson d'automne' (1911)
  'Silken Shoes' (1897)
  'I-Brasîl' (1913)
  'Das Veilchen' (1900)
  'Spielmann' (1890)

Nine Piano pieces (Evlyn Howard-Jones)
  Three Preludes (1923)
  Dance (originally for harpsichord) (1919)
  Five Pieces (1923)
Six Songs for voice and piano (John Armstrong acc. by Evlyn Howard-Jones)
  'Irmelin' (1897)
  'To Daffodils' (1915)
  'The Nightingale has a Lyre of Gold' (1910)
  'Il pleure dans mon coeur' (1895)
  'So white, so soft, so sweet is she' (1915)
  'Let Springtime come then' (1897)
On Hearing the First Cuckoo in Spring (1912)

18 October at Queen's Hall

B.B.C. Orchestra led by Arthur Catterall

Eventyr (1917)
Cynara (First performance) (John Goss) (1907, completed 1929)
Concerto for Piano and Orchestra (Revised 1906) (Evlyn Howard-Jones)
Arabesk (1911) (First performance in London) (John Goss, The London Select Choir)
Appalachia (1902) (Royal College Choral Class and B.B.C. National Chorus)

23 October at Aeolian Hall

Three Unaccompanied Choruses (The London Select Choir)
  'The Splendour Falls' (1923)
  'On Craig Ddu' (1907)
  'A Midsummer Song' (1908)
Four Songs for voice and piano (Dora Labbette acc. by Evlyn Howard-Jones)
  'The Nightingale' (1888)
  'Autumn' (1900)
  'La Lune Blanche' (1910)
  'Kleine Venevil' (1889–90)
Sonata No. 1 for Violin and Piano (1905–15) (Arthur Catterall and Evlyn Howard-Jones)
Three songs: for voice and piano (Heddle Nash acc. by Evlyn Howard-Jones)
  'Indian Love-song' (1891)
  'Love's Philosophy' (1891)
  'To the Queen of my Heart' (1891)
Two Unaccompanied Choruses ('To be sung of a summer night on the water') (The London Select Choir) (1917)
Four Songs for voice and piano (Dora Labbette acc. by Evlyn Howard-Jones)
  'Twilight Fancies' (1889)
  'Am schönsten Sommerabend war's' (1888)

'Margaret's Lullaby' (1889)

'Spring, the sweet Spring' (1915)

String Quartet (1916) (Virtuoso String Quartet: Marjorie Hayward, Edwin Virgo, Raymond Jeremy, Cedric Sharpe)

24 October at Queen's Hall

Royal Philharmonic Society Orchestra

North Country Sketches (1913–14)

Songs of Sunset (1906–7) (Olga Haley, John Goss, The London Select Choir)

Violin Concerto (1916) (Albert Sammons)

Dance Rhapsody No. 1 (1908)

Gerda (First performance in England) (Pauline Maunder, John Goss, The London Select Choir) (1903–10)

1 November at Queen's Hall

B.B.C. Orchestra led by Charles Woodhouse, Philharmonic Choir

A Mass of Life (1904–5) (Miriam Licette, Astra Desmond, Tudor Davies, Roy Henderson)

Select Bibliography

A. Manuscript Sources

British Library, London

Add. MSS 52547–9 and 57962	Letters from Frederick and Jelka Delius to Heseltine
Add. MS 54197	Letters from Heseltine to Taylor
Add. MSS 57794–803	Cecil Gray Papers
Add. MSS 57958–70	Nigel Heseltine Papers
Add. MS 58127	Letters from Heseltine to Olivia Smith
Add. MSS 71167–8	Letters from Heseltine to Delius

Peter Warlock Society Archives
University of Cape Town Library
   Colin Taylor Collection
   South African College of Music Library
University of Melbourne Library
   Grainger Museum
Victoria State Library, Melbourne

B. Secondary Sources

ApIvor, Denis, 'Philip Heseltine: A Psychological Study', *Music Review*, 46 (1985), 118–32.

Backhouse, J. M., 'Delius Letters', *British Museum Quarterly*, 30/1–2 (Autumn 1965), 30–5.

Beecham, Sir Thomas, *A Mingled Chime: Leaves from an Autobiography* (London, 1944).

—— *Frederick Delius* (London, 1959).

Bird, John, *Percy Grainger* (Oxford, 1999).

Carley, Lionel, *Frederick Delius: The Paris Years* (London, 1959).

—— *Delius: A Life in Letters*, i: *1862–1908* (Cambridge, Mass., 1983).

—— *Delius: A Life in Letters*, ii: *1909–1934* (Aldershot, 1988).

—— and Threlfall, Robert, *Delius: A Life in Pictures* (London, 1977).

Chisholm, Alastair, *Bernard van Dieren: An Introduction* (London, 1984).

Collins, Brian, *Peter Warlock: The Composer* (Aldershot, 1996).

Copley, Ian A., 'Warlock in Novels', *Musical Times*, 105 (1964), 739–40.

—— 'Warlock and Delius: A Catalogue', *Music and Letters*, 49 (1968), 213–18.

—— 'The Writings of Peter Warlock (Philip Heseltine) (1894–1930): A Catalogue', *Music Review*, 29 (1968), 288–99.

—— *The Music of Peter Warlock: A Critical Survey* (London, 1979).

—— *A Turbulent Friendship: A Study of the Relationship between D. H. Lawrence and Philip Heseltine ('Peter Warlock')* (London, 1983).

Cox, David, 'What Music Is', *Peter Warlock Society Newsletter*, 19 (1982), 5–8.

—— 'The Balfour Gardiner Connection', *Peter Warlock Society Newsletter*, 34 (1985), 7–8.

Cox, David, and Bishop, John (comps. and eds.), *Peter Warlock: A Centenary Celebration* (London, 1994).

Crowley, Aleister, *The Confessions of Aleister Crowley: An Autohagiography* (London, 1989).

Davies, Hywel, 'Bernard van Dieren, Philip Heseltine and Cecil Gray: A Significant Affiliation', *Music and Letters*, 69 (1988), 30–48.

Delany, Paul, *D. H. Lawrence's Nightmare: The Writer and his Circle in the Years of the Great War* (Hassocks, 1979).

—— 'Halliday's Progress: Letters of Philip Heseltine', *D. H. Lawrence Review*, 13 (1980), 119–33.

Delius, Clare, *Frederick Delius: Memories of my Brother* (London, 1935).

Delius, Frederick, 'At the Cross-Roads', *The Sackbut*, 1/5 (Sept. 1920), 205–8.

—— 'Recollections of Strindberg', *The Sackbut*, 1/8 (Dec. 1920), 353–4.

Dieren, Bernard van, 'Philip Heseltine' (obituary), *Musical Times* (1931), 117–19.

—— 'Frederick Delius: January 29, 1863–June 10, 1934' (obituary), *Musical Times* (1934), 598–604.

Douglas-Home, Jessica, *Violet: The Life and Loves of Violet Gordon Woodhouse* (London, 1996).

Fenby, Eric, *Delius as I Knew Him* (London, 1936).

—— *Delius* (London, 1971).

—— (in conversation with David Cox), 'Warlock as I Knew Him', *Composer*, 82 (1984), 19–23.

—— 'Visitors to Grez', *Delius Society Journal*, 106 (Winter/Spring, 1991); repr. in S. Lloyd (ed.), *Fenby on Delius* (London, 1996), 112–26.

Foreman, Lewis, *From Parry to Britten: British Music in Letters 1900–1945* (London, 1987).

—— *Bax: A Composer and his Times* (London, 1988).

Foss, Hubert, 'Introductions: XIX Philip Heseltine', *Music Bulletin*, 6 (1924), 202–6.

—— 'Cecil Gray: 1895–1951', *Musical Times*, 92 (1951), 496–8.

Gathorne-Hardy, Robert (ed.), *Ottoline at Garsington: Memoirs of Lady Ottoline Morrell 1915–1918* (London, 1974).

Gillies, Malcolm, *Bartók in Britain: A Guided Tour* (Oxford, 1989).

Goldring, Douglas, *Odd Man Out: The Autobiography of a 'Propaganda' Novelist* (London, 1935).

—— *The Nineteen Twenties* (London, 1945).

Goossens, Eugene, *Overture and Beginners: A Musical Autobiography* (London, 1951).

Gray, Cecil, *A Survey of Contemporary Music* (London, 1924).

—— *Peter Warlock: A Memoir of Philip Heseltine* (London, 1934).

—— *Musical Chairs or Between Two Stools: Being the Life and Memoirs of Cecil Gray* (London, 1948).

Gray, Pauline, *Cecil Gray: His Life and Notebooks* (London, 1989).

Hamnett, Nina, *Is She a Lady?* (London, 1955).

Heseltine, Nigel, *Capriol for Mother: A Memoir of Philip Heseltine (Peter Warlock)* (London, 1992).

HESELTINE, PHILIP, *Frederick Delius* (London, 1923).

HUTCHINGS, ARTHUR, *Delius* (London, 1948).

HUXLEY, JULIETTE, *Leaves of the Tulip Tree* (London, 1986).

JEFFERSON, ALAN, *Delius* (London, 1972).

JOHN, AUGUSTUS, *Chiaroscuro: Fragments of Autobiography* (London, 1952).

KINKEAD-WEEKES, MARK, *D. H. Lawrence: Triumph to Exile 1912–1922* (Cambridge, 1996).

LAWRENCE, D. H., *The Letters of D. H. Lawrence*, ii (June 1913–Oct. 1916), ed. George J. Zytaruk and James T. Boulton (Cambridge, 1981).

—— *The Letters of D. H. Lawrence*, iii (October 1916–June 1921), ed. James T. Boulton and Andrew Robertson (Cambridge, 1984).

—— *The Letters of D. H. Lawrence*, iv (June 1921–Mar. 1924), ed. Warren Roberts, James T. Boulton, and Elizabeth Mansfield (Cambridge, 1987).

LINDSAY, JACK, *Fanfrolico and After* (London, 1962).

LLOYD, STEPHEN, *H. Balfour Gardiner* (Cambridge, 1984).

—— 'The Published Writings of Philip Heseltine on Delius', *The Delius Society Journal*, 84 (1987).

—— (ed.), *Fenby on Delius: Collected Writings on Delius to Mark Eric Fenby's 90th Birthday* (London, 1996).

LOWE, RACHEL, *Frederick Delius 1862–1934: A Catalogue of the Music Archive of the Delius Trust, London* (London, 1974).

—— *A Descriptive Catalogue with Checklists of the Letters and Related Documents in the Delius Collection of the Grainger Museum, University of Melbourne* (London, 1981).

MELLERS, WILFRED, 'Delius and Peter Warlock', *Scrutiny*, 5 (1937), 384–97.

MEYERS, JEFFREY, *D. H. Lawrence: A Biography* (London, 1990).

MOORE, HARRY T., *The Priest of Love: A Life of D. H. Lawrence* (Carbondale and Edwardsville, Ill., 1974).

MOORE, JERROLD NORTHROP, *Edward Elgar: A Creative Life* (Oxford, 1984).

NIETZSCHE, FRIEDRICH, *Thus Spoke Zarathustra: A Book for Everyone and No One*, trans. R. J. Hollingdale (Harmondsworth, 1961).

OYLER, PHILIP, 'Delius at Grez', *Musical Times* (1972), 444–7.

PALMER, CHRISTOPHER, *Delius: Portrait of a Cosmopolitan* (London, 1976).

PARROTT, IAN, 'Warlock in Wales', *Musical Times*, 105 (1964), 740–1.

PERLIS, V., 'The Futurist Music of Leo Ornstein', *Music Library Association Notes*, 31 (1975), 735–50.

RAPOPORT, PAUL (ed.), *Sorabji: A Critical Celebration* (Aldershot, 1992).

REDWOOD, CHRISTOPHER (ed.), *A Delius Companion* (London, 1976).

REDWOOD, DAWN, *Flecker and Delius: The Making of Hassan* (London, 1978).

ROSEN, CAROLE, *The Goossens: A Musical Century* (London, 1993).

RUDLAND, MALCOLM, and COX, DAVID, 'Elizabeth Poston (1905–1987)', *Peter Warlock Society Newsletter*, 40 (1988), 15.

SEYMOUR, MIRANDA, *Ottoline Morrell: Life on the Grand Scale* (London, 1992).

SHEAD, RICHARD, *Constant Lambert* (London, 1973).

SHEPHERD, L. (ed.), *Encyclopedia of Occultism and Parapsychology* (Detroit, 1991).

SMITH, BARRY, 'Peter Warlock: A Study of the Composer through the Letters to Colin Taylor between 1911 and 1929' (Ph.D. thesis, Rhodes University, Grahamstown, 1991).

—— 'The Colin Taylor Collection', *Jagger Journal*, 10 (1989/90), 1–5.

—— 'Colin Taylor (1881–1973)', *Peter Warlock Society Newsletter*, 45 (1990), 2–3.

—— *Peter Warlock: The Life of Philip Heseltine* (Oxford, 1994).

—— (ed.), *The Occasional Writings of Philip Heseltine (Peter Warlock)*, 4 vols. (London, 1997–9).

SPENDER, STEPHEN (ed.), *D. H. Lawrence: Novelist, Poet, Prophet* (London, 1973).

TAYLOR, COLIN, 'Peter Warlock at Eton', *Composer*, 4 (1964), 9–10.

THRELFALL, ROBERT, *A Catalogue of the Compositions of Frederick Delius: Sources and References* (London, 1977).

—— 'Delius as They Saw Him: A Further Attempt at an Iconography', *Delius Society Journal*, 83 (1984), 5–18.

—— *Frederick Delius: A Supplementary Catalogue* (London, 1986).

—— *Frederick Delius: Complete Works Issued in Conjunction with the Delius Trust—Editorial report* (London, 1990).

TOMLINSON, FRED, 'Cecil Gray Papers in the British Museum', *Peter Warlock Society Newsletter*, 13 (1973), 7–8.

—— 'Colin Taylor, a Tribute', *Peter Warlock Society Newsletter*, 13 (1973), 3–4.

—— 'Heseltine MSS in the British Museum', *Peter Warlock Society Newsletter*, 14 (1974), 1–5.

—— 'Peter Warlock (1894–1930)', *Music and Musicians*, 23 (1974), 32–4.

—— *A Peter Warlock Handbook*, 2 vols. (London, 1974; Rickmansworth, 1977).

—— *Warlock and Delius* (London, 1976).

—— *Warlock and van Dieren* (London, 1978).

—— 'Philip Heseltine and Kaikhosru Sorabji', *Peter Warlock Society Newsletter*, 42 (1989), 10.

WILSON, COLIN, *The Brandy of the Damned: Discoveries of a Musical Eclectic* (London, 1964).

YOUNG, PERCY M., *A History of British Music* (London, 1967).

Index

Strindberg, Johan August 356
Stuttgart 491
Suhrawardy, Hasan Shahid 152, 156, 180–1,
    188, 361
Sullivan, Sir Arthur 5, 36
    WORKS:
    Mikado, The 5
Sunday Times 328, 345
Surrey 275
Sussex 271
Sussex (liner) 216
Suter, Hermann 100, 118
Sweden 491
Swinburne, Algernon 74
Swiss Cottage 352, 360
Switzerland 293, 297
Symons, Arthur 6, 45, 72, 76, 380, 409
Synge J. M. 231, 310
    WORKS:
    Deidre of the Sorrows 231, 310
Szántó, Theodor 60

Tahiti 190, 192
Tangiers 360
Tate Gallery 402
Tatler, The 312
Taylor, Leonard Campbell 53–4
Taylor, Colin 8, 11, 25, 40, 53–4, 58, 61, 145,
    271, 460
Te Akau, see Collins, Hal
Tertis, Lionel 387, 505
Thames, river 148, 235
Thompson and Son, Joseph 68
Three in Norway, see Lees and Clutterbuck
Times, The 215
Tintoretto, Jacopo Robusti 29
Tischer & Jagenberg 290, 436, 443, 445, 452,
    455, 475–6
Tischer, Gerhard 290, 298, 351
Tite Street 508
Tonkünstlerfest, Basel 315
Tonkünstlerfest, Jena 70, 92–4
Tour Eiffel Hotel, London 300
Tracy, Louis 216
Tredegar, Lord, see Morgan, Evan
Tree, Sir Herbert Beerbohm 242
Trevose Head 244
Trinity College, Dublin 248
Truth 182, 335
Tugwell, Mr 209–10, 220
Tunis 352, 359
Tyrer, Alexander 297
Tyrwhitt-Wilson, Gerald Hugh, see Berners, Lord

Universal Edition 18, 132–3, 136, 230, 280,
    284, 288–9, 295–6, 305, 319–20, 342,

347–8, 352, 361, 374, 376, 381, 384, 391,
    393, 401, 406, 436, 455, 465, 474–6, 483,
    486, 496
University of London 114, 142, 145, 157
University of Oxford 128, 142, 447
University of Wales, Aberystwyth 387, 389

Valdres 271
Vale of Evesham 158
Van Dieren, Bernard, see Dieren, Bernard van
Van Gogh, Vincent 69
Vaughan Williams, Ralph, see Williams, Ralph
    Vaughan
Venice 18, 28–9, 352
Verdi, Giuseppe 301, 409
    WORKS:
    Falstaff 301
Victoria and Albert Museum 207
Victoria Hotel, Christiania 396
Victoria station (London) 48, 281, 305, 308–9,
    368
Victoria station (Manchester) 372
Vienna 1, 70, 101, 132, 284, 288, 290, 295,
    297–8, 300–2, 311, 340, 342, 348, 352,
    359, 361–3, 366–7, 391, 394, 397, 403,
    410–11, 421, 423, 426, 434, 443
Villon, François 252, 255
Vincent, Ruth 235
Virgil 144
Voigt, E. R. 436–7, 442–4, 452, 455, 474,
    483
Vocalion 449
Volkert, Charles G. J. 274, 280–2, 332, 336,
    369, 371
Voules, May (Sackbut business manager) 314,
    332

Wagner, Richard 15–16, 33, 36, 134, 243, 261
    WORKS:
    Götterdämmerung 231
    Lohengrin 56
    Die Meistersinger von Nürnberg 22, 36
    Der Ring des Niebelungen 22
    Tristan und Isolde 56, 134, 300, 361
Wales 6, 10, 12–13, 16, 18–19, 22, 27, 39, 44,
    46, 53, 55, 71, 88, 93–4, 96, 123, 127,
    134, 143, 163, 168–70, 178, 207, 264,
    371, 373, 380, 416
Walden, Lord Howard de (T. E. Ellis) 40
Wallace, William 371
Walton, Sir William 422
Wardour Street 330
Warley, see Great Warley
Warlock, Peter 195, 248, 271, 295, 298, 301,
    387, 410
Warner, Waldo 277